THE UNIVERSITY OF CHICAGO
ORIENTAL INSTITUTE PUBLICATIONS
VOLUME 110

*Thomas A. Holland • Editor*

with the assistance of Richard M. Schoen

THE UNIVERSITY OF CHICAGO
ORIENTAL INSTITUTE PUBLICATIONS
VOLUME 110

# TOWN AND COUNTRY IN SOUTHEASTERN ANATOLIA

Vol. II: The Stratigraphic Sequence at Kurban Höyük

Plates

*Edited by*

GUILLERMO ALGAZE

*with chapters by*

Guillermo Algaze, Mary A. Evins, Michael L. Ingraham,
Leon Marfoe, and K. Aslihan Yener

*and with contributions by*

David S. Reese and Robert M. Whiting, Jr.

THE ORIENTAL INSTITUTE OF THE UNIVERSITY OF CHICAGO
CHICAGO · ILLINOIS

Library of Congress Catalog Card Number: 90–61729

ISBN: 0–918986–64–8

ISSN: 0069–3367

*The Oriental Institute*

©1990 by The University of Chicago. All rights reserved.

Published 1990. Printed in the United States of America.

## LIST OF PLATES

1. Period VIII Pottery From Areas A and C01: Ware Group I Bowls. Scale 2:5.
2. Period VIII Pottery From Areas A and C01: Ware Group I Bowls (*cont.*). Scale 2:5.
3. Period VIII Pottery From Area A: Ware Group I Bowls (*cont.*). Scale 2:5.
4. Period VIII Pottery From Area A: Ware Group I Bowls (*cont.*) and Jars. Scale 2:5.
5. Period VIII Pottery From Area A: Ware Group I Jars (*cont.*). Scale 2:5.
6. Period VIII Pottery From Areas A and C01: Ware Group I Jars (*cont.*). Scale 2:5.
7. Period VIII Pottery From Area A: Ware Group I Decorated Bodies. Scale 2:5.
8. Period VIII Pottery From Areas A and C01: Ware Group I Decorated Bodies (*cont.*). Scale 2:5.
9. Period VIII Pottery From Area A: Ware Group II Bowls. Scale 2:5.
10. Period VIII Pottery From Area A: Ware Group II Bowls (*cont.*) and Holemouth Jars. Scale 2:5.
11. Period VIII Pottery From Area A: Ware Group II Jars. Scale 2:5.
12. Period VII Pottery From Area C01: Dark Faced Burnished Ware and Ware Group I Bowls. Scale 2:5.
13. Period VII Pottery From Area C01: Ware Group I Open Forms, Holemouth Jars, and Decorated Bodies. Scale 2:5.
14. Period VII Pottery From Area C01: Ware Group I Jars and Ware Group II Bowls. Scale 2:5.
15. Period VII Pottery From Area C01: Ware Group II Bowls (*cont.*) and Jars. Scale 2:5.
16. Period VII Pottery From Area C01: Ware Group II Holemouth Jars. Scale 2:5.
17. Period VI Pottery From Pit 203 in Area C01. Scale 2:5.
18. Period VI Pottery From Pit 203 in Area C01 (*cont.*). Scale 2:5.
19. Period VI Pottery From Areas A and C01: Ware Group I Bowls. Scale 2:5.
20. Period VI Pottery From Areas A and C01: Ware Group I Bowls (*cont.*). Scale 2:5.
21. Period VI Pottery From Areas A and C01: Ware Group I Bowls (*cont.*). Scale 2:5.
22. Period VI Pottery From Areas A and C01: Ware Group I Bowls (*cont.*) and Stands. Scale 2:5.
23. Period VI Pottery From Areas A and C01: Ware Group I Holemouth Jars and Decorated Bodies. Scale 2:5.
24. Period VI Pottery From Area A: Plain Simple Ware and Brittle Ware Jars. Scale 2:5.
25. Period VI Pottery From Areas A and C01: Ware Group I Jars and Accessories. Scale 2:5.
26. Period VI Pottery From Areas A and C01: Ware Group I Jars (*cont.*). Scale 2:5.
27. Period VI Pottery From Areas A and C01: Ware Group I Jars (*cont.*) and Stands. Scale 2:5.

28. Period VI Pottery From Areas A and C01: Ware Group II Bowls. Scale 2:5.

29. Period VI Pottery From Areas A and C01: Ware Group II Bowls (*cont.*). Scale 2:5.

30. Period VI Pottery From Areas A and C01: Ware Group II Bowls (*cont.*). Scale 2:5.

31. Period VI Pottery From Areas A and C01: Ware Group II Platters. Scale 2:5.

32. Period VI Pottery From Area A: Ware Group II Platters (*cont.*). Scale 2:5.

33. Period VI Pottery From Areas A and C: Ware Group II Trays, Stands, and Carinated Jars. Scale 2:5.

34. Period VI Pottery From Area A: Ware Group II Carinated Jars (*cont.*). Scale 2:5.

35. Period VI Pottery From Areas A and C01: Ware Group II Jars and Funnel. Scale 2:5.

36. Period VI Pottery From Areas A and C01: Ware Group II Jars (*cont.*). Scale 2:5.

37. Period VI Pottery From Areas A and C01: Ware Group II Jars (*cont.*). Scale 2:5.

38. Period VI Pottery From Areas A and B: Ware Group II Jars (*cont.*). Scale 2:5.

39. Period VI Pottery From Areas A and C01: Ware Group II Jars (*cont.*). Scale 2:5.

40. Period VI Pottery From Area A: Ware Group II Jars (*cont.*). Scale 2:5.

41. Period VI Pottery From Area A: Ware Group II Jars (*cont.*). Scale 2:5.

42. Period VI Pottery From Area A: Ware Group II Jars (*cont.*) and Miscellaneous Karaz Ware Sherds. Scale 2:5.

43. Period V Pottery From Area C01: Ware Group I Bowls. Scale 2:5.

44. Period V Pottery From Area C01: Ware Group I Bowls (*cont.*). Scale 2:5.

45. Period V Pottery From Area C01: Ware Group I Bowls (*cont.*). Scale 2:5.

46. Period V Pottery From Areas C and C01: Ware Group I Bowls (*cont.*). Scale 2:5.

47. Period V Pottery From Area C01: Ware Group I Holemouth Jars. Scale 2:5.

48. Period V Pottery From Area C01: Ware Group I Jars. Scale 2:5.

49. Period V Pottery From Area C01: Ware Group I Jars (*cont.*). Scale 2:5.

50. Period V Pottery From Area C01: Ware Group I Jars (*cont.*). Scale 2:5.

51. Period V Pottery From Areas C and C01: Ware Groups I–II Stands and Pedestal Bases, and Ware Group II Bowls. Scale 2:5.

52. Period V Pottery From Area C01: Ware Group II Jars. Scale 2:5.

53. Period IV Pottery From Areas A, B, and C: Ware Group I Cups. Scale 2:5.

54. Period IV Pottery From Areas A, B, C, C01, and F: Ware Group I Cups (*cont.*) and Bowls. Scale 2:5.

55. Period IV Pottery From Areas A, B, and C: Ware Group I Bowls (*cont.*). Scale 2:5.

56. Period IV Pottery From Areas A, B, C, and F: Ware Group I Bowls (*cont.*). Scale 2:5.

57. Period IV Pottery From Areas A, C, and C01: Ware Group I Bowls (*cont.*). Scale 2:5.

58. Period IV Pottery From Areas A, B, C, and C01: Ware Group I Bowls (*cont.*). Scale 2:5.

## LIST OF PLATES

59. Period IV Pottery From Areas A, B, C, and C01: Ware Group I Bowls (*cont.*). Scale 2:5.
60. Period IV Pottery From Areas A, B, C, C01, and F: Ware Group I Bowls (*cont.*) and Holemouth Jars. Scale 2:5.
61. Period IV Pottery From Areas A, B, C, C01, F, and G: Ware Group I Holemouth Jars (*cont.*). Scale 2:5.
62. Period IV Pottery From Areas A, B, and C: Ware Group I Holemouth Jars (*cont.*). Scale 2:5.
63. Period IV Pottery From Areas A, C, and F: Ware Group I Holemouth Jars (*cont.*). Scale 2:5.
64. Period IV Pottery From Areas A, B, C, C01, and F: Ware Group I Jars. Scale 2:5.
65. Period IV Pottery From Areas A, C, and C01: Ware Group I Jars (*cont.*). Scale 2:5.
66. Period IV Pottery From Areas A, B, C, C01, and F: Ware Group I Jars (*cont.*). Scale 2:5.
67. Period IV Pottery From Areas A, C, C01, and F: Ware Group I Jars (*cont.*). Scale 2:5.
68. Period IV Pottery From Areas A, B, C, and C01: Ware Group I Jars (*cont.*). Scale 2:5.
69. Period IV Pottery From Areas A, C, and C01: Ware Group I Grooved Rim Jars. Scale 2:5.
70. Period IV Pottery From Areas A, B, C, and F: Ware Group I Grooved Rim Jars (*cont.*). Scale 2:5.
71. Period IV Pottery From Areas A, B, and C: Ware Group I Jars (*cont.*). Scale 2:5.
72. Period IV Pottery From Areas A, B, and C: Ware Group I Accessories and Stands. Scale 2:5.
73. Period IV Pottery From Areas A, B, C, C01, and D: Ware Group I Pedestal Bases and Feet. Scale 2:5.
74. Period IV Pottery From Areas A, C, and F: Ware Group I Stands. Scale 2:5.
75. Period IV Pottery From Areas A, B, C, and F: Miscellaneous Ware Group I Bases and Reserved Slip Ware Types. Scale 2:5.
76. Period IV Pottery From Area C: Reserved Slip Ware Jars. Scale 2:5.
77. Period IV Pottery From Areas A, B, C, C01, and F: Metallic Ware Cups and Bowls. Scale 2:5.
78. Period IV Pottery From Areas A, B, C, and F: Metallic Ware Jars. Scale 2:5.
79. Period IV Pottery From Areas A, B, C, and C01: Metallic Ware Pedestal Bases and Stands, and Combed Wash Ware and Painted Band Ware Cups. Scale 2:5.
80. Period IV Pottery From Areas A, B, C, and C01: Combed Wash Ware and Painted Band Ware Bowls and Jars. Scale 2:5.
81. Period IV Pottery From Areas A, C, and C01: Karababa Painted Ware Bowls. Scale 2:5.
82. Period IV Pottery From Areas A, B, C, and C01: Karababa Painted Ware Footed Bowls and Holemouth Jars. Scale 2:5.
83. Period IV Pottery From Areas A, B, and C: Karababa Painted Ware Jars. Scale 2:5.
84. Period IV Pottery From Areas A, B, C, and C01: Karababa Painted Ware Jars (*cont.*). Scale 2:5.
85. Period IV Pottery From Areas A, C, C01, and F: Karababa Painted Ware Jars (*cont.*). Scale 2:5.
86. Period IV Pottery From Areas A and C: Karababa Painted Ware Jars (*cont.*). Scale 2:5.
87. Period IV Pottery From Areas A, C, C01, and D: Karababa Painted Ware Jars (*cont.*). Scale 2:5.

88. Period IV Pottery From Areas A, C, and D: Karababa Painted Ware Jars (*cont.*) and Decorated Bodies. Scale 2:5.

89. Period IV Pottery From Areas A, C, C01, and F: Karababa Painted Ware Jars (*cont.*). Scale 2:5.

90. Period IV Pottery From Areas A, B, C, C01, and F: Miscellaneous Wares. Scale 2:5.

91. Period IV Pottery From Areas A, B, and C: Ware Group II Bowls and Open Forms. Scale 2:5.

92. Period IV Pottery From Areas A, C, and C01: Ware Group II Bowls (*cont.*) and Jars. Scale 2:5.

93. Period IV Pottery From Areas A, B, C, and C01: Ware Group II Jars (*cont.*). Scales: (A–H and K–M) 2:5; (I and J) 1:5.

94. Period IV Pottery From Areas A, B, C, and C01: Ware Group II Jars (*cont.*). Scale 2:5.

95. Period IV Pottery From Areas A, B, and C: Ware Group II Jars (*cont.*). Scales: (A) 1:5; (B–H) 2:5.

96. Period IV Pottery From Areas A, B, C, and C01: Ware Group II Handles, Lids, and Andiron. Scale 2:5.

97. Period III Pottery From Areas A, B, and D: Ware Group I Cups. Scale 2:5.

98. Period III Pottery From Areas A, D, and F: Ware Group I Bowls. Scale 2:5.

99. Period III Pottery From Areas A, B, and D: Ware Group I Bowls (*cont.*). Scale 2:5.

100. Period III Pottery From Areas A and D: Ware Group I Bowls (*cont.*). Scale 2:5.

101. Period III Pottery From Areas A and D: Ware Group I Bowls (*cont.*). Scale 2:5.

102. Period III Pottery From Areas A, B, D, and E: Ware Group I Bowls (*cont.*). Scale 2:5.

103. Period III Pottery From Areas A and D: Ware Group I Bowls (*cont.*). Scale 2:5.

104. Period III Pottery From Areas A and D: Ware Group I Jars. Scale 2:5.

105. Period III Pottery From Areas A and D: Ware Group I Jars (*cont.*). Scale 2:5.

106. Period III Pottery From Areas A, B, and D: Ware Group I Jars (*cont.*). Scale 2:5.

107. Period III Pottery From Areas A, B, D, and F: Ware Group I Jars (*cont.*). Scale 2:5.

108. Period III Pottery From Areas A and D: Ware Group I Jars (*cont.*). Scale 2:5.

109. Period III Pottery From Areas A, B, and D: Ware Group I Jars (*cont.*). Scale 2:5.

110. Period III Pottery From Areas B and D: Ware Group I Jars (*cont.*). Scales: (A–G) 2:5; (H) 1:5.

111. Period III Pottery From Area D: Ware Group I Jars (*cont.*). Scale 2:5.

112. Period III Pottery From Areas A and D: Ware Group I Jars (*cont.*). Scale 2:5.

113. Period III Pottery From Areas D and E: Ware Group I Jars (*cont.*). Scales: (A–E and G–P) 2:5; (F) 1:5.

114. Period III Pottery From Areas A and D: Ware Group I Jars (*cont.*). Scales: (A–E and G–O) 2:5; (F) 1:5.

115. Period III Pottery From Areas B and D: Ware Group I Jars (*cont.*). Scale 2:5.

116. Period III Pottery From Area D: Ware Group I Jars (*cont.*). Scale 2:5.

117. Period III Pottery From Areas A, B, and D: Ware Group I Jars (*cont.*). Scales: (A–C and E–I) 2:5; (D) 1:5.

118. Period III Pottery From Areas A and D: Ware Group I Jars (*cont.*) and Barrels. Scale 2:5.

# LIST OF PLATES

119. Period III Pottery From Areas D and E: Ware Group I Barrels (*cont.*). Scale 2:5.

120. Period III Pottery From Area D: Ware Group I Barrels (*cont.*). Scale 2:5.

121. Period III Pottery From Areas A and D: Ware Group I Barrels (*cont.*).
Scales: (A–D and F–H) 2:5; (E, I, and J) 1:5.

122. Period III Pottery From Area D: Ware Group I Barrels (*cont.*). Scales: (A, E, and F) 2:5; (B–D) 1:5.

123. Period III Pottery From Areas A and D: Ware Group I Barrels (*cont.*). Scales: (A–E) 2:5; (F and G) 1:5.

124. Period III Pottery From Areas B and D: Ware Group I Barrels (*cont.*). Scale 2:5.

125. Period III Pottery From Areas A and D: Ware Group I Barrels and Jars (*cont.*).
Scales: (A and C) 1:5; (B and D–F) 2:5.

126. Period III Pottery From Areas A, B, and D: Ware Group I Holemouth Jars. Scale 2:5.

127. Period III Pottery From Areas A, D, and E: Ware Group I Holemouth Jars (*cont.*). Scale 2:5.

128. Period III Pottery From Areas A, D, and E: Ware Group I Storage-Size Jars. Scale 2:5.

129. Period III Pottery From Areas A and D: Ware Group I Jars (*cont.*) and Stands. Scale 2:5.

130. Period III Pottery From Areas A and D: Ware Group I Stands (*cont.*) and Pedestal Bases. Scale 2:5.

131. Period III Pottery From Areas A and D: Miscellaneous Bases, Feet, Accessories, and Decorated Bodies. Scale 2:5.

132. Period III Pottery From Areas B and D: Decorated Bodies (*cont.*). Scale 2:5.

133. Period III Pottery From Areas A, D, and E: Metallic Ware Bowls and Jars, and Miscellaneous Rare Painted Sherds. Scale 2:5.

134. Period III Pottery From Area D: Ware Group II Bowls. Scale 2:5.

135. Period III Pottery From Areas A, B, and D: Ware Group II Jars. Scale 2:5.

136. Period III Pottery From Areas A and D: Ware Group II Jars (*cont.*). Scale 2:5.

137. Period II Pottery From Area D: Glazed Bowls. Scale 2:5.

138. Period II Pottery From Area D: Glazed Bowls (*cont.*), Jars, and Lamp. Scale 2:5.

139. Period II Pottery From Area D: Plain Simple Ware and Cream Ware Bowls. Scale 2:5.

140. Period II Pottery From Area D: Plain Simple Ware and Cream Ware Jars. Scale 2:5.

141. Period II Pottery From Areas B and D: Plain Simple Ware Amphorae. Scale 2:5.

142. Period II and Early First Millennium A.D. Pottery From Area D: Plain Simple Wares (A–E), "Scroll Painted" (G and H), and Gritty Red (I). Scale 2:5.

143. Period II Pottery From Area D: Cooking Pot Ware Vessels. Scale 2:5.

144. (*A*) Neolithic Washed and Impressed Ware From Areas A and C01 [Extrusive in Periods VIII, VII, V, and IV Deposits].
(*B*) Period VIII, Halaf Painted Pottery [Wares 32 and 38] from Areas A and C01 [Extrusive: top row left, and bottom row].
(*C*) Period VIII, Halaf Painted Pottery from Area A.
(*D*) Period VIII, Halaf Painted Pottery from Area A.
(*E*) Period VII, Middle Chalcolithic Painted Pottery [Ware 31] From Area C01.
(*F*) Period VII, Middle Chalcolithic Chaff/Straw-Tempered Pottery [Ware 13/14] from Area C01.

145. (A) Period VI, Late Chalcolithic Chaff/Straw-Tempered Pottery [Ware 13/14] From Pit 203, Area C01.
(B) Period VI, Late Chalcolithic Chaff/Straw-Tempered Carinated Vessels [Jar 20a] From Area A.
(C) Period VI, Late Chalcolithic Chaff/Straw-Tempered Ware Platters [Bowl 26] From Areas A and C01.
(D) Period VI, Late Chalcolithic Chaff/Straw-Tempered Jars From Area A.
(E) Period VI, Late Chalcolithic Plain Simple Ware [Ware 04] Jars From Areas A and C01.
(F) Period VI, Late Chalcolithic Beveled Rim Bowl [Ware 17] From Area A [= KH 1983/166].
(G) Period VI, Late Chalcolithic Plain Simple Ware Cup From Area C01 [= Plate 19: I].

146. (A) Period VB, Plain Simple Ware [Ware 04] From Area C01, Phases 3 and 4.
(B) Period VA, Plain Simple and Dense Wares [Wares 04 and 03] From Area C01, Phases 8–10.
(C) Comparison of Periods V and IV Reserved Slip Wares. Period V [Top Row]: Diagonal, From Area C01. Period IV [Bottom Row]: Horizontal, From Area A.
(D) Cyma-Recta Cup Found Inside Oven 169 in Area C01, Phases 9 and 10 [= KH 1982/124].
(E) Periods IVA–B, Plain Simple and Karababa Painted Wares [Wares 04 and 08] Grooved Rim Jars.
(F) Period IV, Metallic Ware [Ware 02].

147. (A) Period IV, Plain Simple Ware [Ware 04] Cup [Bowl 1e, = Plate 53: V].
(B) Period IV, White Incrusted Gray Ware [Ware 10] Stand [= Plate 90: H].
(C) Period IV, Metallic Ware [Ware 02] Cup [Bowl 1e, = Plate 77: D].
(D) Period IV, Karababa Painted Ware Sherds [Ware 08].
(E) Period IV, Karababa Painted Ware Sherds.
(F) Period IVA Karababa Painted Ware Tripod From Area B [= Fig. 134: B].
(G) Period IV, Karababa Painted Ware Handled Jar [= Plate 89: B].
(H) Period IVA, Cooking Pot Ware [Ware 18] Tripod From Area B [= Plate 90: B].
(I) Periods IVA–B, Combed Wash Ware [Ware 07] Sherds.
(J) Period IV, Band Painted Ware [Ware 01].

148. (A) Period IV, Cooking Pot Ware [Ware 09] Sherds.
(B) Period IV, Cooking Pot Ware Jar [= KH 1981/105].
(C) Period III, Representative Plain Simple Ware and Cooking Pot Ware [Wares 04 and 09] Sherds From Area D, Building Phase II Deposits.
(D) Period III, Plain Simple Ware Jars [Jar 12b; Left = Plate 111: C, Right = Plate 111: D] From Area D.
(E) Period III, Plain Simple Ware Bowl From Area D [= Plate 98: M].
(F) Period III, Plain Simple Ware Stand From Area D [= Plate 129: N].
(G) Period III, Plain Simple Ware Barrel From Area D [= KH 1981/57].

149. (A) Period III, Cooking Pot Ware [Ware 09] Sherds From Area D.
(B) Period III, Plain Simple Ware [Ware 04] Barrel Shapes From Area D.
(C) Period III, Metallic Ware [Ware 02] Jar From Area D [= Plate 133: O].
(D) Period III, Metallic Ware "Syrian Bottle" From Area D [= Plate 133: I].
(E) Period III, Rare Painted Sherds [Ware 24], and Unique Vegetal-Tempered Ware Sherd [Ware 21] with Punctated Decoration [Bottom Row] From Area D.
(F) Period II, Abbasid Cream Ware [Ware 52].

150. (A) Period II, Plain Simple Ware [Ware 04].
(B) Period II, Glazed Ware [Ware 22].

151. Human (A–C), and Animal Figurines (D–J) From Period IV Levels, Areas A, B, and C. Scale 3:5.

152. Human (A), and Animal Figurines (B–K) From Period III Levels, Areas A and D. Scale 3:5.

153. Figurines From Periods III and IV Levels, Areas A, B, C, and D. Scale Indicated.

154. Theriomorphic Vessels From Periods III and IV Levels, Areas A, C, and D. Scale 2:5.

155. Terracotta Implements From Diverse Periods, Areas A–C, C01, and D: Spindle Whorls (A–C), "Chariot Wheels" (D–L), Beads (M and N), Perforated Roundels (O–W, Y, Z, and BB), and Scrapers (X, AA, and CC–EE). Scale 2:5.

# LIST OF PLATES

156. Terracotta Implements From Diverse Periods, Areas A–C, C01, D, and G: Spools (A and B), Tokens/"Gaming Pieces" (C–E), Stand (H), Spoon (I), Crucibles (J and K), Clay Nails (L–O and Q), Model House (P), and Unassigned (G and M). Scale 2:5.

157. Painted and Unpainted Lids From Periods III and IV Levels, Areas A, C, and D. Scale 3:5.

158. Terracotta Implements From Diverse Periods, Areas A, C, C01, and D: Lids (A and B), Spoon (E), Stand (F), Perforated Brick (G), and Unassigned (C and D). Scale Indicated.

159. Copper Implements From Diverse Periods, Areas C, C01, D, and F: Pins (A–D, F, H, and I), Needles (E and G), and a Lead Coil (J). Scale 4:5.

160. Iron Implements From Period II Levels, Area D. Scale 3:5.

161. Copper Implements (A–J) From Diverse Periods, Areas C, C01, D, and F: Iron Implements (K–LL) From Period II Levels, Areas C and D. Scale Indicated.

162. Bone Implements From Diverse Periods, Areas A, B, C01, and D: Bead (B), Pins (D and E), Horn Core (F), Awls and Awl Fragments (G–I and K–M), Needle (J), Spatula (N), and Unassigned (A and C). Scales: (A, C–I, and K–N) 3:5; (B and J) 6:5.

163. Bone Implements From Diverse Periods, Areas A, B, C, C01, and D. Scales Indicated.

164. Marine and Worked Shells From Diverse Periods, Areas A–D and F–H. Scales: (A–C, E–H, and J) 1:1; (D and I) 2:1; (K–V) Indicated.

165. Stone Vessels From Period VIII Levels, Area A (A–C); Registered Ground Stone (D–U) and Chipped Stone (V–BB) Artifacts From Diverse Periods, Areas A–C, C01, and F. Scales: (A–T and W–BB) 2:5; (U and V) 4:5.

166. Ground and Chipped Stone Artifacts From Diverse Periods, Areas A, B, C01, and D. Scales Indicated.

167. Seals (A–C, H, and I), Sealing (G), Stoppers (D and E), and "Tablet" (F) From Diverse Periods, Areas A, C, C01, D, E, and F. Scales: (A–E and G–I) 3:5; (F) 6:5.

168. Seals and Sealings From Diverse Periods, Areas A, C, C01, D, E, and F.

169. Roman and Ottoman Coins From Area D. Scale Indicated.

# LIST OF ABBREVIATIONS

| | |
|---|---|
| Bns. | Burnish |
| cm | centimeter |
| *cont.* | *continued* |
| *DECO.* | *Decoration* |
| *FCN* | *Find Collection Number* |
| KH | Kurban Höyük |
| Lt. | Light |
| *MRN* | *Master Register Number* |
| Unass. | Unassigned |

Plate 1. Period VIII Pottery From Areas A and C01: Ware Group I Bowls. Scale 2:5.

| | MRN | CONTEXT | FCN | WARE | FORM | TYPE | DECO. | WARE/REMARKS |
|---|---|---|---|---|---|---|---|---|
| A | 17132 | A07-1971/81/91-095 | 919 | 38 | C-49* | Bowl 1 | 978 | Dense, no visible tempering; buff clay, reddish-brownish paint. |
| B | 12506 | A08-14-069 | 704 | 38 | C-46 | Bowl 1 | 910 | Dense, small-sized black grits; grayish clay and reddish-brownish paint. |
| C | 6836 | A07-07-031 | 228 | 38 | 1013 | Bowl 1 | 910 | Dense, no visible tempering; brownish-buff clay; cream slip on exterior surface; reddish-brown paint; out of context in Period VI deposits. |
| D | 12221 | A07-2470-105 | 1053 | 38 | C-46 | Bowl 1 | 977 | Dense, no visible tempering other than a few small white grits; cream slip on surfaces, orangish paint. |
| E | 6837 | A08-07-030 | 224 | 32 | 1132 | Bowl 2 | 978 | Dense, no visible tempering other than a few small white grits; greenish-buff slip on surface, dark brown paint; out of context in Period VI deposits. |
| F | 12488 | A08-12-069 | 686 | 38 | 1132 | Bowl 2 | 921 | Dense, no visible tempering; cream slip on surfaces; dark brown paint. |
| G | 12532 | A08-13-069 | 730 | 38 | 1132 | Bowl 2 | 964 | Dense, scattered small-sized grits; pinkish-reddish clay; red paint on exterior and rim interior; interior surface covered with light reddish wash. |
| H | 11876 | A08-1110/20/30-056 | 552 | 32 | 1132 | Bowl 2 | 926 | Dense, scattered white grits; greenish clay, dark brown paint. |
| I | 11568 | A07-1991/81/089 | 855 | 32 | 1027 | Bowl 3a | 920 | Dense, occasional scattered small black grits; greenish clay, buff slip on exterior surface; dark brown paint; out of context in Period VI deposits. |
| J | 6304 | A09-05-012 | 186 | 38 | 1027 | Bowl 3a | 906 | Dense, occasional small grits; orange-buff clay; cream slip on both surfaces, brownish-red paint; out of context in Period VI deposits. |
| K | 3146 | C01-0167/69-078 | 977 | 38 | 1027 | Bowl 3a | 907 | Dense, occasional small grits; orange-buff clay, cream slip on surface; red paint; out of context in Period V deposits. |
| L | 6360 | A09-05-012 | 192 | 38 | 1027 | Bowl 3a | 980 | Dense, no visible tempering; brownish-buff clay, dark brown paint; out of context in Period VI deposits. |
| M | 12426 | A08-14-068 | 678 | 38 | 1027 | Bowl 3a | 981 | Dense, small-sized grits; brownish-buff clay, dark brown paint. |
| N | 11739 | A08-0511-051 | 499 | 32 | 1027 | Bowl 3a | 902 | Dense, no visible tempering other than a few scattered small-sized red grits; brownish-buff clay and dark brown paint. |
| O | 5639 | C01-09-066 | 1529 | 38 | 941 | Unass. Bowl | 982 | Small-sized black grits; light greenish-buff clay, brown paint; out of context in Period IV deposits. |
| P | 7563 | A07-11-038 | 315 | 32 | 1202 | Unass. Bowl | 983 | Small-sized black grits; light greenish-buff clay, brown paint; out of context in Period IV deposits. |

*A 'C' before the Form Number indicates that the vessel is complete or semi-complete.

PLATE 1

Period VIII Pottery From Areas A and C01: Ware Group I Bowls. Scale 2:5.

Plate 2. Period VIII Pottery From Areas A and C01: Ware Group I Bowls (*cont.*). Scale 2:5.

|   | MRN | Context | FCN | Ware | Form | Type | Deco. | Ware/Remarks |
|---|---|---|---|---|---|---|---|---|
| A | 12496 | A098-12-069 | 694 | 46 | 445 | Bowl 3b | — | Dense, scattered gray and white small- and medium-sized grits; brownish-buff clay with tan core. |
| B | 11739 | A08-0511-051 | 499 | 32 | 445 | Bowl 3b | 907 | Dense, scattered small- and medium-sized white grits; dark greenish clay, brown paint. |
| C | 11568 | A07/1971/81-089 | 655 | 38 | 445 | Bowl 3b | 984 | Dense, small-sized gray and white grits; grayish clay with oxidized core, pinkish; dark brown paint. |
| D | 11623 | A07-19/20-091 | 871 | 32 | 445 | Bowl 3b | 902 | Dense, no visible tempering; greenish clay, olive-brown paint; out of context in Period VI deposits. |
| E | 3894 | C01-0187-095 | 1263 | 32 | 445 | Bowl 3b | 985 | Dense, some scattered white grits and perhaps traces of some chaff as well; brown clay with light-brownish buff slip; dark brown paint. |
| F | 11876 | A08-1110/20/30-056 | 552 | 32 | 445 | Bowl 3b | 927 | Dense, some scattered white grits; buff, somewhat greenish clay; dark brown paint. |
| G | 11711 | A07-1972/82-095 | D913* | 38 | 445 | Bowl 3b | 923 | Somewhat porous orange clay with small-sized white grits; orange paint. |
| H | 1978 | C01-0189-062 | 608 | 38 | 445 | Bowl 3b | 986 | Dense, no visible tempering; brown clay, light brownish-buff slip on surface; brown paint; out of context in Period V/IV deposits. |
| I | 12304 | A08-1142/32-060 | 580 | 38 | 445 | Bowl 3b | 925 | Dense, no visible tempering; brownish clay, brown paint. |
| J | 12532 | A08-13-069 | 730 | 38 | 445 | Bowl 3b | 962 | Dense, small- and medium-sized black grits; grayish-greenish clay, cream slip on surfaces; brown paint. |
| K | 12361 | A08-11-065 | 626 | 38 | 445 | Bowl 3b | 929 | Dense, scattered small-sized white grits; brownish clay; brown paint. |
| L | 12585 | A07-2480-105 | 1029 | 38 | 445 | Bowl 3b | 974 | Dense, no visible tempering other than a few scattered small-sized grits; dark brown paint. |

* A 'D' before the Find Collection Number indicates that the pottery came from sieved remains.

PLATE 2

Period VIII Pottery From Areas A and C01: Ware Group I Bowls (*cont.*). Scale 2:5.

Plate 3. Period VIII Pottery From Area A: Ware Group I Bowls (*cont.*). Scale 2:5.

|   | MRN | CONTEXT | FCN | WARE | FORM | TYPE | DECO. | WARE/REMARKS |
|---|---|---|---|---|---|---|---|---|
| A | 5622 + 6063 | A09-0451-009 + A09-05-012 | D132 + 178 | 38 | 445 | Bowl 3b | 905 | Dense, small white grits; orange-buff clay; cream slip on surfaces; reddish paint; out of context in Period VI deposits. |
| B | 12516 | A08-14-070 | 714 | 38 | 445 | Bowl 3b | 947 | Dense, no visible tempering; brown clay with oxidized purple-colored core; dark brown paint; somewhat irregular. |
| C | 12413 | A08-14-067 | 667 | 38 | 445 | Bowl 3b | 921 | Dense, occasional scattered small red grits; pinkish clay, red paint. |
| D | 12459 | A07-24-102 | 985 | 38 | 445 | Bowl 3b | 934 | Dense, small- and medium-sized white grits; brownish-buff clay; dark brown paint; perhaps a jar neck? |

PLATE 3

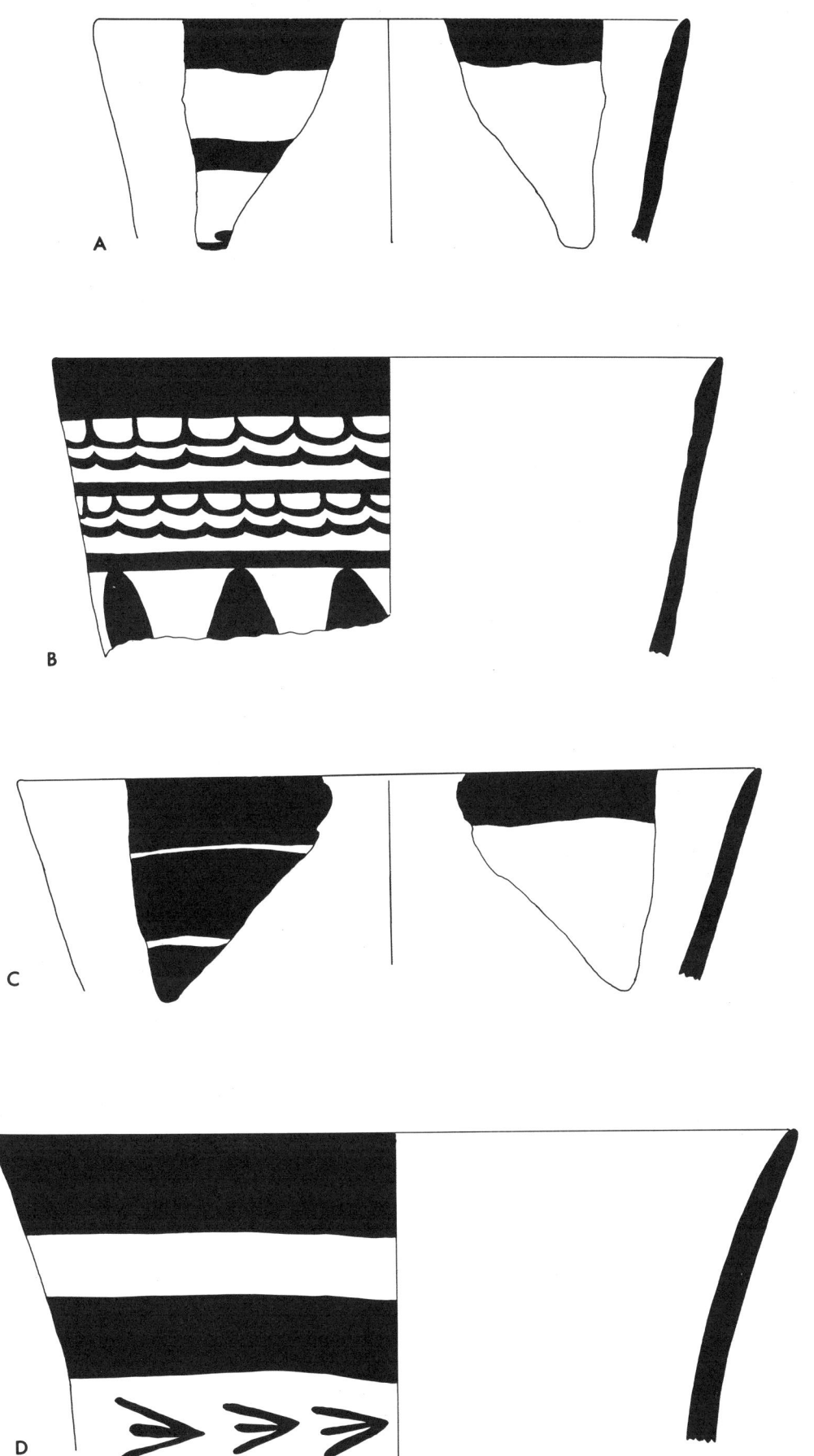

Period VIII Pottery From Area A: Ware Group I Bowls (*cont.*). Scale 2:5.

Plate 4. Period VIII Pottery From Area A: Ware Group I Bowls (*cont.*) and Jars. Scale 2:5.

|   | MRN | CONTEXT | FCN | WARE | FORM | TYPE | DECO. | WARE/REMARKS |
|---|---|---|---|---|---|---|---|---|
| A | 12516 | A08-14-070 | 714 | 32 | 930 | Bowl 4a | 946 | Dense, small-sized grits; greenish-buff clay, dark brown paint. |
| B | 11568 | A07-1971/81-089 | 855 | 38 | 1572 | Bowl 4a | 966 | Dense, small-sized white grits; buff clay, dark brown paint; out of context in Period VI deposits. |
| C | 5694 | A09-0462/72-011 | 142 | 32 | 930 | Bowl 4a | 987 | Dense, no visible tempering; light greenish-buff clay, dark brown paint; out of context in mixed period deposits. |
| D | 11876 | A08-1110/20/30-056 | 552 | 38 | 1471 | Bowl 4c | 906 | Very dense, occasional scattered small-sized white grits; pinkish clay; cream slip on surfaces; reddish paint. |
| E | 11708 | A07-1972/82-095 | 910 | 32 | 1453 | Bowl 4b | 900 | Dense, small-sized grits; greenish clay, somewhat overfired and warped; air bubble on interior body surface; olive green paint. |
| F | 12532 | A08-13-069 | 730 | 38 | 1569 | Jar 1 | 988 | Dense, small-sized grits; brownish-buff clay, somewhat warped; dark brown paint. |
| G | 12480 | A07-24-104 | 1006 | 38 | 1569 | Jar 1 | 943 | Gritty, small- and medium-sized grits; brownish-buff clay, cream slip on surface; brown paint. |
| H | 12242 | A08-13-077 | 777 | 38 | 1546 | Jar 1 | 957 | Dense, occasional small grits; buff clay, orangish paint. |
| I | 12242 | A08-13-077 | 777 | 38 | 1547 | Lid 1 | 958 | Dense, occasional small- and medium-sized gray and white grits; brownish-buff clay, orangish paint. |
| J | 11607 | A07-19-094 | 893 | 46 | 1086 | Jar 2a | — | Dense, small-sized black grits; brownish-buff clay; out of context in Period VI deposits. |
| K | 7638 | A07-10-050 | 383 | 38 | 1086 | Jar 2a | 925 | Dense, no visible tempering; pinkish clay, reddish-brown paint; out of context in Period IV deposits. |

PLATE 4

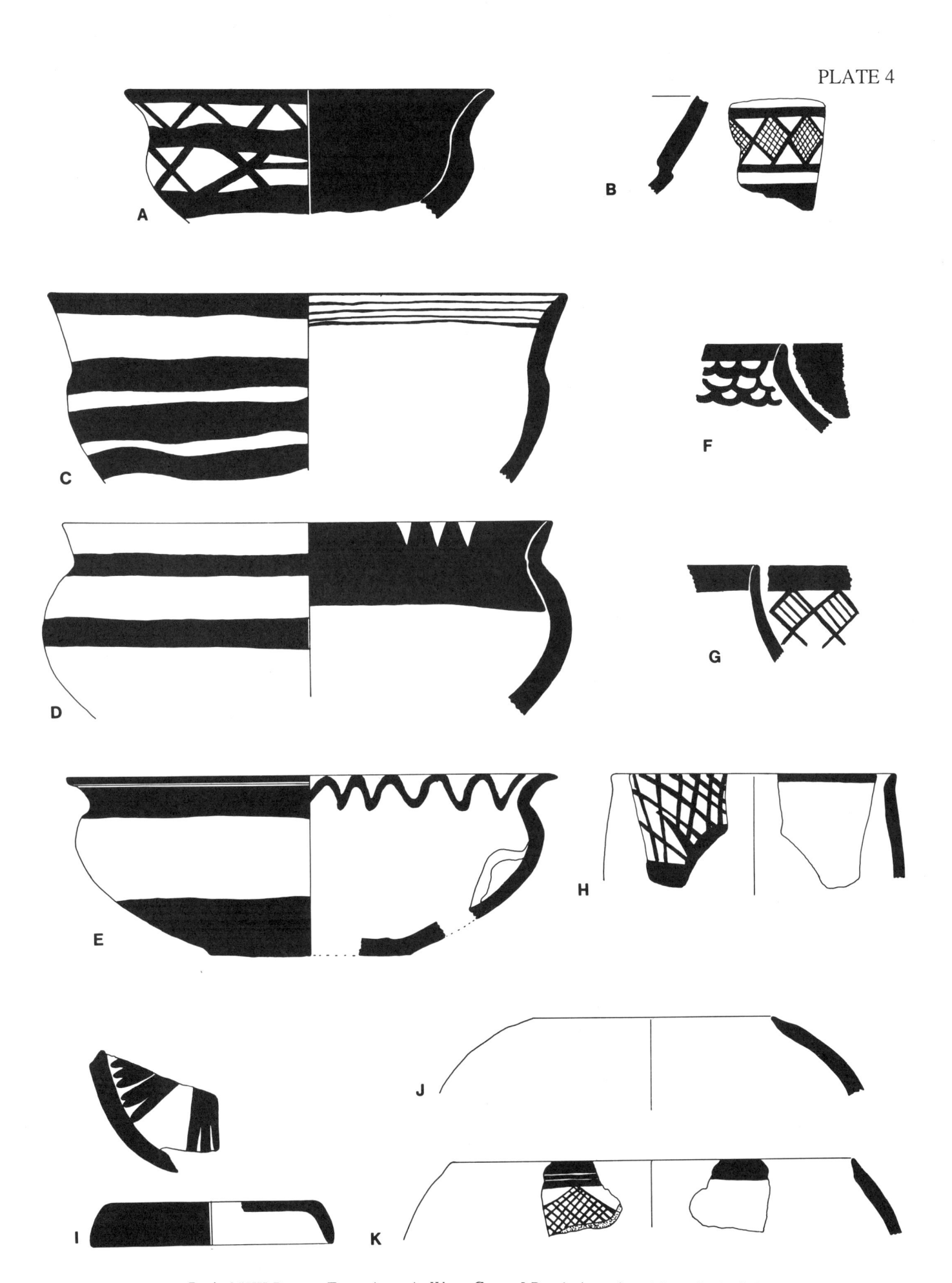

Period VIII Pottery From Area A: Ware Group I Bowls (*cont.*) and Jars. Scale 2:5.

Plate 5. Period VIII Pottery From Area A: Ware Group I Jars (*cont.*). Scale 2:5.

|   | MRN | CONTEXT | FCN | WARE | FORM | TYPE | DECO. | WARE/REMARKS |
|---|---|---|---|---|---|---|---|---|
| A | 12442 | A07-22-101 | 968 | 38 | 1491 | Jar 3a | (?) | Dense, no visible tempering; grayish clay, brownish-buff slip on exterior surface; dark brown paint. |
| B | 12957 | A07-2472/82-119 | 1136 | 38 | 1654 | Jar 3b | 976 | Dense, no visible tempering other than a few scattered white grits; reddish clay; dark brown paint. |
| C | 11739 | A08-0511-051 | 499 | 38 | 1462 | Unass. Jar | 918 | Very dense, no visible tempering; buff clay with grayish oxidized core; dark brown paint. |
| D | 12389 | A08-12-067 | 645 | 38 | 1479 | Jar 4 | 906 | Dense, small white grits; brown clay with gray core; cream slip on exterior surface, brown paint. |
| E | 12413 | A08-14-067 | 667 | 32 | 1479 | Jar 4 | 933 | Dense, small grits; greenish clay, brown paint. |
| F | 12622 | A07-2471/72-112 | 1094 | 32 | 1568 | Jar 5 | 961 | Dense, small grits, some white; greenish clay, dark brown paint. |
| G | 6702 | A09-0870/80-016 | 234 | 32 | 1568 | Jar 5 | 989 | Dense, somewhat overfired; scattered white grits visible; grayish clay, dark brown paint; out of context in Period VI deposits. |
| H | 12434 | A07-21-101 | 960 | 38 | 1488 | Jar 6a | 990 | Dense, scattered white grits; brown clay, dark brown paint. |
| I | 12506 | A08-14-069 | 704 | 38 | 1495 | Jar 6b | 949 | Dense, scattered white grits; brownish-buff clay, cream slip on surfaces; dark brown paint. |
| J | 12304 | A08-1142/32-060 | 580 | 32 | 1495 | Jar 6b | 991 | Dense, no visible tempering; pale greenish buff clay, brown paint. |
| K | 12332 | A09-07-018 | 249 | 32 | 1474 | Jar 7 | 992 | Dense, scattered small red and white grits; greenish-buff clay, dark brown paint; out of context in mixed deposit of Periods VI or VIII. |
| L | — | Area A, Provenience lost | — | 32 | 1081 | Jar 8a | (?) | Dense, grit tempered, greenish-buff clay. |
| M | 12459 | A07-24-102 | 985 | 32 | 1486 | Jar 8b | (?) | Dense, scattered small- and medium-sized white grits; greenish-buff clay, dark brown paint. |
| N | 12438 | A07-21-101 | D964 | 38 | 1486 | Jar 8b | 902 | Dense, no visible tempering other than a few scattered white grits; orange-buff clay; dark brown paint. |
| O | 12532 | A08-13-069 | 730 | 32 | 1486 | Jar 8b | 907 | Dense, small grits; greenish-buff clay, dark brown paint. |

PLATE 5

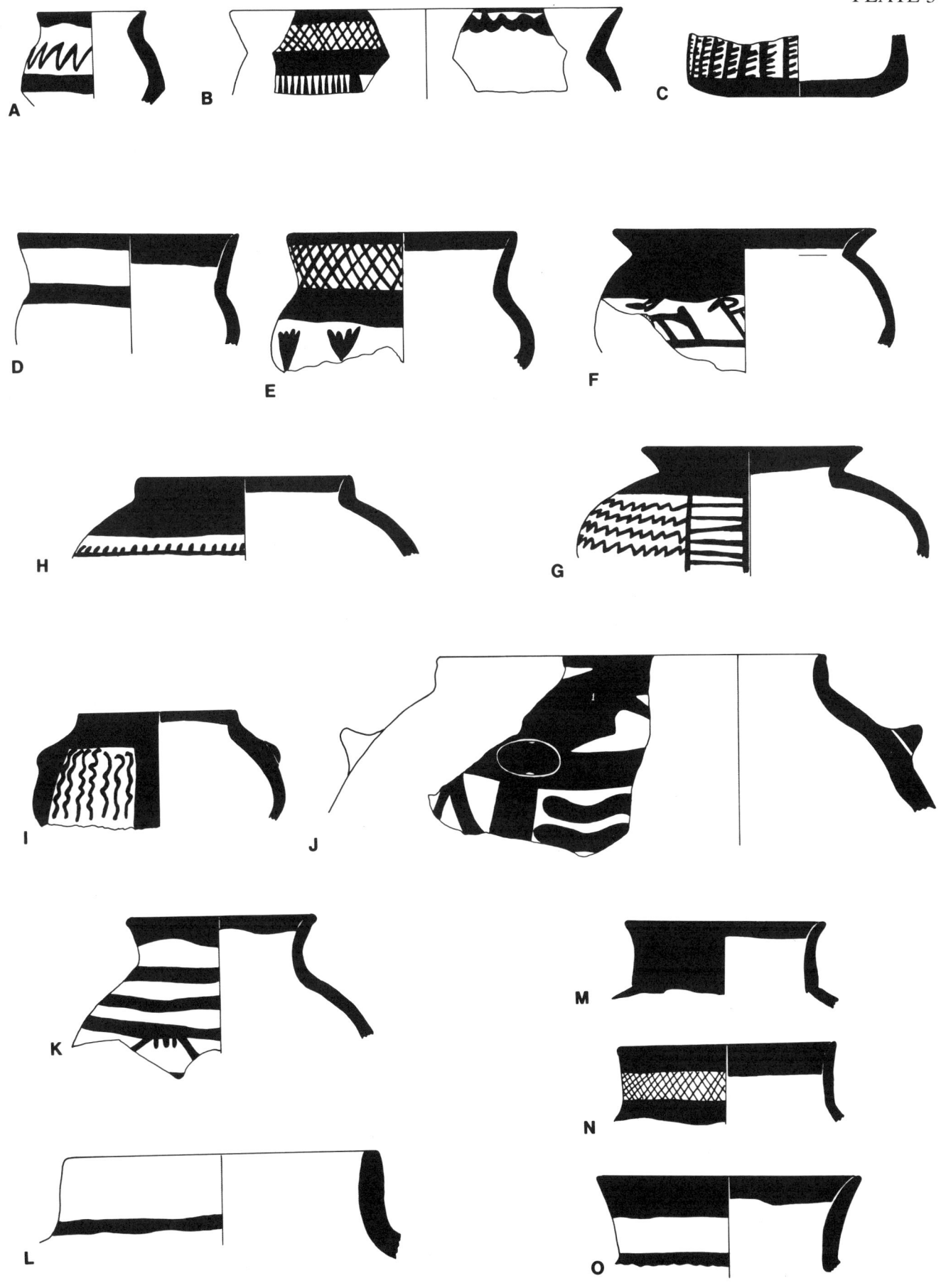

Period VIII Pottery From Area A: Ware Group I Jars (*cont.*). Scale 2:5.

Plate 6. Period VIII Pottery From Areas A and C01: Ware Group I Jars (*cont.*). Scale 2:5.

|   | MRN | CONTEXT | FCN | WARE | FORM | TYPE | DECO. | WARE/REMARKS |
|---|---|---|---|---|---|---|---|---|
| A | 2754 | A07-05-012 | 120 | 38 | 1533 | Jar 8c | 993 | Dense, no visible tempering; pinkish-buff clay, cream slip on exterior; dark brown paint; out of context in Period IV deposits. |
| B | 12488 | A08-12-069 | 686 | 38 | 1533 | Jar 8c | 940 | Dense, no visible tempering; brown clay, dark brown paint. |
| C | 11753 | A07-1970/80/90-095 | 928 | 38 | 1533 | Jar 8c | 903 | Dense, small-sized brown and red grits; brownish-buff clay; brownish-buff slip on exterior surface; dark brown paint. |
| D | 11739 | A08-0511-051 | 499 | 38 | 1533 | Jar 8c | 916 | Dense, small grits; pinkish-buff clay; reddish-brown paint. |
| E | 11769 | A08-10-053 | 518 | 32 | 1533 | Jar 8c | (?) | Dense, no visible tempering; greenish clay; dark brown paint. |
| F | 12571 | A07-2492-105 | 1020 | 38 | 1461 | Jar 8c | 973 | Dense, no visible tempering; brownish-buff clay; dark brown paint. |
| G | 11739 | A08-0511-051 | 499 | 38 | 1461 | Jar 8c | 912 | Dense, no visible tempering; brownish-buff clay; dark brown paint. |
| H | 12459 | A07-24-102 | 985 | 38 | 1461 | Jar 8c | 935 | Dense, small-sized grits. Brownish-buff clay, reddish-brown paint. |
| I | 12434 | A07-21-102 | 960 | 38 | 1461 | Jar 8c | 905 | Dense, small grits; pinkish-buff clay, reddish paint. |
| J | 13641 | C01-0937/39-198 | D3177 | 32 | 1535 | Jar 9 | 951 | Dense, no visible tempering; greenish-buff clay, brown paint; out of context in Period VB deposits. |
| K | 12365 | A08-1101-066 | 630 | 38 | 1461 | Jar 8c | 931 | Dense, no visible tempering; greenish-buff clay; brown paint. |
| L | 12488 | A08-12-069 | 686 | 38 | 1533 | Jar 8c | 939 | Dense, small black and gray grits; brownish-buff clay; brown paint. |

PLATE 6

Period VIII Pottery From Areas A and C01: Ware Group I Jars (*cont.*). Scale 2:5.

Plate 7. Period VIII Pottery From Area A: Ware Group I Decorated Bodies. Scale 2:5.

|   | MRN | CONTEXT | FCN | WARE | FORM | TYPE | DECO. | WARE/REMARKS |
|---|---|---|---|---|---|---|---|---|
| A | 12434 | A07-21-101 | 960 | 38 | — | — | 938 | Dense, no visible tempering other than a few scattered gray grits; light brownish-buff clay; orangish paint. |
| B | 11667 | A07-2091-095 | 888 | 38 | — | — | 994 | Dense, no visible tempering other than a few scattered black grits; light brownish-buff clay; reddish paint. |
| C | 12459 | A07-24-102 | 985 | 38 | — | — | 936 | Dense, small grits; grayish-buff clay, cream slip on exterior surface; reddish paint. |
| D | 11739 | A08-0511-051 | 499 | 38 | — | — | 915 | Dense, no visible tempering; gray clay grading to orange towards surfaces; dark brown paint; out of context in Period VI deposits. |
| E | 11753 | A07-1970/80/90-095 | 928 | 32 | — | — | 904 | Dense, no visible tempering; greenish-buff clay; dark brown paint. |
| F | 11739 | A08-0511-051 | 499 | 32 | — | — | 917 | Dense, small white grits; greenish-buff clay; dark brown paint. |
| G | 11629 | A08-05-049 | 457 | 38 | — | — | 970 | Dense, small grits; brownish-buff clay, mottled orange; cream slip on exterior surface; dark brown paint. |
| H | 11708 | A07-1972/82-095 | 910 | 32 | — | — | 901 | Dense, small white grits; light brownish-buff clay; dark brown paint. |
| I | 11739 | A08-0511-051 | 499 | 38 | — | — | 914 | Dense, no visible tempering other than a few scattered red grits; light brownish buff clay; orangish paint; out of context in Period VI deposits. |
| J | 12532 | A08-13-069 | 730 | 38 | — | — | 963 | Dense, scattered small red grits; pinkish-buff clay, reddish paint. |
| K | 12242 | A08-13/14-077 | 777 | 51 | — | — | 960 | Porous, straw tempered ware; grayish clay, brownish-buff slip on surface; brown paint. |
| L | 12468 | A07-24-103 | 994 | 48 | — | — | 944 | Very dense, no visible tempering other than occasional medium-sized white grits; light brownish-buff clay; breaks in jagged edges. |
| M | 12468 + 12480 | A07-24-103 + A07-24-104 | 994 + 1006 | 38 | — | — | 942 | Dense, small white grits; brownish-buff clay, brownish-buff slip on exterior; dark brown paint. |

PLATE 7

Period VIII Pottery From Area A: Ware Group I Decorated Bodies. Scale 2:5.

Plate 8. Period VIII Pottery From Areas A and C01: Ware Group I Decorated Bodies (*cont.*). Scale 2:5.

| | MRN | CONTEXT | FCN | WARE | FORM | TYPE | DECO. | WARE/REMARKS |
|---|---|---|---|---|---|---|---|---|
| A | 11623 | A07-19/20-091 | 871 | 38 | — | — | 967 | Dense, small-sized white grits; light brownish-buff clay grading towards orange on interior; reddish paint; out of context in Period VI deposits. |
| B | 12459 | A07-24-102 | 985 | 32 | — | — | 937 | Dense, fairly gritty with small white grits predominant; greenish-buff clay; dark brown paint. |
| C | 11182 | A08-0502/12-044 | 387 | 38 | — | — | 969 | Dense, no visible tempering; brownish-buff clay, cream slip on surface; reddish-orange paint; out of context in Period VI deposits. |
| D | 11607 | A07-19-094 | 863 | 32 | — | — | 971 | Dense, small-sized grits; greenish-buff clay; cream slip on exterior surface, brown paint; out of context in Period VI deposits. |
| E | 11739 | A08-0511-051 | 499 | 38 | — | — | 913 | Dense, no visible tempering other than a few scattered small grits; grayish-buff clay; brown paint. |
| F | 11733 | A07-1971/81/91-095 | 919 | 32 | — | — | 909 | Dense, a few scattered small-sized white grits; greenish-buff clay; brown paint. |
| G | 12506 | A08-14-069 | 704 | 32 | — | — | 948 | Dense, small-sized white grits; greenish-buff clay; brown paint. |
| H | 6347 | C01-0189/79/69-122 | 1721 | 32 | — | — | 995 | Dense, small-sized grits; greenish-buff clay; brown paint; out of context in Period VI deposits. |
| I | 12361 | A08-11-065 | 626 | 32 | — | — | 928 | Dense, small-sized white grits; greenish-buff clay; dark brown paint. |
| J | 11028 | A07-17-076 | 628 | 38 | — | — | 968 | Dense, no visible tempering; light brownish-buff clay; dark brown paint; out of context in Period VI deposits. |
| K | 12468 | A07-24-103 | 994 | 38 | — | — | 945 | Dense, small-sized grits; light brownish-buff clay grading to orangish on surfaces; brownish-red paint. |
| L | 11733 | A07-1971/81/91-095 | 919 | 38 | — | — | 908 | Dense, small-sized grits; light brownish-buff clay; cream slip on surface; brown paint. |
| M | 12361 | A08-11-065 | 626 | 38 | — | — | 930 | Dense, small-sized grits; brownish-buff clay grading to orange on surfaces; cream slip; brown paint. |
| N | 12488 | A08-12-069 | 686 | 38 | — | — | 941 | Dense, small-sized grits; light brownish-buff clay; cream slip on surfaces; dark brown paint. |

PLATE 8

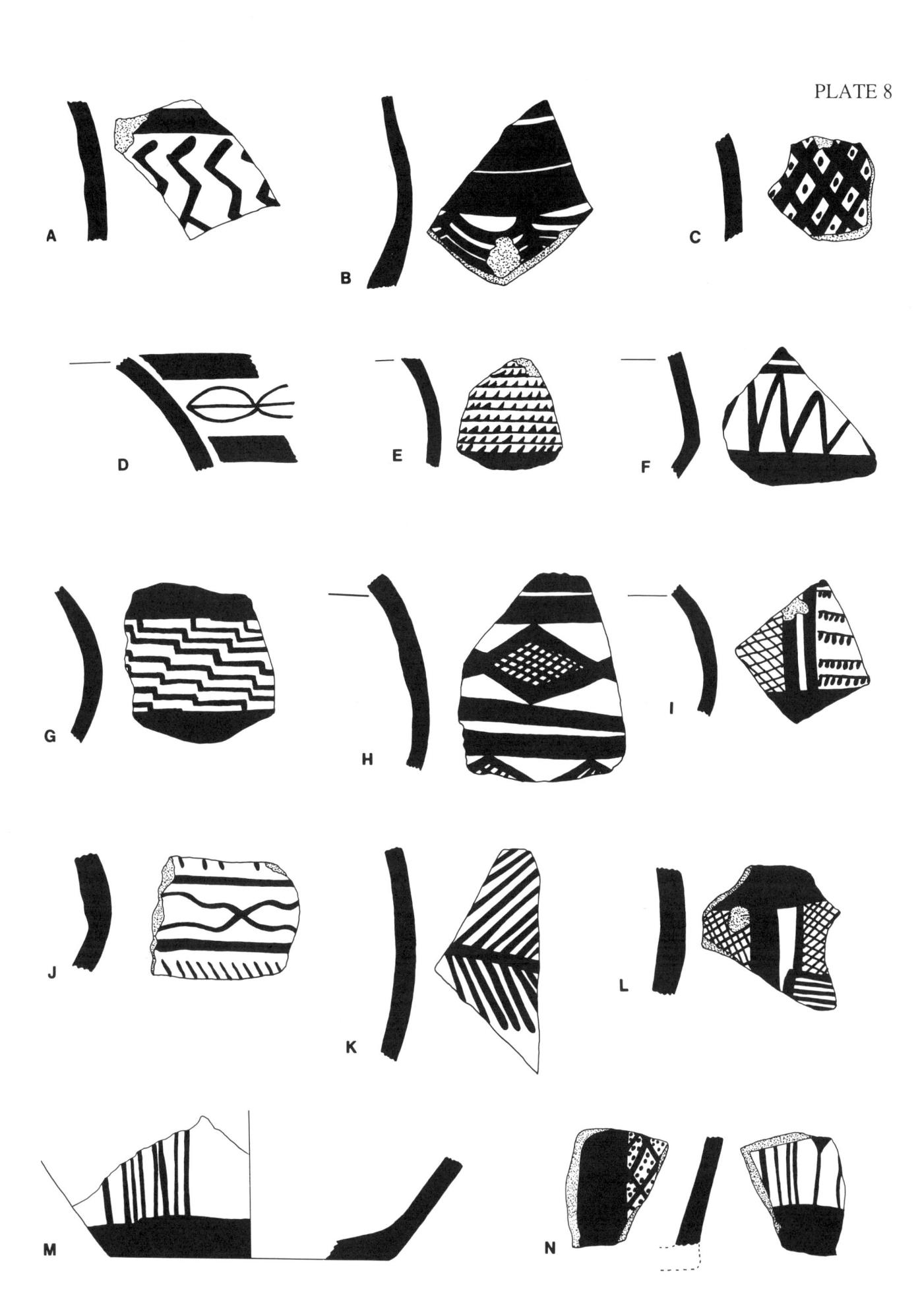

Period VIII Pottery From Areas A and C01: Ware Group I Decorated Bodies (*cont.*). Scale 2:5.

Plate 9. Period VIII Pottery From Area A: Ware Group II Bowls. Scale 2:5.

|   | MRN | CONTEXT | FCN | WARE | FORM | TYPE | DECO. | WARE/REMARKS |
|---|---|---|---|---|---|---|---|---|
| A | 12468 | A07-24-103 | 994 | 14 | 1472 | Bowl 5 | Bns. | Porous, straw-tempered ware; gray clay, surface mottled several shades of gray; irregularly burnished. |
| B | 12389 | A08-12-069 | 645 | 14 | 1472 | Bowl 5 | Bns. | Porous, straw-tempered ware; burnished. |
| C | 12242 | A08-13/14-077 | 774 | 14 | 1544 | Bowl 5 | Bns. | Porous, straw-tempered ware; reddish clay with gray core; exterior surface well burnished. |
| D | 12459 | A07-24-102 | 985 | 14 | 336 | Tray 1 | Bns. | Porous, straw-tempered ware; brown clay with gray core; exterior surface well burnished. |
| E | 11892 | A08-1141-058 | 568 | 14 | 1684 | Tray 2 | Bns. | Porous, straw-tempered ware; orange-brown clay with gray core; exterior surface orangish, mottled and slightly burnished; on interior, two regularly spaced ridges on bottom of tray; fire smudges on interior. |

PLATE 9

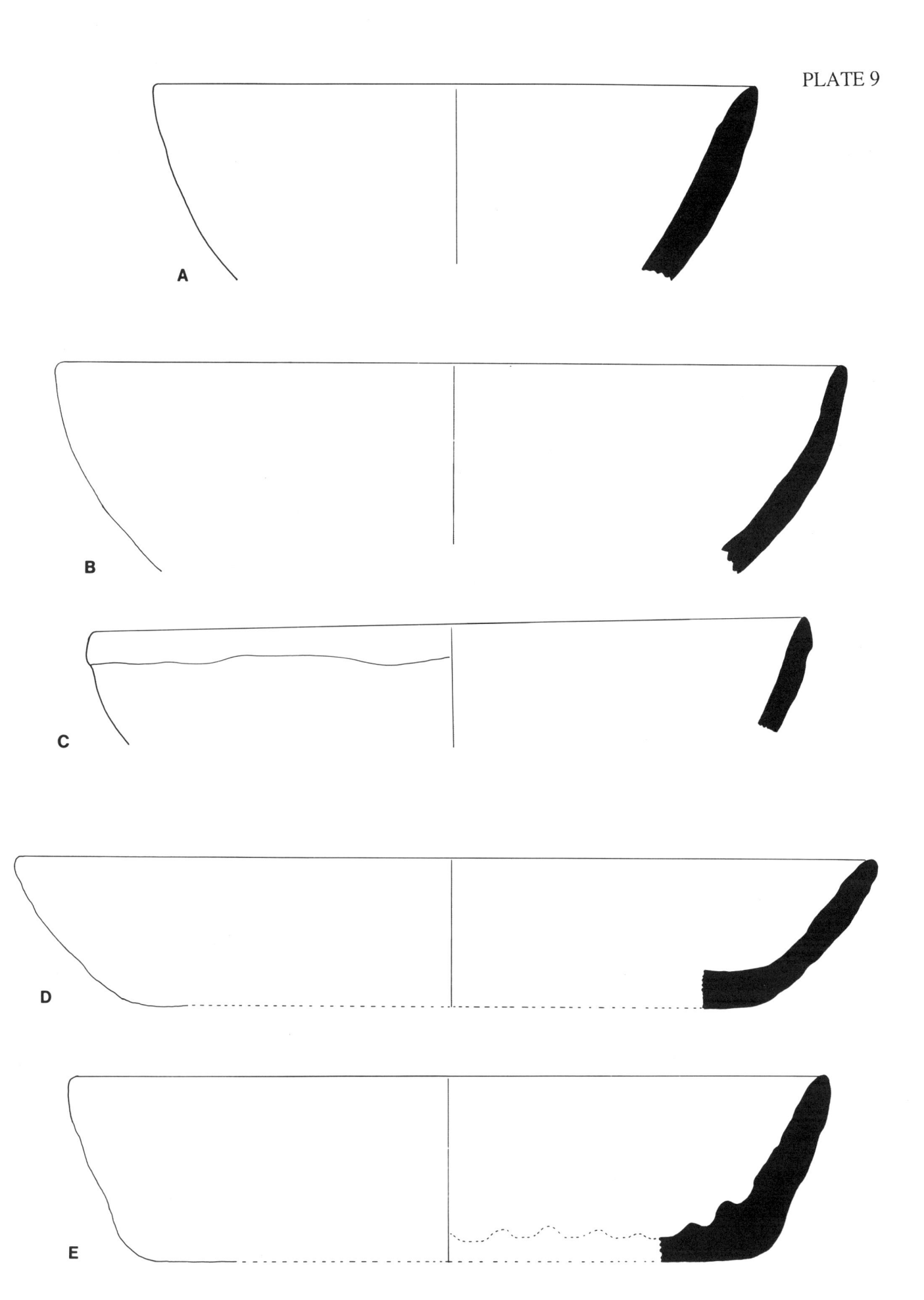

Period VIII Pottery From Area A: Ware Group II Bowls. Scale 2:5.

Plate 10. Period VIII Pottery From Area A: Ware Group II Bowls (*cont.*) and Holemouth Jars. Scale 2:5.

| | MRN | Context | FCN | Ware | Form | Type | Deco. | Ware/Remarks |
|---|---|---|---|---|---|---|---|---|
| A | 11795 | A08-0511-051 | 539 | 14 | 871 | Bowl 6 | Bns. | Porous, straw-tempered ware; brownish-orange clay with prominent gray core; surface well burnished. |
| B | 12234 | A07-2471-108 | 1062 | 14 | 871 | Bowl 6 | Bns. | Relatively dense, straw-tempered ware; small-sized chaff used as tempering; orangish-yellowish clay with prominent dark gray core; on interior surface, black smudges on bottom half of sherd; exterior orangish-yellowish, highly burnished. |
| C | 11733 | A07-1970/80/90-095 | 928 | 14 | 871 | Bowl 6 | Bns. | Porous, straw-tempered ware; brownish-buff clay grading towards grayish on exterior surface; exterior mottled grayish and brown, burnished. |
| D | 12213 | A07-2471-105 | 1048 | 13 | 1143 | Bowl 7 | — | Porous, straw-tempered ware; brownish-buff/orange clay with prominent gray core; faint traces of red wash on exterior surface. |
| E | 11667 | A07-2091-095 | 888 | 13 | C-48 | Lid 1 | — | Porous, straw-tempered ware; brownish clay with gray core; surface is brown mottled grayish. |
| F | 12393 | A08-12-068 | 649 | 14 | 1459 | Jar 10a | Bns. | Fairly dense straw-tempered ware; orange-brown clay with prominent gray core; surface is highly burnished. |
| G | 11753 | A07-1970/80/90-095 | 928 | 13 | 1459 | Jar 10a | — | Fairly dense straw-tempered ware; brownish clay, uniform throughout. |
| H | 11739 | A08-0511-051 | 499 | 14 | 1463 | Jar 10b | Bns. | Fairly dense straw-tempered ware; brownish clay with prominent dark gray core; surface is brown, well burnished. |
| I | 12622 | A07-2471/72-112 | 1094 | 14 | 1567 | Knob | Bns. | Porous, straw-tempered ware; gray clay with darker gray core; black smudges on interior; exterior is well burnished. |
| J | 11708 | A07-1972/82-095 | 910 | 13 | 1490 | Knob | — | Porous, straw-tempered ware; gray clay with darker gray core. |
| K | 12422 | A07-22-101 | 968 | 13 | 1490 | Knob | — | Porous, straw-tempered ware; orange-brownish clay with prominent gray core; occasional scattered white grits also visible. |
| L | 12340 | A09-1111-061 | 604 | 14 | 1476 | Unass. Jar | Bns. | Fairly dense straw-tempered ware; fine chaff tempering; brownish clay grading to orange on surfaces. |
| M | — | Area A, Provenance lost | — | 14 | 597 | Jar 2b | Bns. | Porous, straw-tempered ware; grayish clay grading to brown towards surfaces; darker gray core; exterior well burnished. |
| N | 12506 | A08-14-069 | 704 | 14 | 597 | Jar 2b | Bns. | Porous, straw-tempered ware; very prominent gray core, grades to brown towards surfaces; burnished. |

PLATE 10

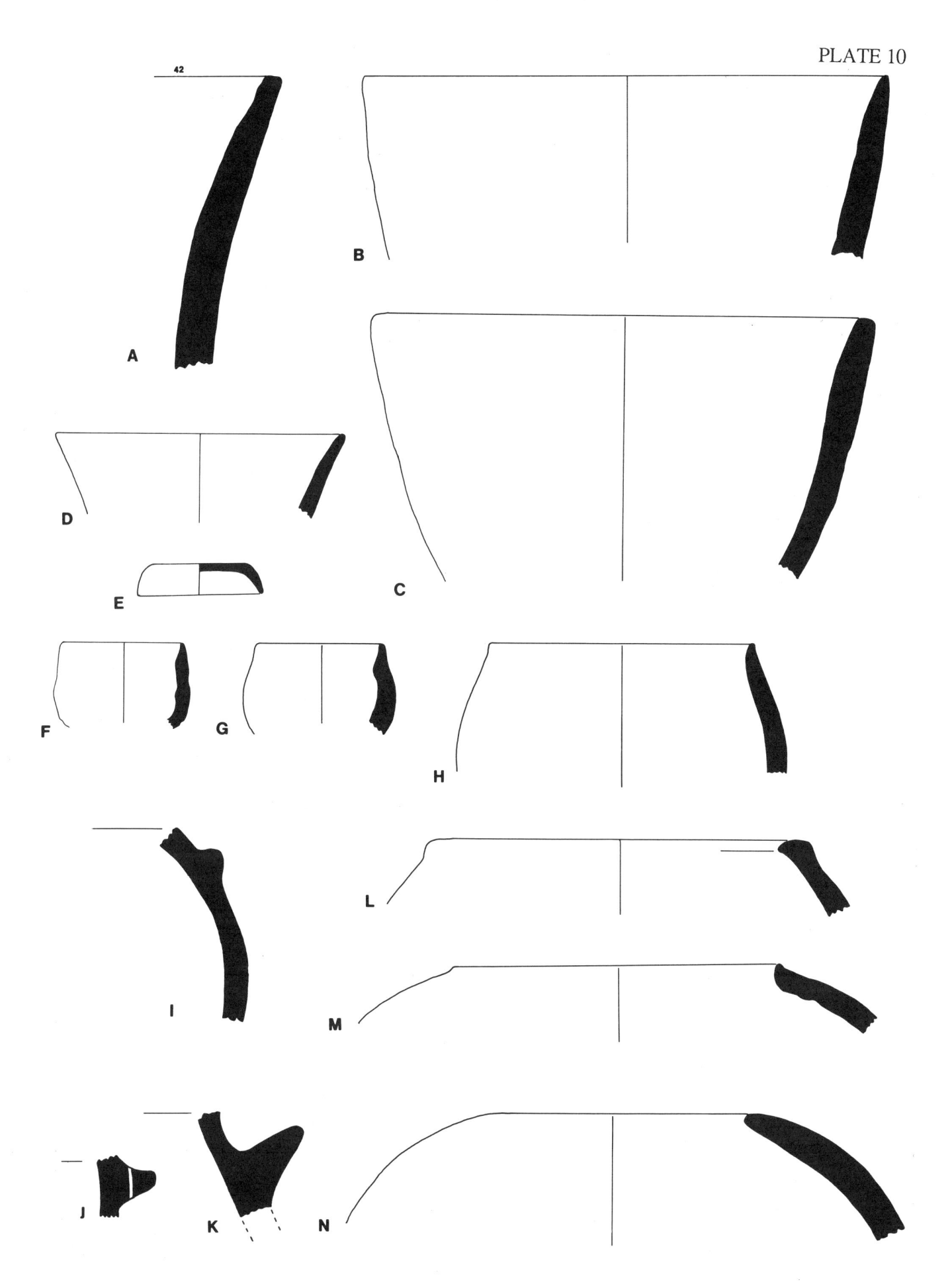

Period VIII Pottery From Area A: Ware Group II Bowls (*cont.*) and Holemouth Jars. Scale 2:5.

Plate 11. Period VIII Pottery From Area A: Ware Group II Jars. Scale 2:5.

|   | MRN | CONTEXT | FCN | WARE | FORM | TYPE | DECO. | WARE/REMARKS |
|---|---|---|---|---|---|---|---|---|
| A | 12459 | A07-24-102 | 985 | 14 | 1533 | Jar 8c | Bns. | Porous, straw-tempered ware; gray clay with darker gray core; exterior lightly burnished. |
| B | 11708 | A07-1972/82-095 | 910 | 13 | 1533 | Jar 8c | — | Porous, straw-tempered ware. |
| C | 12957 | A07-2472/82-119 | 1136 | 13 | 1081 | Jar 8a | — | Porous, straw-tempered ware; gray core grading to brownish-buff towards surface. |
| D | 12459 | A07-24-102 | 985 | 14 | 1480 | Jar 8a | Bns. | Porous, straw-tempered ware; gray clay with prominent darker gray core; both surfaces are burnished. |
| E | 11708 | A07-1972/82-095 | 910 | 14 | 1454 | Jar 11 | Bns. | Fairly dense straw-tempered ware; gray core grading to orange towards surfaces; well burnished. |
| F | 12242 | A08-13/14-077 | 777 | 14 | 1454 | Jar 11 | Bns. | Fairly dense straw-tempered ware; brown clay with light gray core; surface is brown, somewhat mottled, and well burnished. |
| G | 12468 | A07-24-103 | 994 | 14 | 1454 | Jar 11 | Bns. | Porous, straw-tempered ware; prominent gray-black core grading to brown on surfaces; exterior surface lightly burnished. |
| H | 7630 | A04-07-029 | 022 | 14 | 1268 | Jar 11 | Bns. | Porous, straw-tempered ware; orange clay with prominent gray core; surface is mottled orange and brown and burnished; out of context in Period IV deposits. |

PLATE 11

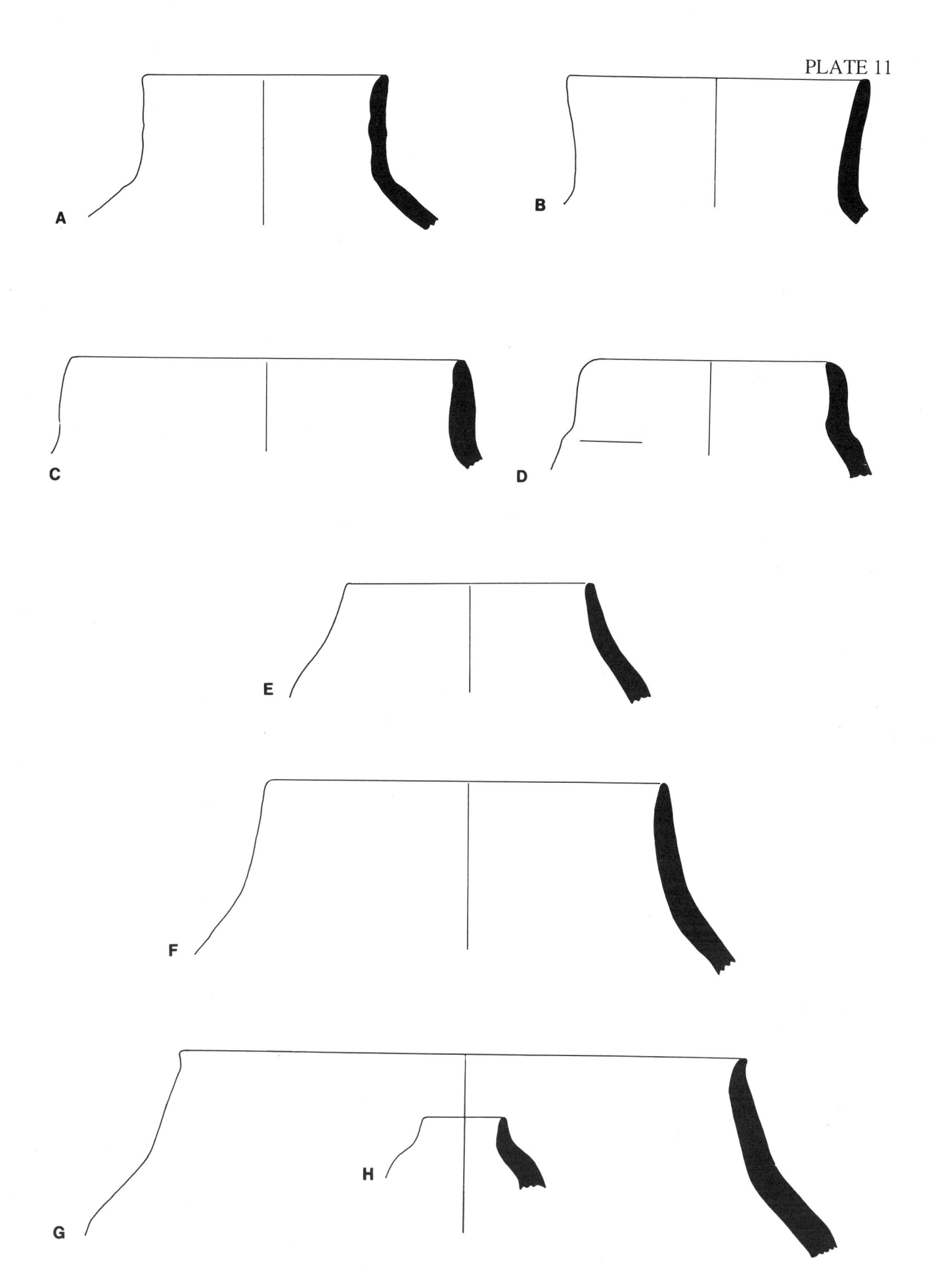

Period VIII Pottery From Area A: Ware Group II Jars. Scale 2:5.

Plate 12. Period VII Pottery From Area C01: Dark Faced Burnished Ware and Ware Group I Bowls. Scale 2:5.

|   | MRN | CONTEXT | FCN | WARE | FORM | TYPE | DECO. | WARE/REMARKS |
|---|---|---|---|---|---|---|---|---|
| A | 7056 | C01-0179-128 | 1897 | 41 | 1138 | Unass. Bowl | 218 | Dense, very fine chaff tempering; brownish-grayish clay grading to gray on surface; well burnished; crosshatched incisions on exterior. |
| B | 6835 | C01-0168/78-130 | 1936 | 41 | 1148 | Unass. Bowl | Bns. | Dense very fine chaff-tempering; gray clay; surface is dark gray, well burnished with close vertical strokes. |
| C | 7043 | C01-0167/77-130 | 1918 | 41 | 1239 | Jar 1 | Bns. | Dense, very fine chaff tempering; occasional scattered white grits also; gray clay surface is burnished. |
| D | 6832 | C01-0168/78-131 | 1939 | 31 | C-25 | Bowl 1 | 210 | Dense vegetal-tempered ware; some air pockets and occasional small-sized grits; orange clay with brown core; reddish paint. |
| E | 6587 | C01-0168/78-126 | 1830 | 31 | 1071 | Bowl 2 | 206 | Dense, vegetal-tempered ware; small-sized grits also used as tempering; greenish-buff clay with olive green paint. |
| F | 6713 | C01-0167/79-127 | 1856 | 31 | 1075 | Bowl 2 | 204 | Dense, vegetal-tempered ware; some grits also; greenish-buff clay; dark brown paint. |
| G | 6835 | C01-0168/78-130 | 1936 | 31 | 1148 | Unass. Bowl | 204 | Dense, vegetal-tempered ware; brownish-buff clay with gray core; brown paint. |
| H | 6543 | C01-0188-128 | 1784 | 31 | 1136 | Bowl 3 | 207 | Dense, vegetal-tempered ware; some grits also; brownish-buff/gray clay; dark brown paint. |
| I | 6713 | C01-0167/77-127 | 1856 | 31 | 1136 | Bowl 3 | 201 | Dense, vegetal-tempered ware; gray core grading to orange on surfaces; red paint. |
| J | 6719 | C01-0168/78-127 | 1864 | 13 | 1136 | Bowl 3 | 228 | Porous, straw-tempered ware; brown clay with gray core; brown paint. |
| K | 7043 | C01-0167/77-130 | 1918 | 31 | 1136 | Bowl 3 | 204 | Dense, vegetal-tempered ware; brownish-buff clay with gray core; light brownish-buff slip on surface; brown paint. |
| L | 6586 | C01-0187/88-131 | 1807 | 31 | 1088 | Bowl 4 | 205 | Dense, vegetal-tempered ware; some small-sized grits also; greenish-buff clay; brown paint. |
| M | 6718 | C01-0189-128 | 1875 | 31 | 1541 | Bowl 4 | 224 | Dense, vegetal-tempered ware; some small-sized white grits also; greenish-buff clay; brown paint. |
| N | 6715 | C01-0178-128 | 1883 | 31 | 1541 | Bowl 4 | 204 | Dense, vegetal-tempered ware; brownish-buff clay; brown paint. |
| O | 6718 | C01-0189-128 | 1875 | 31 | 1542 | Unass. Bowl | Abraded | Dense, vegetal-tempered ware; brown clay; traces of painted decoration on interior and exterior. |
| P | 3894 | C01-0187/88-095 | 1263 | 31 | 1136 | Bowl 3 | 204 | Dense, vegetal-tempered ware; a few small-sized grits also; orange clay with scattered air pockets; reddish-brown clay. |
| Q | 6831 | C01-0169/79/89-130/131 | 1946 | 31 | 1136 | Bowl 3 | 229 | Dense, vegetal-tempered ware; orange clay; reddish paint. |
| R | 7043 | C01-0167/77-130 | 1918 | 31 | 1136 | Bowl 3 | 209 | Dense, vegetal-tempered ware; small-sized grits also; greenish-buff clay with gray core; olive green paint. |
| S | 6715 | C01-0178-128 | 1883 | 31 | 1538 | Unass. Bowl | — | Dense, vegetal-tempered ware; brownish-buff clay; on exterior surface faint traces of painted decoration; eroded. |

PLATE 12

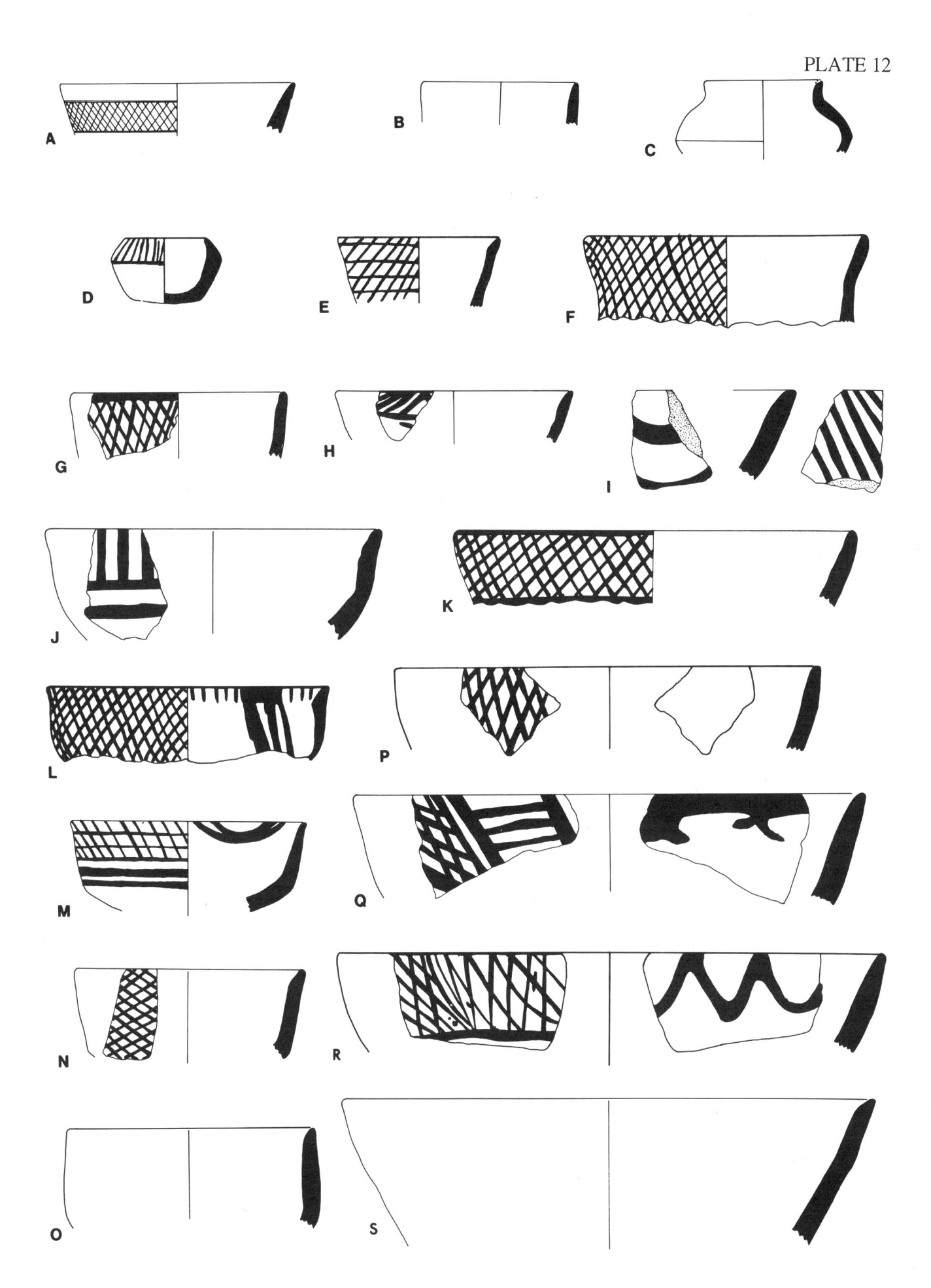

Period VII Pottery From Area C01: Dark Faced Burnished Ware and Ware Group I Bowls. Scale 2:5.

Plate 13. Period VII Pottery From Area C01: Ware Group I Open Forms, Holemouth Jars, and Decorated Bodies. Scale 2:5.

|   | MRN | CONTEXT | FCN | WARE | FORM | TYPE | DECO. | WARE/REMARKS |
|---|-----|---------|-----|------|------|------|-------|--------------|
| A | 7071 | C01-0167/69-128 | 1910 | 31 | 871 | Bowl 5 | 227 | Dense, vegetal-tempered ware; a few small-sized grits also; brownish-grayish clay with gray core; dark brown paint. |
| B | 7044 | C01-0167/77-127 | 1856 | 31 | 1546 | Jar 2 | 208 | Dense, vegetal-tempered ware; a few scattered small grits also; greenish-buff clay; brown paint. |
| C | 3945 | C01-0187/88-096 | 1273 | 31 | 1454 | Jar 3 | 204 | Dense, vegetal-tempered ware. |
| D | 6832 | C01-0168/78-131 | 1939 | 31 | — | — | 220 | Dense, vegetal-tempered ware; a few scattered white grits also; orange/brownish-buff clay with prominent gray core; red paint. |
| E | 3945 | C01-0187/88-096 | 1273 | 31 | — | — | 230 | Dense, vegetal-tempered ware; a few white grits also; grayish clay; brown paint. |
| F | 6551 | C01-0188-128 | 1780 | 32 | — | — | 202 | Somewhat porous gritty ware; small-sized black grits very prominent; greenish-buff clay; brown paint. |
| G | 6258 | C01-0957/59-049/059-060 | 1719 | 31 | 992 | Jar 4a | 226 | Dense, vegetal-tempered ware; brownish-buff clay with gray core; brown paint; out of context in Period IVB deposits. |
| H | 6587 | C01-0188/78-126 | 1830 | 31 | 992 | Jar 4a | 211 | Dense, vegetal-tempered ware; brown clay, brown slip on exterior surface; dark brown paint. |
| I | 3945 | C01-0189/88-096 | 1273 | 31 | 992 | Jar 4a | (?) | Somewhat porous vegetal-tempered ware; chaff imprints clearly visible; orange-buff clay with gray core; dark brown paint. |
| J | 6717 | C01-0189-128 | D1879 | 31 | 992 | Jar 4a | 231 | Dense, vegetal-tempered ware; dark brown clay with lighter brown core; brown paint. |
| K | 6547 | C01-0188-130 | 1795 | 31 | 992 | Jar 4a | (?) | Dense, vegetal-tempered ware; small-sized grits also visible. |
| L | 6551 | C01-0188-128 | 1780 | 31 | 1086 | Jar 5a | 213 | Dense, vegetal-tempered ware; some very small-sized grits also; reddish-buff clay with buff slip on exterior surface; brown paint. |

PLATE 13

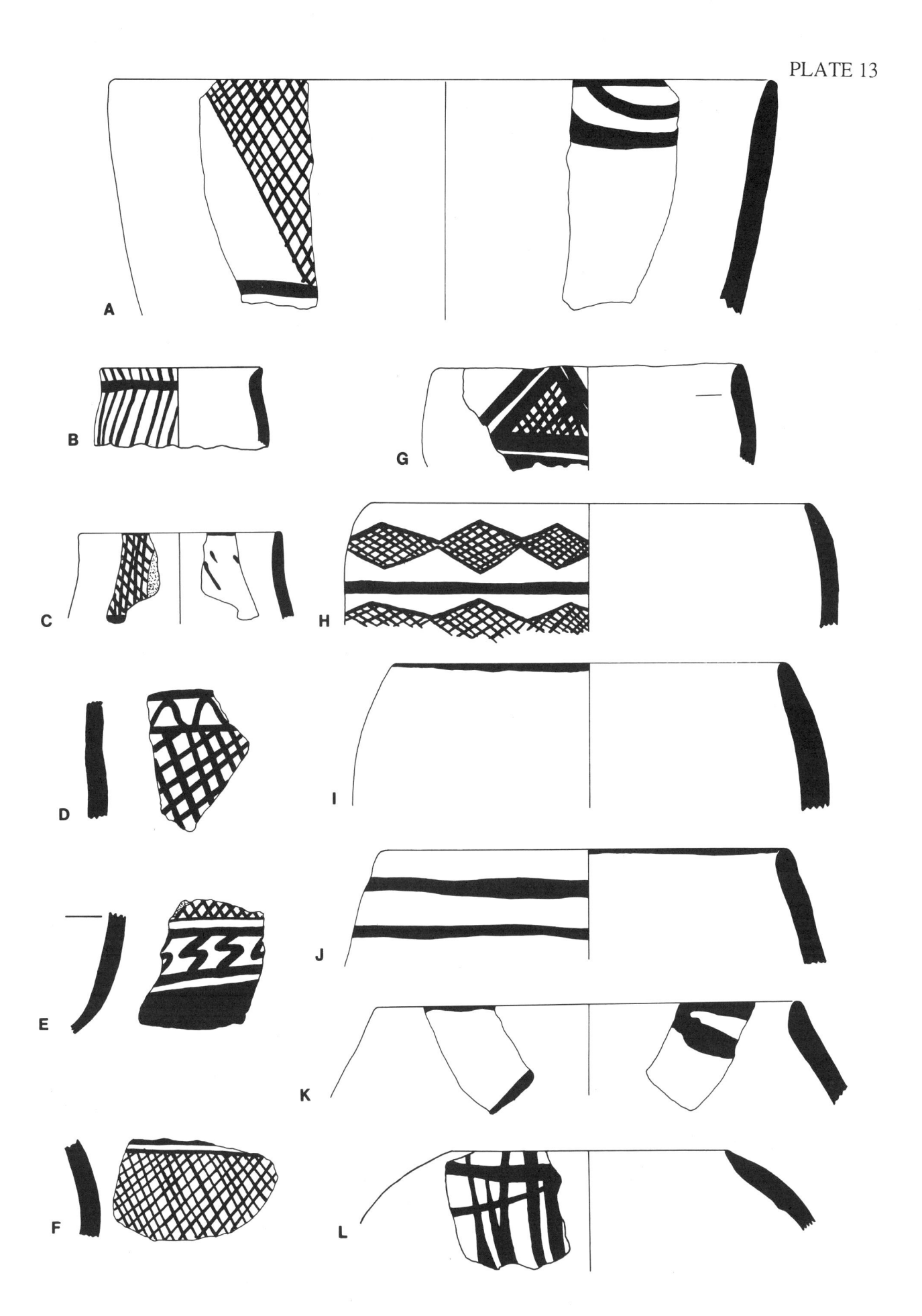

Period VII Pottery From Area C01: Ware Group I Open Forms, Holemouth Jars, and Decorated Bodies. Scale 2:5.

Plate 14. Period VII Pottery From Area C01: Ware Group I Jars and Ware Group II Bowls. Scale 2:5.

|   | MRN | CONTEXT | FCN | WARE | FORM | TYPE | DECO. | WARE/REMARKS |
|---|---|---|---|---|---|---|---|---|
| A | 3945 | C01-0187/88-096 | 1273 | 31 | 801 | Jar 6 | 212 | Dense, vegetal-tempered ware; reddish-brown paint. |
| B | 7043 | C01-0167/77-130 | 1918 | 31 | 1533 | Jar 7a | 214 | Dense, vegetal-tempered ware; some occasional small-sized grits also; brown paint. |
| C | 6266 | C01-0168/78/88-122 | 1690 | 31 | 973 | Jar 8 | 216 | Dense, vegetal-tempered ware; some occasional small-sized white grits also; greenish-buff clay; dark brown paint; out of context in Period VI deposits. |
| D | 6831 | C01-0169/79/89-130/131 | 1946 | 31 | 1533 | Jar 7a | 215 | Dense, vegetal-tempered ware; brownish-buff clay; dark brown clay. |
| E | 6551 | C01-0188-128 | 1780 | 13 | 1081 | Jar 7b | (?) | Porous, straw-tempered ware; brownish-buff clay; design is mostly abraded, may have been more elaborate than represented in the drawing; dark brown paint. |
| F | 6982 | C01-0167/77-128 | 1871 | 13 | C-44 | Bowl 6a | — | Unusually dense, straw-tempered ware; orange-brown clay with prominent gray core; (= KH 1981/112). |
| G | 7068 | C01-0167/77-131 | 1925 | 14 | C-31 | Bowl 6a | Bns. | Porous, straw-tempered ware; dark brown clay grading to lighter brown on surfaces; lightly burnished. |
| H | 3945 | C01-0187/88-096 | 1273 | 13 | 993 | Bowl 6b | — | Porous, straw-tempered ware; orange-brown clay; gray core; exterior mottled orange and brown. |
| I | 6593 | C01-0169/79/89-126 | 1819 | 13 | 1661 | Bowl 7a | — | Porous, straw-tempered ware; brownish-grayish clay with darker gray core; on exterior surface, black fire smudges. |
| J | 7046 | C01-0167/77-130 | 1931 | 13 | 1661 | Bowl 7a | — | Porous, straw-tempered ware; brown clay with gray core prominent; cream slip/wash on exterior surface. |
| K | 6713 | C01-0167/77-127 | 1856 | 13 | 1472 | Bowl 7b | — | Porous, straw-tempered ware; brown clay; gray core prominent. |
| L | 6713 | C01-0167/77-127 | 1856 | 13 | 1472 | Bowl 7b | — | Porous, straw-tempered ware; brown clay; gray core prominent. |

PLATE 14

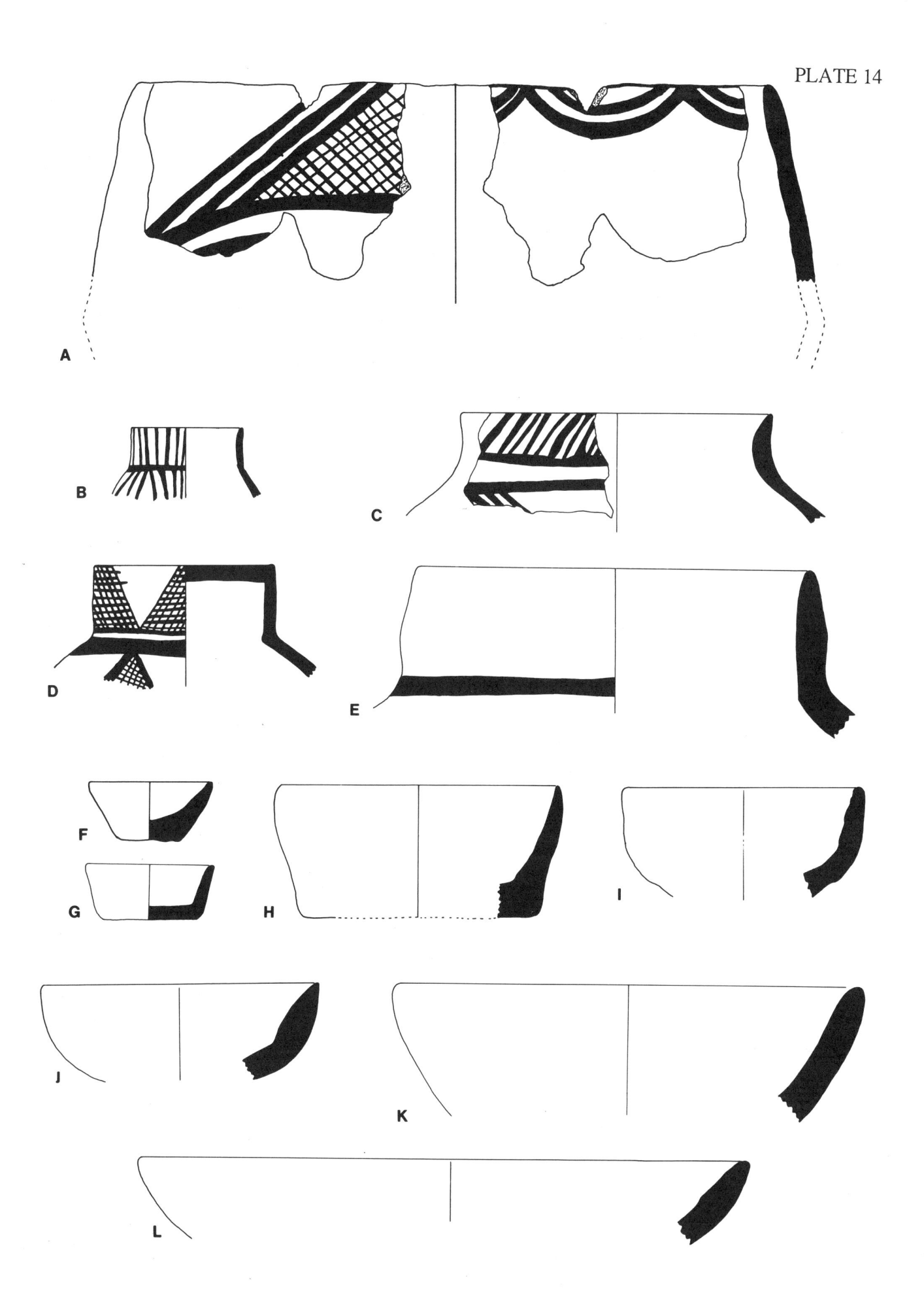

Period VII Pottery From Area C01: Ware Group I Jars and Ware Group II Bowls. Scale 2:5.

Plate 15. Period VII Pottery From Area C01: Ware Group II Bowls (*cont.*) and Jars. Scale 2:5.

|   | MRN | CONTEXT | FCN | WARE | FORM | TYPE | DECO. | WARE/REMARKS |
|---|---|---|---|---|---|---|---|---|
| A | 6831 | C01-0169/79/89-130/131 | 1946 | 13 | 1084 | Tray 1 | — | Coarse, straw-tempered ware; brownish-buff clay. |
| B | 6720 | C01-0167/77-129 | 1872 | 13 | 336 | Tray 1 | — | Coarse, straw-tempered ware. |
| C | 6717 | C01-0189-128 | D1879 | 13 | 1143 | Bowl 8 | — | Fairly dense straw-tempered ware; brownish-orange clay grading to gray on surfaces. |
| D | 6547 | C01-0188-130 | 1795 | 13 | 1143 | Bowl 8 | — | Porous, straw-tempered ware; orange clay with lighter orange core; exterior surface smoothed. |
| E | 7055 | C01-0177-128 | 1897 | 13 | 1143 | Bowl 8 | — | Fairly dense straw-tempered ware; brownish-buff clay; gray core; interior surface is brownish and exterior is grayish; smoothed. |
| F | 6714 | C01-0169/79/89-127 | 1853 | 14 | 871 | Bowl 5 | Bns. | Porous, straw-tempered ware; orange-brown clay; dark gray core; surface is lightly burnished. |
| G | 7053 | C01-0177-128 | D1906 | 14 | 871 | Bowl 5 | Bns. | Somewhat porous straw-tempered ware; gray core; surfaces are mottled grayish; well burnished. |
| H | 6832 | C01-0168/78-131 | 1939 | 14 | 1454 | Jar 3 | Bns. | Porous, straw-tempered ware; burnished. |
| I | 6551 | C01-0188-128 | 1780 | 13 | 973 | Jar 8 | — | Porous, straw-tempered ware; orange clay, very slight gray core; exterior surface smoothed. |
| J | 7043 | C01-0167/77-130 | 1918 | 14 | 1081 | Jar 7b | Lt. Bns. | Porous, straw-tempered ware; brownish-buff clay with prominent gray core; exterior mottled brown and gray; lightly burnished. |
| K | 6835 | C01-0168/78-130 | D1936 | 13 | 1461 | Jar 7a | — | Fairly dense, straw-tempered ware; brownish-gray clay; surface smoothed. |
| L | 6031 | C01-0169/79/89-130/131 | 1946 | 31 | 1533 | Jar 7a | — | Dense, grit and chaff-tempered ware; very finely-chopped chaff visible; no grits visible to the naked eye; orange clay. |
| M | 6547 | C01-0188-130 | 1795 | 14 | 1533 | Jar 7a | Bns. | Porous, straw-tempered ware; gray core grading to orange on surface; exterior is lightly burnished. |
| N | 7043 | C01-0167/77-130 | 1918 | 13 | 1533 | Jar 7a | — | Porous, straw-tempered ware; brownish-buff clay with gray core; exterior surface is smoothed. |

PLATE 15

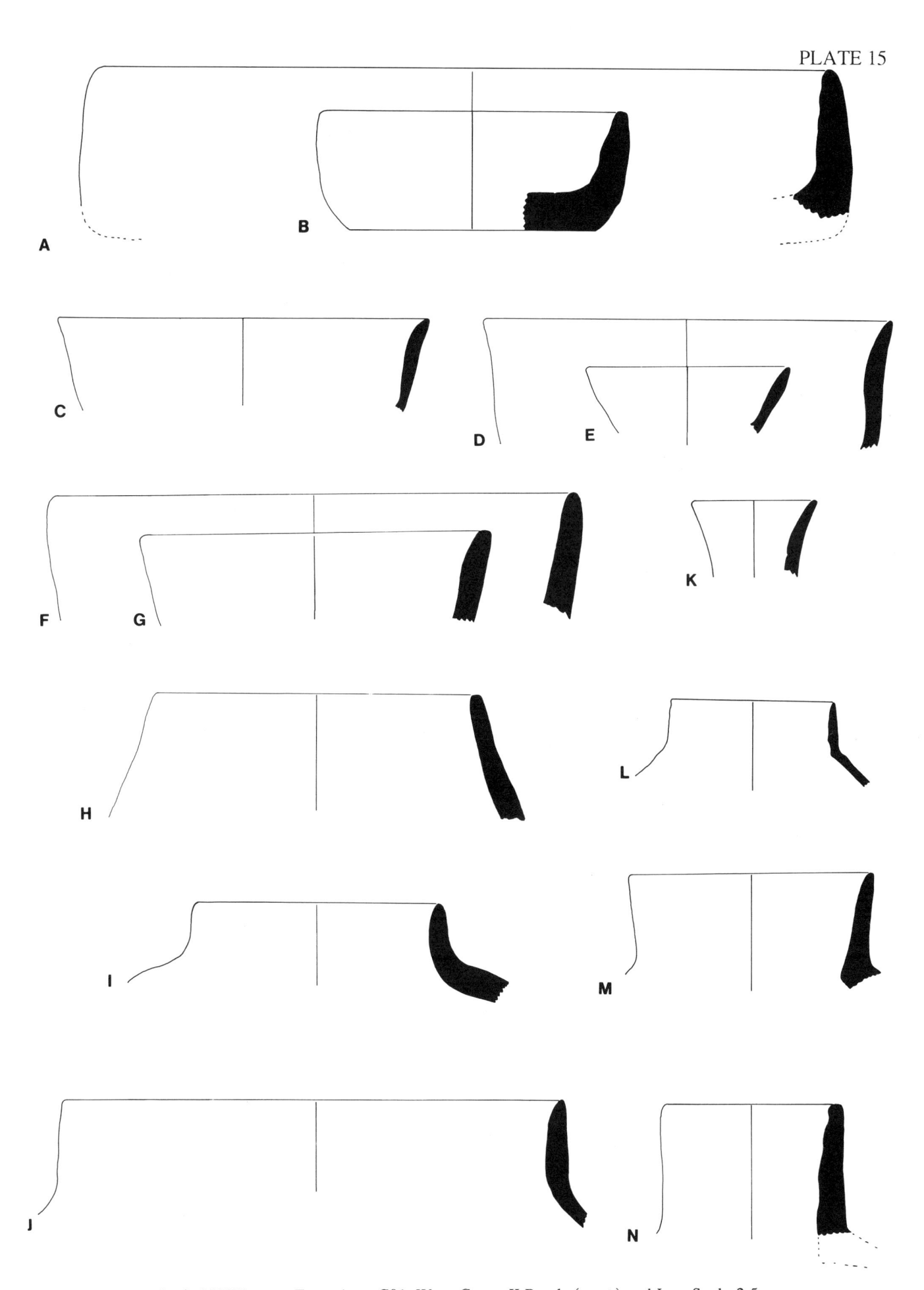

Period VII Pottery From Area C01: Ware Group II Bowls (*cont.*) and Jars. Scale 2:5.

Plate 16. Period VII Pottery From Area C01: Ware Group II Holemouth Jars. Scale 2:5.

|   | MRN | CONTEXT | FCN | WARE | FORM | TYPE | DECO. | WARE/REMARKS |
|---|---|---|---|---|---|---|---|---|
| A | 6551 | C01-0188-128 | 1780 | 31 | 801 | Jar 6 | — | Dense, vegetal-tempered ware; some small-sized white grits also; orange clay. |
| B | 6713 | C01-0167/77-127 | 1856 | 14 | 992 | Jar 4a | Bns. | Somewhat dense straw-tempered ware; a few scattered air holes; also a few scattered small pebbles (accidental?); brownish-buff clay with red slip on both surfaces; burnished. |
| C | 6713 | C01-0167/77-127 | 1856 | 31 | 992a | Jar 4c | — | Dense, vegetal-tempered ware; small-sized white grits quite prominent also; orange clay, exterior surface smoothed. |
| D | 7043 | C01-0168/78-131 | 1918 | 31 | 597a | Jar 5b | — | Dense, vegetal-tempered ware; no visible tempering; brownish-buff clay with gray core prominent. |
| E | 6335 | C01-0189-126 | D1767 | 39 | 1086 | Jar 5a | Bns. | Fairly dense grit- and vegetal-tempered ware; small-sized chaff marks, mica flakes and white grits visible; dark grayish clay; surface mottled brown, orange and gray; well burnished. |
| F | 6831 | C01-0169/79/89-130/131 | 1946 | 13 | 597 | Jar 5a | — | Porous, straw-tempered ware. |
| G | 6718 | C01-0189-128 | 1875 | 13 | 597 | Jar 5a | — | Porous, straw-tempered ware; dark brown clay, somewhat irregular. |
| H | 6718 | C01-0185-128 | 1875 | 13 | 597 | Jar 5a | — | Porous, straw-tempered ware; brownish-buff clay with prominent gray core. |
| I | 13641 | C01-0937/39-198 | D3193 | 14 | 597 | Jar 5a | Bns. | Porous, straw-tempered ware; brownish-buff clay with gray core; exterior surface is burnished; shape somewhat irregular; out of context in Period V deposit. |

PLATE 16

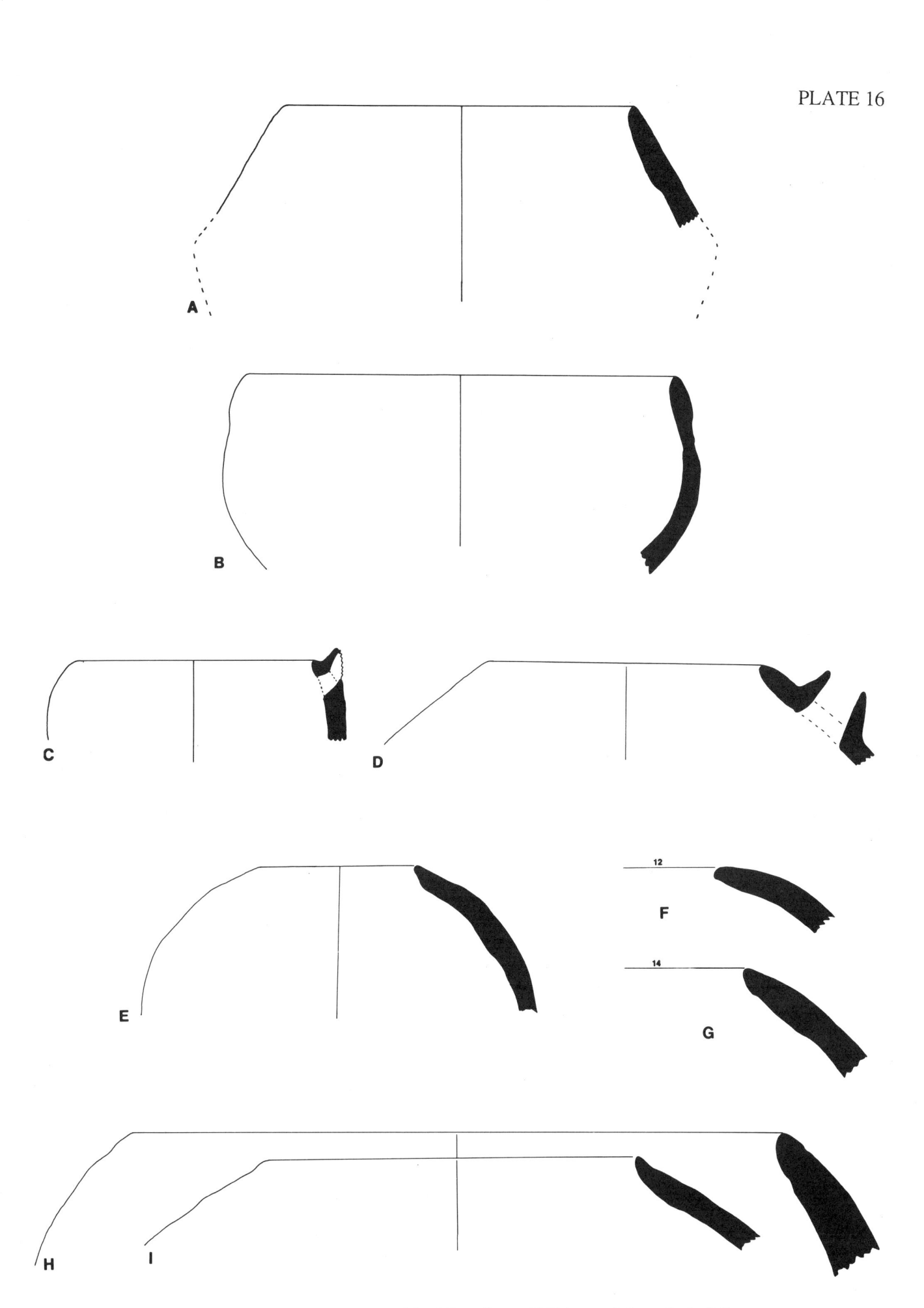

Period VII Pottery From Area C01: Ware Group II Holemouth Jars. Scale 2:5.

Plate 17. Period VI Pottery From Pit 203 in Area C01. Scale 2:5.

|   | MRN | CONTEXT | FCN | WARE | FORM | TYPE | DECO. | WARE/REMARKS |
|---|---|---|---|---|---|---|---|---|
| A | 13731 | C01-0179/89-203 | D3263 | 04 | 1007 | Bowl 3 | — | Plain Simple Ware; occasional small-sized red and gray grits, light brownish-buff clay; exterior black, smudged from fire. |
| B | 13731 | C01-0179/89-203 | D3263 | 13 | 1582 | — | — | Porous, straw-tempered ware; orange clay mottled brownish-buff on exterior; interior surface is burnished. |
| C | 13731 | C01-0179/89-203 | D3263 | 13 | 1584 | — | — | Porous, straw-tempered ware; brownish clay with diffuse, pale gray core; coarse; interior surface black smudged from fire. |
| D | 13731 | C01-0179/89-203 | D3263 | 14 | 1575 | — | Bns. | Fairly dense, straw-tempered ware; a few scattered white grits also; orange clay, exterior surface is mottled orange and yellow, well burnished. |
| E | 13731 | C01-0179/89-203 | D3263 | 13 | 1577 | — | — | Porous, straw-tempered ware; orange-buff clay with prominent gray core; interior surface rather coarse; exterior smoothed, mottled orange and gray. |
| F | 13731 | C01-0179/89-203 | D3263 | 13 | 1537 | Bowl 13 | — | Porous, straw-tempered ware; orange-brown clay with prominent gray core; fairly rough. |
| G | 13731 | C01-0179/89-203 | D3263 | 13 | 1586 | — | — | Porous, straw-tempered ware, brownish-buff clay; fairly rough and irregular; interior surface thoroughly fire blackened. |
| H | 13731 | C01-0179/89-203 | D3263 | 13 | 987 | Bowl 26c | — | Porous, straw-tempered ware; brownish clay with gray core prominent; fairly rough and irregular. |
| I | 13731 | C01-0179/89-203 | D3263 | 13 | 430 | Bowl 26b | — | Porous, straw-tempered ware; brownish-buff clay; surface mottled brown and orange; fairly rough. |
| J | 13731 | C01-0179/89-203 | D3263 | 13 | 901 | Bowl 26b | — | Porous, straw-tempered ware; brownish clay grading to orange towards surface; smoothed. |

PLATE 17

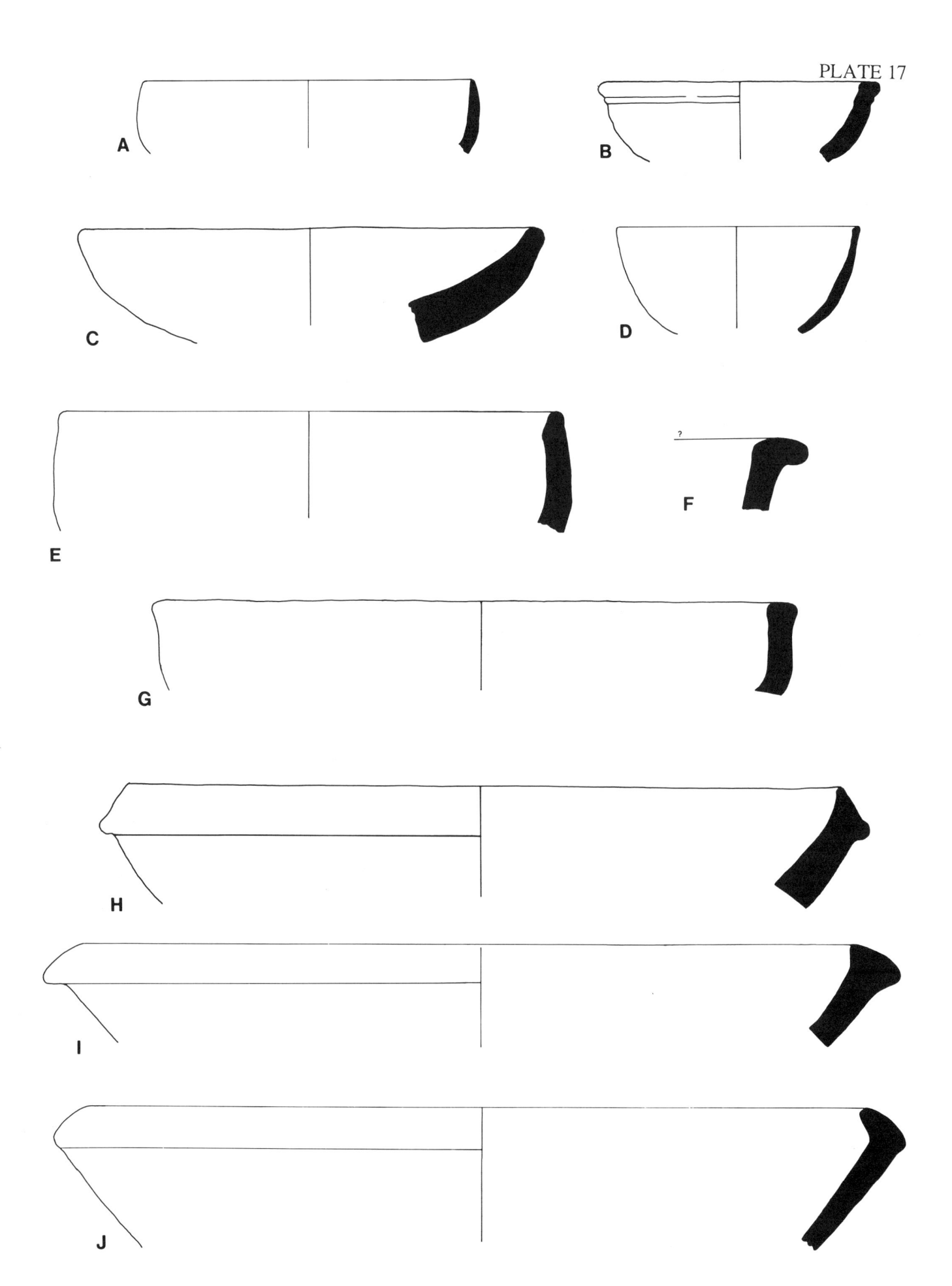

Period VI Pottery From Pit 203 in Area C01. Scale 2:5.

Plate 18. Period VI Pottery From Pit 203 in Area C01 (*cont.*). Scale 2:5.

| | MRN | CONTEXT | FCN | WARE | FORM | TYPE | DECO. | WARE/REMARKS |
|---|---|---|---|---|---|---|---|---|
| A | 13723 | C01-0179/89-203 | D3265 | 13 | 1587 | — | — | Porous, straw-tempered ware; light brownish-buff clay; exterior surface mottled brownish-orange; fairly coarse and irregular. |
| B | 13731 | C01-0179/89-203 | D3263 | 13 | 1579 | — | — | Fairly dense, straw-tempered ware; light brownish-buff clay grading to orange on interior surface and buff on exterior; fairly irregular. |
| C | 13731 | C01-0179/89-203 | D3263 | 13 | 1580 | — | — | Porous, straw-tempered ware; brown clay with diffuse gray core; fairly irregular; traces of fire smudges near rim. |
| D | 13731 | C01-0179/89-203 | D3263 | 13 | 1040 | Jar 35 | — | Porous, straw-tempered ware; brownish-buff clay; somewhat coarse and irregular. |
| E | 13731 | C01-0179/89-203 | D3263 | 13 | 1378 | Jar 24 | — | Fairly dense straw-tempered ware; brownish-buff clay with diffuse gray core; fairly rough and irregular. |
| F | 13731 | C01-0179/89-203 | D3263 | 13 | 1585 | Jar 24 | — | Porous, straw-tempered ware; a few small-sized white grits also; brownish-buff clay; black fire smudges on interior and exterior of neck. |
| G | 13731 | C01-0179/89-203 | D3263 | 13 | 1585 | Jar 24 | — | Porous, straw-tempered ware; yellowish-brown clay; fairly rough and irregular. |
| H | 13731 | C01-0179/89-203 | D3263 | 13 | 1585 | Jar 24 | — | Porous, straw-tempered ware; brownish clay; fairly rough and irregular; black fire smudges on exterior surface. |

PLATE 18

A

B

C

D

E

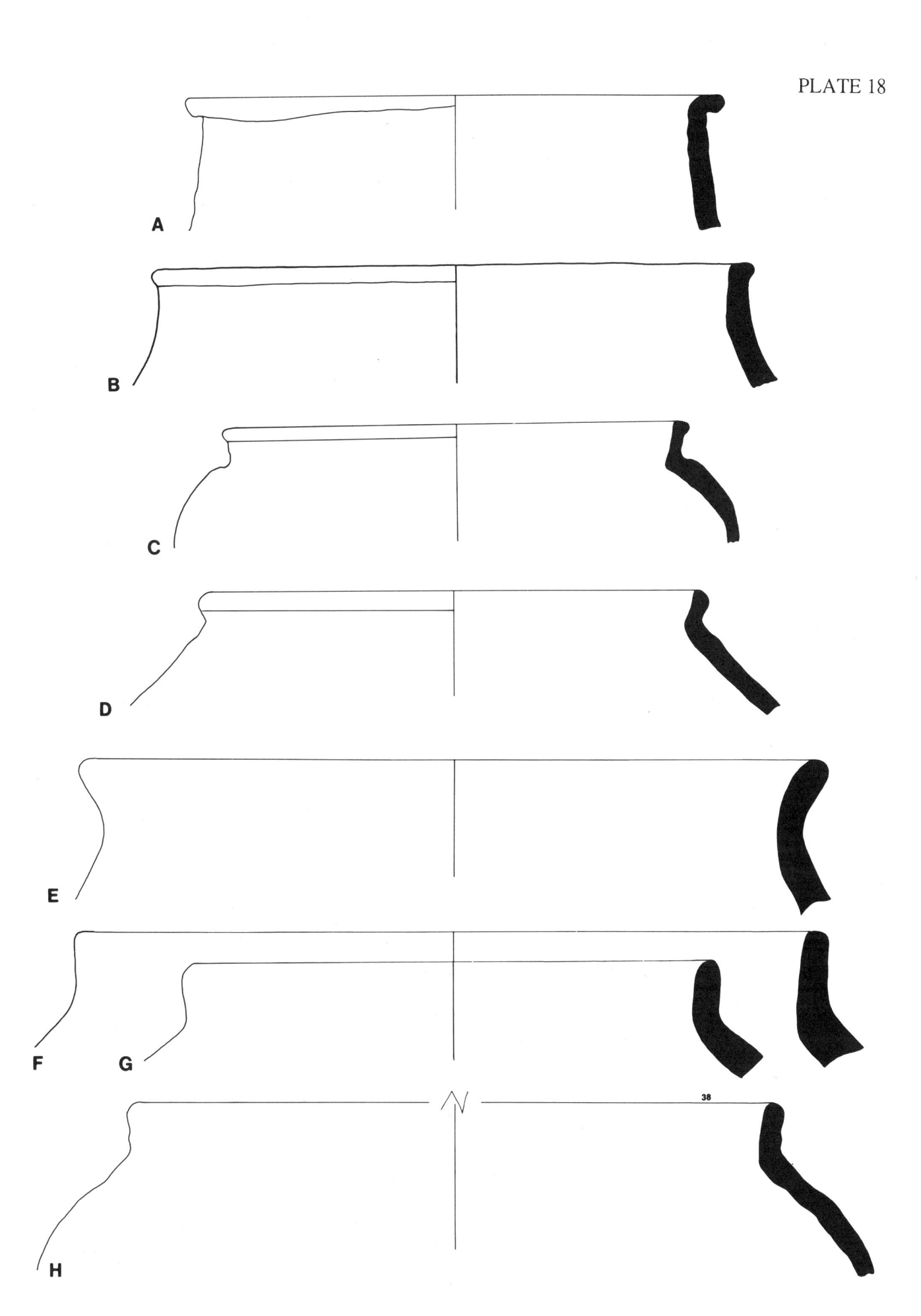

F  G

H

Period VI Pottery From Pit 203 in Area C01 (*cont.*). Scale 2:5.

Plate 19. Period VI Pottery From Areas A and C01: Ware Group I Bowls. Scale 2:5.

| | MRN | Context | FCN | Ware | Form | Type | Deco. | Ware/Remarks |
|---|---|---|---|---|---|---|---|---|
| A | 11045 | A08-0501/02-035 | 310 | 04 | 967 | Bowl 1a | — | Reddish-buff clay; gritty with numerous small- and medium-sized white grits; fast wheel marks visible on interior surface. |
| B | 6063 | A09-05-012 | 178 | 04 | 967 | Bowl 1a | — | Light brownish-buff clay; gritty with numerous small- and medium-sized white grits visible; basal angle is flint-scraped and base itself exhibits concentric marks terminating on a slight protuberance. |
| C | 11045 | A08-051/02-035 | 310 | 04 | 967 | Bowl 1a | — | Buff clay; small-sized black grits visible; basal angle is flint-scraped and base itself is string-cut; hole in base made secondarily, after firing. |
| D | 11185 | A07-19-084 | 734 | 04 | 1435 | Bowl 1b | — | Buff clay; small-sized black grits visible; on exterior and interior surface very regular and evenly spaced wheel mark striations, which also cover the base exterior. |
| E | 11154 | A08-0500-039 | 347 | 04 | 1527 | Bowl 2 | — | Brownish-buff clay; small-sized white grits; on exterior, fast wheel marks visible. |
| F | 11182 | A07-18-083 | 731 | 04 | 1007 | Bowl 3 | 317 | Dense brownish-buff clay with only very small-sized white grits; exterior surface covered with greenish-buff slip. |
| G | 6797 | A09-0870/80-016 | 228 | 04 | 1007 | Bowl 3 | — | Buff clay, grit-tempered. |
| H | 6797 | A09-0870/80-016 | 228 | 04 | 1007 | Bowl 3 | — | Brownish-buff clay; no visible tempering. |
| I | 6255 | C01-0168-123 | 1588 | 04 | C-12 | Bowl 4 | — | Buff clay; small-sized grits; (= KH 1981/95); cf. also plate 145:G. |
| J | 5713 | C01-0167/77-118 | 1570 | 04 | 1097 | Unass. Bowl | — | Brownish-buff clay; small-sized white grits. |
| K | 11170 | A07-18-083 | 724 | 04 | 1442 | Bowl 5 | — | Dense, greenish-buff clay; no visible tempering. |
| L | 11087 | A08-10-037 | 336 | 04 | 02 | Bowl 5 | — | Dense, greenish-buff clay; only occasional scattered minute black grits visible. |
| M | 6085 | A08-05-022 | 204 | 04 | 1390 | Bowl 6a | — | Brownish-buff clay, grit tempered. |
| N | 11059 | A08-0501/02-035 | 323 | 04 | 1390 | Bowl 6a | — | Buff clay, small-sized grits. |
| O | 8316 | A08-05-023 | 247 | 04 | 1329 | Bowl 6a | — | Dense, buff clay; no visible tempering. |
| P | 6587 | C01-0168/78-126 | 1830 | 04 | 1390 | Bowl 6a | — | Buff clay, small-sized grits. |
| Q | 7801 | A07-14-060 | 428 | 04 | 1275 | Bowl 7 | — | Reddish-buff clay; grit-tempered with only small-sized grits visible. |
| R | 17920 | A05-05-076 | 342 | 04 | 1029a | Bowl 8 | — | Grayish clay grading to brownish-buff towards surface; small-sized gray, black, and white grits; out of context in Period IV level. |
| S | 6593 | C01-0169/79/89-126 | 1819 | 04 | 1540 | Bowl 6b | — | Dense, orange-buff clay; no visible tempering other than a few scattered small-sized white grits. |
| T | 11045 | A08-0501/02-035 | 310 | 04 | 935 | Bowl 6a | — | Pinkish-buff clay, small-sized black grits; fast wheel mark striations visible on exterior and interior near base. |
| U | 6836 | A08-07-028 | 218 | 04 | 1015 | Unass. Bowl | — | Light greenish-buff clay; gritty with small- and medium-sized grits visible. |
| V | 6705 | A08-07-028 | 218 | 04 | 1042 | Unass. Bowl | — | Brownish-buff clay; grit-tempered with small- and medium-sized white grits visible; buff slip on both surfaces; irregular, handmade. |

PLATE 19

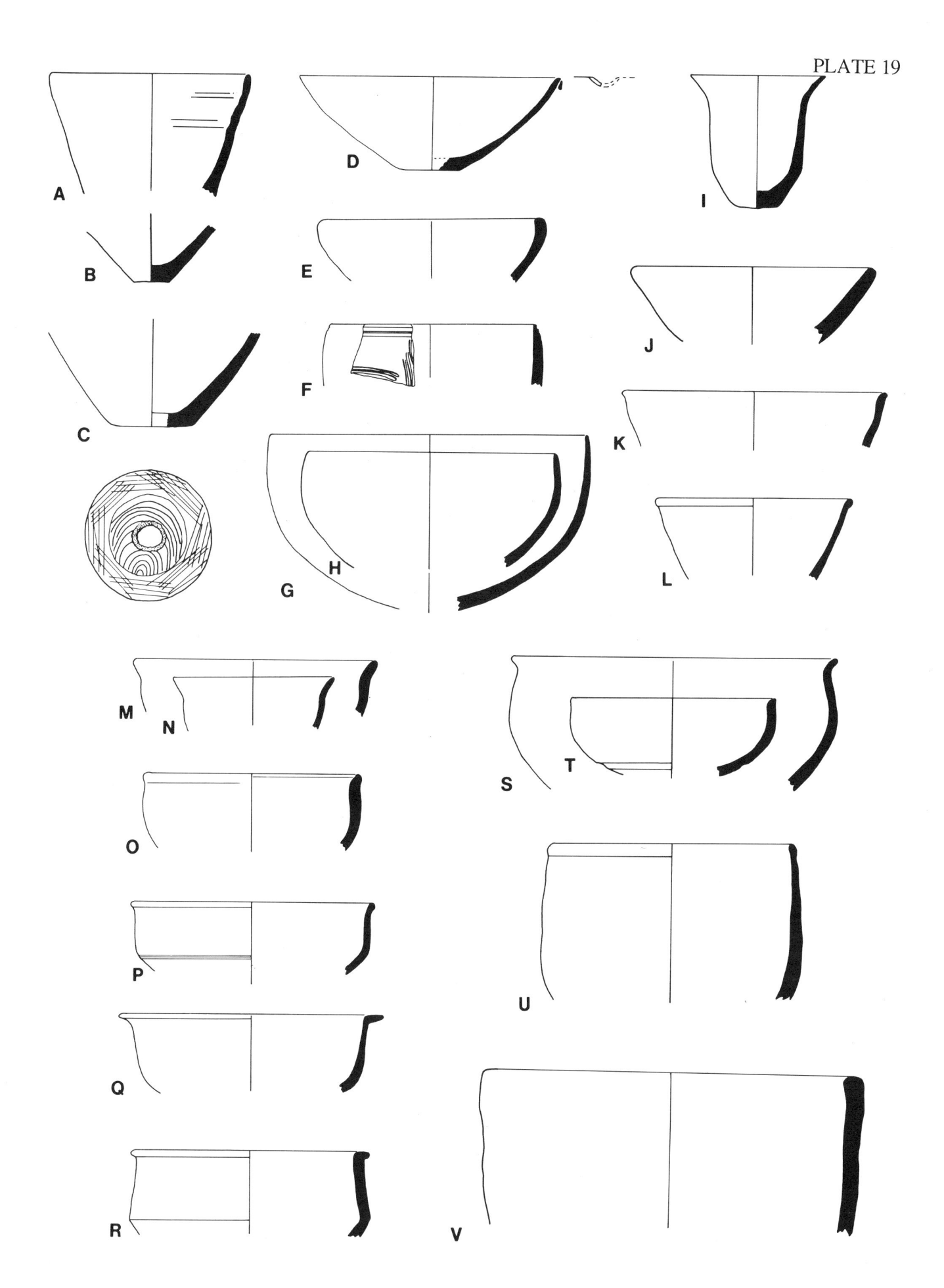

Period VI Pottery From Areas A and C01: Ware Group I Bowls. Scale 2:5.

Plate 20. Period VI Pottery From Areas A and C01: Ware Group I Bowls (*cont.*). Scale 2:5.

|   | MRN | CONTEXT | FCN | WARE | FORM | TYPE | DECO. | WARE/REMARKS |
|---|---|---|---|---|---|---|---|---|
| A | 6347 | C01-0169/79/89-122 | 1721 | 04 | 47e | Bowl 9a | — | Reddish-buff clay; small-sized white grits visible. |
| B | 5946 | C01-0168-120 | 1618 | 04 | 47e | Bowl 9a | — | Fairly dense, orange-buff clay; small-sized grits. |
| C | 1429 | A08-01-002 | 014 | 04 | 47e | Bowl 9a | Bns. | Dense, brownish-buff clay; grit-tempered with white grits visible; orange wash on both surfaces which are lightly burnished; out of context in slope wash. |
| D | 6546 | C01-0169/79-129 | 1788 | 04 | 47e | Bowl 9a | — | Brownish-buff clay with grayish core; exterior surface is buff, interior surface orange; small-sized gray grits. |
| E | 9326 | A08-06-025 | 211 | 04 | 446 | Bowl 9b | Bns. | Very dense orange-buff clay; small-sized white grits visible; orange-buff slip or wash on exterior surface, lightly burnished. |
| F | 11528 | A08-0501-046 | 418 | 04 | 1430 | Bowl 9b | — | Brownish-buff clay, grit-tempered with only small-sized white grits visible; fast wheel marks visible on exterior surface. |
| G | 12372 | A09-07-015 | 255 | 04 | 807 | Bowl 9c | — | Fairly dense orange-buff clay; white grits visible; both surfaces are smoothed. |
| H | 3942 | A07-0750-023 | 221 | 04 | 807 | Bowl 9c | — | Buff clay; small-sized grits; lower exterior surface flint-scraped; out of context in Period IV deposits. |
| I | 13702 | C01-0947/48-202 | D3234 | 04 | 807 | Bowl 9c | — | Dense brownish-buff clay; small-sized grits; exterior covered with light brownish-buff slip; fast wheel marks visible on both surfaces. |
| J | 6063 | A09-05-012 | 178 | 04 | 807 | Bowl 9c | — | Brownish-buff clay; minute white grits; buff slip on surfaces. |
| K | 13364 | C01-0147-120 | D3196 | 04 | 1501 | Bowl 10 | — | Dense buff clay; small-sized white grits; fast wheel striations visible on interior wall near rim. |

PLATE 20

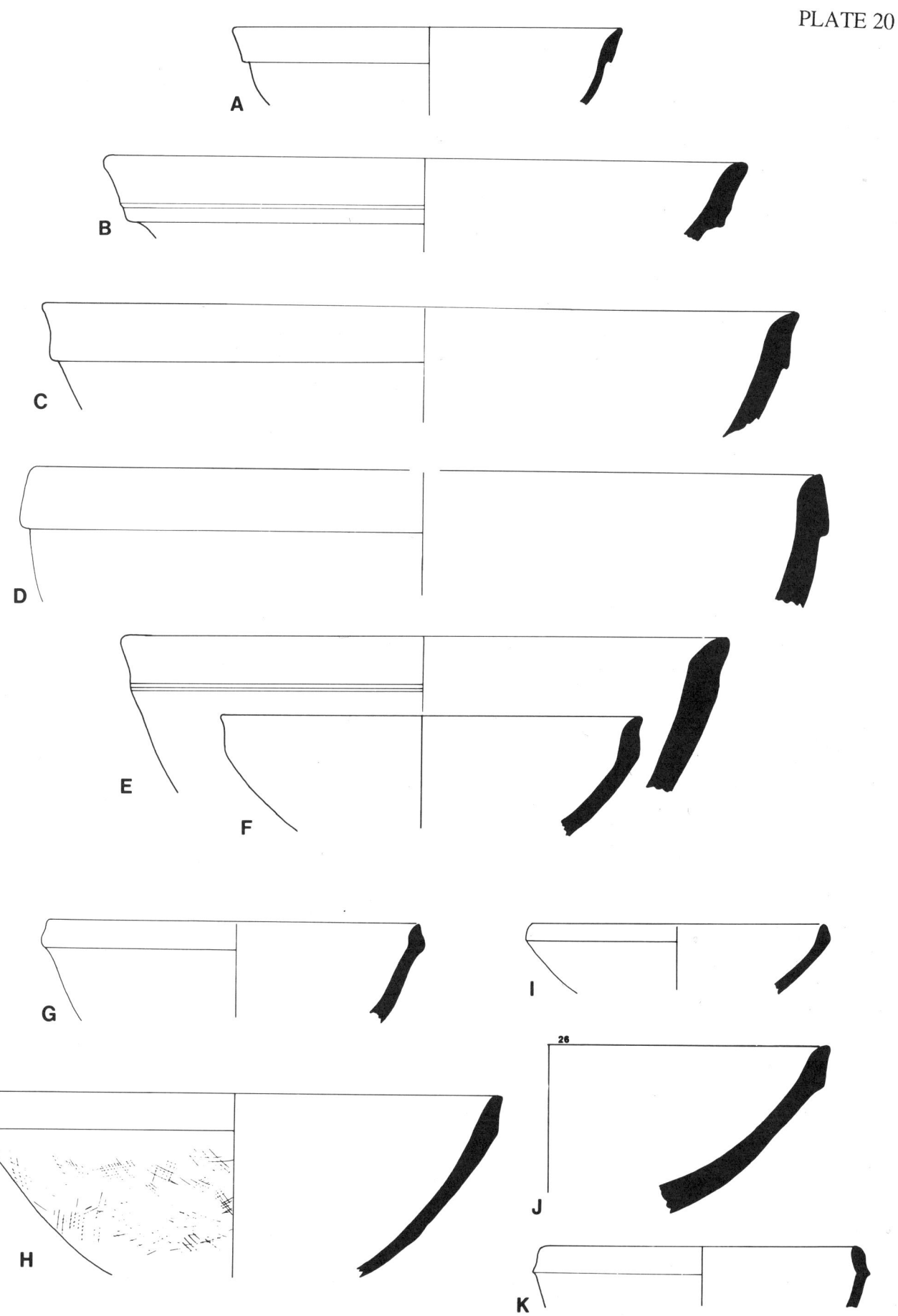

Period VI Pottery From Areas A and C01: Ware Group I Bowls (*cont.*). Scale 2:5.

Plate 21. Period VI Pottery From Areas A and C01: Ware Group I Bowls (*cont.*). Scale 2:5.

|   | MRN | CONTEXT | FCN | WARE | FORM | TYPE | DECO. | WARE/REMARKS |
|---|-----|---------|-----|------|------|------|-------|--------------|
| A | 6266 | C01-0168/78/87/88-122 | 1690 | 04 | 977 | Bowl 11a | — | Orange-buff clay; small-sized white grits visible. |
| B | 1309 | A08-01-002 | 008 | 04 | 479 | Bowl 11a | — | Fairly dense buff clay; small-sized white grits visible; out of context in slope wash. |
| C | 6546 | C01-0169/79-129 | 1788 | 04 | 901a | Bowl 11a | — | Grayish-buff clay; small-sized gray grits visible. |
| D | 11528 | A08-0501-046 | 418 | 04 | 1526 | Bowl 11b | — | Dense, brownish-buff clay; small-sized grits among which white ones are prominent; black fire smudges on exterior surface. |
| E | 11020 | A07-1770/80-076 | 620 | 04 | 1526 | Bowl 11b | — | Buff clay; grit-tempered. |
| F | 11101 | A07-1790-078 | 670 | 04 | 1526 | Bowl 11b | — | Dense, pale greenish-buff clay; no visible tempering other than very small white grits; buff slip on exterior surface. |
| G | 12372 | A09-07-015 | 255 | 04 | 901a | Bowl 11a | — | Dense orange-buff clay; small-sized white grits; fast wheel marks visible on both interior and exterior. |
| H | 11478 | A07-1972-085 | 786 | 04 | 901a | Bowl 11a | — | Dense brownish-buff clay; small-sized white grits. |
| I | 6266 | C01-0168/78/88-122 | 1690 | 04 | 972 | Bowl 12a | — | Brownish-buff clay; small- and medium-sized white grits; buff slip on both surfaces. |
| J | 6836 | A08-07-031 | 228 | 36 | 1018 | Bowl 12b | — | Dense, vegetal-tempered ware; light orange-buff clay with darker gray core; darker orange on surfaces which are smoothed. |
| K | 11060 | A08-0501/02-035 | 324 | 04 | 972 | Bowl 12a | — | Grayish-buff clay grading to orange on surfaces; small-sized black and white grits visible. |

PLATE 21

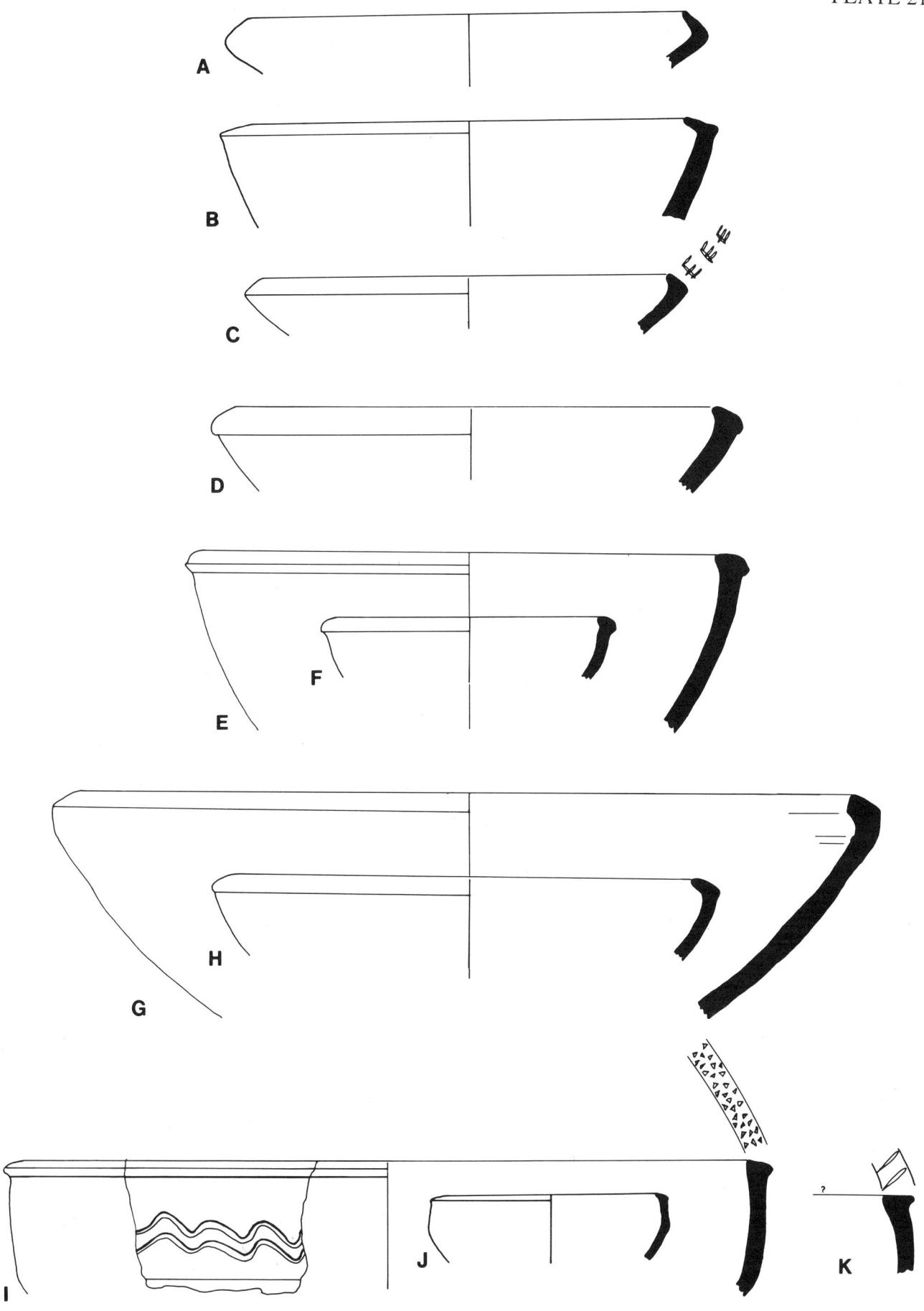

Period VI Pottery From Areas A and C01: Ware Group I Bowls (*cont.*). Scale 2:5.

Plate 22. Period VI Pottery From Areas A and C01: Ware Group I Bowls (*cont.*) and Stands. Scale 2:5.

|   | MRN | CONTEXT | FCN | WARE | FORM | TYPE | DECO. | WARE/REMARKS |
|---|---|---|---|---|---|---|---|---|
| A | 6266 | C01-0168/70/87/88-122 | 1690 | 04 | 979 | Unass. Bowl | — | Brownish-buff clay; gritty with white grits prominent; pinkish slip on interior and exterior. |
| B | 1429 | A08-01-002 | 014 | 04 | 453 | Bowl 13 | — | Reddish-buff clay with light gray core; small-sized white grits are visible; red slip on exterior; out of context in slope wash. |
| C | 6556 | A09-03-013 | 199 | 04 | 1683 | Bowl 13 | — | Fairly dense, orange/brownish-buff clay; primarily grit-tempered with small-sized white grits visible; some finely-chopped chaff also used as tempering. |
| D | 11528 | A08-0501-046 | 418 | 04 | 33 | Bowl 14a | — | Orange-buff clay with gray core; small-sized grits, some finely-chopped chaff also; exterior surface is reddish-buff; interior is buff. |
| E | 3942 | A07-0750-023 | 221 | 04 | 809 | Unass. Bowl | — | Brownish-buff clay; grit-tempered; exterior upper surface smoothed; lower surface roughly pared down; out of context in Period IV deposits. |
| F | 6063 | A09-05-012 | 178 | 04 | 971 | Bowl 15 | — | Reddish-buff clay; grit-tempered with white grits visible; fast wheel marks visible on exterior. |
| G | 6836 | A08-07-031 | 228 | 04 | 1016 | Bowl 15 | — | Reddish-buff clay; grit-tempered with white grits visible; fast wheel marks visible on exterior surface which is also fire smudged. |
| H | 6607 | A08-07-028 | 214 | 04 | 1107 | Unass. Bowl | 022 | Buff clay; small-sized grits; both surfaces covered with thick red slip, burnished. |
| I | 11463 | A08-0502/12-044 | 387 | 04 | 1415 | Stand 1 | — | Pinkish-buff clay; grit-tempered with small- and medium-sized black and white grits; grayish core. |
| J | 6266 | C01-0168/78/87/88-122 | 1690 | 04 | 976 | Stand 2 | — | Dense, grayish-buff clay; very small-sized grits. |

PLATE 22

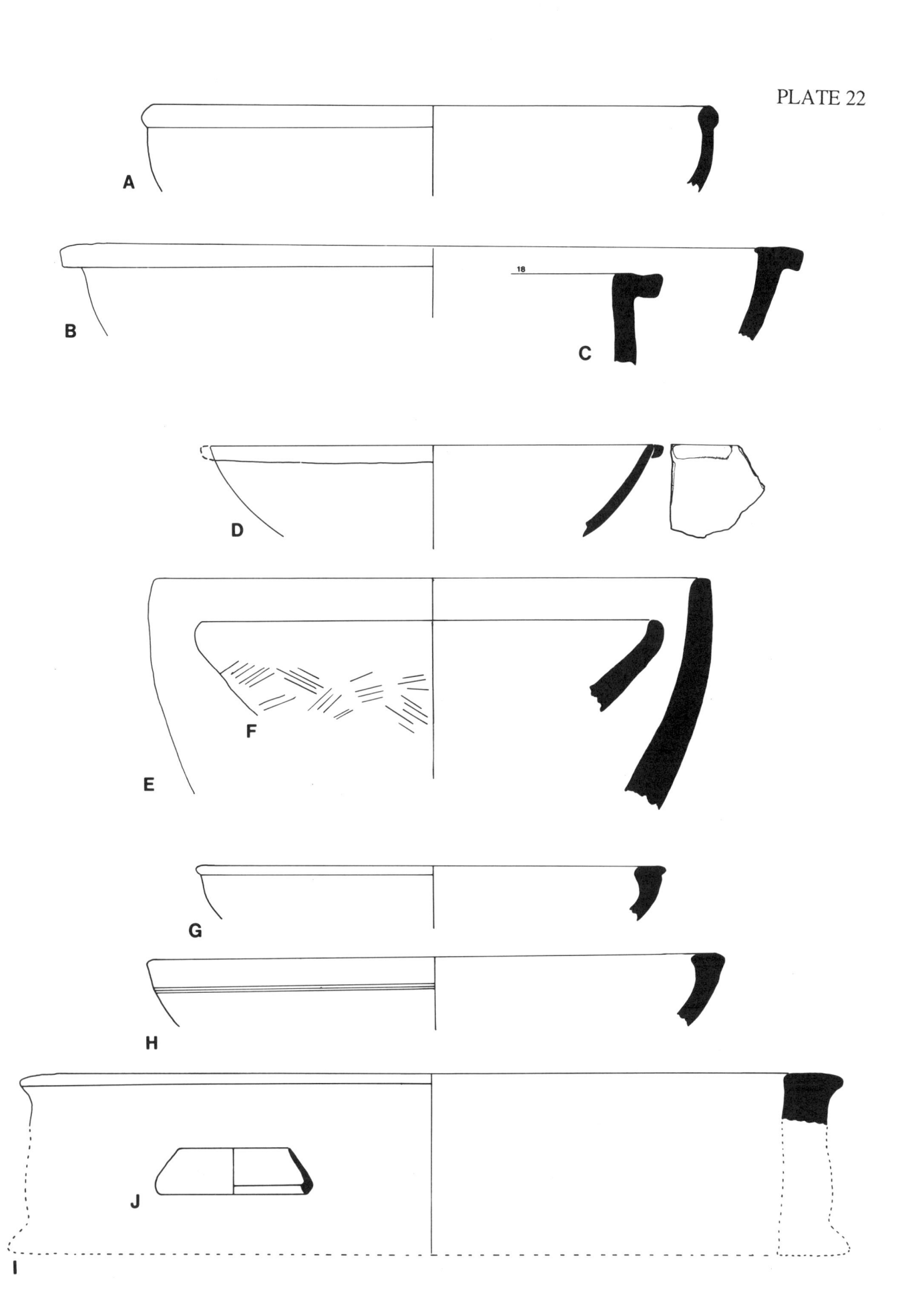

Period VI Pottery From Areas A and C01: Ware Group I Bowls (*cont.*) and Stands. Scale 2:5.

Plate 23. Period VI Pottery From Areas A and C01: Ware Group I Holemouth Jars and Decorated Bodies. Scale 2:5.

|   | MRN | CONTEXT | FCN | WARE | FORM | TYPE | DECO. | WARE/REMARKS |
|---|---|---|---|---|---|---|---|---|
| A | 8147 | A07-1580-072 | D543 | 04 | 1328 | Jar 1a | — | Brownish-buff clay; small grits. |
| B | 8149 | A07-1582-072 | 503 | 04 | 1330 | Jar 1b | — | Dense, pale greenish-yellow clay; no visible tempering. |
| C | 11013 | A07-1691-075 | 613 | 04 | 1363 | Jar 1a | — | Dense, pinkish-buff clay; no visible tempering. |
| D | 5940 | C01-0169-120 | D1634 | 04 | 1363 | Jar 1a | — | Orange-buff clay; small-sized grits. |
| E | 11457 | A07-19-088 | 779 | 04 | 1412 | Jar 1a | — | Light brownish-buff clay grading to reddish-buff on surface; grit-tempered with small-sized white grits; finely-chopped chaff also used as tempering. |
| F | 13711 | C01-0937/39-202 | D3243 | 04 | 1557 | Jar 1b | — | Brownish-buff clay; small-sized white grits. |
| G | 6334 | C01-0188-126 | D1754 | 04 | 1225 | Jar 1a | — | Dense, brownish-buff clay; no visible tempering other than minute white grits. |
| H | 11034 | A07-1770/71/72-077 | 634 | 04 | 1409 | Jar 2a | — | Fairly dense pinkish-buff clay; small-sized white grits visible; on exterior self-slip of same color as clay. |
| I | 11154 | A08-0300-039 | 347 | 04 | 1392 | Jar 2b | — | Dense, pinkish clay; small-sized white grits visible; red paint all over on exterior and interior rim. |
| J | 6593 | C01-0169/79/89-126 | 1819 | 04 | 120 | Jar 3 | — | Greenish-buff clay; gritty with white grits prominent. |
| K | 11013 | A07-1691-075 | 613 | 04 | 1364 | Jar 2b | — | Reddish-buff clay grading to buff on inner surface; small-sized white grits. |
| L | 11090 | A08-0500-036 | 339 | 04 | 1388 | Jar 2b | — | Buff clay; small-sized grits. |
| M | 8147 | A07-1580-072 | 539 | 06 | — | — | 405 | Buff clay; grit-tempered; reserved slip decoration. |
| N | 8315 | A08-05-022 | 244 | 06 | — | — | 407 | Dense orange clay; no visible tempering; reserved slip decoration. |
| O | 5318 | A09-0450-009 | D117 | 06 | — | — | 405 | Buff clay; grit-tempered; reserved slip decoration. |
| P | 8315 | A08-05-022 | 244 | 04 | — | — | 304 | Buff ware; grit-tempered. |
| Q | 11629 | A08-05-049 | 457 | 04 | — | — | 640 | Reddish-buff clay with orange-buff core; small-sized white grits visible; on interior surface, traces of fast wheel marks. |
| R | 823 | C45-0172-005 | D033 | 04 | — | — | 523 | Dense orange clay; small-sized white grits. Buff slip on surface over which red wash was applied; out of context in Period IVB deposits. |
| S | 6304 | A09-05-012 | 186 | 04 | — | — | 306 | Brownish-buff ware; grit-tempered with small-sized white grits prominent. |
| T | 11045 | A08-0501/02-035 | 310 | 04 | — | — | 316 | Dense orangish clay grading to grayish on interior; small-sized white grits visible. |

PLATE 23

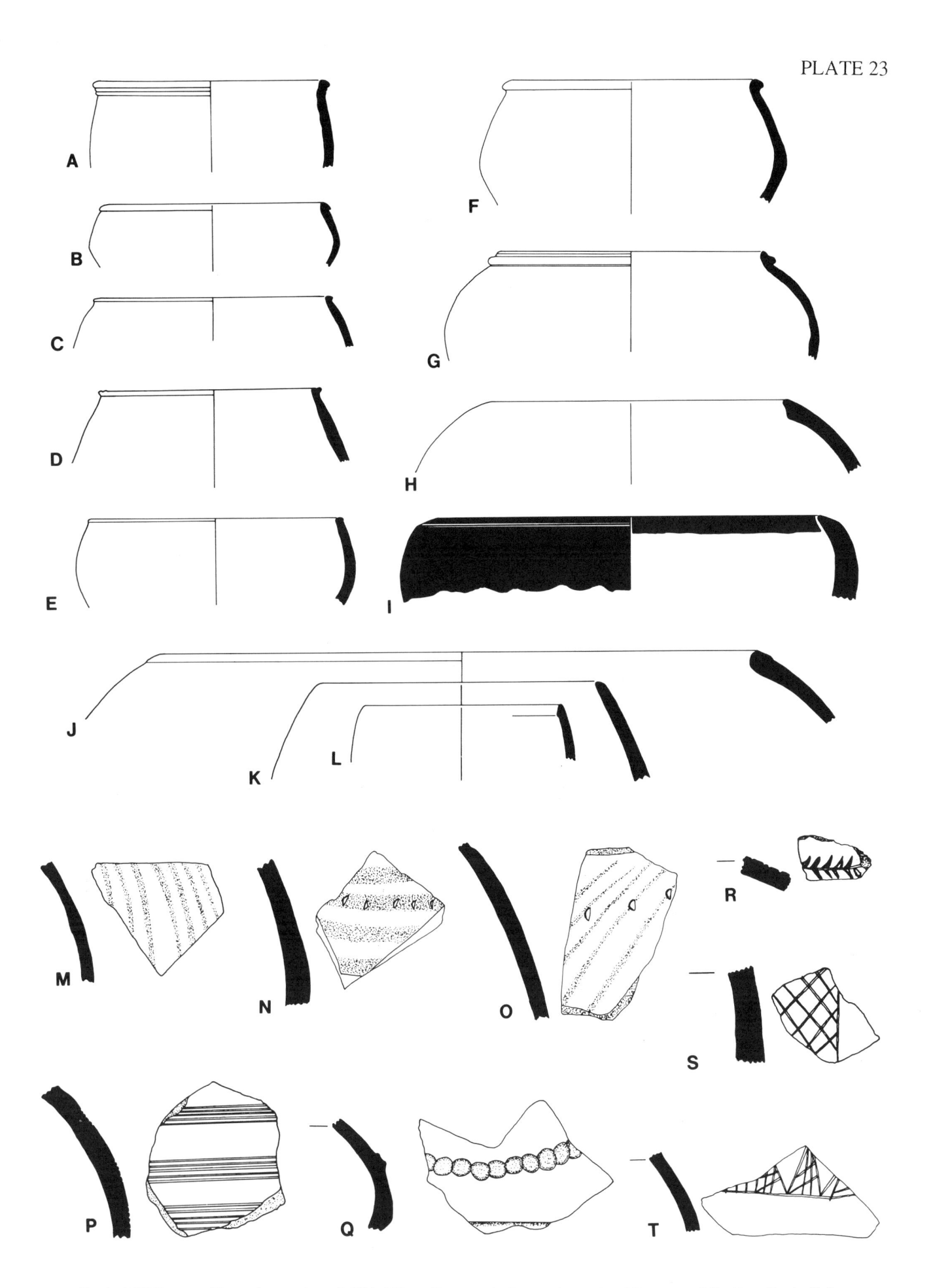

Period VI Pottery From Areas A and C01: Ware Group I Holemouth Jars and Decorated Bodies. Scale 2:5.

Plate 24. Period VI Pottery From Area A: Plain Simple Ware and Brittle Ware Jars. Scale 2:5.

|   | MRN | CONTEXT | FCN | WARE | FORM | TYPE | DECO. | WARE/REMARKS |
|---|---|---|---|---|---|---|---|---|
| A | 11087 | A08-10-037 | 336 | 04 | 1382 | Jar 4a | — | Buff ware; grit-tempered with small-sized white grits prominent. |
| B | 11698 | A08-10-049 | 473 | 04 | 1447 | Jar 4a | — | Buff clay with orange buff patches; small-sized grits; on exterior surface, buff slip. |
| C | 11198 + 11182 | A07-18-083 + A07-18-083 | 731 + 738 | 36 | C-46 | Jar 4a | Bns. | Very dense brownish-buff/tan clay; very fine vegetal-tempering; surface is lightly burnished. |
| D | 11547 | A07-1990/91-089 | 826 | 36 | 326a | Jar 4b | Bns. | Very dense buff clay; very fine vegetal-tempering; exterior surface burnished with horizontal and vertical strokes. |
| E | 929 | A07-04-005 | 019 | 04 | 326 | Jar 4b | — | Buff clay; grit-tempered; out of context in late mixed deposit. |
| F | 11120 | A07-1870/71-082 | 688 | 04 | 1411 | Jar 4b | — | Greenish-buff clay; small- and medium-sized black grits visible. |
| G | 11457 | A07-19-088 | 779 | 04 | 447 | Jar 4c | — | Dense reddish-buff clay with brownish-buff core; no visible tempering other than a few scattered minute white grits; brownish on exterior surface. |
| H | 1724 | A08-0501-051 | D490 | 04 | 1030 | Jar 4c | — | Fairly dense greenish-buff clay; no visible tempering; on interior and exterior surfaces, fast wheel striations visible. |
| I | 11133 | A07-1790-079 | D701 | 04 | 1030a | Jar 4c | — | Dense brownish-buff clay grading to orange on surfaces; small-sized grits. |
| J | 12609 | A07-2490-105 | 1081 | 04? | 1566 | Unass. Jar | — | Dense brownish-buff clay; mixed grit and chaff-tempering; cream slip on surface; mixed Halaf-late Chalcolithic context. |
| K | 7997 | A07-15-070 | 477 | 04 | 1319 | Unass. Jar | — | Dense reddish-buff clay; small-sized white grits. |
| L | 8313 | A07-15-073 | 552 | 04 | 1644 | Jar 5 | — | Light brownish-buff core grading to orangish on surfaces; mixed tempering with very finely-chopped chaff and white grits visible; grits are predominant. |

PLATE 24

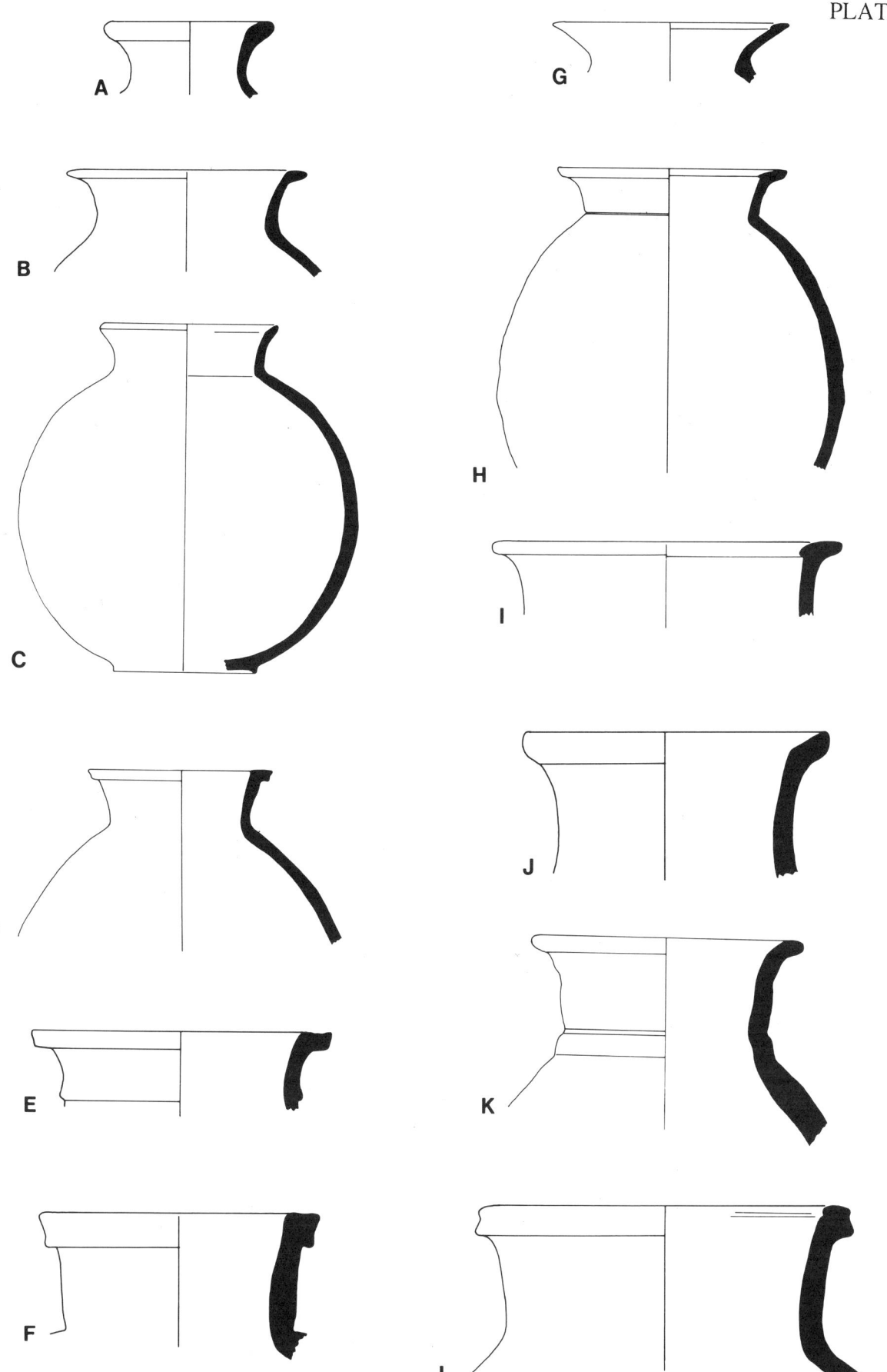

Period VI Pottery From Area A: Plain Simple Ware and Brittle Ware Jars. Scale 2:5.

Plate 25. Period VI Pottery From Areas A and C01: Ware Group I Jars and Accessories. Scale 2:5.

|   | MRN | CONTEXT | FCN | WARE | FORM | TYPE | DECO. | WARE/REMARKS |
|---|---|---|---|---|---|---|---|---|
| A | 1429 | A08-01-002 | 014 | 04 | 452 | Jar 6a | 525 | Dense reddish-buff clay; small-sized white grits; on exterior surface, reddish-orangish wash; lightly burnished; out of context in slope wash. |
| B | 11028 | A07-17-076 | 628 | 04 | 452 | Jar 6a | 525 | Dense pinkish-buff clay; no visible tempering other than minute white grits; on exterior surface, thinly applied red wash, lightly burnished. |
| C | 6063 | A09-05-012 | 178 | 04 | 452a | Jar 6b | 525 | Buff clay; grit-tempered; badly weathered but traces of red wash on exterior can be detected. |
| D | 11185 | A07-19-084 | 734 | 04 | 1371 | Jar 7 | 523 | Buff clay; gritty with small-sized black grits prominent. |
| E | 11045 | A08-0501/02-035 | 310 | 04 | 1371 | Jar 7 | 315 | Brownish-buff clay; small black grits; on shoulder, a band of thinly spaced incisions. |
| F | 6063 | A09-05-012 | 178 | 04 | 420 | Jar 7 | — | Greenish clay, overfired; gritty with white grits visible; fast wheel striations on rim exterior. |
| G | — | A08-06-026 | 205 | 04 | 1044 | Handle 1 | — | Buff clay; grit tempered. |
| H | 11114 | A07-1872-082 | 682 | 04 | 1391 | Jar 7 | — | Buff clay; small- and medium-sized black grits visible; fast wheel striations visible on rim exterior. |
| I | 3664 | C01-0947-120 | D3196 | 04 | 420 | Jar 7 | — | Reddish-buff clay; small-sized white grits. |
| J | 7999 | A07-15-071 | 488 | 04 | 1327 | Jar 8a | — | Orange-buff clay; small-sized white grits. |
| K | 11495 | A08-0502-045 | 400 | 04 | 1414 | Jar 8a | — | Reddish-buff clay; gritty with white grits prominent. |
| L | 5313 | C01-0177-113 | D1484 | 04 | 1414 | Jar 8a | — | Buff clay; small-sized white grits; out of context in Period VB deposits. |
| M | 11120 | A07-1870/71-082 | 688 | 04 | 1413 | Jar 8b | — | Reddish-buff; small-sized white grits. |
| N | 11528 + 11510 + 11525 | A08-0501/02-046 + A08-0502-046 + A08-0502-046 | 407 + 415 + 418 | 04 | 1424 | Jar 8a | 525 | Buff clay grading to pinkish on surface; small-sized grits. |
| O | 5946 + 13626 | C01-0178-120 + C01-0957/58-200 | 1626 | 04 | 949 | Jar 9a | — | Orange-buff ware; small-sized white grits; on interior, clear wheel mark corrugations. |
| P | 13636 | C01-0957/58-120 | D3168 | 04 | 1552 | Jar 9b | — | Buff clay; small-sized white grits; incised line underneath rim. |
| Q | — | C01; Provenance lost | — | 04 | 975 | Spout 1 | — | Orange-brownish buff; grit-tempered with small-sized grits among which white grits are prominent; light reddish-pinkish buff slip on surface. |
| R | 3858 | C01-0187/88-092 | 1241 | 04 | 777 | Jar 9c | — | Orange-buff clay; small-sized white grits; pinkish-buff slip on surface; out of context in Period V deposits. |
| S | 6063 | A09-05-012 | 178 | 04 | 965 | Handle 2 | — | Orange-buff clay; small-sized white grits. |

PLATE 25

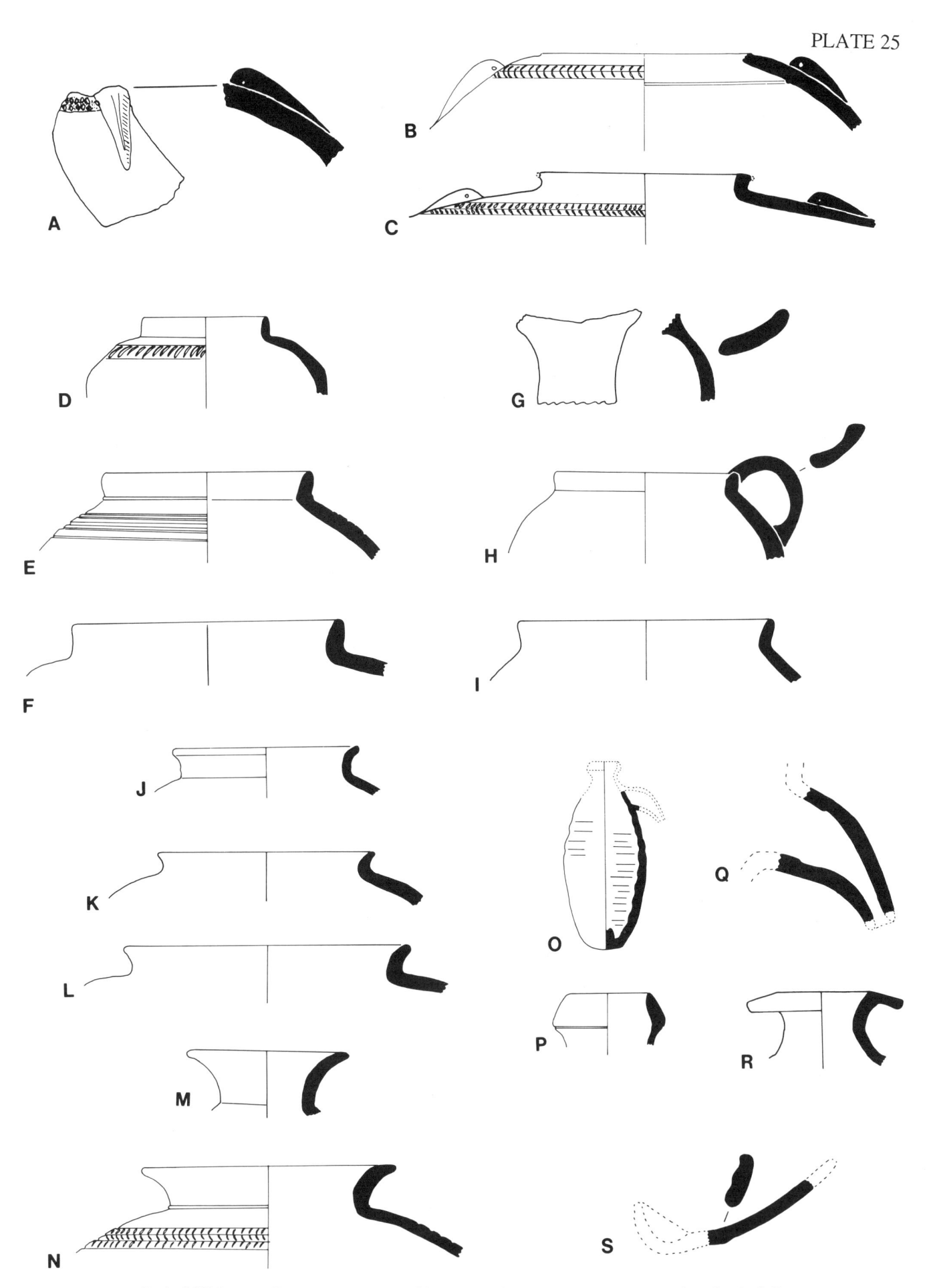

Period VI Pottery From Areas A and C01: Ware Group I Jars and Accessories. Scale 2:5.

Plate 26. Period VI Pottery From Areas A and C01: Ware Group I Jars (*cont.*). Scale 2:5.

|   | MRN | CONTEXT | FCN | WARE | FORM | TYPE | DECO. | WARE/REMARKS |
|---|---|---|---|---|---|---|---|---|
| A | 6063 | A09-05-012 | 178 | 04 | 962 | Jar 10 | 405 | Orange/brownish-buff clay; small-sized white grits; greenish-buff slip on exterior surface; reserved slip decoration. |
| B | 6304 | A09-05-012 | 186 | 04 | 983 | Spout 2 | — | Orange-buff clay; grit-tempered. |
| C | 6541 | A09-06-014 | 214 | 04 | 1059 | Jar 11 | — | Light brownish-buff clay grading to reddish-buff towards surfaces; small-sized white grits. |
| D | 6304 | A09-05-012 | 186 | 04 | 1059a | Jar 11 | — | Greenish-clay, overfired; gritty with white grits prominent. |
| E | 4374 | A08-05-016 | 168 | 04 | 851 | Jar 12 | 304 | Buff clay; small-sized white grits; buff slip on surface. |
| F | 6705 | A08-07-028 | 221 | 04 | 851 | Jar 12 | 304 | Light greenish-buff clay; small-sized grits, some of which are white; buff slip on exterior surface. |
| G | 7896 | A07-15-064 | 463 | 04 | 1267 | Jar 13 | — | Brownish-buff clay; small- and medium-sized white grits; out of context in Period IVC deposit. |
| H | 8315 | A08-05-022 | 244 | 04 | 1324 | Unass. Jar | — | Reddish-buff clay; small-sized white grits. |
| I | 11170 | A07-18-083 | 724 | 04 | 1440 | Unass. Jar | — | Greenish clay, overfired and somewhat warped; small-sized white grits. |
| J | 8147 | A07-1580-072 | 539 | 04 | 1069 | Jar 14 | — | Buff clay; grit-tempered. |
| K | 6587 | C01-0168/78-126 | 1830 | 04 | 1069 | Jar 14 | — | Buff clay; grit-tempered. |
| L | 6836 | A08-07-031 | 228 | 04 | 1014 | Jar 15 | — | Brownish-buff clay; grit-tempered; buff slip on both surfaces. |

PLATE 26

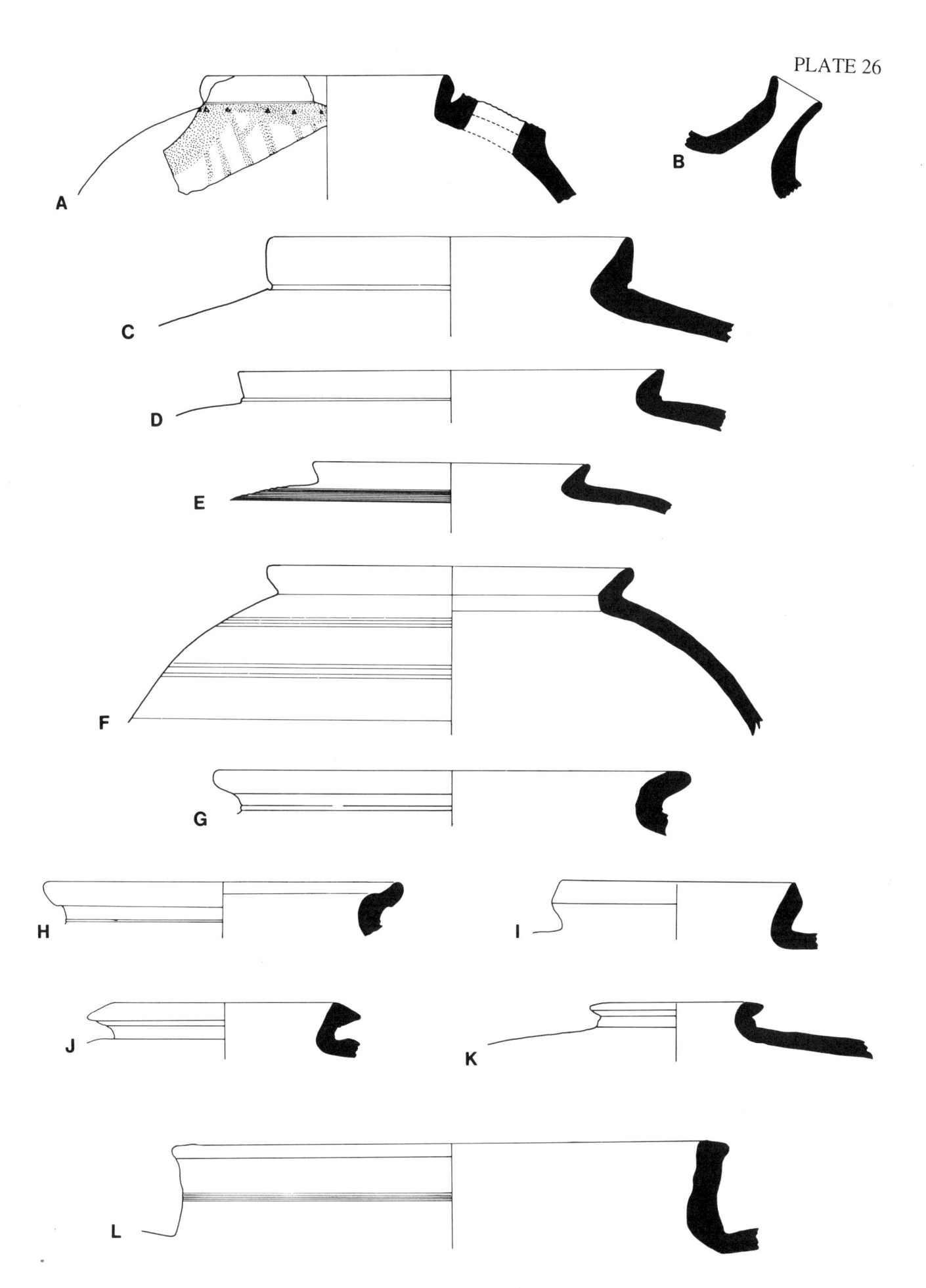

Period VI Pottery From Areas A and C01: Ware Group I Jars (*cont.*). Scale 2:5.

Plate 27. Period VI Pottery From Areas A and C01: Ware Group I Jars (*cont.*) and Stands. Scale 2:5.

|   | MRN | CONTEXT | FCN | WARE | FORM | TYPE | DECO. | WARE/REMARKS |
|---|---|---|---|---|---|---|---|---|
| A | 8141 | A07-15-072 | 506 | 04 | 1326 | Jar 16 | — | Reddish-buff clay; small-sized grits. |
| B | 6837 | A08-07-030 | 224 | 04 | 1325 | Jar 16 | — | Orange/reddish-buff clay; small-sized white grits; buff slip on surface. |
| C | 8152 | A07-1592-072 | D523 | 04 | 1325 | Jar 16 | — | Dense pinkish-buff clay; small-sized white grits visible; buff slip on exterior surface. |
| D | 11154 | A08-0500-039 | 347 | 04 | 492 | Unass. Jar | — | Buff clay; small-sized grits; fast wheel striations on interior and exterior surfaces. |
| E | 6266 | C01-0168/78/87/88-122 | 1690 | 04 | 982 | Unass. Jar | — | Brownish-buff clay; small-sized white grits. |
| F | 6054 | C01-0168/78-121 | D1656 | 04 | 864 | Jar 17 | — | Light brownish-buff clay; grit-tempered. |
| G | 13720 | C01-0958/59-129 | 3252 | 04 | 864 | Jar 17 | — | Dense reddish-buff clay; small-sized grits among which white ones are predominant; buff slip on surfaces. |
| H | 6036 | C01-0169/79/89-121 | 1659 | 04 | 958 | Jar 18 | — | Brownish-buff clay; very small-sized white grits visible. |
| I | 11006 | A07-1692-075 | 606 | 04 | 72 | Jar 18 | — | Buff clay; small-sized black grits. |
| J | 11525 | A08-0502-046 | 415 | 04 | 72 | Jar 18 | — | Dense clay, gray core grading to orange on surfaces; only small-sized white grits visible. |
| K | 712 | C01-6167/77-118 | D1573 | 04 | 928 | Unass. Jar | — | Orange-buff clay; medium-sized grits. |
| L | 11568 | A07-1971/81-089 | 855 | 04 | 1436 | Unass. Jar | — | Pale greenish-buff clay; very small-sized black grits. |
| M | 11182 | A07-18-083 | 731 | 04 | 1402 | Jar 19a | — | Dense orange-buff clay, light gray core; both small-sized grits and finely-chopped chaff used as tempering; grits predominant. |
| N | 5898 | C01-0167/77-118 | 1584 | 04 | 919 | Unass. Pedestal Base | — | Dense brownish-buff clay; small-sized gray grits; red paint on exterior. |
| O | 8149 | A07-1582-072 | D543 | 04 | 1331 | Unass. Pedestal Base | — | Reddish-buff clay; small-sized white grits and some finely-chopped chaff used as tempering, grits predominant; greenish-buff slip on exterior. |

PLATE 27

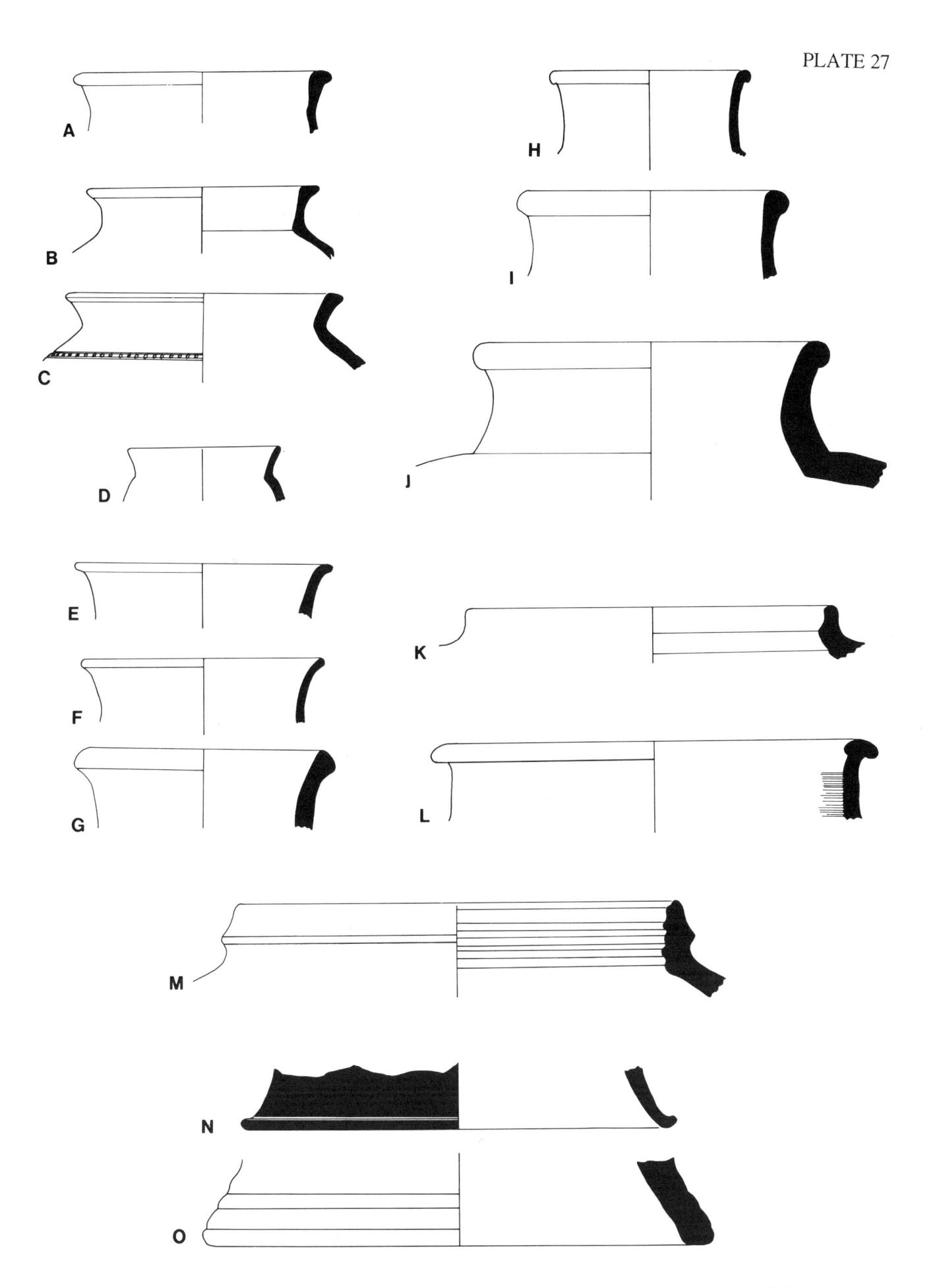

Period VI Pottery From Areas A and C01: Ware Group I Jars (*cont.*) and Stands. Scale 2:5.

Plate 28. Period VI Pottery From Areas A and C01: Ware Group II Bowls. Scale 2:5.

| | MRN | Context | FCN | Ware | Form | Type | Deco. | Ware/Remarks |
|---|---|---|---|---|---|---|---|---|
| A | 6266 | C01-0168/78/88/87-122 | 1690 | 13 | 980 | Bowl 16 | — | Brownish clay, black core; straw/chaff-tempered; surfaces smoothed. |
| B | 13650 | C01-1027/29-198 | D3182 | 13 | C-71 | Bowl 16 | — | Orange-buff clay, gray core; straw/chaff-tempered; out of context in Period V deposits. |
| C | 6053 | C01-0168/78-121 | 1654 | 13 | 1001 | Unass. Bowl | — | Orange clay; chaff-tempered with only fine chaff visible; buff slip on surfaces. |
| D | 6266 | C01-0168/78/88/87-122 | 1690 | 28 | 974 | Bowl 17 | Plum Wash | Dark brownish-buff clay; dense vegetal-tempering with minute silica particles visible (from chaff); plum wash covering both surfaces. |
| E | 6836 | A08-07-031 | 228 | 14 | 1024 | Bowl 14a | Bns. | Orange clay; straw/chaff-tempered; burnished. |
| F | 6606 | A09-06-014 | 222 | 13 | 1055 | Bowl 14b | — | Brownish clay, gray core; straw/chaff-tempered; light brownish-buff slip on surface; out of context in mixed period wash. |
| G | 11151 | A07-1781-079 | 715 | 13 | 1405 | Unass. Bowl | — | Fairly dense chaff-tempered ware; brownish-buff clay with very diffuse gray core; exterior surface smoothed. |
| H | 6266 | C01-0168/78/88/87-122 | 1690 | 14 | 1024 | Bowl 14a | Bns. | Dark brown clay, black core; straw/chaff-tempered; a few scattered white grits too; exterior surface is brown and mottled; burnished. |
| I | 1105 | C45-02-001 | 107 | 13 | 33 | Bowl 14a | — | Orange clay, gray core; straw-tempered; out of context in Period IV deposits. |
| J | 11045 | A08-0501/02-035 | 310 | 13 | 33 | Bowl 14a | — | Fairly dense chaff-tempered ware; brownish-buff clay throughout, no core; traces of brown wash on interior. |
| K | 6606 | A09-06-014 | 222 | 13 | 1057 | Bowl 14a | — | Brownish clay, prominent gray core; surface lighter brownish-buff; straw/chaff-tempered, fairly coarse. |
| L | 6836 | A08-07-031 | 228 | 13 | 1057 | Bowl 14a | — | Brownish clay; straw/chaff-tempered, fairly coarse. |
| M | 5713 | C01-0167/77-118 | 1570 | 13 | 940 | Bowl 18 | — | Orange-brownish clay, prominent gray core; straw/chaff-tempered, somewhat coarse. |
| N | 4987 | A06-05-028 | 130 | 13 | 940 | Bowl 18 | — | Brownish clay, prominent gray core; surface is smoothed and mottled orange; out of context in Period IV deposits. |

PLATE 28

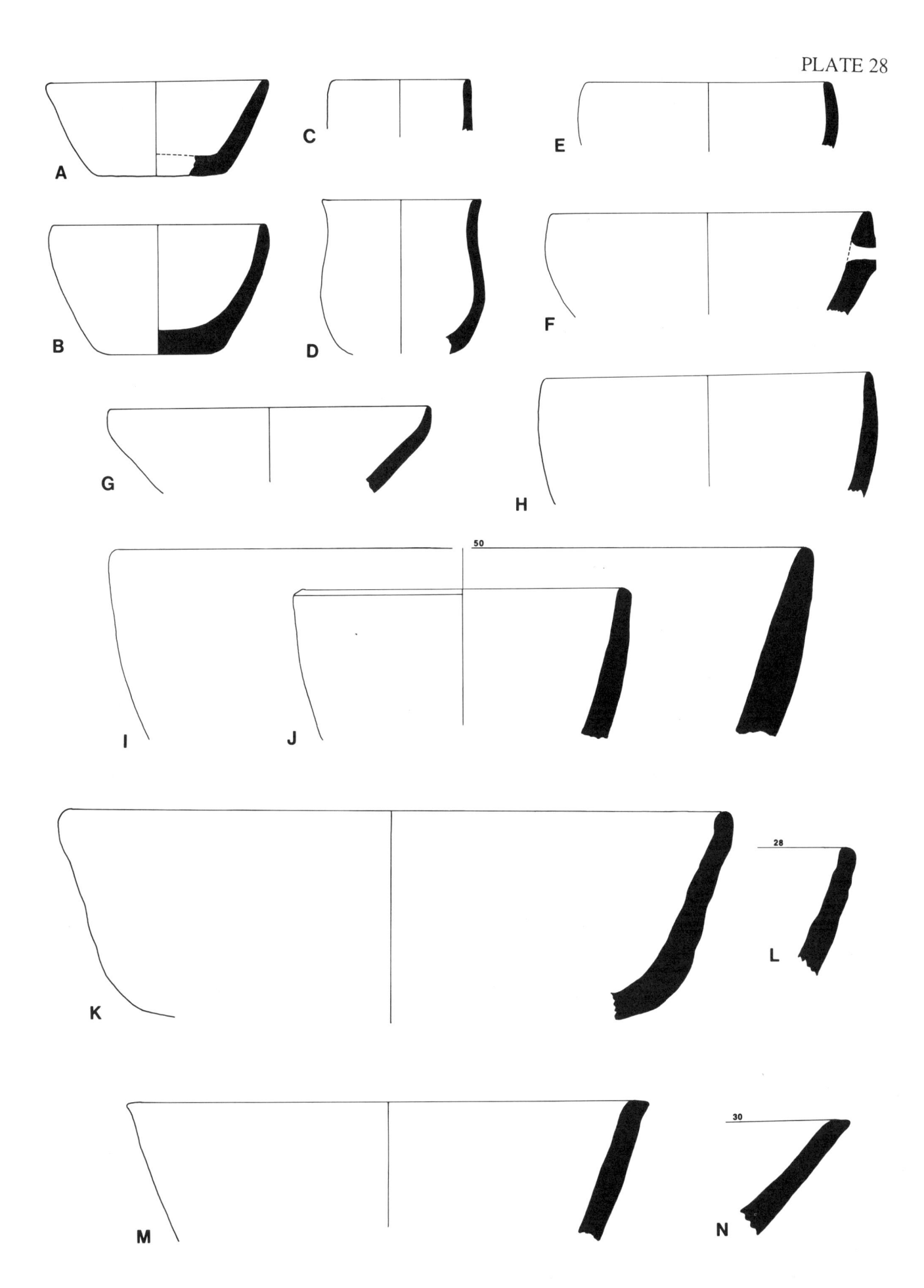

Period VI Pottery From Areas A and C01: Ware Group II Bowls. Scale 2:5.

Plate 29. Period VI Pottery From Areas A and C01: Ware Group II Bowls (*cont.*). Scale 2:5.

|   | MRN | CONTEXT | FCN | WARE | FORM | TYPE | DECO. | WARE/REMARKS |
|---|---|---|---|---|---|---|---|---|
| A | 6399 | A09-0451-009 | 120 | 17 | C-10 | Bowl 19 | — | Beveled Rim Bowl; coarse orange-buff clay, light gray core; straw/chaff-tempered; (= KH 1981/101). |
| B | 16045 | A08-0501/02-035 | 810 | 17 | C-10 | Bowl 19 | — | Beveled Rim Bowl; straw/chaff-tempered; coarse; two finger impressions on bottom of vessel; (= KH 1983/167). |
| C | 11552 | A08-0501-046 | 428 | 17 | 286 | Bowl 19 | — | Unusually large Beveled Rim Bowl; orange-brownish clay; gray core; straw/chaff-tempered, coarse. |
| D | 13482 | C01-10-186 | D2980 | 17 | 1500 | Bowl 20 | — | Beveled Rim Bowl ware; orange-buff clay, prominent gray core; interior surface somewhat smoothed; exterior very rough; out of context in Period V deposits. |
| E | 12459 | A07-24-102 | 185 | 14 | 1485 | Bowl 21 | Bns. | Orange-buff clay; chaff-tempered, no core; very light and irregular burnishing on exterior; out of context, intrusive in Period VIII level. |
| F | 11133 | A07-1790-079 | D701 | 13 | 1397 | Bowl 22 | — | Orange-buff clay, very light gray core; straw/chaff-tempered; exterior surface smoothed. |
| G | 11470 | A08-0512-044 | 394 | 14 | C-47 | Bowl 21 | — | Fairly dense orange-buff clay; chaff-tempered, no visible core; lightly burnished on exterior; (= KH 1983/128). |
| H | 5939 | C01-01-115 | 1580 | 13 | 946 | Bowl 13 | — | Orange-buff clay; straw/chaff-tempered with a few scattered small-sized grits also visible; exterior surface is smoothed. |
| I | 6546 | C01-0469/79-129 | 1788 | 13 | 1537 | Bowl 13 | — | Brownish clay, no visible core; coarse. |

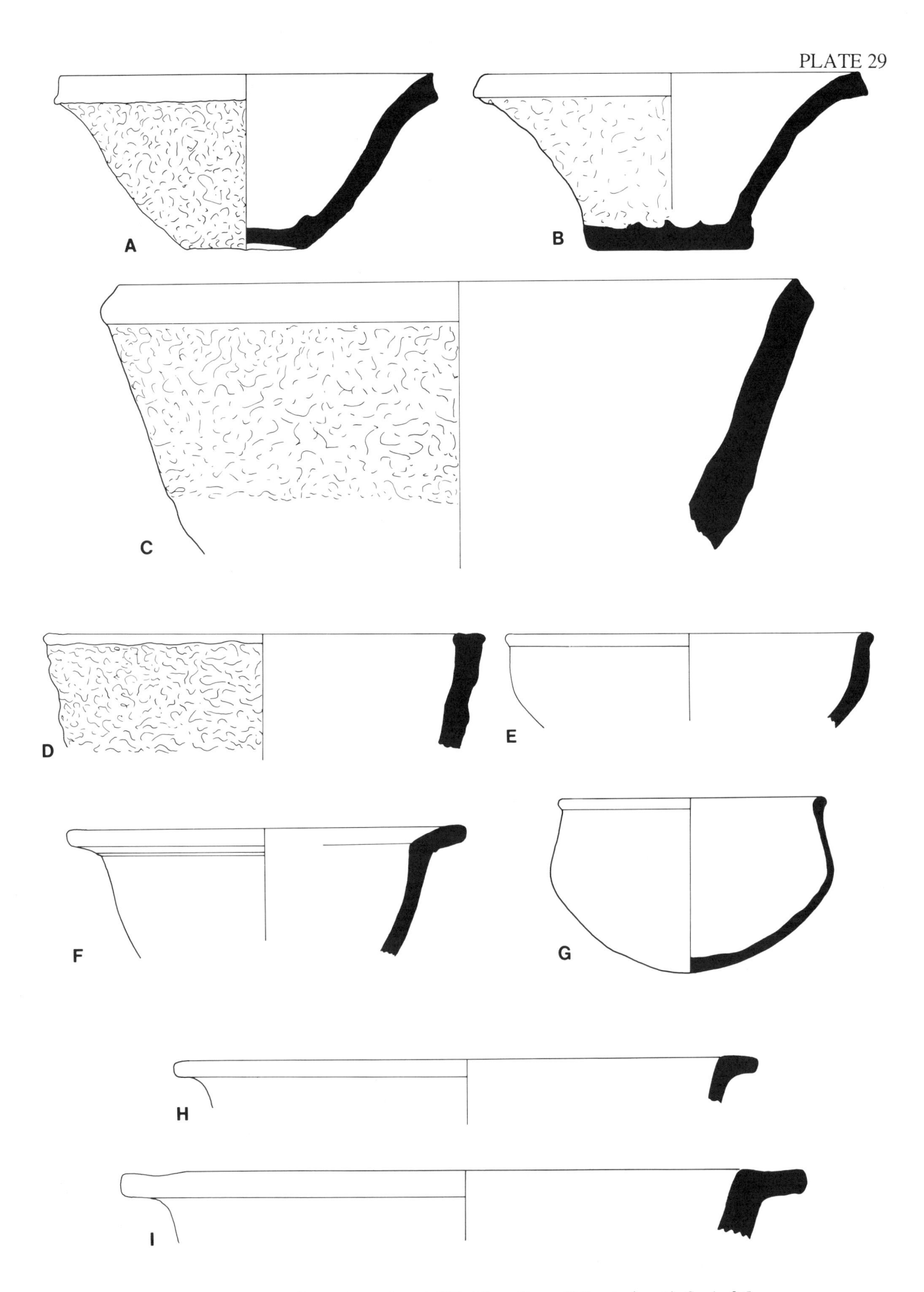

Period VI Pottery From Areas A and C01: Ware Group II Bowls (*cont.*). Scale 2:5.

Plate 30. Period VI Pottery From Areas A and C01: Ware Group II Bowls (*cont.*). Scale 2:5.

|   | MRN | CONTEXT | FCN | WARE | FORM | TYPE | DECO. | WARE/REMARKS |
|---|---|---|---|---|---|---|---|---|
| A | 11087 | A08-10-037 | 336 | 13 | 1686 | Bowl 23 | — | Brownish-buff clay, no core; straw/chaff-tempered; basal angle curves outward suggesting a pedestal base. |
| B | 8315 | A08-05-022 | 244 | 13 | 1686 | Bowl 23 | — | Brownish-buff clay; straw/chaff-tempered. |
| C | 11020 | A07-1770/80-076 | 620 | 13 | 1686 | Bowl 23 | — | Orange-buff clay; straw/chaff-tempered. |
| D | 11059 | A08-0501-02-035 | 323 | 13 | 1693 | Unass. Bowl | — | Orange-buff clay, prominent gray core; straw/chaff-tempered. |
| E | 11481 | A07-1970-085 | 789 | 13 | 1443 | Bowl 24 | — | Brownish clay, prominent gray core; straw/chaff-tempered; flint scraping on lower exterior surface. |
| F | 6063 | A09-05-012 | 178 | 13 | 1093 | Bowl 24 | — | Brownish clay; straw/chaff-tempering, coarse. |
| G | 6702 | A09-0870/80-016 | 234 | 13 | 1005 | Bowl 25 | — | Orange-buff clay, gray core; straw/chaff-tempered; on exterior surface traces of finely-spaced fast wheel marks. |
| H | 11581 | A07-19-090 | 841 | 13 | 1010 | Bowl 25 | — | Brownish clay, gray core; straw/chaff-tempered; top half of vessel interior blackened by fire. |
| I | 6797 | A09-0870/80-016 | 228 | 13 | 1010 | Bowl 25 | — | Orange-buff clay, brown core; straw/chaff-tempered; faint traces of red wash on exterior surface. |
| J | 6347 | C01-0189/79/69-122 | 1721 | 13 | 1062 | Bowl 25 | — | Brownish-buff clay; straw/chaff-tempered; light brownish-buff slip on surface; exterior smoothed. |
| K | 11776 | A08-11-054 | 525 | 13 | 1322 | Bowl 26a | — | Fairly dense greenish-buff clay; chaff-tempered. |
| L | 11882 | A08-11-059 | 558 | 13 | 1322 | Bowl 26a | — | Coarse and porous brownish-orange clay; straw/chaff-tempered; on interior near rim traces of blackened fire smudges. |
| M | 11151 | A07-1781-079 | 715 | 13 | 1322 | Bowl 26a | — | Brownish-buff clay; prominent gray core; straw/chaff-tempered. |
| N | — | Provenance lost | — | 13 | 1322 | Bowl 26a | — | Orange-buff clay; prominent gray core; straw/chaff-tempered; lower exterior surface is flint scraped. |
| O | 11028 | A07-17-076 | 628 | 13 | 1322 | Bowl 26a | — | Light brownish-buff clay, no core; only small-sized chaff used as tempering; smoothed. |

PLATE 30

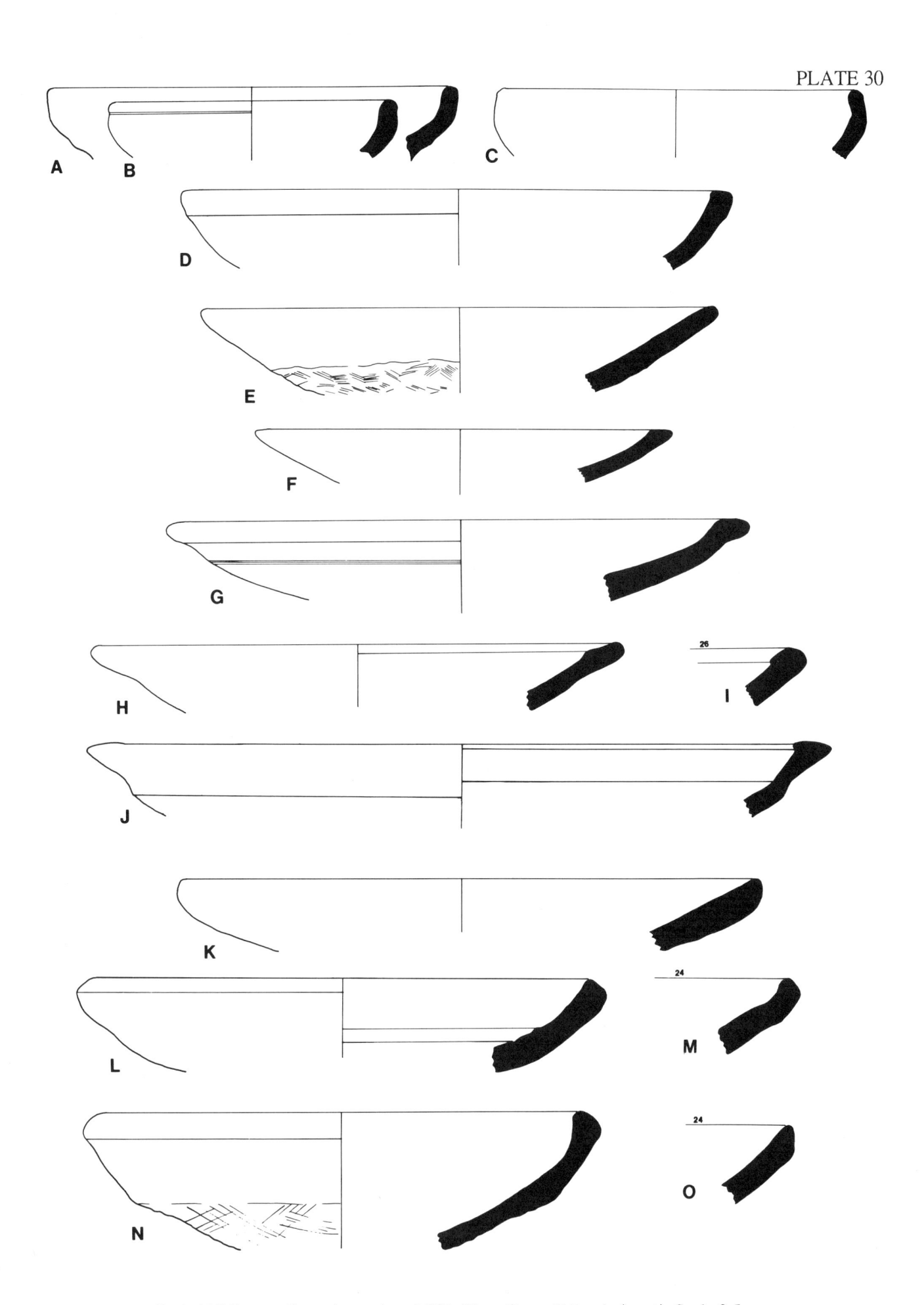

Period VI Pottery From Areas A and C01: Ware Group II Bowls (*cont.*). Scale 2:5.

Plate 31. Period VI Pottery From Areas A and C01: Ware Group II Platters. Scale 2:5.

|   | MRN | CONTEXT | FCN | WARE | FORM | TYPE | DECO. | WARE/REMARKS |
|---|---|---|---|---|---|---|---|---|
| A | 6609 | A08-0751-015 | 214 | 13 | 901 | Bowl 26b | — | Straw/chaff-tempered ware. |
| B | 6704 | A09-0751-015 | 230 | 13 | 901 | Bowl 26b | — | Straw/chaff-tempered ware. |
| C | — | Area C01, Provenance lost | — | 13 | 901 | Bowl 26b | — | Orange-buff clay, prominent gray core; straw/chaff-tempered; on interior, fast wheel striations; exterior lower half flint-scraped. |
| D | 5320 | A09-0451-009 | D114 | 13 | 901 | Bowl 26b | — | Brownish clay, prominent gray core; straw/chaff-tempered; some small-sized grits visible also; buff slip on both surfaces. |
| E | — | Area A, Provenance lost | — | 13 | 901 | Bowl 26b | — | Fairly dense brownish clay, gray core; straw/chaff-tempered; buff slip on both surfaces. |
| F | 11525 | A08-0502-046 | 415 | 13 | 901 | Bowl 26b | — | Dense reddish-buff clay; tempered with finely-chopped chaff; scattered small-sized grits also visible. |
| G | 6266 | C01-0168/78/88-122 | 1690 | 14 | 978 | Bowl 26c | Bns. | Orange-buff clay, gray core; straw/chaff-tempered; a few scattered small-sized grits also visible; buff slip on exterior, horizontally burnished; red slip on interior. |
| H | 11128 | A07-1780-079 | D696 | 13 | 978 | Bowl 26c | — | Straw/chaff-tempered ware. |
| I | 11141 | A08-0500-038 | D343 | 13 | 1467 | Bowl 26c | — | Brownish clay, gray core; straw/chaff-tempered; exterior lower half flint scraped. |
| J | 11657 | A07-19-091 | D879 | 13 | 1456 | Bowl 26b | — | Dense brownish clay, no core; straw/chaff-tempered; on interior, fast wheel striations; exterior smoothed. |
| K | 11629 | A08-05-049 | 457 | 13 | 1456 | Bowl 26b | — | Orange-buff clay, no core; straw/chaff-tempered; black fire smudges on rim; lower exterior flint scraped. |
| L | 11721 | A08-0511-051 | 487 | 13 | 1451 | Bowl 26d | — | Brownish clay, prominent gray core; straw/chaff-tempered. |
| M | 7898 | A07-15-062 | 440 | 13 | 1293 | Bowl 26d | — | Brownish-buff clay, no core; straw/chaff-tempered. |
| N | 8543 | C01-0938/39-156 | 2297 | 13 | 1336 | Bowl 26d | — | Orange-buff clay, prominent gray core; somewhat irregular and coarse; out of context in Period V deposits. |

PLATE 31

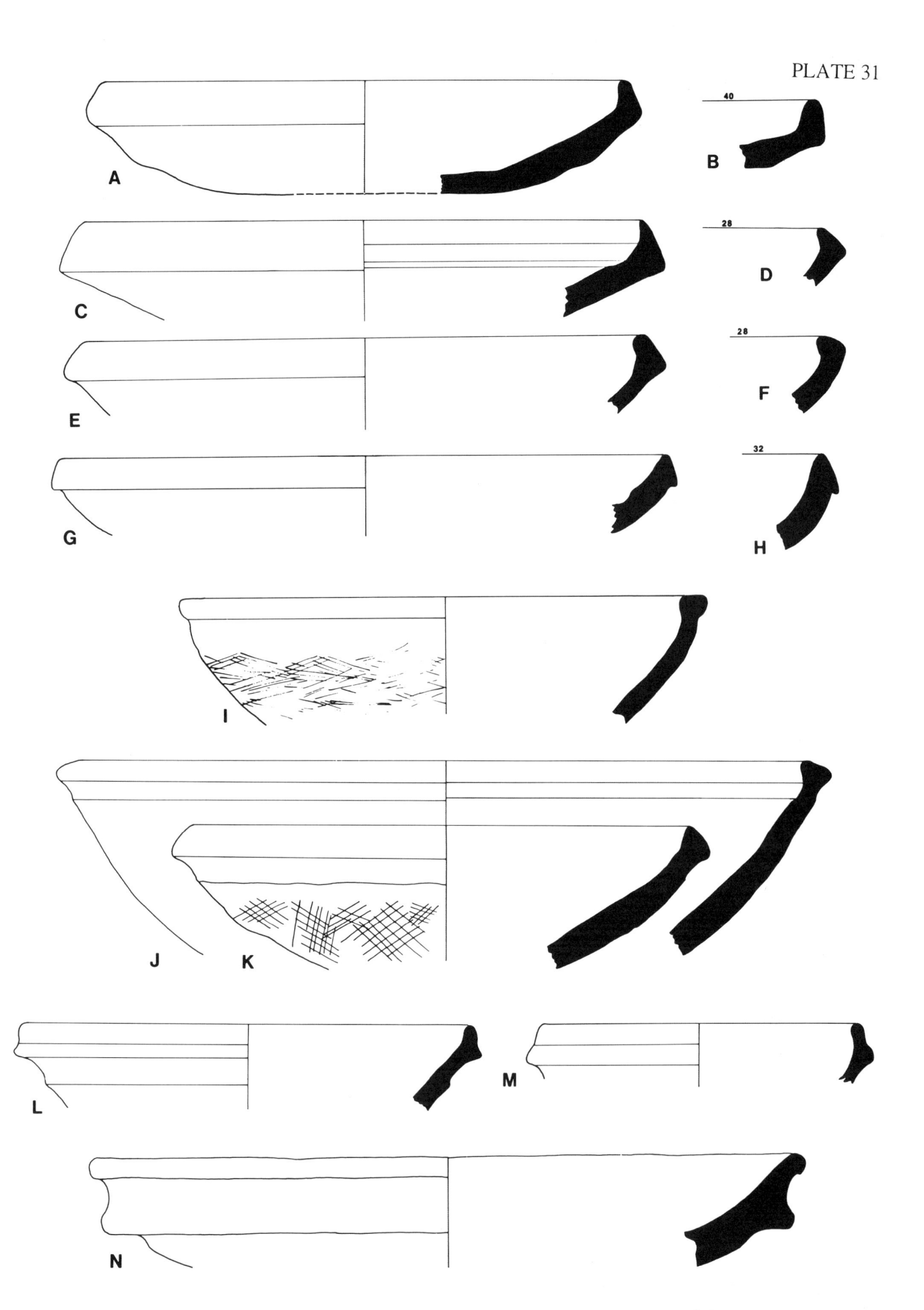

Period VI Pottery From Areas A and C01: Ware Group II Platters. Scale 2:5.

Plate 32. Period VI Pottery From Area A: Ware Group II Platters (*cont.*). Scale 2:5.

|   | MRN | CONTEXT | FCN | WARE | FORM | TYPE | DECO. | WARE/REMARKS |
|---|---|---|---|---|---|---|---|---|
| A | 11060 | A08-0501/02-035 | 324 | 14 | 987 | Bowl 26c | Bns. | Brownish-orangish clay; straw/chaff-tempered; on exterior, traces of horizontal burnish on rim; on interior, traces or irregular vertical burnishing strokes. |
| B | 6304 | A09-05-012 | 186 | 13 | 987 | Bowl 26c | — | Orange-buff clay, prominent gray core; straw/chaff-tempered; smoothed. |
| C | 6704 | A09-0751-015 | 230 | 14 | 1012 | Bowl 26c | Bns. | Orange-buff clay, prominent gray core; straw/chaff-tempered; light burnishing on surfaces. |
| D | 11619 | A07-19-094 | D867 | 13 | 1475 | Bowl 26c | — | Brownish clay, prominent gray core; straw/chaff-tempered. |
| E | 1378 | A08-01-002 | 011 | 14 | 430 | Bowl 26c | Bns. | Brownish-orange clay, prominent gray core; straw/chaff-tempered; exterior surface covered with buff slip; interior surface is mottled orange and burnished; out of context in slope wash. |
| F | 6063 | A09-05-012 | 178 | 13 | 430 | Bowl 26c | — | Straw/chaff-tempered ware. |
| G | 1310 | A08-01-002 | 011 | 13 | 396 | Bowl 26b | — | Orange-buff clay, prominent buff core; straw/chaff-tempered; a few white grits visible also; surfaces are smoothed; out of context in slope wash. |
| H | 11133 | A07-1790-079 | — | 13 | 901 | Bowl 26b | — | Straw/chaff-tempered ware. |
| I | 1378 | A08-01-002 | 011 | 14 | 427 | Bowl 26e | Bns. | Brownish clay, gray core; tempered with finely-chopped chaff; a few scattered small-sized grits also visible; on exterior surface, traces of horizontal burnishing strokes; out of context in slope wash. |
| J | 11721 | A08-0511-051 | 487 | 13 | 1450 | Bowl 26e | — | Orange-buff clay, prominent gray core; straw/chaff-tempered; somewhat irregular. |
| K | 11629 | A08-05-049 | 457 | 13 | 427 | Bowl 26e | — | Brownish-orange clay, prominent gray core; straw/chaff-tempered; coarse. |
| L | 11133 | A07-1790-079 | D701 | 13 | 1396 | Bowl 26e | — | Orange-buff clay, very light gray core; straw/chaff-tempered; occasional small-sized pebbles also visible; lower exterior surface is flint-scraped. |
| M | 11629 | A08-05-049 | 457 | 13 | 427 | Bowl 26e | — | Orange-buff clay, prominent gray core; straw/chaff-tempered; lower exterior surface is flint-scraped. |

PLATE 32

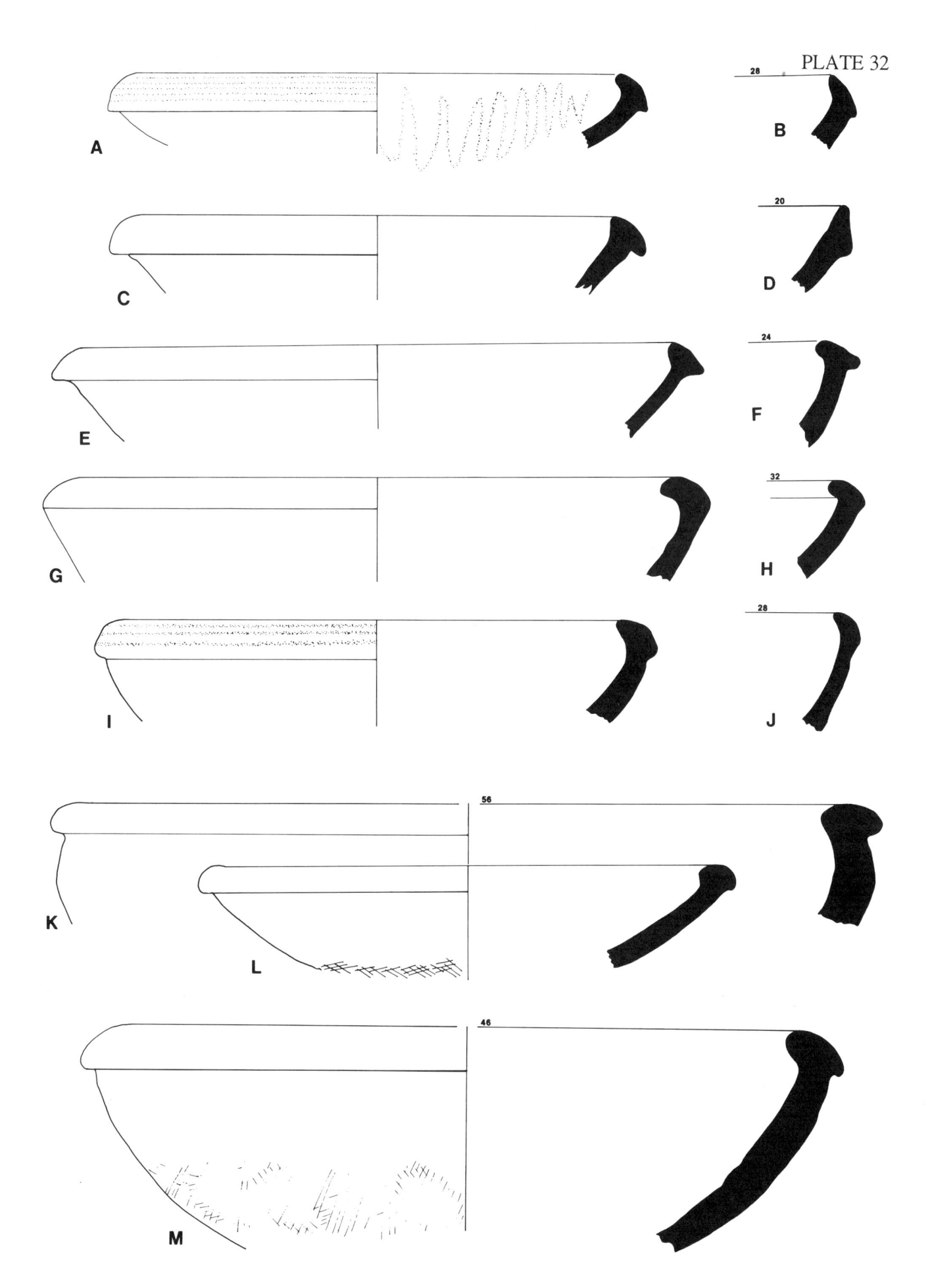

Period VI Pottery From Area A: Ware Group II Platters (*cont.*). Scale 2:5.

Plate 33. Period VI Pottery From Areas A and C: Ware Group II Trays, Stands, and Carinated Jars. Scale 2:5.

|   | MRN | CONTEXT | FCN | WARE | FORM | TYPE | DECO. | WARE/REMARKS |
|---|---|---|---|---|---|---|---|---|
| A | 3882 | C46-04-003 | 043 | 13 | 731 | Tray 1 | — | Straw/chaff-tempered ware; out of context in Period IV deposits. |
| B | 5322 | A09-0462-009 | D121 | 13 | 939 | Tray 2 | — | Orange-buff clay, gray core; straw/chaff-tempered; some small-sized white grits also visible; buff slip on bottom side. |
| C | 11463 | A08-0502/12-044 | 397 | 13 | 1415 | Stand 1 | — | Orange/reddish-buff clay, prominent gray core; flint-scraped on exterior middle and whole of interior surface. |
| D | 11427 | A08-1032/42-042 | 375 | 13 | 1029 | Jar 20a | — | Fairly dense orange-brownish clay; prominent dark gray core; straw/chaff-tempered; exterior surface smoothed and mottled orange and brown. |
| E | 6702 | A09-0870/80-016 | 234 | 13 | 1006 | Jar 20a | — | Orange-brownish clay; straw/chaff-tempered; exterior surface is smoothed and fire blackened. |
| F | 11407 | A08-1032/42-040 | 365 | 14 | 1006 | Jar 20a | Bns. | Orange-buff clay, prominent gray core; straw/chaff-tempered; both surfaces irregularly burnished. |
| G | 7039 | A08-07-028 | 221 | 13 | 913 | Jar 20a | — | Brownish clay; prominent gray core; straw/chaff-tempered; a few scattered small-sized pebbles also visible; exterior surface smoothed. |
| H | 1378 | A08-01-002 | 011 | 13 | 428 | Jar 20a | — | Straw/chaff-tempered ware; out of context in slope wash. |
| I | 11581 | A07-19-090 | 841 | 14 | 1029 | Jar 20a | Bns. | Brownish clay, prominent gray core; straw/chaff-tempered; a few scattered small-sized pebbles and crushed pieces of flint visible also; exterior surface above carination is smoothed and irregularly burnished; below carination, surface is rough. |
| J | 11054 | A08-0501/02-035 | D318 | 13 | 1029 | Jar 20a | — | Orange-buff clay, no core; straw/chaff-tempered; occasional large-sized gray and small-sized white grits visible. |

PLATE 33

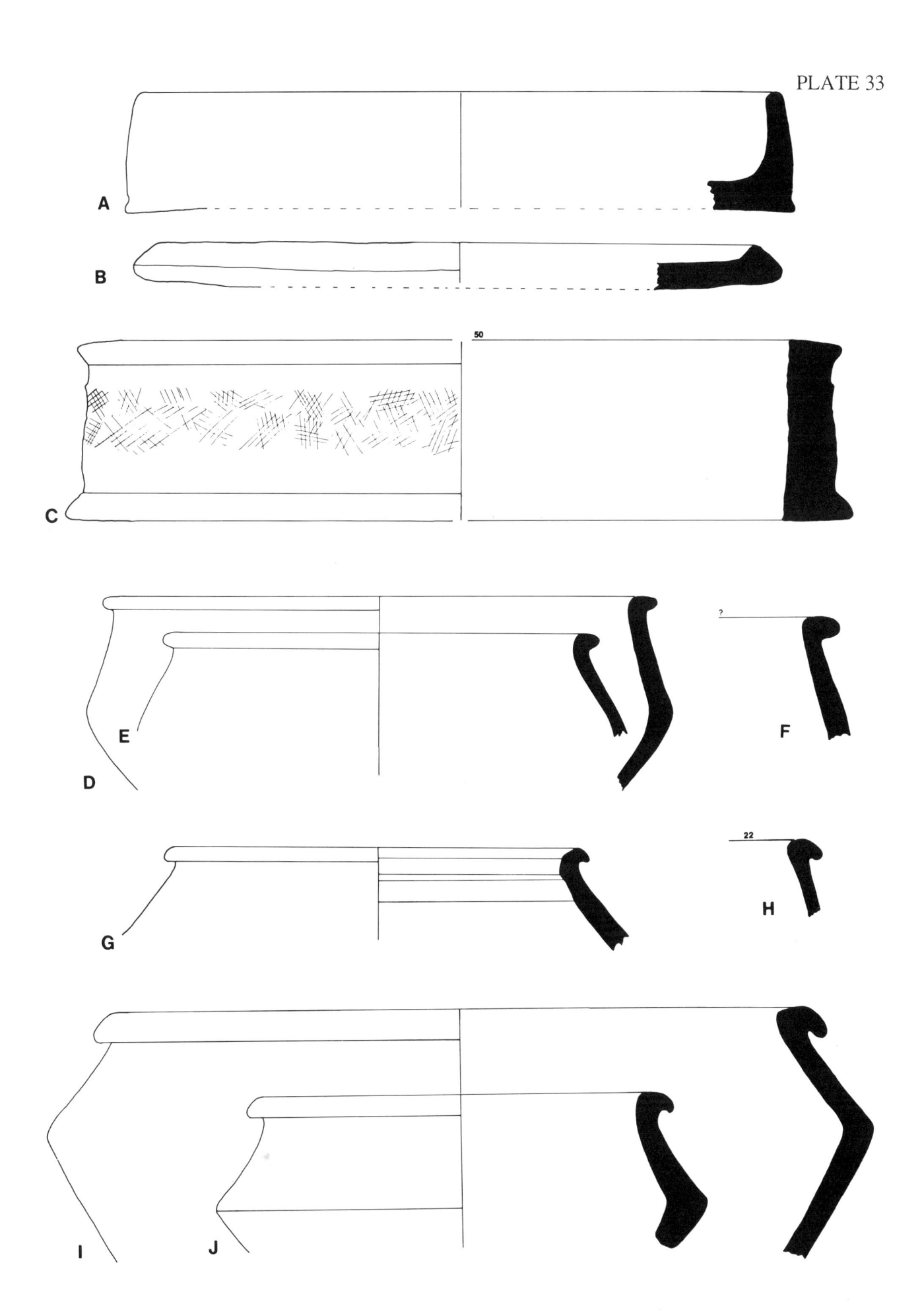

Period VI Pottery From Areas A and C: Ware Group II Trays, Stands, and Carinated Jars. Scale 2:5.

Plate 34. Period VI Pottery From Area A: Ware Group II Carinated Jars (*cont.*). Scale 2:5.

|   | MRN | CONTEXT | FCN | WARE | FORM | TYPE | DECO. | WARE/REMARKS |
|---|---|---|---|---|---|---|---|---|
| A | 6837 | A08-07-030 | 224 | 13 | 1029 | Jar 20a | — | Brownish clay, prominent gray core; straw/chaff-tempered; a few scattered small-sized pebbles also visible; red wash on uneven surface; exterior mottled brown and black from fire smudges. |
| B | 12434 | A07-21-101 | 960 | 13 | 1006 | Jar 20a | — | Reddish-buff clay; straw/chaff-tempered; out of context, intrusive into Period VIII level. |
| C | 6797 | A09-0270/80-016 | 228 | 13 | 1008 | Jar 20b | — | Brownish-orange clay; straw/chaff-tempered; exterior smoothed. |
| D | 6837 | A08-07-030 | 224 | 13 | 1008 | Jar 20b | — | Brownish-buff clay; straw/chaff-tempered; exterior smoothed. |
| E | 6836 | A08-07-031 | 228 | 13 | 1019 | Jar 20b | — | Orange-buff clay, brown core; straw/chaff-tempered; a few scattered small-sized pebbles also visible; smoothed. |
| F | 11185 | A07-19-084 | 734 | 13 | 1403 | Jar 20c | — | Orange-brownish clay, prominent gray core; straw/chaff-tempered; smoothed. |
| G | 11753 | A07-1970/80/90-095 | 928 | 13 | 1403 | Jar 20c | — | Light brown clay, darker brown core; straw/chaff-tempered; exterior smoothed and fire smudged on spots; out of context, intrusive into Period VIII deposit. |
| H | 11721 | A08-0511-051 | 487 | 13 | 1258 | Jar 20c | — | Orange clay, prominent gray core; straw/chaff-tempered. |
| I | 7638 | A07-10-050 | 383 | 13 | 1258 | Jar 20c | — | Orange clay, prominent dark gray core; straw/chaff-tempered; out of context in Period IV deposits. |

PLATE 34

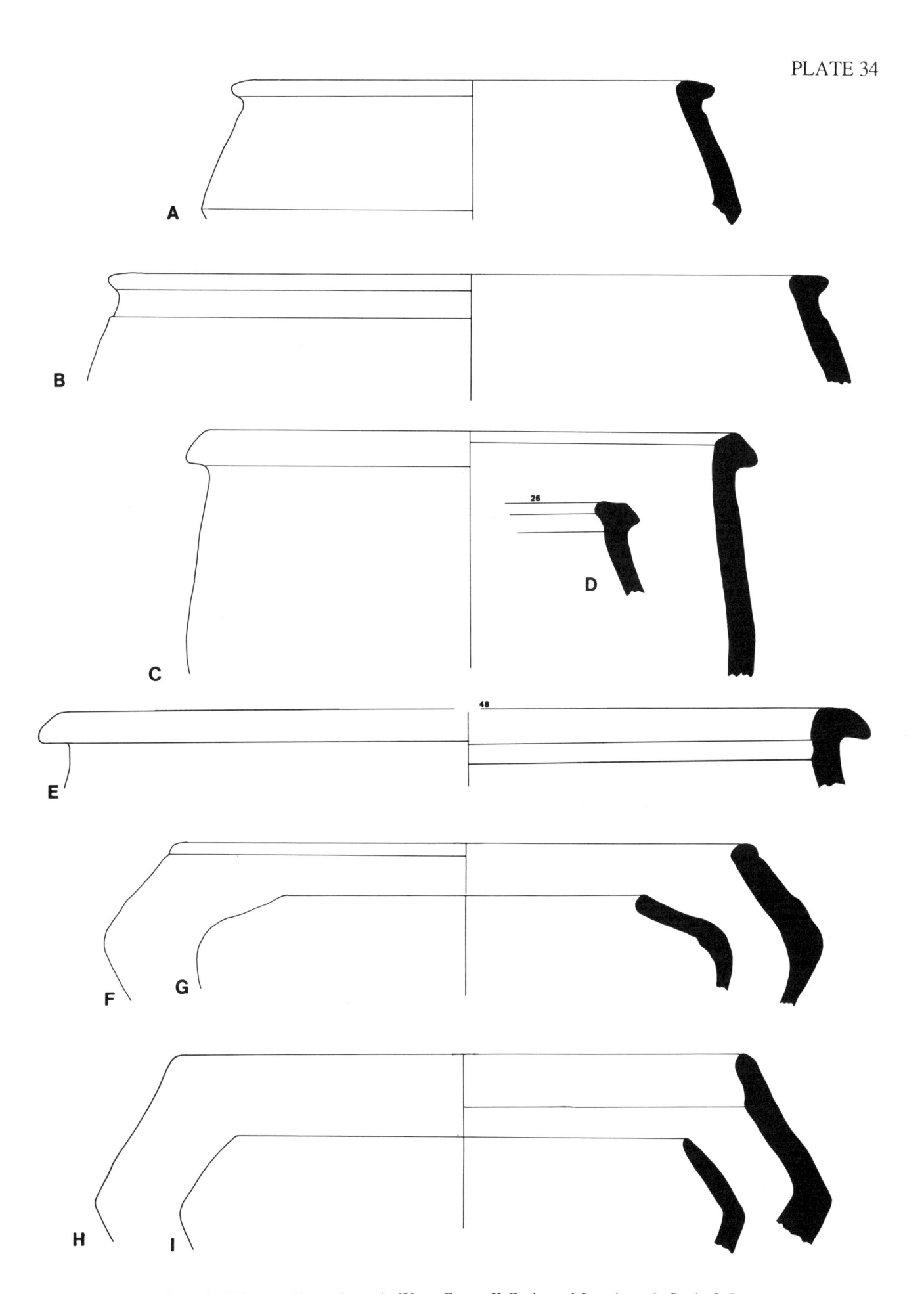

Period VI Pottery From Area A: Ware Group II Carinated Jars (*cont.*). Scale 2:5.

Plate 35. Period VI Pottery From Areas A and C01: Ware Group II Jars and Funnel. Scale 2:5.

|   | MRN | CONTEXT | FCN | WARE | FORM | TYPE | DECO. | WARE/REMARKS |
|---|---|---|---|---|---|---|---|---|
| A | 11407 | A08-1632/42-040 | 305 | 14 | 1427 | Jar 21 | Bns. | Orange-buff clay, prominent gray core; straw/chaff-tempered; exterior surface lightly burnished. |
| B | 11478 | A07-1972-085 | 786 | 13 | 1427 | Jar 21 | — | Brownish clay, prominent gray core; fast wheel striations visible on interior and exterior. |
| C | 5632 | A09-0462-009 | D132 | 13 | 933 | Unass. Jar | — | Orange clay, light brownish-buff core; straw/chaff-tempered; exterior smoothed. |
| D | 11739 | A08-0511-051 | 499 | 13 | 808 | Jar 2a | — | Orange-buff clay, gray core; straw/chaff-tempered; exterior smoothed. |
| E | 3942 | A07-0750-023 | 221 | 13 | 808 | Jar 2a | — | Orange-buff clay, gray core; straw/chaff-tempered; a few scattered grits also visible; buff slip on both surfaces; out of context in Period IV deposit. |
| F | 11060 | A08-0501/02-035 | 324 | 13 | 129 | Jar 3 | — | Brownish clay, prominent gray core; straw/chaff-tempered. |
| G | 11013 | A07-1691-075 | 613 | 13 | 1367 | Unass. Jar | — | Brownish-buff clay, prominent gray core. |
| H | — | Area A, Provenance lost | — | 13 | — | Funnel | — | Brownish clay, prominent gray core; straw/chaff-tempered; wheel striations visible near rim interior. |
| I | 6347 | C01-0169/79/89-122 | 1721 | 13 | 1061 | Jar 22 | — | Straw/chaff-tempered ware. |
| J | 11000 | A07-1680-075 | 600 | 13 | 1373 | Jar 22 | — | Dense brownish-buff clay, diffuse light gray core; straw/chaff-tempered; pinkish-buff slip on exterior. |
| K | 11090 | A08-0500-086 | 339 | 13 | 1385 | Jar 22 | — | Orange clay, gray core; straw/chaff-tempered. |
| L | 11120 | A07-1870/71-082 | 688 | 13 | 1385 | Jar 22 | — | Orange-buff clay, brown core; straw/chaff-tempered. |

PLATE 35

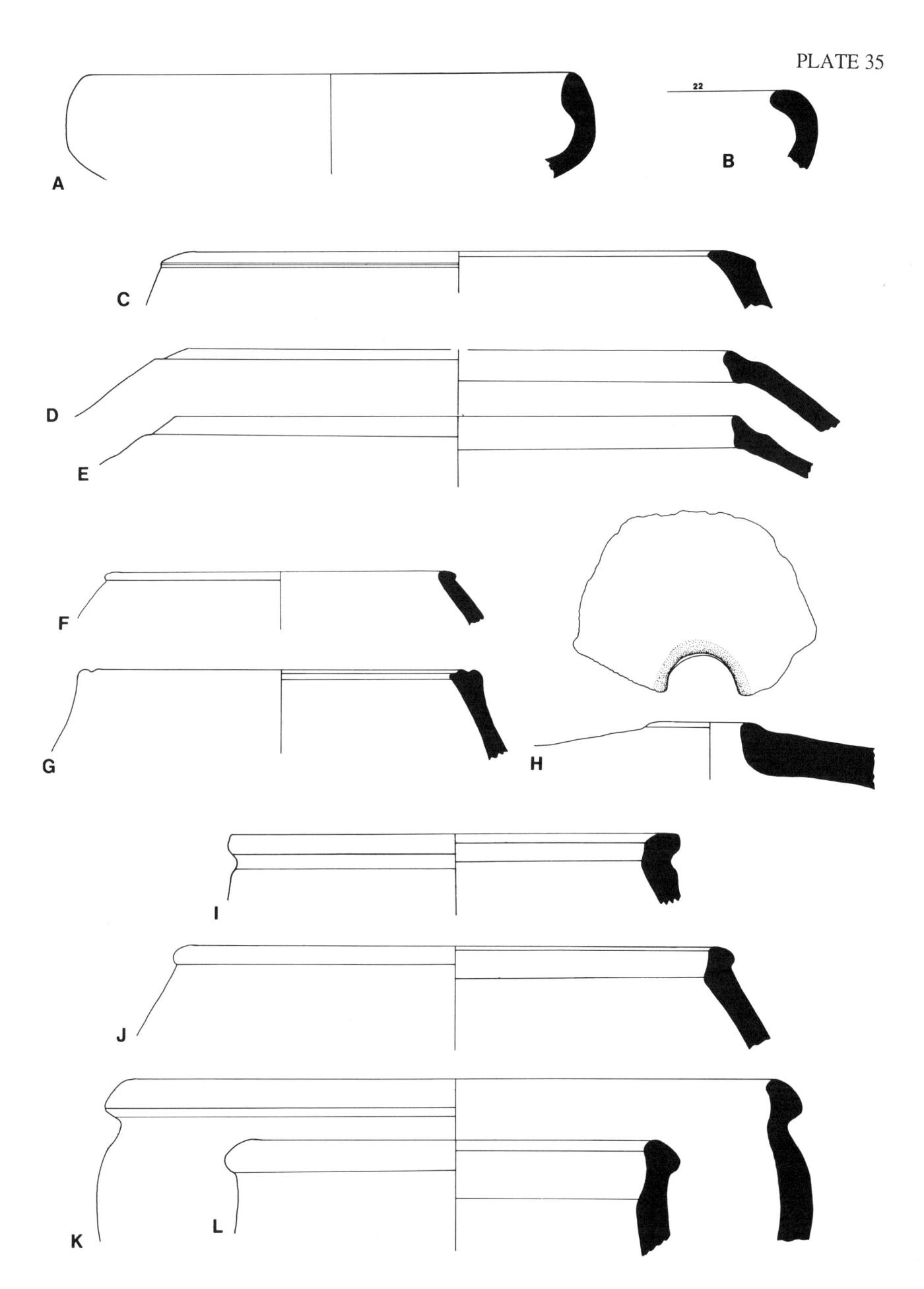

Period VI Pottery From Areas A and C01: Ware Group II Jars and Funnel. Scale 2:5.

Plate 36. Period VI Pottery From Areas A and C01: Ware Group II Jars (*cont.*). Scale 2:5.

|   | MRN | CONTEXT | FCN | WARE | FORM | TYPE | DECO. | WARE/REMARKS |
|---|-----|---------|-----|------|------|------|-------|--------------|
| A | 6063 | A09-05-012 | 178 | 28 | 970 | Jar 22 | — | Dark brown clay; tempered with a combination of finely-chopped chaff, some small-sized grits and mica flakes. |
| B | 1169 | A08-10-053 | 518 | 13 | 1466 | Jar 23 | — | Orange-brownish clay, gray core; straw/chaff-tempered; exterior surface smoothed; buff slip on interior surface. |
| C | 12459 | A07-24-102 | 985 | 14 | 1483 | Jar 23 | Bns. | Brownish clay, light gray core; irregular horizontal burnishing marks. |
| D | 11028 | A07-17-076 | 628 | 13 | 1267 | Jar 13 | — | Orange-brownish clay, prominent gray core; straw/chaff-tempered. |
| E | 11133 | A07-1790-079 | 0701 | 14 | 1398 | Jar 24 | Bns. | Orange-buff clay, prominent gray core; straw/chaff-tempered; exterior surface lightly burnished. |
| F | 6347 | C01-0189/79/69-122 | 1721 | 29 | 1064 | Jar 24 | Bns. | Dark brown-black clay, mixed finely-chopped chaff and grit-tempering; light burnishing on exterior surface which is mottled grayish. |
| G | 11407 | A08-1032/42-040 | 365 | 13 | 1445 | Jar 24 | — | Brown clay, prominent gray core; fire smudges on both interior and exterior surfaces; faint traces of flint scraping on exterior lower body. |
| H | 11629 | A08-05-049 | 457 | 13 | 1445 | Jar 24 | — | Fairly dense orange clay; finely-chopped chaff used as tempering; a few small-sized grits also visible. |
| I | 11573 | A08-05-046 | 430 | 13 | 1445 | Jar 24 | — | Brownish-buff clay, prominent gray core; somewhat porous; straw/chaff-tempered; coarse. |

PLATE 36

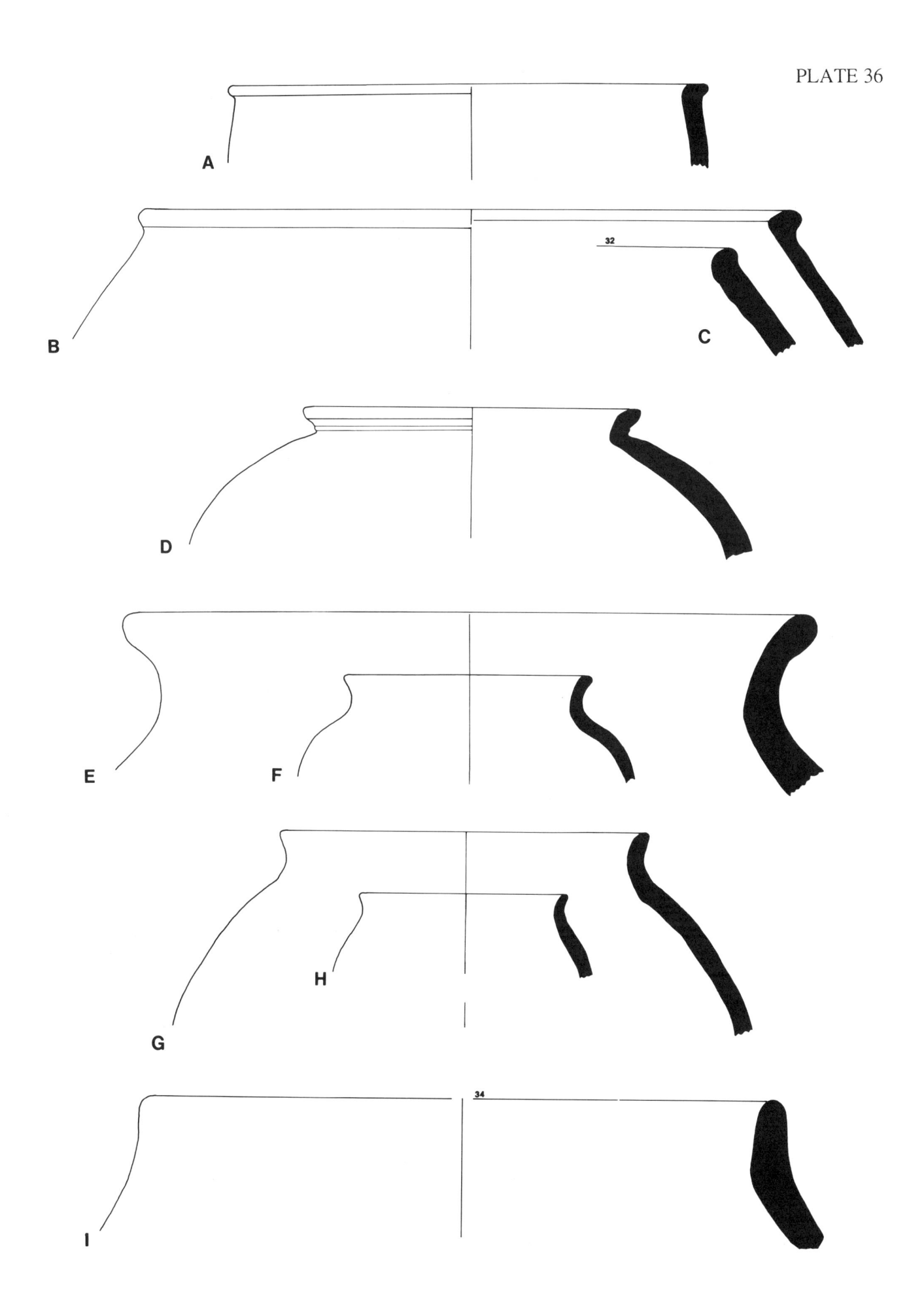

Period VI Pottery From Areas A and C01: Ware Group II Jars (*cont.*). Scale 2:5.

Plate 37. Period VI Pottery From Areas A and C01: Ware Group II Jars (*cont.*). Scale 2:5.

|   | MRN | Context | FCN | Ware | Form | Type | Deco. | Ware/Remarks |
|---|---|---|---|---|---|---|---|---|
| A | 6837 | A08-07-030 | 224 | 13 | 1028 | Jar 25 | — | Orange-buff clay, gray core; straw/chaff-tempered; exterior surface well smoothed. |
| B | 6837 | A08-07-030 | 224 | 13 | 1028 | Jar 25 | — | Brownish clay, gray core; straw/chaff-tempered; interior surface somewhat rough. |
| C | 11739 | A08-0511-051 | 499 | 13 | 508 | Jar 25 | — | Orange clay, prominent gray core; straw/chaff-tempered; exterior surface is well smoothed. |
| D | 11059 | A08-0501/02-035 | 323 | 13 | 1333 | Jar 25 | — | Orange clay, no core; straw/chaff-tempered; a few scattered large-sized grits also used as tempering. |
| E | 11172 | A07-17-083 | 727 | 13 | 1406 | Jar 26 | — | Brownish clay; light gray core; straw/chaff-tempered; exterior surface is smoothed. |
| F | 11698 | A08-10-049 | 473 | 13 | 1446 | Jar 26 | — | Orange/brownish-buff clay, prominent gray core; straw/chaff-tempered. |
| G | 6837 | A08-07-030 | 224 | 13 | 1033 | Jar 26 | — | Brownish clay; no core; straw/chaff-tempered; exterior surface smoothed and covered with a buff slip. |
| H | 2326 | C01-0167/68/69-063 | 764 | 14 | 113 | Jar 27 | — | Orange clay, prominent gray core; straw/chaff-tempered; exterior surface is orange and burnished, interior is gray; out of context in Period V–IV deposit. |
| I | 487 | A07-02-002 | 003 | 13 | 112 | Jar 27 | — | Orange clay, prominent gray core; straw/chaff-tempered; irregular; out of context in later mixed period wash. |

PLATE 37

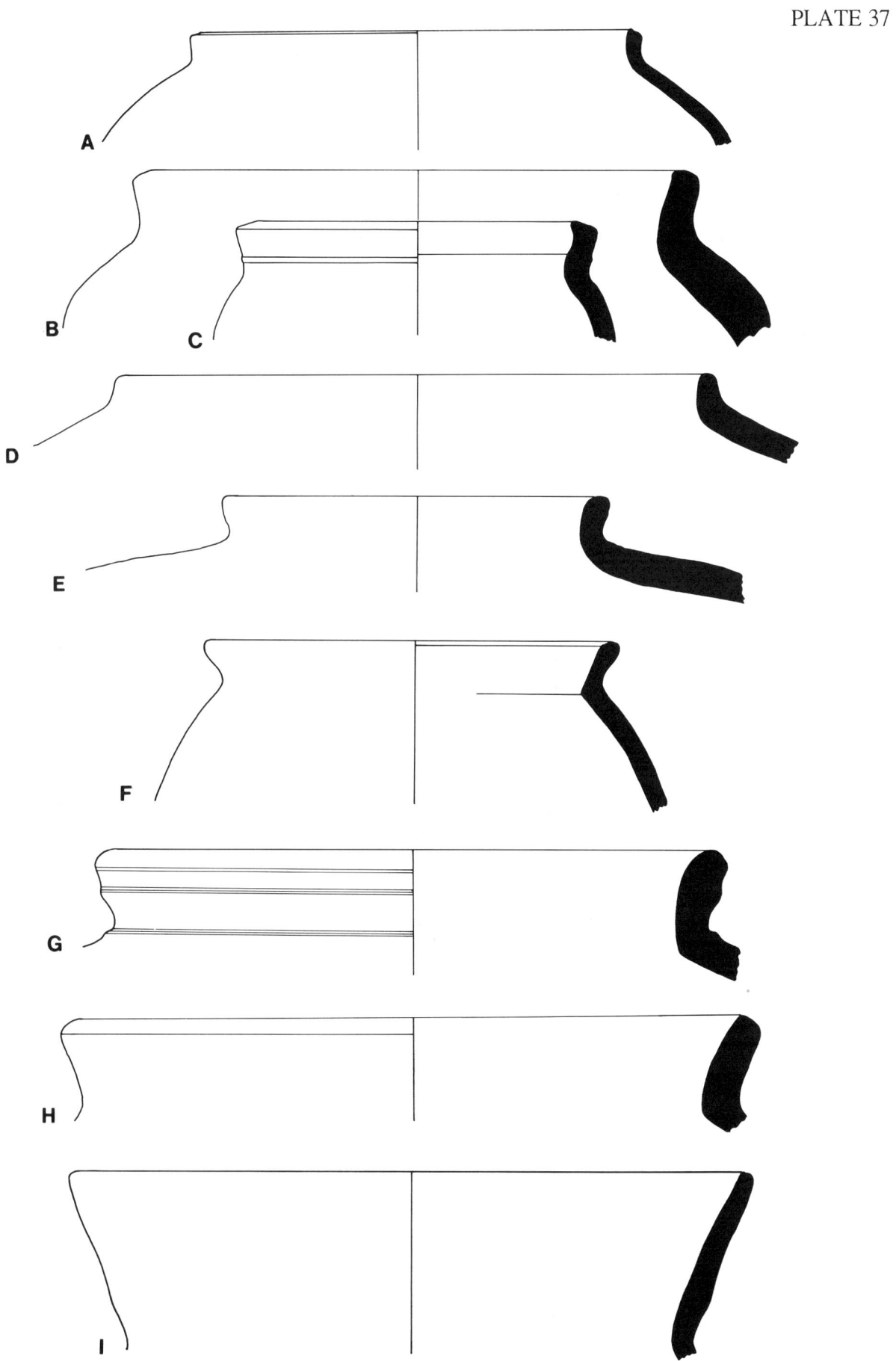

Period VI Pottery From Areas A and C01: Ware Group II Jars (*cont.*). Scale 2:5.

Plate 38. Period VI Pottery From Areas A and B: Ware Group II Jars (*cont.*). Scale 2:5.

|   | MRN | CONTEXT | FCN | WARE | FORM | TYPE | DECO. | WARE/REMARKS |
|---|---|---|---|---|---|---|---|---|
| A | 5322 | A09-0462-009 | D121 | 14 | 937 | Jar 28 | Bns. | Orange-brownish clay, no core; tempered with finely-chopped chaff and scattered small-sized gray and white grits; exterior surface covered with brownish-red wash; irregularly burnished with horizontal strokes. |
| B | 11607 | A07-19-094 | 863 | 14 | 1437 | Jar 28 | Bns. | Orange-buff clay, prominent gray core; straw/chaff-tempered; red wash on both surfaces; exterior burnished. |
| C | 6836 | A08-07-031 | 228 | 14 | 1437 | Jar 28 | Bns. | Orange clay; straw/chaff-tempered; exterior burnished. |
| D | 11764 | A08-05-032 | 513 | 13 | 1043 | Jar 29 | — | Brownish-buff clay, gray core; straw/chaff-tempered; exterior surface mottled orange and brown. |
| E | 11133 | A07-1790-079 | D701 | 13 | 79 | Jar 29 | — | Brownish-orangish clay, prominent gray core; straw/chaff-tempered. |
| F | 11604 | A08-0500/01-042 | 446 | 13 | 1043 | Jar 29 | — | Light brownish-buff clay, prominent gray core; straw/chaff-tempered; a few scattered large-sized grits also visible. |
| G | 11141 | A08-0500-038 | D343 | 14 | 1043 | Jar 29 | Bns. | Brownish clay, prominent gray core; straw/chaff-tempered; exterior smoothed and lightly burnished. |
| H | 11154 | A08-0500-039 | 347 | 13 | 1043 | Jar 29 | — | Brownish clay, light gray core; straw/chaff-tempered. |
| I | 11028 | A07-1691-075 | 613 | 13 | 1043 | Jar 29 | — | Brownish-buff clay, prominent gray core; straw/chaff-tempered. |
| J | 445 | B01-05-014 | 167 | 13 | 79 | Jar 29 | — | Brownish clay, prominent gray core; straw/chaff-tempered; a few scattered small-sized white grits also visible; out of context in Period IV deposits. |
| K | 11154 | A08-0500-039 | 347 | 13 | 79 | Jar 29 | — | Orange-buff clay, prominent gray core; straw/chaff-tempered; rim interior and top fire smudged. |

PLATE 38

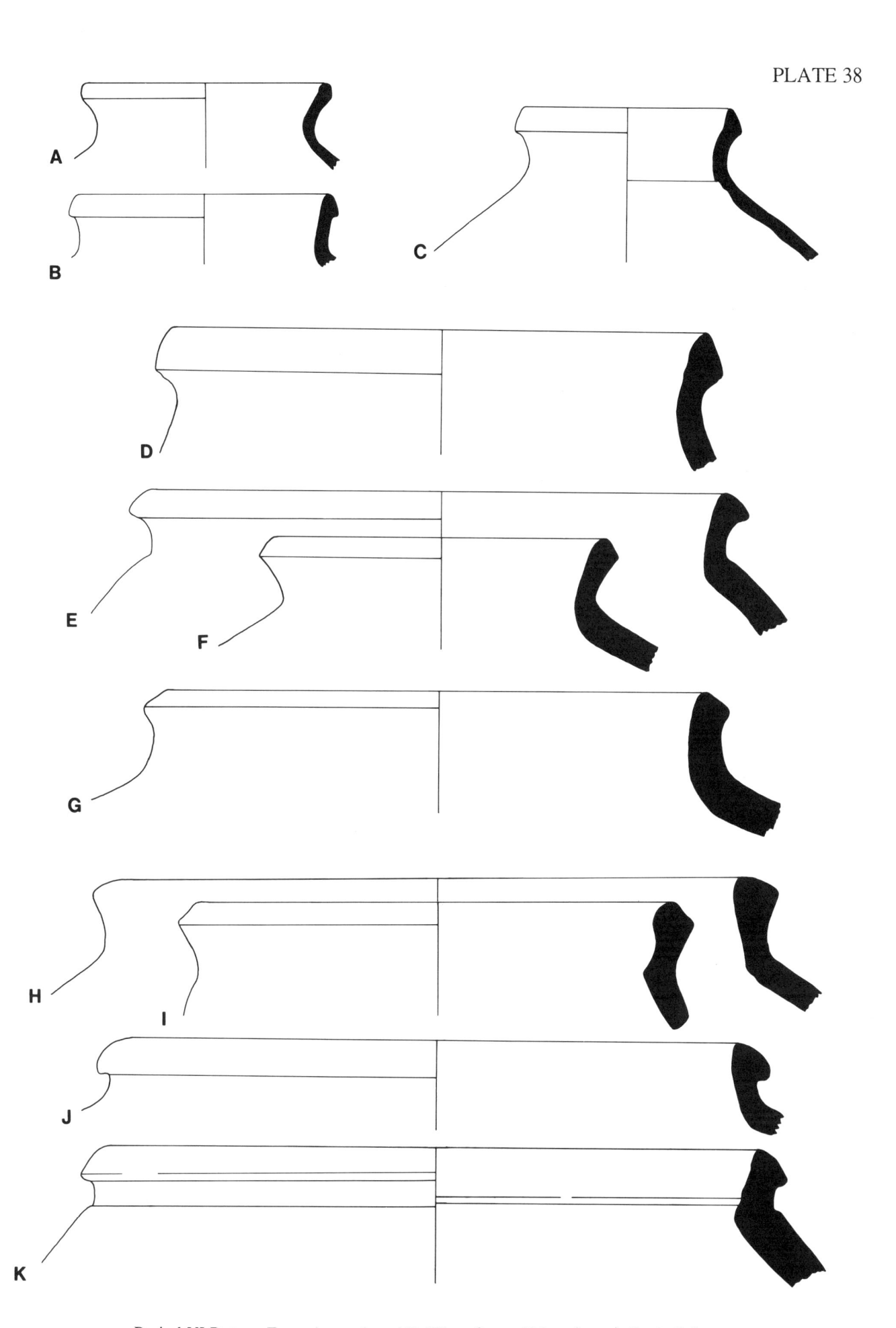

Period VI Pottery From Areas A and B: Ware Group II Jars (*cont.*). Scale 2:5.

Plate 39. Period VI Pottery From Areas A and C01: Ware Group II Jars (*cont.*). Scale 2:5.

|   | MRN | CONTEXT | FCN | WARE | FORM | TYPE | DECO. | WARE/REMARKS |
|---|---|---|---|---|---|---|---|---|
| A | 11170 | A07-18-083 | 724 | 13 | 1441 | Jar 30 | — | Brownish clay, prominent gray core; straw/chaff-tempered. |
| B | 11607 | A07-19-094 | 863 | 13 | 1438 | Jar 30 | — | Brownish clay, prominent gray core; straw/chaff-tempered. |
| C | 11074 | A08-0500/01-036 | 333 | 13 | 1030 | Jar 4c | — | Dense orange-buff clay, prominent gray core; straw/chaff-tempered. |
| D | 4935 | C01-01-093 | 1414 | 13 | 889 | Jar 4c | — | Light brownish-buff clay; straw/chaff-tempered; occasional scattered large-sized grits also visible; out of context in Period V deposits. |
| E | 11138 | A07-1781-079 | D706 | 13 | 1473 | Jar 31 | — | Orange clay grading to gray on interior surface; straw/chaff-tempered. |
| F | 6063 | A09-05-012 | 178 | 13 | 963 | Jar 31 | — | Fairly dense brownish clay, light gray core; straw/chaff-tempered; a few scattered small-sized grits also visible; buff slip on exterior. |
| G | 6837 | A08-07-030 | 224 | 13 | 1034 | Jar 19b | — | Orange-brownish clay; straw/chaff-tempered. |
| H | 6797 | A09-0870/80-016 | 228 | 13 | 1009 | Jar 19a | — | Orange-buff clay; straw/chaff-tempered; fast wheel striations on interior. |
| I | 11547 | A07-1990/91-089 | 826 | 13 | 1433 | Jar 19c | — | Greenish-buff clay, diffuse light gray core; clay grades to orange on inner surface; straw/chaff-tempered. |
| J | 12325 | A09-07-019 | 247 | 13 | 1532 | Jar 19c | — | Brownish-buff clay, prominent gray core; straw/chaff-tempered; exterior smoothed. |

PLATE 39

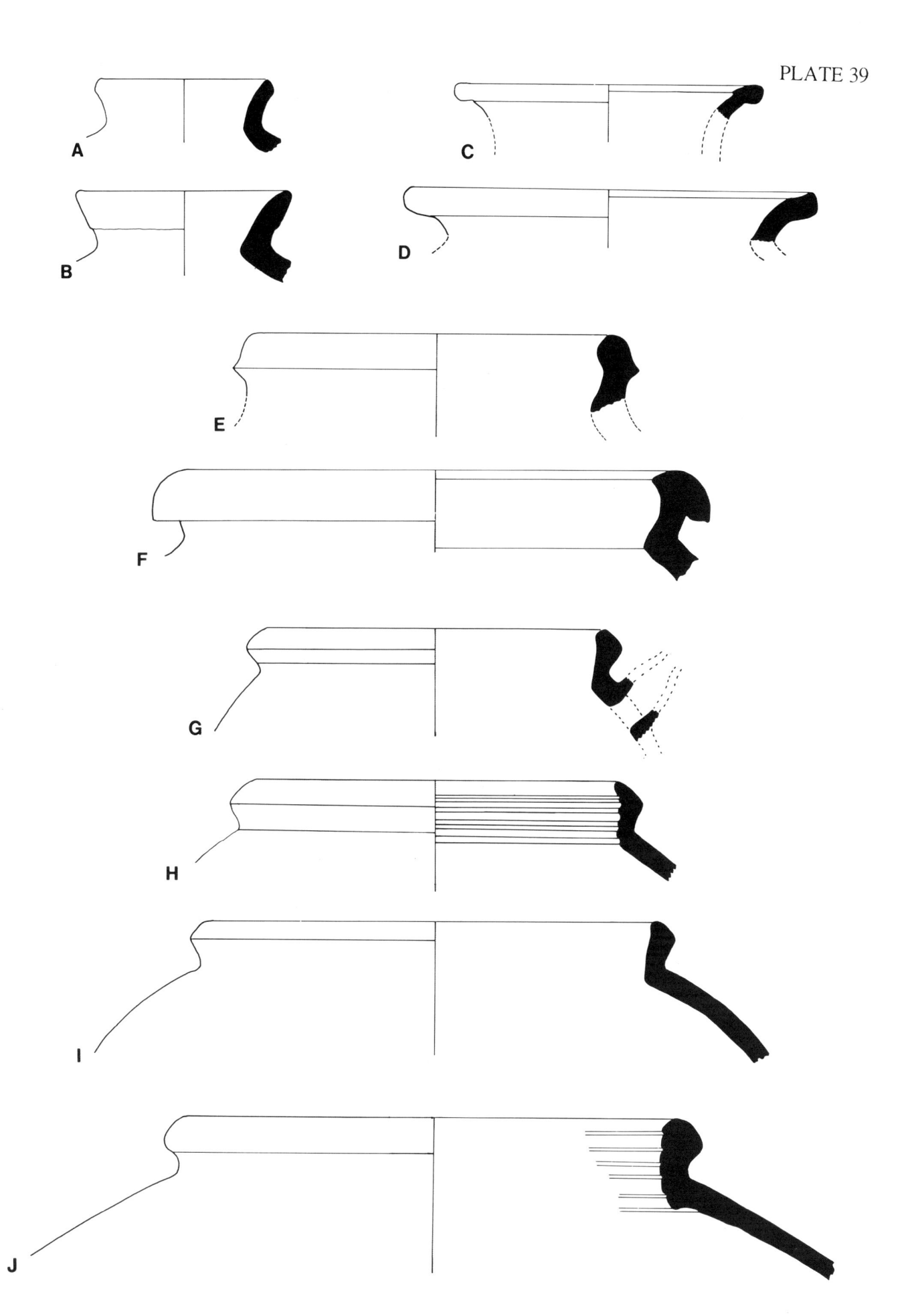

Period VI Pottery From Areas A and C01: Ware Group II Jars (*cont.*). Scale 2:5.

Plate 40. Period VI Pottery From Area A: Ware Group II Jars (*cont.*). Scale 2:5.

|   | MRN | CONTEXT | FCN | WARE | FORM | TYPE | DECO. | WARE/REMARKS |
|---|---|---|---|---|---|---|---|---|
| A | 866 | A07-05-003 | 014 | 13 | 366 | Jar 32 | — | Orange-buff clay, gray core; straw/chaff-tempered; out of context in slope wash. |
| B | 5322 | A09-0462-009 | D121 | 13 | 938 | Jar 32 | — | Brownish clay, gray core; straw/chaff-tempered; some small-sized white grits also visible; fire smudges on exterior. |
| C | 6837 | A08-07-030 | 224 | 13 | 1035 | Jar 32 | — | Brownish clay, gray core; straw/chaff-tempered; interior surface coarse, exterior smoothed and covered with brown wash. |
| D | 11182 | A07-18-083 | 731 | 13 | 1393 | Jar 32 | — | Orange-buff clay, prominent gray core; straw/chaff-tempered. |
| E | 8149 | A07-1582-072 | 503 | 13 | 1382 | Jar 32 | — | Brownish clay, prominent gray core; straw/chaff-tempered; some occasional small-sized pebbles also visible. |
| F | 9326 | A08-06-025 | 211 | 13 | 1045 | Jar 32 | — | Orange-buff clay, prominent gray core; straw/chaff-tempered; exterior smoothed. |
| G | 11090 | A08-0500-036 | 339 | 13 | 1386 | Jar 32 | — | Orange-buff clay, prominent gray core; straw/chaff-tempered. |
| H | 7738 | A07-14-058 | 422 | 13 | 1270 | Jar 32 | — | Orange-buff clay, prominent dark gray core; straw/chaff-tempered; out of context in Period IV deposits. |

PLATE 40

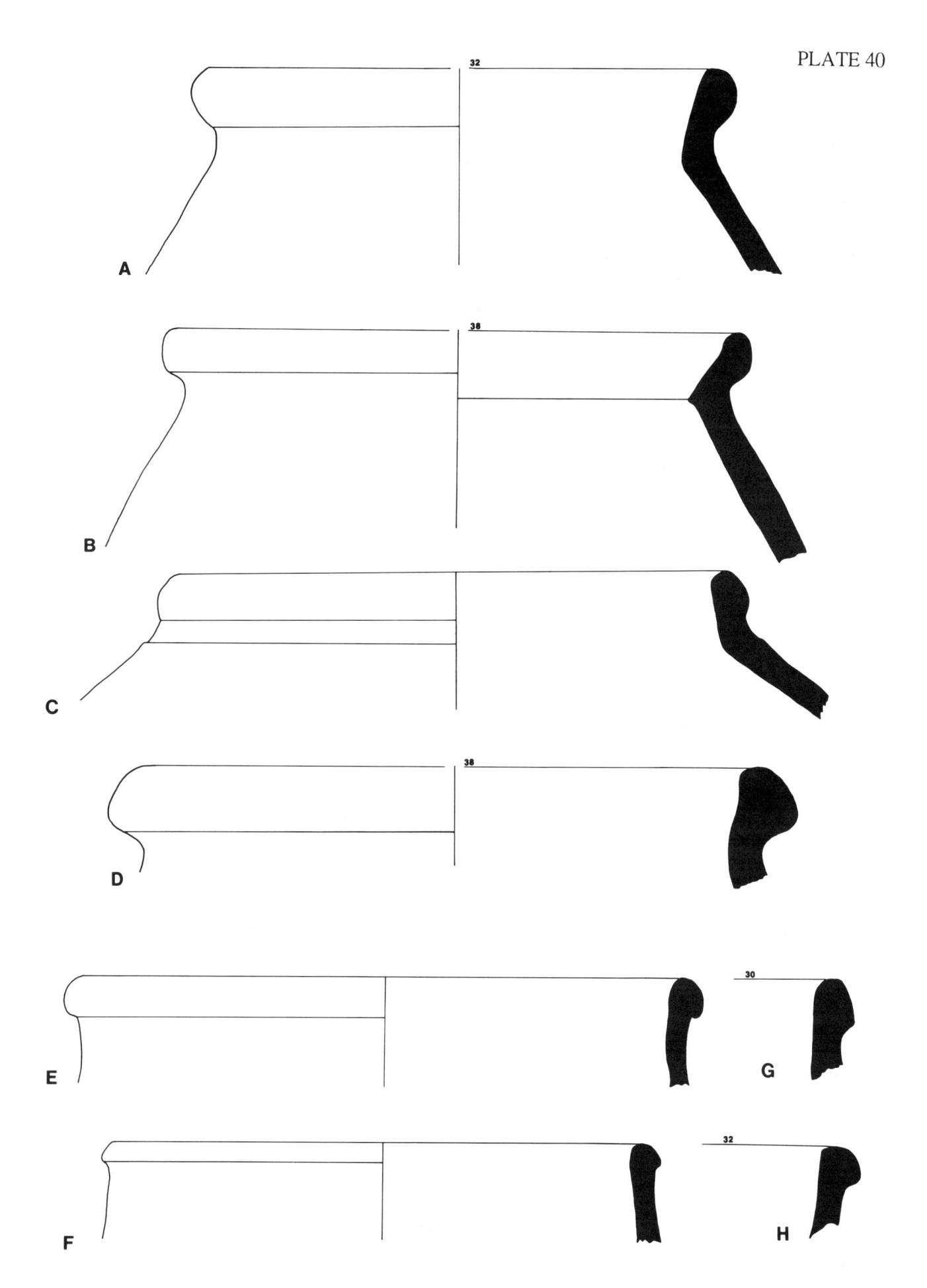

Period VI Pottery From Area A: Ware Group II Jars (*cont.*). Scale 2:5.

Plate 41. Period VI Pottery From Area A: Ware Group II Jars (*cont.*). Scale 2:5.

|   | MRN | CONTEXT | FCN | WARE | FORM | TYPE | DECO. | WARE/REMARKS |
|---|---|---|---|---|---|---|---|---|
| A | 1782 | A08-02-002 | D044 | 13 | 506 | Jar 33 | — | Orange-buff clay; prominent gray core; straw/chaff-tempered; out of context in slope wash. |
| B | 6702 | A09-0870/80-016 | 234 | 14 | 1004 | Jar 33 | Bns. | Orange-buff clay; prominent gray core; straw/chaff-tempered; lightly burnished on exterior and top of rim. |
| C | 11478 | A07-1972-085 | 786 | 13 | 506a | Jar 33 | — | Brownish clay, prominent gray core; straw/chaff-tempered; a few scattered small-sized grits also visible. |
| D | 11618 | A08-0501-048 | 456 | 13 | 1432 | Jar 34 | — | Greenish-buff clay, light gray core; straw/chaff-tempered. |
| E | 11020 | A07-1770/80-076 | 620 | 13 | 1368 | Unass. Jar | — | Brownish clay, no core; straw/chaff-tempered; some small-sized grits also visible. |
| F | 6063 | A09-05-012 | 178 | 13 | 964 | Jar 34 | — | Brownish clay, light gray core; straw/chaff-tempered; some small-sized grits also visible. |
| G | 7079 | A08-07-028 | 221 | 13 | 1040 | Jar 35 | — | Orange clay, prominent gray core; straw/chaff-tempered; faint traces of red wash on surface. |
| H | 11721 | A08-0511-051 | 487 | 13 | 1448 | Jar 36 | — | Orange clay, thick and prominent dark gray core; straw/chaff-tempered. |

PLATE 41

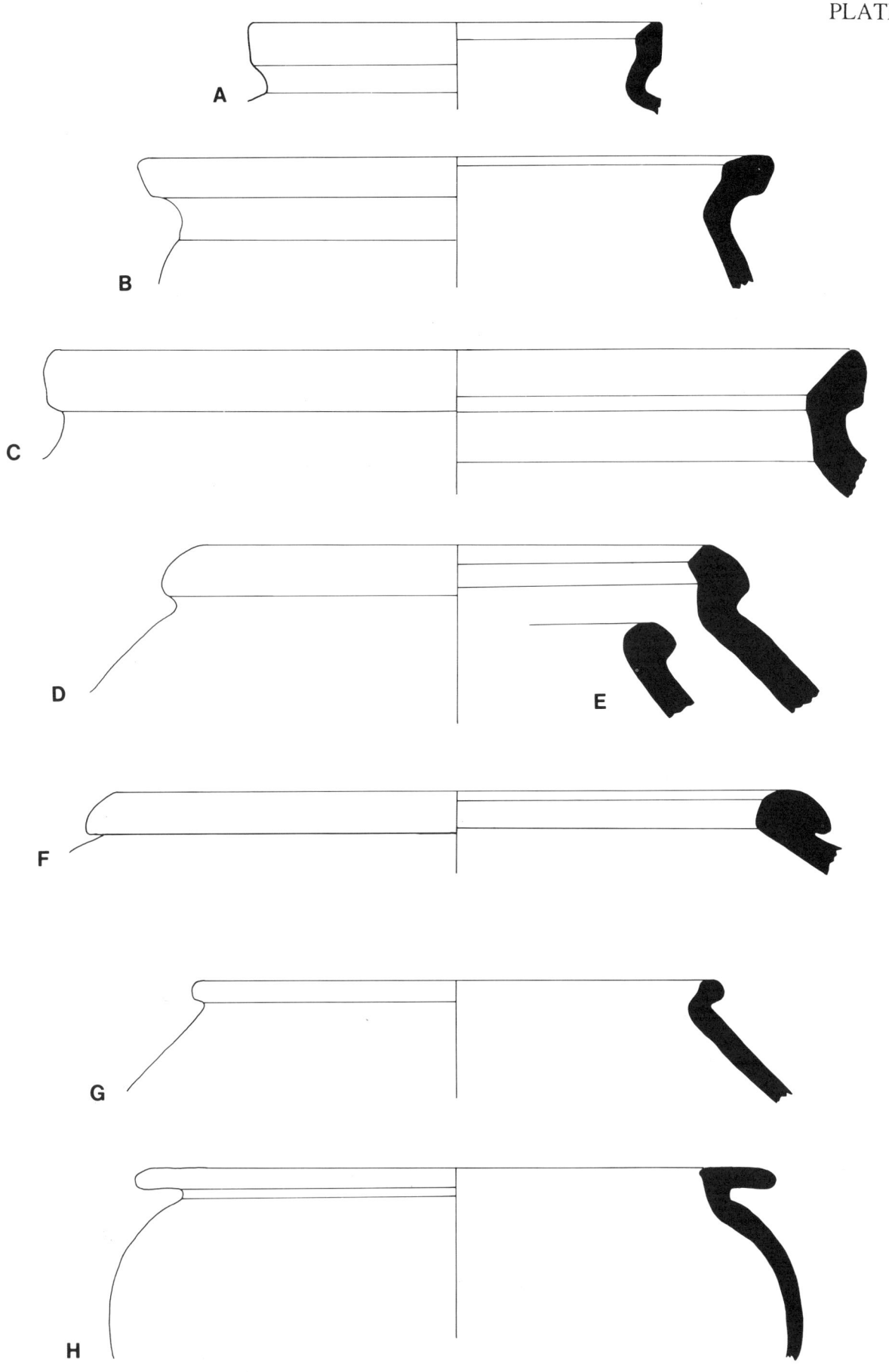

Period VI Pottery From Area A: Ware Group II Jars (*cont.*). Scale 2:5.

Plate 42. Period VI Pottery From Area A: Ware Group II Jars (*cont.*) and Miscellaneous Karaz Ware Sherds. Scale 2:5.

|   | MRN | Context | FCN | Ware | Form | Type | Deco. | Ware/Remarks |
|---|---|---|---|---|---|---|---|---|
| A | 11090 | A08-0500-036 | 339 | 13 | 1387 | Unass. Jar | — | Brownish clay, straw/chaff-tempered, very prominent straw imprints; surface smoothed. |
| B | 6837 | A08-07-030 | 224 | 13 | 1031 | Unass. Jar | — | Brownish clay, no core; straw/chaff-tempered; a few scattered large-sized grits also visible; exterior fire blackened in spots. |
| C | 7997 | A07-15-070 | 477 | 13 | 1321 | Unass. Jar | — | Brownish-buff clay, no core; straw/chaff-tempered. |
| D | 11133 | A07-1790-079 | D701 | 13 | 963a | Unass. Jar | — | Brownish-buff clay, prominent gray core; straw/chaff-tempered. |
| E | 11074 | A08-0500/01-035 | 333 | 13 | 866 | Unass. Jar | — | Brownish-buff clay; straw/chaff-tempered. |
| F | 6362 | A08-06-024 | 205 | 37 | 1039 | Unass. Jar | Bns. | Karaz Ware; dense brownish clay, gray core; finely-chopped chaff used as tempering; exterior is brownish on bottom, orange on top; interior is orange; both surfaces are well burnished and horizontal burnishing strokes may be distinguished on the interior. |
| G | 6558 | A09-03-013 | 200 | 37 | 807 | Bowl 9c | Bns. | Karaz Ware; dense brownish clay; tempered with both finely-chopped chaff and small-sized grits, including some white ones; exterior and interior are black; highly burnished with horizontal strokes. |
| H | 6609 | A08-07-028 | 214 | 37 | 1690 | Unass. Jar | Bns. | Karaz Ware; dense brownish clay; exterior is black, interior is orange; slightly burnished. |

PLATE 42

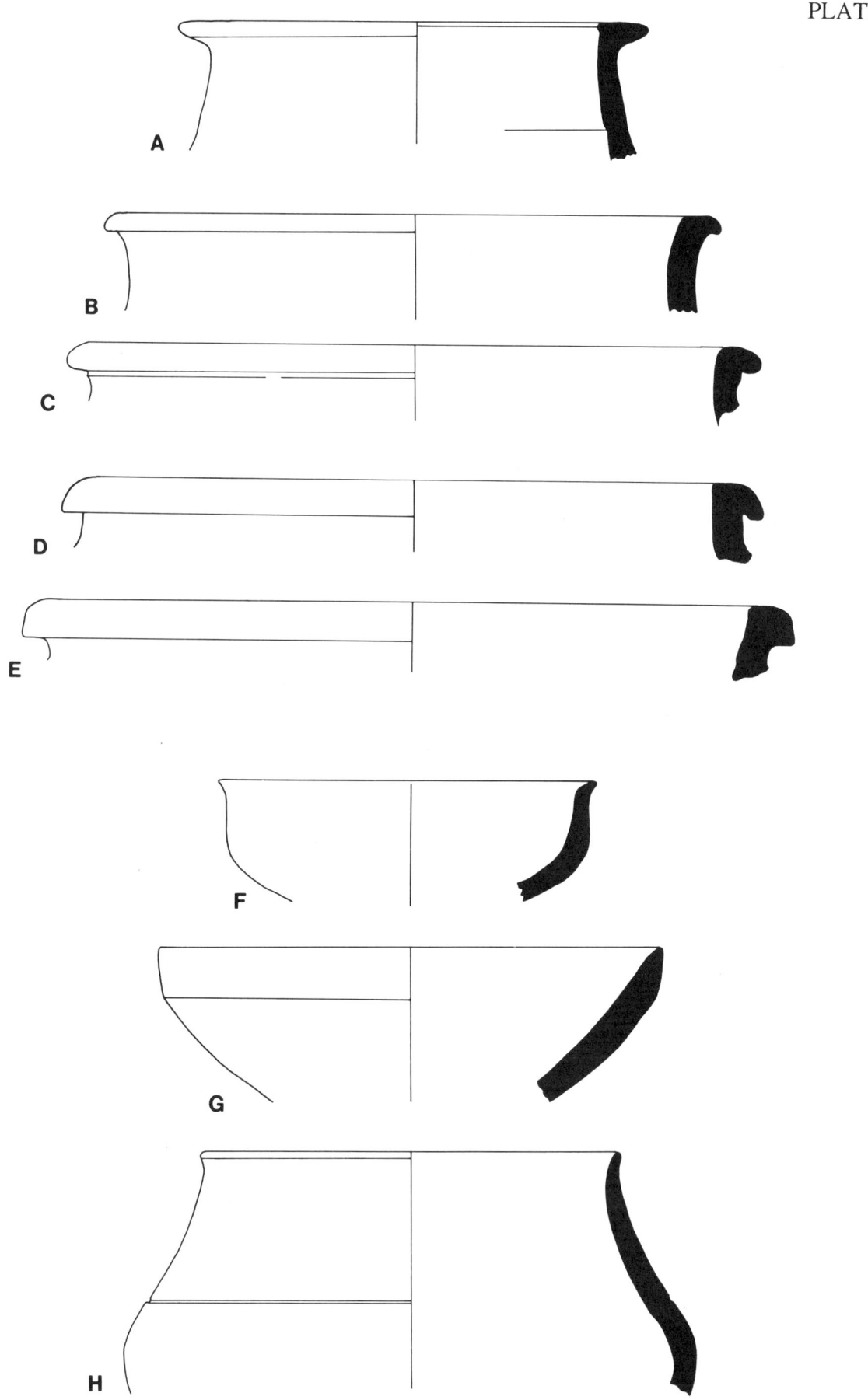

Period VI Pottery From Area A: Ware Group II Jars (*cont.*) and Miscellaneous Karaz Ware Sherds. Scale 2:5.

Plate 43. Period V Pottery From Area C01: Ware Group I Bowls. Scale 2:5.

|   | MRN | Context | FCN | Ware | Form | Type | Deco. | Ware/Remarks |
|---|---|---|---|---|---|---|---|---|
| A | 3366 | C01-0177/78/79-078 | 1006 | 04 | 727 | Bowl 1 | — | Orange-buff clay; small-sized white grits; deep fast wheel corrugations visible on interior. |
| B | 5240 | C01-0169/79/89-110 | 1466 | 04 | 985 | Bowl 2 | — | Light greenish-buff clay; small-sized grits. |
| C | 13496 | C01-0937/38/39-101 | D2994 | 04 | 1275 | Bowl 3 | — | Brownish-buff clay; small-sized grits. |
| D | 3860 | C01-0177-090 | 1225 | 04 | 781 | Bowl 3 | — | Fairly dense grayish-buff clay; small-sized white grits. |
| E | 13541 | C01–1027/28/29-188 | D3088 | 04 | 1506 | Unass. Bowl | — | Fairly dense light greenish-buff clay; small-sized grits. |
| F | 13586 | C01-1007/08/09-195 | D3088 | 04 | 5 | Bowl 4a | — | Buff clay; small-sized grits. |
| G | 3078 | C01-0177/79-074 | 923 | 03 | 5a | Bowl 4b | — | Greenish-buff clay; no visible tempering. |
| H | 13017 | C01-1007-168 | 2516 | 04 | 5a | Bowl 4b | — | Fairly dense buff clay; small-sized grits. |
| I | 13586 | C01-1007/08/09-195 | D3088 | 04 | 1524 | Bowl 4a | — | Fairly dense brownish-buff clay; small-sized grits. |
| J | 2770 | C01-0187/88-074 | 898 | 03 | C-2 | Bowl 4a | — | Dense greenish-buff clay; no visible tempering. |
| K | 13063 | C01-0958-078 | 2560 | 03 | C-2 | Bowl 4a | — | Dense greenish-buff clay; no visible tempering; (= KH 1983/165). |
| L | 13436 | C01-1007/08/17/18-187 | D2933 | 03 | C-2 | Bowl 4a | — | Dense greenish clay; no visible tempering. |
| M | 13300 | C01-0947/48/49-088 | D2997 | 03 | C-50 | Bowl 4a | — | Dense greenish clay; no visible tempering. |
| N | 9027 | C01-1019-169 | 2476 | 03 | C-2 | Bowl 4a | — | Dense greenish clay; no visible tempering; (= KH 1983/124). |
| O | 4931 | C01-0187-093 | 1420 | 03 | C-2 | Bowl 4a | — | Dense greenish clay; no visible tempering; warped; (= KH 1981/82). |
| P | 13332 | C01-1007/08/17/18-182 | D2829 | 04 | C-2 | Bowl 4a | — | Dense buff clay; small-sized grits. |

PLATE 43

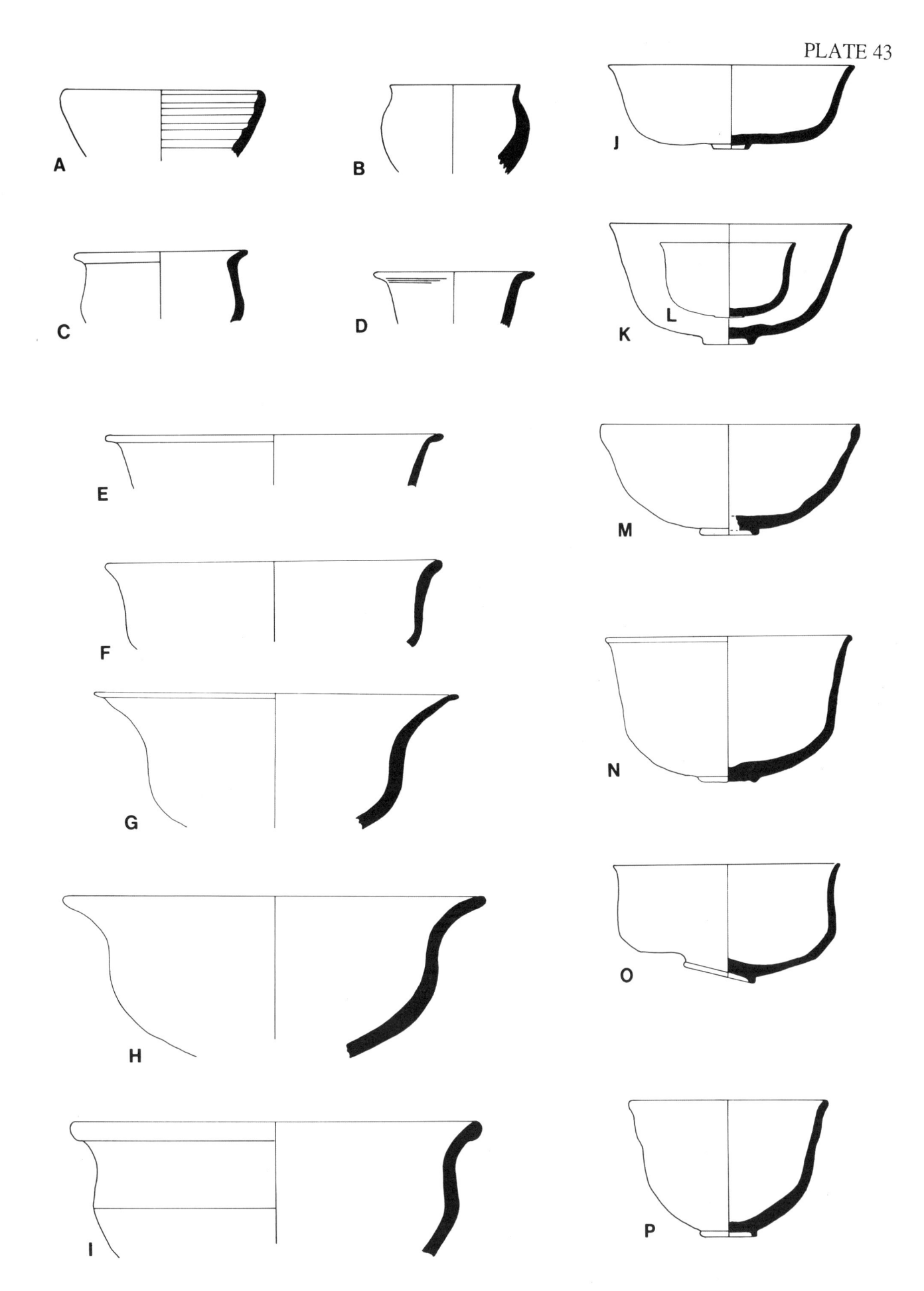

Period V Pottery From Area C01: Ware Group I Bowls. Scale 2:5.

Plate 44. Period V Pottery From Area C01: Ware Group I Bowls (*cont.*). Scale 2:5.

|   | MRN | CONTEXT | FCN | WARE | FORM | TYPE | DECO. | WARE/REMARKS |
|---|-----|---------|-----|------|------|------|-------|--------------|
| A | 5240 | C01-0169/79/89-110 | 1466 | 04 | 909 | Bowl 5a | — | Fairly dense, buff clay; small-sized grits. |
| B | 13386 | C01-09-183 | D2883 | 03 | 1503 | Bowl 5a | — | Dense grayish-buff clay; no visible tempering. |
| C | 13386 | C01-09-183 | D2883 | 04 | C-51 | Bowl 5a | — | Dense pinkish-buff clay; small-sized grits. |
| D | 5021 | C01-0167/77-108 | D1454 | 04 | 904 | Bowl 5b | — | Buff clay; small-sized grits. |
| E | 13626 | C01-0957/58-200 | D3158 | 04 | C-55 | Bowl 5c | — | Somewhat porous greenish-buff clay; small-sized black and white grits. |
| F | 13626 | C01-0957/58-200 | D3158 | 04 | 728 | Bowl 5c | — | Fairly dense buff clay; small-sized grits. |
| G | 13506 | C01-0937/38/39-188 | D3004 | 04 | 1503 | Bowl 5c | — | Greenish-buff clay; small-sized black grits. |
| H | 13251 | C01-0939-178 | D2748 | 04 | 909 | Bowl 5a | — | Buff, small-sized grits. |
| I | 13449 | C01-09-101 | — | 04 | 728 | Bowl 5c | — | Dense buff clay; no visible tempering. |
| J | 13599 | C01-0957/58/47/48-112 | D3101 | 04 | 1503 | Bowl 5c | — | Buff clay; small-sized grits. |
| K | 3366 | C01-0177/78/79-078 | 1006 | 04 | 728 | Bowl 5c | — | Buff clay; small-sized grits. |
| L | 13626 | C01-0957/58-200 | D3158 | 04 | 650 | Bowl 6a | — | Fairly dense buff clay; small-sized black grits; fast wheel mark striations visible on both surfaces. |
| M | 13684 | C01-1017/18/19-198 | D3216 | 04 | 650 | Bowl 6a | — | Buff clay; small-sized grits. |
| N | 8158 | C01-0957/59-062 | 2128 | 03 | 650 | Bowl 6a | — | Dense light greenish clay; no visible tempering. |
| O | 2700 | C01-0189-074 | 843 | 03 | 650 | Bowl 6a | — | Dense greenish-buff clay; no visible tempering. |
| P | 3078 | C01-1077/78-074 | 923 | 03 | 650 | Bowl 6a | — | Dense greenish clay; no visible tempering. |
| Q | 4935 | C01-01-093 | 1414 | 03 | C-9 | Bowl 6b | — | Dense greenish clay; no visible tempering; fast wheel striations visible on interior. |
| R | 9016 | C01-09-144/066 | 2240 | 03 | 1355 | Bowl 6b | — | Dense greenish clay; no visible tempering. |
| S | 2770 | C01-0189-074 | 843 | 14 | 697 | Bowl 6b | — | Dense buff clay; no visible tempering. |
| T | 13552 | C01-1007/08/09-195 | D3088 | 04 | 697 | Bowl 6b | — | Buff clay; light orange-buff core; small-sized white and black grits; buff slip on exterior. |

PLATE 44

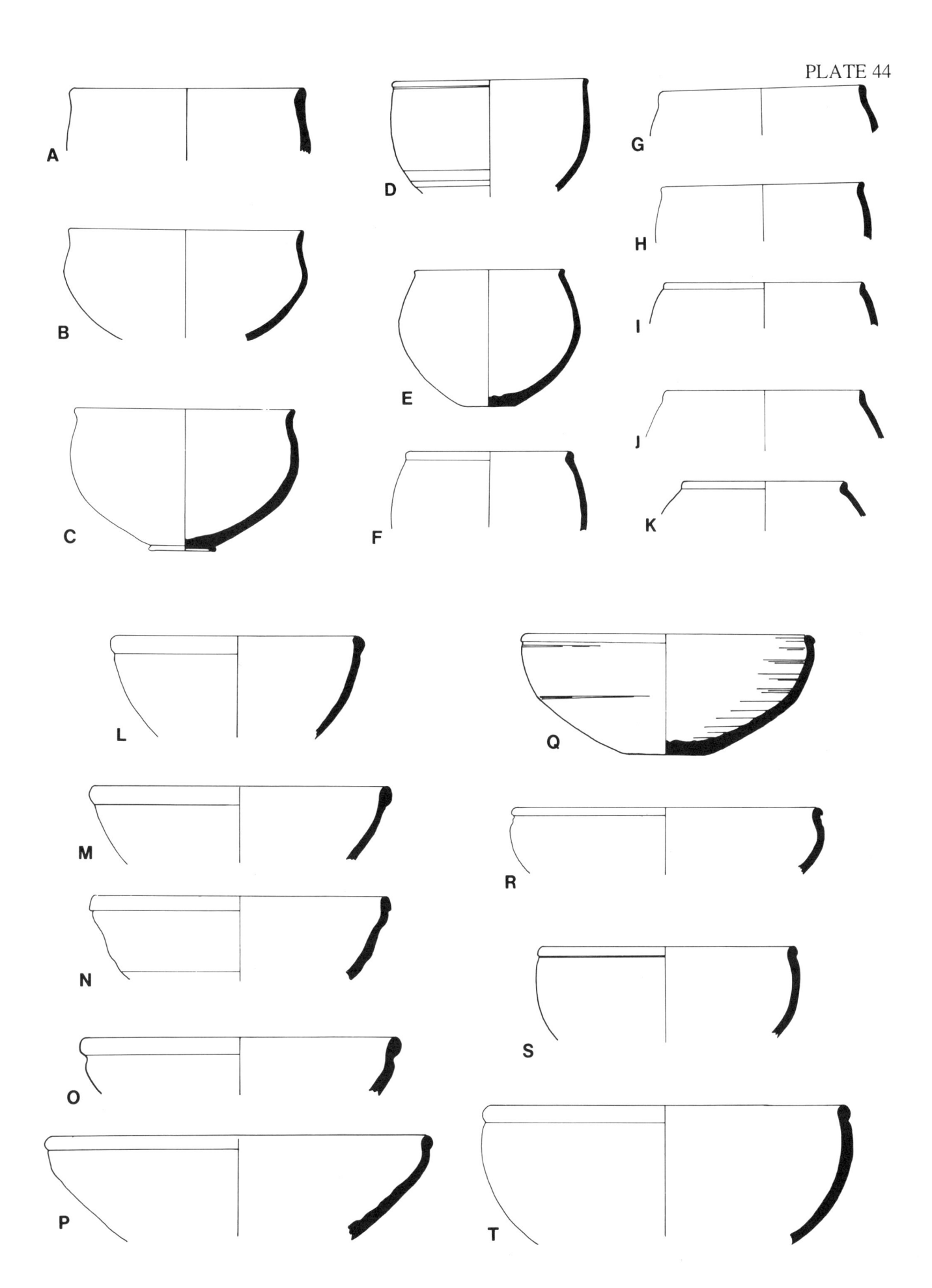

Period V Pottery From Area C01: Ware Group I Bowls (*cont.*). Scale 2:5.

Plate 45. Period V Pottery From Area C01: Ware Group I Bowls (*cont.*). Scale 2:5.

|   | MRN | CONTEXT | FCN | WARE | FORM | TYPE | DECO. | WARE/REMARKS |
|---|---|---|---|---|---|---|---|---|
| A | 13541 | C01-1027/28/29-188 | D3038 | 04 | 1507 | Bowl 7 | — | Pinkish-buff clay grading to buff on exterior; small-sized white grits; buff slip. |
| B | 13586 | C01-1007/08/09-195 | D3088 | 04 | 1507 | Bowl 7 | — | Brownish-buff clay; fairly gritty but only small-sized grits are visible; self slip of same color of clay on exterior. |
| C | 13541 | C01-1027/28/29-188 | D3038 | 04 | 1527 | Bowl 7 | — | Light greenish-buff clay; small-sized grits. |
| D | 13599 | C01-0957/58/47/48-112 | D3101 | 04 | 1507 | Bowl 7 | — | Dense buff clay; no visible tempering. |
| E | 13552 | C01-1017/18/19-191 | D3050 | 04 | 1523 | Bowl 8 | — | Brownish-buff clay; small-sized grits. |
| F | 4831 | C01-1017/27-106 | D1361 | 04 | 883 | Bowl 8 | — | Buff clay; very small white and gray grits; out of context in Period IVB deposits. |
| G | 3078 | C01-1077/78/79-074 | 923 | 03 | 679 | Bowl 9 | — | Greenish clay, somewhat more porous than normal; small-sized grits. |
| H | 3535 | C35-06-003 | 086 | 03 | 756 | Bowl 9 | — | Dense greenish clay; no visible tempering; out of context in Period IVB deposits. |
| I | 3858 | C01-0187/88-092 | 1241 | 04 | 779 | Bowl 10 | — | Dense pinkish-buff clay; no visible tempering. |
| J | 3859 | C01-0187/88-092 | 1247 | 03 | 779 | Bowl 10 | — | Dense greenish clay; no visible tempering. |
| K | 3078 | C01-0177/78/79-074 | 923 | 03 | 698 | Unass. Bowl | — | Dense greenish clay; no visible tempering. |
| L | 13684 | C01-1017/18/19-198 | D3216 | 04 | 1592 | Unass. Bowl | — | Fairly porous brownish-buff clay; small-sized white grits; pinkish slip on surface. |
| M | 3363 | C01-0167/68/69-073 | 1018 | 04 | 807 | Bowl 11 | — | Buff clay; small-sized grits. |
| N | 13065 | C01-0957/58/59-078 | 2562 | 04 | 47e | Bowl 11 | — | Brownish-buff clay; grit tempered. |
| O | 3863 | C01-0188-091 | 1226 | 04 | 1099 | Unass. Bowl | — | Light greenish-buff clay; gritty with small-sized white grits visible. |
| P | 13541 | C01-1027/28/29-188 | D3038 | 04 | 47e | Bowl 11 | — | Brownish-buff clay; small-sized white grits. |
| Q | 5238 | C01-0169/79/89-110 | D1471 | 04 | 479 | Bowl 11 | — | Buff clay; small-sized grits. |

PLATE 45

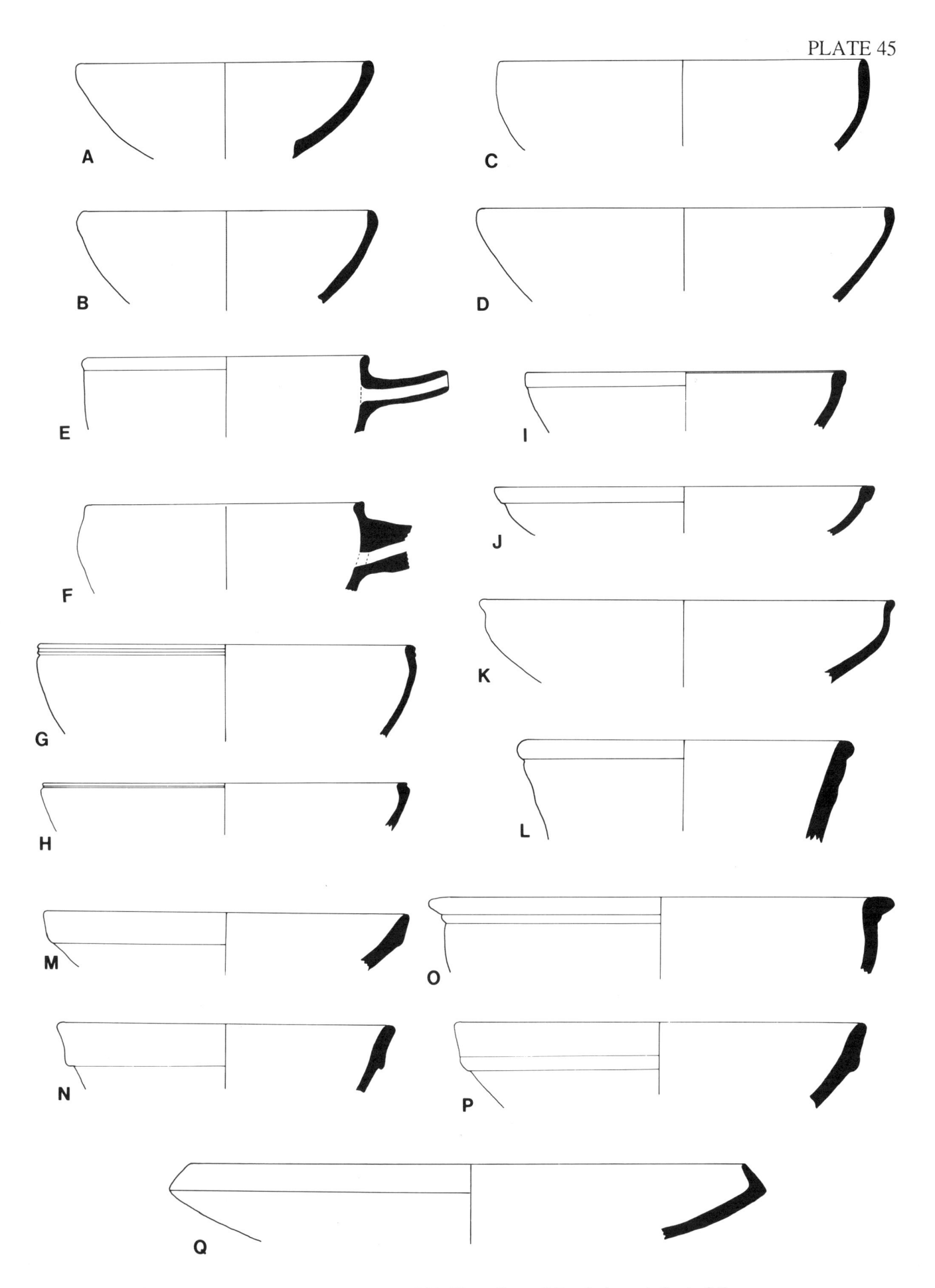

Period V Pottery From Area C01: Ware Group I Bowls (*cont.*). Scale 2:5.

Plate 46. Period V Pottery From Areas C and C01: Ware Group I Bowls (*cont.*). Scale 2:5

|   | MRN | CONTEXT | FCN | WARE | FORM | TYPE | DECO. | WARE/REMARKS |
|---|---|---|---|---|---|---|---|---|
| A | 5724 | C01-0179/69-117 | 1553 | 04 | 47c | Bowl 12a | — | Buff clay; small-sized grits, white predominant. |
| B | 13691 | C01-1007/08-198 | D3223 | 04 | 47d | Bowl 12a | — | Buff clay; small-sized grits. |
| C | 13626 | C01-0957/58-200 | D3158 | 04 | 47d | Bowl 12a | — | Fairly dense buff clay; small-sized grits; fast wheel striations visible on interior and exterior. |
| D | 5219 | C01-01-115 | 1539 | 04 | 47c | Bowl 12a | — | Buff clay; small-sized grits. |
| E | 5715 | C01-01-116 | 1565 | 04 | 47d | Bowl 12a | — | Buff clay; small-sized grits. |
| F | 13122 | C01-0937/38/39-171 | 2619 | 03 | 47d | Bowl 12b | — | Dense greenish clay; no visible tempering. |
| G | 3520 | C01-0167/68/087 | 1106 | 03 | 47d | Bowl 12b | — | Dense greenish clay; no visible tempering. |
| H | 3529 | C01-0177/78/79-082 | 1094 | 04 | 47d | Bowl 12b | — | Buff clay; small-sized grits. |
| I | 872 | C45-0172-005 | 030 | 03 | 47a | Bowl 12b | — | Dense greenish clay; no visible tempering; out of context in Period IVB deposits. |
| J | 12975 | C01-0947-188 | 3107 | 04 | 1526 | Bowl 13 | — | Greenish-buff clay; gritty with small- and medium-sized white and black grits visible. |
| K | 13599 | C01-0957/58/47/48-112 | D3101 | 04 | 1526 | Bowl 13 | — | Pinkish-buff clay; gritty with small-sized white grits prominent; buff slip on exterior. |
| L | 3884 | C01-0187/88-093 | 1255 | 04 | 793 | Bowl 14a | — | Pinkish-buff clay; small-sized grits. |
| M | 3863 | C01-0188-091 | 1226 | 03 | 780 | Bowl 14a | — | Dense light greenish-buff clay; no visible tempering; light greenish-buff slip on both surfaces. |
| N | 13512 | C01-10-191 | D3010 | 04 | 1501 | Bowl 14b | — | Dense grayish clay; small-sized grits; exterior covered with brownish-buff slip. |

PLATE 46

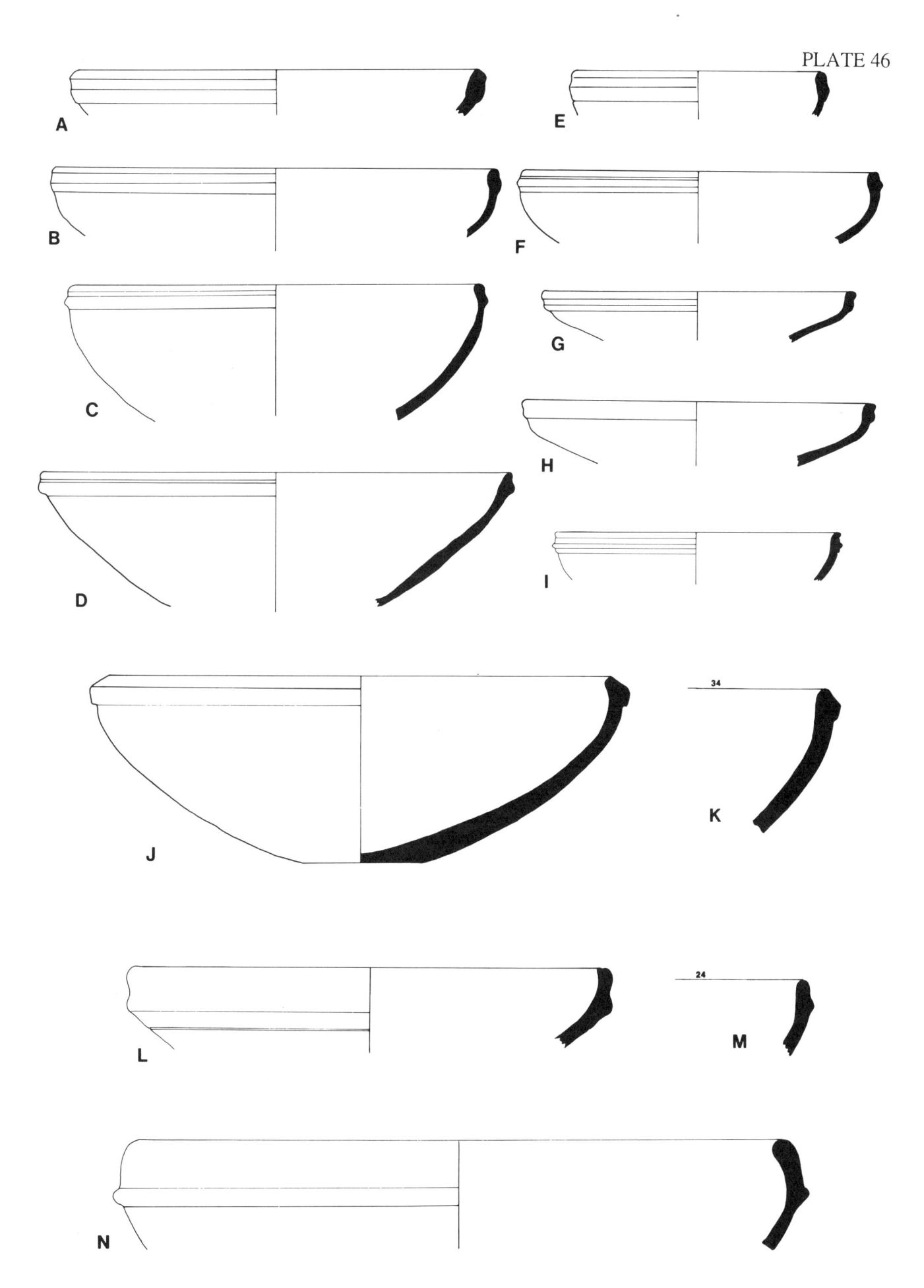

Period V Pottery From Areas C and C01: Ware Group I Bowls (*cont.*). Scale 2:5.

Plate 47. Period V Pottery From Area C01: Ware Group I Holemouth Jars. Scale 2:5.

|   | MRN | Context | FCN | Ware | Form | Type | Deco. | Ware/Remarks |
|---|---|---|---|---|---|---|---|---|
| A | 13706 | C01-1099-198 | D3238 | 04 | 1510 | Jar 1 | Bns. | Brownish-buff clay; very small-sized white grits; exterior covered with red slip; burnished. |
| B | 13065 | C01-0957/58/59-078 | 2562 | 04 | 1662 | Jar 2a | — | Greenish-buff clay; small-sized grits. |
| C | 13078 | C01-0959-135 | 2575 | 04 | 1662 | Jar 2a | — | Light grayish-buff clay; a few minute white grits. |
| D | 13386 | C01-09-183 | D2883 | 03 | 1364 | Jar 3a | — | Greenish-buff clay; no visible tempering. |
| E | 13575 | C01-1017/18/19-195 | D3072 | 04 | 769 | Jar 3b | — | Brownish-buff clay; very small white grits. |
| F | 3858 | C01-0187/88-092 | 1241 | 03 | 778 | Jar 3b | — | Greenish clay; no visible tempering. |
| G | 3748 | C01-0167/68/69-087 | 1118 | 03 | 769 | Jar 3b | — | Greenish clay; no visible tempering. |
| H | 13305 | C01-0957/57/47-101 | D2802 | 04 | 126 | Jar 2a | — | Dense buff clay; small-sized grits. |
| I | 8537 | C01-1017-145 | D2310 | 03 | 1337 | Jar 2a | — | Dense greenish clay; no visible tempering. |
| J | 9016 | C01-09-144/066 | 2240 | 04 | 1356 | Jar 2a | — | Orangish-buff clay; small-sized grits. |
| K | 13332 | C01-1007/08/17/18-182 | D2829 | 04 | 1355 | Jar 2a | — | Fairly dense greenish-buff clay; small-sized grits. |
| L | 13506 | C01-0937/38/39-188 | D3004 | 04 | 1356 | Jar 2a | — | Light greenish-buff clay. Very small-sized grits. |
| M | 13122 | C01-0937/38/39-171 | 2619 | 04 | 120 | Jar 2b | — | Light greenish-buff clay; gritty with white and gray grits. |
| N | 13453 | C01-0947/48-188 | D2950 | 04 | 120 | Jar 2b | — | Light greenish-buff clay, somewhat porous; small-sized white grits. |
| O | 13523 | C01-1027/28-101 | D3021 | 04 | 120 | Jar 2b | — | Dense buff clay; small-sized white and black grits. |
| P | 8404 | C01-0957-155 | D2205 | 04 | 120 | Jar 2b | — | Buff clay; small-sized grits. |
| Q | 13188 | C01-1017/18/19-173 | D2685 | 06 | 1660 | Unass. Jar | 406 | Grayish-buff clay; gritty, white grits prominent; on exterior, traces of reserved slip but very eroded. |
| R | 13122 | C01-0937/38/39-171 | 2619 | 04 | 1657 | Unass. Jar | — | Light brownish-buff clay; small-sized gray and white grits; buff slip on surface. |

PLATE 47

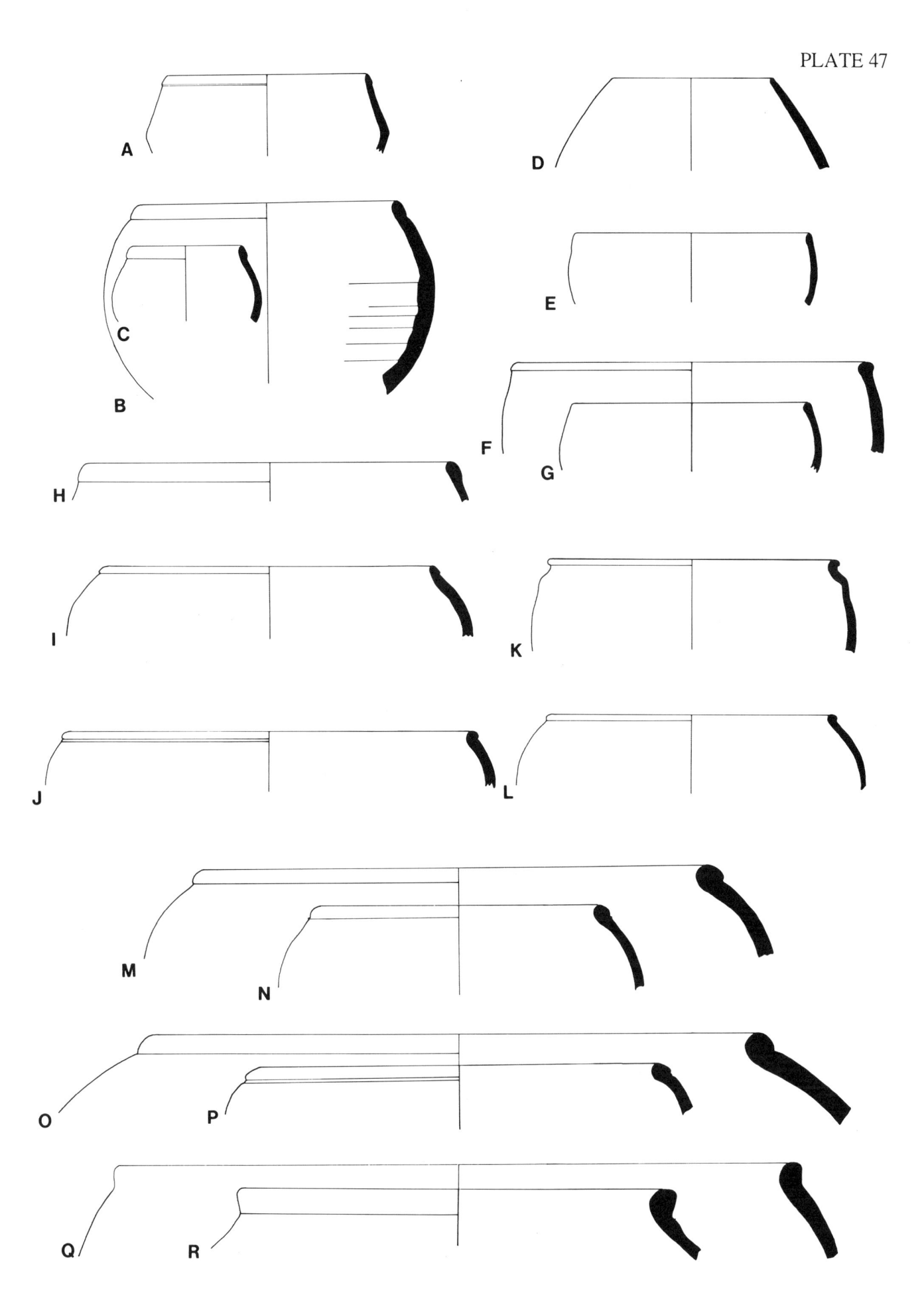

Period V Pottery From Area C01: Ware Group I Holemouth Jars. Scale 2:5.

Plate 48. Period V Pottery From Area C01: Ware Group I Jars. Scale 2:5.

|   | MRN | CONTEXT | FCN | WARE | FORM | TYPE | DECO. | WARE/REMARKS |
|---|---|---|---|---|---|---|---|---|
| A | 13122 | C01-0937/38/39-171 | 2619 | 04 | 1528 | Jar 4 | — | Handmade; dense greenish-buff clay; small- and medium-sized black and white grits; exterior covered with cream slip. |
| B | 13599 | C01-0957/58/47/48-112 | D3101 | 04 | 492 | Jar 4 | — | Dense buff clay; no visible tempering. |
| C | 13280 | C01-0957/58/59-088 | D2782 | 04 | 401 | Unass. Jar | — | Brownish-buff clay; small-sized grits; a few quartz flakes also visible. |
| D | 13367 | C01-09-183 | D2864 | 04 | 864 | Jar 5 | — | Buff clay; small-sized white and red grits visible. |
| E | 4444 | C01-0169/79/89-101 | 1305 | 04 | 864 | Jar 5 | — | Orange-buff clay; small-sized white grits. |
| F | 4826 | C01-01-093 | 1400 | 03 | 884 | Jar 6 | — | Greenish clay; no visible tempering. |
| G | 4444 | C01-0169/79/89-101 | 1305 | 04 | 884 | Jar 6 | — | Greenish-buff clay; small-sized white grits. |
| H | 4929 | C01-01-093 | D1407 | 03 | 886 | Jar 7 | — | Greenish clay; no visible tempering. |
| I | 4935 | C01-01-093 | 1414 | 03 | 888 | Jar 7 | — | Greenish clay; no visible tempering. |
| J | 3885 | C01-0187/88-093 | D1258 | 03 | 888a | Jar 7 | — | Greenish clay; no visible tempering. |
| K | 3078 | C01-0177/78/79-074 | 923 | 03 | 528 | Jar 8a | — | Greenish-buff clay; no visible tempering. |
| L | 3149 | C01-0177/78/79-078 | 1000 | 03 | 528 | Jar 8a | — | Greenish clay; no visible tempering. |
| M | 13506 | C01-0937/38/39-188 | D3004 | 04 | 1502 | Jar 8b | — | Greenish-buff clay; small-sized white grits; fast wheel striations visible on exterior. |
| N | 4826 | C01-01-093 | 1400 | 03 | 737 | Jar 9 | — | Greenish-grayish clay; no visible tempering. |
| O | 13541 | C01-1027/28/29-188 | D3038 | 04 | 737 | Jar 9 | — | Light greenish-buff clay; small-sized grits. |
| P | 3859 | C01-0187/88-092 | D1247 | 04 | 783 | Jar 10 | — | Brownish-buff clay; small-sized white and gray grits. |
| Q | 2771 | C01-0187/88-074 | D904 | 04 | 679 | Jar 10 | — | Buff clay; small-sized grits; light buff slip on surfaces. |
| R | 3527 | C01-0187/88/89-085 | 1084 | 06 | 758 | Jar 10 | 406 | Greenish-buff clay; small-sized grits; lighter greenish-buff slip on exterior. |
| S | 13122 | C01-0937/38/39-171 | 2619 | 04 | 1656 | Jar 11 | — | Light greenish-buff clay; small-sized white and gray grits. |
| T | 13289 | C01-1027/28/29-175 | D2791 | 04 | 1497 | Jar 11 | — | Buff clay; small-sized white and black grits. |
| U | 13332 | C01-1007/08/17/18-182 | D2829 | 04 | 304 | Jar 11 | — | Pinkish-buff clay; small-sized white grits. |

PLATE 48

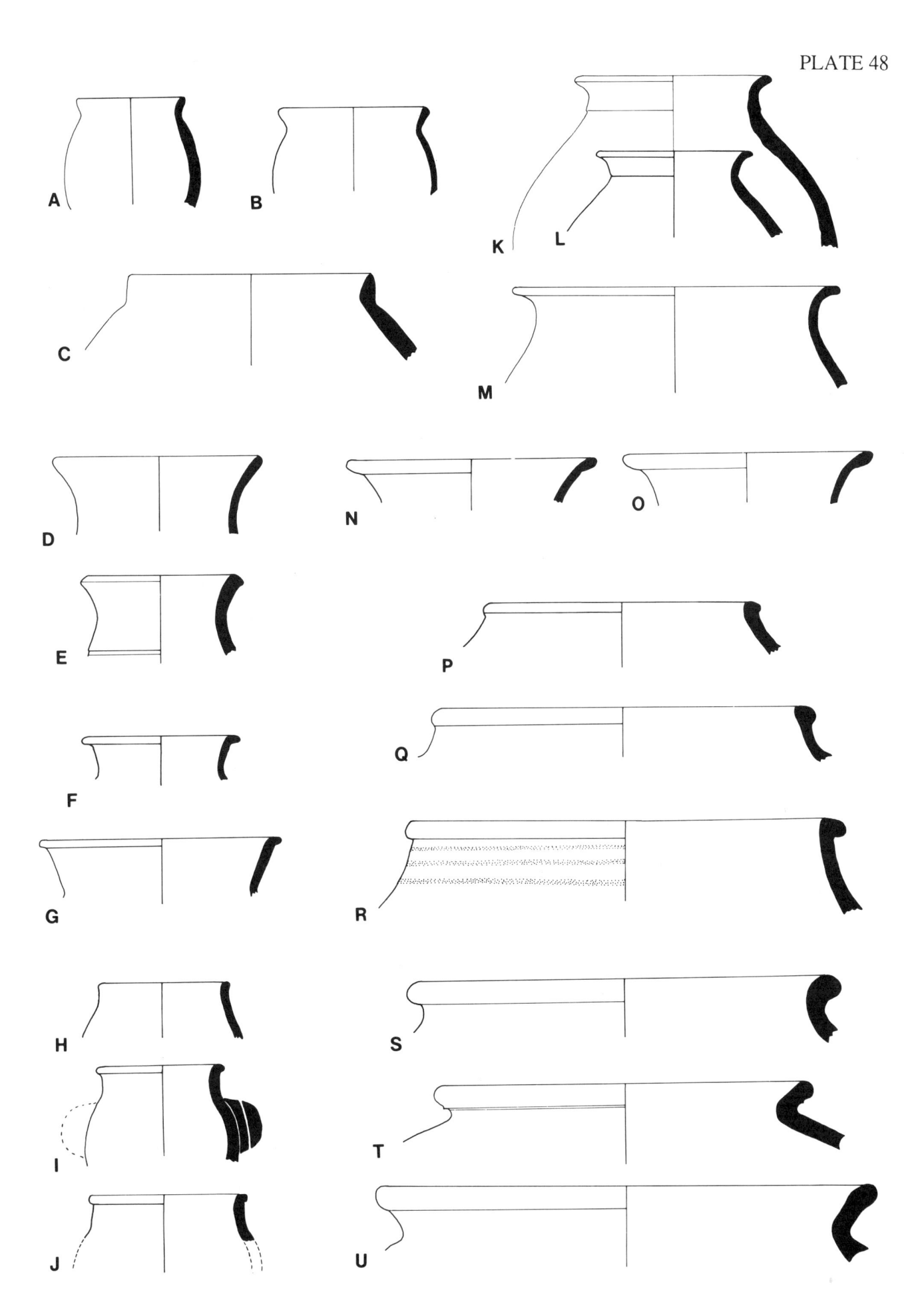

Period V Pottery From Area C01: Ware Group I Jars. Scale 2:5.

Plate 49. Period V Pottery From Area C01: Ware Group I Jars (*cont.*). Scale 2:5.

|   | MRN | CONTEXT | FCN | WARE | FORM | TYPE | DECO. | WARE/REMARKS |
|---|---|---|---|---|---|---|---|---|
| A | 4444 | C01-0169/79/89-101 | 1305 | 04 | 863 | Jar 12 | — | Light greenish-buff clay; small-sized grits. |
| B | 3078 | C01-0177/78/79-074 | 923 | 03 | 701 | Jar 12 | — | Greenish-buff clay; no visible tempering. |
| C | 2459 | C01-0169-072 | 732 | 03 | 1120 | Unass. Jar | — | Greenish clay; no visible tempering. |
| D | 13606 | C01-0957/58-117 | D3138 | 04 | 918 | Jar 13 | — | Buff clay; small-sized grits. |
| E | 5642 | C01-0169/79/89-111 | 1506 | 04 | 918 | Jar 13 | — | Light greenish-buff clay; small-sized black grits. |
| F | 13078 | C01-0959-135 | 2575 | 04 | 1692 | Jar 14 | — | Light greenish-buff clay; small-sized grits among which black are prominent. |
| G | 13401 | C01-0939/29/19-175 | D2898 | 04 | 1492 | Jar 14 | — | Buff clay; gritty with small-sized grits. |
| H | 13078 | C01-0959-135 | 2575 | 04 | 702 | Jar 15 | — | Light greenish-buff clay; small-sized grits with white grits prominent. |
| I | 3878 | C01-0177/78/79-074 | 923 | 04 | 702 | Jar 15 | — | Buff clay; small-sized grits with white ones prominent. |
| J | 13599 | C01-0957/58/47/48-112 | D3101 | 04 | 752 | Jar 15 | — | Buff to light greenish-buff clay; small-sized grits. |
| K | 3529 | C01-0177/78/79-082 | 1094 | 06 | 752 | Jar 15 | 406 | Fairly dense brownish-buff clay; small-sized grits with white ones prominent; buff slip on exterior, reserved. |
| L | 13590 | C01-09/1037/38/27/28-196 | D3077 | 06 | 752 | Jar 15 | 406 | Fairly dense light greenish-buff clay; small-sized grits; buff slip on exterior, reserved. |
| M | 3858 + 3796 | C01-01-092 + C01-0178-089 | 1241 + D1159 | 06 | 775 | Jar 14 | 406 | Greenish-buff clay; small-sized grits; greenish-buff slip on exterior, reserved; two joining pieces. |
| N | 3078 | C01-0177/78/75-074 | 923 | 04 | 700 | Jar 16 | Bns. | Dense orange clay; no visible tempering; exterior covered with red slip, burnished. |
| O | 3152 | C01-0187/88/89-078 | D963 | 06 | — | — | 405 | Orange-buff clay; small-sized grits; buff slip on exterior, reserved. |
| P | 3862 | C01-0187-090 | 1235 | 06 | — | — | 406 | Reddish-buff clay; small-sized grits with white ones predominant; buff slip on exterior, reserved. |

PLATE 49

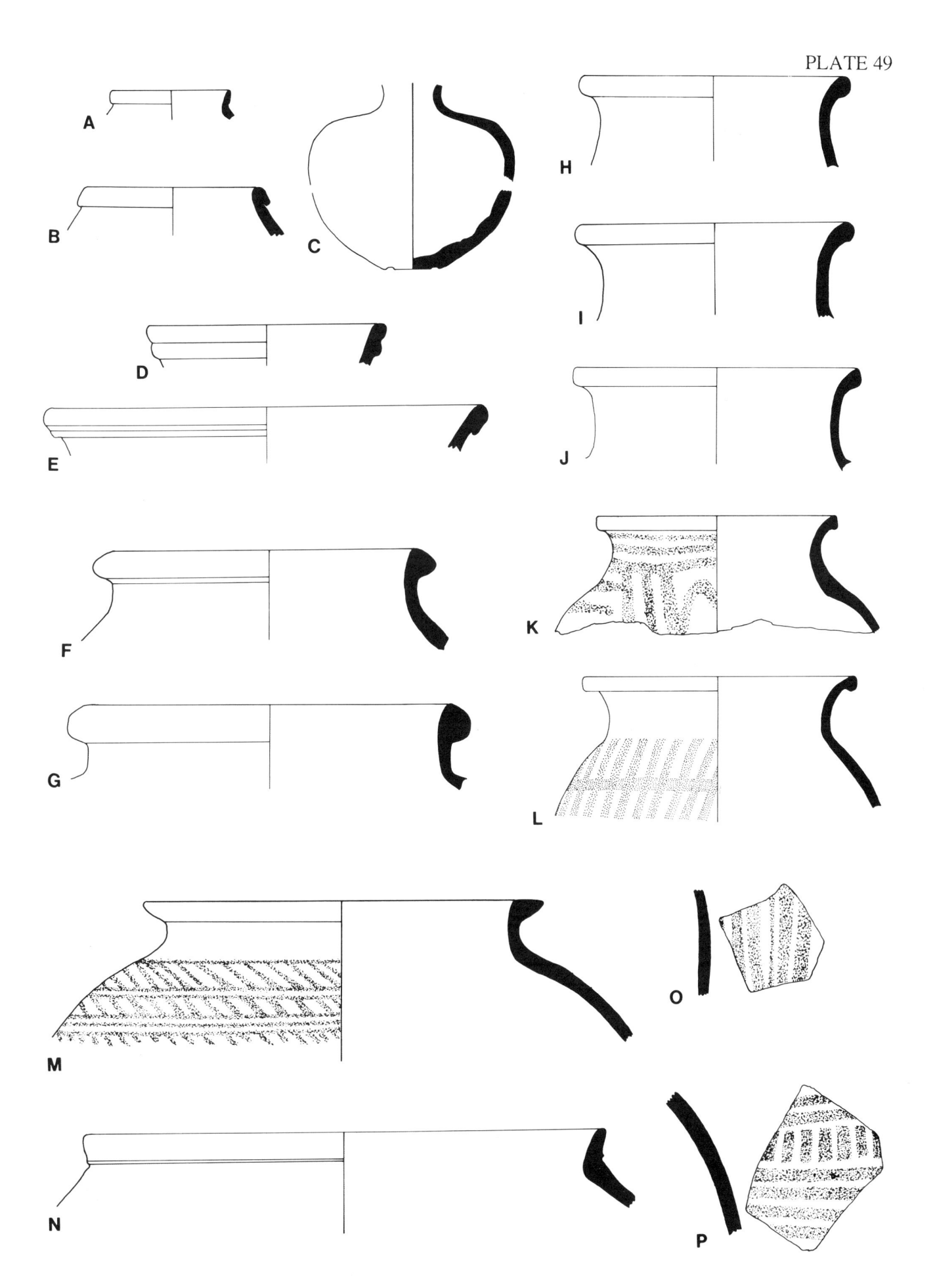

Period V Pottery From Area C01: Ware Group I Jars (*cont.*). Scale 2:5.

Plate 50. Period V Pottery From Area C01: Ware Group I Jars (*cont.*). Scale 2:5.

|   | MRN | CONTEXT | FCN | WARE | FORM | TYPE | DECO. | WARE/REMARKS |
|---|---|---|---|---|---|---|---|---|
| A | 13496 | C01-0937/38/39-101 | D2994 | 04 | 1507 | Jar 17a | — | Dense reddish-buff clay; small-sized grits, mostly white; buff slip on exterior, reserved. |
| B | 13711 | C01-0937/38/39-202 | D3243 | 06 | 69a | Jar 17a | 406 | Brownish-buff clay; small-sized grits; buff slip on surface, reserved; found intrusive in Period VIA deposits. |
| C | 13523 | C01-1027/28-101 | D3021 | 06 | 69a | Jar 17a | 406 | Fairly dense buff clay; small-sized grits; buff slip on exterior, reserved. |
| D | 8992 | C01-1007/08/17/18-164 | D2393 | 04 | 69a | Jar 17a | — | Buff clay; small-sized white grits. |
| E | 13367 | C01-09-183 | D2864 | 04 | 69a | Jar 17a | — | Fairly dense buff clay; small-sized white grits. |
| F | 13496 | C01-0937/38/39-101 | D2994 | 04 | 69a | Jar 17a | — | Dense reddish-buff clay; small-sized black grits; buff slip on surface. |
| G | 13065 | C01-0957/58/59-078 | 2562 | 04 | 72 | Jar 17b | — | Grayish-buff clay; gritty with small- and medium-sized grits; exterior smudged by burning. |
| H | 8404 | C01-0957-155 | D2205 | 04 | 72 | Jar 17b | — | Greenish-buff clay; small-sized grits with white ones prominent. |
| I | 8988 | C01-0937/38-159 | 2420 | 04 | 72 | Jar 17b | — | Buff clay; small- and medium-sized grits. |
| J | 13523 | C01-1027/28-101 | D3121 | 04 | 72 | Jar 17b | — | Buff clay; small- and medium-sized grits. |
| K | 13541 | C01-1027/28/29-188 | D3038 | 04 | 1508 | Unass. Jar | — | Greenish-buff clay; gritty with medium-sized black grits prominent. |
| L | 13150 | C01-1027/28/29-173 | D2623 | 04 | — | — | 318 | Greenish-buff clay; gritty with small- and medium-sized white grits predominant. |

PLATE 50

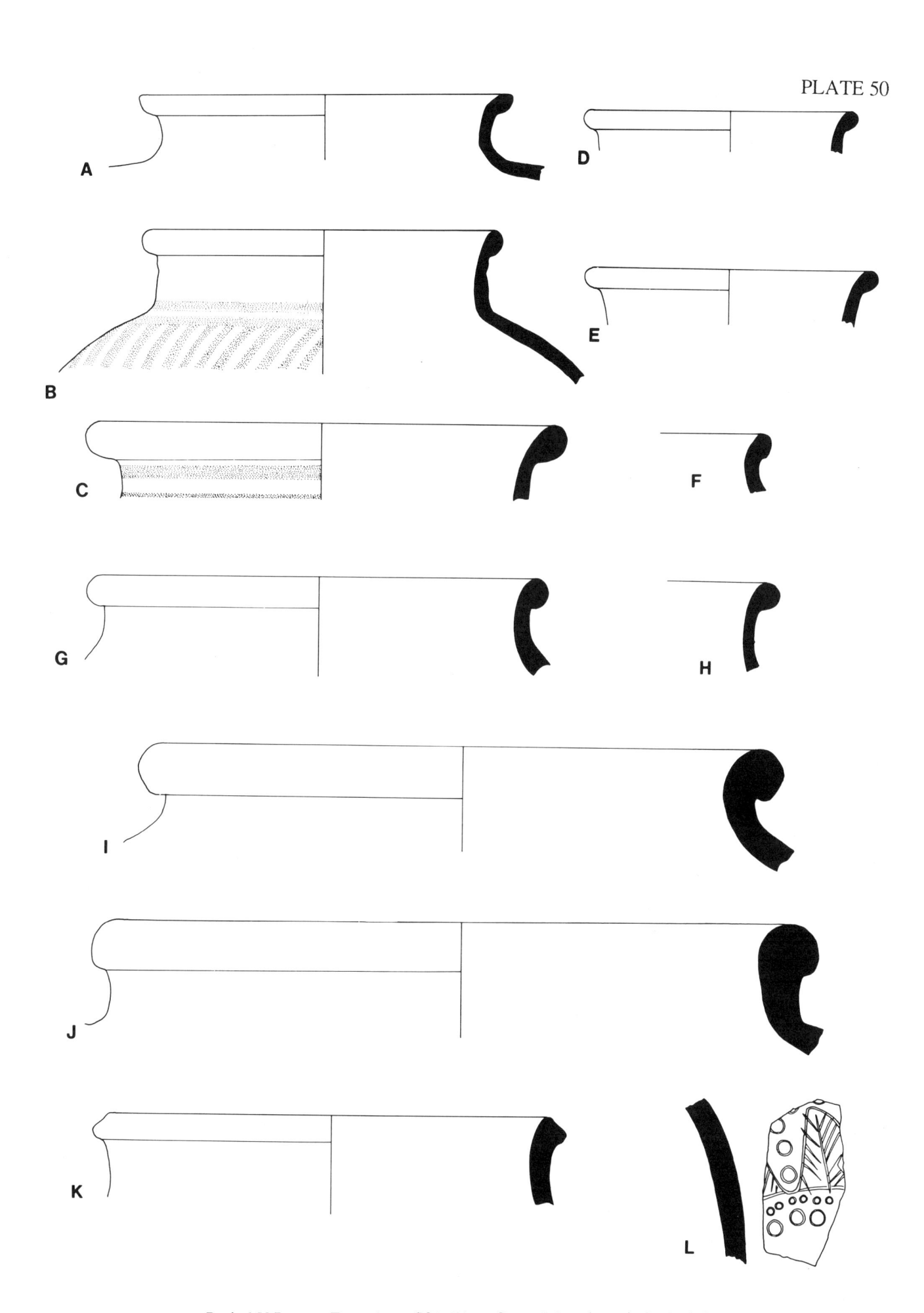

Period V Pottery From Area C01: Ware Group I Jars (*cont.*). Scale 2:5.

Plate 51. Period V Pottery From Areas C and C01: Ware Groups I–II Stands and Pedestal Bases, and Ware Group II Bowls. Scale 2:5.

|   | MRN | CONTEXT | FCN | WARE | FORM | TYPE | DECO. | WARE/REMARKS |
|---|---|---|---|---|---|---|---|---|
| A | 3885 | C01-0187/88/89-093 | D1258 | 04 | 787 | Stand 1 | — | Tubular "fruit stand" pedestal; orange-buff clay; small-sized grits; buff slip on exterior. |
| B | 13305 | C01-0957/58/47/48-101 | D2802 | 04 | 976 | Stand 2 | — | Greenish-buff clay; small-sized grits. |
| C | 13401 | C01-0939/29/19-175 | D2898 | 04 | 1360 | Pedestal Base | — | Buff clay; small-sized white grits. |
| D | 3507 | C35-02-006 | 070 | 04 | 743 | Pedestal Base | — | Orange-buff clay; small-sized white grits; on exterior, very faint traces of horizontal smoothing or burnishing; out of context in Period IVB deposits. |
| E | 13626 | C01-0957/58-200 | D3158 | 04 | 173 | Pedestal Base | — | Buff clay; small-sized white and black grits. |
| F | 13289 | C01-1027/28/29-175 | D2721 | 29 | 1498 | Unass. Bowl | Bns. | Orange clay, prominent gray core; chaff-tempered with quartz flakes visible; porous; exterior mottled gray and orange; interior orange; burnished. |
| G | 13150 | C01-1027/29-173 | 2623 | 29 | 792 | Bowl 15 | Bns. | Rather dense brown clay, gray core; tempered with a combination of chaff and small-sized grits with chaff predominant; exterior mottled brownish-orange and gray; interior is brown; lightly burnished. |
| H | 13150 | C01-1027/29-173 | 2623 | 29 | 1659 | Bowl 15 | Bns. | Fairly dense brown clay, gray core; tempered with a combination of finely-chopped chaff and small-sized white grits; mottled gray and brown; burnished. |
| I | 8991 | C01-1007/08/17/18-164 | 2390 | 29 | 792 | Bowl 15 | Bns. | Orange clay, gray core; tempered with a combination of chaff and small-sized grits; surfaces orange and burnished. |
| J | 8404 | C01-0957-155 | D2205 | 28 | 1333 | Jar 18 | — | Orange clay, gray core; tempered with a combination of chaff and small-sized grits; exterior smoothed. |
| K | 5719 | C01-01-115 | 1539 | 29 | 923 | Jar 18 | Bns. | Dark brown clay; tempered with a combination of chaff and small white grits; quartz flakes visible also; exterior is brown and burnished. |
| L | 4935 | C01-01-093 | 1414 | 29 | 890 | Stand 3 | Bns. | Orange clay; tempered with a combination of small-sized grits and chaff, grits predominant; exterior is orange and burnished; interior is mottled orange and black. |
| M | 13522 | C01-1017/18/19-191 | D3050 | 29 | 890 | Stand 3 | Bns. | Brownish clay; tempered with a combination of small- and medium-sized gray grits and chaff, grits predominant; exterior is orangish and burnished; interior is mottled orange and black. |

PLATE 51

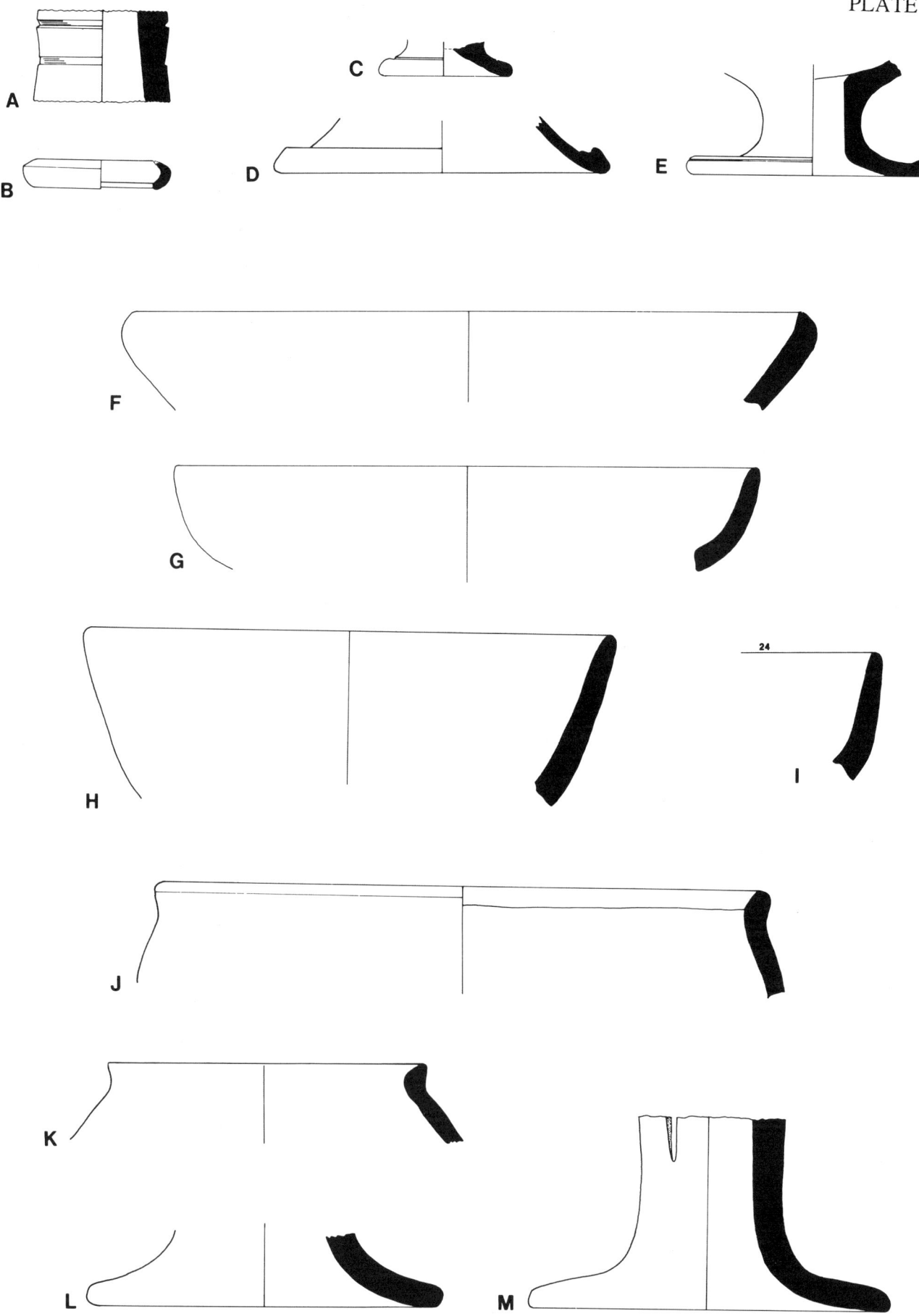

Period V Pottery From Areas C and C01: Ware Groups I–II Stands and Pedestal Bases, and Ware Group II Bowls. Scale 2:5.

Plate 52. Period V Pottery From Area C01: Ware Group II Jars. Scale 2:5.

|   | MRN | CONTEXT | FCN | WARE | FORM | TYPE | DECO. | WARE/REMARKS |
|---|-----|---------|-----|------|------|------|-------|--------------|
| A | 13599 | C01-0957/58/47/48-112 | D3101 | 30 | 495 | Jar 19a | — | Brownish clay, prominent gray core; gritty with medium-sized white grits prominent; fire smudges on exterior near rim; coarse. |
| B | 5315 | C01-0169/79/89-111 | 1492 | 28 | 495 | Jar 19a | — | Brownish clay; tempered with a combination of small-sized grits and chaff, grits predominant; brownish wash on exterior; smoothed. |
| C | 13039 | C01-1009/19/2-169 | 2538 | 29 | 495a | Jar 19a | Bns. | Brown clay, prominent gray core; tempered with a combination of chaff and small-sized gray grits, chaff predominant; burnished. |
| D | 13615 | C01-0947/48-117 | D3147 | 30 | 495 | Jar 19a | — | Brown clay; prominent gray core; gritty with medium-sized grits mostly white; exterior mottled brown and orange; fire smudges on shoulder near rim; coarse. |
| E | 8539 | C01-097-157 | D2286 | 13 | 495 | Jar 19a | — | Brownish-buff clay; prominent gray core; porous with straw/chaff impressions very visible; smoothed. |
| F | 8698 | C01-09-159 | 2346 | 28 | 495 | Jar 19b | — | Black clay; tempered with a combination of chaff and large-sized grits; exterior is black and not smoothed. |
| G | 13541 | C01-1027/28/29-188 | D3038 | 29 | 112 | Jar 19b | Bns. | Dense gray clay; tempered with a combination of small-sized white grits and chaff, grits predominant; exterior mottled gray and very lightly burnished; interior is brown. |
| H | 2326 | C01-0167/68/69-063 | 764 | 28 | 495 | Jar 19b | — | Brown clay, prominent gray core; tempered with a combination of chaff and small-sized grits; exterior smoothed and mottled orange and brown. |
| I | 13541 | C01-1027/28/29-188 | D3038 | 29 | 495 | Jar 19b | Bns. | Brownish clay, prominent gray core; tempered with a combination of small- and medium-sized white grits and chaff; grits predominant; exterior is mottled brown and burnished. |
| J | 3078 | C01-1077/78/79-074 | 923 | 29 | 495 | Jar 19b | Bns. | Brown clay, gray core; tempered with a combination of chaff and small-sized grits, grits predominant; exterior covered with a brownish wash; burnished. |
| K | 2770 | C01-0187/88-074 | 898 | 30 | 696 | Jar 17b | — | Reddish-brown/buff clay; prominent gray core; gritty; exterior covered with brown wash; smoothed. |

PLATE 52

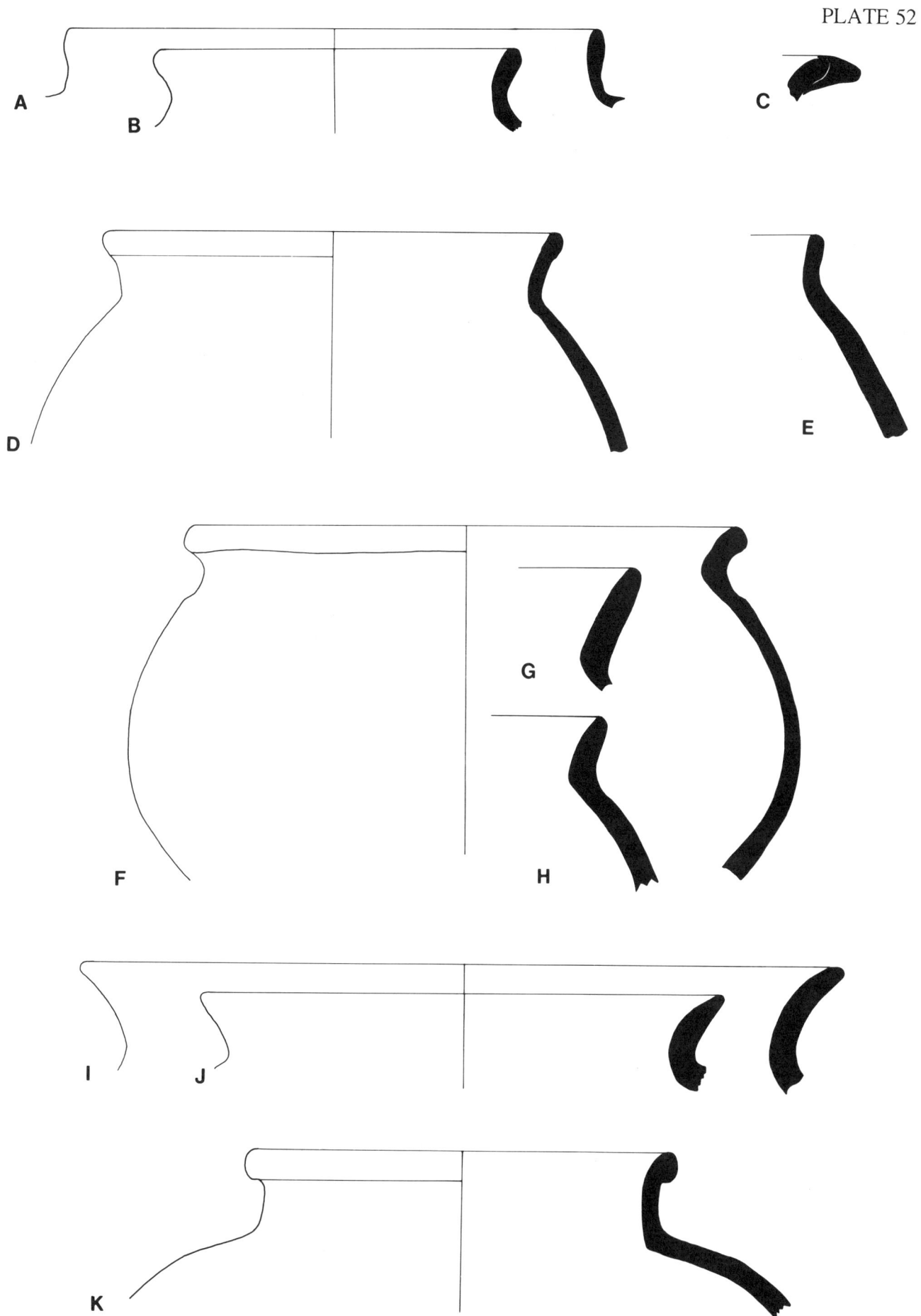

Period V Pottery From Area C01: Ware Group II Jars. Scale 2:5.

Plate 53. Period IV Pottery From Areas A, B, and C: Ware Group I Cups. Scale 2:5.

|   | *MRN* | *Context* | *FCN* | *Ware* | *Form* | *Type* | *Deco.* | *Ware/Remarks* |
|---|---|---|---|---|---|---|---|---|
| A | 526 | B03-06-002 | 011 | 04 | C-20 | Bowl 1a | — | Greenish-buff clay; small-sized white grits. |
| B | 1983 | C01-09-024 | 578 | 04 | 11 | Bowl 1b | — | Buff clay; small-sized grits. |
| C | 7561 | A07-11-039 | D317 | 04 | 11 | Bowl 1b | — | Fairly dense buff clay; small-sized grits; wheel mark corrugations visible on exterior and interior. |
| D | 4760 | C55-05-014 | 310 | 04 | 11 | Bowl 1b | — | Buff clay; small-sized grits. |
| E | 5728 | C55-07-020 | 467 | 04 | 11 | Bowl 1b | — | Buff clay; small-sized white grits; some wheel mark corrugations visible on exterior. |
| F | 374 | B02-04-004 | 009 | 04 | 11 | Bowl 1b | — | Fairly dense brownish-buff clay; no visible tempering other than small-sized grits. |
| G | 3388 | C56-1095-017 | D157 | 04 | 1310 | Bowl 1b | — | Fairly dense light greenish-buff paste; small-sized grits. |
| H | 19286 | B72-0141-006 | 049 | 04 | C-8a | Bowl 1c | — | Brownish-buff clay, mottled orange in spots; small-sized grits, white ones prominent. |
| I | 500 | B03-05-002 | 007 | 04 | 261 | Bowl 1d | — | Buff clay; small-sized grits. |
| J | 2559 | C45-06-031 | 287 | 04 | 261 | Bowl 1d | — | Fairly dense light brownish-buff clay; small-sized grits. |
| K | 841 | C45-01-001 | 001 | 04 | 261 | Bowl 1d | — | Light greenish-buff clay; small-sized grits; slight wheel mark corrugations on interior. |
| L | 3938 | C55-08-009 | 202 | 04 | 1109 | Bowl 1d | — | Buff clay; small-sized grits. |
| M | 4761 | C55-05-014 | 319 | 04 | C-5 | Bowl 1e | — | Dense light brownish-buff clay; small-sized white grits. |
| N | 1108 | C45-04-001 | 094 | 04 | 02 | Bowl 1e | — | Light greenish-buff clay; small-sized grits, white ones prominent. |
| O | 6700 | A04-05-016 | 065 | 04 | 02 | Bowl 1e | — | Buff clay; small-sized grits. |
| P | 544 | A05-03-006 | 016 | 04 | 02 | Bowl 1e | — | Light reddish-buff clay; small-sized grits; buff slip on both surfaces. |
| Q | 111 | B02-03-004 | 083 | 04 | 02 | Bowl 1e | — | Brownish-buff clay; small-sized grits, white ones predominant; light greenish-buff slip on both surfaces. |
| R | 190 | B02-02-006 | 119 | 04 | 02 | Bowl 1e | — | Fairly dense brownish-buff clay; small-sized grits, white ones predominant; buff slip on surface. |
| S | 3915 | A06-0742-019 | 076 | 04 | C-7 | Bowl 1e | — | Light brownish-buff clay; small-sized white grits; (= KH 1981/67). |
| T | 7272 | A07-0750-023 | 548 | 04 | C-7 | Bowl 1e | — | Buff clay; small-sized grits; (= KH 1982/118). |
| U | 604 | B03-06-002 | 023 | 04 | C-7 | Bowl 1e | — | Fairly dense buff clay; small-sized grits. |
| V | 3888 | A07-0750-023 | 206 | 04 | C-5 | Bowl 1e | — | Buff clay; grit-tempered; fast wheel mark striations visible on exterior; cf. also plate 147:A. |

PLATE 53

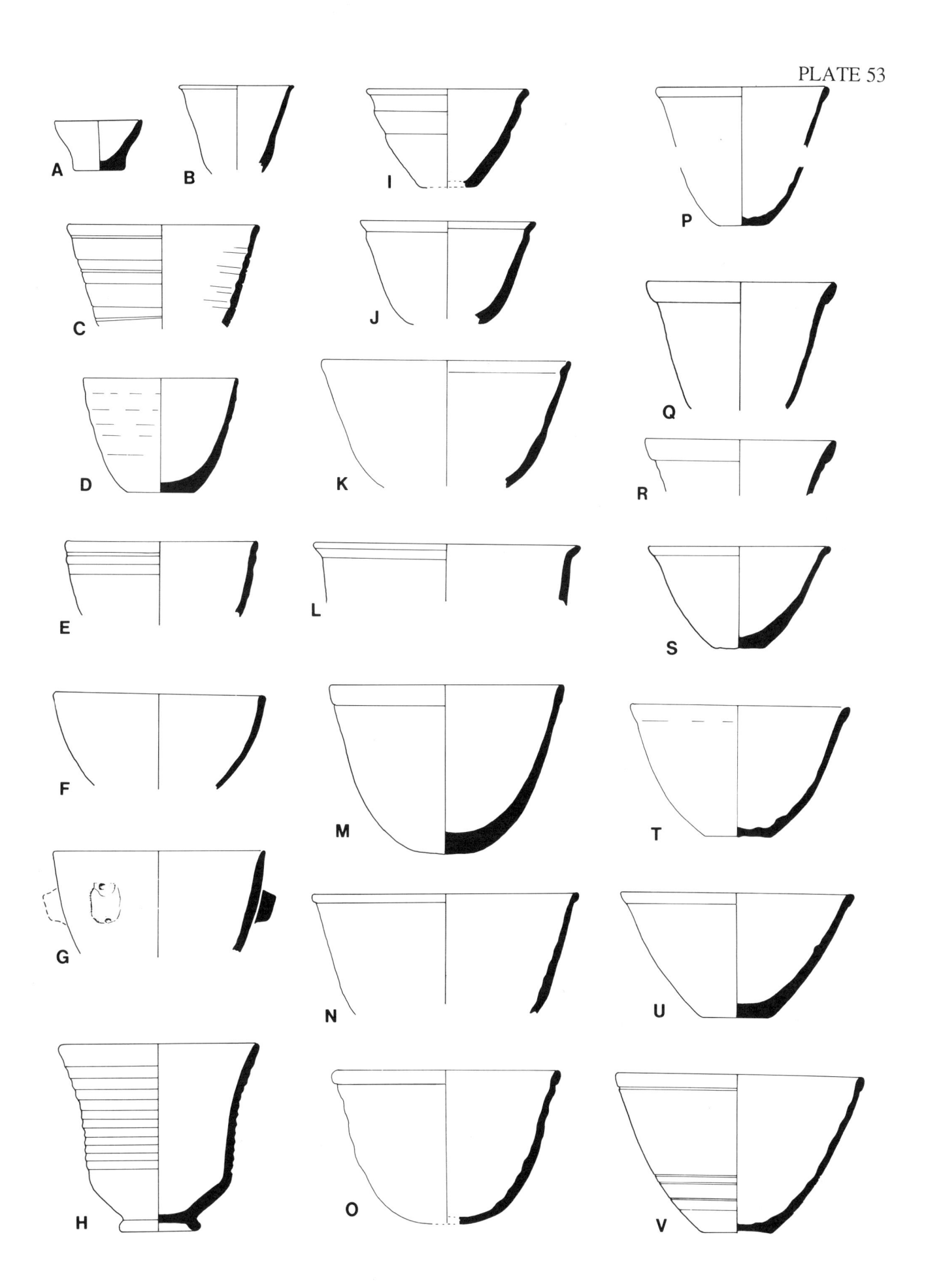

Period IV Pottery From Areas A, B, and C: Ware Group I Cups. Scale 2:5.

Plate 54. Period IV Pottery From Areas A, B, C, C01, and F: Ware Group I Cups (*cont.*) and Bowls. Scale 2:5.

|   | MRN | CONTEXT | FCN | WARE | FORM | TYPE | DECO. | WARE/REMARKS |
|---|---|---|---|---|---|---|---|---|
| A | 333 | B02-04-002 | 006 | 04 | 178 | Base 1 | — | Reddish-buff clay; small-sized grits. |
| B | 280 | B02-02-006 | 131 | 04 | 178 | Base 1 | — | Buff clay; small-sized grits; wheel mark corrugations visible on interior. |
| C | 814 | C01-10-013 | 190 | 04 | 211 | Base 1 | — | Buff clay; small-sized grits. |
| D | 007 | B01-02-001 | 003 | 04 | 211 | Base 1 | — | Buff clay; small-sized grits. |
| E | 3941 | A06-07-020 | 084 | 04 | 591 | Base 2 | — | Fairly dense greenish-buff clay; small-sized white grits. |
| F | 7506 | A07-05-035 | 243 | 04 | 1181 | Base 1 | — | Fairly dense buff clay; small-sized grits. |
| G | 2684 | A08-04-010 | 107 | 04 | 685 | Bowl 2a | — | Buff clay; small-sized grits. |
| H | 695 | C01-01-008 | 128 | 04 | 07 | Bowl 2a | 023 | Fairly dense brownish-buff clay; occasional white grits. |
| I | 373 | B02-04-010 | 010 | 04 | 01 | Bowl 2b | — | Dark brownish-buff clay; small-sized white grits; brownish-buff slip on exterior. |
| J | 373 | B02-04-010 | 010 | 04 | 01 | Bowl 2b | — | Buff clay; small-sized grits. |
| K | 483 | A05-04-008 | 014 | 04 | 16 | Bowl 3 | — | Brownish-buff clay; small-sized white grits. |
| L | 6327 | C35-0361-005 | 235 | 04 | 10 | Bowl 3 | — | Grayish clay; small-sized white grits. |
| M | 6588 | C55-05-025 | 591 | 04 | 1318 | Unass. Bowl | — | Fairly dense buff clay; small-sized black grits. |
| N | 1092 | A07-04-005 | 032 | 04 | 14 | Bowl 4a | — | Fairly dense brownish-buff clay; small-sized white grits. |
| O | 532 | B02-13-015 | 181 | 04 | 14 | Bowl 4a | — | Fairly dense brownish-buff clay; small-sized white grits. |
| P | 163 | B02-03-004 | 091 | 04 | 12 | Bowl 4b | — | Brownish-buff clay; small-sized white grits. |
| Q | 236 | B02-03-010 | 127 | 04 | 12 | Bowl 4b | — | Buff clay; small-sized grits. |
| R | 5031 | C55-0217-011 | 375 | 04 | 1260 | Unass. Bowl | — | Greenish-buff clay; small-sized black grits. |
| S | 152 | C01-01-002 | 004 | 04 | 21 | Bowl 5 | — | Greenish-buff clay; small-sized grits. |
| T | 691 | C01-08-011 | 004 | 04 | 21 | Bowl 5 | — | Buff clay; small-sized grits. |
| U | 041 | B01-04-007 | 026 | 04 | C-37 | Bowl 5 | — | Buff clay; small-sized grits. |
| V | 12127 | F01-05-049 | 267 | 04 | C-37 | Bowl 5 | — | Buff clay; small-sized grits. |
| W | 6359 | C55-08-010 | 570 | 04 | C-64a | Bowl 6 | — | Buff clay; small-sized grits. |
| X | 19453 | B72-872-03-007 | 127 | 04 | C-64 | Bowl 6 | — | Grayish-greenish buff clay; small-sized white grits. |
| Y | 532 | B02-03-015 | 181 | 04 | 49 | Bowl 6 | — | Buff clay; small-sized grits. |

PLATE 54

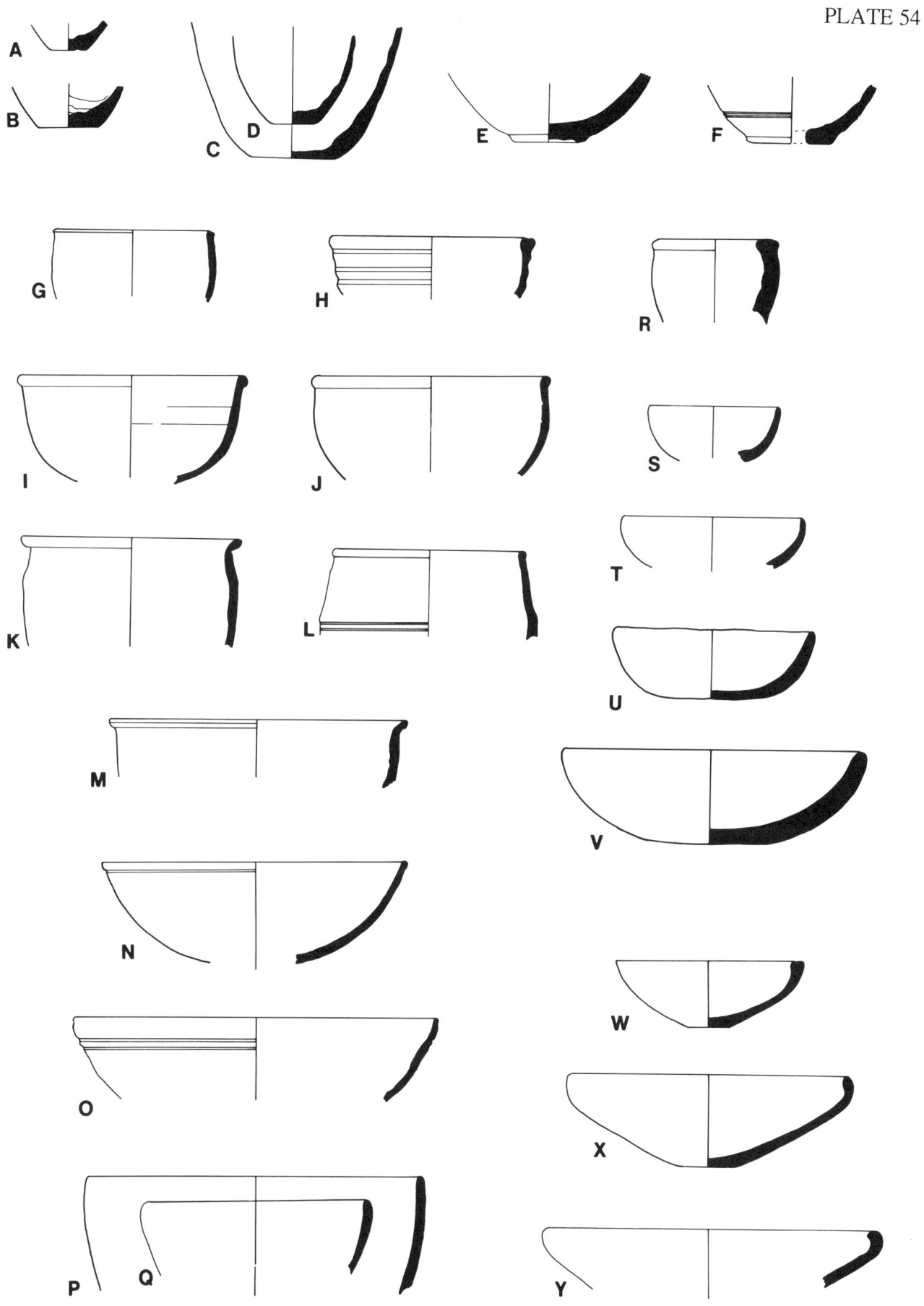

Period IV Pottery From Areas A, B, C, C01, and F: Ware Group I Cups (*cont.*) and Bowls. Scale 2:5.

Plate 55. Period IV Pottery From Areas A, B, and C: Ware Group I Bowls (*cont.*). Scale 2:5.

|   | MRN | CONTEXT | FCN | WARE | FORM | TYPE | DECO. | WARE/REMARKS |
|---|---|---|---|---|---|---|---|---|
| A | 5665 | C56-07-029 | 348 | 04 | C-33 | Bowl 7a | — | Light greenish-buff clay; small-sized grits. |
| B | 5032 | C55-0765-011 | 356 | 04 | C-33 | Bowl 7a | — | Fairly dense buff clay; small-sized grits. |
| C | 5041 | C55-0316-011 | — | 04 | 43a | Bowl 7a | — | Buff clay; small-sized grits. |
| D | 3497 | A07-05/06-021 | 157 | 04 | 43a | Bowl 7b | — | Buff clay; small-sized grits. |
| E | — | Provenance lost | — | 04 | 43a | Bowl 7b | — | Buff clay; small-sized grits; "potter's mark" on exterior. |
| F | 531 | A06-02-004 | 019 | 04 | 43 | Bowl 8a | — | Grayish-buff clay; small-sized white grits; exterior fire blackened. |
| G | 6839 | C55-02-029 | 648 | 04 | 43 | Bowl 8a | — | Buff clay; small-sized grits. |
| H | 1127 | A07-05-006 | 037 | 04 | 291 | Bowl 8a | — | Fairly dense reddish-buff clay; small-sized white grits. |
| I | 2758 | A07-0591-014 | 116 | 04 | 291 | Bowl 8a | — | Buff clay; small-sized grits. |
| J | 487 | A07-02-002 | 003 | 04 | 42 | Bowl 8b | — | Buff clay; small-sized grits. |
| K | 1780 | A05-04-019 | 057 | 04 | 42 | Bowl 8b | — | Buff clay; small-sized grits. |
| L | 19033 | B72-0144-006 | 107 | 04 | 1638 | Bowl 8c | — | Grayish-buff clay; small-sized grits, white ones prominent. |
| M | 1780 | A05-04-019 | 057 | 04 | 42 | Bowl 8b | — | Buff clay; small-sized grits. |
| N | 4451 | C55-0449-011 | 238 | 04 | 869 | Bowl 8c | — | Buff clay; small-sized grits. |
| O | 3517 | C56-10-017 | 168 | 04 | 869 | Bowl 8c | — | Reddish-buff clay; small-sized white grits. |

PLATE 55

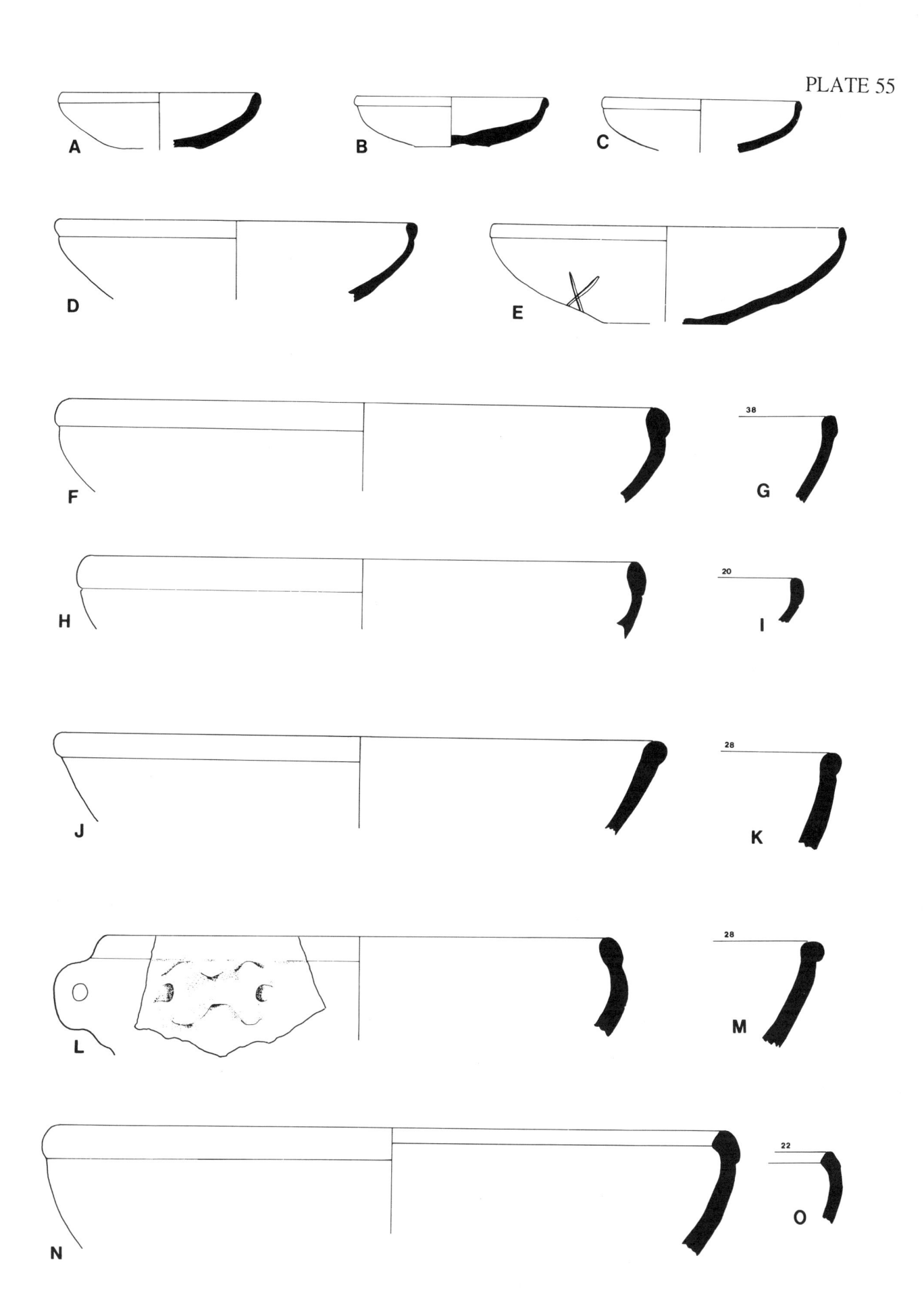

Period IV Pottery From Areas A, B, and C: Ware Group I Bowls (*cont.*). Scale 2:5.

Plate 56. Period IV Pottery From Areas A, B, C, and F: Ware Group I Bowls (*cont.*). Scale 2:5.

|   | MRN | CONTEXT | FCN | WARE | FORM | TYPE | DECO. | WARE/REMARKS |
|---|---|---|---|---|---|---|---|---|
| A | 3165 | C56-10-001 | 136 | 04 | 712 | Bowl 8d | — | Buff clay; small-sized white grits. |
| B | 2799 | C35-02-003 | 016 | 04 | 712 | Bowl 8d | — | Fairly dense orange-buff clay, gray core; small-sized white grits. |
| C | 1967 | A08-0222-007 | 058 | 04 | 600 | Bowl 9a | — | Orange-buff clay; small-sized white grits. |
| D | 4533 | C55-05-011 | — | 04 | 1280 | Bowl 9a | — | Buff clay; small-sized grits. |
| E | 7040 | C55-02-033 | 638 | 04 | 1314 | Bowl 9a | — | Fairly dense brownish-buff clay grading to orange towards surface; small-sized grits. |
| F | 5932 | C56-07-031 | 366 | 04 | 1309 | Bowl 9a | 023 | Fairly dense orange clay; small-sized grits. |
| G | 2436 | A05-04-020 | 064 | 04 | 650 | Bowl 9a | — | Brownish-buff clay; small-sized white grits. |
| H | 12036 | F01-05-032 | 175 | 04 | 650 | Bowl 9a | — | Buff clay; small-sized grits. |
| I | 7590 | A07-13-047 | 349 | 04 | 1237 | Bowl 9a | — | Fairly dense buff clay grading to orangish on surface; small-sized grits; mottled orange buff on exterior. |
| J | 7563 | A07-11-038 | 315 | 04 | 1237 | Bowl 9a | — | Greenish-buff clay; small-sized black grits. |
| K | 17903 | A04-10-101 | 587 | 04 | 697 | Bowl 9b | — | Grayish-buff clay; gray and white grits visible; fast wheel striations visible on interior. |
| L | 17903 | A04-10-101 | 587 | 04 | 697 | Bowl 9b | — | Buff clay; small-sized grits. |
| M | 4227 | A08-05-017 | 182 | 04 | 1051 | Bowl 9b | — | Reddish-buff clay; small-sized white grits; buff slip on exterior. |
| N | 0475 | B01-02-014 | 135 | 04 | 0697 | Bowl 9b | — | Buff clay; small-sized grits. |

PLATE 56

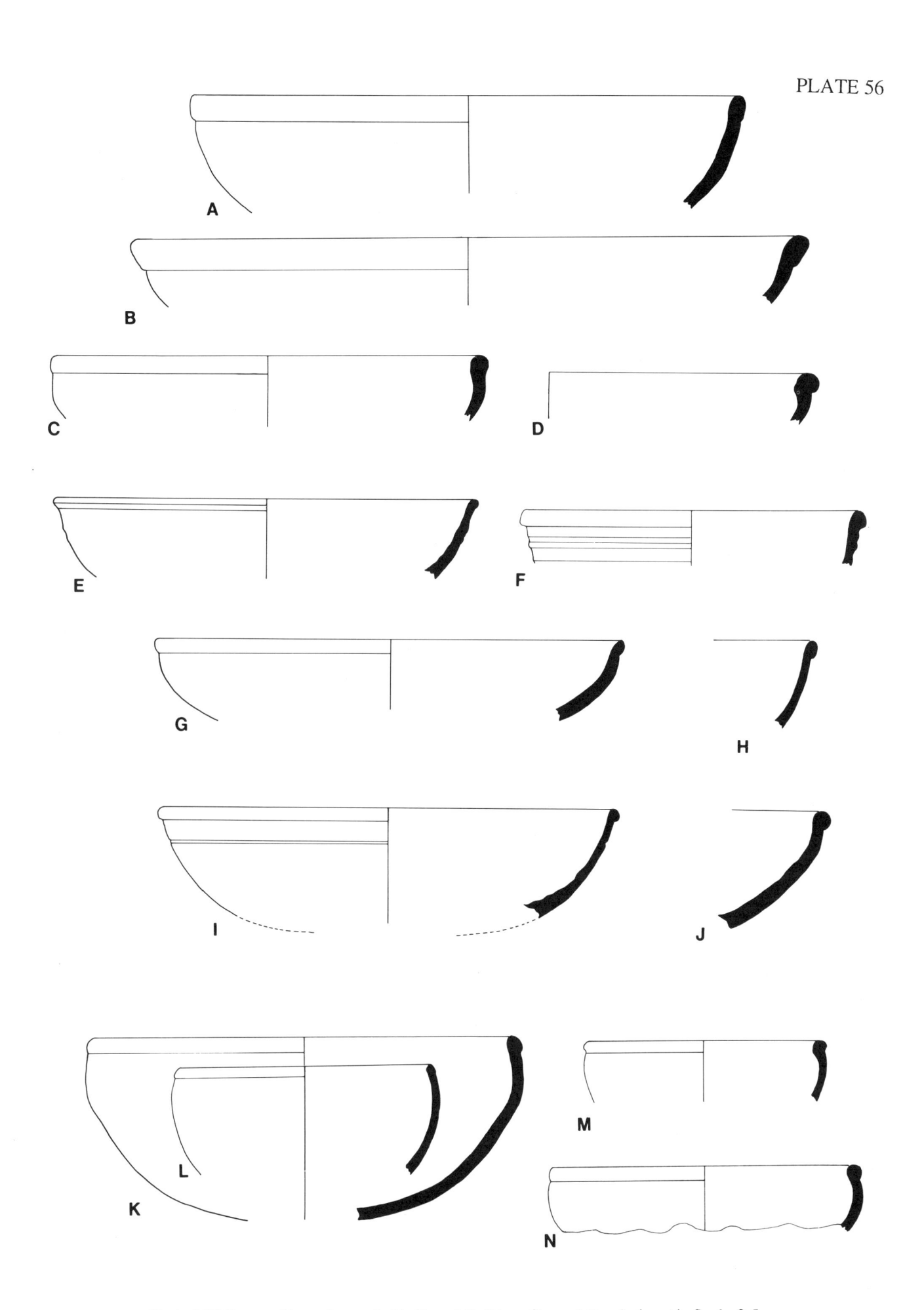

Period IV Pottery From Areas A, B, C, and F: Ware Group I Bowls (*cont.*). Scale 2:5.

Plate 57. Period IV Pottery From Areas A, C, and C01: Ware Group I Bowls (*cont.*). Scale 2:5.

|   | MRN | CONTEXT | FCN | WARE | FORM | TYPE | DECO. | WARE/REMARKS |
|---|---|---|---|---|---|---|---|---|
| A | 268 | C01-01-005 | 041 | 04 | 47b | Bowl 10a | — | Buff clay; small-sized grits. |
| B | 4650 | A05-05-017 | 069 | 04 | 1140 | Bowl 10a | — | Greenish-buff clay; small-sized grits. |
| C | 11394 | A04-07-079 | 443 | 04 | C-52 | Bowl 10a | — | Reddish-buff clay grading to light brownish-buff on exterior; fairly gritty with white grits predominant; buff slip on exterior. |
| D | 936 | A07-04-005 | 018 | 04 | 47b | Bowl 10a | — | Light brownish-buff clay; small-sized white grits. |
| E | 871 | C45-0181-006 | 055 | 04 | 47c | Bowl 10b | — | Buff clay; small-sized grits. |
| F | 6268 | C35-0361-005 | 229 | 04 | 47b | Bowl 10a | — | Buff clay; small-sized grits. |
| G | 248 | C01-02-006 | 028 | 04 | 47b | Bowl 10a | — | Light brownish-buff clay; small-sized grits; buff slip on exterior. |
| H | 3881 | C46-07-006 | 086 | 04 | 798 | Bowl 10a | — | Buff clay; small-sized grits. |
| I | 7899 | A07-15-065 | 456 | 04 | 1298 | Bowl 10b | — | Fairly dense buff clay; small-sized white grits. |
| J | 7667 | A07-14-054 | 389 | 04 | 1298 | Bowl 10b | — | Reddish-buff clay; small-sized grits. |
| K | 12824 | A05-08-019 | 232 | 04 | 1291 | Bowl 11a | — | Brownish-buff clay, reddish-buff core; small-sized grits, white ones predominant; buff slip on both surfaces. |
| L | 6623 | C35-0382-005 | 282 | 04 | 1291 | Bowl 11a | — | Fairly porous orange-buff clay; small-sized white grits; buff slip on exterior. |
| M | 919 | C45-01-004 | 014 | 04 | 207 | Bowl 11b | — | Dense reddish-buff clay; small-sized white grits; traces of red wash on both surfaces. |
| N | 4953 | C55-0785-011 | D338 | 04 | 1195 | Bowl 11b | — | Buff clay; small-sized grits. |
| O | 8135 | A04-08-042 | 206 | 04 | 723 | Bowl 11c | — | Buff clay; small-sized grits. |
| P | 11248 | A04-08-059 | 298 | 04 | 723 | Bowl 11c | — | Brownish-buff clay grading to orange on inner surface; small-sized white grits. |

PLATE 57

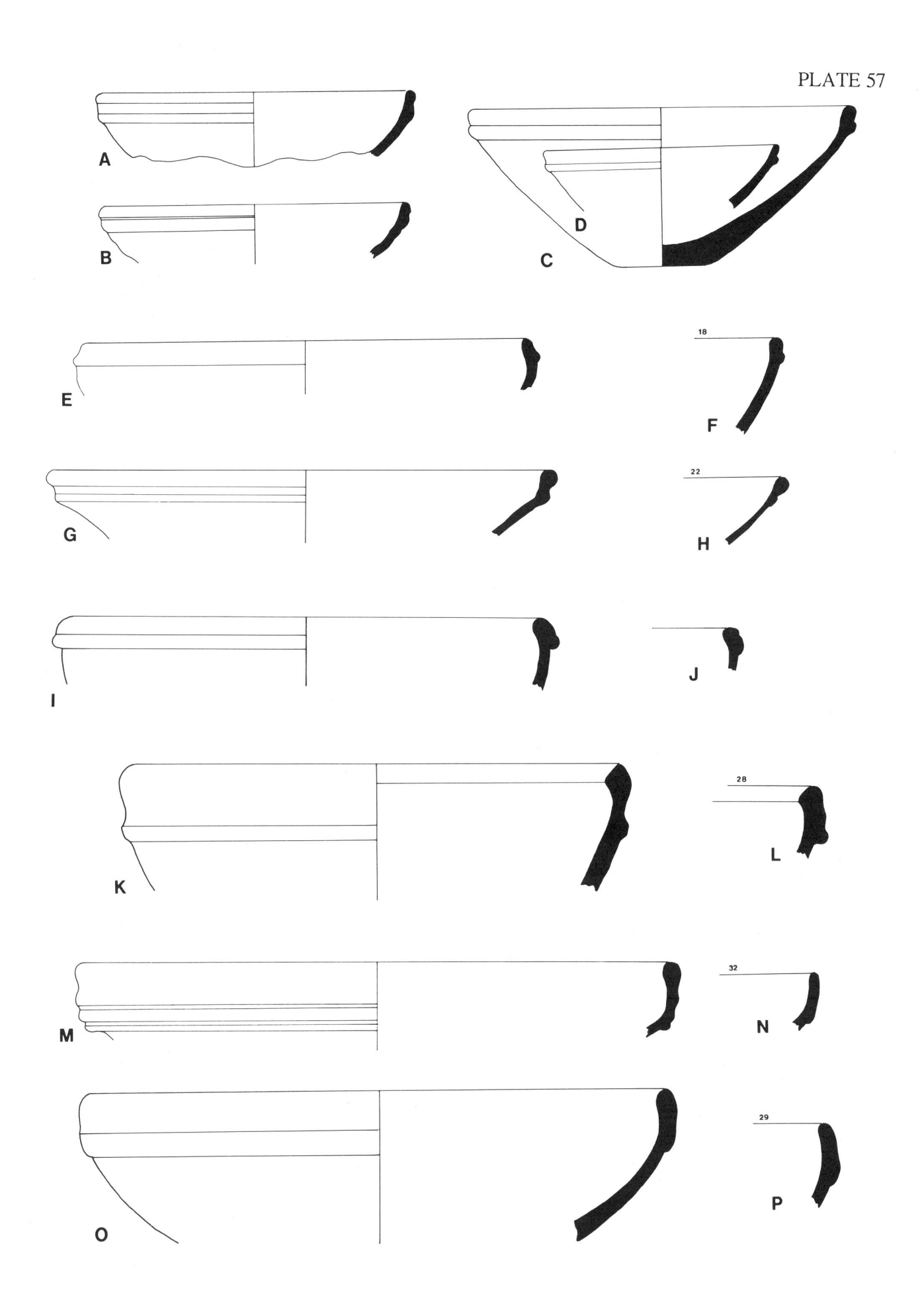

Period IV Pottery From Areas A, C, and C01: Ware Group I Bowls (*cont.*). Scale 2:5.

Plate 58. Period IV Pottery From Areas A, B, C, and C01: Ware Group I Bowls (*cont.*). Scale 2:5.

|   | MRN | CONTEXT | FCN | WARE | FORM | TYPE | DECO. | WARE/REMARKS |
|---|---|---|---|---|---|---|---|---|
| A | 12700 | A05-05-046 | 150 | 04 | 1599 | Unass. Bowl | — | Dense light buff clay; no visible tempering. |
| B | 4655 | A08-05-018 | 185 | 04 | 1050 | Unass. Bowl | — | Brownish-buff clay; white grits. |
| C | 4631 | C56-0361-024 | 257 | 04 | 770 | Bowl 12 | — | Brownish-buff clay; small-sized grits; buff slip on surfaces. |
| D | 3742 | C56-03-004 | — | 04 | 770 | Bowl 12 | — | Brownish-buff clay; small-sized white grits. |
| E | 7663 | A04-07-027 | 113 | 04 | 052 | Bowl 13 | — | Buff clay; small-sized grits. |
| F | 6706 | A04-05-013 | 071 | 04 | 052 | Bowl 13 | — | Buff clay; small-sized grits. |
| G | 1574 | C01-1017-053 | 424 | 04 | 052 | Bowl 13 | — | Fairly dense orange-buff clay; small-sized white grits. |
| H | 369 | C01-03-002 | 073 | 04 | 052 | Bowl 13 | — | Fairly dense brownish-buff clay; no visible tempering other than a few scattered white grits. |
| I | 1023 | A07-04-005 | 030 | 04 | 310 | Bowl 14 | — | Buff clay; small-sized white grits. |
| J | 2204 | A08-0220-007 | 074 | 04 | 592 | Bowl 14 | — | Orange-buff clay; small-sized white grits; buff slip on exterior. |
| K | 500 | B03-05-002 | 007 | 04 | 051 | Bowl 14 | — | Reddish-buff clay; small-sized grits. |
| L | 533 | B02-05-002 | 019 | 04 | 051 | Bowl 14 | — | Reddish-buff clay; small-sized white grits; brown wash on interior. |
| M | 823 | C45-0172-005 | D033 | 04 | 330 | Bowl 15 | — | Brownish-buff clay; small-sized white grits; brown wash on interior. |
| N | 4759 | C35-02-012 | 176 | 04 | 879 | Bowl 15 | — | Orange-buff clay; small-sized white grits. |
| O | 176 | A04-05-003 | 013 | 04 | 019 | Bowl 15 | — | Fairly dense reddish-buff clay; no visible tempering other than scattered white grits. |
| P | 3161 | C35-04-003 | D043 | 04 | 719 | Bowl 15 | — | Brownish-buff clay; small-sized white grits; buff slip on surface. |

PLATE 58

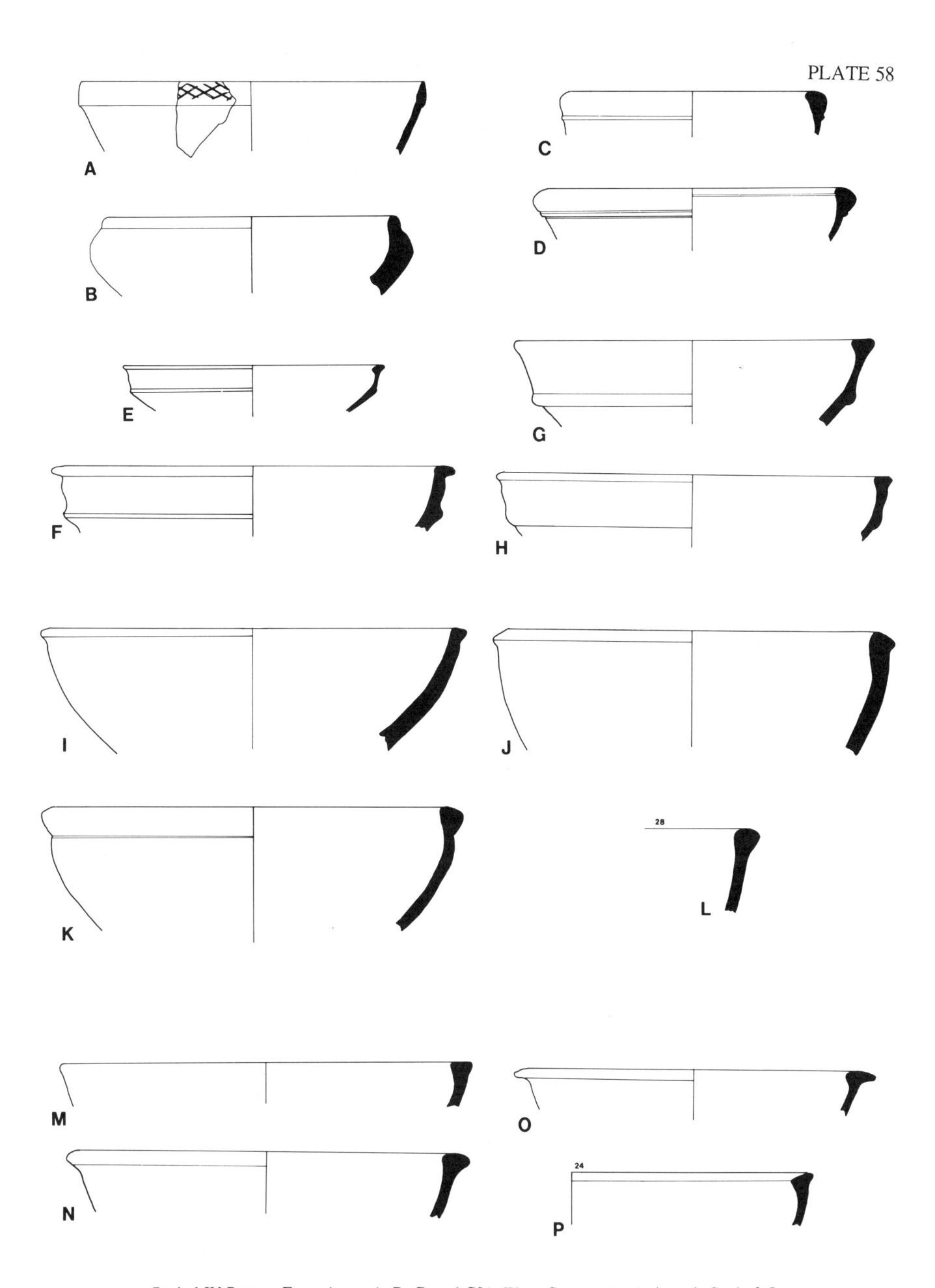

Period IV Pottery From Areas A, B, C, and C01: Ware Group I Bowls (*cont.*). Scale 2:5.

Plate 59. Period IV Pottery From Areas A, B, C, and C01: Ware Group I Bowls (*cont.*). Scale 2:5

|   | MRN | CONTEXT | FCN | WARE | FORM | TYPE | DECO. | WARE/REMARKS |
|---|---|---|---|---|---|---|---|---|
| A | 691 | C01-08-011 | 131 | 04 | 779 | Unass. Bowl | — | Reddish-buff clay; small-sized grits. |
| B | 6621 | C35-04-009 | — | 04 | 34 | Bowl 16 | — | Buff clay; small-sized grits. |
| C | 041 | B01-04-007 | 026 | 04 | 34 | Bowl 16 | — | Brownish-buff clay; small-sized white grits. |
| D | 7602 | A07-1392-047 | D353 | 04 | 1265 | Unass. Bowl | — | Greenish-buff clay; small-sized grits. |
| E | 5264 | A08-05-019 | 198 | 04 | 1119 | Unass. Bowl | — | Fairly dense grayish-buff clay; small-sized white grits. |
| F | 815 | C01-09-020 | 171 | 04 | 1119 | Unass. Bowl | — | Fairly dense brownish-buff clay; small-sized grits. |
| G | 1235 | C45-03-012 | 145 | 04 | 1119 | Unass. Bowl | — | Brownish-buff clay; medium-sized white grits prominent. |
| H | 490 | B02-04-016 | 016 | 04 | 38 | Bowl 17 | — | Reddish-buff clay; small-sized grits. |
| I | 2631 | A07-0591-010 | 091 | 04 | 846 | Bowl 17 | — | Greenish-buff clay, somewhat overfired; small-sized white grits. |
| J | 163 | B02-03-004 | 091 | 04 | 39 | Bowl 17 | — | Reddish-buff clay; small-sized white grits; faint traces of cream slip on exterior. |

PLATE 59

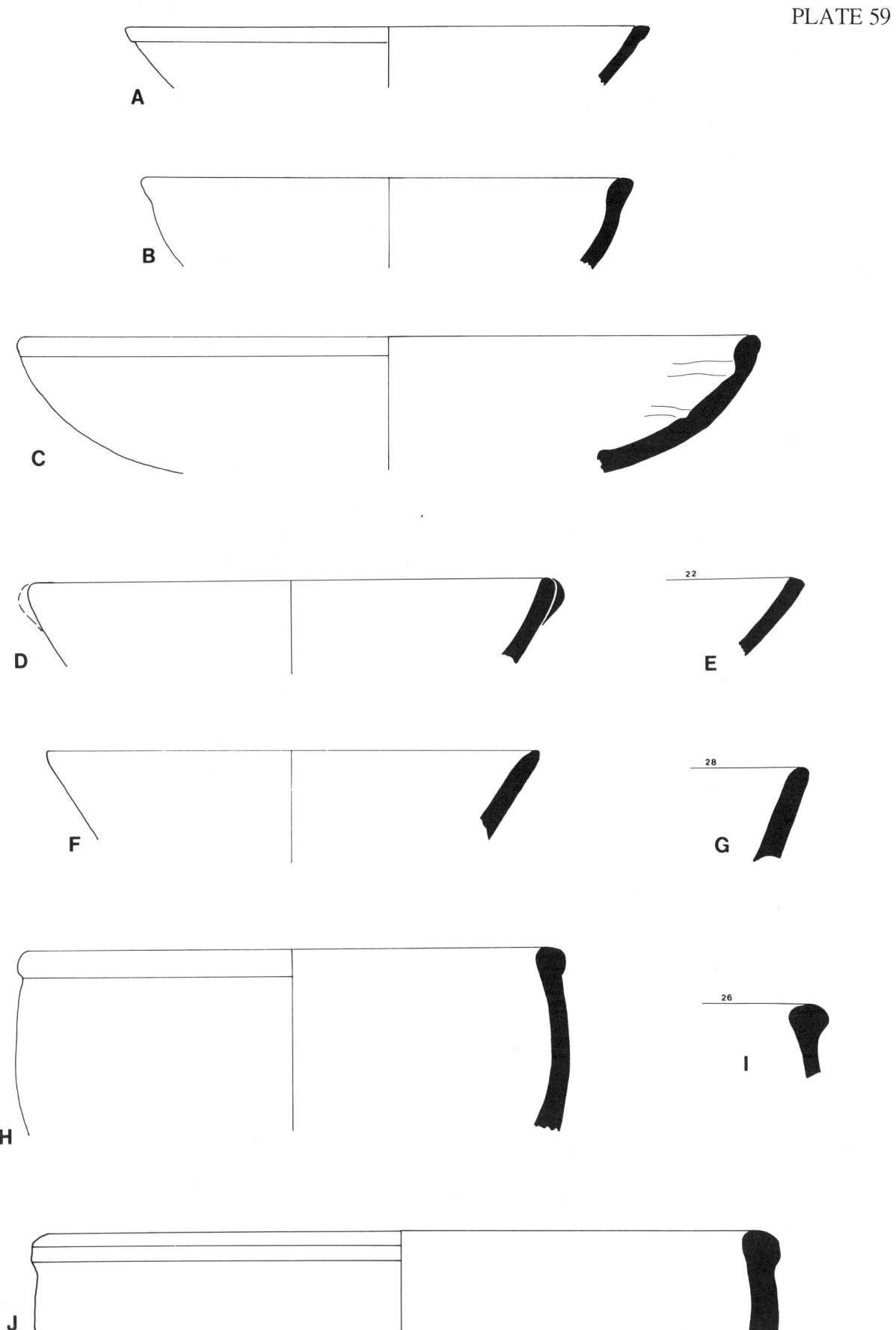

Period IV Pottery From Areas A, B, C, and C01: Ware Group I Bowls (*cont.*). Scale 2:5.

Plate 60. Period IV Pottery From Areas A, B, C, C01, and F: Ware Group I Bowls (*cont.*) and Holemouth Jars. Scale 2:5.

|   | MRN | CONTEXT | FCN | WARE | FORM | TYPE | DECO. | WARE/REMARKS |
|---|---|---|---|---|---|---|---|---|
| A | 6700 | A04-05-016 | 065 | 04 | 1283 | Bowl 18 | — | Buff clay; small-sized grits. |
| B | 6707 | C35-04-009 | 295 | 04 | 1287 | Jar 1a | — | Buff clay; small-sized white grits. |
| C | 1714 | C01-0167-059 | 507 | 04 | 497 | Jar 1a | — | Light brownish-buff clay; small-sized white grits; light greenish-buff slip on exterior; slight wheel mark corrugations on exterior. |
| D | — | Area C01, Provenance lost | — | 04 | 497 | Jar 1a | — | Light brownish-buff clay; fairly gritty with small white grits prominent. |
| E | 16107 | A01-0600/10-036 | 231 | 04 | 1560 | Jar 1b | Bns. | Fairly dense brownish-buff clay; small-sized white grits; on exterior, faint traces of horizontal burnishing strokes. |
| F | 11636 | A04-08-038 | 118 | 04 | 1598 | Unass. Jar | — | Brownish/orangish-buff clay; medium-sized white grits prominent; exterior pinkish; faint traces of burnishing or smoothing. |
| G | 17926 | A04-10-103 | 605 | 04 | 1120 | Unass. Jar | — | Buff clay; small-sized grits. |
| H | 7513 | A07-05-035 | 246 | 04 | 1202 | Unass. Jar | 023 | Dense reddish-buff clay; small-sized white grits. |
| I | 1309 | A08-01-002 | 008 | 04 | 1364 | Jar 2 | 023 | Dense buff clay; no visible tempering other than a few small-sized grits. |
| J | 532 | B02-03-015 | 181 | 04 | 1364 | Jar 2 | — | Buff clay; small-sized grits. |
| K | 4758 | C35-02-013 | D180 | 04 | 540 | Jar 2 | — | Light greenish-buff clay; small-sized grits. |
| L | 1993 | C55-06-003 | 093 | 04 | 540 | Jar 2 | — | Buff clay; small-sized grits; light greenish-buff slip on surface. |
| M | 12155 | F01-05-051 | 295 | 04 | 1662 | Jar 3a | — | Buff clay; small-sized grits. |
| N | 656 | B02-03-015 | 187 | 04 | 126 | Jar 3b | — | Buff clay; small-sized grits. |

PLATE 60

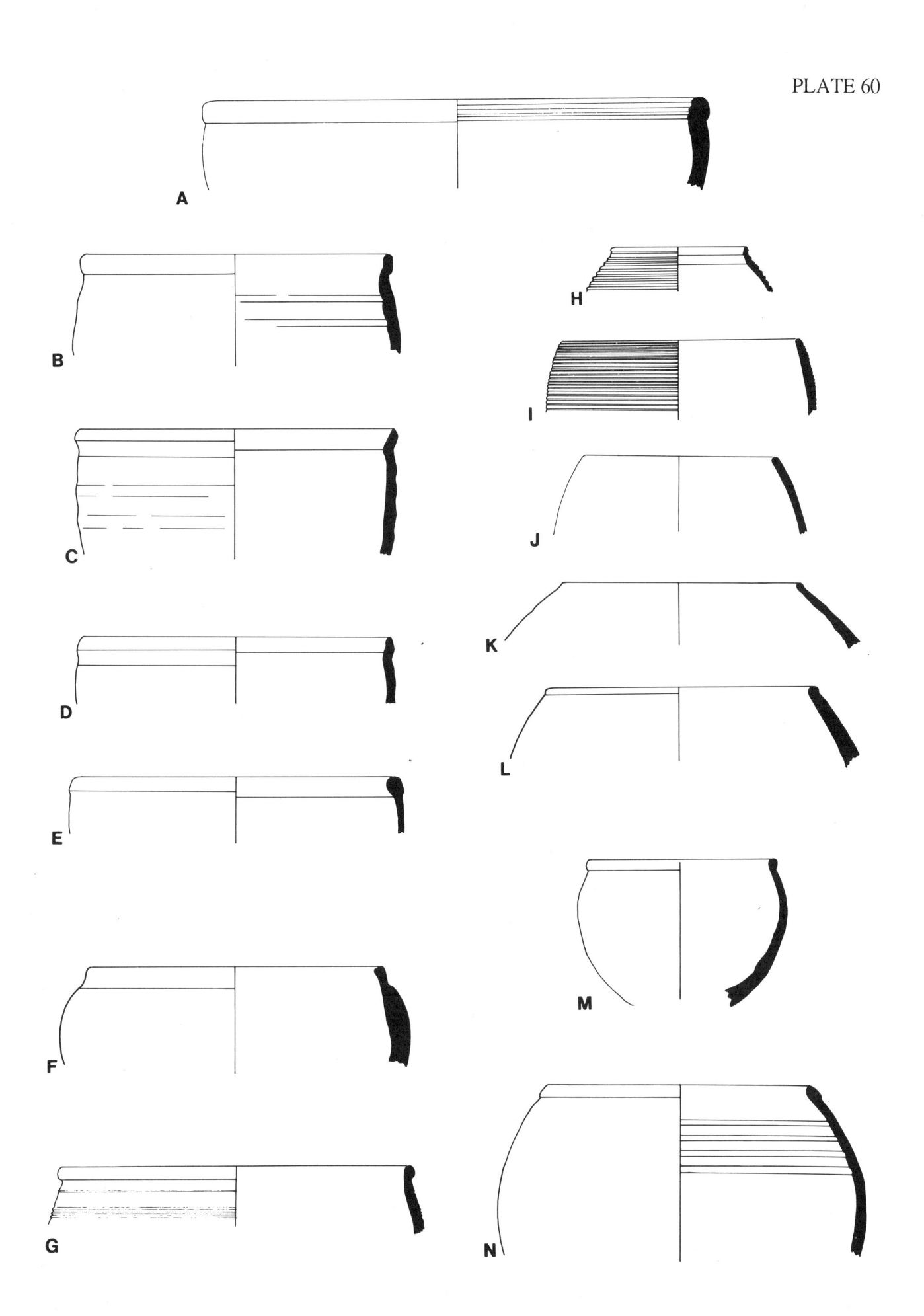

Period IV Pottery From Areas A, B, C, C01, and F: Ware Group I Bowls (*cont.*) and Holemouth Jars. Scale 2:5.

Plate 61. Period IV Pottery From Areas A, B, C, C01, F, and G: Ware Group I Holemouth Jars (*cont.*). Scale 2:5.

|   | MRN | CONTEXT | FCN | WARE | FORM | TYPE | DECO. | WARE/REMARKS |
|---|---|---|---|---|---|---|---|---|
| A | 1057 | C01-10-031 | 236 | 04 | 126 | Jar 3b | — | Fairly dense light, greenish-buff clay; small-sized grits. |
| B | 373 | B02-04-010 | 010 | 04 | 120 | Jar 3c | — | Greenish-buff clay; small-sized grits. |
| C | 3716 | A06-07-019 | 072 | 04 | 1658 | Jar 3c | — | Fairly dense greenish clay, somewhat overfired; white and black medium-sized grits visible. |
| D | 3881 | C46-07-006 | 086 | 04 | 797 | Jar 3c | — | Pinkish-buff clay; small-sized white grits. |
| E | 11253 | A04-08-059 | 303 | 04 | 121 | Jar 3d | — | Greenish-buff clay; small-sized white grits prominent. |
| F | 1717 | C01-0167-059 | D516 | 04 | 121 | Jar 3d | — | Buff clay; small-sized grits; white ones are prominent. |
| G | 005 | B01-04-002 | 007 | 04 | 121 | Jar 3d | — | Fairly dense brownish-buff clay; small-sized grits; buff slip on exterior. |
| H | 6049 | G64-01-006 | 017 | 04 | 1282 | Jar 3c | — | Fairly dense brownish-buff clay; small-sized white grits. |
| I | 4549 | C56-08-022 | 241 | 04 | 1282 | Jar 3c | — | Buff clay; small-sized grits. |
| J | 0039 | B02-01-002 | 039 | 04 | 120 | Jar 3c | — | Reddish-buff clay; small- and medium-sized white grits. |
| K | 034 | F01-01-001 | 001 | 04 | 124 | Jar 3c | — | Greenish-buff clay; medium-sized grits, white ones predominant; out of context in slope wash. |
| L | 008 | B01-05-002 | 015 | 04 | 120 | Jar 3c | — | Brownish-buff clay; small-sized white grits. |
| M | 1018 | C45-04-001 | 091 | 04 | 303 | Jar 3c | — | Light greenish-buff clay; small- and medium-sized grits. |
| N | 3355 | A07-05/06-019 | 148 | 04 | 303 | Jar 3c | — | Dense orange/reddish-buff clay; small-sized white grits. |

PLATE 61

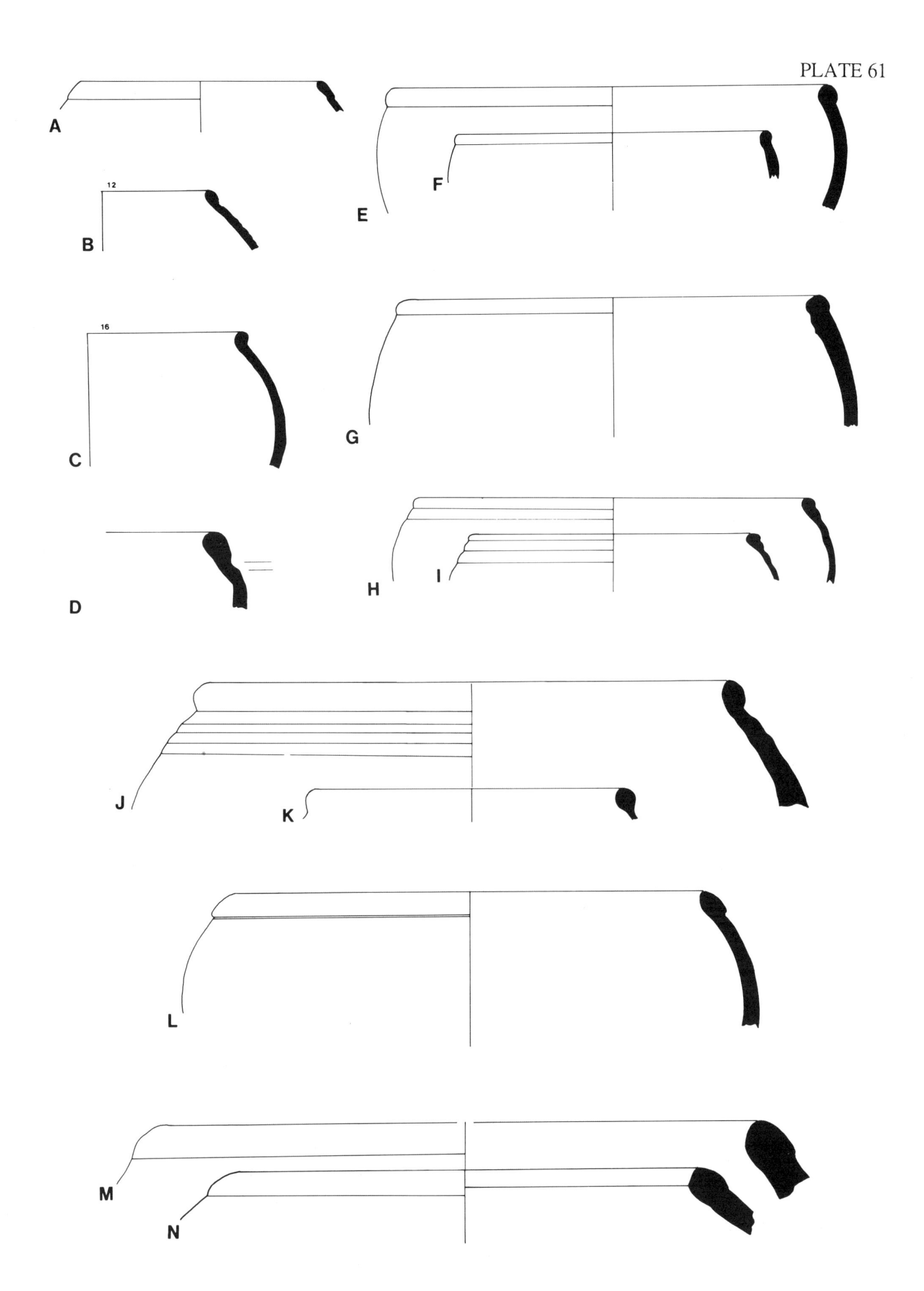

Period IV Pottery From Areas A, B, C, C01, F, and G: Ware Group I Holemouth Jars (*cont.*). Scale 2:5.

Plate 62. Period IV Pottery From Areas A, B, and C: Ware Group I Holemouth Jars (*cont.*). Scale 2:5.

|   | MRN  | CONTEXT       | FCN | WARE | FORM | TYPE   | DECO. | WARE/REMARKS |
|---|------|---------------|-----|------|------|--------|-------|--------------|
| A | 7052 | C56-04-025    | 425 | 04   | 1302 | Jar 4a | —     | Fairly dense reddish-buff clay; small-sized grits. |
| B | 7971 | A01-14-066    | 460 | 04   | 1307 | Jar 4a | —     | Reddish-buff clay; small-sized white grits. |
| C | 7130 | C55-0457-034  | 658 | 04   | 1278 | Jar 4a | —     | Buff clay grading to brown-buff towards surfaces; small-sized white grits. |
| D | 4533 | C55-05-011    | 275 | 04   | 1278 | Jar 4a | —     | Fairly dense grayish-buff clay; small-sized grits. |
| E | 3139 | A07-05/06-018 | 140 | 04   | 717  | Jar 4a | —     | Buff clay; small-sized grits. |
| F | 5031 | C55-0217-011  | 375 | 04   | 1259 | Jar 4a | —     | Buff clay; small-sized grits. |
| G | 1625 | C55-02-003    | 025 | 04   | 114  | Jar 4a | —     | Reddish-buff clay; small-sized white grits; circular incisions filled with white paste. |
| H | 3517 | C56-10-017    | 165 | 04   | 116  | Jar 4a | —     | Orange-buff clay; small-sized white grits; traces of red wash on exterior. |
| I | 3160 | C35-04-003    | 040 | 04   | 722  | Jar 4a | —     | Fairly dense orange-buff clay, brownish core; small-sized white grits. |
| J | 788  | A06-03-010    | 029 | 04   | 215  | Jar 4a | —     | Brownish-buff clay; small- and medium-sized white grits; greenish-buff slip on exterior. |
| K | 045  | B02-01-001    | 088 | 04   | 215  | Jar 4a | —     | Buff clay; small-sized white grits; impressed triangles on shoulder. |

PLATE 62

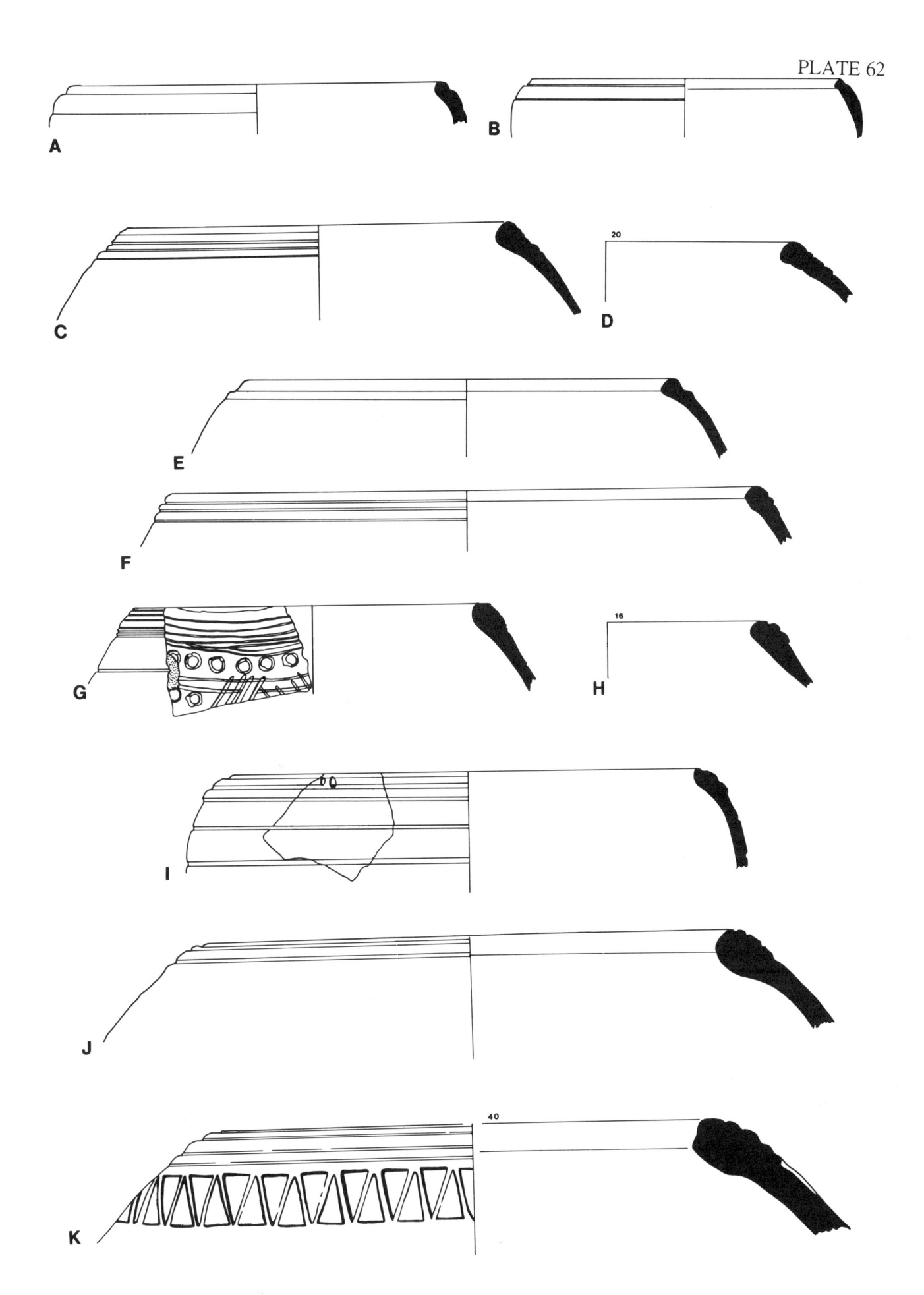

Period IV Pottery From Areas A, B, and C: Ware Group I Holemouth Jars (*cont.*). Scale 2:5.

Plate 63. Period IV Pottery From Areas A, C, and F: Ware Group I Holemouth Jars (*cont.*). Scale 2:5.

|   | MRN | CONTEXT | FCN | WARE | FORM | TYPE | DECO. | WARE/REMARKS |
|---|---|---|---|---|---|---|---|---|
| A | 937 | A07-04-005 | 020 | 04 | 114 | Jar 4a | — | Buff clay; small-sized white grits. |
| B | 1126 | A07-05-006 | 086 | 04 | 337 | Jar 4a | — | Buff clay; small- and medium-sized grits. |
| C | 12764 | A02-0552/53-032 | D096 | 04 | 414 | Jar 4b | — | Buff clay; small-sized grits. |
| D | 7566 | A07-13-043 | 330 | 04 | 1231 | Jar 4b | — | Grayish clay grading to orange-buff towards surface; small-sized grits. |
| E | 7590 | A07-13-047 | 349 | 04 | 1231 | Jar 4b | — | Buff clay; small-sized grits. |
| F | 6375 | C35-0371-005 | 250 | 04 | 414 | Jar 4b | — | Orange-buff clay; small- and medium-sized white grits. |
| G | 1625 | C55-02-003 | 025 | 04 | 524 | Jar 4c | — | Orange-buff clay; small- and medium-sized white grits. |
| H | 12104 | F01-05-044 | 244 | 04 | 1681 | Unass. Jar | — | Fairly dense light brownish-buff clay; white grits; at least one triangular-shaped lug preserved. |

PLATE 63

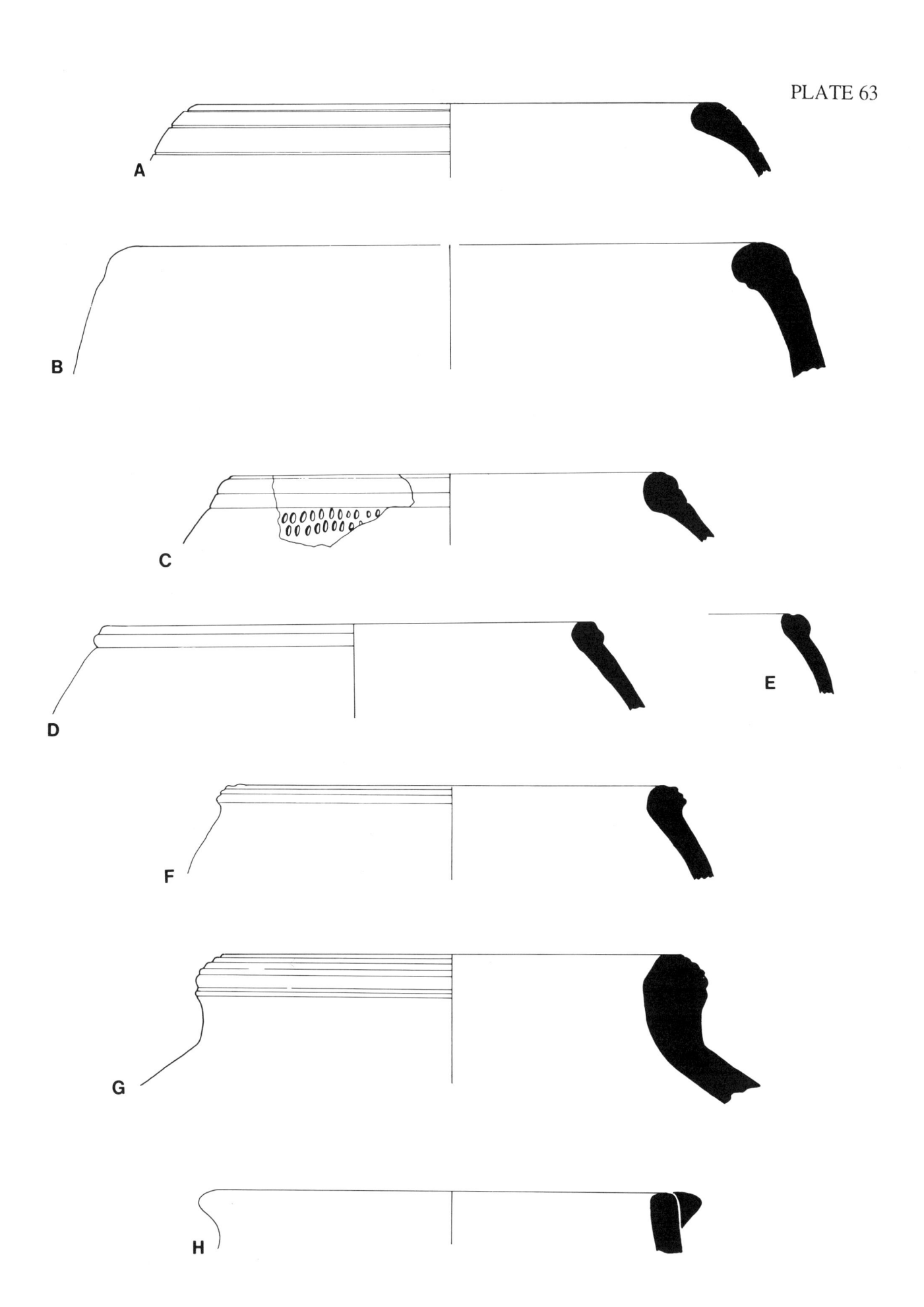

Period IV Pottery From Areas A, C, and F: Ware Group I Holemouth Jars (*cont.*). Scale 2:5.

Plate 64. Period IV Pottery From Areas A, B, C, C01, and F: Ware Group I Jars. Scale 2:5.

|   | MRN | CONTEXT | FCN | WARE | FORM | TYPE | DECO. | WARE/REMARKS |
|---|---|---|---|---|---|---|---|---|
| A | 7590 | A07-13-047 | 349 | 04 | 107 | Jar 5a | — | Fairly dense brownish-buff clay, orangish core; small-sized white grits; hole on jar shoulder bored secondarily. |
| B | 19301 | B03-03-011/022 | 284 | 04 | C-76 | Jar 5a | — | Reddish-buff clay, orangish core; small-sized white grits; buff slip on exterior; (= KH 1984/175). |
| C | 1104 | C45-01-007 | 097 | 04 | 107 | Jar 5a | — | Buff clay; small-sized grits. |
| D | — | Provenance lost | — | 04 | 107 | Jar 5a | — | Brownish-buff clay; small-sized grits. |
| E | 6331 | C55-04-014 | 536 | 04 | 107 | Jar 5a | — | Buff clay; small-sized white grits. |
| F | 4386 | C01-1017/27-098 | D1288 | 04 | 852 | Jar 5b | — | Dense buff clay; no visible tempering. |
| G | 12196 | F01-05-060 | D327 | 04 | 852 | Jar 5b | — | Buff clay; small-sized grits. |
| H | 4454 | C55-0459-011 | D230 | 04 | 870 | Unass. Jar | — | Reddish-buff clay; small-sized grits. |
| I | 7694 | A07-14-056 | D409 | 04 | 1264 | Unass. Jar | — | Orange-buff clay; small-sized white grits; handmade, somewhat irregular; a series of oval depressions near rim exterior. |
| J | 1236 | C45-03-012 | D148 | 04 | 106 | Jar 6 | — | Light brownish-buff clay; small-sized grits. |
| K | 1688 | C55-04-003 | 036 | 04 | 488 | Jar 6 | — | Buff clay; small-sized white grits. |
| L | 1945 | C55-07-003 | 073 | 04 | 519 | Jar 6 | — | Brownish-buff clay; small-sized grits; buff slip on surface. |
| M | 3096 | C56-08-001 | 122 | 04 | 705 | Jar 6 | — | Buff clay; small-sized grits. |
| N | 1698 | A08-01-004 | 032 | 04 | 492 | Jar 7 | — | Dense orange-buff clay; small-sized white grits; brownish-buff slip on surface. |
| O | 1322 | C45-03-016 | 181 | 04 | 401 | Jar 7 | — | Greenish-buff clay; small- and medium-sized white inclusions; handmade, irregular. |
| P | 1945 | C55-07-003 | 073 | 04 | 102 | Jar 8a | — | Greenish-buff clay; small-sized grits. |
| Q | 12790 | A01-0500/03-028 | D172 | 04 | 1562 | Jar 8b | — | Brownish-buff clay grading to gray towards surfaces; small-sized white grits. |
| R | 12790 | A01-0500/03-028 | D172 | 04 | 1562 | Jar 8b | — | Brownish-buff clay; small-sized white grits. |
| S | 337 | B02-04-012 | 006 | 04 | 104 | Jar 9 | — | Reddish-buff clay; small-sized white grits. |
| T | 106 | A02-02-004 | 016 | 04 | 103 | Jar 9 | — | Fairly dense reddish-buff clay; small-sized white grits; buff slip on exterior surface. |
| U | 2141 | C01-0187/88-062 | D652 | 04 | 573 | Unass. Jar | — | Reddish-buff clay; gritty with white grits prominent; exterior covered with thick bone-white slip; handmade, irregular. |
| V | 2684 | A08-04-010 | 107 | 04 | 684 | Jar 10 | — | Orange-buff clay; small- and medium-sized white grits; buff slip on exterior. |
| W | 3559 | A07-0761-022 | 165 | 04 | 774 | Jar 10 | — | Orange-buff clay; small-sized white grits. |

PLATE 64

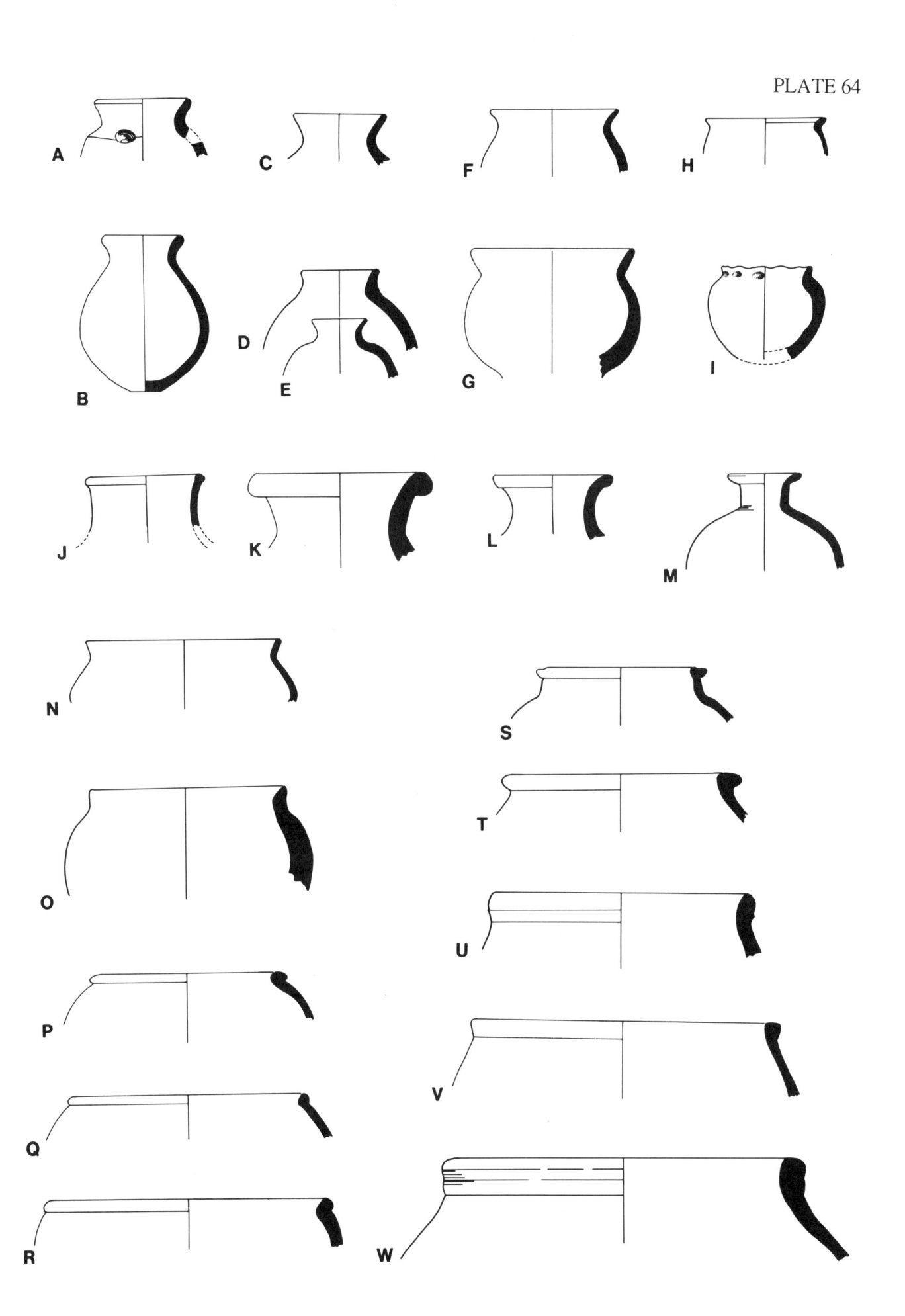

Period IV Pottery From Areas A, B, C, C01, and F: Ware Group I Jars. Scale 2:5.

Plate 65. Period IV Pottery From Areas A, C, and C01: Ware Group I Jars (*cont.*). Scale 2:5.

|   | MRN | CONTEXT | FCN | WARE | FORM | TYPE | DECO. | WARE/REMARKS |
|---|---|---|---|---|---|---|---|---|
| A | 12790 | A01-0500/03-028 | D172 | 04 | 1563 | Jar 11 | — | Dense greenish-buff clay; small-sized grits; exterior surface covered with lighter greenish-buff slip. |
| B | 12790 | A01-0500/03-028 | D172 | 04 | 1563 | Jar 11 | — | Brownish-buff clay; small-sized white grits. |
| C | 1416 | C01-0187/89-049 | 411 | 04 | 391 | Jar 12 | — | Brownish-buff clay; gritty with small- and medium-sized grits; exterior smoothed, interior coarse. |
| D | 1092 | A07-04-005 | 032 | 04 | 391 | Jar 12 | Bns. | Brownish-buff clay; small-sized white grits; orange-buff slip on surface, very slightly burnished. |
| E | 3788 | C56-0646-021 | D224 | 04 | 656 | Jar 13 | — | Buff clay; small-sized grits. |
| F | 1698 | A08-01-004 | 032 | 04 | 304 | Jar 13 | — | Somewhat porous greenish-buff clay; gritty. |
| G | 3374 | C01-1008/09/19/29-080 | 1043 | 04 | 1255 | Jar 13 | — | Brownish-buff clay; small-sized white grits. |
| H | 8158 | C01-0957/59-062 | 2128 | 04 | 1335 | Jar 13 | — | Dense orange-buff clay; small white and larger-sized black grits visible; pinkish-buff slip on exterior. |
| I | 1236 | C45-03-012 | D148 | 04 | 656 | Jar 13 | — | Greenish/grayish-buff clay; small-sized white grits. |
| J | 7616 | A04-07-023 | 095 | 04 | 1251 | Jar 13 | — | Buff clay; small-sized black and white grits. |
| K | 944 | C45-01-006 | 068 | 04 | 304 | Jar 13 | — | Greenish-buff clay; small-sized white grits. |
| L | 1429 | A08-01-002 | 014 | 04 | 444 | Jar 13 | — | Brownish-buff clay; gritty with small- and medium-sized white grits; greenish-buff slip on exterior; out of context in slope wash. |
| M | 17916 | A04-1032/42-102 | 601 | 04 | 1677 | Unass. Jar | — | Reddish-buff clay; small-sized grits. |
| N | 3717 | A08-05-013 | 145 | 04 | 837 | Unass. Jar | — | Orange-buff clay; small-sized gray grits. |

PLATE 65

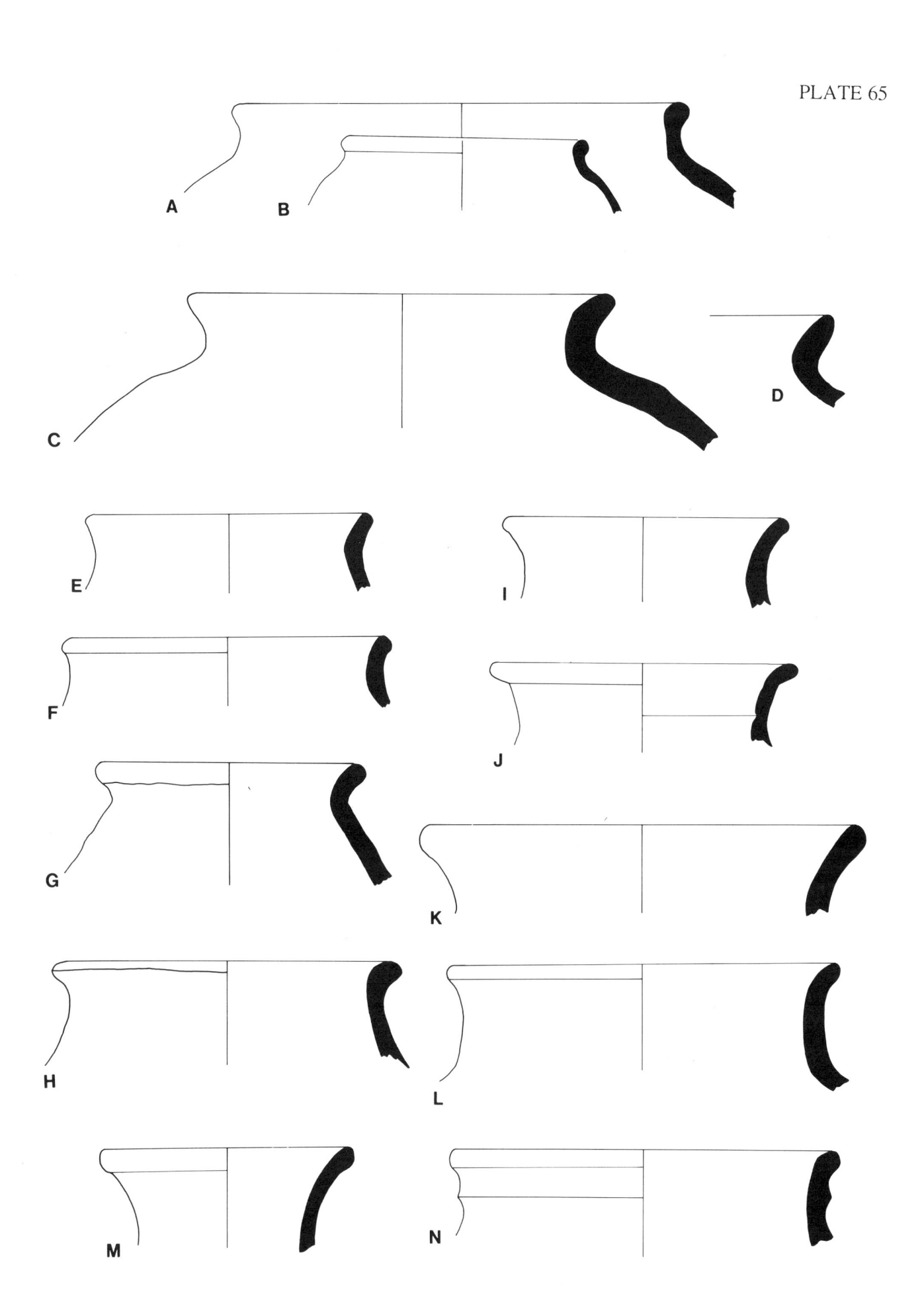

Period IV Pottery From Areas A, C, and C01: Ware Group I Jars (*cont.*). Scale 2:5.

Plate 66. Period IV Pottery From Areas A, B, C, C01, and F: Ware Group I Jars (*cont.*). Scale 2:5.

|   | MRN | CONTEXT | FCN | WARE | FORM | TYPE | DECO. | WARE/REMARKS |
|---|---|---|---|---|---|---|---|---|
| A | 930 | A05-04-013 | 031 | 04 | 276 | Jar 14a | — | Greenish-buff clay; small-sized grits. |
| B | 1697 | A08-01-004 | 031 | 04 | 504 | Jar 14a | — | Brownish-buff clay; small-sized white grits. |
| C | 1994 | C55-07-003 | 088 | 04 | 535 | Jar 14a | — | Buff clay; small-sized white grits. |
| D | 1305 | A06-06-013 | 049 | 04 | 737 | Jar 14b | — | Brownish-buff clay; small-sized grits. |
| E | 5260 | C55-0219-011 | 399 | 04 | 1261 | Jar 14b | — | Orange-buff clay; small-sized grits. |
| F | 3490 | C56-07-015 | 166 | 04 | 841 | Jar 14b | — | Grayish/greenish-buff clay; grit-tempered, small-sized grits. |
| G | 282 | B02-03-010 | 130 | 04 | 084 | Jar 23 | — | Fairly dense brownish-buff clay; small-sized white grits; buff slip on exterior. |
| H | 2201 | A07-05-008 | 066 | 04 | 086 | Jar 15 | — | Brownish-buff clay, reddish core; small-sized white grits; buff slip on exterior and interior rim. |
| I | 543 | F01-04-004 | 025 | 04 | 086 | Jar 15 | — | Reddish-buff clay, darker brown core; small-sized white grits; buff slip on exterior. |
| J | 17916 | A04-1032/42-102 | 601 | 04 | 1676 | Jar 15 | Bns. | Reddish clay; gritty, medium-sized grits very prominent; pinkish slip on surfaces, exterior lightly burnished. |
| K | 19831 | B81-01-002 | 013 | 04 | 084 | Jar 15 | — | Brownish-buff clay; small-sized white grits. |
| L | 129 | A02-03-011 | 031 | 04 | 087 | Jar 16a | — | Buff clay; small-sized grits. |
| M | 369 | C01-03-002 | 073 | 04 | 087 | Jar 16a | — | Buff clay; small-sized grits. |
| N | 493 | C01-03-002 | 084 | 04 | 087 | Jar 16a | — | Buff clay, orange-buff core; small-sized white grits; buff slip on exterior. |
| O | 1235 | C45-03-012 | 1012 | 04 | 087 | Jar 16a | — | Buff clay; small- and medium-sized grits. |

PLATE 66

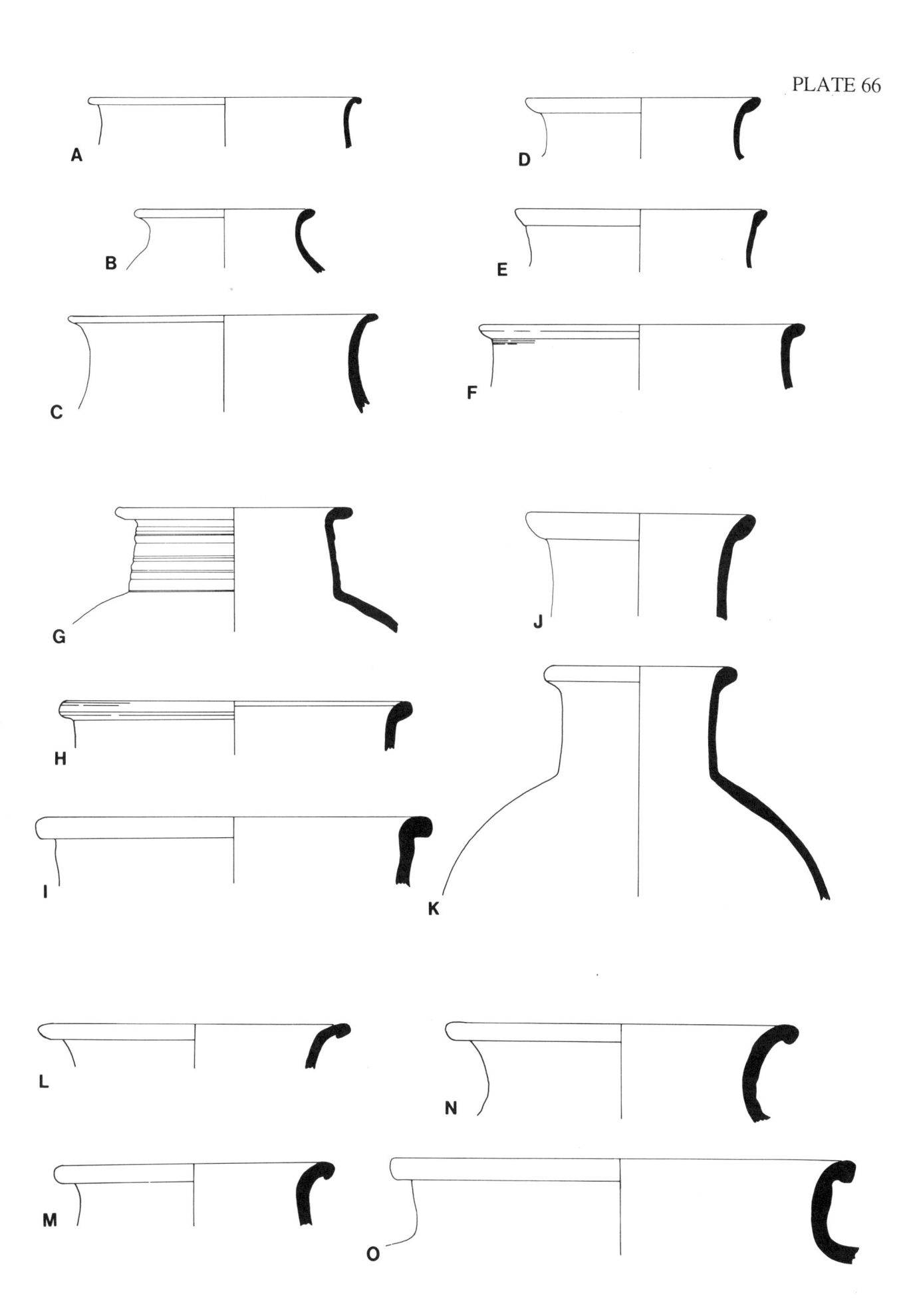

Period IV Pottery From Areas A, B, C, C01, and F: Ware Group I Jars (*cont.*). Scale 2:5.

Plate 67. Period IV Pottery From Areas A, C, C01, and F: Ware Group I Jars (*cont.*). Scale 2:5.

|   | MRN | CONTEXT | FCN | WARE | FORM | TYPE | DECO. | WARE/REMARKS |
|---|---|---|---|---|---|---|---|---|
| A | 0814 | C01-10-013 | 190 | 04 | 69 | Jar 16b | — | Buff clay; small-sized grits. |
| B | 12157 | F01-05-052 | 297 | 04 | 69 | Jar 16b | — | Brownish-buff clay; small-sized grits. |
| C | 363 | A06-02-003 | 012 | 04 | 69 | Jar 16b | — | Buff clay; small-sized grits; buff slip on surface. |
| D | 17703 | A05-05-073 | 321 | 04 | 69 | Jar 16b | — | Fairly dense greenish-buff clay, reddish core; small-sized black and white grits visible. |
| E | 1967 | A08-0222-007 | 058 | 04 | 69 | Jar 16b | — | Light brownish-buff clay; small-sized gray and white grits; buff slip on surface. |
| F | 813 | C01-02-007 | 173 | 04 | 69 | Jar 16b | — | Brownish-buff clay; fairly gritty, small- and medium-sized white grits. |
| G | 3888 | A07-0750-023 | 206 | 04 | 69 | Jar 16b | — | Buff clay; small-sized grits. |
| H | 576 | C01-03-006 | 117 | 04 | 69 | Jar 16b | — | Buff clay; small- and medium-sized grits. |
| I | 4447 | C55-0439-011 | 249 | 04 | 69 | Jar 16b | — | Grayish-buff clay; small-sized white grits. |
| J | 2208 | A10-01-001 | 001 | 04 | 587 | Jar 16b | — | Buff clay; small- and medium-sized grits; light greenish-buff slip on exterior; "potter's mark" on interior near rim; out of context in slope wash. |

PLATE 67

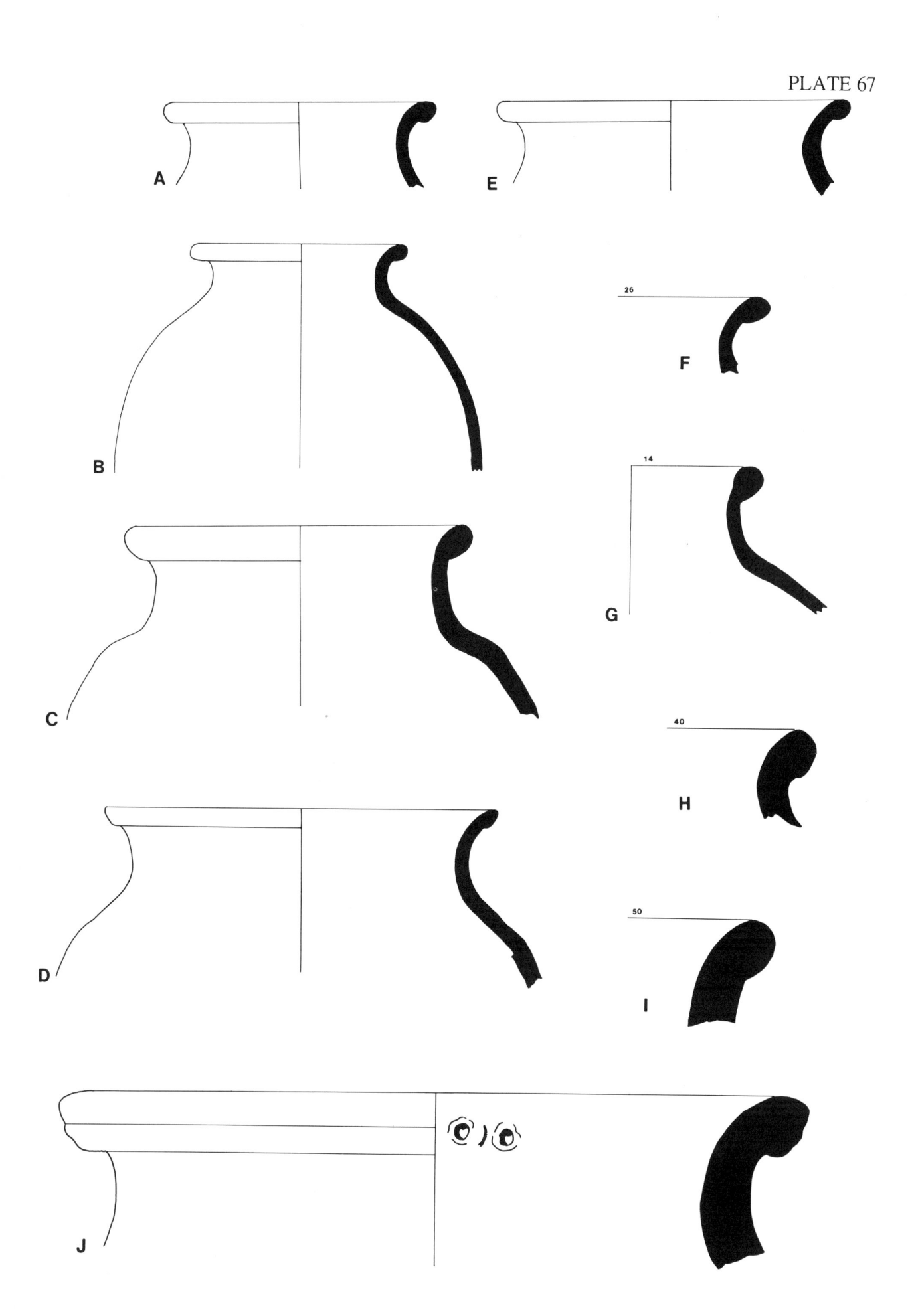

Period IV Pottery From Areas A, C, C01, and F: Ware Group I Jars (*cont.*). Scale 2:5.

Plate 68. Period IV Pottery From Areas A, B, C, and C01: Ware Group I Jars (*cont.*). Scale 2:5.

|   | MRN | CONTEXT | FCN | WARE | FORM | TYPE | DECO. | WARE/REMARKS |
|---|---|---|---|---|---|---|---|---|
| A | 1127 | A07-05-006 | 037 | 04 | 334 | Jar 16c | — | Brownish-buff clay; small-sized white grits. |
| B | 7136 | C55-04-036 | 668 | 04 | 72 | Jar 16c | — | Buff clay; small-sized grits; "potter's mark" on rim interior. |
| C | 532 | B02-03-015 | 181 | 04 | 68 | Jar 16c | — | Reddish-buff clay; small- and medium-sized white grits. |
| D | 680 | B01-05-019 | 192 | 04 | 72 | Jar 16c | — | Buff clay; small-sized grits. |
| E | 302 + 268 | C01-187/89-005 + C01-01-005 | 044 + 041 | 04 | 72 | Jar 16c | — | Buff clay; small- and medium-sized black and white grits. |
| F | 003 | B01-03-001 | 004 | 04 | 72 | Jar 16c | — | Buff clay; small- and medium-sized grits. |

PLATE 68

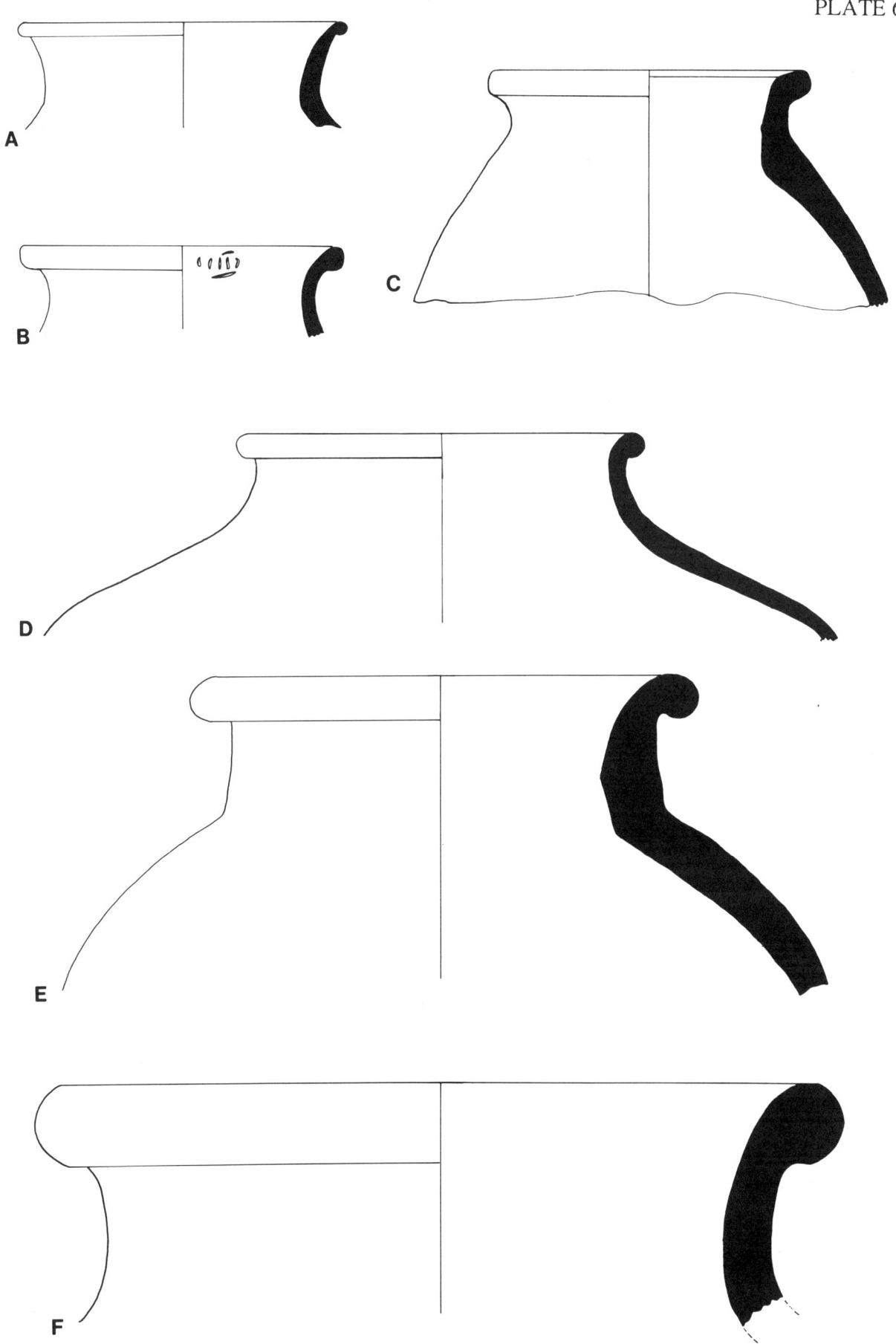

Period IV Pottery From Areas A, B, C, and C01: Ware Group I Jars (*cont.*). Scale 2:5.

Plate 69. Period IV Pottery From Areas A, C, and C01: Ware Group I Grooved Rim Jars. Scale 2:5.

|   | MRN | CONTEXT | FCN | WARE | FORM | TYPE | DECO. | WARE/REMARKS |
|---|---|---|---|---|---|---|---|---|
| A | 7692 | A07-14-054 | 402 | 04 | 1266 | Jar 17 | — | Buff clay; small-sized grits. |
| B | 2631 | A07-0591-010 | 091 | 04 | 062 | Jar 17 | — | Buff clay; small-sized grits. |
| C | 2679 | A07-0591-010 | 101 | 04 | 669 | Jar 17 | — | Buff clay; small-sized white grits. |
| D | 365 | C01-04-002 | 081 | 04 | 062 | Jar 17 | — | Buff clay; small-sized grits. |
| E | 3158 | A07-0760-022 | 167 | 04 | 753 | Jar 18a | — | Brownish-buff clay; small- and medium-sized grits; buff slip on surface. |
| F | 1943 | C55-06-003 | D069 | 04 | 521 | Jar 18a | — | Fairly porous greenish-buff clay; small-sized grits. |
| G | 2220 | C56-01-001 | 019 | 04 | 062 | Jar 17 | — | Grayish-buff clay; small-sized grits; buff slip on surfaces. |
| H | 2128 | A07-05-006 | 056 | 04 | 0753 | Jar 18a | — | Grayish-buff clay; small-sized white grits; buff slip on exterior. |
| I | 860 | A07-03-004 | 011 | 04 | 0352 | Jar 18a | — | Light pinkish-buff clay; small-sized white grits; greenish-buff slip on exterior and interior. |
| J | 640 | C01-01-005 | 124 | 04 | 521 | Jar 18a | — | Buff clay; small-sized white grits. |
| K | 6840 | C55-02-016 | 644 | 04 | 1682 | Jar 18a | — | Buff clay; small-sized white grits; presumably a jar rim but perhaps a pedestal base. |

PLATE 69

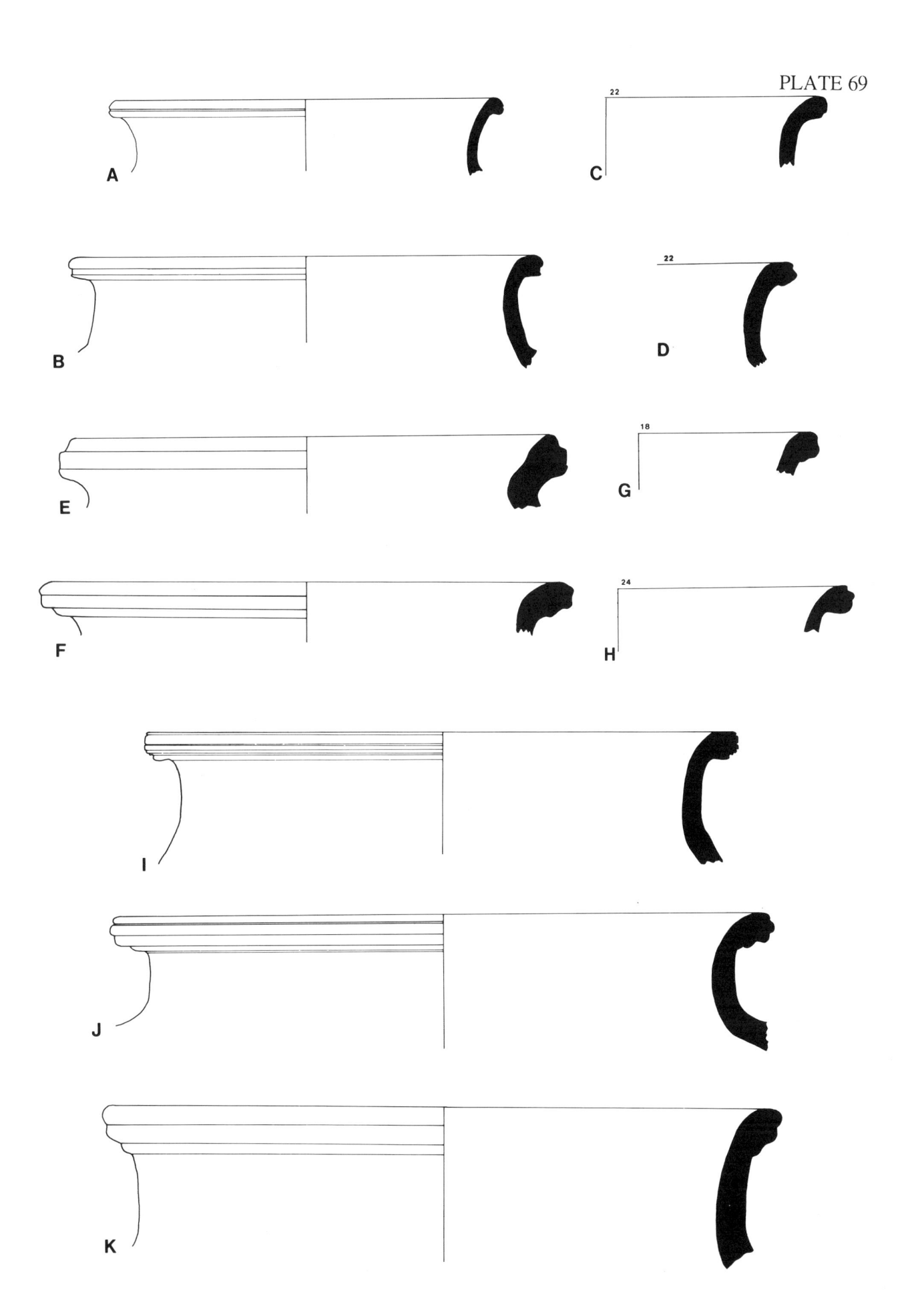

Period IV Pottery From Areas A, C, and C01: Ware Group I Grooved Rim Jars. Scale 2:5.

Plate 70. Period IV Pottery From Areas A, B, C, and F: Ware Group I Grooved Rim Jars (*cont.*). Scale 2:5.

|   | MRN | CONTEXT | FCN | WARE | FORM | TYPE | DECO. | WARE/REMARKS |
|---|---|---|---|---|---|---|---|---|
| A | 322 | F01-03-009 | 019 | 04 | 065 | Jar 18b | — | Buff clay; small-sized grits; "potter's mark" on rim interior. |
| B | 936 | A07-04-005 | 018 | 04 | 480 | Jar 18a | — | Buff clay; small-sized grits; impressed and excised decoration on exterior. |
| C | 1309 | A08-01-002 | 008 | 04 | 480 | Jar 18a | — | Brownish-buff clay; small- and medium-sized white grits; light greenish-buff slip on exterior; out of context in slope wash. |
| D | 2157 | C55-09-003 | 113 | 04 | 590 | Jar 18a | — | Orange-buff clay; white grits; air pocket in rim fold. |
| E | 3517 | C56-10-017 | 168 | 04 | 762 | Jar 18a | — | Brownish-buff clay; small-sized grits. |
| F | 656 | B02-03-015 | 187 | 04 | 065 | Jar 18b | — | Orange-buff clay; occasional scattered small-sized grits. |
| G | 3743 | C56-0514-013 | 190 | 04 | 065 | Jar 18b | — | Orange-buff clay; occasional scattered small-sized grits. |
| H | 4954 | C55-0785-011 | 336 | 04 | 065 | Jar 18b | — | Light greenish-buff clay; small-sized white grits. |

PLATE 70

A

B  C 24

D  E

F

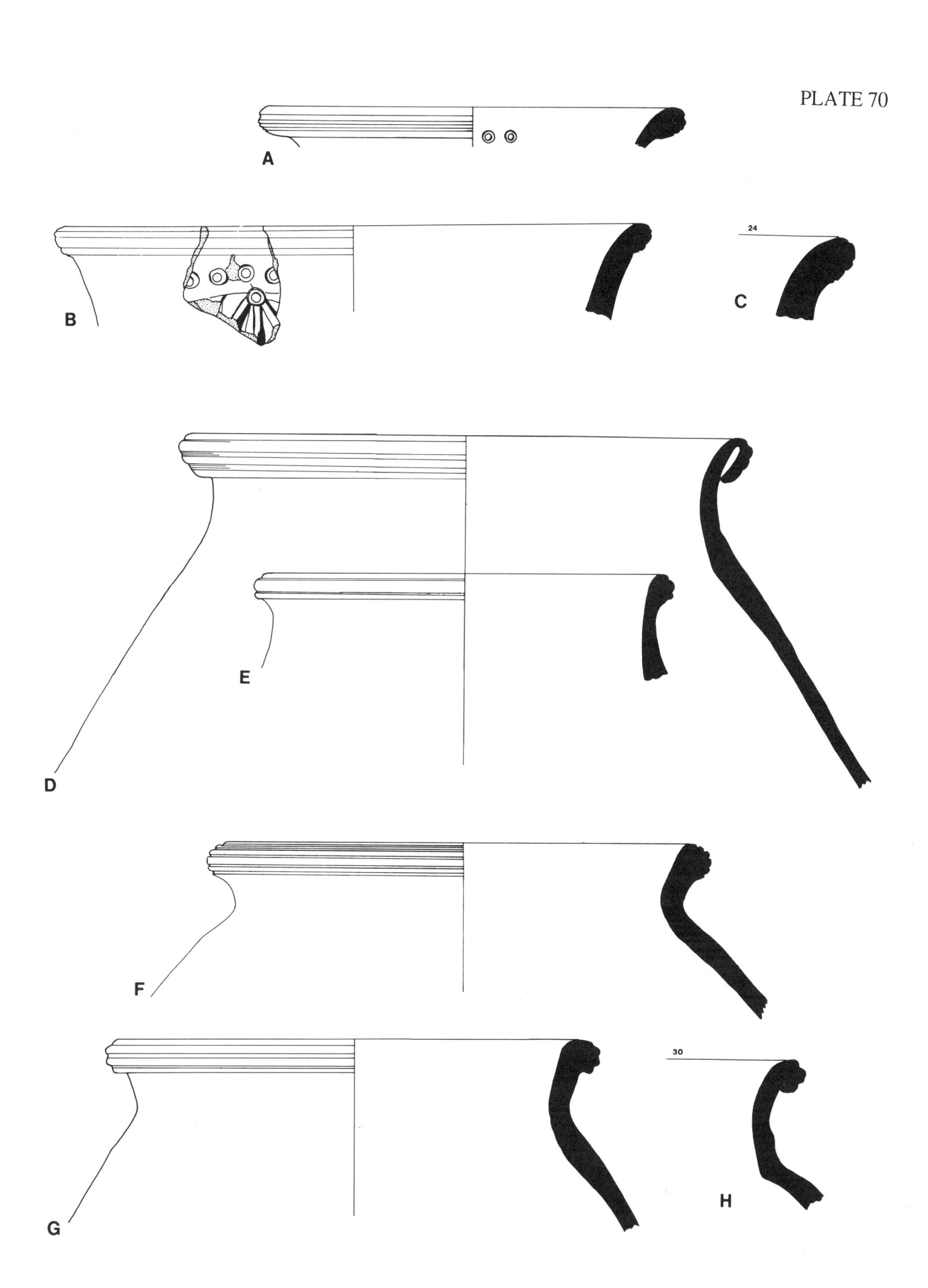

G  H 30

Period IV Pottery From Areas A, B, C, and F: Ware Group I Grooved Rim Jars (*cont.*). Scale 2:5.

Plate 71. Period IV Pottery From Areas A, B, and C: Ware Group I Jars (*cont.*). Scale 2:5.

|   | MRN | CONTEXT | FCN | WARE | FORM | TYPE | DECO. | WARE/REMARKS |
|---|---|---|---|---|---|---|---|---|
| A | 3694 | A07-0750-022 | 182 | 04 | 66 | Jar 18b | — | Light greenish-buff clay; small- and medium-sized white grits. |
| B | 4559 | A08-05-015 | 175 | 04 | 460 | Unass. Jar | Ring Bns. | Dense orange-buff clay; small-sized white grits; exterior burnished with horizontal strokes. |
| C | 5682 | A09-0470-010 | D145 | 04 | 942 | Jar 19 | — | Brownish-buff clay; small-sized white grits. |
| D | 3388 | C56-1095-017 | D157 | 04 | 66 | Jar 18b | — | Buff clay; small- and medium-sized grits. |
| E | 6808 | C56-04-025 | D437 | 04 | 66 | Jar 18b | — | Buff clay; small- and medium-sized grits. |
| F | 1723 | A06-06-013 | 045 | 04 | 374 | Jar 19 | Bns. | Fairly dense orange-buff clay; small-sized white grits; exterior lightly burnished. |
| G | 7899 | A07-15-065 | 456 | 04 | 1295 | Jar 20 | — | Buff clay; small-sized black grits. |
| H | 19287 | B72-0142-006 | 050 | 04 | 1640 | Jar 20 | — | Dense reddish clay; medium-sized white grits; buff slip on exterior. |
| I | 5263 | C56-08-030 | 319 | 04 | 1315 | Unass. Jar | — | Dense grayish-buff clay; small-sized grits. |
| J | 943 | C45-03-001 | 058 | 04 | 323 | Unass. Jar | — | Greenish-buff clay; small-sized white grits. |

PLATE 71

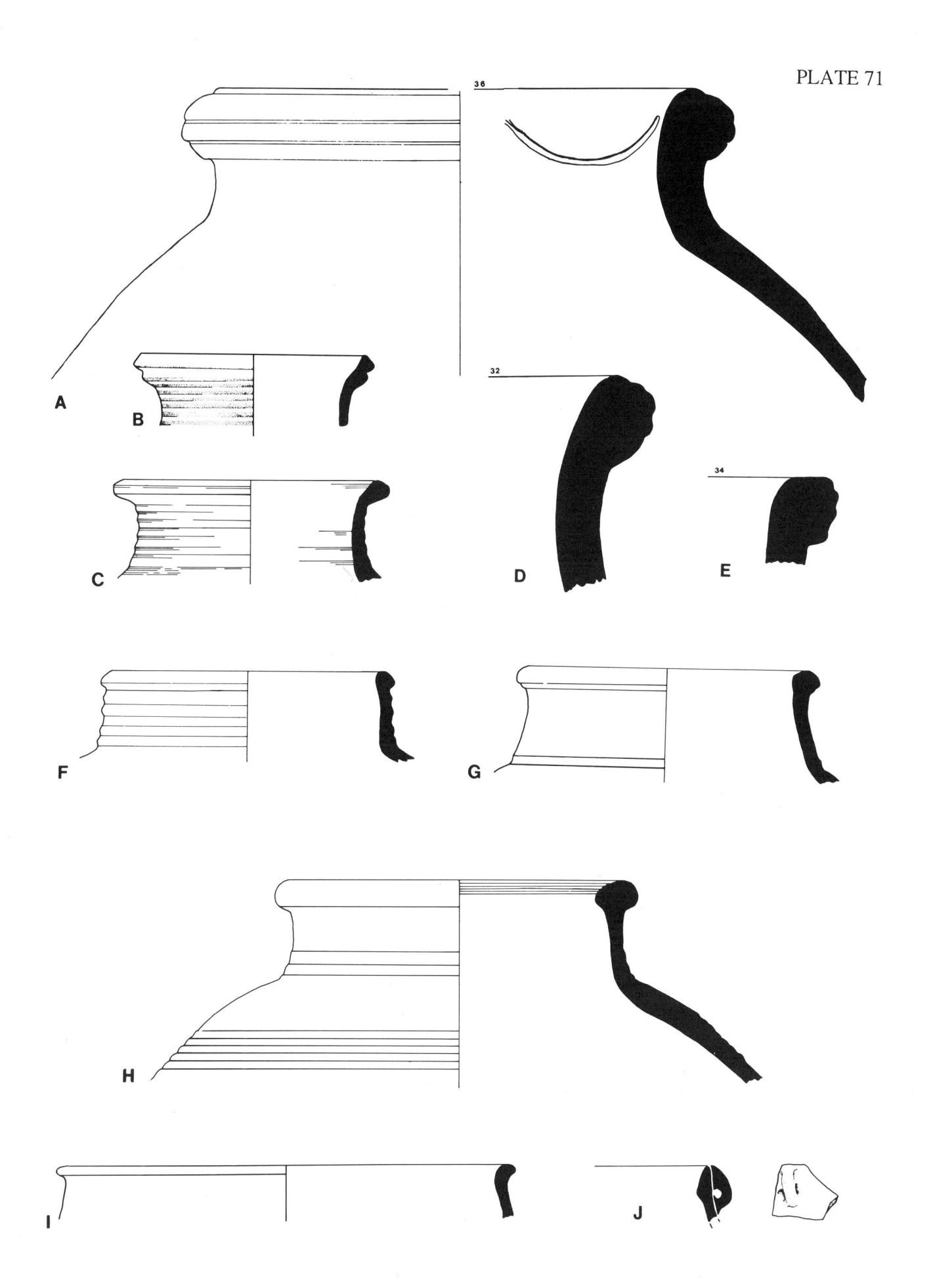

Period IV Pottery From Areas A, B, and C: Ware Group I Jars (*cont.*). Scale 2:5.

Plate 72. Period IV Pottery From Areas A, B, and C: Ware Group I Accessories and Stands. Scale 2:5.

|   | MRN | CONTEXT | FCN | WARE | FORM | TYPE | DECO. | WARE/REMARKS |
|---|---|---|---|---|---|---|---|---|
| A | 1807 | C55-0449-003 | 045 | 04 | — | — | 521 | Light brownish-buff clay; small-sized grits; light greenish-buff slip on surface. |
| B | 4529 | C55-04-012 | 285 | 04 | — | — | 525 | Buff clay; small-sized white grits. |
| C | 7563 | A07-11-038 | 315 | 04 | — | — | 023 | Dense orange-buff clay towards interior, buff towards exterior; small-sized white grits. |
| D | 3792 | C56-1076-020 | D212 | 04 | 816 | Unass. Lug | — | Buff clay; small-sized white grits. |
| E | 008 | B01-05-002 | 015 | 04 | 1616 | Unass. Spout | — | Fairly dense greenish-buff clay; small-sized grits. |
| F | 4377 | C55-0457-011 | 209 | 04 | 1262 | Unass. Spout | — | Fairly dense orange-buff clay; small-sized white grits. |
| G | 7617 | A07-10-049 | 360 | 04 | C-6 | Stand 1a | — | Buff clay; small-sized grits. |
| H | 7537 | A07-12-041 | 298 | 04 | 341 | Stand 1a | — | Fairly dense light greenish-buff clay; small-sized grits. |
| I | 3888 | A07-0750-023 | 206 | 04 | C-6 | Stand 1a | — | Fairly dense light greenish-buff clay; small-sized black grits. |
| J | 071 | B01-0210-012 | D064 | 04 | C-6 | Stand 1a | — | Dense buff clay, red oxidized core; no visible tempering; buff slip on exterior. |
| K | 12778 | A01-0540/42-026 | 159 | 04 | 1595 | Stand 1a | — | Dense brownish-buff clay; no visible tempering. |
| L | 371 | A06-03-003 | 008 | 04 | 205 | Stand 1b | — | Greenish clay, somewhat overfired; small-sized grits. |
| M | 861 | A06-02-008 | 026 | 04 | 976 | Stand 1b | — | Buff clay; small-sized white grits. |
| N | 2282 | A08-0201-006 | 083 | 04 | 1694 | Stand 2 | — | Light brownish-buff clay; small-sized grits; found as illustrated in situ on a floor (cf. fig. 18 "pot"); presumably a stand; secondarily cut across shoulder while still at the leather-hard stage; (= KH 1981/025). |
| O | 3888 | A07-0750-023 | 206 | 04 | 795 | Pedestal Base 1 | — | Brownish-buff clay; small-sized white grits; buff slip on exterior. |
| P | 3727 | C46-07-006 | 068 | 04 | 743 | Pedestal Base 1 | — | Dense reddish-buff clay grading to brownish towards surfaces; small-sized white grits. |
| Q | 095 | B01-04-002 | 075 | 04 | 94 | Pedestal Base 1 | — | Buff clay; small-sized grits. |

PLATE 72

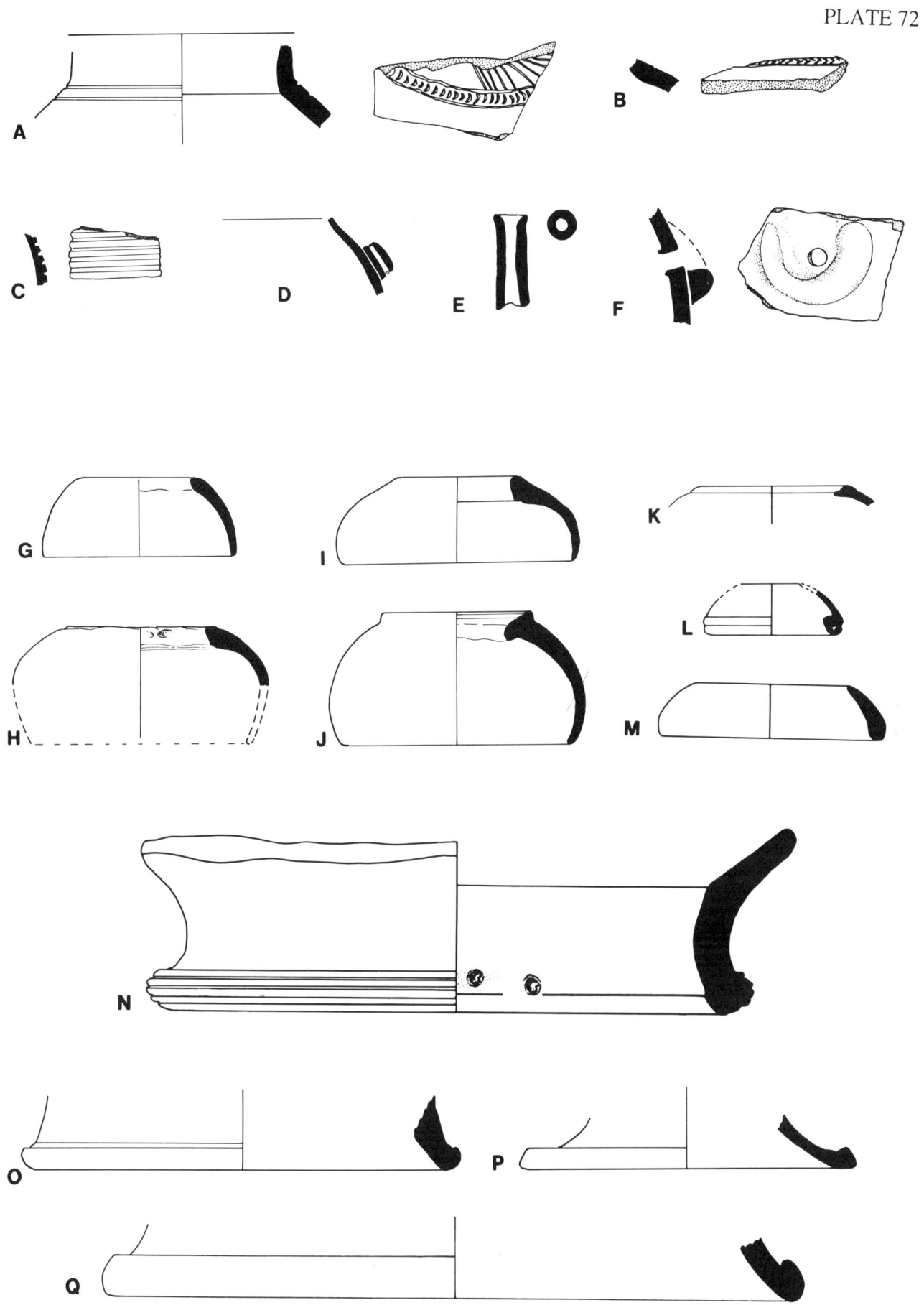

Period IV Pottery From Areas A, B, and C: Ware Group I Accessories and Stands. Scale 2:5.

Plate 73. Period IV Pottery From Areas A, B, C, C01, and D: Ware Group I Pedestal Bases and Feet. Scale 2:5.

|   | MRN | CONTEXT | FCN | WARE | FORM | TYPE | DECO. | WARE/REMARKS |
|---|-----|---------|-----|------|------|------|-------|--------------|
| A | 1235 | C45-03-012 | 145 | 04 | 350 | Pedestal Base 2 | — | Buff clay; small-sized grits. |
| B | 3069 | A07-0591-014 | 127 | 04 | 230 | Pedestal Base 2 | — | Dense reddish-buff clay; small-sized white grits. |
| C | 499 | B03-05-002 | 009 | 04 | 170 | Pedestal Base 2 | — | Reddish-buff clay; small-sized white grits; light brownish-buff slip on exterior. |
| D | 493 | C01-03-002 | 084 | 04 | 171 | Pedestal Base 2 | — | Fairly dense reddish-buff clay; small-sized grits. |
| E | 497 | C01-04-002 | 088 | 04 | 171 | Pedestal Base 2 | — | Buff clay; small-sized grits. |
| F | 2216 | C55-08-003 | 124 | 04 | 586 | Pedestal Base 1 | — | Buff clay; small-sized grits. |
| G | 3387 | C56-10-007 | 151 | 04 | 850 | Pedestal Base 1 | — | Brownish-buff clay, gray core; small-sized white and gray grits. |
| H | 4378 | C55-0458-011 | 214 | 04 | 853 | Pedestal Base 1 | — | Orange/brownish-buff clay; small-sized white grits. |
| I | 268 | C01-01-005 | 041 | 04 | 27 | Foot 1 | — | Brownish-buff clay; small-sized white grits. |
| J | 7513 | A07-05-035 | 246 | 04 | 1204 | Foot 1 | — | Reddish-buff clay; small-sized white grits; light cream slip on exterior. |
| K | 676 | B03-06-009 | 032 | 04 | 194 | Foot 1 | — | Buff clay; small-sized grits; wheel corrugations visible on exterior. |
| L | 3165 | C56-10-001 | 136 | 04 | 713 | Stand 3 | — | Reddish-buff clay; small-sized white grits. |
| M | 1688 | C55-04-003 | 036 | 04 | 487 | Foot 1 | — | Fairly dense orange-buff clay; small-sized white grits. |
| N | 3927 | A07-0750-023 | 217 | 04 | 309 | Foot 2 | — | Dense reddish-buff clay; small-sized white grits. |
| O | 369 | C01-03-002 | 073 | 04 | 174 | Foot 2 | — | Fairly dense reddish-buff clay; small-sized grits; buff slip on surface. |
| P | 7821 | D75-02-005 | 093 | 04 | 174a | Foot 2 | — | Fairly dense orange-buff clay; small-sized grits, some are white; exterior covered with greenish-buff slip; out of context in Period III deposit. |
| Q | 232 | A06-01-001 | 001 | 04 | 175 | Foot 2 | — | Grayish-buff clay grading to reddish on surface; small-sized white grits; out of context in slope wash. |
| R | 1780 | A05-04-019 | 057 | 04 | 217 | Foot 2 | — | Brownish-buff clay grading to orange-buff on surface; small-sized white grits. |

PLATE 73

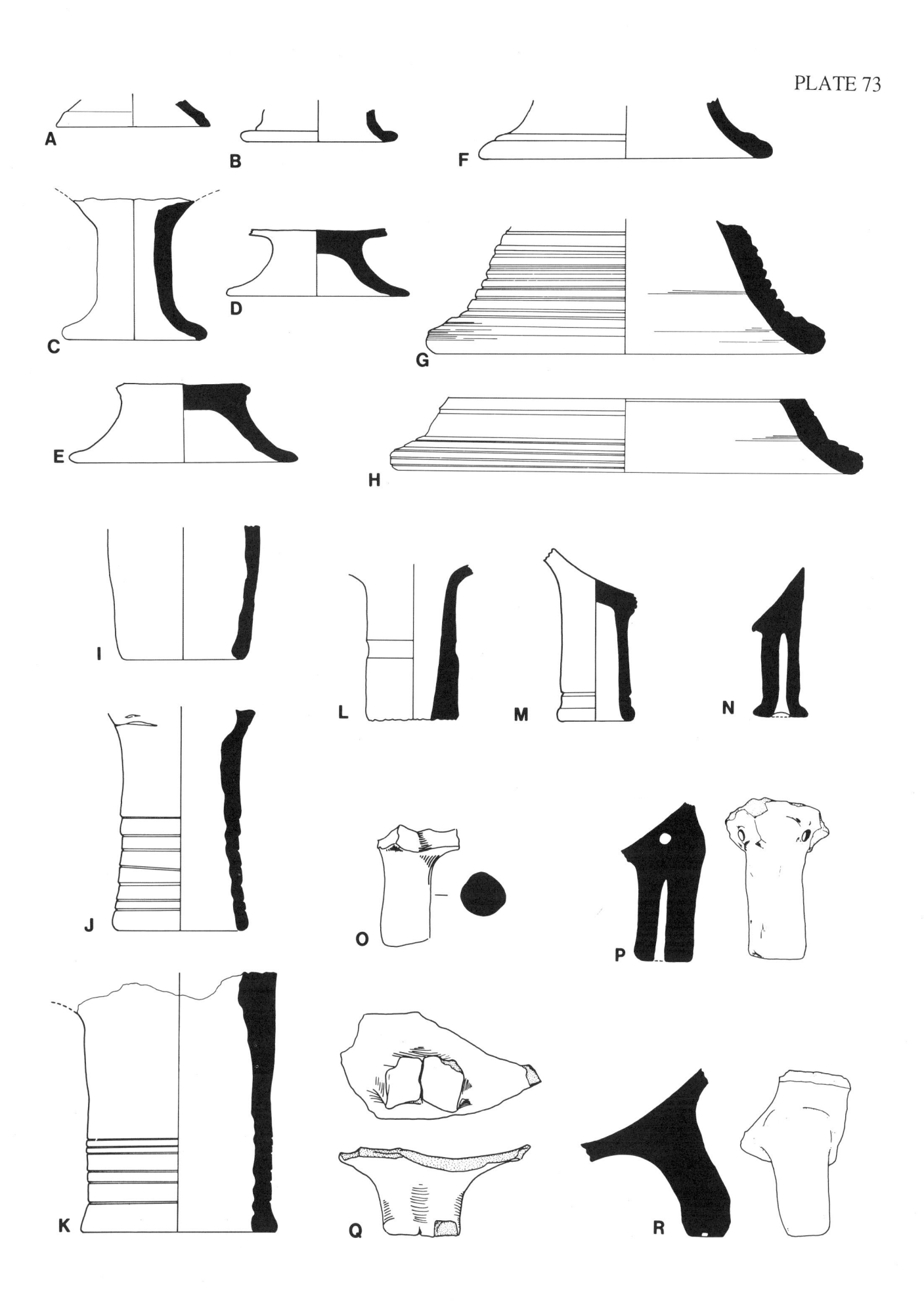

Period IV Pottery From Areas A, B, C, C01, and D: Ware Group I Pedestal Bases and Feet. Scale 2:5.

Plate 74. Period IV Pottery From Areas A, C, and F: Ware Group I Stands. Scale 2:5.

|   | *MRN* | *Context* | *FCN* | *Ware* | *Form* | *Type* | *Deco.* | *Ware/Remarks* |
|---|---|---|---|---|---|---|---|---|
| A | 3405 | C35-05-003 | 065 | 04 | 988 | Stand 4 | — | Buff clay; small-sized grits; (= KH 1981/72). |
| B | 2557 | C35-01-001 | 001 | 04 | 643 | Stand 4 | — | Greenish-buff clay; small-sized grits. |
| C | 12003 | F01-05-031 | 143 | 04 | 1697 | Stand 4 | — | Greenish-buff clay; small-sized grits; (= KH 1983/135). |
| D | 1430 | A08-01-002 | D018 | 04 | 435 | Stand 4 | — | Orange-buff clay; small-sized white grits; lighter orange-buff slip on exterior; traces of fenestration; out of context in slope wash. |
| E | 1994 | C55-07-003 | 088 | 04 | 535 | Stand 4 | — | Buff clay; small-sized grits. |
| F | 2207 | A09-01-002 | 005 | 04 | 595 | Stand 4 | — | Fairly dense grayish-buff clay grading to orange on surfaces; small-sized white grits; out of context in slope wash. |

PLATE 74

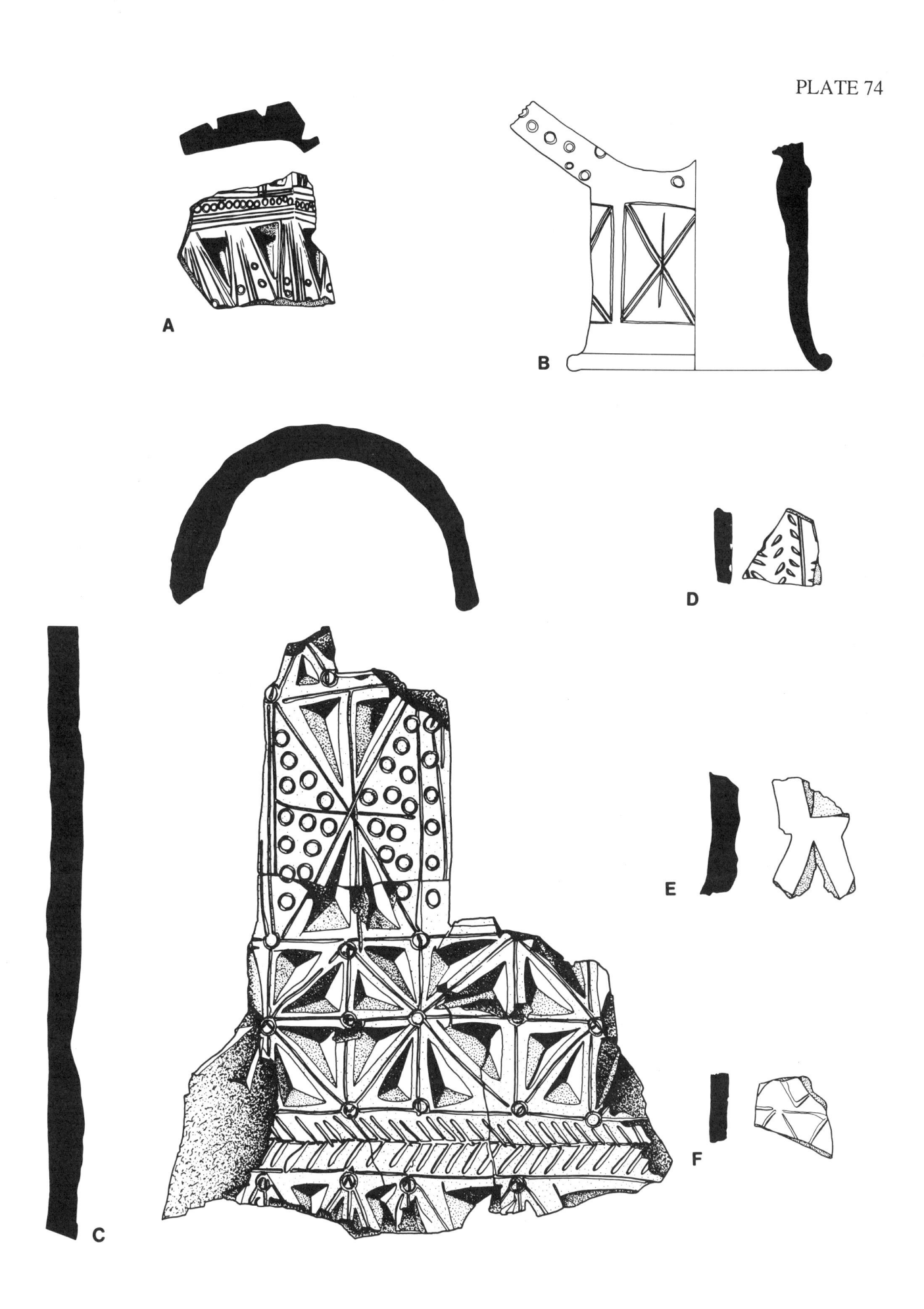

Period IV Pottery From Areas A, C, and F: Ware Group I Stands. Scale 2:5.

Plate 75. Period IV Pottery From Areas A, B, C, and F: Miscellaneous Ware Group I
Bases and Reserved Slip Ware Types. Scale 2:5.

|   | MRN | CONTEXT | FCN | WARE | FORM | TYPE | DECO. | WARE/REMARKS |
|---|---|---|---|---|---|---|---|---|
| A | 111 | B02-03-004 | 083 | 04 | 186 | Unass. Ring Base | — | Reddish-buff clay; small-sized white grits. |
| B | 532 | B02-03-015 | 181 | 04 | 186 | Unass. Ring Base | — | Buff clay; small-sized grits. |
| C | 1092 | A07-04-005 | 032 | 04 | 1121 | Unass. Base | — | Grayish-buff clay grading to orange-buff towards exterior; small-sized white grits. |
| D | 929 | A07-04-005 | 019 | 04 | 325 | Unass. Base | — | Dense reddish-buff clay; small-sized white grits. |
| E | 2567 | C56-03-007 | 073 | 04 | 615 | Unass. Base | — | Grayish-buff clay grading to orange on surfaces; small-sized grits. |
| F | 16107 | A01-0600/01-036 | 231 | 05 | 291 | Bowl 8a | 402 | Reddish-buff clay; small-sized white grits; exterior covered with greenish-buff slip, horizontally reserved. |
| G | 224 | F01-02-007 | 016 | 05 | 102 | Jar 8a | 402 | Buff clay; small-sized grits. |
| H | 475 | B01-02-012 | 135 | 05 | 72 | Jar 16c | 402 | Reddish-buff clay; small- and medium-sized grits; greenish-buff slip horizontally reserved on exterior. |
| I | 656 | B01-03-015 | 187 | 05 | 69 | Jar 16b | 402 | Buff clay; small- and medium-sized grits; greenish-buff slip, horizontally reserved on exterior. |
| J | 3356 | A07-05/0650-019 | 153 | 05 | 72 | Jar 16c | 402 | Brownish-buff clay, reddish core; small-sized white grits; buff slip, horizontally reserved on exterior. |
| K | 12863 | A01-05-032 | 052 | 05 | — | — | 401 | Buff clay; small-sized grits; greenish-buff slip on exterior, horizontally reserved; out of context in Period III pit. |
| L | 3854 | A06-07-020 | 077 | 05 | — | — | 404 | Fairly dense reddish-buff clay; small-sized white grits; greenish-buff slip on exterior, horizontally reserved. |
| M | 936 | A07-04-005 | 018 | 05 | — | — | 404 | Brownish-buff clay; small-sized white grits; buff slip on exterior horizontally reserved. |
| N | 658 | B02-03-015 | 185 | 05 | — | — | 403 | Buff clay; small-sized grits; greenish-buff on exterior. |

PLATE 75

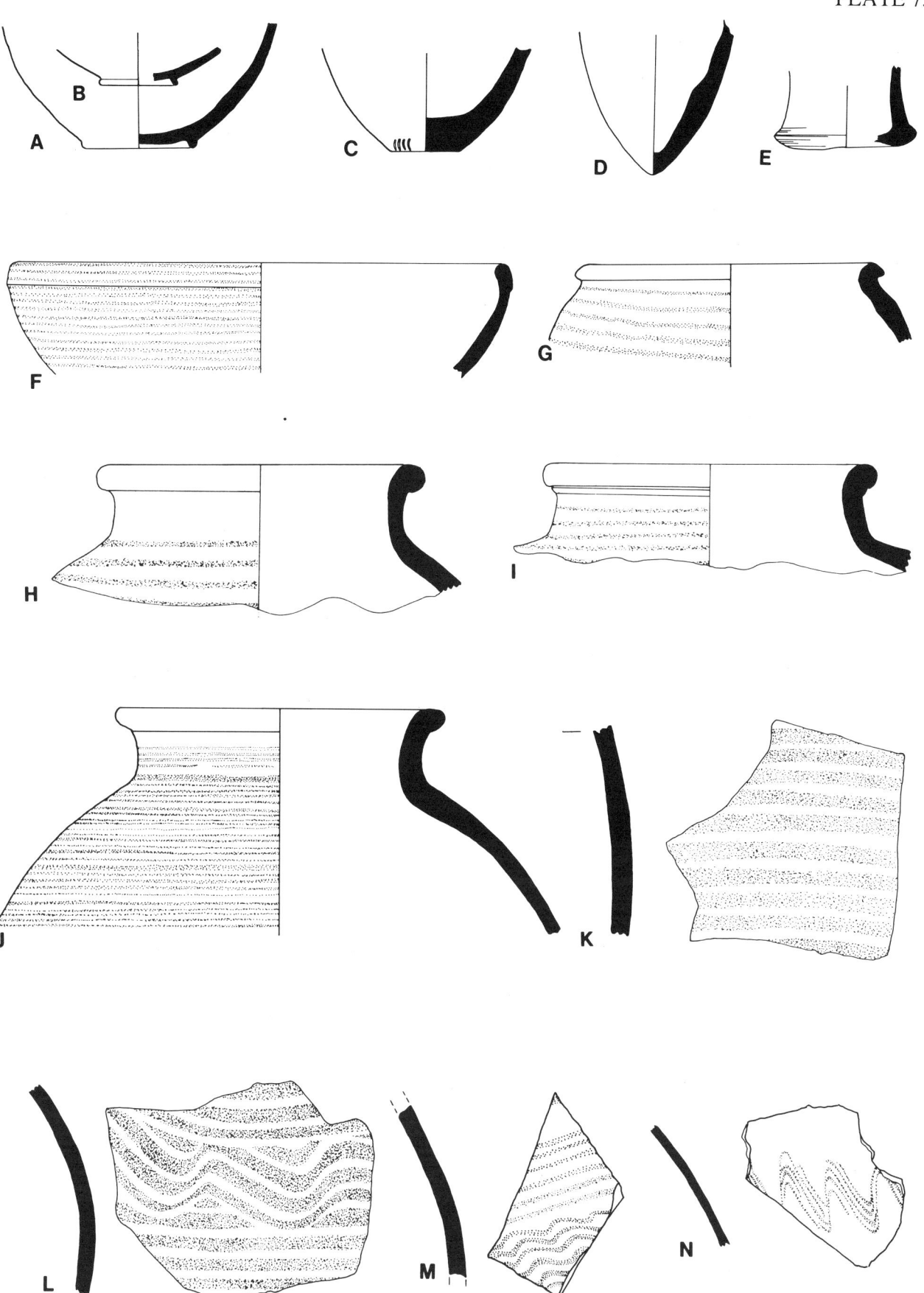

Period IV Pottery From Areas A, B, C, and F: Miscellaneous Ware Group I Bases and Reserved Slip Ware Types. Scale 2:5.

Plate 76. Period IV Pottery From Area C: Reserve Slip Ware Jars. Scale 2:5.

|   | *MRN* | *Context* | *FCN* | *Ware* | *Form* | *Type* | *Deco.* | *Ware/Remarks* |
|---|---|---|---|---|---|---|---|---|
| A | 7129 | C55-09-023 | 602 | 05 | 065 | Jar 18b | 402 | Buff clay; small-sized grits; buff slip on exterior, horizontally reserved. |
| B | 4750 | C35-02-014 | 182 | 05 | C-87 | Jar 16b | 402 | Buff clay; small-sized grits; greenish-buff slip on exterior, horizontally reserved. |

PLATE 76

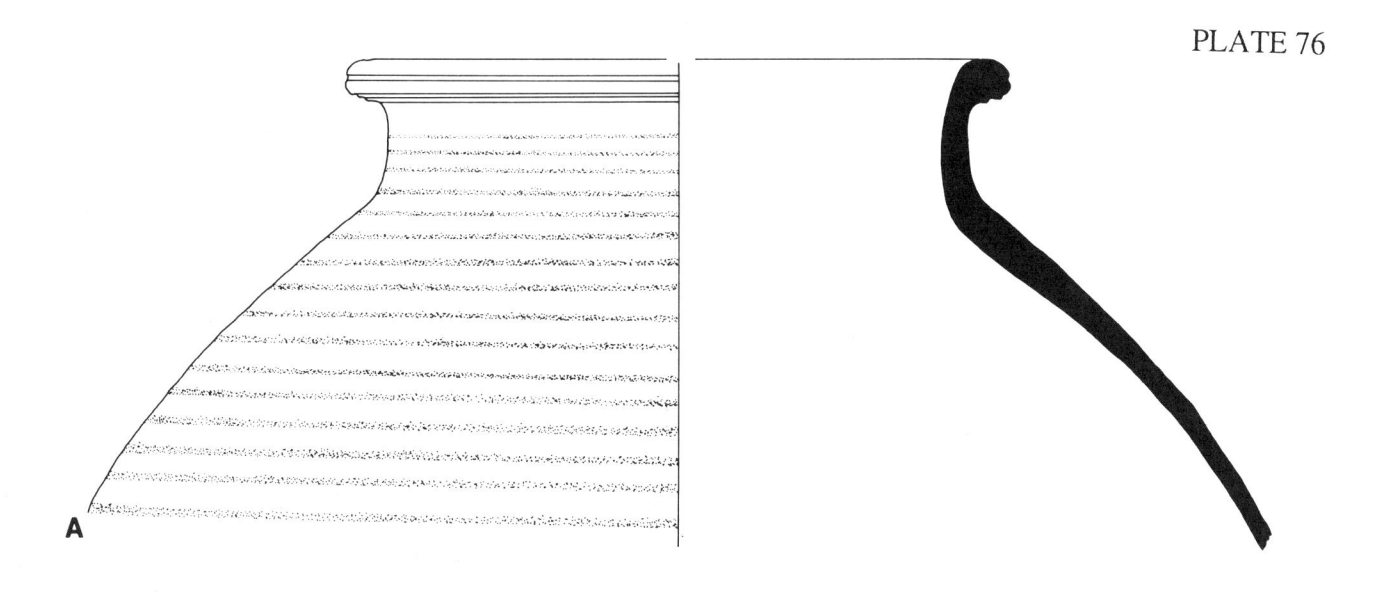

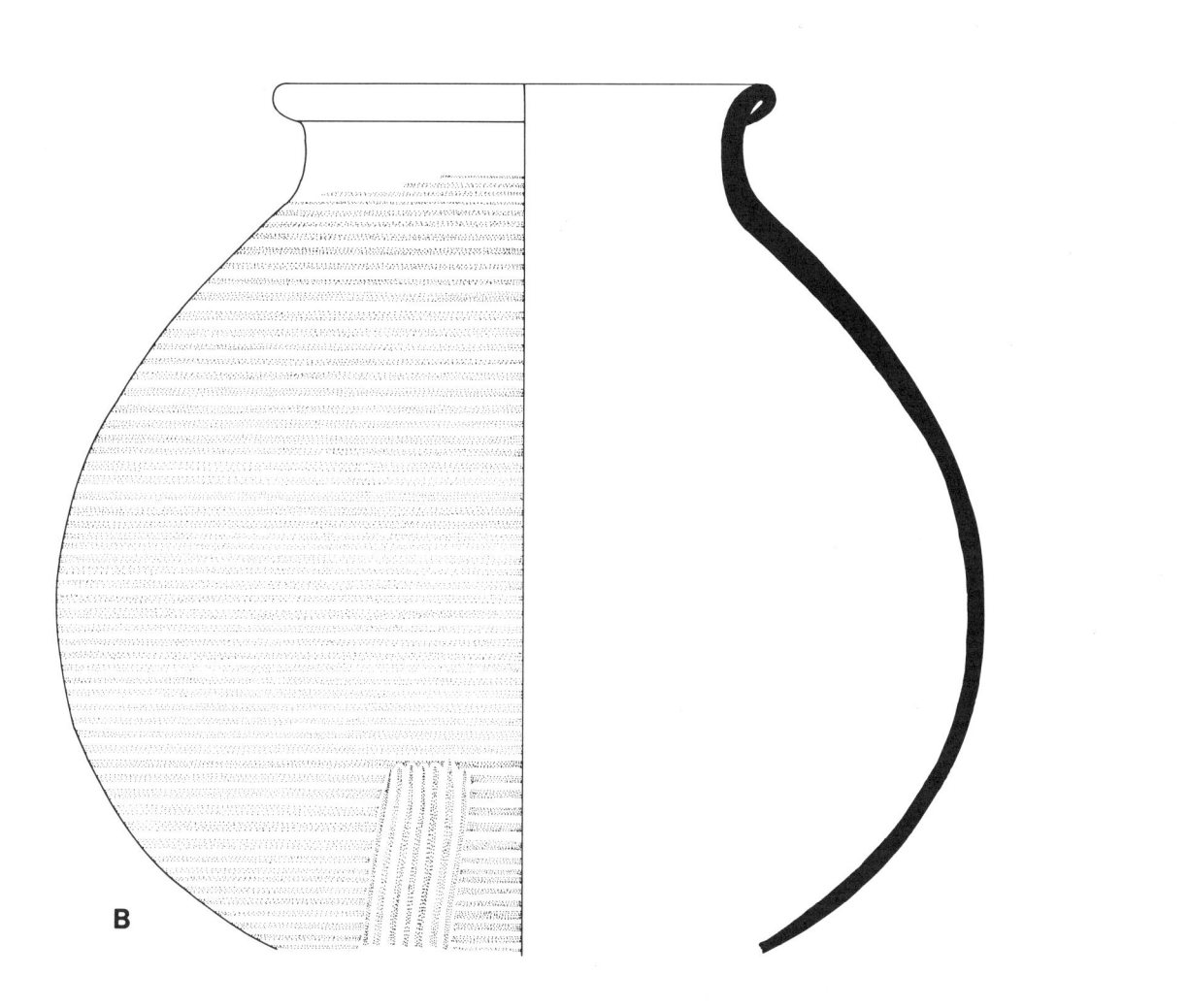

Period IV Pottery From Area C: Reserved Slip Ware Jars. Scale 2:5.

Plate 77. Period IV Pottery From Areas A, B, C, C01, and F: Metallic Ware Cups and Bowls. Scale 2:5.

|   | MRN | Context | FCN | Ware | Form | Type | Deco. | Ware/Remarks |
|---|---|---|---|---|---|---|---|---|
| A | 337 | B02-04-012 | 006 | 02 | C-3 | Bowl 1e | — | Dense reddish-buff clay; no visible tempering; buff slip on exterior near rim. |
| B | 4754 | C35-02-014 | 184 | 02 | C-8 | Bowl 1c | 023 | Dense light brownish-buff clay, gray core; a few scattered small-sized white grits visible. |
| C | 691 | C01-08-011 | 131 | 02 | 02 | Bowl 1e | — | Dense black clay, reddish core; no visible tempering other than a few scattered small-sized grits. |
| D | 7275 | A07-04-005 | 553 | 02 | C-5 | Bowl 1e | — | Red clay; no visible tempering; exterior is gray-black close to rim, reddish below; (= KH 1982/119); cf. also plate 147:C. |
| E | 2204 | A08-0220-009 | 074 | 02 | 1090 | Base 2 | 023 | Red clay; no visible tempering; exterior is brownish. |
| F | 6542 | A08-06-024 | 208 | 02 | 1047 | Base 1 | — | Dense gray clay; small-sized white grits; "clinky." |
| G | 7738 | A07-14-058 | 422 | 02 | 02 | Bowl 1e | — | Dense orange clay; no visible tempering. |
| H | 500 | B03-05-002 | 007 | 02 | 03 | Bowl 1e | 023 | Dense greenish-buff clay; occasional scattered small-sized grits. |
| I | 3517 | C56-10-017 | 168 | 02 | 761 | Bowl 1d | 023 | Dense brownish-buff clay, gray core; occasional scattered white grits; exterior reddish. |
| J | 111 | B02-03-004 | 083 | 02 | 03 | Bowl 1e | 023 | Dense reddish clay; occasional scattered small-sized grits; on exterior: top is blackish, bottom is reddish. |
| K | 1222 | A07-05-006 | 041 | 02 | 372 | Unass. Bowl | 023 | Dense grayish clay; occasional scattered white grits. |
| L | 476 | B02-04-010 | 012 | 02 | 014 | Bowl 4a | — | Dense orange clay; no visible tempering other than occasional minute white grits; exterior: red near rim, lower part is orange. |
| M | 2495 | A07-05-009 | 083 | 02 | 211 | Base 1 | — | Dense grayish clay; occasional small-sized white grits. |
| N | 2157 | C55-09-003 | 113 | 02 | 591 | Base 2 | — | Dense gray clay; no visible tempering; "clinky." |
| O | 4932 | C01-1009-073 | 1432 | 02 | 887 | Unass. Ring Base | — | Brownish-orange clay; occasional white and gray grits; wheel striations visible on bottom of base. |
| P | 111 | B02-03-004 | 083 | 02 | 183 | Base 2 | — | Reddish clay; small-sized white grits; exterior is black. |
| Q | 818 | A02-0390-024 | 074 | 02 | C-33 | Bowl 7a | — | Dense brownish-buff clay; no visible tempering; buff slip on surface. |
| R | 7599 | A07-13-044 | 338 | 02 | C-33 | Bowl 7a | — | Purplish clay; occasional scattered minute white grits. |
| S | 862 | A06-04-010 | 035 | 02 | C-1 | Bowl 6 | Ring Bns. | Dense gray ware; no visible tempering except occasional minute white grits; ring burnished on both surfaces. |
| T | 648 | F01-04-009 | 031 | 02 | 291 | Bowl 8a | — | Dense reddish clay. |
| U | 2436 | A05-04-020 | 064 | 02 | 661 | Bowl 15 | Bns. | Dense brownish clay; occasional scattered small-sized white grits; exterior lightly burnished. |
| V | 11917 | F01-05-017 | 057 | 02 | 1612 | Bowl 6 | Ring Bns. | Dense grayish clay; irregular traces of ring burnish on exterior. |
| W | 4530 | C56-08-023 | 248 | 02 | 049 | Bowl 6 | — | Fairly dense brownish clay grading to gray on exterior; occasional scattered white grits. |
| X | 488 | A07-03-002 | 006 | 02 | 229 | Unass. Bowl | Bns. | Very dense clay, orange towards exterior and grayish towards interior; no visible tempering other than occasional white grits; burnished; out of context in slope wash. |

PLATE 77

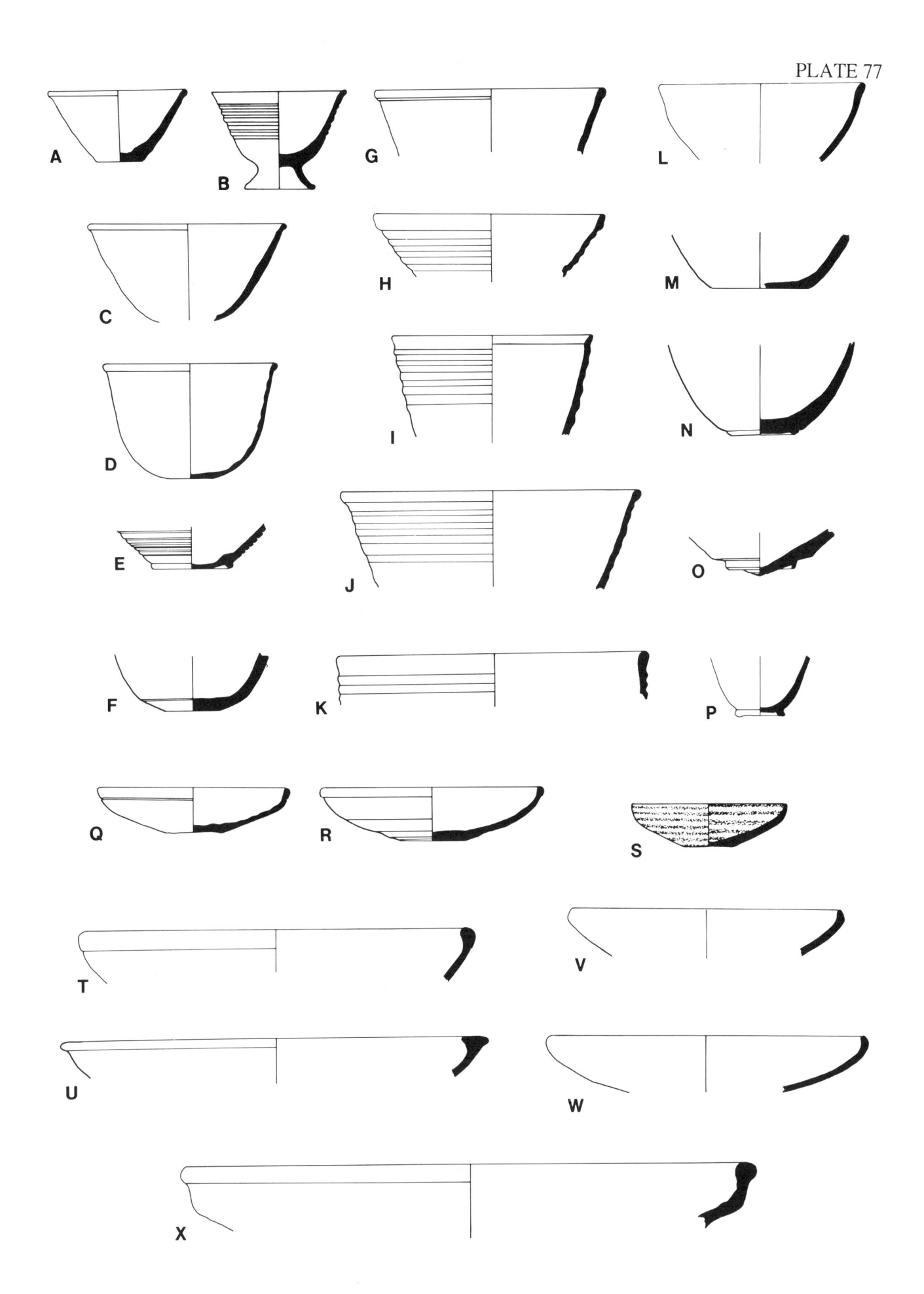

Period IV Pottery From Areas A, B, C, C01, and F: Metallic Ware Cups and Bowls. Scale 2:5.

Plate 78. Period IV Pottery From Areas A, B, C, and F: Metallic Ware Jars. Scale 2:5.

|   | MRN | CONTEXT | FCN | WARE | FORM | TYPE | DECO. | WARE/REMARKS |
|---|---|---|---|---|---|---|---|---|
| A | 4760 | C55-05-014 | 310 | 02 | 902 | Jar 21 | — | Dense brownish-grayish clay; no visible tempering; gray exterior. |
| B | 4524 | C55-08-009 | 269 | 02 | 873 | Jar 21 | — | Dense red clay; occasional small-sized white grits. |
| C | 17916 | A04-1032/42-102 | 601 | 02 | 195 | Jar 22 | Ring Bns. | Dense gray clay; no visible tempering; traces of burnish on exterior. |
| D | 656 | B02-03-015 | 187 | 02 | 105 | Unass. Jar | Ring Bns. | Dense dark brown clay; no visible tempering; ring burnish on exterior. |
| E | 252 | F01-02-006 | 014 | 02 | — | — | 023 | Dense reddish clay; no visible tempering other than occasional scattered small-sized white grits. |
| F | 532 | B02-03-015 | 181 | 02 | 1364 | Jar 2 | 023 | Dense reddish clay; exterior is burnished. |
| G | 4748 | C55-05-014 | D312 | 02 | 1364 | Jar 2 | 023 | Dense reddish clay; occasional small-sized white grits. |
| H | 494 | B01-05-14 | 166 | 02 | 126 | Jar 3b | — | Dense clay, grayish towards interior, and reddish towards exterior; no visible tempering. |
| I | 860 | A07-03-004 | 011 | 02 | 126 | Jar 3b | — | Dense brownish clay grading to grayish on interior; no visible tempering. |
| J | 535 | B03-04-002 | 013 | 02 | 126 | Jar 3b | 023 | Dense clay gray on exterior, orange-reddish on interior; no visible tempering other than scattered minute white grits. |
| K | 530 | A02-02-004 | 058 | 02 | 123 | Jar 3c | — | Dense clay, orange towards exterior and grayish towards interior; no visible tempering. |
| L | 039 | B02-01-002 | 039 | 02 | 78 | Unass. Jar | Ring Bns. | Brownish clay; no visible tempering other than minute white grits; traces of ring burnish on exterior. |
| M | 1024 | A05-04-013 | 036 | 02 | 287 | Unass. Jar | — | Reddish clay; no visible tempering other than minute white grits; reddish towards exterior and black towards interior. |
| N | 2739 | A07-0592-014 | 106 | 02 | C-4 | Jar 23 | — | Brownish-orange clay; occasional white grits; exterior badly abraded; (= KH 1981/68). |
| O | 7506 | A07-05-035 | 243 | 02 | 695 | Jar 23 | Ring Bns. | Dense gray clay; no visible tempering other than occasional white grits; ring burnish on exterior. |
| P | 3066 + 2739 + 2758 | A07-0590-014 + A07-0592-014 + A07-0591-014 | 126 + 106 + 116 | 02 | 695 | Jar 23 | Bns. | Dense orange clay grading to gray on interior, reddish on exterior; neck and rim are gray; lightly burnished with horizontal strokes. |
| Q | 488 | A07-03-002 | 006 | 02 | 85 | Jar 23 | — | Dense reddish clay; no visible tempering other than occasional scattered white grits. |
| R | 3517 | C56-10-017 | 168 | 02 | 737 | Jar 14b | — | Dense gray clay; scattered small-sized white grits; wheel striations visible on interior near rim. |

PLATE 78

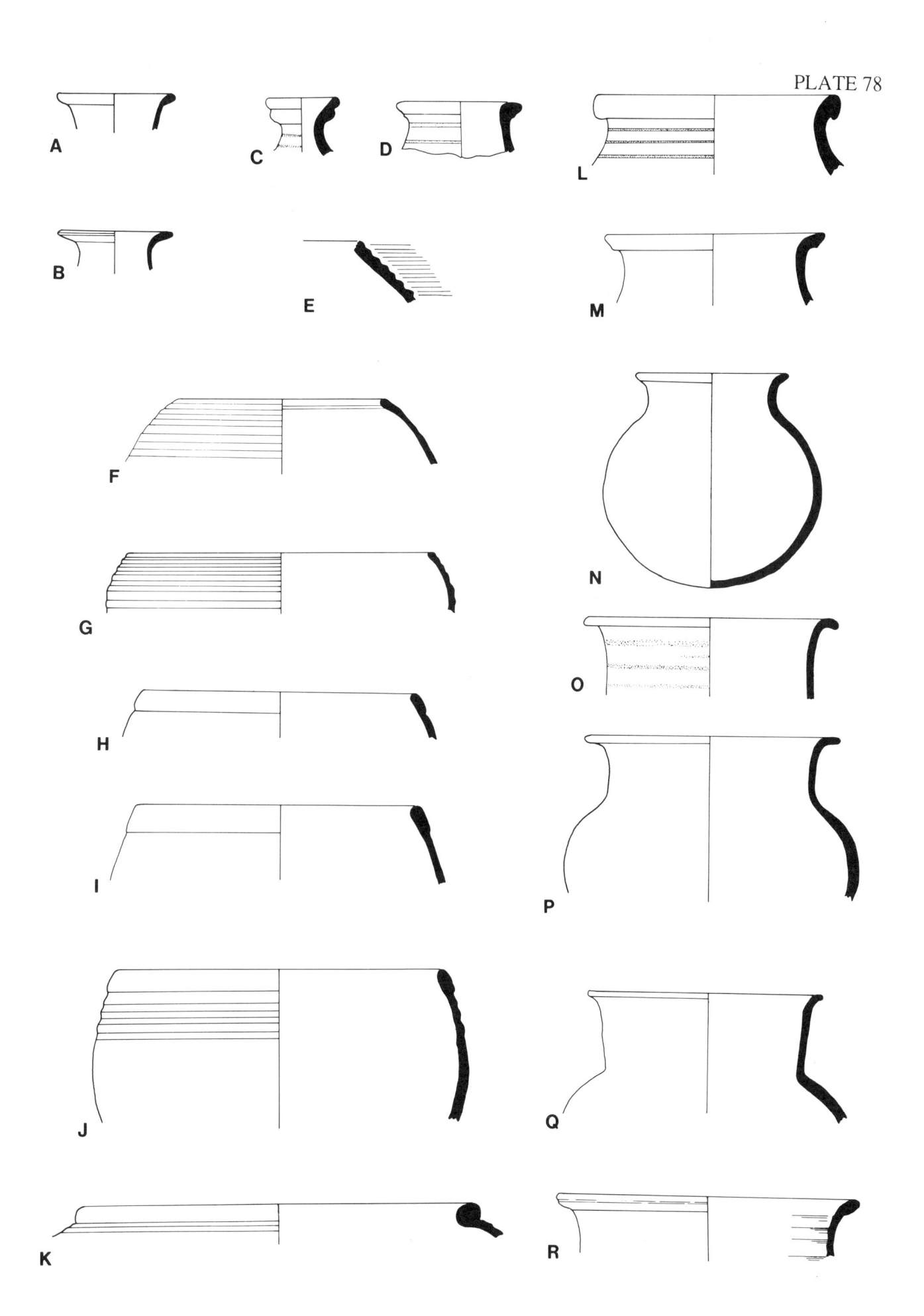

Period IV Pottery From Areas A, B, C, and F: Metallic Ware Jars. Scale 2:5.

Plate 79. Period IV Pottery From Areas A, B, C, and C01: Metallic Ware Pedestal Bases and Stands, and Combed Wash Ware and Band Painted Ware Cups. Scale 2:5.

|   | MRN | CONTEXT | FCN | WARE | FORM | TYPE | DECO. | WARE/REMARKS |
|---|---|---|---|---|---|---|---|---|
| A | 3517 | C56-10-017 | 168 | 02 | 763 | Pedestal Base 2 | Bns. | Dense red clay; small-sized white grits; very light horizontal burnishing strokes on exterior. |
| B | 500 | B03-05-002 | 007 | 02 | 173 | Pedestal Base 2 | — | Dense gray clay; no visible tempering other than occasional white grits. |
| C | 6621 | C35-04-009 | 291 | 02 | 1288 | Pedestal Base 2 | — | Dense gray clay; no visible tempering other than occasional white grits. |
| D | 7619 | A07-1060-050 | 362 | 02 | 1250 | Stand 3 | — | Dense gray clay; no visible tempering; on exterior, orange wash left horizontally reserved in places. |
| E | 4959 | C55-0775-011 | 340 | 02 | 1250 | Stand 3 | — | Dense gray clay; no visible tempering; exterior is orange. |
| F | 813 | C01-02-007 | 173 | 02 | 230 | Pedestal Base 2 | — | Dense gray clay; no visible tempering. |
| G | 258 | B02-02-011 | 132 | 02 | 23 | Stand 1b | — | Dense reddish clay; no visible tempering other than minute white grits; surface is black-gray with red. |
| H | 532 | B02-03-015 | 181 | 07 | C-89 | Bowl 4b | 450 | Dense orange-reddish clay; very small-sized white grits; red paint. |
| I | 258 | B02-02-011 | 132 | 01 | 12 | Bowl 4b | 013 | Dense reddish clay; no visible tempering other than small-sized white grits; brown paint. |
| J | 374 | B02-04-004 | 009 | 07 | 12 | Bowl 4b | 450 | Dense brownish-buff clay; small-sized grits; brown paint. |
| K | 5040 | C56-08-029 | 314 | 07 | C-34 | Bowl 1e | 451 | Light greenish-buff clay; small-sized grits; brown paint. |
| L | 7207 | C55-05-035 | 681 | 07 | C-34 | Bowl 1e | 451 | Light greenish-buff clay; small-sized grits; on exterior, paint is reddish but brownish where thick; (= KH 1982/116). |
| M | 3888 | A07-0750-023 | 206 | 07 | C-5 | Bowl 1e | 450 | Buff clay; small-sized white grits; brownish-reddish paint; traces of bitumen stain on base of interior. |
| N | 6373 | C55-04-014 | 553 | 01 | C-34 | Bowl 1e | 013 | Light greenish-buff clay; small-sized grits; reddish paint. |
| O | 282 | B02-03-010 | 130 | 01 | 02 | Bowl 1e | 013 | Greenish-buff clay; small-sized grits; reddish-brownish paint. |
| P | 7130 | C55-0457-034 | 658 | 01 | 02 | Bowl 1e | 013 | Buff clay; small-sized grits; reddish paint. |
| Q | 788 | A06-03-010 | 029 | 07 | 02 | Bowl 1e | 450 | Dense brownish-buff clay; no visible tempering; brown paint. |
| R | 3871 | C56-1096-020 | D240 | 12 | 02 | Bowl 1e | 013 | Dense gray clay; no visible tempering other than minute white grits; exterior reddish, paint is black; slight corrugations on exterior. |
| S | 865 | A07-04-005 | 015 | 07 | 591 | Base 2 | 450 | Reddish clay; small-sized grits; brown paint. |
| T | 7537 | A07-12-041 | 298 | 07 | 591 | Base 2 | 451 | Dense buff clay; small-sized grits; paint is reddish towards bottom, blackish on top. |
| U | 6542 | A08-06-024 | 208 | 07 | 591 | Base 2 | 451 | Dense pinkish ware; small-sized white grits; reddish painted bands. |
| V | 211 | B01-04-013 | 114 | 07 | 178 | Base 1 | 450 | Dense clay; small-sized grits; brownish-buff ware. |
| W | 531 | A06-02-004 | 019 | 12 | 179 | Base 1 | 013 | Dense gray clay; no visible tempering; gray paint. |

PLATE 79

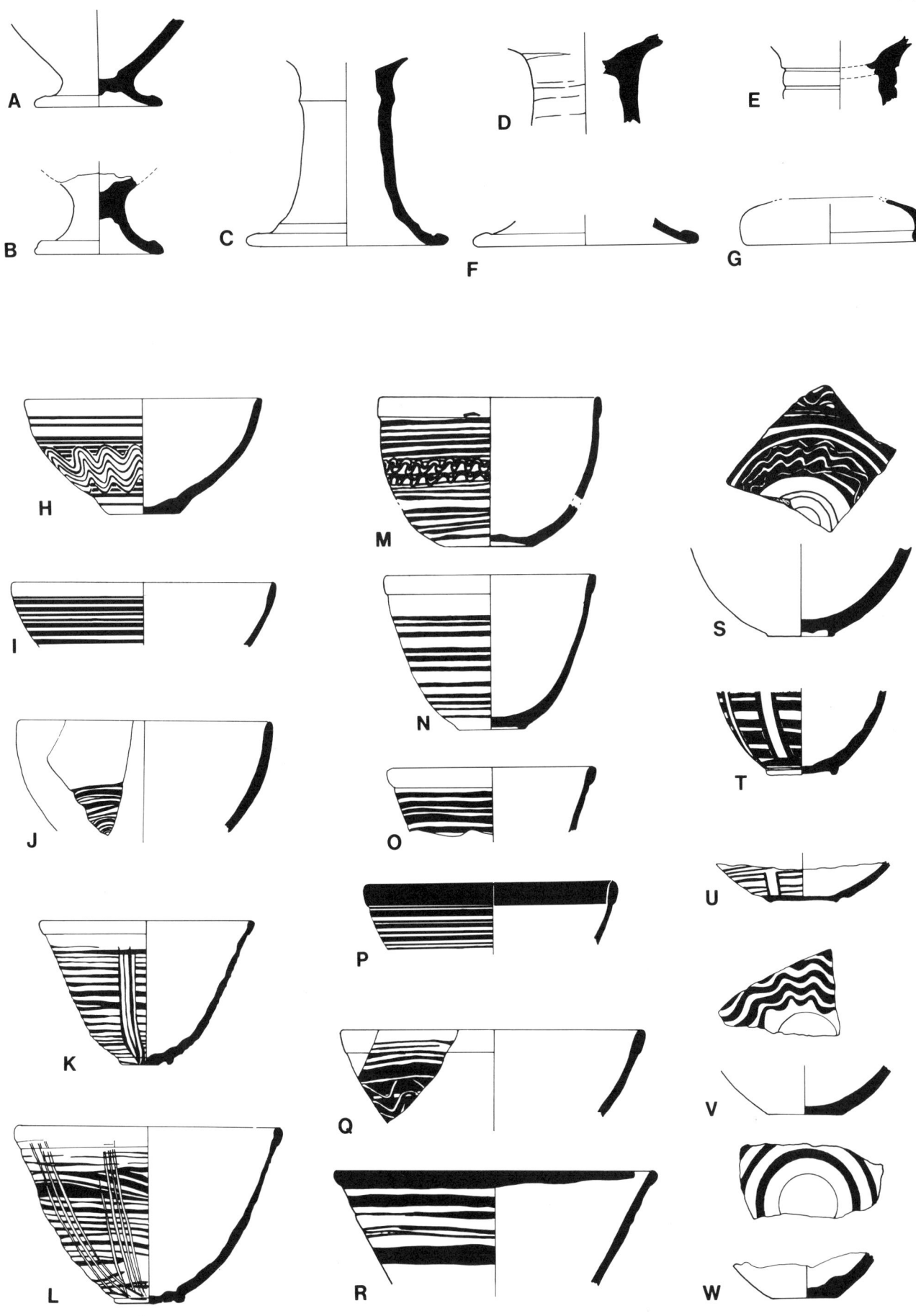

Period IV Pottery From Areas A, B, C, and C01: Metallic Ware Pedestal Bases and Stands, and Combed Wash Ware and Band Painted Ware Cups. Scale 2:5.

Plate 80. Period IV Pottery From Areas A, B, C, and C01: Combed Wash Ware and Band Painted Ware Bowls and Jars. Scale 2:5.

|   | MRN | CONTEXT | FCN | WARE | FORM | TYPE | DECO. | WARE/REMARKS |
|---|---|---|---|---|---|---|---|---|
| A | 282 | B02-03-010 | 130 | 01 | 43 | Bowl 8a | 013 | Greenish-buff clay; small-sized grits; black paint. |
| B | 813 | C01-02-007 | 173 | 01 | 291 | Bowl 8a | 013 | Brownish-buff clay, irregular reddish core; small-sized white grits; buff slip on exterior; black paint. |
| C | 696 | B01-0213-015 | 150 | 01 | 126 | Jar 3b | 013 | Greenish-buff clay; small-sized grits; brown paint. |
| D | 937 | A07-04-005 | 020 | 01 | 120 | Jar 3c | 013 | Reddish-buff clay; small-sized white grits; greenish-buff slip on exterior; plum colored paint. |
| E | 1093 | A07-04-005 | 033 | 01 | 335 | Jar 3d | 013 | Buff clay; small-sized white grits; brownish paint. |
| F | 1629 | C55-05-002 | 031 | 01 | 579 | Jar 16c | 013 | Greenish-buff clay; small-sized white grits; brown paint. |
| G | 531 | A06-02-004 | 019 | 01 | 1120 | Unass. Jar | 013 | Buff clay; small-sized grits; brown paint. |
| H | 2784 | C46-03-003 | 021 | 12 | 488 | Jar 6 | 013 | Dense gray clay; occasional scattered white grits; buff slip on exterior; "clinky." |
| I | 2221 | C45-0182-011 | 163 | 12 | 632 | Jar 24 | 013 | Dense orange clay; no visible tempering other than occasional scattered small-sized grits; pinkish-buff slip on exterior; brownish-purplish paint. |
| J | 7506 | A07-05-035 | 243 | 12 | 632 | Jar 24 | 013 | Dense brownish-buff clay; a few scattered white grits; light burnish on exterior; brown paint. |
| K | 3495 | A08-05-010 | 135 | 07 | 742 | Unass. Jar | 450 | Dense light brownish-buff clay; small-sized grits; dark brown paint. |
| L | 7130 | C55-0457-034 | 658 | 01 | 1312 | Jar 25 | 013 | Greenish-buff clay; small-sized white grits; olive green paint. |
| M | 532 + 656 | B02-03-015 + B02-03-015 | 181 + 187 | 07 | 1000 | Jar 25 | 450 | Dense greenish-buff clay; small-sized grits; olive-brown paint. |
| N | 008 | B01-05-002 | 015 | 01 | 1121 | Unass. Base | 013 | Fairly dense light greenish-buff clay; small-sized white grits; buff slip on interior and exterior; orange paint. |
| O | 3066 | A07-0590-014 | 126 | 07 | — | — | 450 | Dense reddish clay, brownish core; small-sized white grits; brownish-buff slip on surface. |

PLATE 80

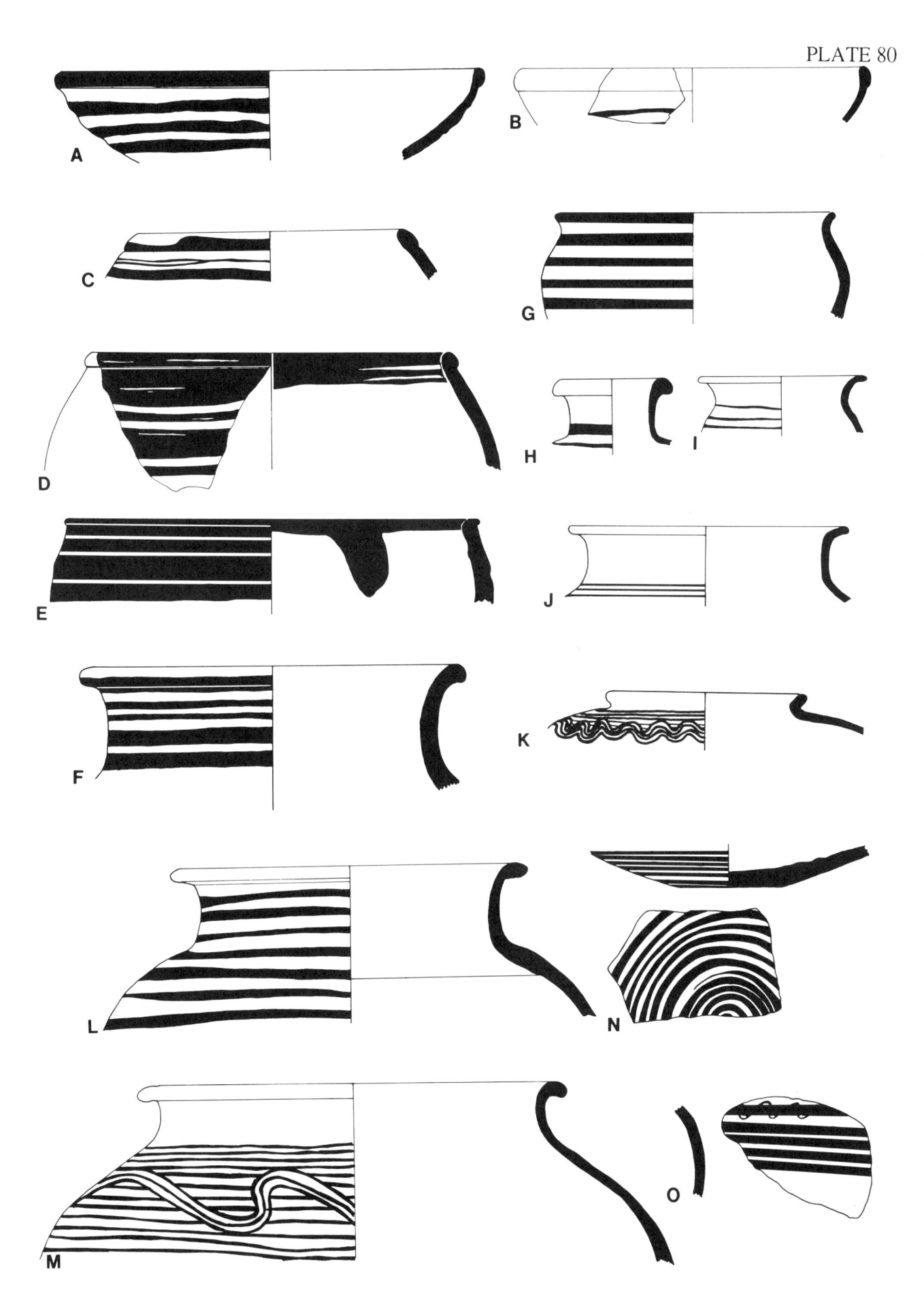

Period IV Pottery From Areas A, B, C, and C01: Combed Wash Ware and Band Painted Ware Bowls and Jars. Scale 2:5.

Plate 81. Period IV Pottery From Areas A, C, and C01: Karababa Painted Ware Bowls. Scale 2:5.

|   | MRN | CONTEXT | FCN | WARE | FORM | TYPE | DECO. | WARE/REMARKS |
|---|---|---|---|---|---|---|---|---|
| A | 1309 | A09-01-002 | 008 | 08 | 482 | Bowl 19 | 049 | Greenish-buff clay; small-sized grits; brown paint. |
| B | 11832 | A04-07-080 | 477 | 08 | 1603 | Bowl 19 | 049 | Rather soft and porous brownish-buff clay; gritty, white grits easily visible; brown paint. |
| C | 7788 | A07-14-058 | 422 | 08 | 1271 | Bowl 19 | 049 | Red clay; gritty with white grits prominent; brownish-buff slip on surface. |
| D | 6707 | C35-04-009 | 295 | 08 | 1286 | Bowl 20 | 049 | Buff clay; small-sized white and red grits; red paint. |
| E | 1722 | C01-0188-059 | 492 | 08 | 499 | Bowl 20 | 049 | Light brownish-buff clay; small-sized white grits; brown paint. |
| F | 4458 | C55-0578-011 | D256 | 08 | 861 | Unass. Bowl | — | Greenish-buff clay; small-sized gray grits; red paint. |
| G | 7738 | A07-14-058 | 422 | 08 | 712 | Bowl 8e | 049 | Dense reddish clay; small-sized white grits; plum colored paint. |
| H | 6574 | C35-0382-005 | 273 | 08 | 1283 | Bowl 18 | 024 | Dense buff clay; small-sized grits; scarlet red paint or wash. |
| I | 17911 | A04-1032/42-101 | 596 | 08 | 1670 | Bowl 21 | 049 | Dense reddish clay; small black grits; red paint. |
| J | 5267 | A06-05-029 | 140 | 08 | 1128 | Unass. Bowl | 024 | Dense buff clay; small-sized black grits; traces of red wash on interior and exterior, largely abraded. |

PLATE 81

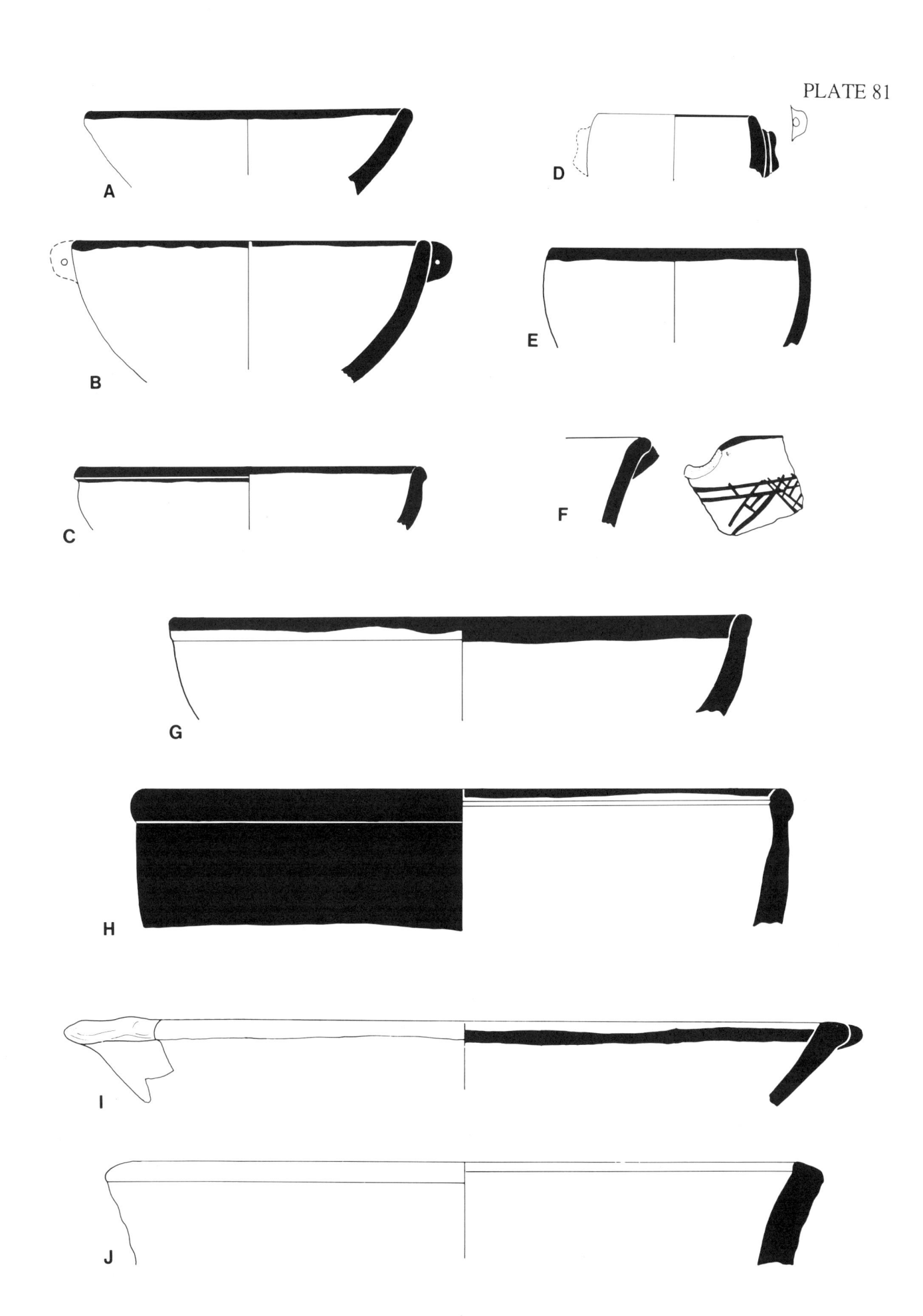

Period IV Pottery From Areas A, C, and C01: Karababa Painted Ware Bowls. Scale 2:5.

Plate 82. Period IV Pottery From Areas A, B, C, and C01: Karababa Painted Ware Footed Bowls and Holemouth Jars. Scale 2:5.

|   | MRN | CONTEXT | FCN | WARE | FORM | TYPE | DECO. | WARE/REMARKS |
|---|-----|---------|-----|------|------|------|-------|--------------|
| A | 2783 | C46-02-005 | 018 | 08 | 688 | Footed Bowl 1 | — | Dense brownish-buff clay; small-sized white grits; red paint. |
| B | 3535 | C35-06-003 | 086 | 08 | 757 | Footed Bowl 2 | — | Dense brownish-buff clay; small-sized grits; red paint, largely abraded. |
| C | 11312 | A04-07-067 | 367 | 08 | 1286 | Unass. Jar | — | Brownish-buff clay; gritty with medium-sized white grits prominent; reddish-brown paint. |
| D | 6544 | A05-07-034 | 100 | 08 | 1214 | Jar 3d | — | Fairly dense clay; small-sized white grits; red paint. |
| E | 7970 | A04-08-038 | 182 | 08 | 1308 | Jar 3c | — | Buff clay; small-sized grits. |
| F | 179 | A04-04-003 | 010 | 08 | 169 | Jar 3d | — | Dense brownish-buff clay; no visible tempering other than occasional small-sized grits; surface covered with olive green slip; brown paint. |
| G | 7537 | A07-12-041 | 298 | 08 | 1205 | Jar 3e | — | Brownish-buff clay; small-sized white grits; brown paint. |
| H | 8015 | C01-1009/19/29-150 | 2075 | 08 | 1303 | Jar 2 | 049 | Greenish-buff clay; fairly gritty with black grits visible; olive green paint. |
| I | 1969 | A08-04-017 | 194 | 08 | 1364 | Jar 2 | 049 | Buff clay; small-sized grits; red paint. |
| J | 17977 | A04-10-105 | 616 | 08 | 120 | Jar 3c | 150 | Fairly dense grayish-buff clay; small-sized black and medium-sized white grits visible; reddish paint. |
| K | 7802 | A07-15-061 | 432 | 08 | 120 | Jar 3c | — | Greenish-buff clay; small-sized white grits; black paint. |
| L | 1978 | C01-0178-060 | 583 | 08 | 120 | Jar 3c | — | Orange-buff clay; small-sized white grits; red paint within incisions on shoulder. |
| M | 007 | B01-02-001 | 003 | 08 | 303 | Jar 3c | — | Brownish-buff clay; small-sized white grits; lighter brownish-buff slip on exterior; reddish-brown paint. |

PLATE 82

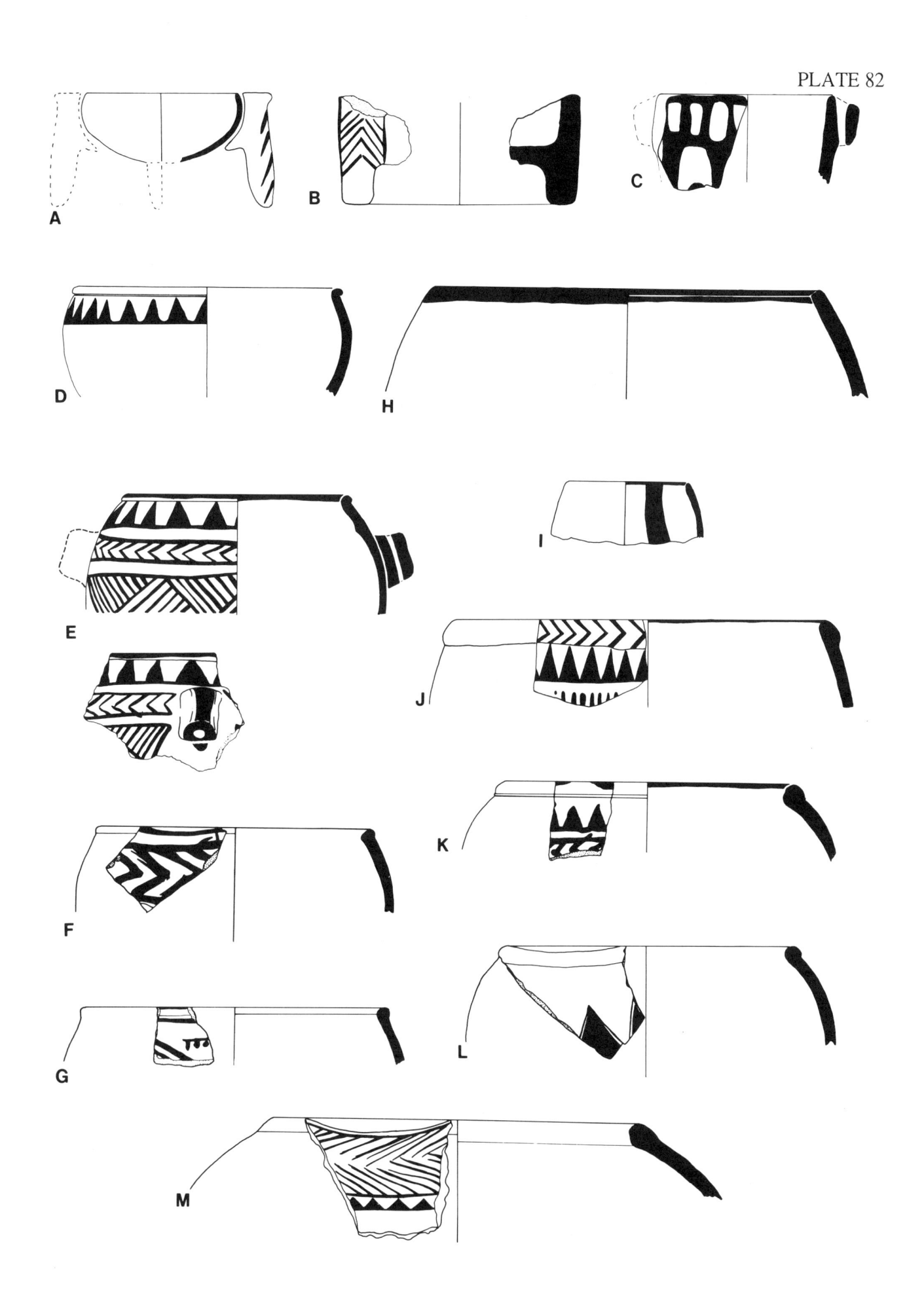

Period IV Pottery From Areas A, B, C, and C01: Karababa Painted Ware Footed Bowls and Holemouth Jars. Scale 2:5.

Plate 83. Period IV Pottery From Areas A, B, and C: Karababa Painted Ware Jars. Scale 2:5.

|   | MRN | CONTEXT | FCN | WARE | FORM | TYPE | DECO. | WARE/REMARKS |
|---|---|---|---|---|---|---|---|---|
| A | 656 | B02-03-015 | 187 | 08 | 414 | Jar 4b | 504 | Buff clay; small-sized grits; scarlet red paint within incisions on shoulder. |
| B | 1992 | C55-03-004 | 086 | 08 | 1231 | Jar 4b | — | Orange-buff clay; small-sized grits. |
| C | 374 | B02-04-004 | 009 | 08 | 167 | Jar 26a | — | Dense brownish-buff clay; no visible tempering; lighter buff slip of same color on surface; brownish paint. |
| D | 3491 | A07-05/06-021 | 156 | 08 | 842 | Jar 26a | 027 | Greenish-buff clay; small-sized white grits; exterior covered with black paint. |
| E | 8930 | C56-07-032 | 371 | 08 | 1695 | Jar 26b | — | Brownish-buff clay; small-sized grits; reddish-brownish paint. |
| F | 12790 | A01-0500/03-028 | D172 | 08 | 1564 | Jar 26b | 027 | Dense brownish-buff clay; medium-sized white grits; plum-brownish paint. |
| G | 2756 | A07-0591-013 | 117 | 08 | 677 | Jar 26b | — | Orange-buff clay; small-sized white grits; buff slip on exterior; dark brown-black paint. |
| H | 936 | A07-04-005 | 018 | 08 | 320 | Unass. Lug | — | Buff clay; small-sized grits; brown paint. |
| I | 391 | A06-07-020 | 084 | 08 | 814 | Unass. Handle | — | Brownish-buff clay; small-sized white grits; brown paint. |
| J | 6035 | C55-09-010 | 494 | 08 | 814 | Unass. Handle | — | Buff clay; small-sized grits; brown paint. |
| K | 1450 | C45-07-020 | 199 | 08 | 171 | Pedestal Base 2 | — | Buff clay; small-sized grits; red paint. |

PLATE 83

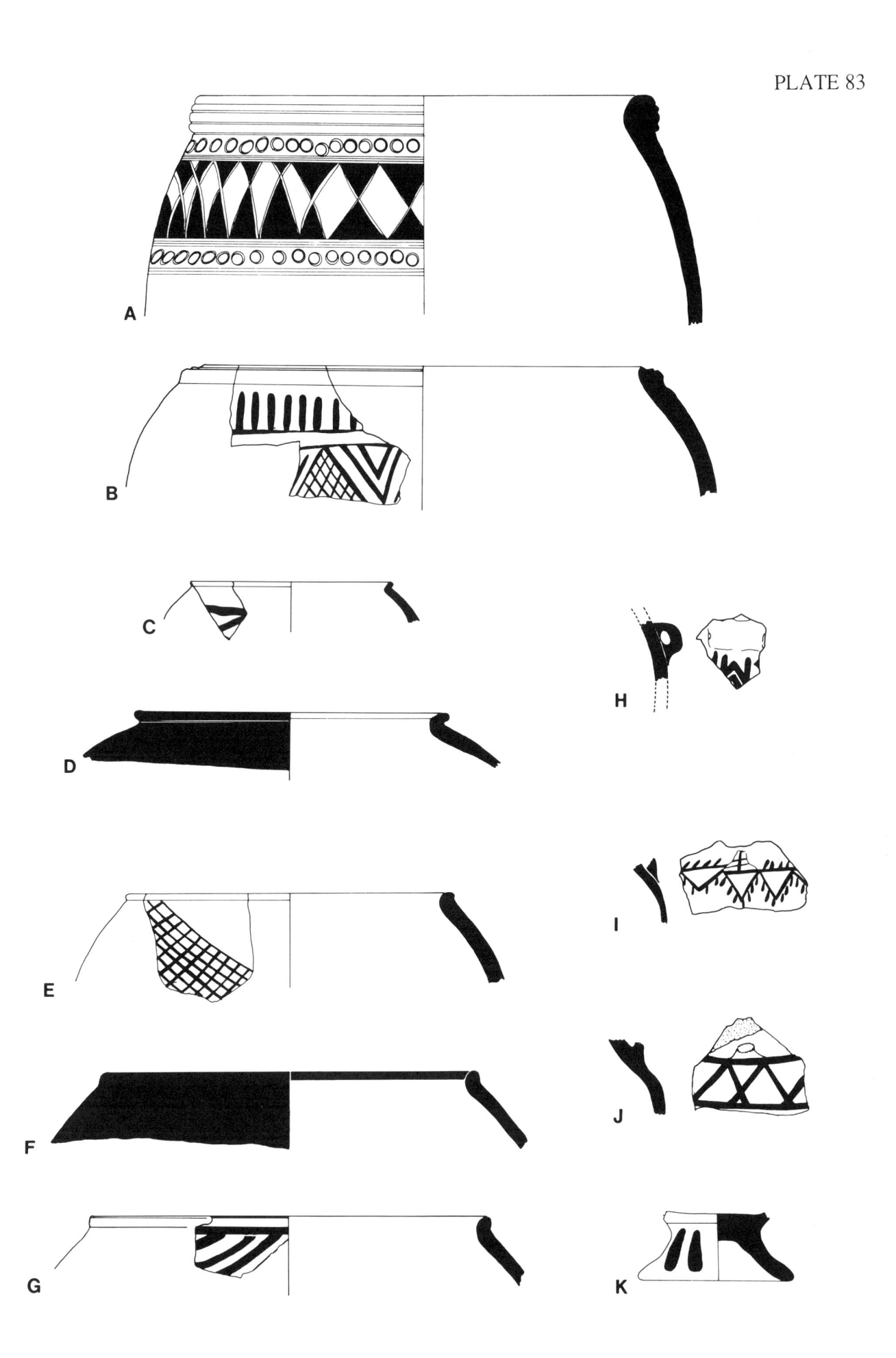

Period IV Pottery From Areas A, B, and C: Karababa Painted Ware Jars. Scale 2:5.

Plate 84. Period IV Pottery From Areas A, B, C, and C01: Karababa Painted Ware Jars (*cont.*). Scale 2:5.

|   | MRN | CONTEXT | FCN | WARE | FORM | TYPE | DECO. | WARE/REMARKS |
|---|---|---|---|---|---|---|---|---|
| A | 1025 | C01-01-005 | 232 | 08 | 322 | Jar 27 | — | Brownish-buff clay; small-sized white grits; exterior covered with thick bone-white slip; irregular, handmade. |
| B | 2436 | A05-04-020 | 064 | 08 | 322 | Jar 27 | 049 | Brownish-buff clay; small-sized white grits; dark brown-black paint. |
| C | 573 | C01-067/69-005 | 114 | 08 | 165 | Jar 27 | 049 | Buff clay; small-sized grits; plum colored paint. |
| D | 1128 | C01-1008-030 | 285 | 08 | 476 | Jar 27 | — | Orange-buff clay; small-sized white and red grits; plum paint. |
| E | 1131 | C01-1009-030 | 273 | 08 | 660 | Jar 27 | 049 | Buff clay; small-sized grits; Brownish-plum colored paint. |
| F | 152 | C01-01-002 | 004 | 08 | 164 | Jar 28 | — | Brownish-buff clay; small-sized white grits; greenish-buff slip on surfaces; black paint. |
| G | 19871 | B72-05-017 | 182 | 08 | 903 | Jar 28 | 142 | Brownish-buff clay; medium-sized white grits; thick cream slip on surface over which black paint was applied. |
| H | 2473 | C55-07-003 | 163 | 08 | 668 | Jar 28 | — | Fairly dense gray clay; small-sized white grits; buff slip on surfaces; brownish-plum colored paint. |
| I | 4637 | C55-05-014 | 305 | 08 | 903 | Jar 28 | 027 | Orange-buff clay; small-sized white grits; dark brown paint. |
| J | 2200 | C56-01-001 | 003 | 08 | 668 | Jar 28 | 027 | Orange-buff clay; small-sized grits; dark red paint on exterior. |
| K | 3089 | C46-03-003 | 026 | 08 | — | — | 117 | Greenish-buff clay; small-sized white grits; buff slip on surfaces; dark brown paint; probably joins jar on plate 84:L, below. |
| L | 2714 | C46-03-003 | 015 | 08 | 668 | Jar 28 | 117 | Greenish-buff clay; small-sized white grits; buff slip on both surfaces; dark brown paint; probably joins jar on plate 84:K, above. |

PLATE 84

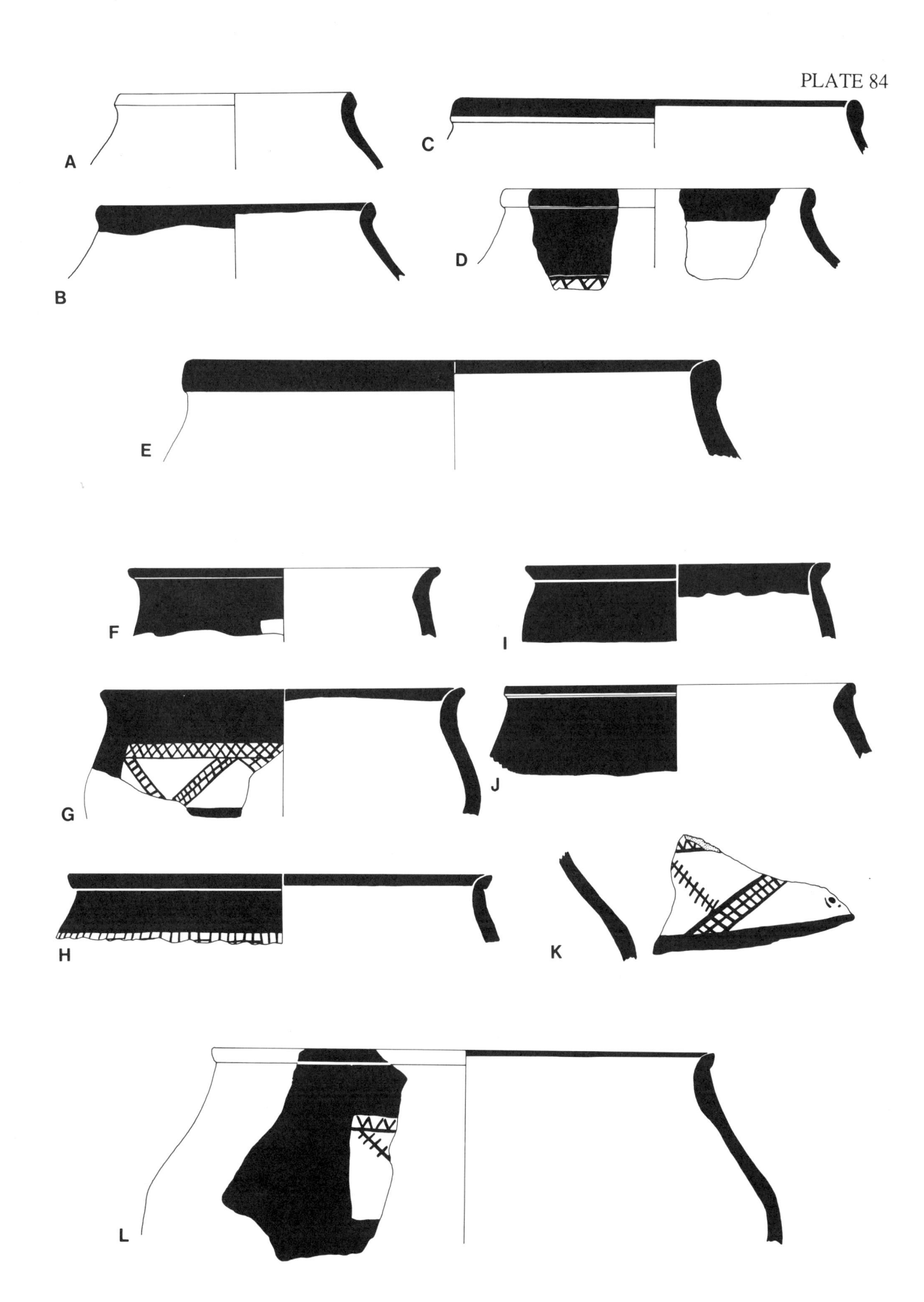

Period IV Pottery From Areas A, B, C, and C01: Karababa Painted Ware Jars (*cont.*). Scale 2:5.

Plate 85. Period IV Pottery From Areas A, C, C01, and F: Karababa Painted Ware Jars (*cont.*). Scale 2:5.

|   | MRN | CONTEXT | FCN | WARE | FORM | TYPE | DECO. | WARE/REMARKS |
|---|---|---|---|---|---|---|---|---|
| A | 6040 | C55-05-014 | 496 | 08 | 316 | Unass. Jar | 027 | Dense grayish-buff core grading to orange on surfaces; small-sized white grits; plum colored wash or paint, lightly burnished. |
| B | 12144 | F01-05-051 | 284 | 08 | 1680 | Unass. Jar | 049 | Grayish-buff clay; gritty, white, and black grits visible; reddish paint. |
| C | 483 | A05-04-008 | 014 | 08 | 163 | Jar 29a | — | Reddish-buff clay; small-sized white grits; buff slip on exterior; black paint. |
| D | 17916 | A04-1032/42-102 | 601 | 08 | 1675 | Jar 29a | 149 | Brownish-buff clay grading to orange on inner surface; small-sized white grits; dark brown paint. |
| E | 1315 | C01-09-022 | 324 | 08 | 437 | Jar 29a | — | Light greenish-buff clay; small-sized white grits; plum colored paint. |
| F | 3545 | C56-06-013 | 177 | 08 | 1292 | Jar 29a | 027 | Dense brownish clay; no visible tempering other than occasional scattered small grits; orange paint. |
| G | 6621 | C35-04-009 | 291 | 08 | 672 | Jar 29a | 049 | Brownish-buff clay; small-sized grits; buff slip; brown paint. |
| H | 2644 | C46-04-001 | 005 | 08 | 672 | Jar 29a | 049 | Brownish-buff clay; small-sized grits; buff slip; red paint; exterior slightly burnished. |
| I | 8322 | C01-09-066 | 2152 | 08 | 437 | Jar 29a | 104 | Buff clay; small-sized grits; reddish paint. |
| J | 11368 | A04-08-079 | 423 | 08 | 437a | Jar 29a | *027 | Buff clay; gritty, small- and medium-sized grits visible; brownish-red paint. |
| K | 0682 | C01-01-009 | 152 | 08 | 1160 | Jar 29b | — | Fairly dense brownish-buff clay; small gray, red and white grits; plum red paint. |

PLATE 85

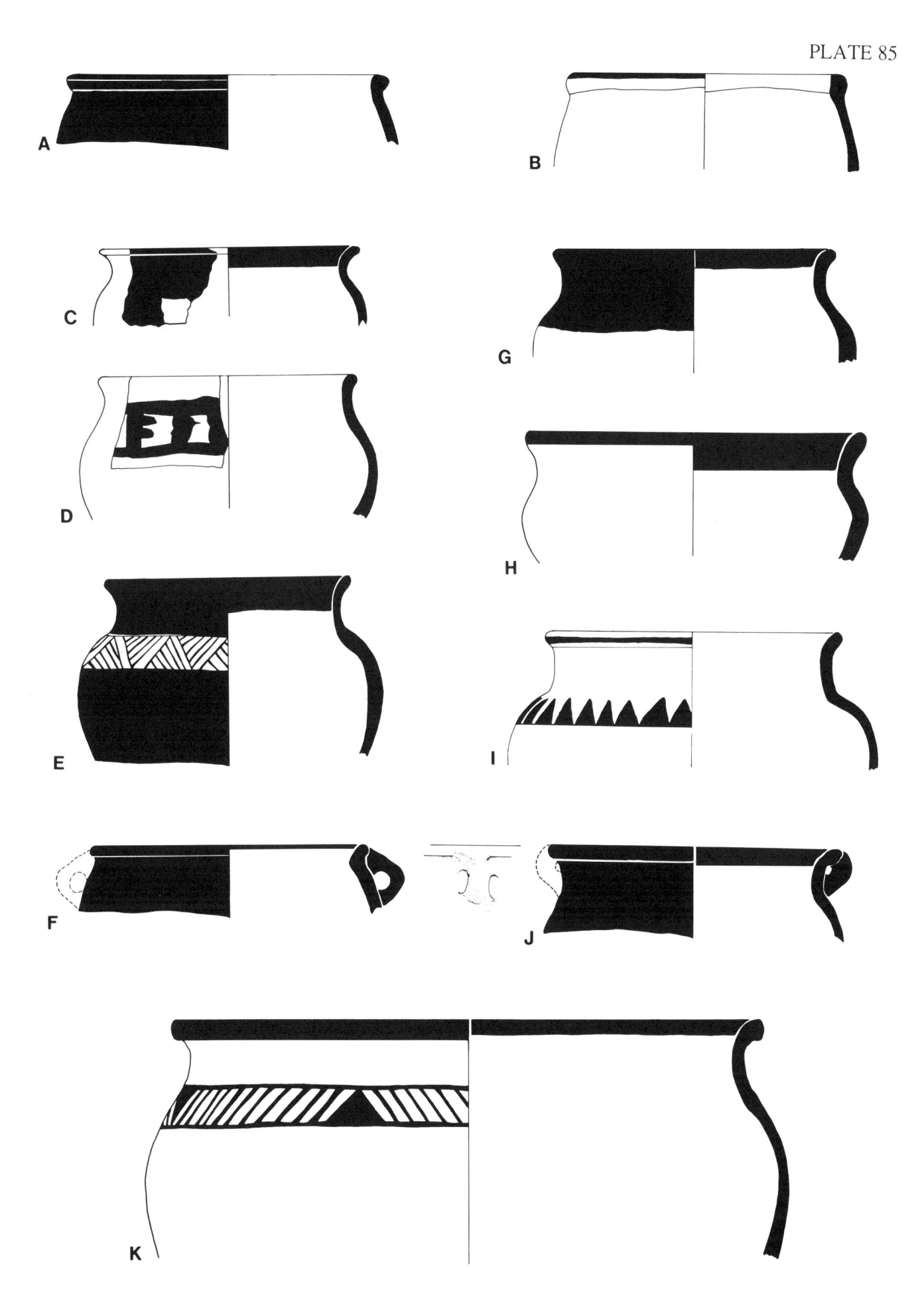

Period IV Pottery From Areas A, C, C01, and F: Karababa Painted Ware Jars (*cont.*). Scale 2:5.

Plate 86. Period IV Pottery From Areas A and C: Karababa Painted Ware Jars (*cont.*). Scale 2:5.

|   | *MRN* | *Context* | *FCN* | *Ware* | *Form* | *Type* | *Deco.* | *Ware/Remarks* |
|---|---|---|---|---|---|---|---|---|
| A | 11312 | A04-07-067 | 367 | 08 | 437 | Jar 29a | 145 | Reddish-buff clay; fairly gritty and porous, white grits prominent; cream-buff slip on surfaces; purple paint. |
| B | 1104 | C45-01-007 | 097 | 08 | 378 | Jar 29a | — | Greenish-buff ware; small-sized grits, some white; plum colored paint. |
| C | 1320 | C45-01-017 | 171 | 08 | 437 | Jar 29a | — | Greenish-buff clay; small-sized grits; plum colored paint. |
| D | 11074 | A08-0500/01-036 | 333 | 08 | 437a | Jar 29a | 029 | Greenish-buff clay; gritty, small-sized white grits prominent; plum colored paint over cream slip; found intrusive in Period VIA level. |
| E | 2700 | C35-03-003 | 023 | 08 | 676 | Jar 5c | — | Orange-buff clay; small-sized white grits; reddish paint. |
| F | 1926 | A05-04-019 | 061 | 08 | 351 | Jar 5 | — | Orange-buff clay; small- and medium-sized grits; brown paint. |
| G | 1998 | A07-05-006 | 053 | 08 | 107 | Jar 5a | — | Buff clay; fairly gritty, small-sized grits; brown paint. |
| H | 5704 | C56-07-029 | 352 | 08 | 107 | Jar 5a | — | Buff clay; small-sized grits; reddish-plum colored paint. |
| I | 3898 | C55-08-009 | 198 | 08 | 819 | Jar 5c | — | Light greenish-buff clay; small-sized grits. |
| J | 4741 | A07-0951-022 | 225 | 08 | 351 | Jar 5 | — | Buff clay; small-sized grits; reddish paint. |
| K | 17903 | A04-10-101 | — | 08 | 1674 | Jar 30 | 148 | Dense buff clay; small-sized white grits; red paint. |
| L | 4445 | C55-0438-011 | 244 | 08 | 1052 | Jar 30 | — | Buff clay; small-sized gray grits; red paint. |
| M | 4227 | A08-05-017 | 182 | 08 | 1052 | Jar 30 | — | Brownish clay; gritty, white grits prominent; on exterior, pinkish-buff slip; interior, buff slip; dark red paint. |

PLATE 86

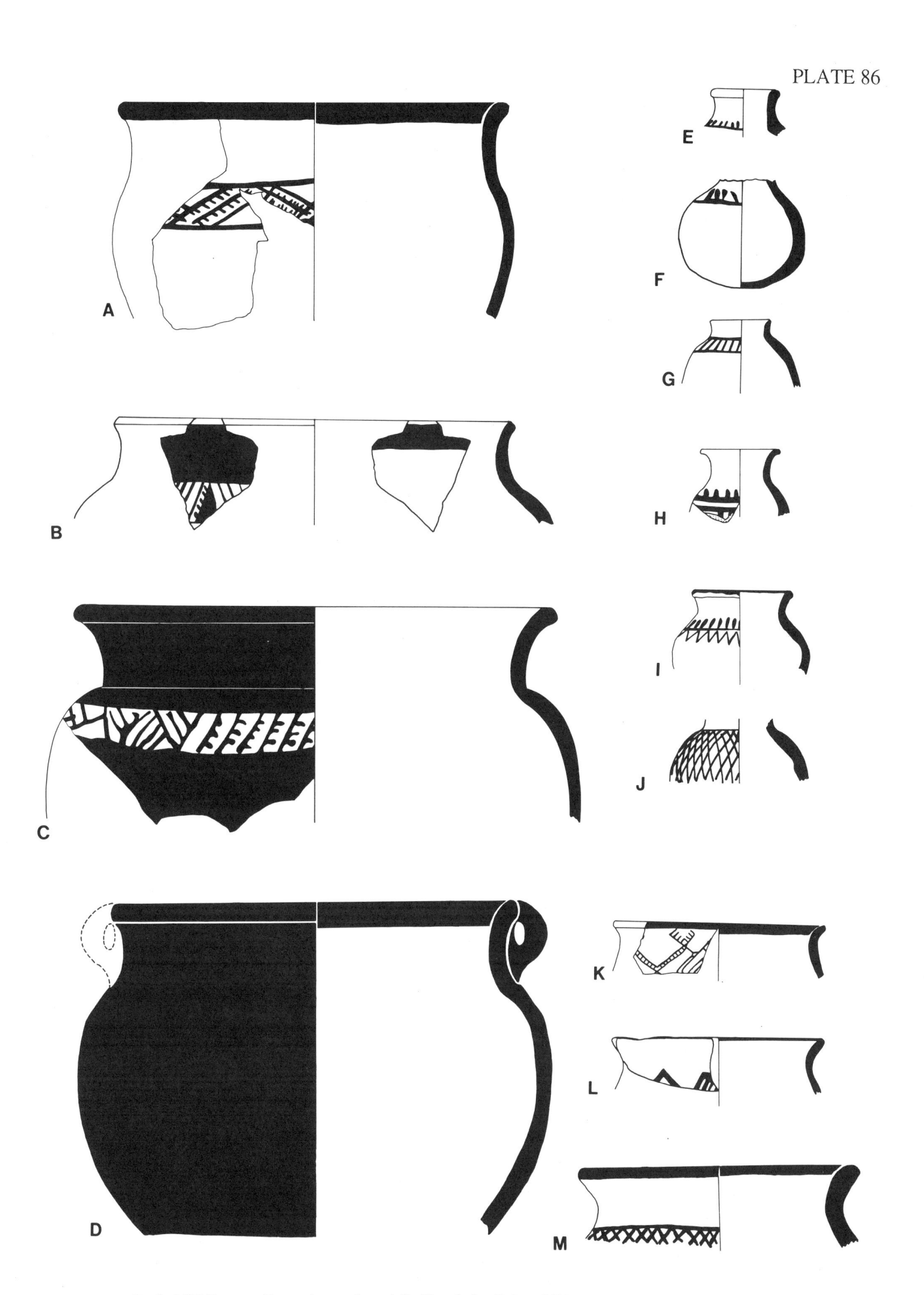

Period IV Pottery From Areas A and C: Karababa Painted Ware Jars (*cont.*). Scale 2:5.

Plate 87. Period IV Pottery From Areas A, C, C01, and D: Karababa Painted Ware Jars (*cont.*). Scale 2:5.

|   | MRN | Context | FCN | Ware | Form | Type | Deco. | Ware/Remarks |
|---|---|---|---|---|---|---|---|---|
| A | 6538 | C35-0372-005 | 264 | 08 | 402 | Jar 29b | — | Buff clay; small-sized white grits; plum colored paint. |
| B | 1131 | C01-1009-030 | 273 | 08 | 402 | Jar 29b | — | Light greenish-buff clay; small-sized white grits; dark brown paint. |
| C | 1698 | A08-01-004 | 032 | 08 | 314 | Jar 31 | — | Buff clay; small-sized white grits; plum colored paint. |
| D | 6840 | C55-02-016 | 644 | 08 | 314 | Jar 31 | — | Buff clay; small-sized grits; reddish paint. |
| E | 1016 | C45-01-007 | 076 | 08 | 314 | Jar 31 | — | Buff clay; small-sized grits; reddish-brownish paint. |
| F | 1602 | A06-07-015 | 065 | 08 | 601 | Unass. Jar | — | Fairly dense brownish-buff clay; small-sized white grits; buff slip on exterior; red paint. |
| G | 11268 | A04-07-061 | 318 | 08 | — | — | 142 | Grayish-buff clay; fairly gritty, small-sized grits prominent; plum colored paint. |
| H | 1779 | A05-0411-019 | 060 | 08 | — | — | — | Buff clay; small-sized grits; plum-reddish paint. |
| I | — | Area A, Provenance lost | — | 08 | — | — | — | Buff clay; small-sized grits; plum-reddish paint. |
| J | 1926 | A05-04-019 | 061 | 08 | — | — | 102 | Buff clay; small-sized grits; brownish-reddish paint. |
| K | 8032 | D44-01-026 | 209 | 08 | 314 | Jar 31 | 147 | Greenish-buff clay; small-sized black grits and medium-sized white grits visible; plum colored paint; out of context in Period III deposit. |
| L | 5685 | A06-05-031 | 150 | 08 | 314 | Jar 31 | — | Buff clay; small-sized grits; plum paint. |

PLATE 87

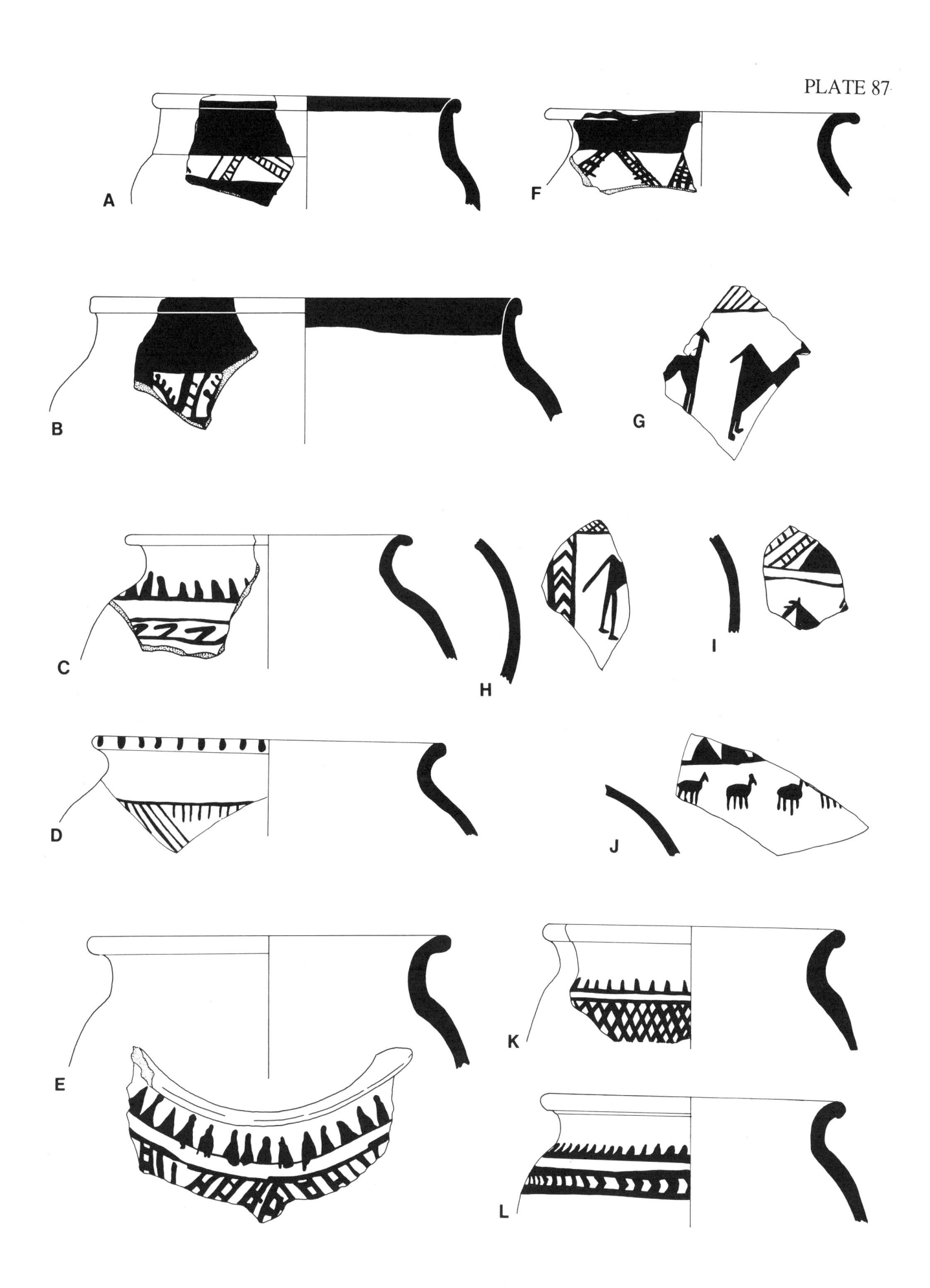

Period IV Pottery From Areas A, C, C01, and D: Karababa Painted Ware Jars (*cont.*). Scale 2:5.

Plate 88. Period IV Pottery From Areas A, C, and D: Karababa Painted Ware Jars (*cont.*) and Decorated Bodies. Scale 2:5.

|   | MRN | CONTEXT | FCN | WARE | FORM | TYPE | DECO. | WARE/REMARKS |
|---|---|---|---|---|---|---|---|---|
| A | 794 | A06-02-009 | 028 | 08 | 314 | Jar 31 | — | Reddish-buff clay; small-sized white grits; reddish-brownish paint. |
| B | 7802 | A07-05-061 | 432 | 08 | 314 | Jar 31 | — | Buff clay; small-sized white grits; reddish-plum colored paint. |
| C | 3765 | D53-02-005 | 024 | 08 | 314 | Jar 31 | 143 | Fairly dense grayish-buff clay; small-sized red, white and gray grits visible; reddish-brown paint; out of context in Period III level. |
| D | 11342 | A04-08-031 | 389 | 08 | — | Jar 31 | 140 | Fairly dense brownish-buff clay; small-sized black grits. |
| E | 6329 | C35-06-017 | 233 | 08 | — | Jar 31 | — | Buff clay; small-sized grits; plum colored paint. |
| F | 788 | A06-03-010 | 029 | 08 | — | Jar 31 | 106 | Fairly dense brownish-buff clay; buff slip over surfaces; red paint. |
| G | 11368 | A04-08-077 | 423 | 08 | — | Jar 31 | 139 | Buff clay; small-sized white grits; plum colored paint. |
| H | 11327 | A04-08-069 | 382 | 08 | — | Jar 31 | 141 | Fairly dense buff clay; small-sized white grits; red paint. |
| I | 17722 | A04-10-097 | 569 | 08 | — | Jar 31 | 144 | Light greenish-buff clay; gritty with medium-sized white grits; brown paint. |
| J | 1780 | A05-04-019 | 057 | 08 | — | Jar 31 | 108 | Buff clay; small-sized white grits; reddish paint. |
| K | 7734 | A04-07-032 | 138 | 08 | — | Jar 31 | — | Buff clay; small-sized grits; plum paint. |

PLATE 88

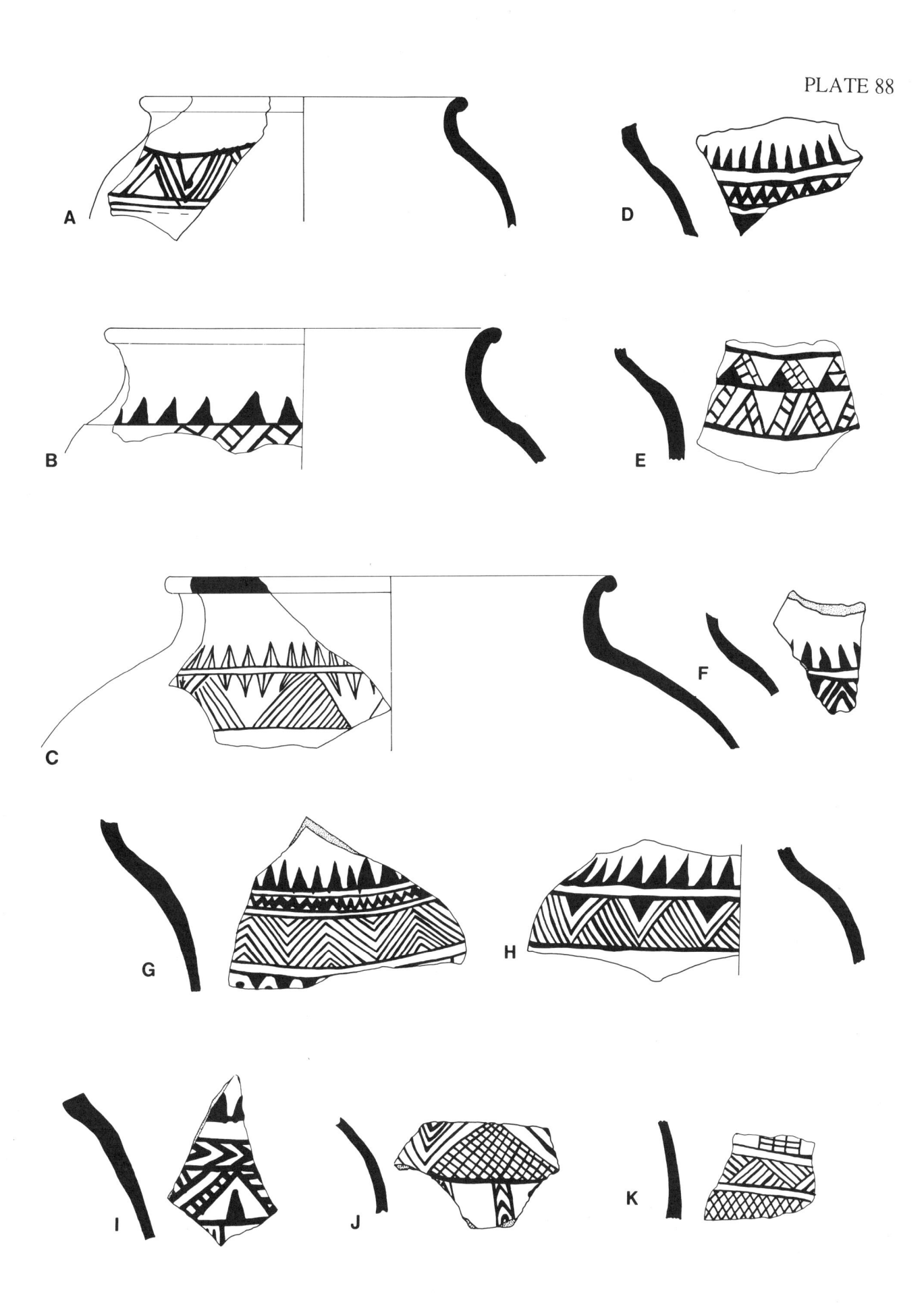

Period IV Pottery From Areas A, C, and D: Karababa Painted Ware Jars (*cont.*) and Decorated Bodies. Scale 2:5.

Plate 89. Period IV Pottery From Areas A, C, C01, and F: Karababa Painted Ware Jars (*cont.*). Scale 2:5.

|   | *MRN* | *Context* | *FCN* | *Ware* | *Form* | *Type* | *Deco.* | *Ware/Remarks* |
|---|---|---|---|---|---|---|---|---|
| A | 7653 | A04-07-023 | 099 | 08 | 1256 | Jar 32a | 049 | Brownish-buff clay; small-sized white grits; black paint. |
| B | 17650 | A05-0582/92-067 | 292 | 08 | C-75 | Jar 32b | 146 | Brownish-buff clay; gritty; small-sized white grits, brownish-reddish paint; (= KH 1984/181). |
| C | 6707 | C35-04-009 | 295 | 08 | 1285 | Jar 32b | 049 | Dense greenish clay, overfired; small-sized white grits; olive-brown paint. |
| D | 865 | A07-04-005 | 015 | 08 | 365 | Unass. Handle | 013 | Brownish-buff clay; small-sized white grits; brownish paint. |
| E | 819 | C45-01-004 | 014 | 08 | 208 | Jar 31 | 049 | Buff clay; small-sized grits; brown paint. |
| F | 576 | C01-03-006 | 117 | 08 | 159 | Jar 31 | 104 | Buff clay; small-sized grits; reddish paint. |
| G | 1127 | A07-05-006 | 037 | 08 | 87 | Jar 16a | 027 | Fairly dense buff clay; small-sized white grits; scarlet red paint. |
| H | 300 | C01-0187/89-008 | 050 | 08 | 69 | Jar 16b | 049 | Buff clay; small-sized grits; red paint. |
| I | 1306 | A06-05-014 | 051 | 08 | 72 | Jar 16c | — | Buff clay; small-sized grits; orange-brownish paint. |
| J | 6623 | C35-0382-005 | 282 | 08 | 72 | Jar 16c | 049 | Greenish-buff clay; small-sized white grits; olive green paint. |
| K | 12196 | F01-05-060 | 337 | 08 | 1696 | Jar 33 | — | Fairly dense brownish-buff clay; small-sized grits; brown paint. |

PLATE 89

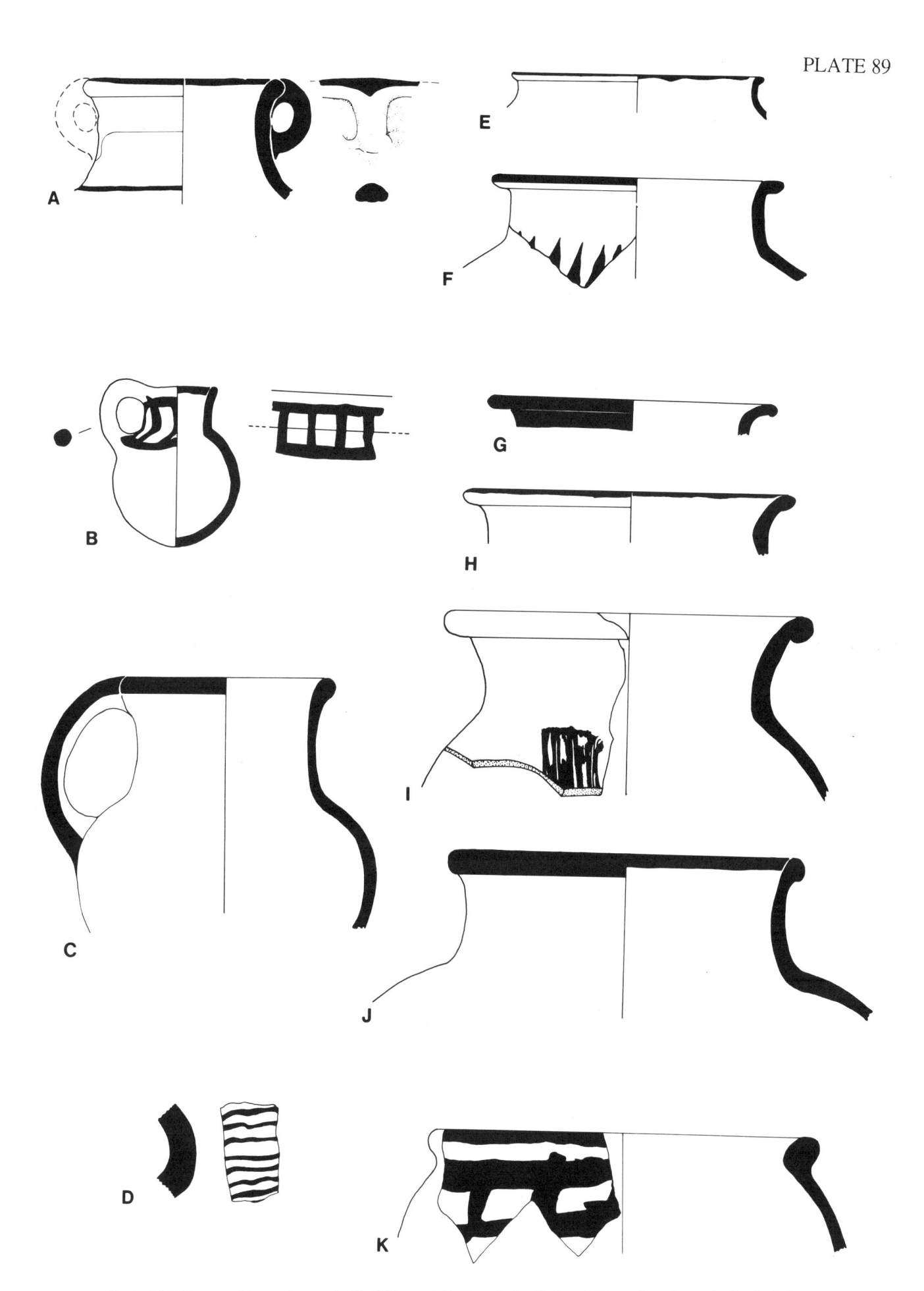

Period IV Pottery From Areas A, C, C01, and F: Karababa Painted Ware Jars (*cont.*). Scale 2:5.

Plate 90. Period IV Pottery From Areas A, B, C, C01, and F: Miscellaneous Wares. Scale 2:5.

|   | MRN | CONTEXT | FCN | WARE | FORM | TYPE | DECO. | WARE/REMARKS |
|---|---|---|---|---|---|---|---|---|
| A | 057 | B01-0464-007 | 052 | 18 | C-43 | Footed Bowl 3 | Bns. | Dense orange-buff/brownish clay; primarily grit-tempered, but a few scattered chaff imprints visible; exterior mottled brownish-orange, lightly burnished and smudged black presumably from fire; one leg missing; handmade; (= KH 1980/2). |
| B | 054 | B01-0464-007 | 037 | 18 | C-43 | Footed Bowl 3 | Bns. | Description as above (A); (= KH 1980/1). |
| C | 865 | A07-04-005 | 015 | 18 | 362 | Footed Bowl 3 | — | Gray core grading to orange on surfaces; traces of grit tempering with white grits predominant; irregular; handmade. |
| D | 861 | A06-02-008 | 026 | 21 | 340 | Unass. Bowl | — | Dense brownish clay; tempered with very fine chaff; a few occasional scattered small-sized white grits (accidental?) visible; exterior smoothed, mottled brown and black; irregular; handmade. |
| E | 4987 | A06-05-028 | 130 | 21 | 895 | Unass. Jar | — | Dense brownish-gray clay; vegetal-tempered but a few scattered small-sized white grits; irregular; handmade. |
| F | 3875 | C35-04-009 | 153 | 21 | 799 | Unass. Jar | — | Dense dark brown clay; vegetal-tempered, a few scattered grits; light brownish-buff surface, smoothed; irregular; handmade. |
| G | 6352 | C55-05-025 | 562 | 10 | 997 | Stand 5 | 505 | Rather porous dark brown clay; shiny quartz(?) flakes prominent; grayish exterior; irregular incisions some of which bear traces of white paste incrustation. |
| H | 111 | B02-03-004 | 083 | 10 | 997 | Stand 5 | 502 | Gray clay; shiny quartz(?) flakes quite prominent; a few white grits visible; exterior gray and smoothed; white paste still visible as filling of exterior decoration; cf. also plate 147:B. |
| I | 11980 | F01-05-023 | 120 | 10 | 1655 | Unass. Jar | Bns. | Grayish clay; small-sized grits visible as well as a few shiny quartz flakes; badly abraded but traces of burnishing remain; also traces of white paste filling incisions. |
| J | 3710 | A07-0592-014 | 198 | 37 | 856 | Unass. Bowl | Bns. | Brown clay; fairly gritty with numerous medium-sized red grits and shiny quartz flakes visible; exterior is black and highly burnished. |
| K | 1935 | C01-1017-046 | 580 | 37 | 1190 | Unass. Jar | Bns. | Dense gray clay; no visible tempering other than a few scattered small-sized white grits; surface is gray, mottled orange in spots; highly burnished. |
| L | 4536 | A08-05-017 | 177 | 13 | 1058 | Stand 5 | — | Brownish clay; chaff impressions easily visible; exterior mottled brown and black. |
| M | 7902 | A04-08-037 | 172 | 13 | 1296 | Unass. Handle | — | Orange clay, well-marked gray core; predominantly tempered with chaff but numerous white grits visible. |
| N | 11248 | A04-08-059 | 298 | 13 | 146 | Unass. Handle | — | Brownish-orange clay, well-marked gray core; chaff and straw imprints prominent; no traces of mineral tempering. |

PLATE 90

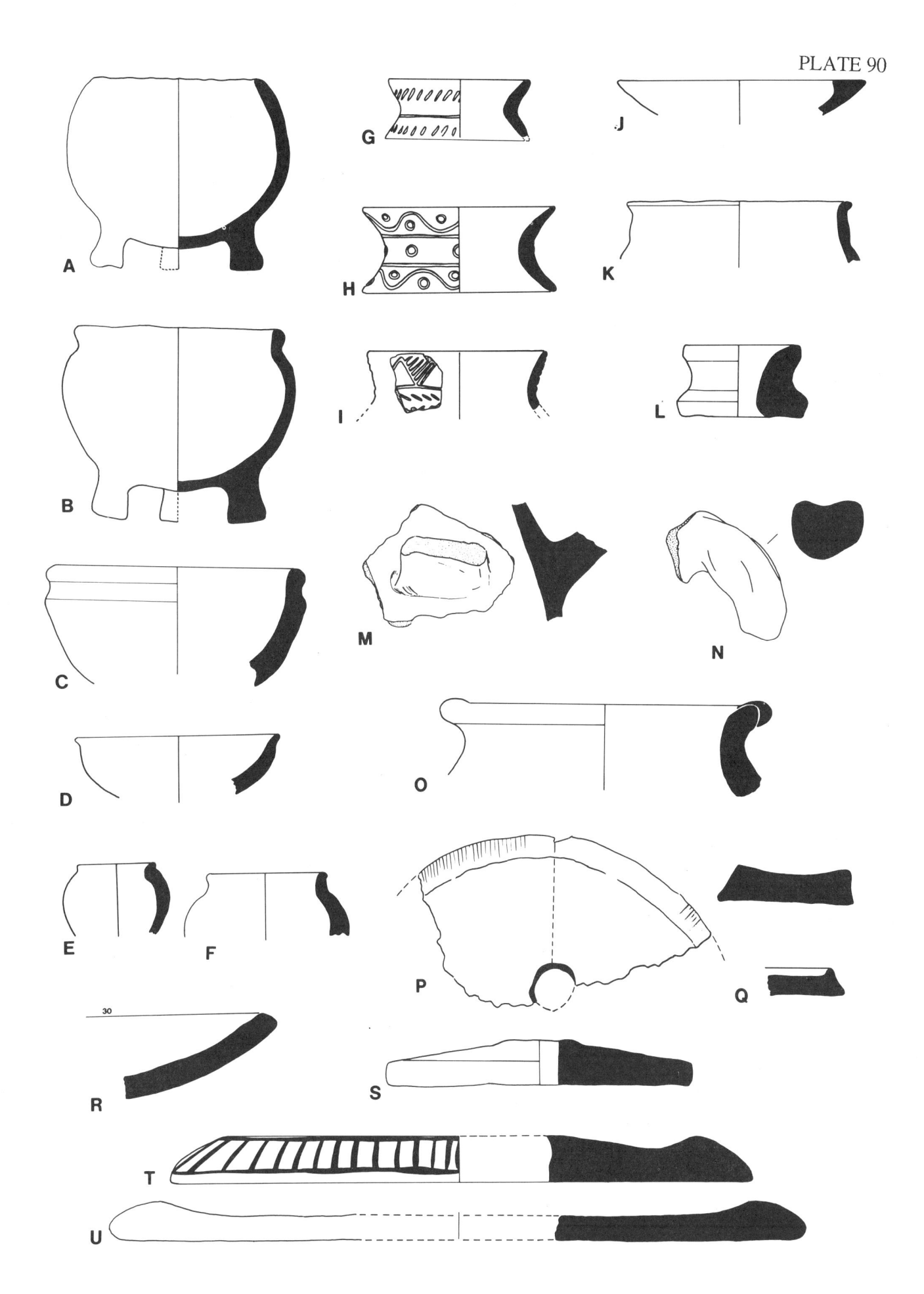

Period IV Pottery From Areas A, B, C, C01, and F: Miscellaneous Wares. Scale 2:5.

Plate 90. Period IV Pottery From Areas A, B, C, C01, and F: Miscellaneous Wares. Scale 2:5. (*cont.*).

|   | MRN | Context | FCN | Ware | Form | Type | Deco. | Ware/Remarks |
|---|---|---|---|---|---|---|---|---|
| O | 17749 | A04-10-100 | 584 | 13 | 152 | Jar 34b | — | Brownish clay, well-marked gray core; straw/chaff imprints prominent; no traces of mineral tempering; a small triangular ledge handle on rim. |
| P | 1016 | C45-01-007 | 076 | 13 | 156b | Lid 1b | — | Brownish clay, gray core; straw/chaff imprints prominent; no traces of mineral tempering. |
| Q | 1016 | C45-01-007 | 076 | 13 | 317 | Lid 1a | — | Orange clay, gray core; straw/chaff imprints prominent; a few scattered grits visible; exterior covered with thin brown wash. |
| R | 5331 | A06-05-029 | 144 | 13 | 792 | Bowl 23 | — | Brownish-buff clay; chaff imprints predominant but a few small-sized grits visible. |
| S | 6371 | C35-0372-005 | D259 | 14 | 156b | Lid 1b | Bns. | Brownish-buff clay, gray core; straw/chaff imprints prominent; no traces of mineral tempering; exterior brownish-buff, mottled grayish; burnished. |
| T | 5323 | A05-05-026 | 079 | 13 | 917 | Tray 2 | — | Brownish clay; gray core; straw/chaff imprints prominent; reddish-brownish paint. |
| U | 17973 | A04-10-104 | 612 | 13 | 917 | Tray 2 | — | Fairly dense, extensive gray core grading to thin orange clay layer on surface; interior bottom smudged black from fire. |

Plate 91. Period IV Pottery From Areas A, B, and C: Ware Group II Bowls and Open Forms. Scale 2:5.

|   | MRN | Context | FCN | Ware | Form | Type | Deco. | Ware/Remarks |
|---|---|---|---|---|---|---|---|---|
| A | 6040 | C55-05-014 | 496 | 09 | C-37 | Bowl 5 | — | Reddish-brownish clay; large-sized white grits visible; exterior mottled black-brownish; smoothed but unburnished. |
| B | 3788 | C56-0646-021 | D224 | 09 | 829 | Unass. Bowl | — | Orange clay; gritty with numerous medium- and large-sized grits visible; handmade, rather rough. |
| C | 1104 | C45-01-007 | 097 | 09 | 380 | Unass. Bowl | Bns. | Red clay; white grits visible; exterior mottled grayish-brown; smoothed; interior burnished. |
| D | 1605 | A08-01-003 | 029 | 09 | 996 | Unass. Bowl | Bns. | Reddish clay; gritty; exterior reddish, mottled and burnished; out of context in slope wash. |
| E | 19409 | B72-0141-008 | 065 | 09 | C-65 | Bowl 22 | Bns. | Rather coarse brownish clay grading to dark brown on surfaces; large-sized black and white grits visible; surface very lightly burnished; friable. |
| F | — | Provenance lost | — | 09 | 155 | Bowl 23 | Bns. | Black clay; medium-sized grits, some black, visible; surfaces are mottled black and gray; burnished. |
| G | 1779 | A05-04-019 | 060 | 09 | 845 | Bowl 23 | Bns. | Fairly dense gray-brownish clay grading to orange on inner surface; white grits visible; exterior surface mottled brownish-buff and black; burnished. |
| H | 3786 | C56-0646-019 | 220 | 09 | 792 | Bowl 23 | Bns. | Brownish-reddish clay; large white and gray grits; quartz flakes prominent; surface mottled; burnished. |
| I | 4533 | C55-05-011 | 275 | 09 | 1279 | Bowl 23 | Bns. | Reddish clay, light brownish-buff core; exterior mottled brownish-black; lightly burnished. |

PLATE 91

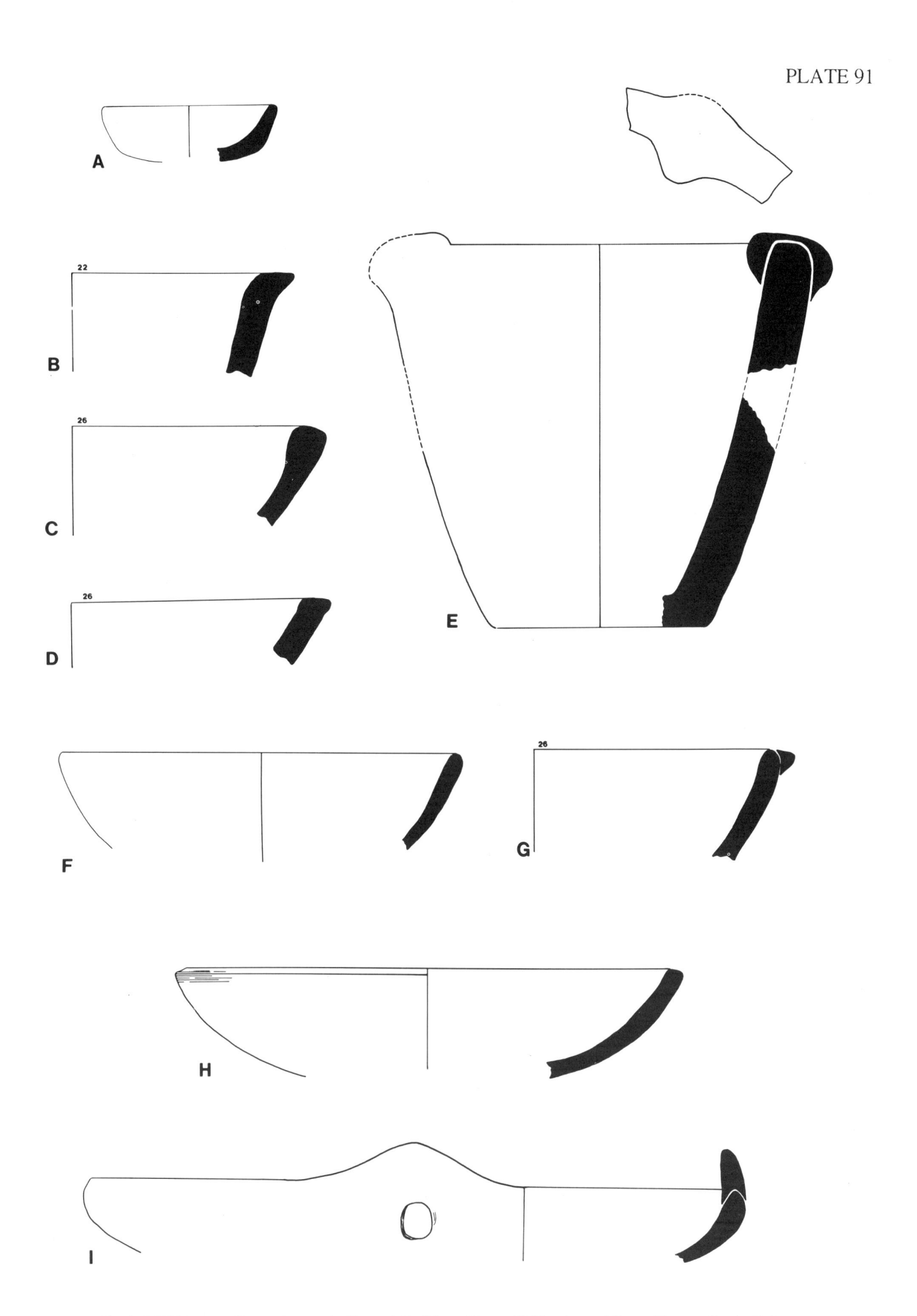

Period IV Pottery From Areas A, B, and C: Ware Group II Bowls and Open Forms. Scale 2:5.

Plate 92. Period IV Pottery From Areas A, C, and C01: Ware Group II Bowls (*cont.*) and Jars. Scale 2:5.

|   | MRN | CONTEXT | FCN | WARE | FORM | TYPE | DECO. | WARE/REMARKS |
|---|-----|---------|-----|------|------|------|-------|--------------|
| A | 531 | A06-02-004 | 019 | 09 | 154 | Unass. Bowl | Bns. | Brownish clay; tempered with white grits and shiny quartz flakes; gray exterior, well burnished. |
| B | 4435 | A06-07-021 | 090 | 09 | 1108 | Unass. Bowl | Bns. | Orange clay; large-sized gray grits; both surfaces gray; lower exterior lightly burnished; upper body above carination is rough. |
| C | 7513 | A07-05-035 | 246 | 09 | 1203 | Unass. Bowl | Bns. | Orange clay; large-sized white grits and quartz flakes visible; exterior mottled brown and black; well burnished. |
| D | 2756 | A07-0591-013 | 117 | 09 | 678 | Unass. Jar | Bns. | Reddish clay; large-sized white grits visible; surface mottled reddish-black; lightly burnished. |
| E | 4076 | C56-0973-016 | 239 | 09 | 1178 | Unass. Jar | — | Reddish clay; large-sized white grits and quartz flakes visible. |
| F | 2130 | A08-0221-007 | 071 | 09 | 574 | Unass. Jar | Bns. | Gray clay; rather porous with large- and medium-sized white grits visible; exterior mottled brown and black; lightly burnished. |
| G | 300 | C01-0187-89-008 | 050 | 09 | 153 | Jar 34a | — | Brown clay; gritty with large-sized white grits visible; exterior is smoothed and mottled brown and black. |
| H | 6554 | A05-07-034 | 100 | 09 | 153 | Jar 34a | Bns. | Dense gray clay; quartz flakes visible; exterior is mottled brown and black; lightly burnished. |

PLATE 92

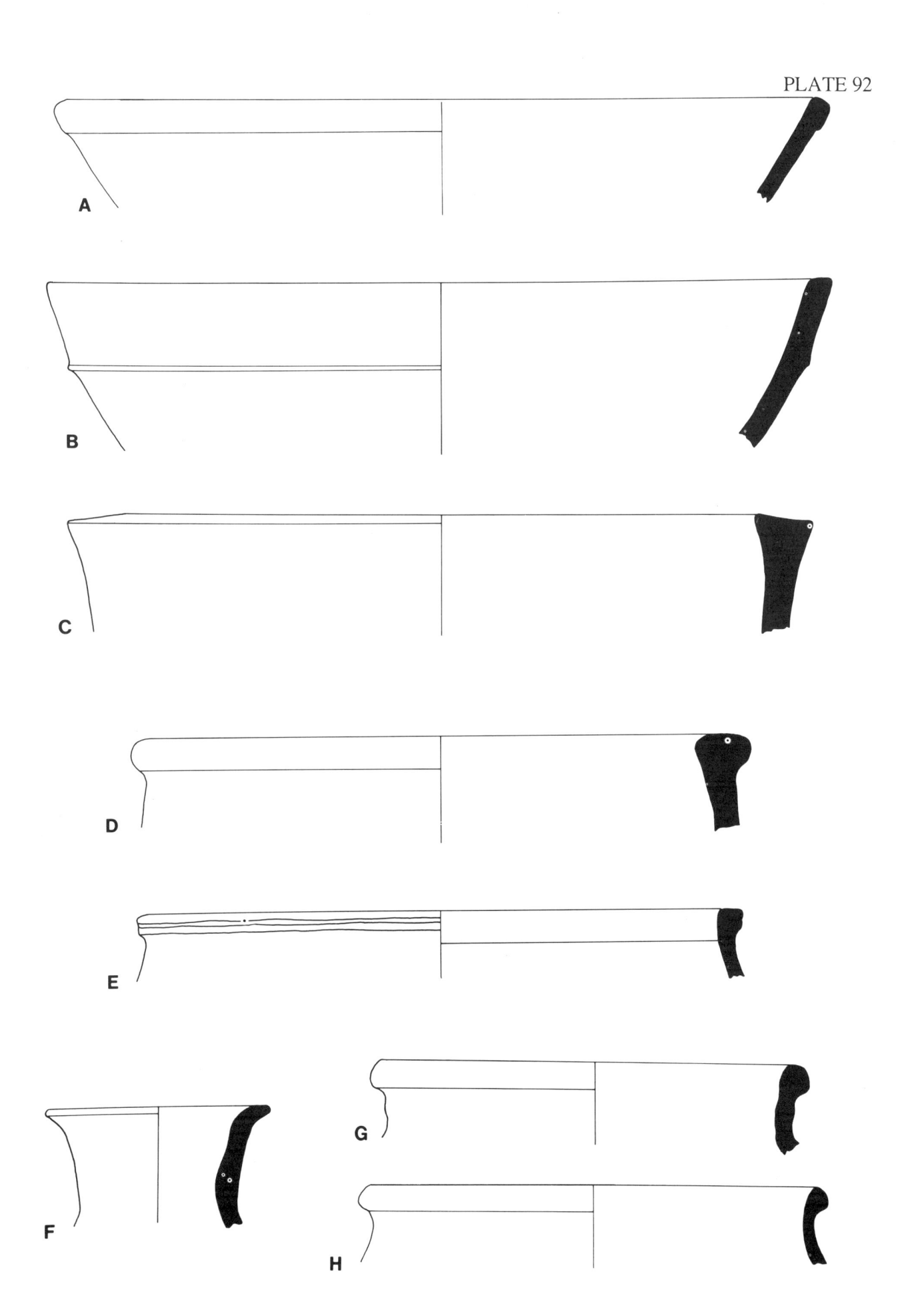

Period IV Pottery From Areas A, C, and C01: Ware Group II Bowls (*cont.*) and Jars. Scale 2:5.

Plate 93. Period IV Pottery From Areas A, B, C, and C01: Ware Group II Jars (*cont.*). Scales: (A–H and K–M) 2:5; (I and J) 1:5.

|   | MRN | CONTEXT | FCN | WARE | FORM | TYPE | DECO. | WARE/REMARKS |
|---|-----|---------|-----|------|------|------|-------|--------------|
| A | 938 | C01-09-028 | 230 | 09 | 152 | Jar 34b | Bns. | Grayish clay; medium-sized white grits and quartz flakes visible; exterior is mottled black and brown, interior is grayish; both surfaces lightly burnished. |
| B | 4632 | C56-0362-024 | 253 | 09 | 880 | Jar 34b | — | Orange-buff clay, brownish core; large-sized white grits visible; somewhat rough. |
| C | 696 | B01-0213-015 | 150 | 09 | 152 | Jar 34b | Bns. | Brownish clay; gritty with white grits and quartz flakes visible; interior is orange, exterior is mottled brown and black; lightly burnished. |
| D | 268 | C01-01-005 | 041 | 09 | 152 | Jar 34b | Bns. | Grayish clay; exterior mottled gray, brown, and black; burnished. |
| E | 840 | C01-06/02/08/07 (Found during clean up.) | 169 | 09 | 112 | Jar 34b | Bns. | Brownish clay; gritty with large grits and quartz flakes visible; surface mottled brown and black; lightly burnished. |
| F | 17725 | A05-05-075 | 330 | 09 | 112 | Jar 34b | Bns. | Brownish clay, grayish core; medium-sized white grits visible; exterior mottled black and brown; lightly burnished. |
| G | 5267 | A06-05-029 | 140 | 40 | 152 | Jar 34b | — | Dark brown clay; tempered with grits and chaff; exterior mottled brown and black; somewhat rough. |
| H | 6700 | A04-05-016 | 065 | 09 | 152 | Jar 34b | Bns. | Cooking Pot Ware; burnished. |
| I | 3757 | A07-0752-025 | 197 | 09 | C-24 | Jar 34d | Bns. | Dark gray clay grading to brown towards surfaces; medium-sized grits and quartz flakes visible; exterior is mottled orange, brown, and black; burnished. |
| J | — | Area B Provenance lost | — | 09 | C-24 | Jar 34b | Bns. | Brown clay; gritty with large-sized white grits and quartz flakes visible; exterior mottled orange, brown, and black; burnished. |
| K | 5930 | C56-07-032 | 371 | 04 | 151 | Jar 34c | Bns. | Cooking Pot Ware; burnished. |
| L | 6035 | C55-09-010 | 494 | 09 | 152 | Jar 34b | Bns. | Gray clay; medium-sized grits and quartz flakes visible; exterior mottled and burnished. |
| M | 6035 | C55-09-010 | 494 | 09 | 152 | Jar 34b | Bns. | Cooking Pot Ware; burnished. |

PLATE 93

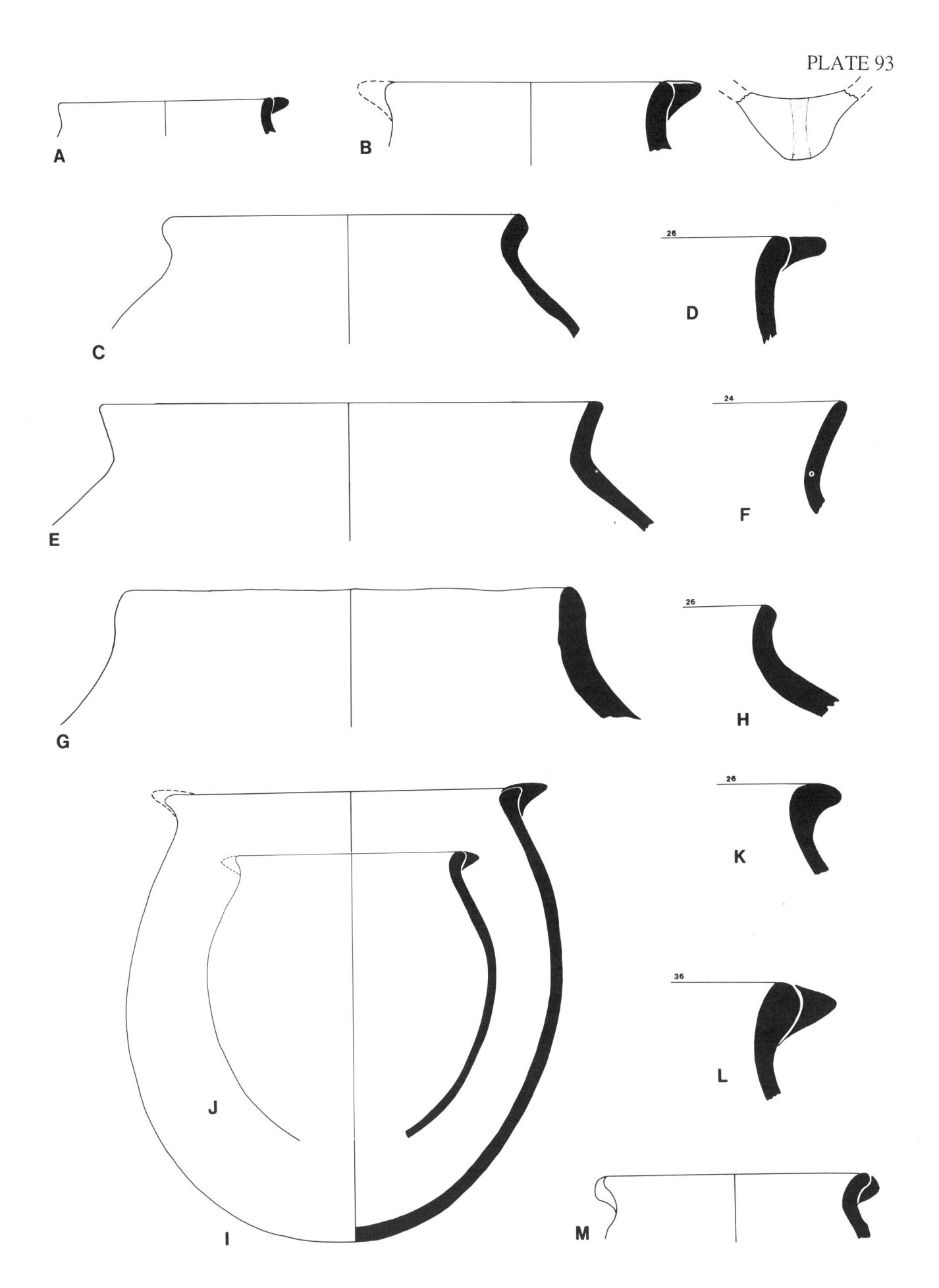

Period IV Pottery From Areas A, B, C, and C01: Ware Group II Jars (*cont.*). Scales: (A–H and K–M) 2:5; (I and J) 1:5.

Plate 94. Period IV Pottery From Areas A, B, C, and C01: Ware Group II Jars (*cont.*). Scale 2:5.

|   | *MRN* | *Context* | *FCN* | *Ware* | *Form* | *Type* | *Deco.* | *Ware/Remarks* |
|---|---|---|---|---|---|---|---|---|
| A | 3560 | A07-0762-022 | 171 | 09 | 151 | Jar 34c | Bns. | Cooking Pot Ware; burnished. |
| B | 0680 | B01-05-019 | 192 | 09 | 151 | Jar 34c | Bns. | Brownish clay; medium-sized grits and quartz flakes visible; exterior mottled brown and black, lightly burnished. |
| C | 7128 | C55-05-035 | 660 | 09 | 151 | Jar 34c | Bns. | Cooking Pot Ware; burnished; possibly same jar as plate 94:D, below. |
| D | 7128 | C55-05-035 | 660 | 09 | 151 | Jar 34c | Bns. | Cooking Pot Ware; burnished; possibly same jar as plate 94:C, above. |
| E | 1514 | A06-07-015 | 64 | 09 | 150 | Jar 34d | Bns. | Brownish-buff clay; very large gray and white grits (miniature pebbles); exterior brown; burnished. |
| F | 0824 | C01-09-020 | 184 | 09 | 150 | Jar 34d | Bns. | Cooking Pot Ware; burnished. |

PLATE 94

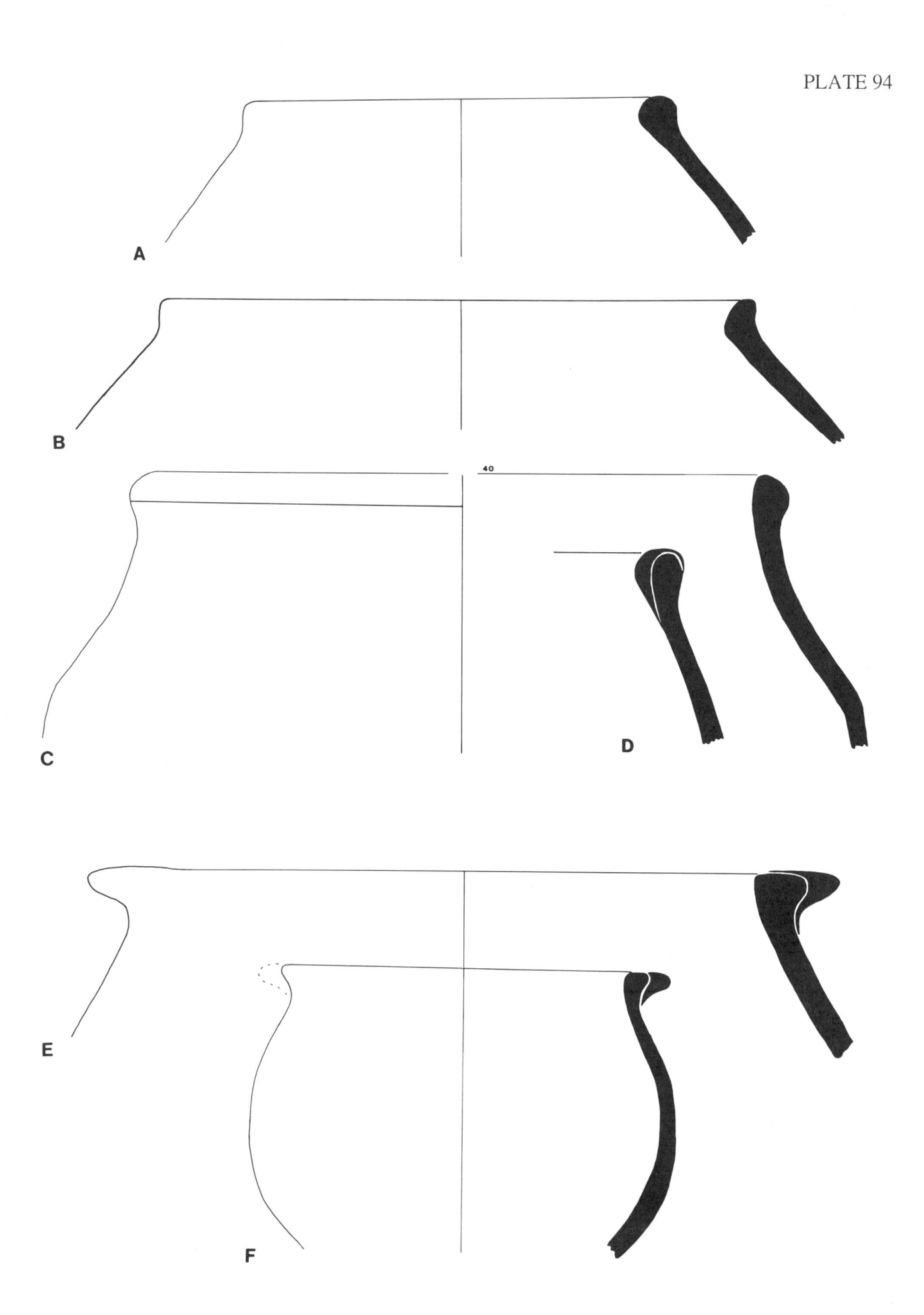

Period IV Pottery From Areas A, B, C, and C01: Ware Group II Jars (*cont.*). Scale 2:5.

Plate 95. Period IV Pottery From Areas A, B, and C: Ware Group II Jars (*cont.*). Scales: (A) 1:5; (B–H) 2:5.

|   | MRN | CONTEXT | FCN | WARE | FORM | TYPE | DECO. | WARE/REMARKS |
|---|---|---|---|---|---|---|---|---|
| A | 7190 | A04-05-018 | 077 | 09 | C-30 | Jar 34d | — | Coarse brown clay; gritty with white grits visible; exterior mottled brown and somewhat coarse. |
| B | 0007 | B01-01-001 | 003 | 09 | 149 | Jar 35 | Bns. | Orange clay; medium- to large-sized grits; exterior mottled orange, brown, and black; lightly burnished. |
| C | 0604 | B03-06-002 | 023 | 09 | 148 | Jar 36 | — | Reddish clay; medium-sized white grits; exterior gray-brown. |
| D | 3739 | C56-0615-013 | 185 | 09 | 773 | Jar 36 | Bns. | Fairly dense brownish-buff clay; exterior mottled brown and black; burnished. |
| E | 0620 | B01-04-007 | 182 | 09 | 147 | Jar 36 | Bns. | Brownish-buff clay grading to orange on surfaces; burnished. |
| F | 7566 | A07-13-043 | 330 | 09 | 1230 | Unass. Handle | — | Somewhat porous gray clay; quartz flakes prominent; gray smoothed surface. |
| G | 5930 | C56-07-032 | 371 | 09 | 148 | Jar 36 | Bns. | Cooking Pot Ware; burnished. |
| H | 19121 | B72-0131-006 | 026 | 09 | 148 | Jar 36 | — | Rather dense reddish clay; small-sized gray and black grits; quartz flakes also visible; exterior very rough. |

PLATE 95

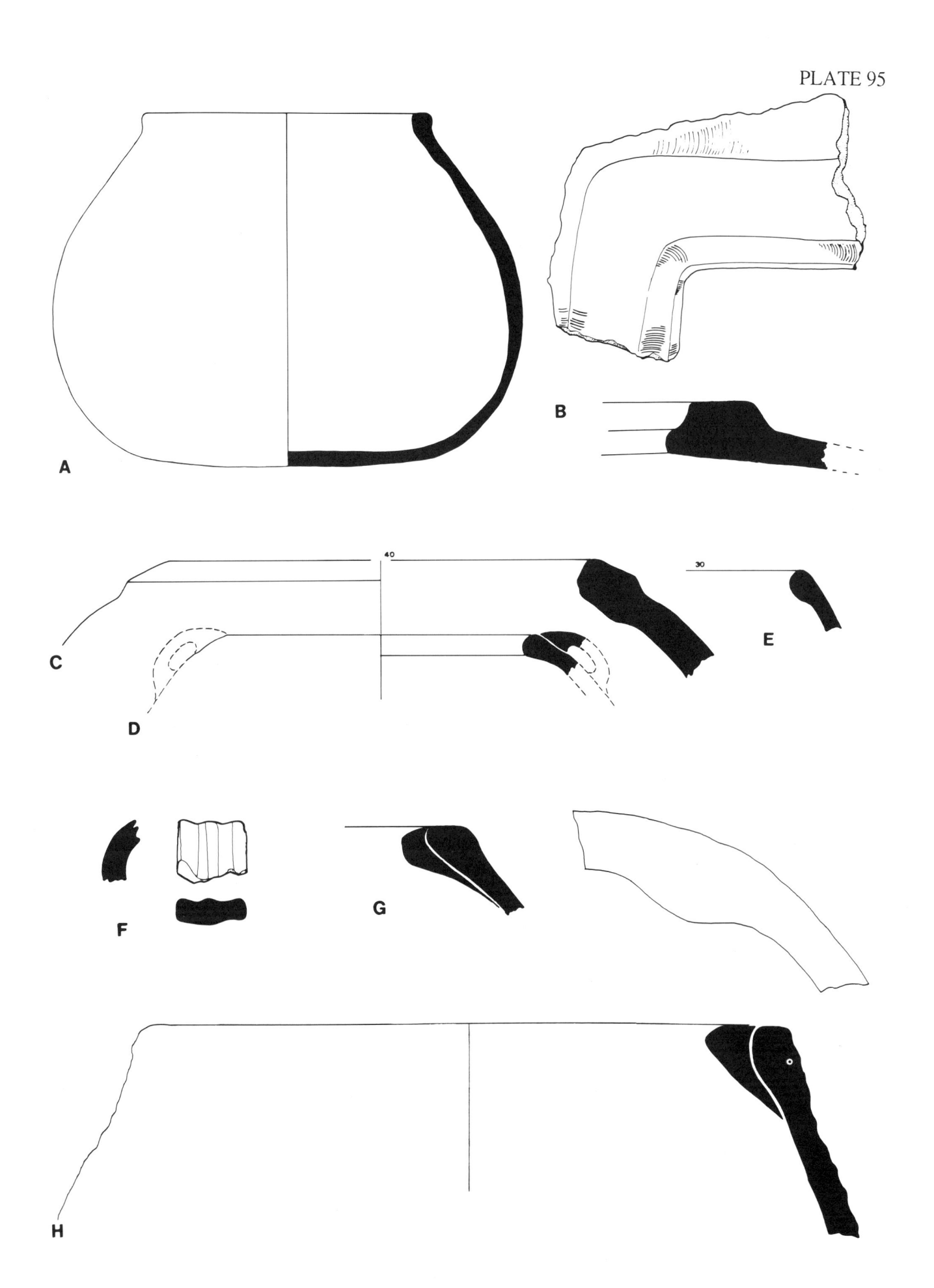

Period IV Pottery From Areas A, B, and C: Ware Group II Jars (*cont.*). Scales: (A) 1:5; (B–H) 2:5.

Plate 96. Period IV Pottery From Areas A, B, C, and C01: Ware Group II Handles, Lids, and Andiron. Scale 2:5.

|   | MRN | CONTEXT | FCN | WARE | FORM | TYPE | DECO. | WARE/REMARKS |
|---|---|---|---|---|---|---|---|---|
| A | 0656 | B02-03-015 | 187 | 09 | 146 | Unass. Handle | — | Brownish clay; gritty with large-sized grits; exterior mottled brown; rough. |
| B | — | A05-04-012 | 025 | 09 | 145 | Unass. Handle | — | Rather porous black clay grading to orange towards exterior surface; medium-sized white grits visible. |
| C | 0280 | B02-02-006 | 131 | 09 | 157 + 580 | Andiron | — | Reddish clay; large-sized white grits; exterior grayish, mottled, and not smoothed. |
| D | 1983 | C01-09-024 | 578 | 09 | 360 | Lid 1a | Bns. | Grayish clay; white grits visible; exterior gray; burnished. |
| E | 1108 | C45-04-001 | 094 | 09 | 360 | Lid 1a | Bns. | Brown clay grading to black towards exterior; grit-tempered but some chaff added; exterior mottled gray, brown, and black; burnished. |
| F | 4227 | A08-05-017 | 182 | 09 | 156 | Lid 1a | Bns. | Fairly dense reddish clay; medium-sized white grits and quartz flakes visible; upper surface is reddish and not burnished; lower surface mottled brownish-gray and well burnished. |
| G | 4811 | C56-05-014 | — | 09 | 156b | Lid 1b | Bns. | Cooking Pot Ware; burnished. |
| H | 0823 | C45-0162-005 | 024 | 09 | 917 | Tray 2 | Bns. | Gray clay; gritty; exterior surface is gray; smoothed on interior; burnished on bottom of tray. |
| I | 7506 | A07-12-041 | D306 | 09 | 1362 | Unass. Ring Base | Bns. | Orange clay, gray core; large-sized white grits; surface is orange; burnished. |

PLATE 96

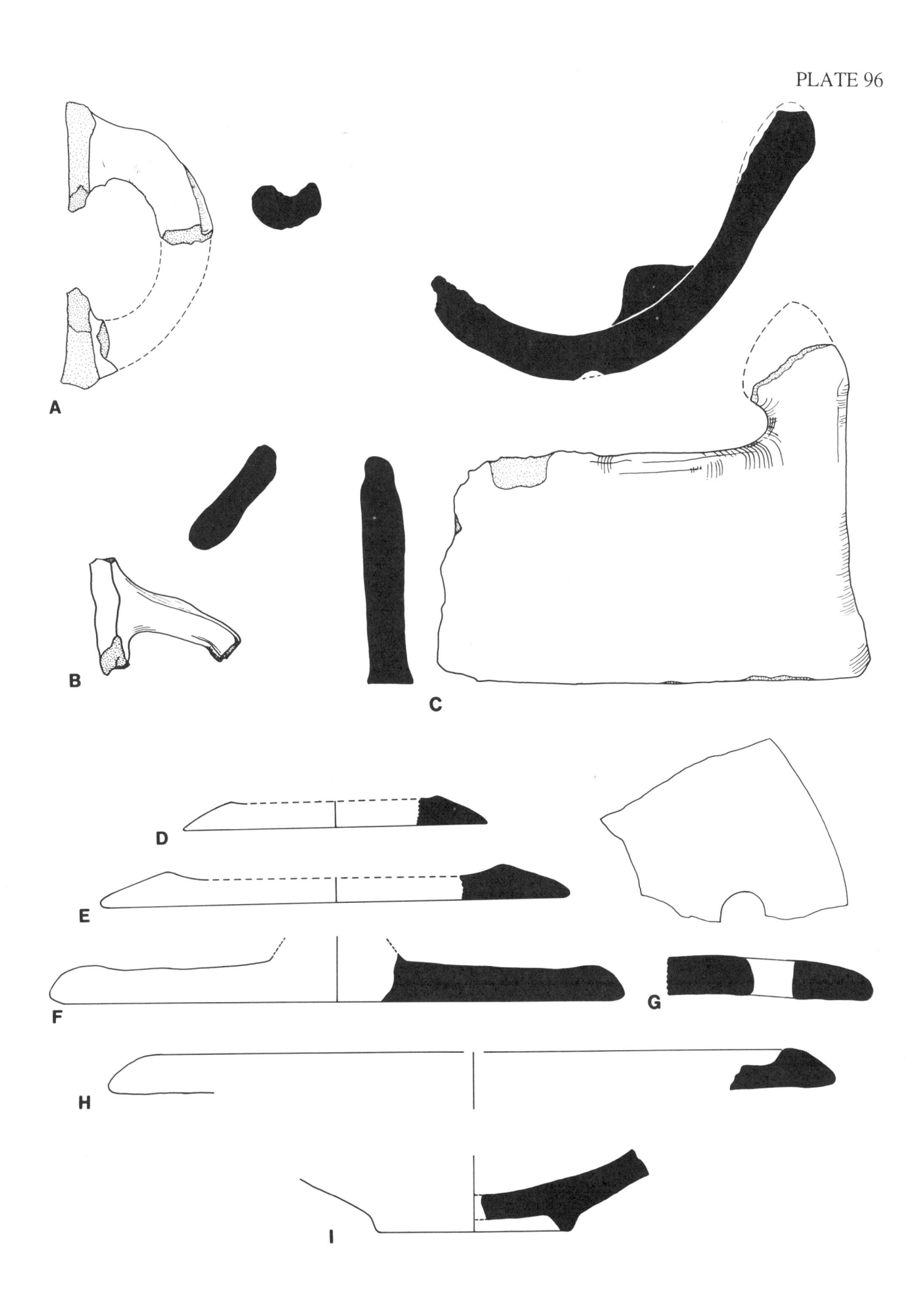

Period IV Pottery From Areas A, B, C, and C01: Ware Group II Handles, Lids, and Andiron. Scale 2:5.

Plate 97. Period III Pottery From Areas A, B, and D: Ware Group I Cups. Scale 2:5.

|   | MRN | CONTEXT | FCN | WARE | FORM | TYPE | DECO. | WARE/REMARKS |
|---|---|---|---|---|---|---|---|---|
| A | 14762 | D23-03-016 | 089 | 04 | C-54 | Bowl 1a | — | Buff clay; small-sized grits; (= KH 1983/147). |
| B | 14851 | D23-0275/85/95-004 | 128 | 04 | 11 | Bowl 1b | — | Fairly dense gray clay; small-sized grits, white ones prominent; fast wheel corrugations visible on exterior. |
| C | 1951 | D54-02-006 | 11 | 04 | 536 | Unass. Bowl | — | Reddish-buff clay; small-sized white grits. |
| D | 17152 | D76-0119/29-050 | 282 | 04 | 6a | Bowl 2 | — | Brownish-buff clay; small-sized grits. |
| E | 084 | A01-01-008 | 023 | 04 | 17 | Unass. Bowl | — | Buff clay; small-sized grits. |
| F | 1310 | A08-01-002 | 011 | 04 | 395 | Unass. Bowl | — | Buff clay; small-sized grits. |
| G | 7156 | D76-02-036 | 197 | 04 | 6b | Bowl 2 | 023 | Fairly dense reddish-buff clay; small-sized white grits; exterior and interior corrugated. |
| H | 14813 | D25-0343-011 | D177 | 04 | 6a | Bowl 2 | 023 | Reddish-buff clay; small-sized white grits; exterior and interior corrugated. |
| I | 12882 | A01-05-032 | 071 | 04 | 6a | Bowl 2 | 023 | Brownish-buff clay; small-sized grits; exterior corrugations. |
| J | 013 | B01-01-001 | 001 | 04 | 185 | Base 1 | — | Dense reddish-buff clay; small-sized white grits. |
| K | 0084 | A01-04-008 | 023 | 04 | 6a | Bowl 2 | 023 | Fairly dense clay, reddish towards exterior and brownish towards interior; small-sized white grits. |
| L | 17645 | D66-1075-097 | 897 | 04 | 185 | Base 1 | 023 | Fairly dense brownish-buff clay; no visible tempering other than scattered minute white grits. |
| M | 12882 | A01-05-032 | 071 | 04 | 6a | Bowl 2 | — | Greenish-buff clay; minute black grits. |
| N | 10259 | D37-0792-016 | — | 04 | 6a | Bowl 2 | 023 | Reddish-buff clay; small-sized white grits. |
| O | 12904 | A01-05-016 | 092 | 04 | 6b | Bowl 2 | — | Orange-buff clay; small-sized grits. |
| P | 7156 | D76-02-036 | 197 | 04 | 6a | Bowl 2 | — | Brownish-buff clay; small-sized white grits. |
| Q | 6614 | D76-02-032 | 177 | 04 | 6a | Bowl 2 | — | Dense grayish clay; small-sized grits. |
| R | 1159 | D66-04-032 | 165 | 04 | 6b | Bowl 2 | — | Reddish-buff clay; small-sized grits; corrugations on interior and exterior. |
| S | 5259 | D45-030-07 | 049 | 04 | 6b | Bowl 2 | — | Dense orange/brownish-buff clay; small-sized grits. |
| T | 17856 | D66-1095-096 | D876 | 04 | 1645 | Unass. Bowl | — | Fairly dense buff clay; small-sized grits. |
| U | 7156 | D76-02-036 | 197 | 04 | 1124 | Unass. Bowl | — | Buff/brownish-buff clay; small-sized grits, some white. |
| V | 15643 | D66-0989-087 | D568 | 04 | 1601 | Unass. Bowl | — | Dense brownish-buff clay; minute grits, some white; buff slip over both surfaces. |
| W | 4521 | D44-03-012 | 099 | 04 | 1247 | Bowl 3 | — | Reddish clay; small-sized white grits. |
| X | 12882 | A01-05-032 | 071 | 04 | 1247 | Bowl 3 | — | Orange-buff/brownish-buff clay; small-sized grits; traces of perforation near base. |

PLATE 97

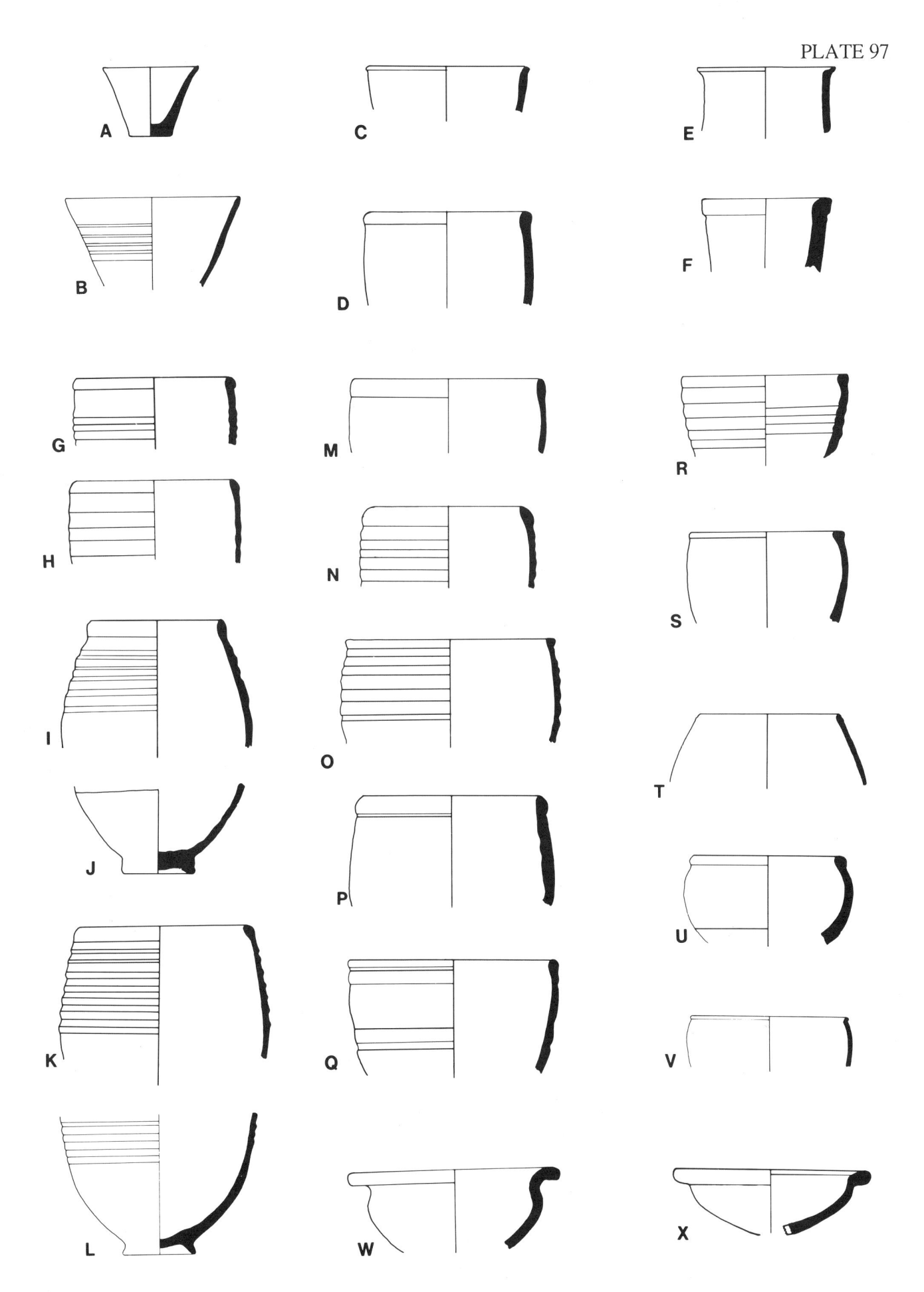

Period III Pottery From Areas A, B, and D: Ware Group I Cups. Scale 2:5.

Plate 98. Period III Pottery From Areas A, D, and F: Ware Group I Bowls. Scale 2:5.

|   | MRN | CONTEXT | FCN | WARE | FORM | TYPE | DECO. | WARE/REMARKS |
|---|---|---|---|---|---|---|---|---|
| A | 12892 | A01-05-016 | 081 | 04 | 50 | Bowl 4 | — | Brownish-buff clay; small-sized white grits; brownish-buff slip on exterior. |
| B | 488 | A07-03-002 | 006 | 04 | 50 | Bowl 4 | — | Reddish-buff clay; small-sized grits, white ones predominant; out of context in slope wash. |
| C | 15346 | D66-0826/36-083 | D474 | 04 | 50a | Bowl 4 | — | Dense grayish-buff clay grading to brownish-buff on exterior; small-sized grits. |
| D | 1156 | D66-04-031 | 161 | 04 | 400 | Bowl 4 | — | Brownish-buff clay; small-sized grits. |
| E | 826 | D66-04-014 | 079 | 04 | 247 | Bowl 4 | — | Brownish-buff clay; small-sized grits. |
| F | 480 | F01-04-002 | 024 | 04 | 247 | Bowl 4 | — | Buff clay; small-sized grits; out of context in slope wash. |
| G | 7156 | D76-02-036 | 197 | 04 | 456 | Bowl 4 | — | Dense reddish-buff clay; small-sized grits, white predominant. |
| H | 936 | A07-04-005 | 018 | 04 | 456 | Bowl 4 | — | Reddish-buff clay; small-sized grits. |
| I | 12877 | A01-05-015 | 066 | — | 456 | Bowl 4 | 456 | Fairly dense grayish clay; small-sized gray and white grits. |
| J | 1635 | D66-06-041 | 205 | 04 | 50 | Bowl 4 | — | Buff clay; small-sized grits. |
| K | 17642 | D66-1076-097 | 893 | 04 | C-73 | Bowl 4 | — | Reddish-buff clay; small-sized grits, white ones predominant; lighter reddish-buff slip on surface. |
| L | — | Area D Provenance lost | — | 04 | 49a | Bowl 5a | — | Brownish-buff clay; small-sized grits, some white. |
| M | 7274 | D44-0846-024 | 210 | 04 | C-31 | Bowl 5a | — | Buff clay; small-sized grits; (= KH 1982/120). |
| N | 10924 | D35-0945/49-033 | D676 | 04 | 49 | Bowl 5b | — | Buff clay; small-sized grits. |
| O | 15989 | D66-09-087 | 588 | 04 | 49 | Bowl 5b | — | Buff clay; small-sized grits. |
| P | 15715 | D23-0183-026 | 275 | 04 | C-64 | Bowl 5b | — | Greenish-buff clay, somewhat warped from overfiring; small-sized black and white grits; (= KH 1983/171). |

PLATE 98

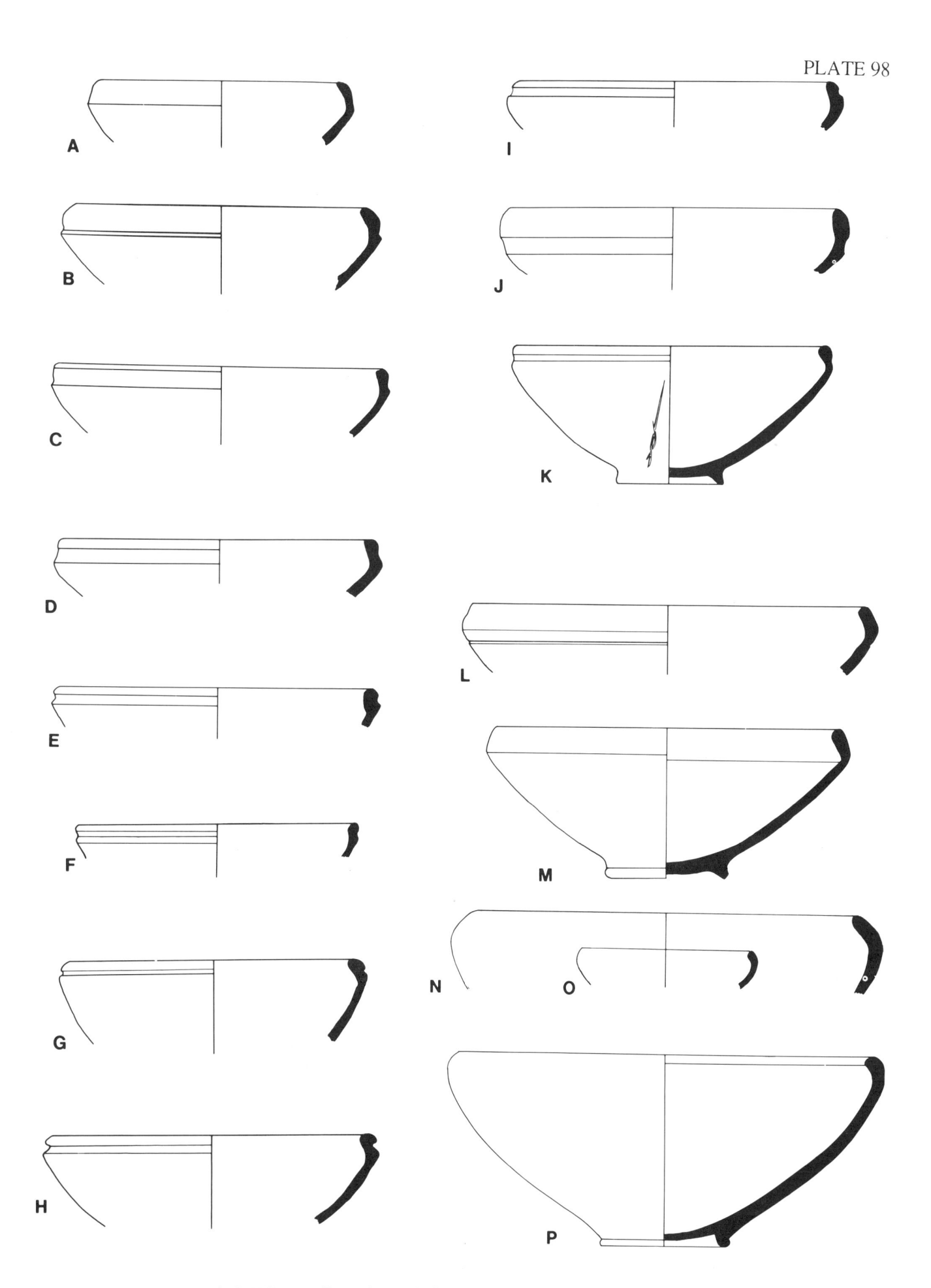

Period III Pottery From Areas A, D, and F: Ware Group I Bowls. Scale 2:5.

Plate 99. Period III Pottery From Areas A, B, and D: Ware Group I Bowls (*cont.*). Scale 2:5.

|   | MRN | CONTEXT | FCN | WARE | FORM | TYPE | DECO. | WARE/REMARKS |
|---|---|---|---|---|---|---|---|---|
| A | 9111 | D45-0413-015 | 137 | 04 | 1650 | Bowl 6 | — | Fairly porous light grayish clay; small-sized grits. |
| B | 15850 | D23-03-014 | D277 | 04 | 1609 | Bowl 6 | — | Greenish-buff clay; small-sized grits, black and white visible. |
| C | 2586 | D76-02-001 | 005 | 04 | 622 | Bowl 6 | — | Dense orange-buff clay; small-sized white grits; buff slip on exterior. |
| D | 065 | A01-04-006 | 019 | 04 | 28 | Bowl 7 | — | Brownish-buff clay; small-sized grits. |
| E | 12877 | A01-05-015 | 066 | 04 | 1191 | Bowl 7 | — | Dense brownish-buff clay; small-sized grits, some white. |
| F | 12892 | A01-05-016 | 081 | 04 | 1520 | Bowl 7 | — | Reddish-buff clay; small-sized grits; pinkish slip on surface. |
| G | 19210 | B62-03-002 | 071 | 04 | 1191 | Bowl 7 | — | Dense brownish-buff clay; small- and medium-sized scattered white grits. |
| H | 2485 | D44-03-012 | 029 | 04 | 1191 | Bowl 7 | — | Fairly dense grayish clay; small-sized grits, some white. |
| I | 5202 | D54-07-001 | 101 | 04 | C-19 | Bowl 8a | — | Buff clay; small-sized black grits; (= KH 1981/80). |
| J | 3321 | D53-0129-002 | 011 | 04 | C-19 | Bowl 8a | — | Buff clay; small-sized grits; (= KH 1981/40). |
| K | 12895 | A01-05-016 | 084 | 04 | 1518 | Bowl 8b | — | Brownish-buff clay; small-sized white grits; light buff slip on exterior. |
| L | 15657 | D25-0353-011 | 287 | 04 | 1171 | Bowl 8b | — | Buff clay; small-sized grits. |
| M | 5269 | D45-03-007 | 049 | 04 | 1171 | Bowl 8b | — | Greenish-buff clay; fairly porous; small-sized grits; traces of chaff. |
| N | 492 | D66-02-007 | 030 | 04 | 39 | Bowl 8c | — | Brownish clay; small-sized white grits. |
| O | 8659 | D35-0394-010 | 235 | 04 | 291 | Bowl 8c | — | Buff clay; small-sized grits. |
| P | 002 | B01-02-001 | 005 | 04 | 40 | Bowl 8c | — | Dense brownish clay grading to reddish-buff towards surfaces. |
| Q | 541 | D66-03-002 | 049 | 04 | 039 | Bowl 8c | — | Dense brownish-buff clay; small-sized grits. |
| R | 6567 | Area D Provenance lost | — | 04 | 291 | Bowl 8c | — | Fairly dense orange-buff clay; small-sized grits; buff slip on exterior. |
| S | 6614 | D76-02-032 | 177 | 04 | 1111 | Bowl 8d | — | Greenish-buff clay; small-sized grits, some white. |
| T | 6365 | D76-02-028 | 164 | 04 | 52 | Bowl 8d | — | Fairly dense buff clay; small-sized grits, some white; buff slip on exterior. |
| U | 7156 | D76-02-036 | 197 | 04 | 1195 | Bowl 8d | — | Buff clay; small-sized grits. |
| V | — | Area D Provenance lost | — | 04 | 291 | Bowl 8c | — | Reddish-buff clay; small-sized grits, some white; buff slip on exterior. |

PLATE 99

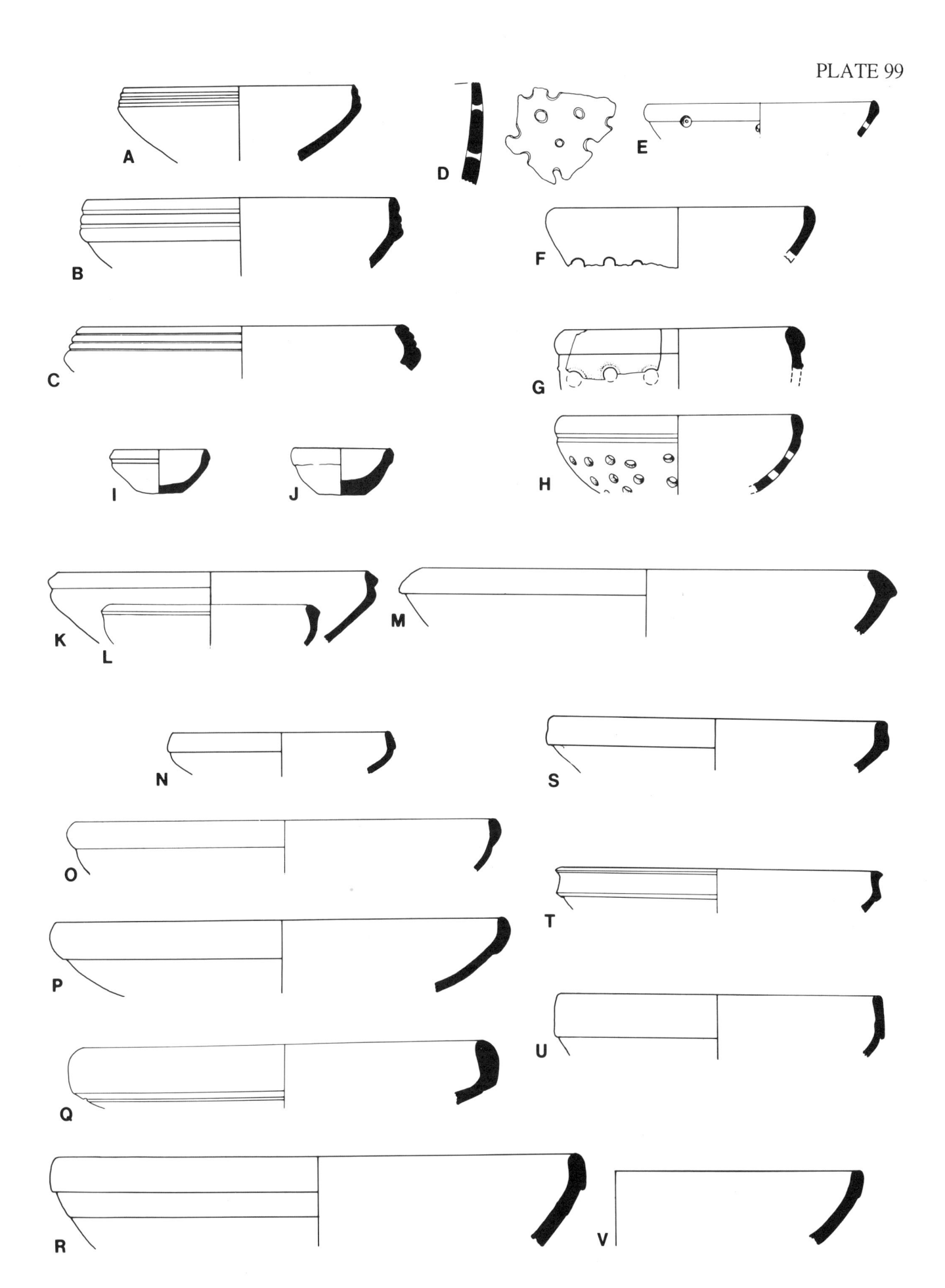

Period III Pottery From Areas A, B, and D: Ware Group I Bowls (*cont.*). Scale 2:5.

Plate 100. Period III Pottery From Areas A and D: Ware Group I Bowls (*cont.*). Scale 2:5.

|   | MRN | CONTEXT | FCN | WARE | FORM | TYPE | DECO. | WARE/REMARKS |
|---|-----|---------|-----|------|------|------|-------|--------------|
| A | 3392 | D53-01-002 | 013 | 04 | 42 | Bowl 9a | — | Fairly dense orange-buff clay; small-sized white grits. |
| B | 065 | A01-04-006 | 019 | 04 | 29 | Bowl 9a | — | Reddish-buff clay; small- and medium-sized grits. |
| C | 12882 | A01-05-032 | 071 | 04 | 44 | Bowl 9b | — | Buff clay; small-sized black and white grits. |
| D | 12933 | A01-05-018 | 117 | 04 | 43 | Bowl 9b | — | Brownish-buff clay; small-sized grits; buff slip on exterior. |
| E | 086 | A02-03-002 | 006 | 04 | 45 | Bowl 9b | — | Fairly dense reddish-buff clay; small-sized grits, white ones prominent. |
| F | 12933 | A01-05-018 | 117 | 04 | 44 | Bowl 9b | — | Buff clay; small-sized grits. |
| G | 2001 | D44-02-007 | 014 | 04 | 398 | Bowl 9b | — | Light orange-buff clay; small-sized grits, some white. |
| H | 065 | A01-04-006 | 019 | 04 | 44 | Bowl 9b | — | Reddish-buff clay; small-sized grits. |
| I | 12877 | A01-05-015 | 066 | 04 | 398 | Bowl 9b | — | Dense gray clay grading to orange towards surface; exterior covered with buff slip. |
| J | 1517 | A08-01-003 | 021 | 04 | 398 | Bowl 9b | Bns. | Fairly dense grayish clay; small-sized grits, white ones prominent; gray slip on exterior; lightly burnished with irregular horizontal strokes; out of context in slope wash. |
| K | 15710 | D23-0193-026 | 278 | 04 | C-86 | Bowl 9b | — | Fairly dense brownish-buff clay; small-sized white grits; buff slip on exterior. |
| L | 1378 | A08-01-002 | 011 | 04 | 398 | Bowl 9b | — | Brownish-buff clay; small-sized grits; out of context in slope wash. |
| M | 15673 | D26-0250/60-006 | 030 | 04 | 398 | Bowl 9b | — | Brownish-buff clay; small-sized grits. |

PLATE 100

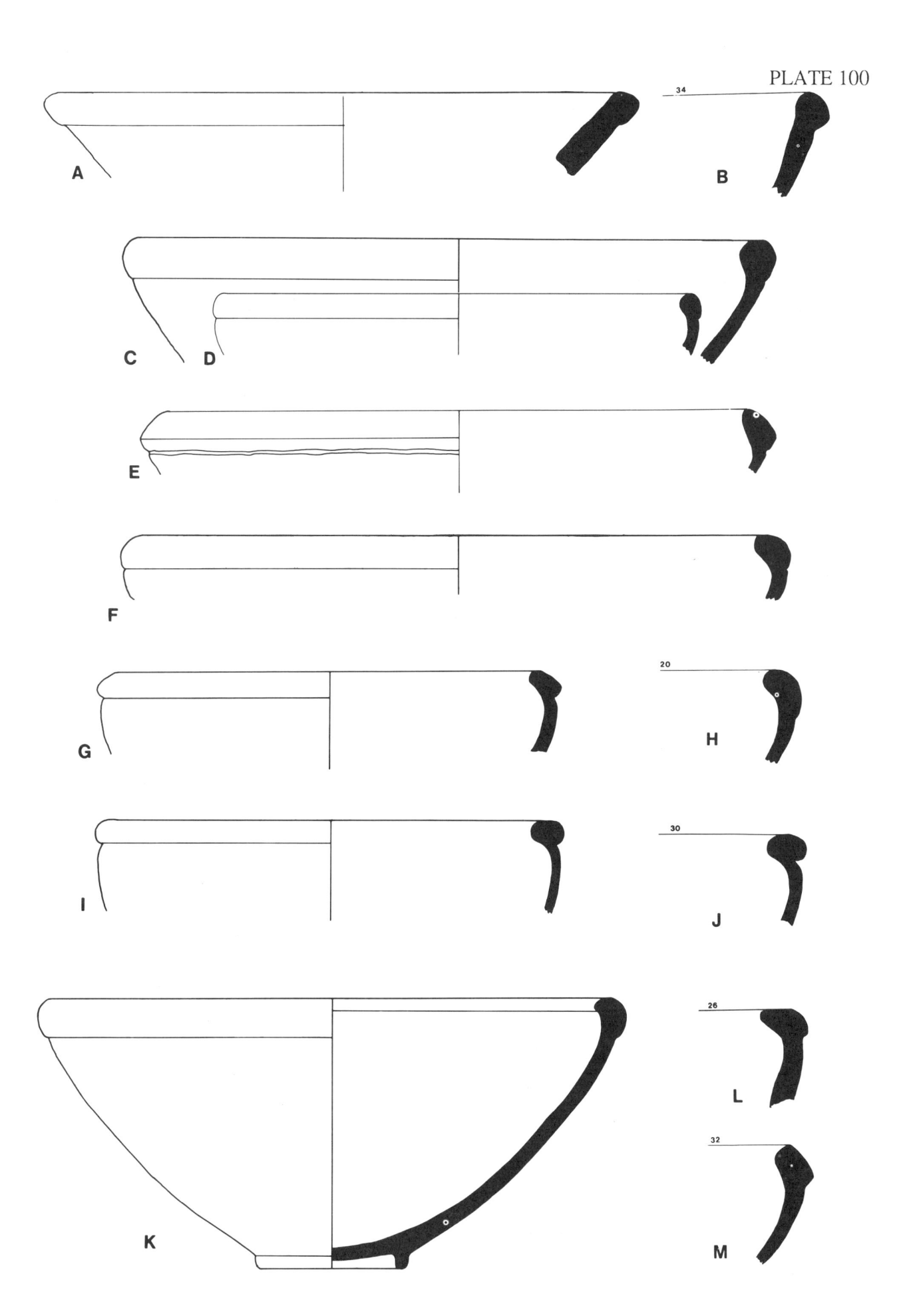

Period III Pottery From Areas A and D: Ware Group I Bowls (*cont.*). Scale 2:5.

Plate 101. Period III Pottery From Areas A and D: Ware Group I Bowls (*cont.*). Scale 2:5.

|   | MRN | CONTEXT | FCN | WARE | FORM | TYPE | DECO. | WARE/REMARKS |
|---|---|---|---|---|---|---|---|---|
| A | 15184 | D56-05-019 | D170 | 04 | 1652 | Bowl 9d | — | Dense grayish clay; small-sized gray grits; buff slip on exterior; lug attached to rim. |
| B | 4802 | D55-01-004 | 057 | 04 | 1193 | Bowl 9d | — | Fairly dense reddish-buff clay; small-sized grits, white predominant; fragmentary remains of strap handle attached to body and rim. |
| C | 14215 | D43-07-020 | D136 | 04 | 398a | Bowl 9d | — | Fairly dense brownish-buff clay; small-sized grits, white ones prominent; fragmentary loop handle attached to body. |
| D | 2582 | D66-06-001 | 265 | 04 | 618 | Bowl 9c | — | Greenish-buff clay; small-sized grits; slightly warped from firing; greenish-buff slip on exterior. |
| E | 487 | A07-02-002 | 003 | 04 | 618 | Bowl 9c | — | Dense gray clay; no visible tempering other than a few scattered white grits; buff slip on exterior. |
| F | 14856 | D23-0352/53-020 | D133 | 04 | 398 | Bowl 9b | — | Brownish-buff clay; small-sized grits. |
| G | 3185 | D76-04-020 | 042 | 04 | 723 | Bowl 9e | — | Dense brownish-buff clay grading to reddish on exterior; small-sized grits. |
| H | 15295 | D25-0557-011 | D279 | 04 | 723 | Bowl 9e | — | Buff clay; small-sized grits. |
| I | 5808 | D34-02-003 | 013 | 04 | 1238 | Bowl 10 | — | Orange-buff clay; small-sized grits; incisions on exterior. |
| J | 616 | D66-02-005 | 060 | 04 | 030 | Bowl 10 | — | Greenish-buff clay, slightly overfired; small-sized grits. |

PLATE 101

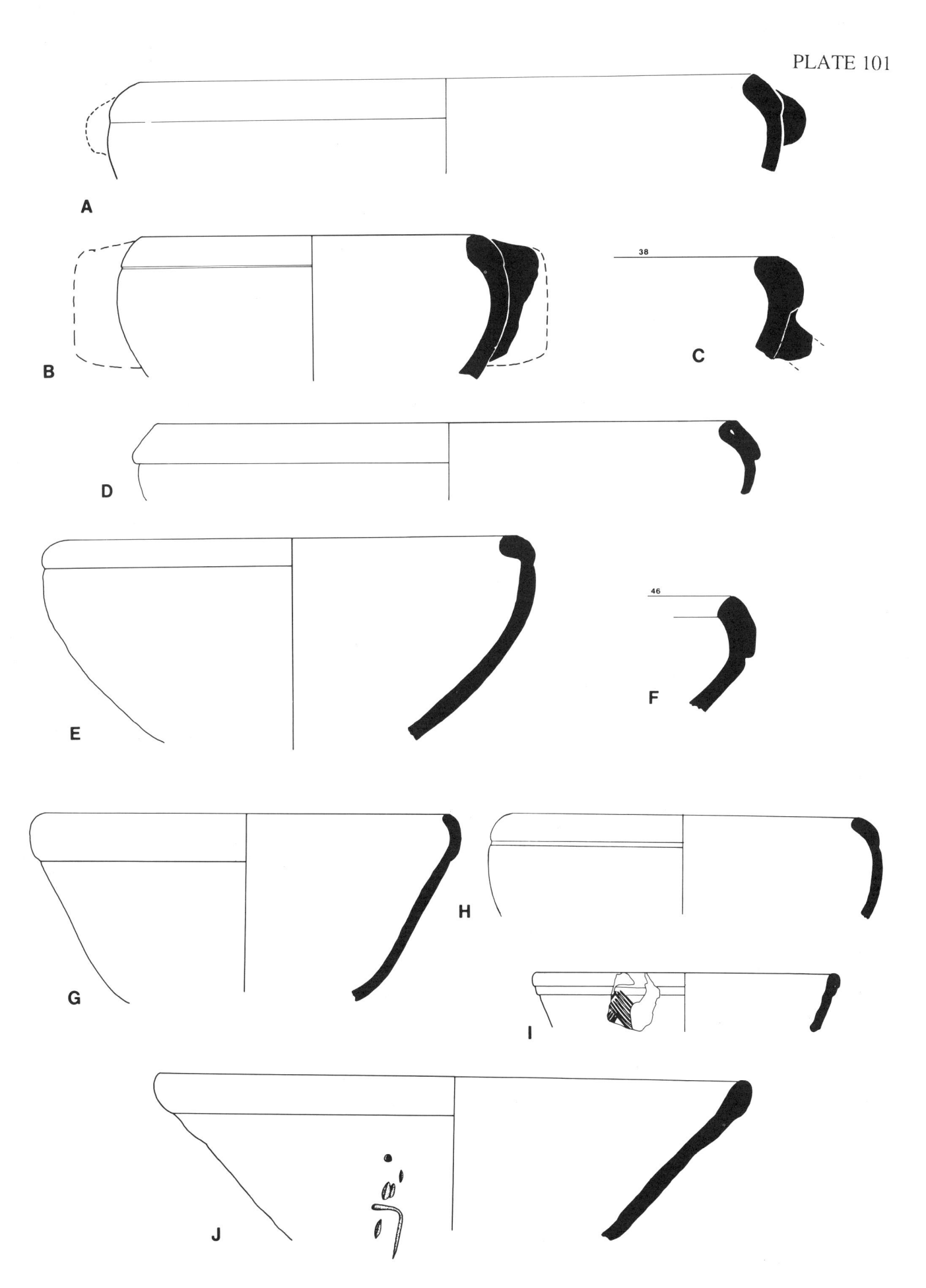

Period III Pottery From Areas A and D: Ware Group I Bowls (*cont.*). Scale 2:5.

Plate 102. Period III Pottery From Areas A, B, D, and E: Ware Group I Bowls (*cont.*). Scale 2:5.

|   | MRN | CONTEXT | FCN | WARE | FORM | TYPE | DECO. | WARE/REMARKS |
|---|---|---|---|---|---|---|---|---|
| A | 4804 | E54-01-002 | 004 | 04 | 905 | Unass. Bowl | — | Orange-buff clay; small-sized grits. |
| B | 3393 | D54-05-014 | 053 | 04 | 1186 | Unass. Bowl | — | Fairly dense reddish-buff clay; small-sized white grits. |
| C | 257 | B02-04-002 | 003 | 04 | 054 | Bowl 11 | — | Buff clay; small-sized grits; buff slip on exterior. |
| D | 3389 | D24-01-002 | 020 | 04 | 734 | Bowl 11 | — | Brownish-buff clay; small-sized grits, white ones predominant. |
| E | 16522 | D36-0331-006 | 423 | 04 | 822 | Bowl 11 | — | Rather porous brownish-buff clay; small-sized grits, white predominant; lighter brownish-buff slip on exterior. |
| F | 3912 | D44-01-010 | 072 | 04 | 822 | Bowl 11 | — | Brownish-buff clay; small-sized white grits; lighter brownish-buff slip on exterior. |
| G | 14850 | D23-0362/63-020 | 127 | 04 | 46 | Bowl 12 | — | Rather porous grayish clay; small-sized grits, white prominent; brownish-buff slip on exterior. |
| H | 370 | B01-03-002 | 163 | 04 | 46 | Bowl 12 | — | Buff clay; small-sized grits. |
| I | 3940 | D65-05-002 | 113 | 04 | 818 | Unass. Bowl | — | Reddish-buff clay; small-sized grits; brownish-buff slip on exterior. |
| J | 5345 | D45-0190-008 | 052 | 04 | 915 | Unass. Bowl | — | Brownish-buff clay; small-sized grits. |
| K | 13924 | A01-05-016 | 108 | 04 | 1517 | Unass. Bowl | — | Fairly dense gray clay grading to brownish-buff on exterior; small-sized white grits. |
| L | 6368 | D76-02-030 | 166 | 04 | 1199 | Bowl 13 | — | Fairly dense reddish-buff clay; small-sized grits. |
| M | 2487 | D55-02-006 | 026 | 04 | 38 | Bowl 13 | — | Brownish-buff clay; small-sized grits. |
| N | 2712 | D55-04-018 | 097 | 04 | 38 | Bowl 13 | — | Orange clay; small-sized grits. |

PLATE 102

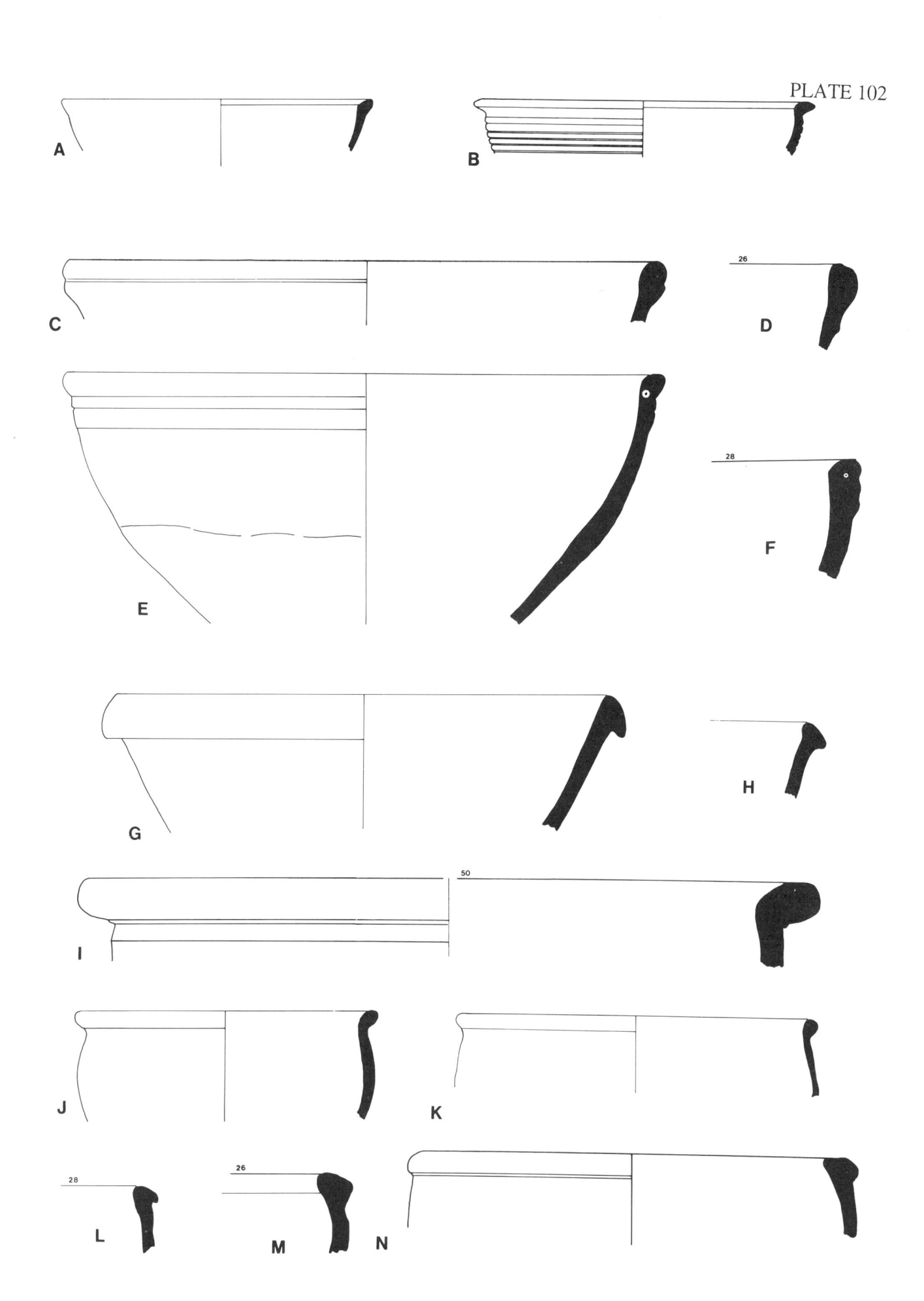

Period III Pottery From Areas A, B, D, and E: Ware Group I Bowls (*cont.*). Scale 2:5.

Plate 103. Period III Pottery From Areas A and D: Ware Group I Bowls (*cont.*). Scale 2:5.

|   | *MRN* | *Context* | *FCN* | *Ware* | *Form* | *Type* | *Deco.* | *Ware/Remarks* |
|---|---|---|---|---|---|---|---|---|
| A | 5289 | D54-05-021 | 126 | 04 | 1156 | Bowl 14 | — | Orange-buff clay; small-sized black and white grits. |
| B | 2493 | D76-01-001 | 001 | 04 | 1169 | Bowl 14 | — | Brownish-buff clay; small-sized grits, white ones prominent; buff slip on both surfaces. |
| C | 5016 | D54-03-007 | 044 | 04 | 1169 | Bowl 14 | — | Light brownish-buff clay; small-sized grits, white ones prominent. |
| D | 12917 | A01-0522/23-016 | 105 | 04 | 1169 | Bowl 14 | — | Brownish-buff clay; small-sized white grits; buff slip on exterior. |
| E | 7888 | D44-05-017 | 208 | 04 | 1299 | Bowl 14 | — | Dense orange-buff clay; small-sized white grits. |
| F | 501 | D66-03-001 | 033 | 04 | 33 | Bowl 14 | — | Reddish-buff clay; small- and medium-sized grits, white ones prominent; buff slip on exterior. |
| G | 4521 | D44-03-012 | 099 | 04 | 33 | Bowl 14 | — | Greenish-buff clay; small- and medium-sized grits. |
| H | 1451 | D46-01-002 | 012 | 04 | 465 | Unass. Bowl | — | Brownish-buff clay; small- and medium-sized grits; irregular impressions on exterior. |
| I | 12942 | A01-05-021 | 124 | 04 | 33 | Bowl 14 | — | Reddish-buff clay; small- and medium-sized grits. |
| J | 2657 | D66-06-042 | 268 | 04 | 671 | Bowl 15 | Bns. | Orange-buff clay; small-sized grits; buff slip on exterior and interior; exterior burnished with irregular horizontal strokes; interior burnished in a carelessly drawn pattern. |

PLATE 103

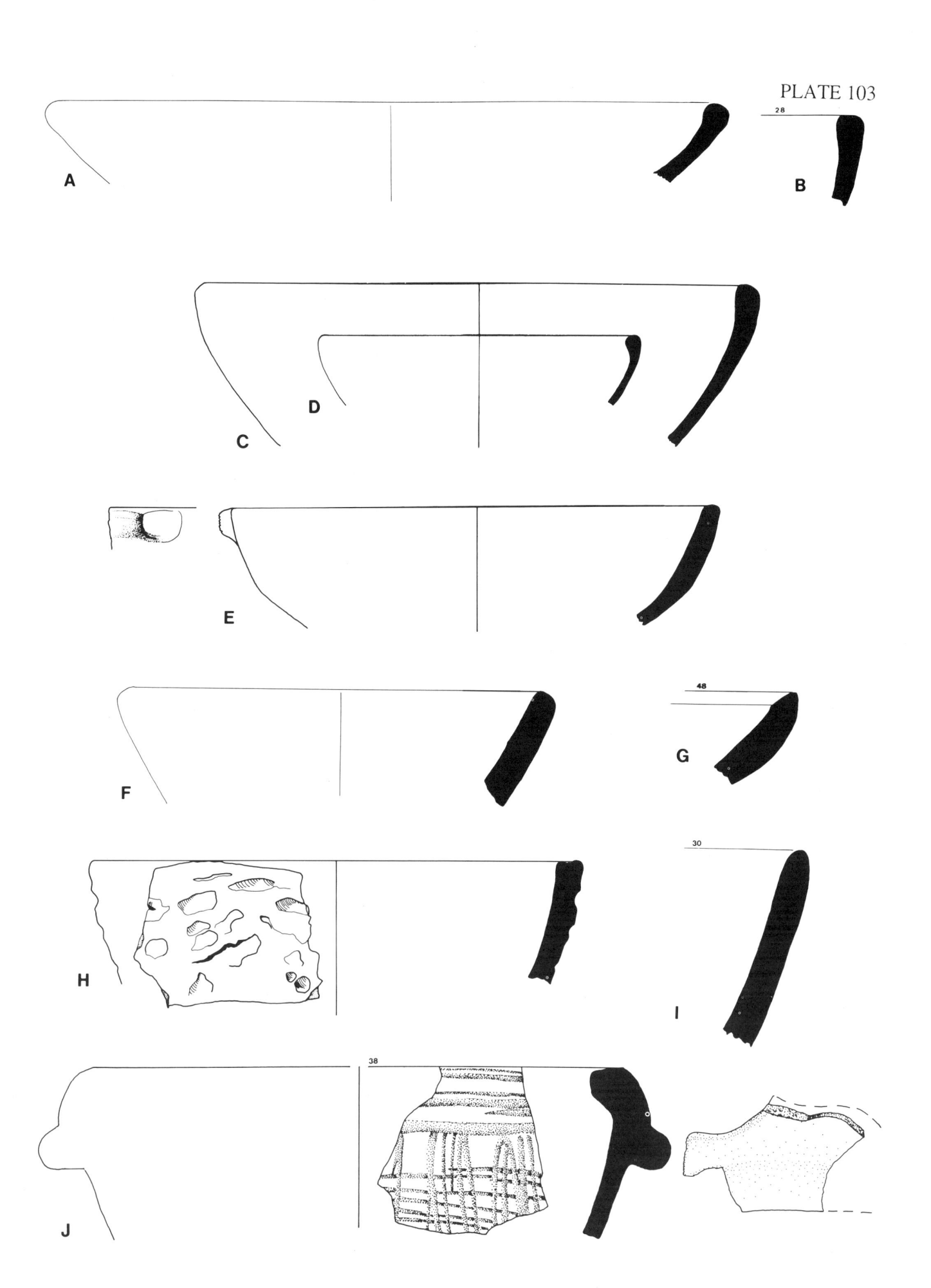

Period III Pottery From Areas A and D: Ware Group I Bowls (*cont.*). Scale 2:5.

Plate 104. Period III Pottery From Areas A and D: Ware Group I Jars. Scale 2:5.

|   | MRN | CONTEXT | FCN | WARE | FORM | TYPE | DECO. | WARE/REMARKS |
|---|---|---|---|---|---|---|---|---|
| A | 12882 | A01-05-032 | 071 | 04 | 1510 | Jar 1 | — | Brownish-buff clay; small-sized white grits; fast wheel striations visible on interior. |
| B | 17454 | D66-1361-102 | D839 | 04 | 1643 | Jar 1 | — | Light brownish-buff clay; small-sized grits, white ones prominent. |
| C | 10779 | D34-0543-015 | 416 | 04 | 1645 | Unass. Jar | — | Rather porous greenish-buff clay; small-sized grits, gray and white ones visible. |
| D | 6571 | D76-02-032 | 173 | 04 | 1115 | Unass. Jar | — | Reddish-buff clay; small-sized white grits; buff slip on exterior. |
| E | 3914 | A07-00-000 | 203 | 04 | C-18 | Jar 2a | — | Light brownish-buff clay; small-sized grits; out of context in slope wash; (= KH 1981/66). |
| F | 5204 | D55-0121-004 | 065 | 04 | C-18 | Jar 2a | — | Grayish-buff clay; small-sized white grits; (= KH 1981/83). |
| G | 5203 | D44-0516-017 | 128 | 04 | C-18a | Jar 2a | — | Brownish-buff clay; small-sized white grits; buff slip on exterior; (= KH 1981/81). |
| H | 15073 | D25-0191-003 | 190 | 04 | C-18 | Jar 2a | — | Fairly dense reddish-buff clay grading to brownish-buff towards surfaces; small-sized black grits. |
| I | 3947 | D34-01-002 | 030 | 04 | 1164 | Jar 2a | — | Orange-buff clay; small-sized white grits. |
| J | 2487 | D55-02-006 | 026 | 04 | 606 | Jar 2b | — | Orange-buff clay; small-sized white grits. |
| K | 2721 | D44-03-012 | 037 | 04 | 811 | Jar 2b | — | Orange-buff clay; small-sized black grits. |
| L | 17854 | D66-1094-096 | D874 | 04 | 811 | Jar 2b | — | Buff clay; small-sized grits. |
| M | 3941 | D34-01-007 | 047 | 04 | 811 | Jar 2b | — | Brownish-buff clay; small-sized white grits. |
| N | 2663 | D34-01-003 | 015 | 04 | 101 | Jar 2b | — | Brownish-buff clay; small-sized grits. |
| O | 5164 | D25-0184-003 | 199 | 04 | C-82 | Jar 2c | — | Dense gray clay, reddish core; small-sized grits and occasional larger-sized white inclusions; exterior is gray, interior is red. |
| P | 5345 | D45-0190-008 | 052 | 04 | 916 | Jar 2c | — | Greenish-buff clay; small-sized grits. |
| Q | 540 | D66-03-042 | 042 | 04 | 492 | Jar 3 | — | Buff clay; grit-tempered with small-sized grits. |
| R | 14364 | D55-05-042 | D436 | 04 | 492 | Jar 3 | — | Reddish-buff clay; small-sized white grits; light brownish-buff slip on exterior. |

PLATE 104

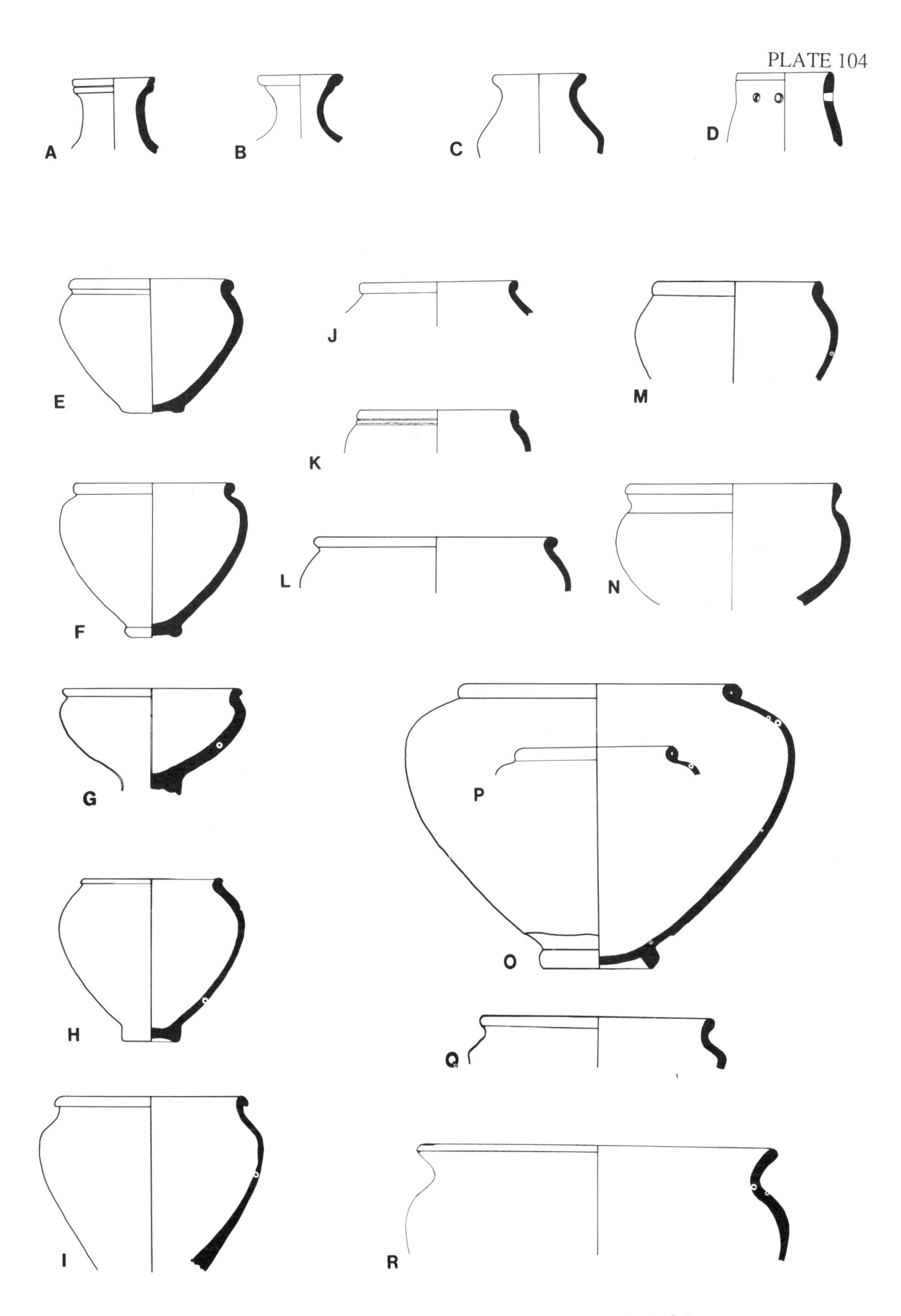

Period III Pottery From Areas A and D: Ware Group I Jars. Scale 2:5.

Plate 105. Period III Pottery From Areas A and D: Ware Group I Jars (*cont.*). Scale 2:5.

|   | *MRN* | *Context* | *FCN* | *Ware* | *Form* | *Type* | *Deco.* | *Ware/Remarks* |
|---|---|---|---|---|---|---|---|---|
| A | 7920 | D75-01-010 | 091 | 04 | 1301 | Jar 4a | 307 | Brownish-buff clay; small-sized white grits. |
| B | 083 | A02-03-003 | 008 | 04 | 1301 | Jar 4a | 023 | Reddish-clay; small-sized grits. |
| C | 001 | A01-02-002 | 003 | 04 | 18 | Jar 4a | 023 | Fairly dense reddish-buff clay; small-sized grits, some white; greenish-buff slip on exterior. |
| D | 10070 | D35-0513-018 | D316 | 04 | 1159 | Jar 4b | 023 | Brownish-buff clay; small-sized grits. |
| E | 6273 | D44-0394-030 | 172 | 04 | 1159 | Jar 4b | 307 | Somewhat porous brownish-buff clay; small-sized black grits; buff slip on exterior. |
| F | 7620 | D34-01-002 | 061 | 04 | 1226 | Jar 4b | — | Brownish-buff clay; small-sized white grits. |
| G | 6104 | D54-06-026 | 131 | 04 | 1224 | Jar 4b | — | Fairly dense brownish-buff clay; small-sized white grits. |
| H | 830 | D66-05-001 | 080 | 04 | 58b | Jar 5a | — | Dense brownish-buff clay; small-sized white grits. |
| I | 5807 | D34-01-002 | 010 | 04 | 58b | Jar 5a | — | Buff clay; small-sized grits. |
| J | 001 | A01-02-002 | 003 | 04 | 58a | Jar 5b | — | Buff clay; small-sized grits. |
| K | 12858 | A01-05-015 | 047 | 04 | 58a | Jar 5b | — | Brownish-buff clay; small-sized white grits. |
| L | 17538 | D38-0458-018 | 061 | 04 | C-67 | Jar 5b | — | Dark brownish-buff clay; small-sized grits, white ones prominent. |
| M | 084 | A01-01-008 | 023 | 04 | 58a | Jar 5b | — | Dense brownish-buff clay; small-sized white grits. |
| N | 5807 | D34-01-002 | 010 | 04 | 58a | Jar 5b | — | Grayish-buff clay; small-sized white grits. |
| O | 018 | A01-02-004 | 007 | 04 | 58a | Jar 5b | — | Dense reddish-buff clay; small-sized white grits; lighter reddish-pink slip on exterior. |
| P | 12751 | A01-05-023 | 138 | 04 | 58a | Jar 5b | — | Brownish-buff clay; small-sized grits. |

PLATE 105

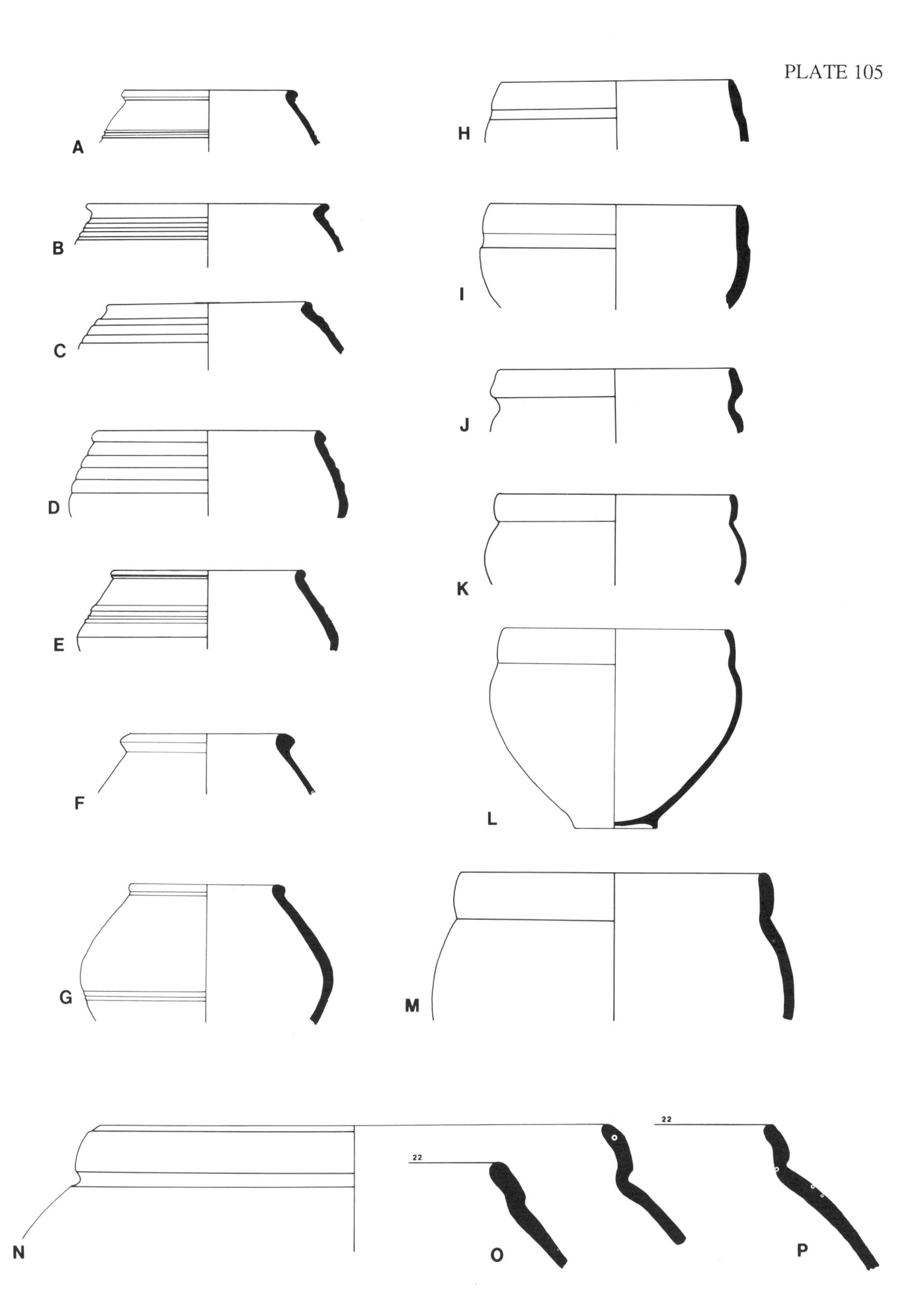

Period III Pottery From Areas A and D: Ware Group I Jars (*cont.*). Scale 2:5.

Plate 106. Period III Pottery From Areas A, B, and D: Ware Group I Jars (*cont.*). Scale 2:5.

|   | MRN | CONTEXT | FCN | WARE | FORM | TYPE | DECO. | WARE/REMARKS |
|---|---|---|---|---|---|---|---|---|
| A | 039 | B02-01-002 | 039 | 04 | 59 | Jar 5c | — | Dense brownish-buff clay; small-sized white grits. |
| B | 116 | B02-02-004 | 082 | 04 | 59 | Jar 5c | — | Dense brownish/reddish-buff clay; small-sized white grits; buff slip on exterior. |
| C | 4737 | D44-03-012 | 105 | 04 | 59 | Jar 5c | — | Dense gray clay; small-sized white grits; buff slip on exterior. |
| D | 12895 | A01-05-016 | 084 | 04 | 59 | Jar 5c | — | Dense gray clay grading to reddish-buff towards surfaces; small-sized grits, white prominent. |
| E | 069 | A02-02-002 | 003 | 04 | 109 | Jar 6 | — | Dense grayish clay; small-sized grits. |
| F | 3766 | D53-02-003 | 027 | 04 | 1209 | Jar 6 | — | Buff clay; small-sized grits. |
| G | 4936 | D44-05-017 | 122 | 04 | 1187 | Jar 6 | — | Grayish clay; small-sized grits. |
| H | 1968 | A09-01-001 | 001 | 04 | 0538 | Jar 6 | — | Grayish-brownish-buff clay; small-sized white grits; out of context in slope wash. |
| I | 936 | A07-04-005 | 018 | 04 | 455 | Jar 7 | — | Brownish-buff clay; small-sized grits, some white; greenish-buff slip on surface. |
| J | 15899 | D23-01/02-020 | 261 | 04 | 277 | Jar 7 | — | Very dense clay, gray towards interior and reddish towards exterior; small-sized white grits. |
| K | 15899 | D23-01/02-020 | 261 | 04 | 076 | Jar 7 | — | Dense clay ranging from brown in interior and reddish towards exterior; pinkish slip on exterior. |
| L | 15899 | D23-01/02-020 | 261 | 04 | 076 | Jar 7 | — | Dense brownish-buff clay grading to reddish on exterior; small-sized black grits; light brownish-buff slip on exterior. |
| M | — | B03-06-001 | 010 | 04 | 076 | Jar 7 | — | Brownish-buff clay; small-sized grits, some white; greenish slip on exterior. |

PLATE 106

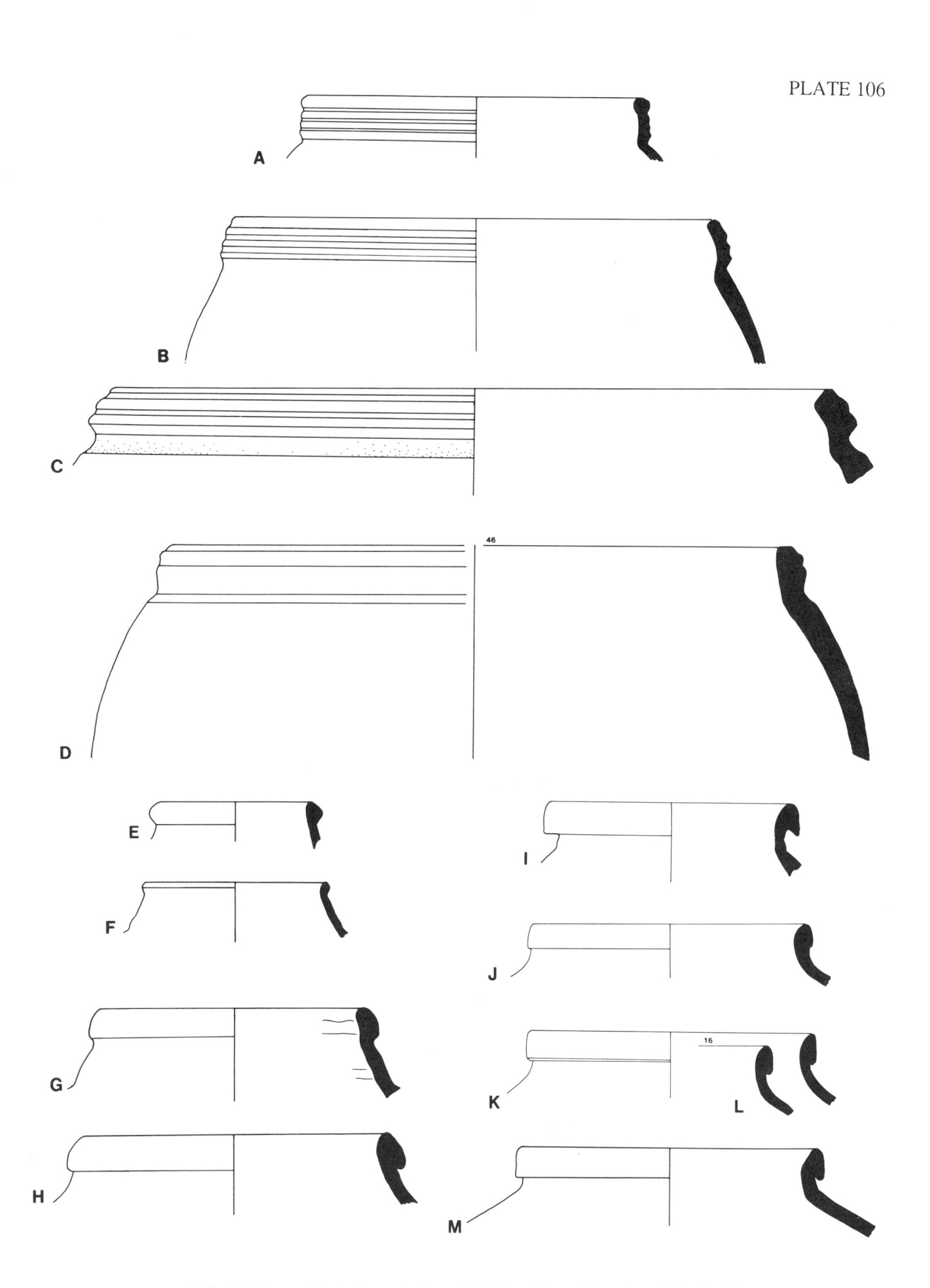

Period III Pottery From Areas A, B, and D: Ware Group I Jars (*cont.*). Scale 2:5.

Plate 107. Period III Pottery From Areas A, B, D, and F: Ware Group I Jars (*cont.*). Scale 2:5.

|   | MRN | CONTEXT | FCN | WARE | FORM | TYPE | DECO. | WARE/REMARKS |
|---|-----|---------|-----|------|------|------|-------|--------------|
| A | 14910 | D36-0567-012 | D288 | 04 | 81 | Jar 8 | — | Light brownish-buff clay; small-sized grits, some white; light greenish-buff clay on exterior. |
| B | 12756 | A01-0531/32-024 | 141 | 04 | 81 | Jar 8 | — | Dense brownish-buff clay grading to orange on surface; small-sized white grits; pinkish slip on exterior. |
| C | 12933 | A01-05-018 | 117 | 04 | 1513 | Jar 8 | — | Brownish-buff clay; small-sized white grits; buff slip on both surfaces. |
| D | 480 | F01-04-002 | 024 | 04 | 81 | Jar 8 | — | Fairly dense brownish-buff clay; small-sized white grits; out of context in slope wash. |
| E | 3110 | D76-04-002 | 035 | 04 | 81 | Jar 8 | — | Dense grayish-buff clay; small-sized grits, some white; buff slip on exterior. |
| F | 011 | A01-03-003 | 010 | 04 | 81 | Jar 8 | — | Brownish-buff clay; small-sized grits, some white. |
| G | 336 | A06-03-002 | 004 | 04 | 75 | Jar 8 | — | Reddish-buff clay; small-sized grits; greenish-buff slip on surface; out of context in slope wash. |
| H | 12756 | A01-0531/32-024 | 141 | 04 | 81 | Jar 8 | — | Dense brownish-buff clay; small-sized grits. |
| I | 003 | B01-03-001 | 004 | 04 | 81 | Jar 8 | — | Dense brownish-buff clay; small-sized grits; grayish slip on exterior; out of context in slope wash. |
| J | 001 | A01-02-002 | 003 | 04 | 81 | Jar 8 | — | Fairly dense light brownish-buff clay; small-sized grits; greenish-buff slip on exterior. |
| K | 2795 | D44-03-012 | 044 | 04 | 81 | Jar 8 | Red Wash | Dense brownish-buff clay; small sized grits; red wash on exterior. |
| L | 5864 | D44-05-017 | 063 | 04 | 81 | Jar 8 | — | Dense orange clay; small-sized grits, some white; reddish-buff slip on exterior. |
| M | 6294 | D44-0176-026 | 191 | 04 | 81 | Jar 8 | — | Fairly dense reddish-buff clay; small-sized grits, some white; buff slip on exterior. |
| N | 15991 | D66-0847-083 | 585 | 04 | C-61 | Jar 8 | Bns. | Fairly dense light brownish-buff clay; small-sized grits, some white; very light traces of light burnish applied in spiral fashion over body of exterior; base hole was made while clay was still wet. |
| O | 12907 | A01-05-016 | 092 | 04 | 81 | Jar 8 | — | Dense brownish-buff clay; small-sized grits, some white; greenish-buff slip on exterior; fast wheel striations visible on interior. |
| P | 011 | A01-03-003 | 010 | 04 | 77 | Jar 8 | — | Fairly dense reddish/brownish-buff clay; small-sized grits, some white. |

PLATE 107

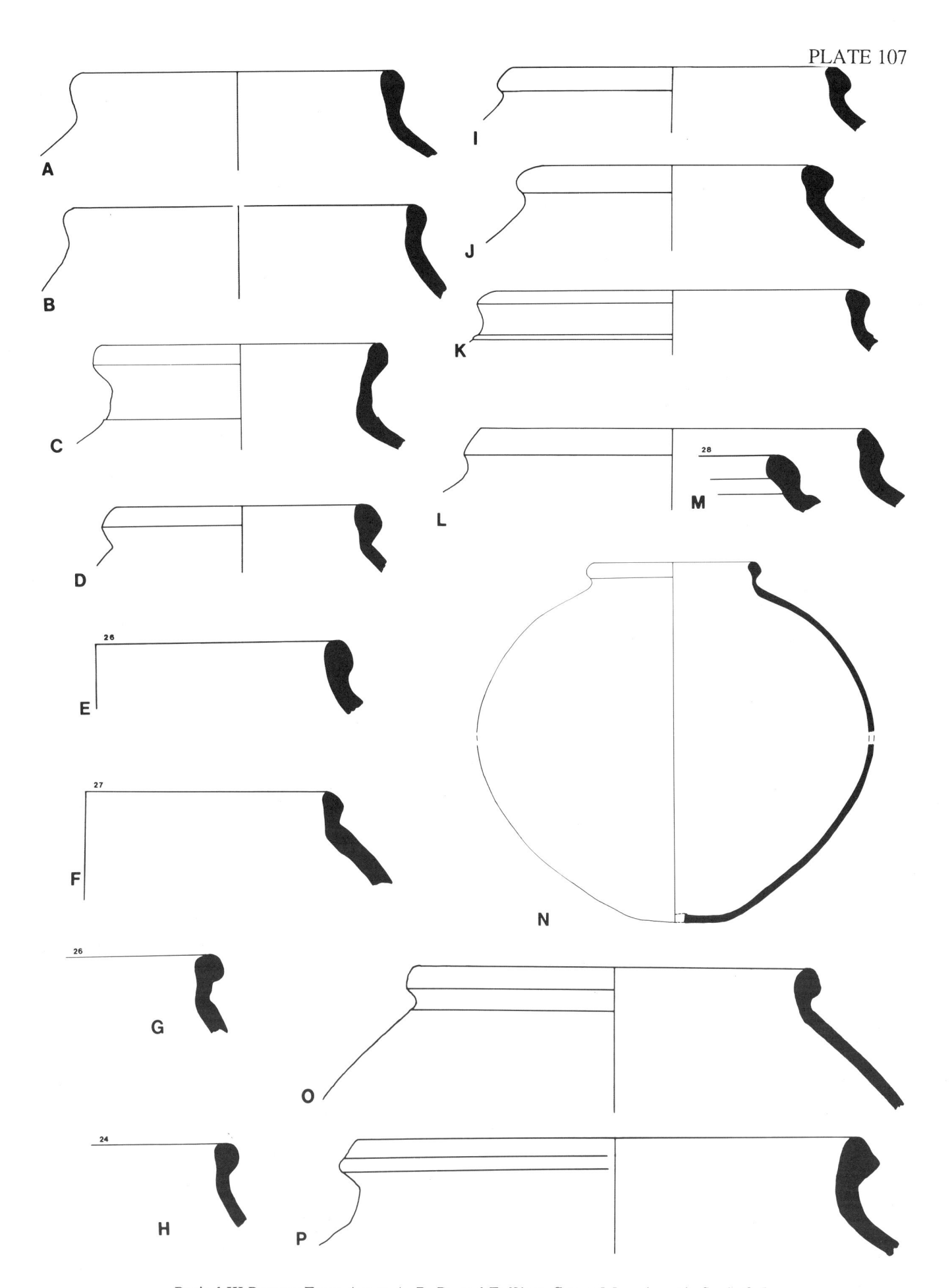

Period III Pottery From Areas A, B, D, and F: Ware Group I Jars (*cont.*). Scale 2:5.

Plate 108. Period III Pottery From Areas A and D: Ware Group I Jars (*cont.*). Scale 2:5.

|   | MRN | CONTEXT | FCN | WARE | FORM | TYPE | DECO. | WARE/REMARKS |
|---|---|---|---|---|---|---|---|---|
| A | 15717 | D23-0183-026 | 278 | 04 | C-88 | Jar 9 | — | Fairly dense brownish-buff clay, reddish core; small-sized grits, some white; greenish-buff slip on exterior. |
| B | 10546 + 15199 | D25-0184-003 + D25-0199-003 | 021 + 227 | 04 | 1688 | Jar 9 | 319 | Buff clay; small-sized grits; black ones prominent. |
| C | 1630 | D46-01-004 | 017 | 04 | 567 | Jar 9 | 309 | Buff clay; small-sized grits. |
| D | 15705 | D23-1092/93-026 | 267 | 04 | 073 | Jar 9 | — | Fairly dense brownish-buff clay; small-sized black grits; buff slip on exterior. |
| E | 12933 | A01-05-018 | 117 | 04 | 073 | Jar 9 | — | Dense orange clay grading to gray on interior; small-sized grits, some white. |
| F | 1698 | A08-01-004 | 032 | 04 | 73 | Jar 9 | — | Dense orange clay; small-sized grits; pinkish slip on exterior; out of context in slope wash. |
| G | 12877 | A01-05-015 | 066 | 04 | 73 | Jar 9 | — | Gray clay; small-sized grits. |
| H | 5269 | D45-03-007 | 049 | 04 | 1173 | Jar 9 | — | Fairly dense brownish-buff clay; small-sized grits, some white. |
| I | 1784 | A08-01-004 | 036 | 04 | 1095 | Jar 9 | — | Buff clay; small-sized black grits; out of context in slope wash. |
| J | 12904 | A01-05-016 | 092 | 04 | 535 | Jar 9 | — | Buff clay; small-sized grits; some white. |
| K | 103 | A02-04-005 | 021 | 04 | 88 | Jar 9 | — | Buff clay; small-sized grits, some white; greenish-buff slip on exterior. |

PLATE 108

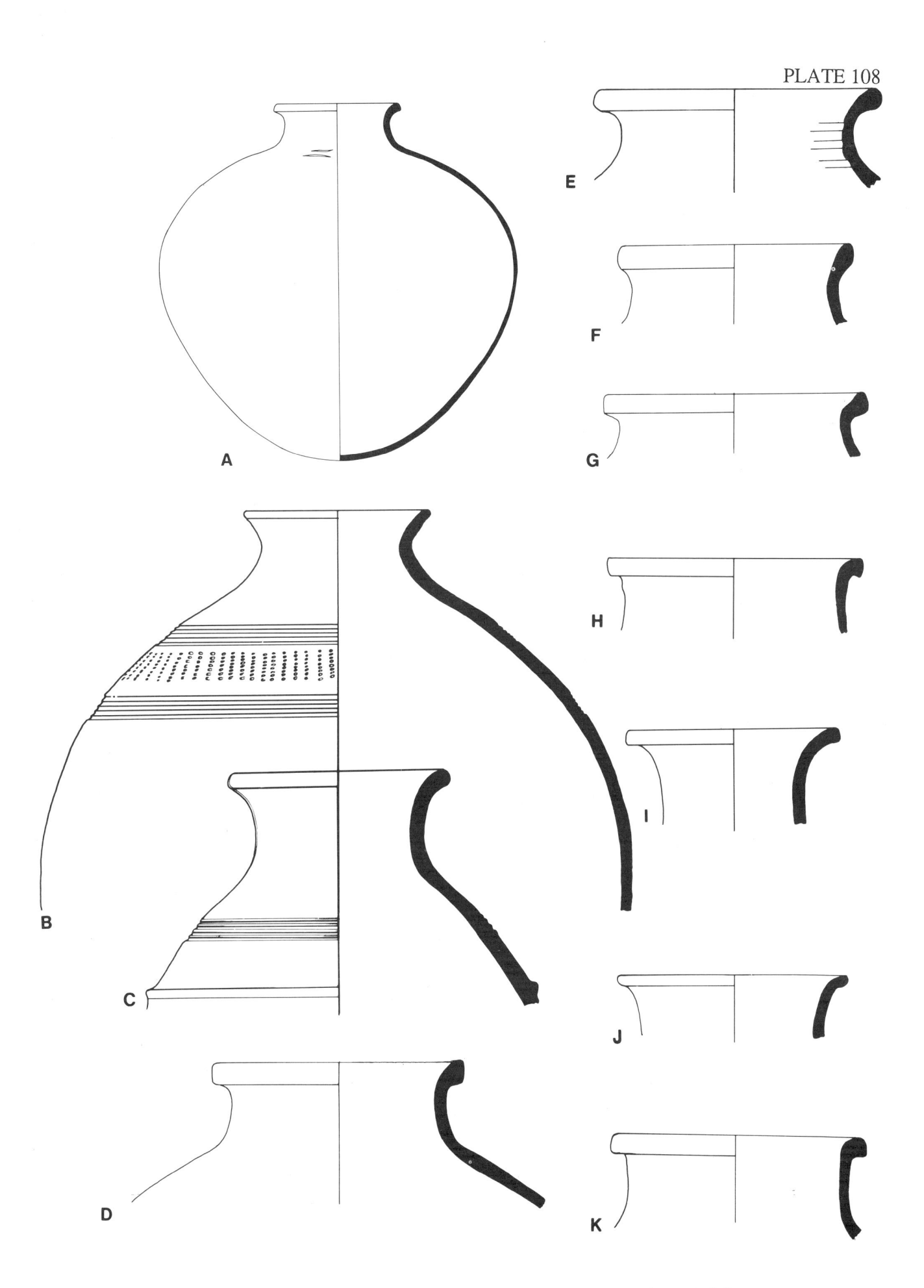

Period III Pottery From Areas A and D: Ware Group I Jars (*cont.*). Scale 2:5.

Plate 109. Period III Pottery From Areas A, B, and D: Ware Group I Jars (*cont.*). Scale 2:5.

|   | MRN | CONTEXT | FCN | WARE | FORM | TYPE | DECO. | WARE/REMARKS |
|---|---|---|---|---|---|---|---|---|
| A | 6116 | D43-0418-011 | 076 | 04 | 1161 | Jar 10 | — | Dense reddish/brownish-buff clay; small-sized grits. |
| B | 15321 | D66-0846-083 | D460 | 04 | 1597 | Jar 10 | — | Light brownish-buff clay; small-sized grits, some white. |
| C | 1698 | A08-01-004 | 032 | — | 490 | Jar 10 | — | Orange-buff clay; small-sized grits, some white; out of context in slope wash. |
| D | 042 | B03-01-002 | 048 | 04 | 89 | Jar 10 | — | Buff clay; small-sized grits. |
| E | 14243 | D23-01-005 | D021 | 04 | 1608 | Jar 10 | — | Dense brownish-buff clay; small-sized white grits. |
| F | 12933 | A01-05-018 | 117 | 04 | 72 | Jar 11 | — | Fairly dense brownish-buff clay; small-sized buff grits; lighter brownish-buff slip on exterior. |
| G | 12968 | A01-0521/23-025 | 147 | 04 | 942 | Jar 11 | — | Light brownish-buff clay; small-sized grits, some white; corrugations on neck exterior. |
| H | 6571 | D76-02-032 | 173 | 04 | 72 | Jar 11 | — | Fairly dense brownish-buff clay; small-sized white grits; buff slip on exterior. |
| I | — | Area D Provenance lost | — | 04 | 72 | Jar 11 | — | Rather porous greenish-buff clay; small-sized black grits. |
| J | 4837 | D55-03-009 | 055 | 04 | 072 | Jar 11 | — | Grayish clay; small-sized grits, some white. |
| K | 1457 | D66-06-001 | 194 | 04 | 72 | Jar 11 | — | Buff clay; small-sized gray grits. |
| L | 8709 | D34-0373-010 | 140 | 04 | 72 | Jar 11 | — | Buff clay; small-sized grits, some black. |
| M | 12858 | A01-05-015 | 047 | 04 | 72 | Jar 11 | — | Buff clay; small-sized white grits; buff slip on surface. |
| N | 17152 | D76-0119/29-050 | 282 | 04 | 72 | Jar 11 | — | Buff clay; small-sized grits. |
| O | 17886 | D38-04-019 | D073 | 04 | 72 | Jar 11 | — | Light brownish-buff clay; small-sized black and gray grits. |

PLATE 109

Period III Pottery From Areas A, B, and D: Ware Group I Jars (*cont.*). Scale 2:5.

Plate 110. Period III Pottery From Areas B and D: Ware Group I Jars (*cont.*). Scales: (A–G) 2:5; (H) 1:5.

|   | *MRN* | *Context* | *FCN* | *Ware* | *Form* | *Type* | *Deco.* | *Ware/Remarks* |
|---|---|---|---|---|---|---|---|---|
| A | 5201 | D54-0239-006 | 099 | 04 | C-15 | Jar 12a | 307 | Brownish-buff clay; small-sized white grits; buff slip on exterior; (= KH 1981/79). |
| B | 19438 | B62-0193-002 | 022 | 04 | C-80 | Jar 12b | — | Fairly dense brownish-buff clay; small- and medium-sized white grits; lighter brownish-buff slip on exterior; (= KH 1984/176). |
| C | 6400 | D44-05-017 | 139 | 04 | C-11 | Jar 12b | — | Brownish-buff clay; small-sized grits; (= KH 1981/102). |
| D | 15072 | D25-0192-003 | 193 | 04 | 1667 | Jar 12b | — | Rather porous gray clay; small-sized black grits; light buff slip on exterior with traces of black fire smudges near bottom. |
| E | 7156 | D76-02-036 | 197 | 04 | 1125 | Jar 12b | — | Greenish-buff clay; small-sized black grits. |
| F | 17798 | D65-0766/65-050 | D334 | 04 | 69c | Jar 12b | — | Brownish-buff clay; small-sized grits. |
| G | 17601 | D38-03/04-028 | 094 | 04 | 69c | Jar 12b | — | Light brownish-buff clay; small-sized gray grits and medium-sized white ones. |
| H | 4156 | D34-01-007 | 040 | 04 | C-23 | Jar 12b | — | Light brownish-buff clay; small-sized grits; (= KH 1981/58). |

PLATE 110

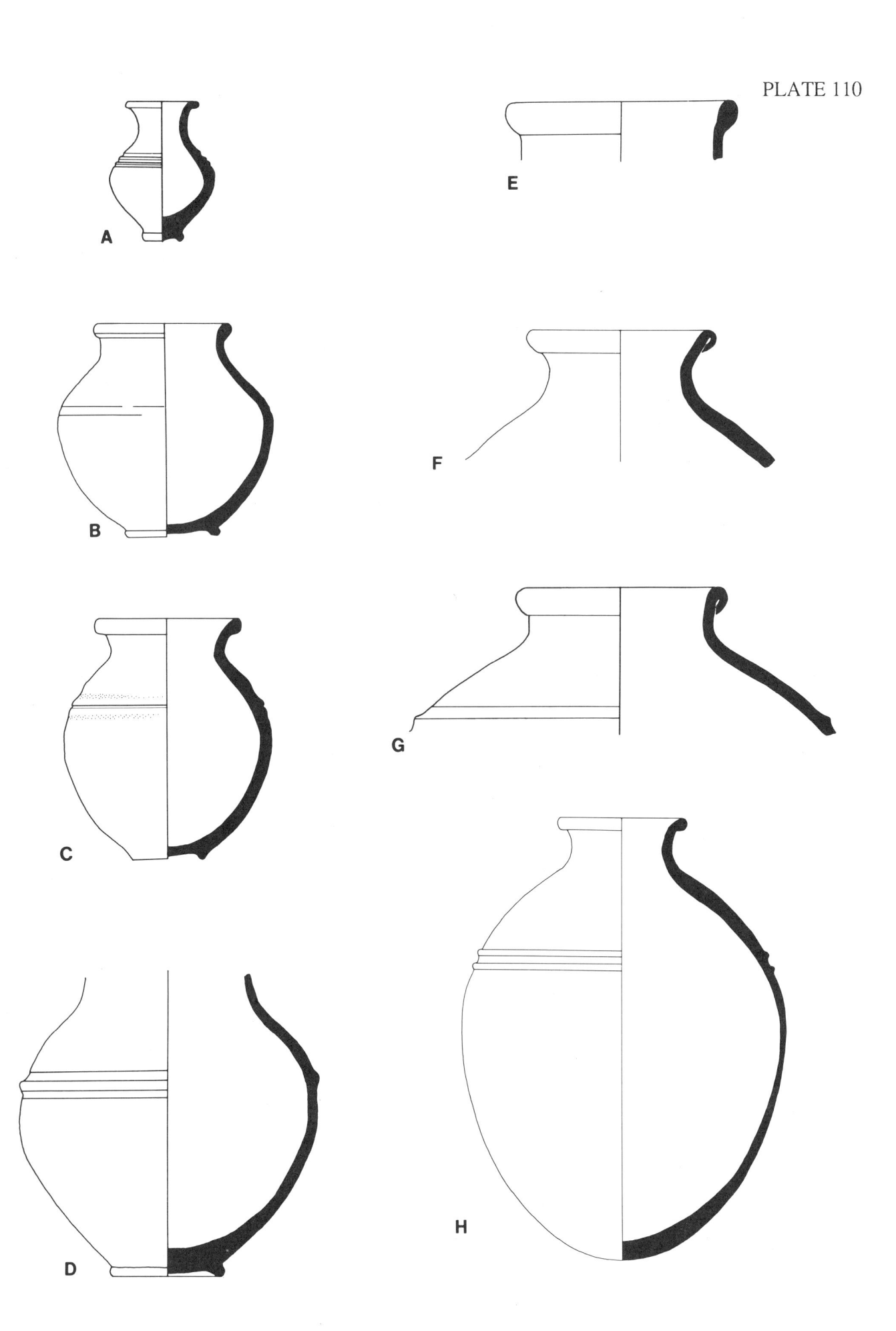

Period III Pottery From Areas B and D: Ware Group I Jars (*cont.*). Scales: (A–G) 2:5; (H) 1:5.

Plate 111. Period III Pottery From Area D: Ware Group I Jars (*cont.*). Scale 2:5.

|   | *MRN* | *Context* | *FCN* | *Ware* | *Form* | *Type* | *Deco.* | *Ware/Remarks* |
|---|---|---|---|---|---|---|---|---|
| A | 5874 | D45-0310-007 | 278 | 04 | C-23 | Jar 12b | 604 | Light brownish-buff clay; small-sized grits, some white; (= KH 1981/103). |
| B | 15079 | D35-0501-028 | 763 | 04 | C-23 | Jar 12b | 603 | Gritty reddish-buff clay; small- and medium-sized grits, black ones visible but white ones prominent. |
| C | 15088 | D25-0193-003 | 198 | 04 | C-23 | Jar 12b | 604 | Brownish-buff clay; small-sized grits; (= KH 1983/151). |
| D | 16498 | D38-01-004 | 019 | 04 | C-23 | Jar 12b | 604 | Light brownish-buff clay; small-sized grits; (= KH 1983/172). |

PLATE 111

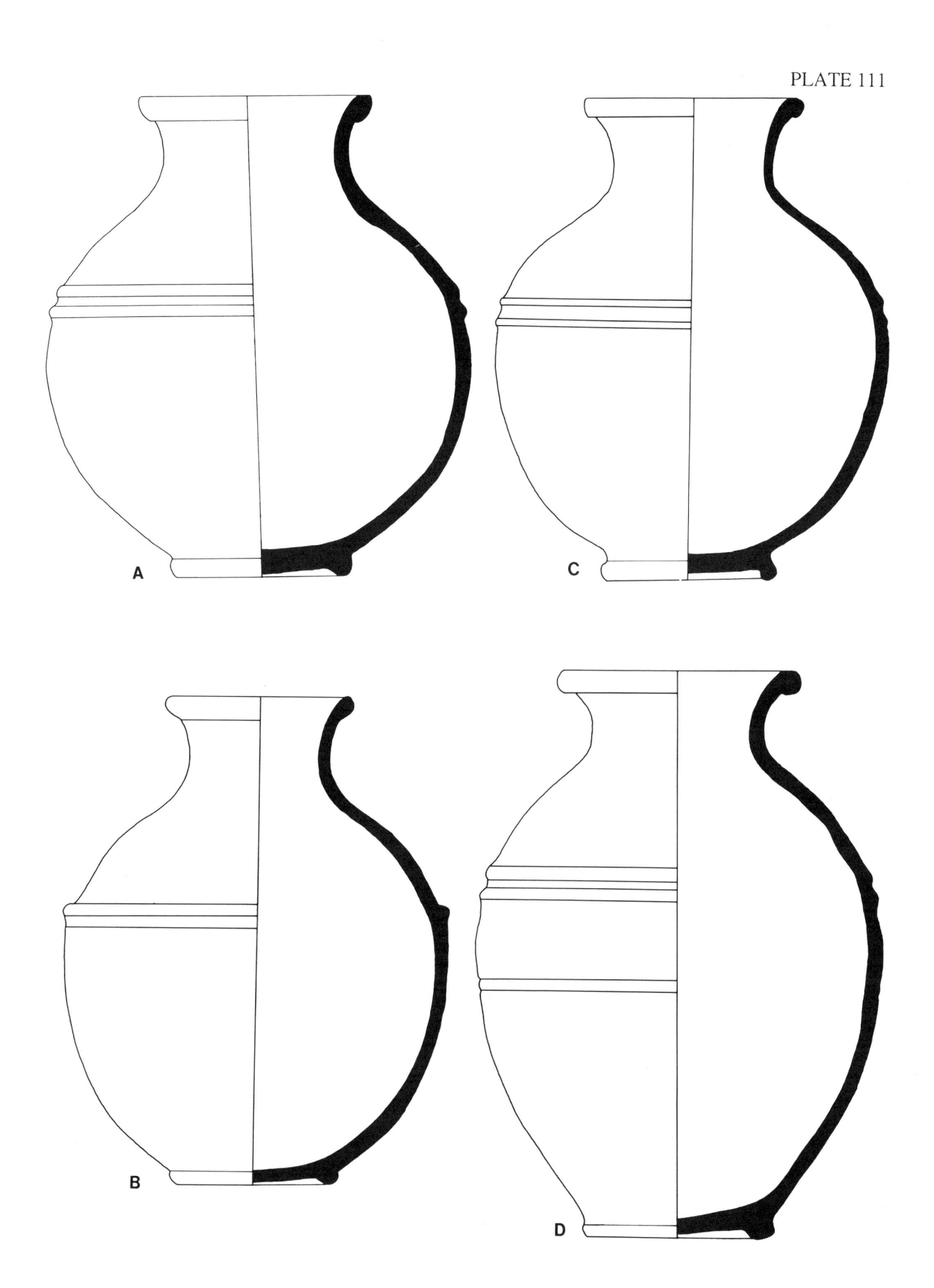

Period III Pottery From Area D: Ware Group I Jars (*cont.*). Scale 2:5.

Plate 112. Period III Pottery From Areas A and D: Ware Group I Jars (*cont.*). Scale 2:5.

|   | *MRN* | *Context* | *FCN* | *Ware* | *Form* | *Type* | *Deco.* | *Ware/Remarks* |
|---|---|---|---|---|---|---|---|---|
| A | 2311 | D42-01-001 | 006 | 04 | 629 | Jar 13 | — | Fairly dense grayish-buff ware; small-sized white grits. |
| B | 1451 | D46-01-002 | 012 | 04 | 463 | Jar 13 | — | Greenish-buff clay; small-sized grits; lighter greenish-buff slip on exterior. |
| C | 10687 | D25-0190-005 | 086 | 04 | 66 | Jar 13 | — | Brownish-buff clay; small-sized grits. |
| D | 6571 | D76-02-032 | 173 | 04 | 65 | Jar 13 | — | Brownish-buff clay; small-sized grits. |
| E | 2722 | D44-03-012 | 041 | 04 | 66 | Jar 13 | — | Brownish-buff clay; small-sized grits, some white. |
| F | 12917 | A01-0522/23-016 | 105 | 04 | 463 | Jar 13 | — | Gritty brownish-buff clay, light gray core; small- and medium-sized grits visible. |
| G | 6294 | D44-0176-026 | 191 | 04 | 66 | Jar 13 | — | Fairly dense grayish clay; small-sized grits; buff slip on surfaces. |
| H | 12882 | A01-05-032 | 071 | 04 | 66 | Jar 13 | — | Brownish-buff clay; small-sized grits. |
| I | 14855 | D55-0617-044 | D383 | 04 | 66 | Jar 13 | — | Light grayish-buff clay; small-sized grits, white ones prominent. |

PLATE 112

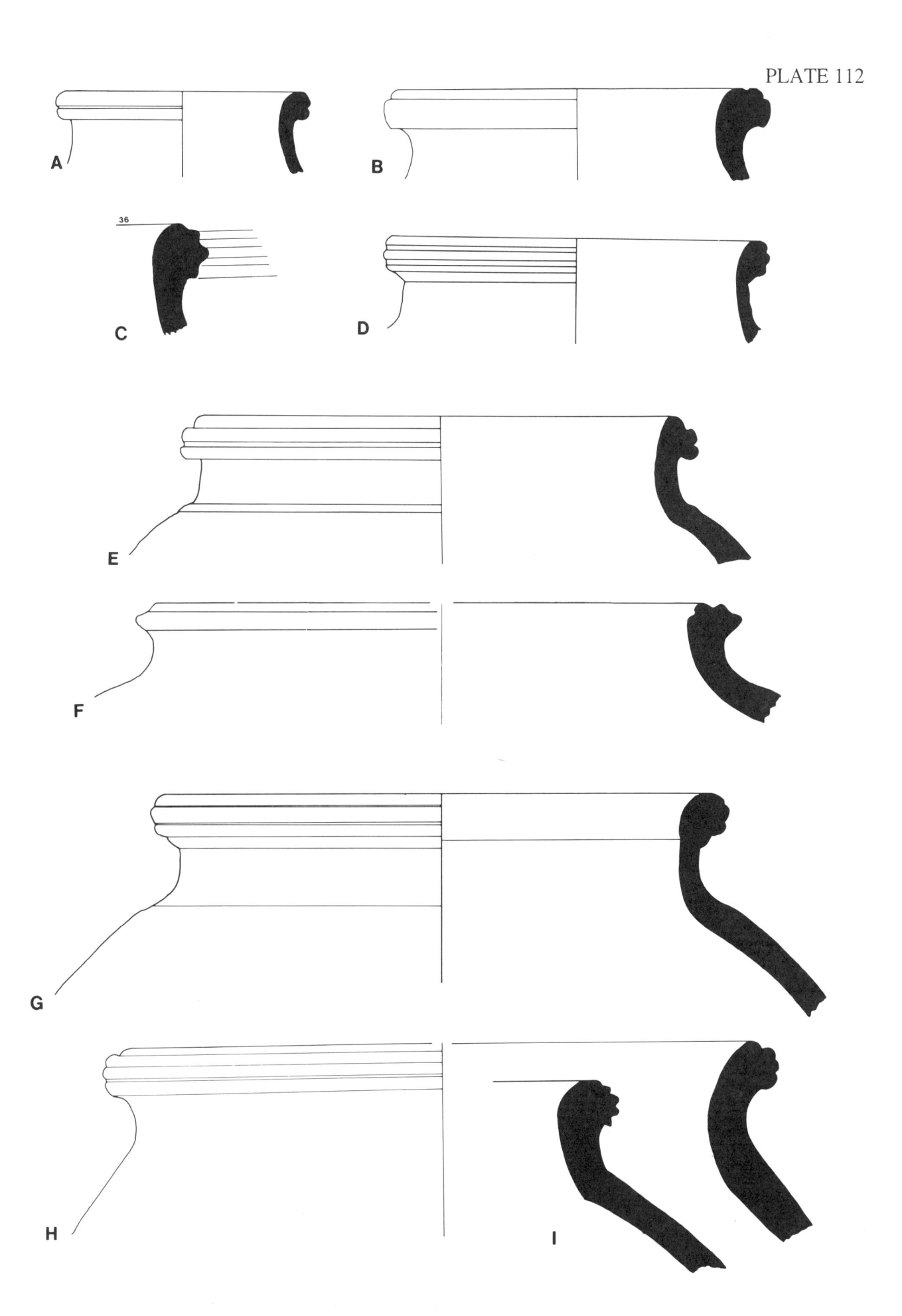

Period III Pottery From Areas A and D: Ware Group I Jars (*cont.*). Scale 2:5.

Plate 113. Period III Pottery From Areas D and E: Ware Group I Jars (*cont.*). Scales: (A–E and G–P) 2:5; (F)1:5.

|   | MRN | CONTEXT | FCN | WARE | FORM | TYPE | DECO. | WARE/REMARKS |
|---|---|---|---|---|---|---|---|---|
| A | 15687 | D36-0559-022 | D337 | 04 | 599 | Jar 14 | — | Light grayish-buff clay; small-sized grits, some white. |
| B | 14707 | D23-01-004 | D034 | 04 | 599 | Jar 14 | — | Brownish-buff clay; small-sized grits. |
| C | 15841 | D23-0352/62-014 | 219 | 04 | 599 | Jar 14 | — | Brownish-buff clay; small-sized grits. |
| D | 5364 | E44-01-006 | — | 04 | 599 | Jar 14 | — | Brownish-buff clay; small-sized grits. |
| E | 15711 | D23-0193-026 | 274 | 04 | C-57 | Jar 14 | — | Fairly dense brownish-buff clay; small-sized white grits. |
| F | 15718 | D23-0183-026 | 272 | 04 | C-57 | Jar 14 | — | Fairly dense brownish-buff clay; small-sized black grits; buff slip on exterior; brown painted bands. |
| G | 15703 | D23-0194-026 | 265 | 04 | C-57 | Jar 14 | — | Greenish-buff clay; small-sized white grits; fast wheel striations visible on exterior; potter's mark on shoulder; (= KH 1983/169). |
| H | 2568 | D76-02-001 | 005 | 04 | 620 | Jar 15a | — | Reddish-buff clay; small-sized grits. |
| I | 15190 | D66-0827-083 | D485 | 04 | 620 | Jar 15a | — | Brownish-buff clay; small-sized grits. |
| J | 17187 | D76-0128/38-051 | 294 | 04 | 960 | Jar 15b | — | Fairly dense orange/brownish-buff clay; small-sized grits, some white. |
| K | 1820 | D66-07-001 | 230 | 04 | 960 | Jar 15b | — | Light grayish clay; small-sized white grits. |
| L | 5017 | D54-02-006 | 098 | 04 | 687 | Jar 16a | — | Reddish-buff clay, dark brown core; small-sized grits, some white. |
| M | 0172 | D66-02-002 | 003 | 04 | 60 | Jar 16a | — | Fairly dense reddish-buff clay; small-sized white grits; buff slip on exterior. |
| N | 2804 | D76-04-001 | 025 | 04 | 687 | Jar 16a | — | Brownish-buff clay; small-sized grits, some white; buff slip on exterior. |
| O | 3108 | D76-03-002 | 029 | 04 | 735 | Jar 16b | — | Brownish-buff clay; small-sized white grits. |
| P | 7156 | D76-02-036 | 197 | 04 | 1126 | Jar 16b | — | Reddish/brownish-buff clay; small-sized grits, some white. |

PLATE 113

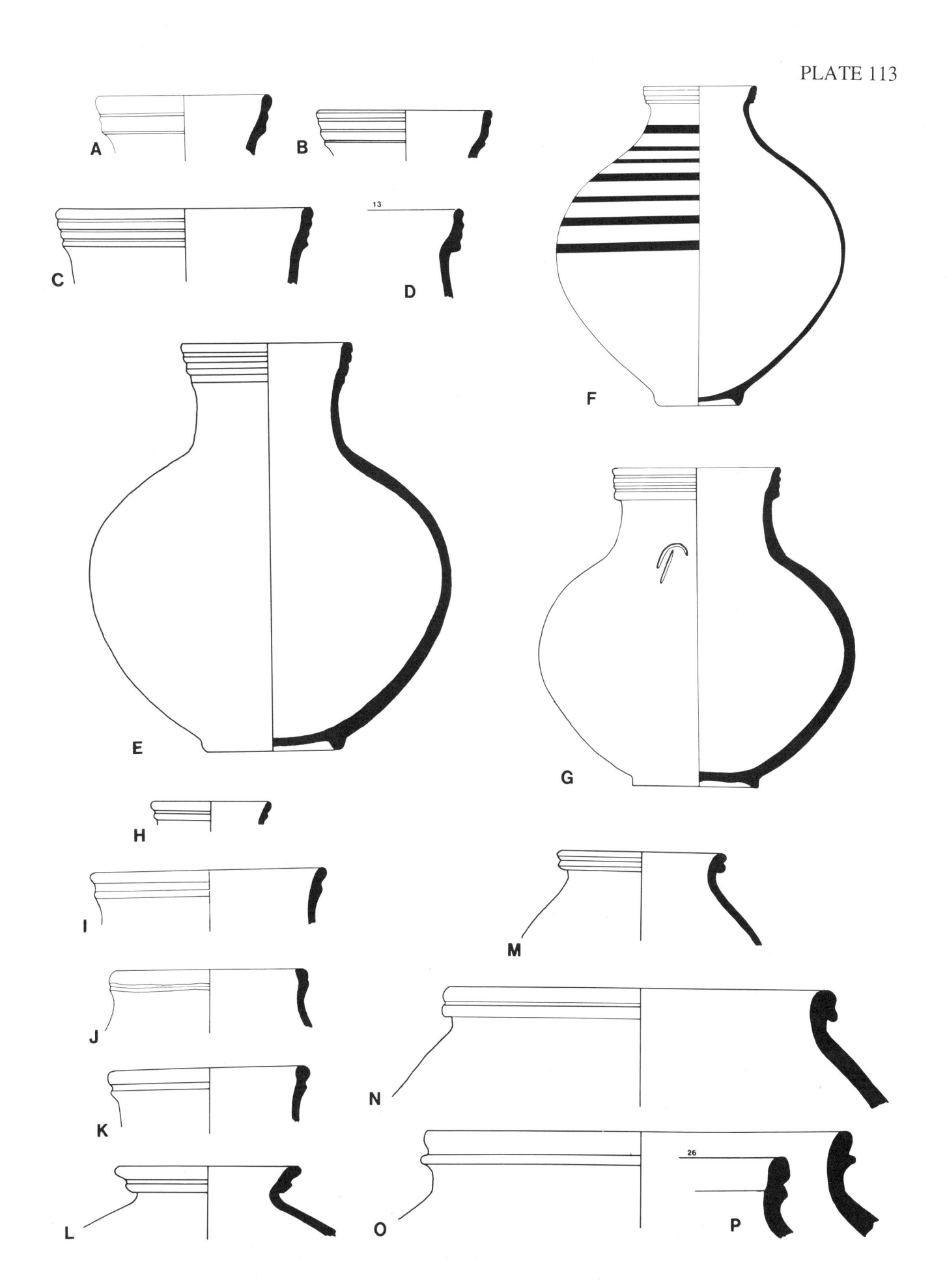

Period III Pottery From Areas D and E: Ware Group I Jars (*cont.*). Scales: (A–E and G–P) 2:5; (F) 1:5.

Plate 114. Period III Pottery From Areas A and D: Ware Group I Jars (*cont.*). Scales: (A–E and G–O) 2:5; (F) 1:5.

|   | MRN | CONTEXT | FCN | WARE | FORM | TYPE | DECO. | WARE/REMARKS |
|---|---|---|---|---|---|---|---|---|
| A | 5689 | D43-04-009 | 067 | 04 | 1242 | Jar 17 | — | Brownish-buff clay; small-sized grits, some white. |
| B | 3392 | D53-01-002 | 013 | 04 | 1242 | Jar 17 | — | Dense grayish clay; small-sized grits; buff slip on exterior. |
| C | 059 | A01-03-003 | 017 | 04 | 1242 | Jar 17 | — | Buff clay; small-sized grits. |
| D | — | Provenance lost | — | 04 | 514 | Jar 17 | — | Dense orange-buff clay; small-sized grits, some white; greenish-buff slip on both surfaces. |
| E | 1820 | D66-07-001 | 230 | 04 | 514 | Jar 17 | — | Light greenish-buff clay; small-sized grits. |
| F | 15156 | D35-0504-018 | 765 | 04 | C-83 | Jar 17 | 308 | Fairly gritty dark gray clay; small- and medium-sized grits, white ones prominent but black ones visible. |
| G | 4466 | D44-05-017 | 092 | 04 | 514a | Jar 17 | 308 | Grayish clay; small-sized grits. |
| H | 17010 | D66-1097-096 | D609 | 04 | 514b | Jar 17 | — | Fairly dense brownish-buff clay; small-sized grits; lighter brownish-buff slip on exterior. |
| I | 17454 | D66-1361-102 | D839 | 04 | 514 | Jar 17 | — | Light brownish-buff clay; small-sized white grits. |
| J | 17886 | D38-04-019 | D173 | 04 | 1646 | Jar 17 | — | Reddish/pinkish-buff clay; small-sized grits, white ones prominent. |
| K | 3896 | D76-04-002 | 060 | 04 | 821 | Jar 17 | — | Orange-buff clay; small-sized white grits. |
| L | 1956 | D66-07-050 | 238 | 04 | 821a | Jar 17 | — | Brownish-buff clay; small-sized grits, some white. |
| M | 14410 | D36-0353-006 | D168 | 04 | 514 | Jar 17 | — | Brownish-buff clay; small-sized grits. |
| N | 3176 | D54-04-013 | 049 | 04 | 748 | Jar 17 | — | Brownish-buff clay; small- and medium-sized grits, some white. |
| O | 879 | D66-05-017 | 106 | 04 | 821a | Jar 17 | — | Fairly dense reddish-buff clay; small-sized grits, some white. |

PLATE 114

Period III Pottery From Areas A and D: Ware Group I Jars (*cont.*). Scales: (A–E and G–O) 2:5; (F) 1:5.

Plate 115. Period III Pottery From Areas B and D: Ware Group I Jars (*cont.*). Scale 2:5.

|   | MRN | CONTEXT | FCN | WARE | FORM | TYPE | DECO. | WARE/REMARKS |
|---|---|---|---|---|---|---|---|---|
| A | 1326 | D46-01-002 | 003 | 04 | 399 | Unass. Jar | — | Buff clay; small-sized white grits. |
| B | 17541 | D35-04-015 | 265 | 04 | 617 | Jar 18 | — | Orange-buff clay; small-sized white grits. |
| C | 17541 | D38-04-018 | 064 | 04 | 617 | Jar 18 | — | Dense reddish clay grading to brownish-buff on exterior; small-sized grits, white prominent. |
| D | 007 | B01-02-001 | 003 | 04 | 56 | Unass. Jar | — | Dense reddish/brownish-buff clay; small-sized grits, white prominent; out of context in slope wash. |
| E | 15714 | D23-0193-026 | 280 | 04 | 1571 | Unass. Jar | 307 | Reddish-buff clay; small-sized grits; potter's mark on shoulder; (= KH 1983/171). |
| F | 4409 | D44-0549-017 | 096 | 04 | — | Unass. Jar | — | Brownish-buff clay; small-sized grits; (= KH 1981/73). |
| G | 3918 | D34-0188-002 | 021 | 04 | C-63 | Unass. Jar | — | Brownish-buff clay; small-sized grits; neck broken in antiquity and secondarily reground; neck hole made after clay was dry, probably at time of regrinding; (= KH 1981/45). |
| H | 17501 | D65-07-051 | D364 | 04 | 1671 | Unass. Jar | — | Fairly dense greenish-buff clay; small-sized white grits; hole by neck secondarily cut after clay was dry. |
| I | 15702 | D23-0192-026 | 264 | 04 | 1572 | Unass. Jar | — | Brownish-buff clay; small-sized grits; (= KH 1983/170). |
| J | 045 | B02-01-001 | 038 | 04 | 80 | Jar 19 | — | Dense reddish-buff clay; small-sized grits, some white; out of context in slope wash. |
| K | 5318 | D66-0837-083 | D460 | 04 | 80 | Jar 19 | — | Dense buff clay; small-sized grits, some white; self slip of same color as clay on exterior. |
| L | 1700 | D44-01-001 | 001 | 04 | 80 | Jar 19 | — | Buff clay; small-sized grits; potter's mark on rim interior. |
| M | 5688 | D44-08-024 | 143 | 04 | 1165 | Unass. Jar | — | Fairly dense greenish-buff clay; small-sized grits. |
| N | 0595 | D66-02-008 | 053 | 04 | 103 | Unass. Jar | — | Brownish-buff clay; small-sized grits. |
| G | 17513 | D38-04-016 | D053 | 04 | 1669 | Unass. Jar | — | Dense grayish clay; small-sized black grits; grayish/greenish-buff slip on exterior. |
| P | 2651 | D42-03-001 | 023 | 04 | 690 | Unass. Jar | — | Brownish-buff clay; small-sized white grits; greenish-buff slip on exterior. |
| Q | 15085 | D35-0501-028 | 776 | 04 | 1664 | Unass. Jar | Painted Bands | Dense grayish clay; small-sized black grits; exterior covered with horizontal dark brown painted bands; upper part of exterior and interior fire blackened. |

PLATE 115

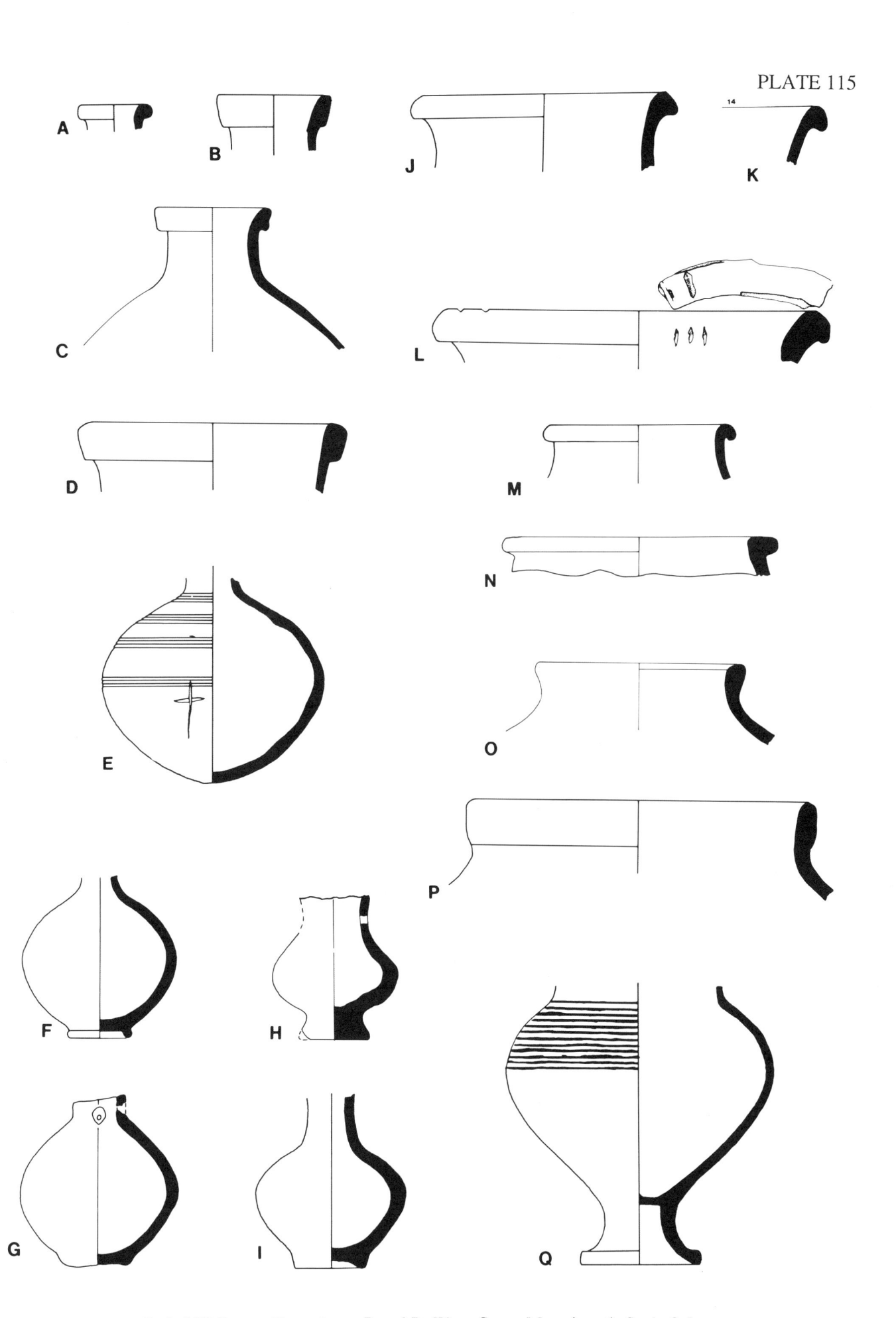

Period III Pottery From Areas B and D: Ware Group I Jars (*cont.*). Scale 2:5.

Plate 116. Period III Pottery From Area D: Ware Group I Jars (*cont.*). Scale 2:5.

|   | MRN | CONTEXT | FCN | WARE | FORM | TYPE | DECO. | WARE/REMARKS |
|---|---|---|---|---|---|---|---|---|
| A | 15264 | D35-0949-033 | 790 | 04 | 1574 | Jar 20 | — | Brownish-buff clay; small-sized grits; body and neck made separately and joined after clay was dry. |
| B | 15257 | D35-0949-033 | 786 | 04 | 1572 | Jar 20 | — | Brownish-buff clay; small-sized grits; body and neck made separately and joined after clay was dry. |
| C | 15701 | D23-0192-026 | 263 | 04 | 1570 | Jar 20 | — | Buff clay; small-sized grits; body and neck made separately and joined after clay was dry; (= KH 1983/168). |
| D | 1951 | D54-02-006 | 011 | 04 | 537 | Handle 1 | — | Dense orange clay; small-sized grits, some white; greenish-buff slip on exterior. |
| E | 5012 | D54-06-015 | 105 | 04 | 1100 | Jar 20 | — | Dense grayish clay; small-sized grits; orange-buff slip on exterior. |
| F | 3940 | D65-05-002 | 113 | 04 | 1100 | Jar 20 | — | Orange-buff clay; small-sized grits; buff slip on exterior. |

PLATE 116

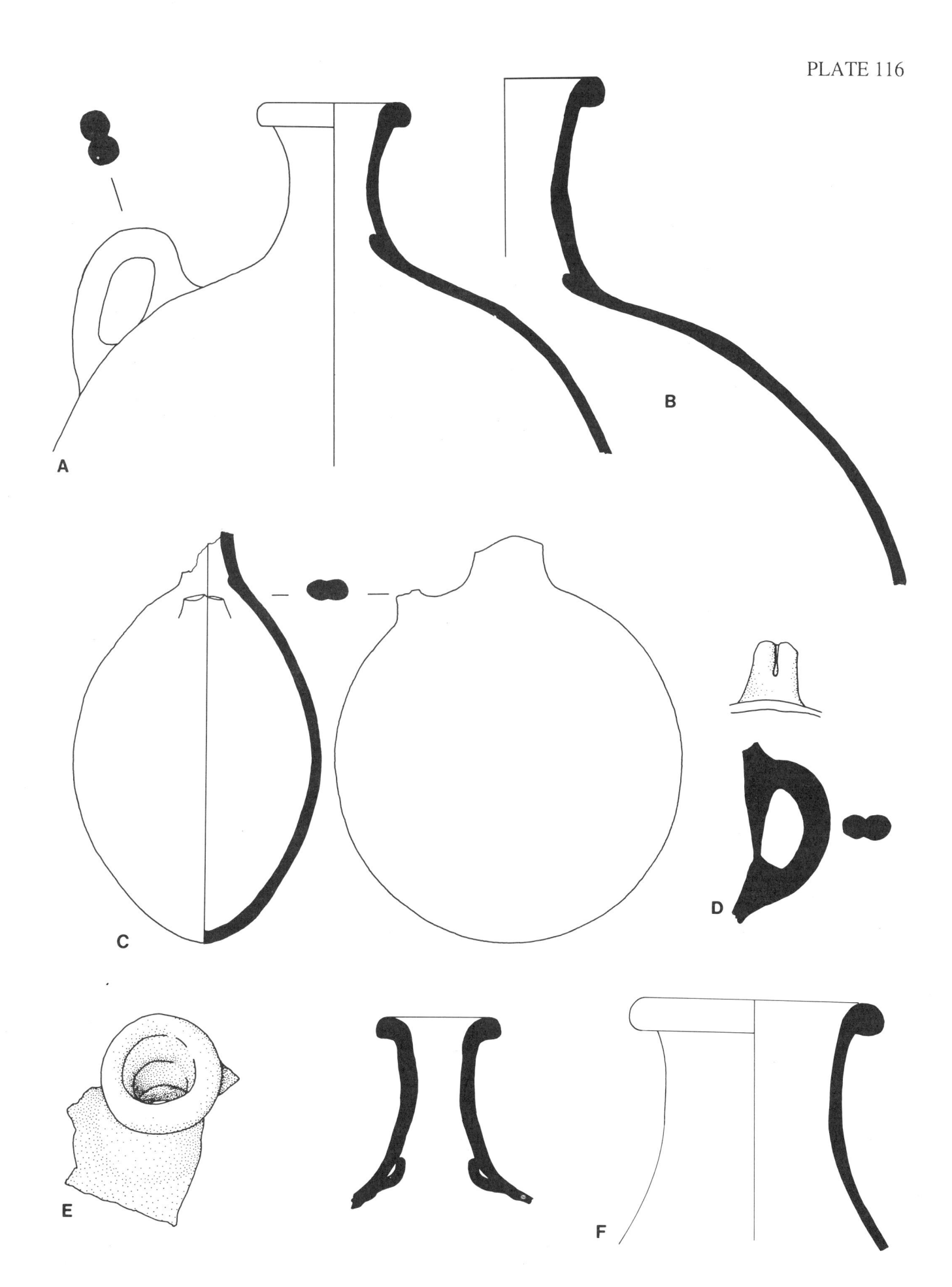

Period III Pottery From Area D: Ware Group I Jars (*cont.*). Scale 2:5.

Plate 117. Period III Pottery From Areas A, B, and D: Ware Group I Jars (*cont.*). Scales: (A–C and E–I) 2:5; (D) 1:5.

|   | MRN | CONTEXT | FCN | WARE | FORM | TYPE | DECO. | WARE/REMARKS |
|---|---|---|---|---|---|---|---|---|
| A | 9233 | D55-0579-027 | 283 | 04 | 448 | Jar 21 | — | Reddish-buff clay; small-sized grits. |
| B | 116 | B02-02-004 | 082 | 04 | 55 | Jar 21 | — | Dense reddish-buff clay; small-sized grits; buff slip on exterior. |
| C | 1429 | A08-01-002 | 014 | 04 | 442 | Jar 21 | — | Dense orange-buff clay; small-sized grits; out of context in slope wash. |
| D | 17146 | D76-0108-043 | 297 | 04 | C-70 | Jar 21 | — | Gritty brownish-buff clay; small-sized black and white grits; fast wheel striations visible on exterior. |
| E | 19450 | B72-0122-009 | 124 | 04 | 1613 | Jar 21 | — | Dense brownish-buff clay; small-sized grits, some white. |
| F | 1429 | A08-01-002 | 014 | 04 | 448 | Jar 21 | — | Reddish-buff clay; small-sized grits; out of context in slope wash. |
| G | 10676 | D36-0193-005 | 042 | 04 | 1613 | Jar 21 | — | Dense orange/brownish-buff clay; small-sized grits, some white. |
| H | 6101 | D44-04-018 | 150 | 04 | 1163 | Jar 21 | — | Yellowish-buff clay; small-sized grits, some quartz flakes visible. |
| I | 4985 | D54-02-006 | 082 | 04 | 1613 | Jar 21 | — | Fairly dense buff clay; small-sized grits, some white. |

PLATE 117

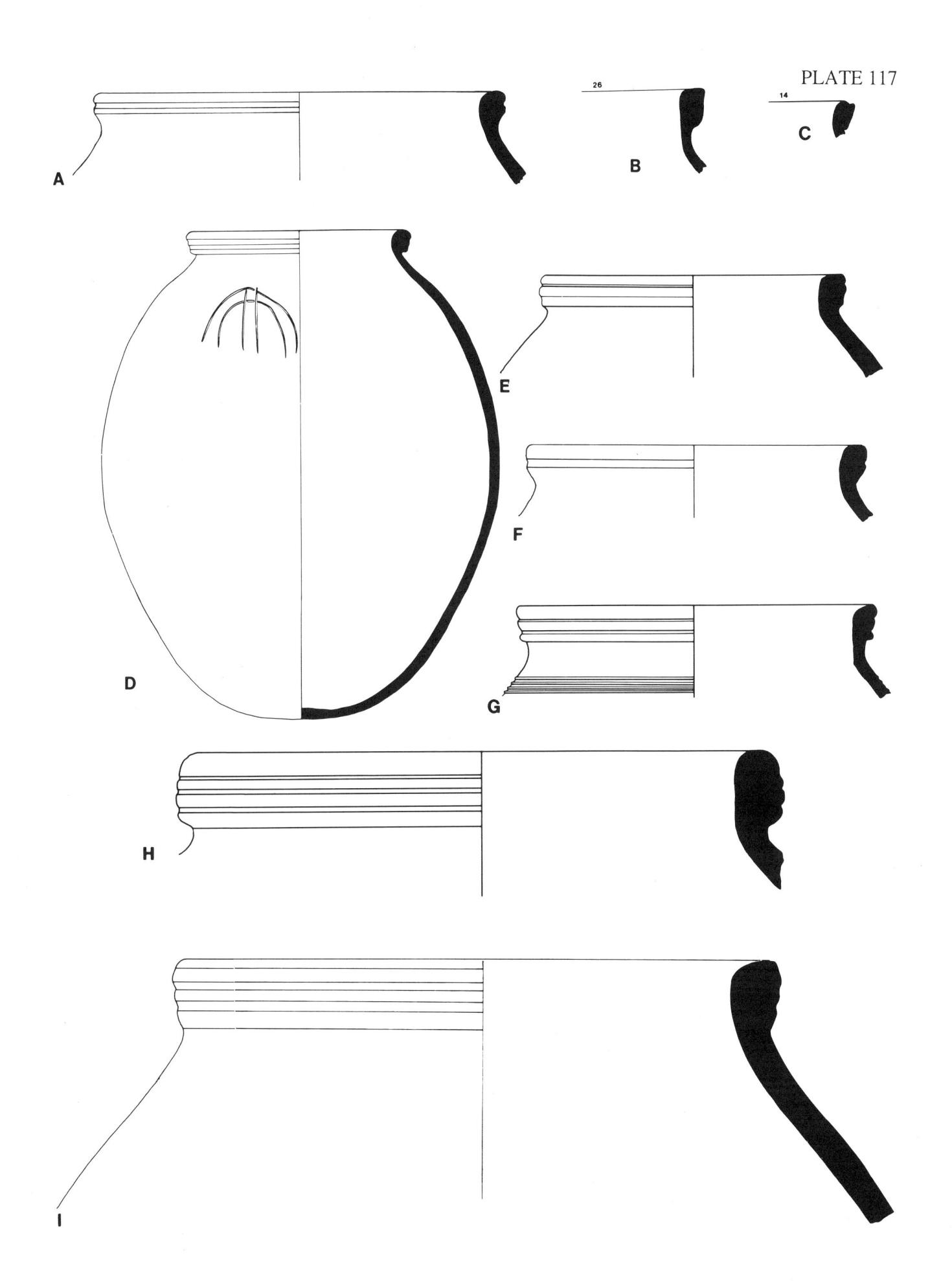

Period III Pottery From Areas A, B, and D: Ware Group I Jars (*cont.*). Scales: (A–C and E–I) 2:5; (D) 1:5.

Plate 118. Period III Pottery From Areas A and D: Ware Group I Jars (*cont.*) and Barrels. Scale 2:5

|   | MRN | CONTEXT | FCN | WARE | FORM | TYPE | DECO. | WARE/REMARKS |
|---|---|---|---|---|---|---|---|---|
| A | 12904 | A01-05-016 | 092 | 04 | 1515 | Jar 22 | — | Brownish-buff clay; small-sized grits; buff slip on exterior. |
| B | 17359 | D66-1240/41-102 | D789 | 04 | 813 | Jar 22 | — | Dense pinkish-buff clay; occasional scattered small-sized grits; buff slip on exterior. |
| C | 6571 | D76-02-032 | 173 | 04 | 1112 | Jar 22 | — | Dense orange-buff clay; small-sized grits, some white. |
| D | 1397 | D46-01-002 | 007 | 04 | 416 | Barrel 1c | — | Orange buff clay; small-sized white grits; buff slip on exterior. |
| E | 1378 | A08-01-002 | 011 | 04 | 550 | Barrel 1c | — | Reddish-buff clay; small-sized grits, some white; out of context in slope wash. |
| F | 17466 | D66-1361-104 | D841 | 04 | 550 | Barrel 1c | — | Light brownish-buff clay; small-sized grits, some white; light greenish-buff slip on surface. |
| G | 17878 | D38-03-023 | 081 | 04 | 461 | Barrel 1a | 603 | Rather porous light greenish-buff clay; small-sized black and white grits. |
| H | 4153 | D34-01-007 | 037 | 04 | 461 | Barrel 1a | — | Light greenish-buff clay; small-sized grits; (= KH 1981/56). |
| I | 2003 | D45-01-001 | 003 | 04 | 461 | Barrel 1a | 604 | Grayish clay; small-sized white grits. |
| J | 9038 | D45-0403-015 | 117 | 04 | 1651 | Barrel 1a | 604 | Light brownish-buff clay; small-sized white grits. |
| K | 15620 | D66-0959-087 | D538 | 04 | C-59 | Barrel 1a | 307 | Fairly porous greenish-buff clay; small-sized black and white grits and larger-sized white grits visible. |
| L | 1630 | D46-01-004 | 017 | 04 | 461 | Barrel 1a | 603 | Orange-buff clay; small-sized white grits; buff slip on exterior. |

PLATE 118

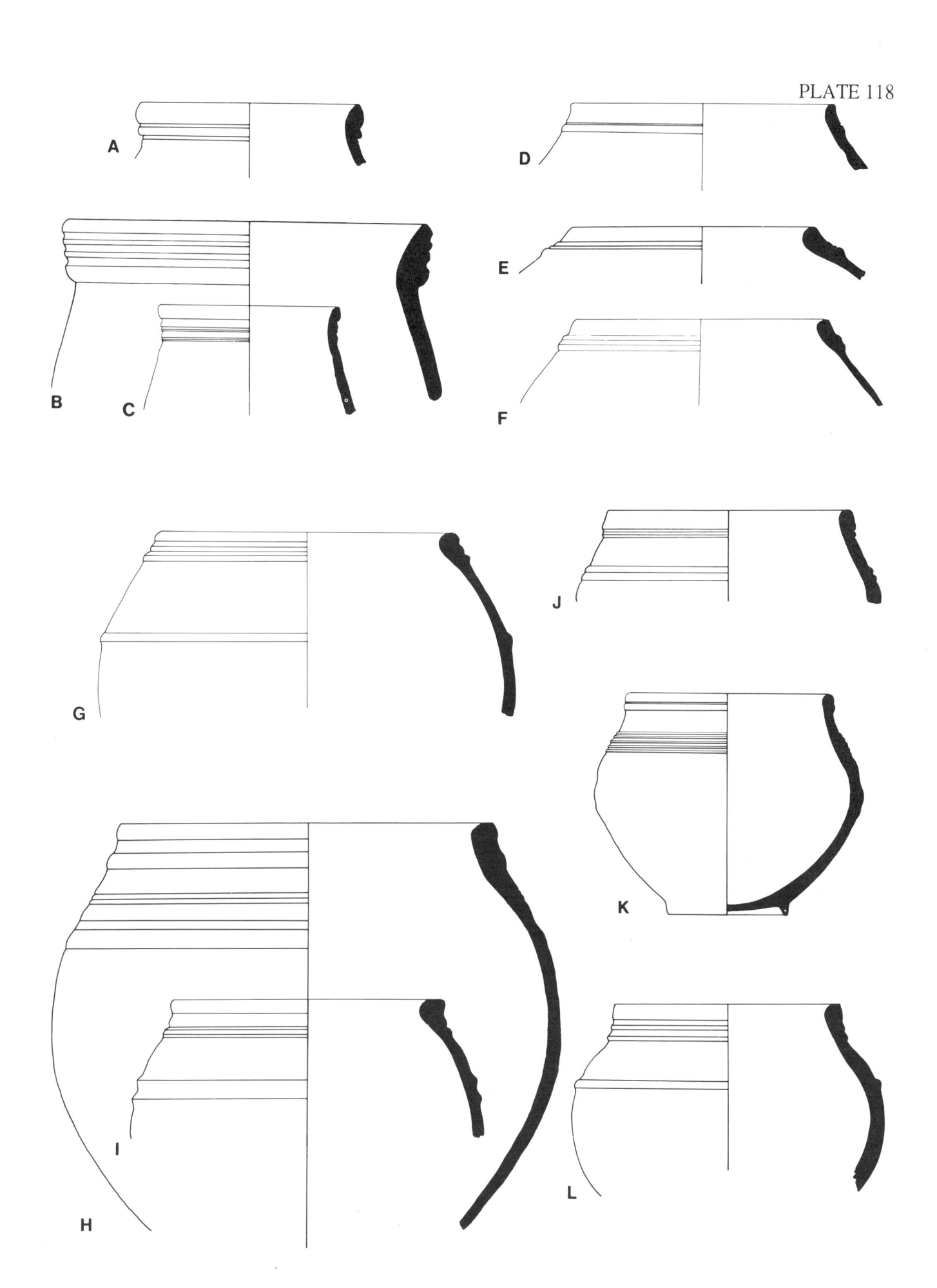

Period III Pottery From Areas A and D: Ware Group I Jars (*cont.*) and Barrels. Scale 2:5.

Plate 119. Period III Pottery From Areas D and E: Ware Group I Barrels (*cont.*). Scale 2:5

|   | MRN | CONTEXT | FCN | WARE | FORM | TYPE | DECO. | WARE/REMARKS |
|---|-----|---------|-----|------|------|------|-------|--------------|
| A | 15083 | D25-0182-003 | 192 | 04 | C-84 | Barrel 1a | 311 | Light brownish-orangish clay; small-sized red, black, and white grits; fire smudges on exterior near rim. |
| B | 16603 | D36-0819-022 | 512 | 04 | C-62 | Barrel 1b | 311 | Porous greenish-buff clay; small-sized black and white grits. |
| C | 16612 | D36-0714-021 | 521 | 04 | 118 | Barrel 1b | 604 | Brownish-buff clay; small-sized grits. |
| D | 14469 | D35-0152-037 | D748 | 04 | 118 | Barrel 1b | 311 | Grayish-buff clay; small-sized black and white grits. |
| E | 14269 | D35-0172-037 | D719 | 04 | 118 | Barrel 1b | — | Brownish-buff clay; small-sized grits. |
| F | 4986 | E44-01-004 | 013 | 04 | 118 | Barrel 1b | — | Brownish-buff clay; small-sized grits. |
| G | 15989 | D66-09-087 | 588 | 04 | 118 | Barrel 1b | 307 | Greenish-buff clay; small-sized grits. |

PLATE 119

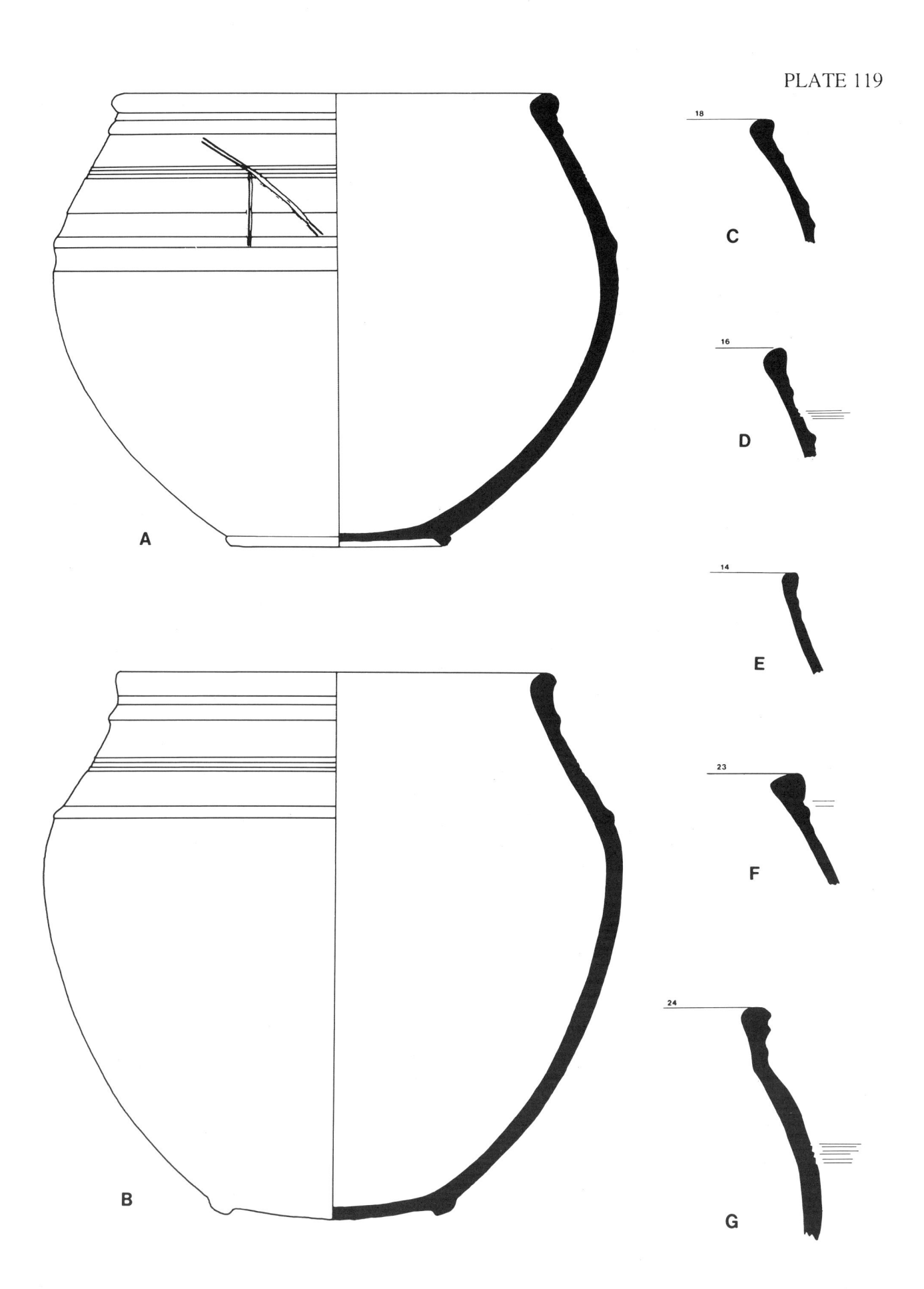

Period III Pottery From Areas D and E: Ware Group I Barrels (*cont.*). Scale 2:5.

Plate 120. Period III Pottery From Area D: Ware Group I Barrels (*cont.*). Scale 2:5

|   | MRN | CONTEXT | FCN | WARE | FORM | TYPE | DECO. | WARE/REMARKS |
|---|---|---|---|---|---|---|---|---|
| A | 7695 | D35-01-001 | 003 | 04 | 118 | Barrel 1b | 331 | Dense brownish-clay, lighter gray core; small-sized grits. |
| B | 6393 | D54-0237-019 | 142 | 04 | 118 | Barrel 1b | — | Reddish-buff clay; small-sized grits. |
| C | 4152 | D34-01-007 | 036 | 04 | 118 | Barrel 1b | — | Greenish-buff clay; small-sized grits; (= KH 1981/55). |
| D | 15071 | D35-0501-028 | 784 | 04 | C-22 | Barrel 1b | 311 | Fairly dense grayish clay; small-sized grits, some white; buff slip on exterior; hole in base made while clay was still wet. |
| E | 4152 | D34-01-007 | 036 | 04 | C-22 | Barrel 1b | 307 | Fairly dense buff clay; small-sized black grits, some larger-sized white ones visible; (= KH 1981/55). |

PLATE 120

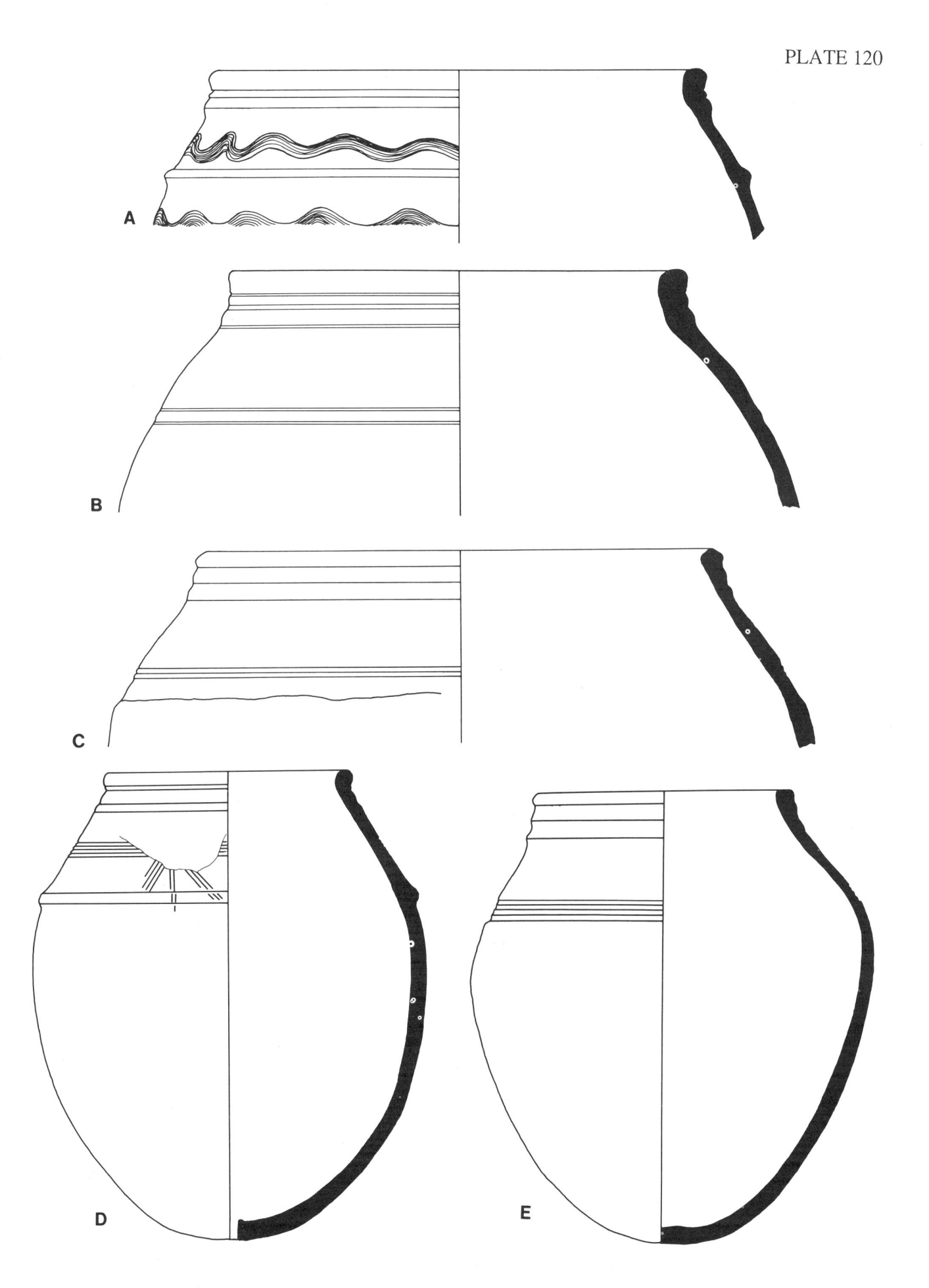

Period III Pottery From Area D: Ware Group I Barrels (*cont.*). Scale 2:5.

Plate 121. Period III Pottery From Areas A and D: Ware Group I Barrels (*cont.*). Scales: (A–D and F–H) 2:5; (E, I, and J) 1:5.

|   | MRN | CONTEXT | FCN | WARE | FORM | TYPE | DECO. | WARE/REMARKS |
|---|---|---|---|---|---|---|---|---|
| A | 617 | D66-03-001 | 064 | 04 | 118 | Barrel 1b | 307 | Fairly dense reddish-buff clay; small-sized white grits. |
| B | 4936 | D44-05-017 | 122 | 04 | 118 | Barrel 1b | — | Grayish clay; small-sized grits. |
| C | 830 | D66-05-001 | 090 | 04 | — | Barrel 1b | 308 | Greenish-buff clay; small-sized black and white grits. |
| D | 3912 | D44-01-010 | 072 | 04 | 823 | Barrel 1b | — | Brownish-buff clay; small-sized grits, some white. |
| E | 16500 + 16483 + 16485 | D35-0859-033 + D35-0949-033 (ditto) | 803 + 797 + 757 | 04 04 04 | C-22 | Barrel 1b | 308 | Brownish-buff clay; small-sized black and white grits. |
| F | 3774 | D66-07-052 | D293 | 04 | 63 | Barrel 1b | — | Greenish-buff clay; small-sized grits. |
| G | 086 | A02-03-002 | 006 | 04 | 63 | Barrel 1b | — | Reddish-buff clay; small-sized grits, some white; buff slip on exterior. |
| H | 133 | D66-01-001 | 001 | 04 | 118 | Barrel 1b | — | Brownish-buff clay; small-sized grits. |
| I | 15521 | D35-0929-033 | 754 | 04 | C-22 | Barrel 1b | 308 | Gritty, light brownish-buff clay; small-sized grits, some white; greenish-buff slip on exterior. |
| J | 15150 | D35-0514-018 | 766 | 04 | C-22 | Barrel 1b | 308 | Fairly dense, light brownish-buff clay; very pale reddish core; small-sized grits and medium-sized white inclusions visible; light brownish-buff slip on exterior. |

PLATE 121

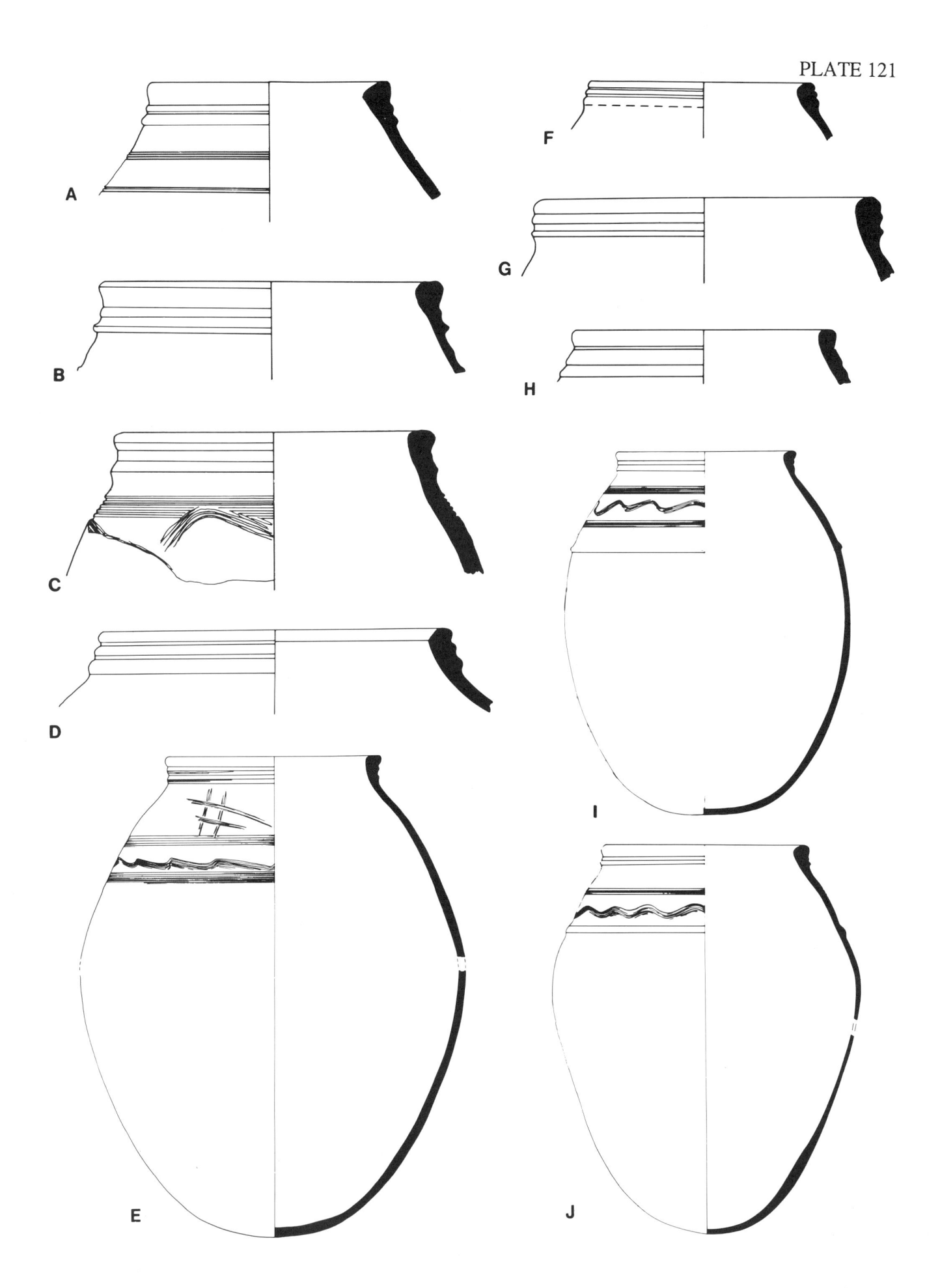

Period III Pottery From Areas A and D: Ware Group I Barrels (*cont.*). Scales: (A–D and F–H) 2:5; (E, I, and J) 1:5.

Plate 122. Period III Pottery From Area D: Ware Group I Barrels (*cont.*). Scales: (A, E, and F) 2:5; (B–D) 1:5.

|   | MRN | CONTEXT | FCN | WARE | FORM | TYPE | DECO. | WARE/REMARKS |
|---|---|---|---|---|---|---|---|---|
| A | 5807 | D34-01-002 | 010 | 04 | 118 | Barrel 1b | 308 | Fairly gritty buff clay; small-sized black and white grits. |
| B | 16522 | D36-0331-006 | 423 | 04 | C-22 | Barrel 1b | 308 | Greenish clay, slightly overfired; small-sized grits, black ones prominent. |
| C | 15162 | D25-0182-003 | 195 | 04 | C-62 | Barrel 1b | 311 | Light greenish-buff/grayish clay; small-sized black and white grits. |
| D | 16538 | D36-0253/54/63/64-006 | 448 | 04 | C-85 | Barrel 1b | 331 | Gritty brownish-buff clay; small- and medium-sized grits prominent on exterior; lighter brownish-buff slip. |
| E | 4840 | D55-03-009 | 060 | 04 | 1184 | Barrel 1b | 622 | Grayish-buff clay; small-sized grits. |
| F | 3766 | D53-02-003 | 023 | 04 | 1207 | Barrel 1b | 308 | Grayish clay; small-sized grits. |

PLATE 122

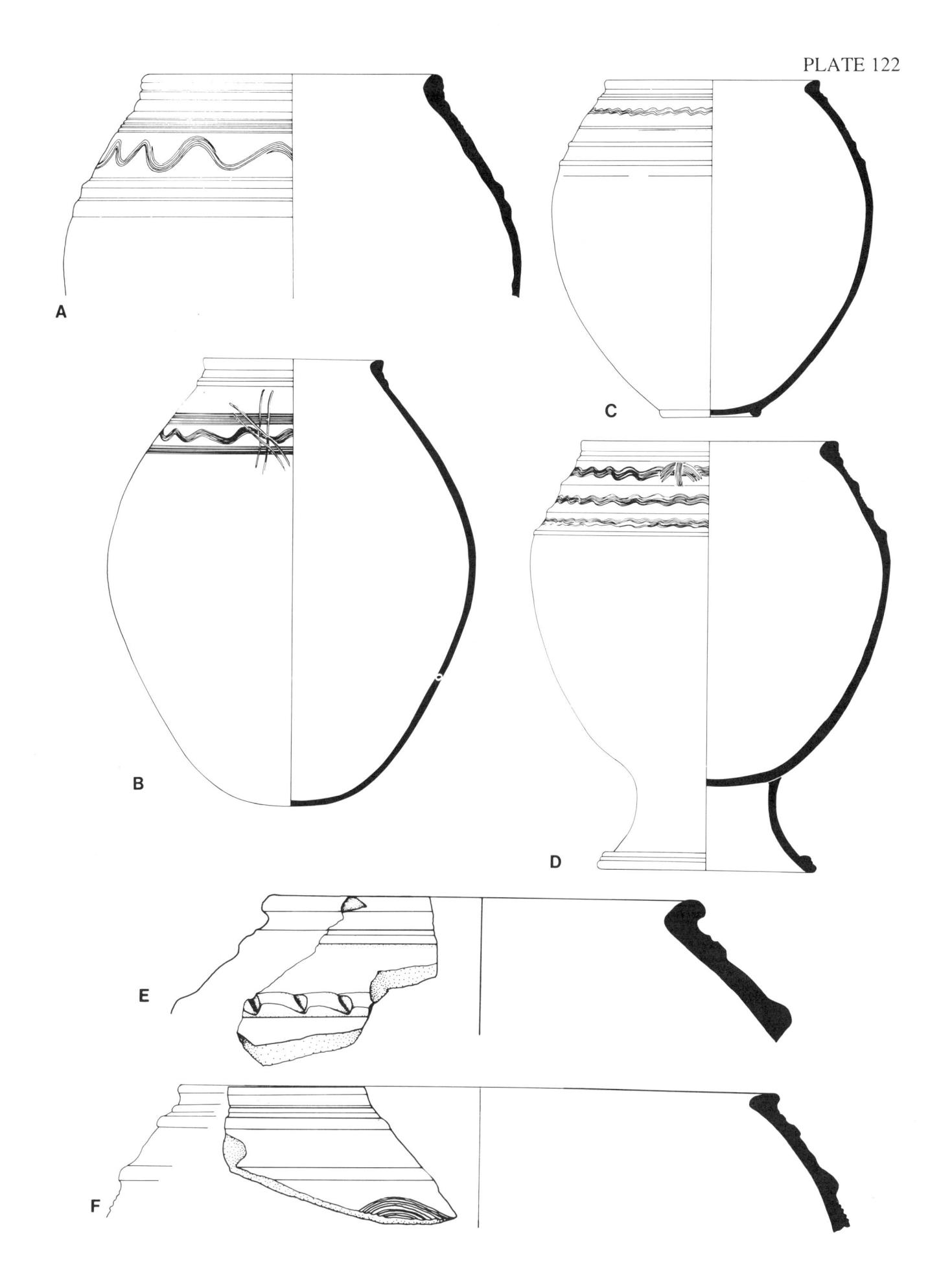

Period III Pottery From Area D: Ware Group I Barrels (*cont.*). Scales: (A, E, and F) 2:5; (B–D) 1:5.

Plate 123. Period III Pottery From Areas A and D: Ware Group I Barrels (*cont.*). Scales: (A–E) 2:5; (F and G) 1:5.

|   | MRN | CONTEXT | FCN | WARE | FORM | TYPE | DECO. | WARE/REMARKS |
|---|---|---|---|---|---|---|---|---|
| A | 15850 | D23-03-014 | D227 | 04 | 1610 | Barrel 1b | — | Brownish-buff clay; small-sized grits, some white. |
| B | 6610 | D65-04-039 | 201 | 04 | 1117 | Barrel 1b | — | Grayish clay; fairly dense small white grits; buff slip on exterior. |
| C | 2656 | D65-02-006 | 053 | 04 | 641 | Barrel 1b | 308 | Brownish-buff clay; small-sized grits. |
| D | 001 | A01-02-002 | 003 | 04 | 117 | Barrel 1b | — | Fairly dense brownish-buff clay; small-sized grits. |
| E | 4838 | D55-01-004 | 061 | 04 | 1197 | Barrel 1b | — | Grayish clay; small-sized grits. |
| F | 16493 | D35-0479/69-033 | 760 | 04 | C-72 | Barrel 1b | 622 | Reddish clay, brownish-buff core; small-sized grits, some white. |
| G | 16550 | D36-0242-006 | 459 | 04 | C-58 | Barrel 1b | 308 | Orange-buff clay, grayish core; small-sized grits, some white; buff slip on exterior. |

PLATE 123

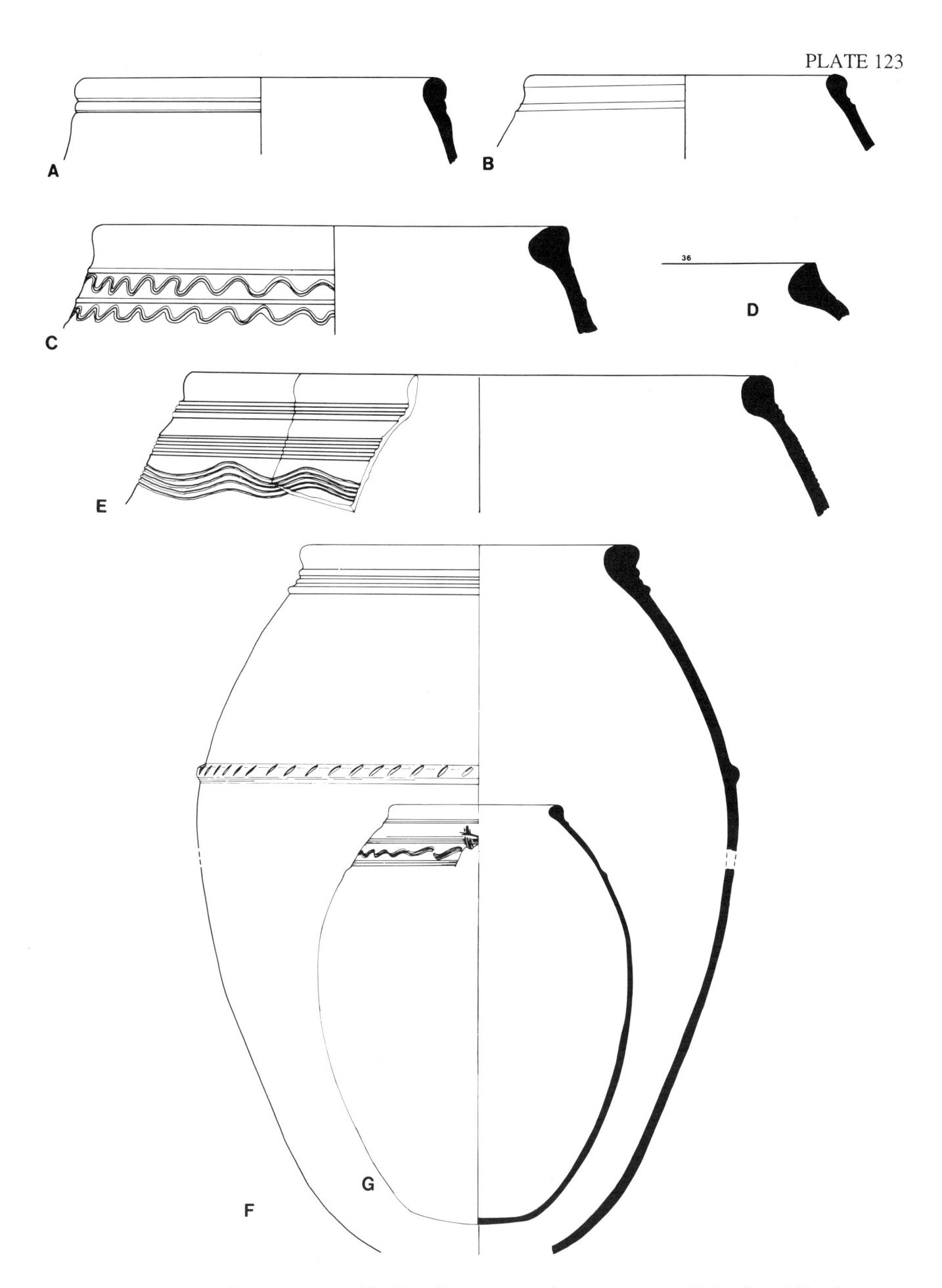

Period III Pottery From Areas A and D: Ware Group I Barrels (*cont.*). Scales: (A–E) 2:5; (F and G) 1:5.

Plate 124. Period III Pottery From Areas B and D: Ware Group I Barrels (*cont.*). Scale 2:5.

|   | MRN | CONTEXT | FCN | WARE | FORM | TYPE | DECO. | WARE/REMARKS |
|---|---|---|---|---|---|---|---|---|
| A | 5014 | D44-08-023 | 125 | 04 | 1167 | Barrel 1b | — | Fairly dense grayish clay; small- and medium-sized white grits; small pebbles also used as tempering; on exterior, a buff slip. |
| B | 19831 | B81-01-002 | 013 | 04 | 1641 | Barrel 1b | — | Brownish-buff clay; small-sized grits, gray and white ones visible; buff slip on exterior. |
| C | 1952 | D55-01-001 | 007 | 04 | 520 | Barrel 2 | — | Gritty grayish clay; small- and medium-sized white grits. |
| D | 5272 | D54-06-022 | 114 | 04 | 944 | Barrel 2 | 622 | Brownish-buff clay; small- and medium-sized gray and white grits. |
| E | 5848 | D53-02-003 | 030 | 04 | 624 | Barrel 2 | — | Buff clay; small- and medium-sized grits. |

PLATE 124

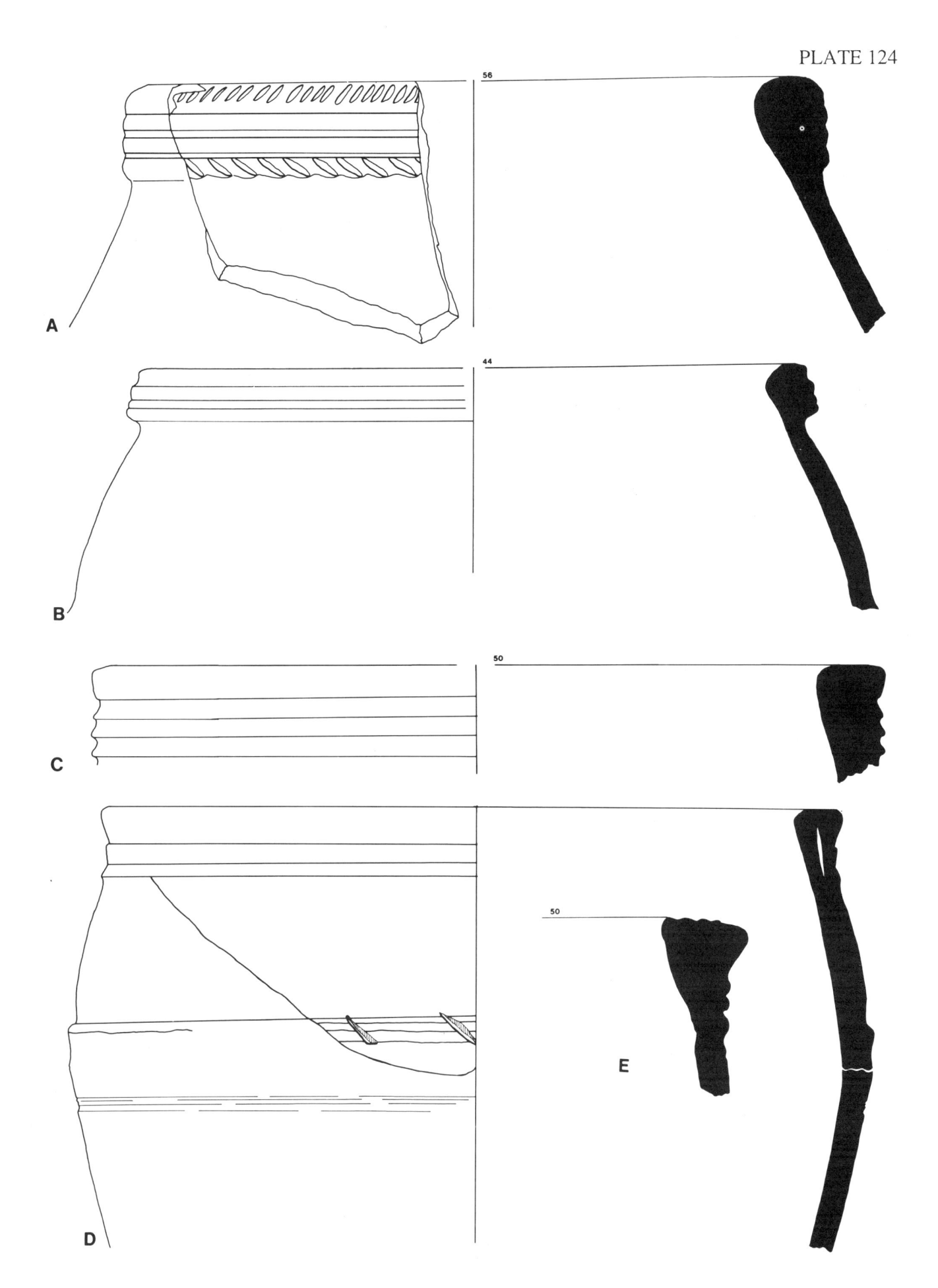

Period III Pottery From Areas B and D: Ware Group I Barrels (*cont.*). Scale 2:5.

Plate 125. Period III Pottery From Areas A and D: Ware Group I Barrels and Jars (*cont.*). Scales: (A and C) 1:5; (B and D–F) 2:5.

|   | *MRN* | *Context* | *FCN* | *Ware* | *Form* | *Type* | *Deco.* | *Ware/Remarks* |
|---|---|---|---|---|---|---|---|---|
| A | 6803 | D54-0560-021 | 158 | 04 | C-69 | Barrel 2 | 622 | Light brownish-buff clay; small- and medium-sized grits. |
| B | 15208 | D35-0948/49-033 | 755 | 04 | C-69 | Barrel 2 | 622 | Brownish-buff clay; small- and medium-sized grits, black and white ones prominent; traces of fire smudges near base on interior. |
| C | 16500 | D35-0859-033 | 803 | 04 | 1663 | Unass. Jar | 622 | Brownish-buff clay; small-sized grits, some white. |
| D | 2315 | A07-05-008 | 069 | 04 | 377 | Jar 23 | — | Dense orange clay; small-sized grits; out of context in slope wash. |
| E | 12904 | A01-05-016 | 092 | 04 | 377 | Jar 23 | — | Orange clay, brownish-buff core; small-sized white grits; exterior grooved. |
| F | 1378 | A08-01-001 | 004 | 04 | 377 | Jar 23 | — | Grayish clay; small- and medium-sized grits, some white; buff slip on exterior; out of context in slope wash. |

PLATE 125

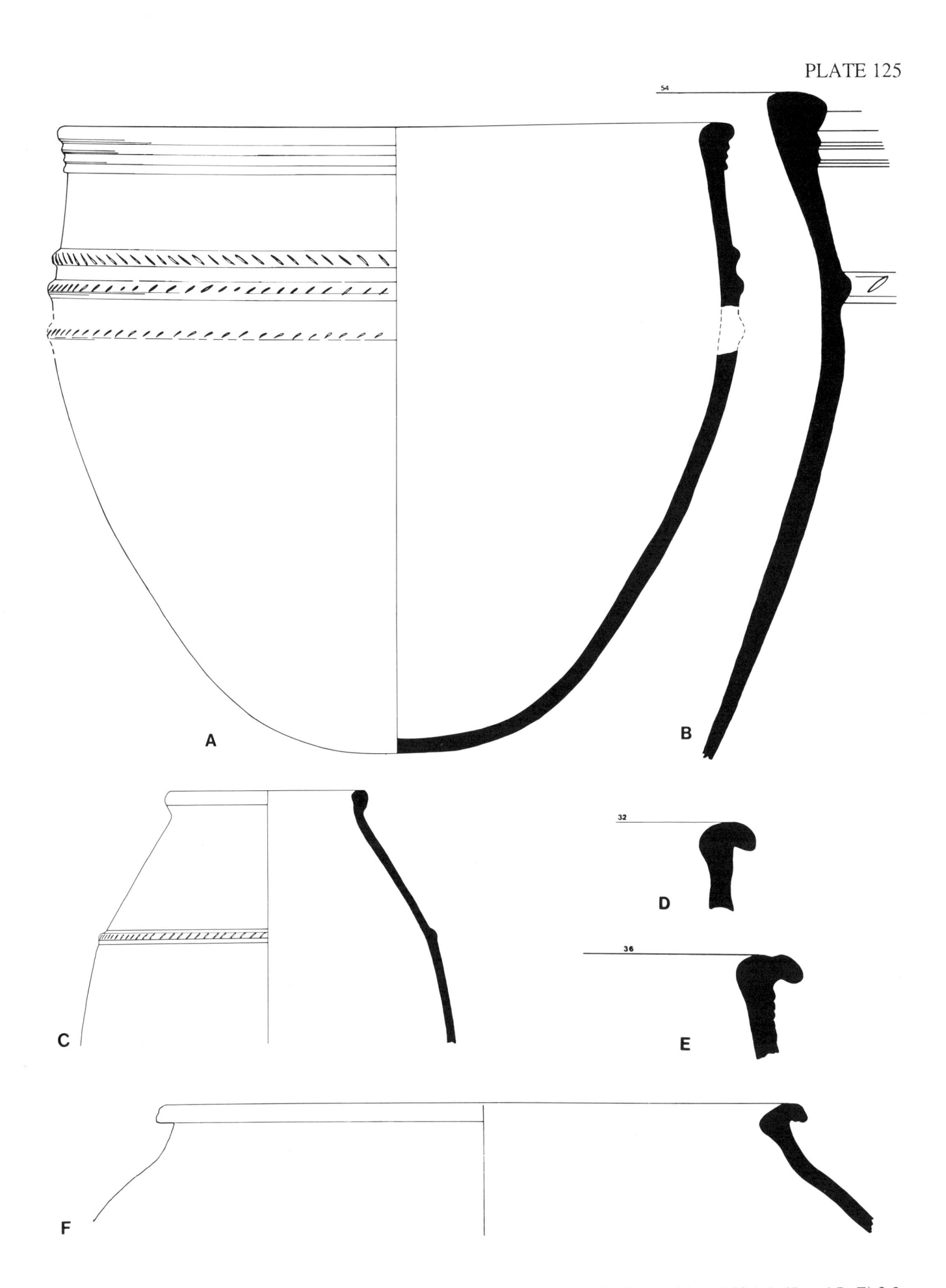

Period III Pottery From Areas A and D: Ware Group I Barrels and Jars (*cont.*). Scales: (A and C) 1:5; (B and D–F) 2:5.

Plate 126. Period III Pottery From Areas A, B, and D: Ware Group I Holemouth Jars. Scale 2:5.

|   | MRN | CONTEXT | FCN | WARE | FORM | TYPE | DECO. | WARE/REMARKS |
|---|---|---|---|---|---|---|---|---|
| A | 19210 | B62-03-002 | 071 | 04 | 116 | Jar 24a | — | Dense grayish clay; small-sized grits, white ones prominent. |
| B | 12878 | A01-05-015 | 069 | 04 | 116 | Jar 24a | — | Fairly dense brownish-buff clay; small-sized grits. |
| C | 1397 | D46-01-002 | 007 | 04 | 415 | Jar 24a | — | Brownish-buff clay; small-sized grits, some white. |
| D | 3913 | D44-03-013 | 068 | 04 | 415 | Jar 24a | — | Dense grayish clay with orange layer on exterior; small-sized white grits. |
| E | 2001 | D44-02-007 | 014 | 04 | 415 | Jar 24a | — | Dense brownish-buff clay; small-sized grits, white ones prominent; exterior covered with lighter brownish-buff slip. |
| F | 14338 | D56-04-013 | 105 | 04 | 215 | Jar 24a | — | Light brownish-buff clay; small-sized grits. |
| G | 3110 | D76-04-002 | 035 | 04 | 414 | Jar 24b | — | Dense reddish clay, brownish-buff core; small-sized grits, some white. |
| H | 1630 | D46-01-004 | 017 | 04 | 414 | Jar 24b | — | Light brownish-buff clay; small-sized grits, white ones prominent; buff slip on exterior. |
| I | 5338 | D44-08-024 | 138 | 04 | 215 | Jar 24a | — | Brownish-buff clay; small- and medium-sized grits. |
| J | 1397 | D46-01-002 | 007 | 04 | 414 | Jar 24b | — | Buff clay; small-sized grits, some white. |
| K | 3660 | D76-01-002 | 010 | 04 | 414 | Jar 24b | — | Dense brownish-buff clay; small-sized grits. |
| L | 3500 | D45-02-005 | 021 | 04 | 524 | Jar 24b | — | Greenish-buff clay, somewhat overfired; small- and medium-sized grits. |
| M | 12904 | A01-05-016 | 092 | 04 | 524 | Jar 24b | — | Buff clay grading to orange-buff on exterior; small-sized white grits; buff slip on exterior. |

PLATE 126

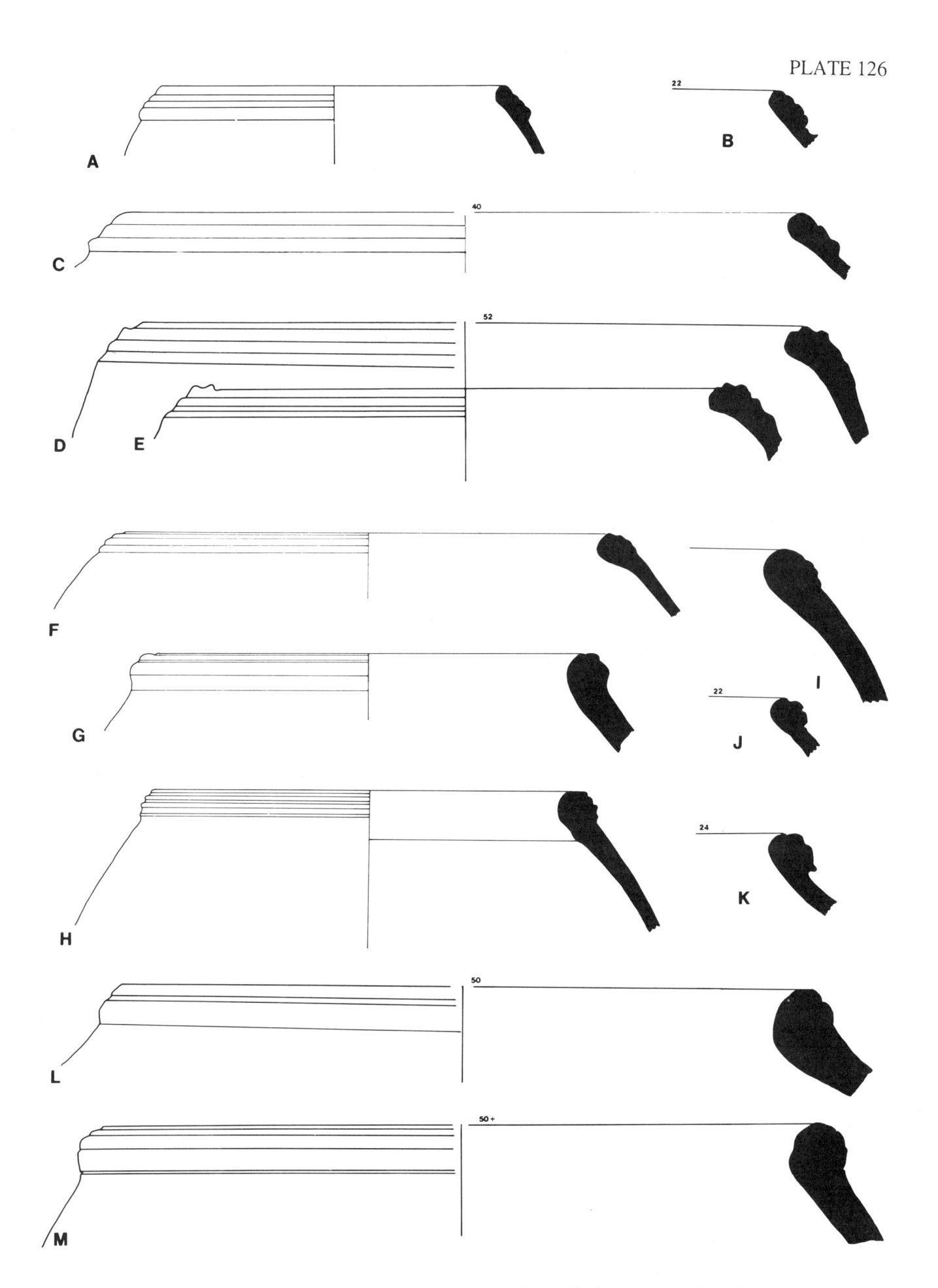

Period III Pottery From Areas A, B, and D: Ware Group I Holemouth Jars. Scale 2:5.

Plate 127. Period III Pottery From Areas A, D, and E: Ware Group I Holemouth Jars (*cont.*). Scale 2:5.

|   | MRN | CONTEXT | FCN | WARE | FORM | TYPE | DECO. | WARE/REMARKS |
|---|---|---|---|---|---|---|---|---|
| A | 5364 | E44-01-006 | 020 | 04 | 943 | Jar 25a | — | Orange/reddish-buff clay; small-sized white grits; buff slip on exterior. |
| B | 2493 | D76-01-001 | 001 | 04 | 691 | Jar 25a | — | Dense brownish-buff clay; small-sized white grits; greenish-buff slip on exterior. |
| C | 0265 | D66-02-004 | 014 | 04 | 1116 | Jar 25b | — | Orange/reddish-buff clay; small-sized grits, white ones prominent; reddish-buff slip on exterior. |
| D | 6571 | D76-02-032 | 173 | 04 | 1116 | Jar 25b | — | Buff clay; small-sized grits. |
| E | 15809 | D23-0192-013 | D186 | 04 | 1364 | Jar 25b | — | Brownish-buff clay; small-sized grits. |
| F | 12904 | A01-05-016 | 092 | 04 | 303 | Jar 25b | — | Brownish-buff clay; small-sized grits, white ones prominent. |
| G | 1451 | D46-01-002 | 012 | 04 | 303 | Jar 25b | — | Brownish-buff clay; small-sized grits, white ones prominent; buff slip on exterior. |
| H | 6368 | D76-02-030 | 166 | 04 | 1201 | Jar 26a | — | Grayish-buff clay; small-sized grits. |
| I | 15643 | D66-0989-087 | D568 | 04 | 1601 | Jar 26a | — | Dense red clay; small-sized white grits. |
| J | 3564 | D65-04-023 | 091 | 04 | 120 | Jar 26b | — | Buff clay; small-sized grits. |
| K | 084 | A01-01-008 | 023 | 04 | 123 | Jar 26b | — | Buff clay; small-sized grits. |
| L | 12877 | A01-05-015 | 066 | 04 | 120 | Jar 26b | — | Buff clay; small-sized grits. |
| M | 5654 | E44-01-006 | 021 | 04 | 120 | Jar 26b | — | Brownish-buff clay; small-sized grits, some white. |
| N | 12877 | A01-05-015 | 066 | 04 | 120 | Jar 26b | — | Orange-buff clay grading to brownish-buff towards interior; small-sized grits. |
| O | 1636 | D66-06-041 | D207 | 04 | 553 | Unass. Jar | — | Greenish-buff clay; small-sized grits; lighter greenish-buff slip on exterior. |
| P | 2585 | D76-01-001 | 003 | 04 | 623 | Unass. Jar | — | Greenish clay, overfired; small-sized grits, white prominent. |

PLATE 127

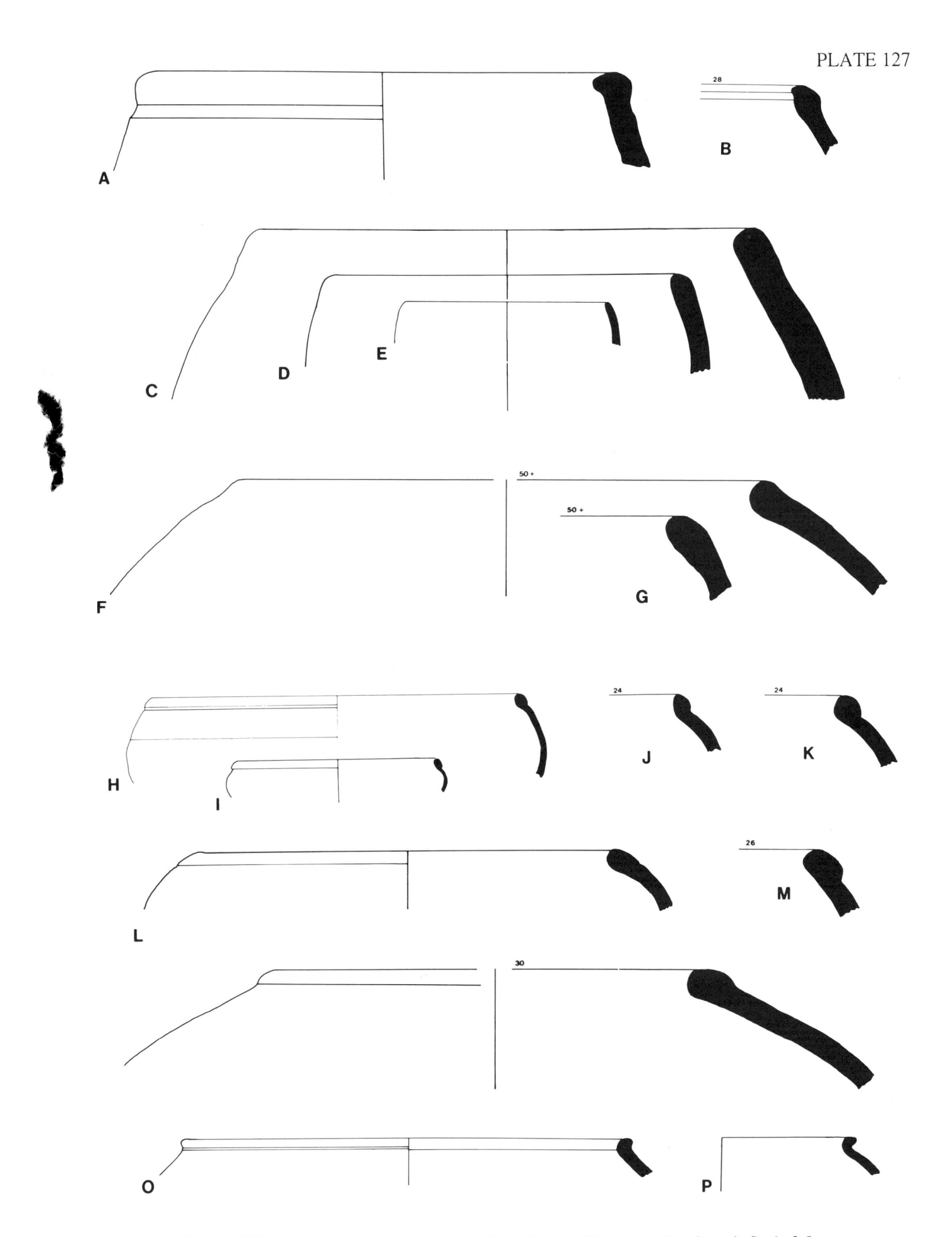

Period III Pottery From Areas A, D, and E: Ware Group I Holemouth Jars (*cont.*). Scale 2:5.

Plate 128. Period III Pottery From Areas A, D, and E: Ware Group I Storage-Sized Jars. Scale 2:5.

| | MRN | CONTEXT | FCN | WARE | FORM | TYPE | DECO. | WARE/REMARKS |
|---|---|---|---|---|---|---|---|---|
| A | 15873 | D34-06-023 | 470 | 04 | 1629 | Jar 27 | — | Fairly dense brownish-buff clay; small- and medium-sized grits, white ones prominent; light greenish-buff slip on exterior. |
| B | 012 | A01-02-003 | 012 | 04 | 131 | Jar 27 | — | Brownish/reddish-buff clay; small- and medium-sized grits, white ones prominent; brownish-buff slip on exterior. |
| C | 3929 | D76-04-002 | 065 | 04 | 830 | Jar 27 | — | Fairly dense brownish-buff clay; small-sized grits. |
| D | 2722 | D44-03-012 | 041 | 04 | 1248 | Jar 27 | — | Brownish-buff clay; small- and medium-sized grits. |
| E | 4737 | D44-03-012 | 105 | 04 | 1218 | Jar 27 | — | Porous reddish clay; medium- and large-sized grits, white ones prominent. |
| F | 6610 | D65-04-039 | 201 | 04 | 1118 | Jar 27 | — | Brownish-buff clay; medium- to large-sized grits, white ones prominent; orange-buff slip on exterior. |
| G | 4469 | E44-01-004 | 007 | 04 | 1227 | Jar 27 | — | Fairly dense brownish-buff clay; small- and medium-sized grits. |
| H | 15846 | D23-03-014 | D223 | 04 | 1611 | Jar 27 | — | Fairly dense greenish clay, overfired; small- and medium-sized grits. |

PLATE 128

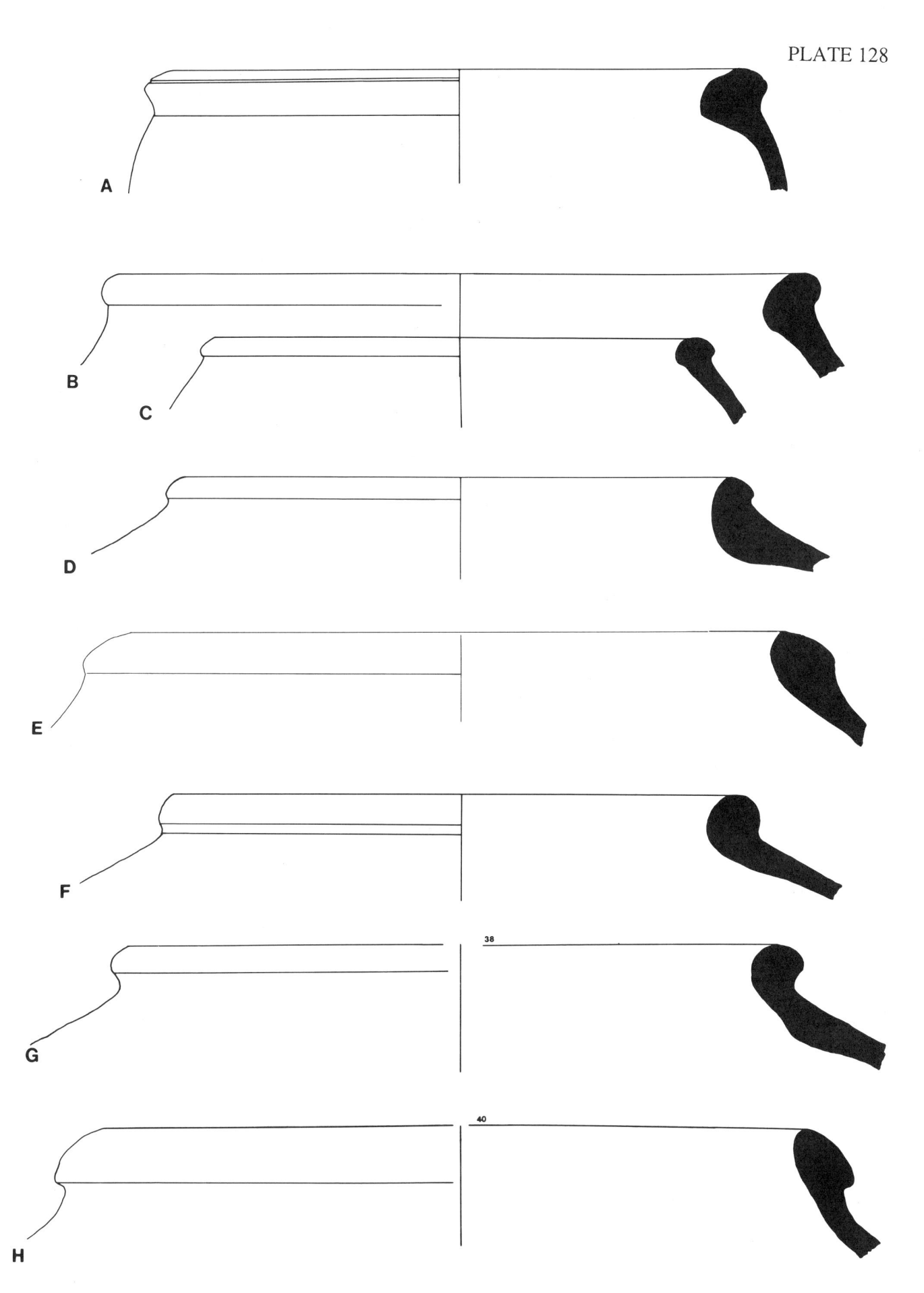

Period III Pottery From Areas A, D, and E: Ware Group I Storage-Sized Jars. Scale 2:5.

Plate 129. Period III Pottery From Areas A and D: Ware Group I Jars (*cont.*) and Stands. Scale 2:5.

|   | MRN | CONTEXT | FCN | WARE | FORM | TYPE | DECO. | WARE/REMARKS |
|---|---|---|---|---|---|---|---|---|
| A | 14920 | D36-0566-012 | D295 | 04 | 464 | Jar 28 | — | Dense reddish-buff clay; occasional scattered small-sized grits; lighter reddish-buff slip on exterior. |
| B | 2169 | D66-07-053 | 250 | 04 | 464 | Jar 28 | — | Brownish/orange-buff clay; small-sized white grits. |
| C | 10924 | D35-0948/49-033 | D676 | 04 | 464 | Jar 28 | — | Brownish-buff clay, reddish core; light brownish-buff slip on exterior. |
| D | 1451 | D46-01-002 | 012 | 04 | 464 | Jar 28 | — | Orange-buff clay; small-sized grits; buff slip on exterior. |
| E | 6104 | D43-0437-011 | 080 | 04 | C-32 | Stand 1 | — | Dense greenish-buff clay; small-sized grits. |
| F | 15853 | D23-02-013 | D230 | 04 | C-32 | Stand 1 | — | Dense light greenish-buff clay; small-sized grits. |
| G | 14233 | D23-01-005 | 011 | 04 | 976 | Stand 1 | — | Grayish-buff clay; small-sized grits. |
| H | 12886 | A01-05-016 | 075 | 04 | 205 | Stand 1 | — | Dense brownish-buff clay; small-sized grits. |
| I | 5019 | D54-05-014 | 102 | 04 | 898 | Stand 2 | — | Brownish-buff clay; small-sized grits; buff slip on exterior. |
| J | 0825 | A02-02-026 | 079 | 04 | 225 | Stand 2 | — | Fairly dense light brownish-buff clay; small-sized white grits. |
| K | 1398 | D56-03-002 | 029 | 04 | 749a | Stand 2 | — | Buff clay; small- and medium-sized grits, white ones prominent. |
| L | 5687 | D44-05-017 | 145 | 04 | 1168 | Stand 2 | — | Gritty brownish-buff clay; small- and medium-sized black and white grits. |
| M | 3176 | D54-04-013 | 049 | 04 | 749 | Stand 2 | — | Buff clay; small- and medium-sized grits, white ones prominent. |
| N | 15076 | D25-0191-003 | 189 | 04 | C-56 | Stand 2 | — | Buff clay mottled orange in patches; small-sized grits; somewhat irregular; (= KH 1983/152). |

PLATE 129

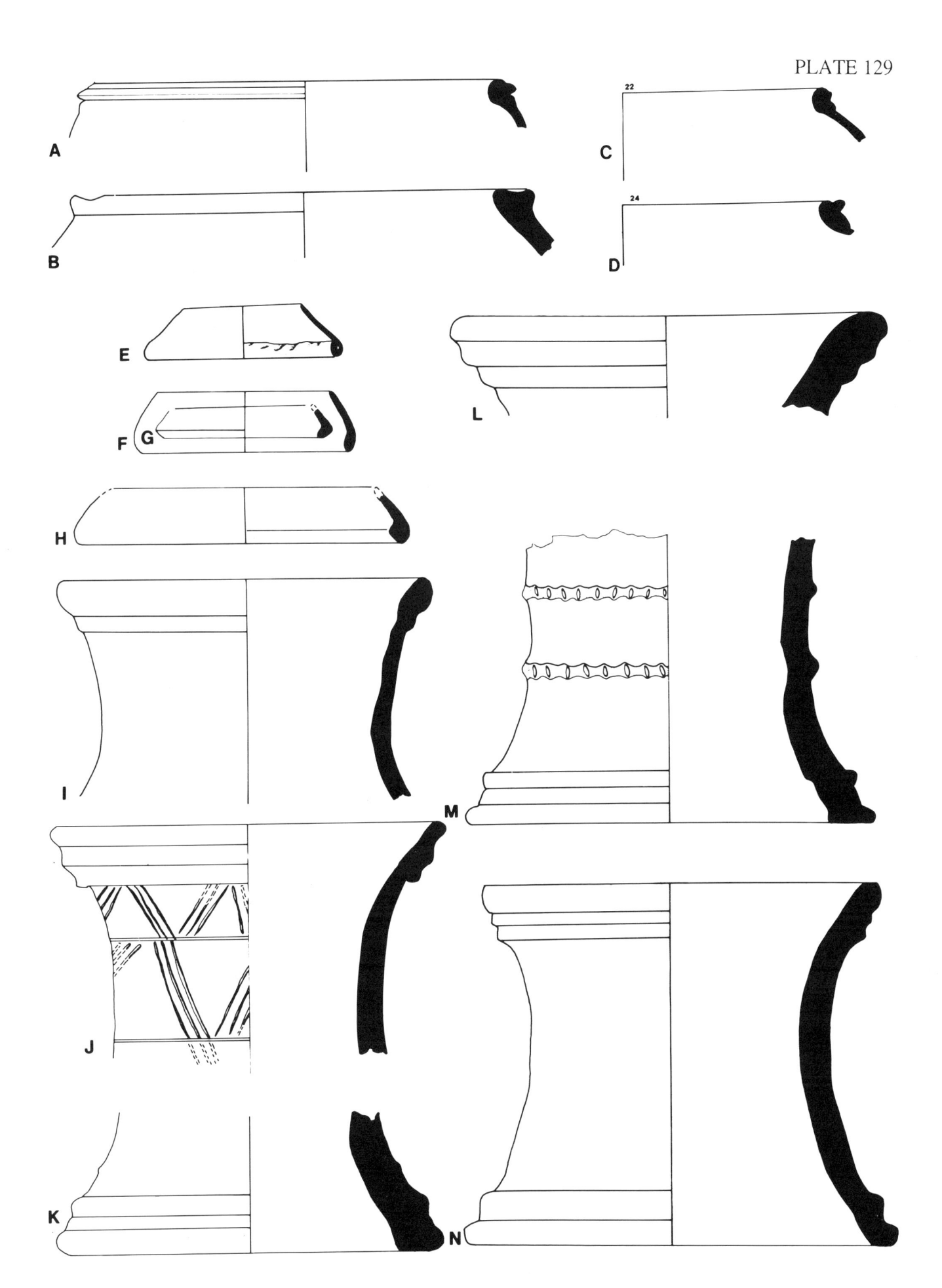

Period III Pottery From Areas A and D: Ware Group I Jars (*cont.*) and Stands. Scale 2:5.

Plate 130. Period III Pottery From Areas A and D: Ware Group I Stands (*cont.*) and Pedestal Bases. Scale 2:5.

|   | MRN | CONTEXT | FCN | WARE | FORM | TYPE | DECO. | WARE/REMARKS |
|---|---|---|---|---|---|---|---|---|
| A | 1221 | D56-03-001 | 022 | 04 | 368 | Stand 3 | — | Buff clay; small-sized grits. |
| B | 0825 | A02-02-026 | 079 | 04 | 227 | Stand 3 | — | Reddish-buff clay; small-sized grits, some white; note rectangular-shaped fenestration on body. |
| C | 16513 + 17517 | D36-0250-006 (ditto) | 425 + 423 | 04 | 173 | Pedestal Base 1 | — | Gritty orange-buff clay, slight brownish-buff core; small- and medium-sized grits visible, white ones prominent; orange-buff slip on exterior. |
| D | 5654 | D76-03-020 | D135 | 04 | 1153 | Pedestal Base 1 | — | Dense brownish-buff clay; small-sized grits, some white; greenish-buff slip on exterior. |
| E | 5863 | D53-02-003 | 028 | 04 | 1211 | Pedestal Base 1 | — | Light brownish-buff clay; small-sized black grits with some quartz flakes visible. |
| F | 5863 | D53-02-003 | 028 | 04 | 1210 | Pedestal Base 1 | — | Buff clay; small- and medium-sized grits. |
| G | 7813 | D35-0171-002 | 055 | 04 | 173 | Pedestal Base 1 | — | Dense brownish-buff clay; small-sized white grits; pedestal base attached secondarily to ring based jar. |
| H | 16604 | D36-0808-022 | 513 | 04 | 173 | Pedestal Base 1 | Bns. | Dense orange clay; small-sized white grits; exterior burnished with irregular but patterned vertical strokes. |
| I | 4802 | D55-01-004 | D57 | 04 | 1192 | Pedestal Base 1 | 308 | Gritty pinkish-buff clay; small-sized white grits; incised decoration. |
| J | 16552 | D36-0242-006 | 461 | 04 | 1615 | Pedestal Base 1 | 307 | Fairly dense orange-buff clay, grayish core; small-sized black grits. |

PLATE 130

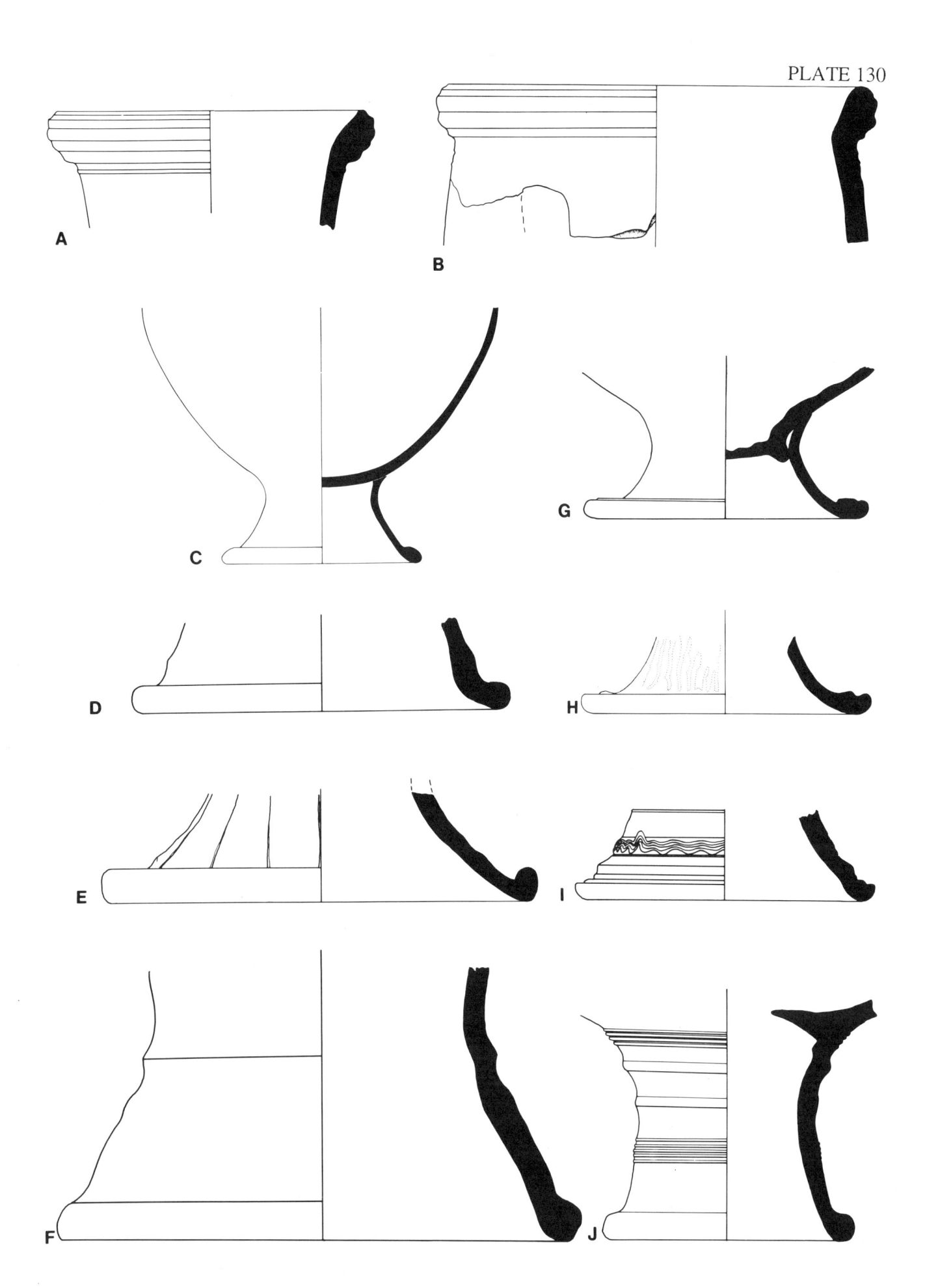

Period III Pottery From Areas A and D: Ware Group I Stands (*cont.*) and Pedestal Bases. Scale 2:5.

Plate 131. Period III Pottery From Areas A and D: Miscellaneous Bases, Feet, Accessories, and Decorated Bodies. Scale 2:5.

|   | MRN | CONTEXT | FCN | WARE | FORM | TYPE | DECO. | WARE/REMARKS |
|---|---|---|---|---|---|---|---|---|
| A | 6284 | D44-0710-027 | 152 | 04 | 1162 | Unass. Ring Base | — | Dense grayish-buff clay; small-sized gray grits. |
| B | 1110 | D65-01-003 | 015 | 04 | 1157 | Unass. Ring Base | — | Fairly dense orange-buff clay; small-sized grits. |
| C | 1429 | A08-01-002 | 014 | 04 | 441 | Unass. Ring Base | — | Brownish-buff clay; small-sized white grits; out of context in slope wash. |
| D | 1429 | A08-01-002 | 014 | 04 | 440 | Unass. Ring Base | — | Dense brownish-buff clay; small-sized grits; fast wheel corrugations clearly visible on interior; out of context in slope wash. |
| E | 2734 | D76-04-001 | 019 | 04 | 653 | Unass. Ring Base | — | Brownish-buff clay; small-sized white grits; spout by base. |
| F | 2734 | D76-04-001 | 019 | 04 | 652 | Unass. Ring Base | — | Brownish-buff clay; small-sized grits; buff slip on exterior. |
| G | 1542 | D66-06-041 | 199 | 04 | 441 | Unass. Ring Base | — | Brownish-buff clay; small-sized grits. |
| H | 3485 | D75-02-001 | 008 | 04 | 747 | Unass. Ring Base | 622 | Dense grayish-buff clay; small-sized grits, some white. |
| I | 6368 | D76-02-030 | 1661 | 04 | 309 | Foot | — | Dense reddish-buff clay; small-sized white grits. |
| J | 2586 | D76-02-001 | 005 | 04 | 242 | Foot | — | Buff clay; small-sized grits. |
| K | 3109 | D76-04-001 | 031 | 04 | 716 | Foot | — | Brownish-buff clay; small-sized grits, some white; exterior, fire smudged. |
| L | — | Area D Provenance lost | — | 04 | 716 | Foot | — | Brownish clay; small-sized white grits. |
| M | 16581 | D36-0565-012 | 490 | 04 | — | Unass. Body | 327 | Dense greenish-buff clay mottled orange in places. |
| N | 0274 | D66-02-003 | 009 | 04 | — | Unass. Body | 313 | Buff clay; small-sized grits. |
| O | 0265 | D66-02-004 | 012 | 04 | — | Unass. Body | 622 | Brownish-buff clay; small-sized grits. |
| P | 3187 | D76-0401-006 | 041 | 04 | — | Unass. Body | 701 | Buff clay; small-sized grits; impressed raised band, perhaps a snake. |
| Q | 5847 | D43-0198-010 | 068 | 04 | — | Unass. Body | 702 | Gritty greenish clay, overfired; small-sized black grits; relief decoration of winged(?) animal, possibly a lion or griffin; feathers indicated by vertical incisions; (=KH 1981/93). |

PLATE 131

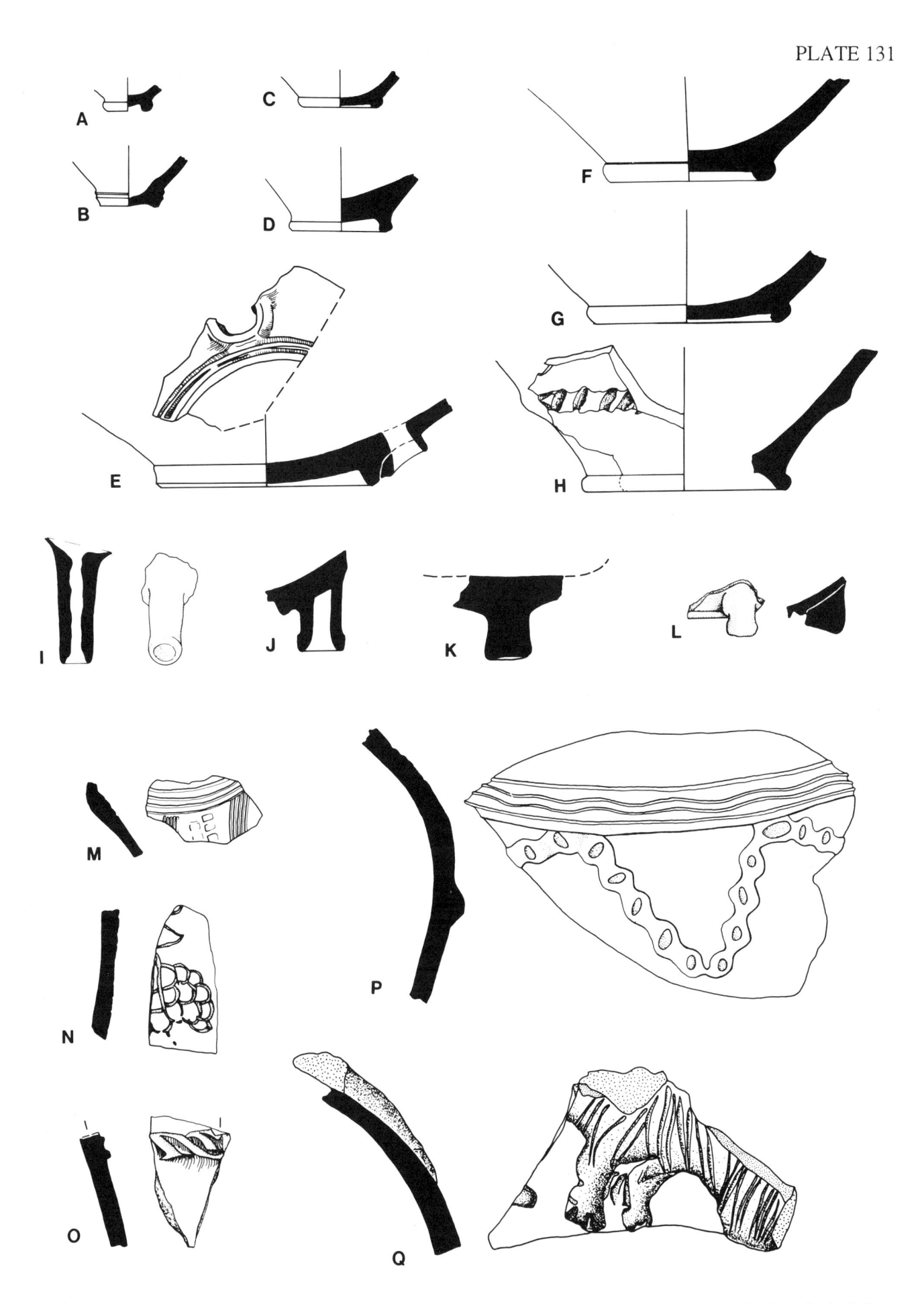

Period III Pottery From Areas A and D: Miscellaneous Bases, Feet, Accessories, and Decorated Bodies. Scale 2:5.

Plate 132. Period III Pottery From Areas B and D: Decorated Bodies (*cont.*). Scale 2:5.

|   | MRN | CONTEXT | FCN | WARE | FORM | TYPE | DECO. | WARE/REMARKS |
|---|---|---|---|---|---|---|---|---|
| A | 7813 | D35-0171-002 | 055 | 04 | — | Unass. Body | 330 | Brownish-buff clay; small-sized grits. |
| B | 15215 | D36-07-021 | D335 | 04 | — | Unass. Body | 329 | Grayish-buff clay; small-sized gray grits. |
| C | 17010 | D66-1097-096 | D609 | 04 | — | Unass. Body | 328 | Rather porous greenish-buff clay; small- and medium-sized grits visible. |
| D | 0003 | B01-03-001 | 004 | 04 | — | Unass. Body | 308 | Reddish-buff clay; small-sized grits. |
| E | 3889 | D34-01-003 | 016 | 04 | — | Unass. Body | 309 | Pinkish-buff clay; small-sized grits. |
| F | 3179 | D65-03-018 | 079 | 04 | — | Unass. Body | — | Cream paste; small-sized grits. |
| G | 5864 | D44-05-017 | 063 | 04 | — | Unass. Body | — | Reddish clay; small- and medium-sized white grits. |
| H | 5019 | D54-05-014 | 102 | 04 | — | Unass. Body | — | Grayish clay; small- and medium-sized white grits. |
| I | 5274 | D44-04-018 | 134 | 04 | — | Unass. Body | 622 | Reddish-buff clay; small-sized grits. |
| J | 10623 | D25-0183-003 | 032 | 04 | — | Unass. Body | 308 | Buff clay; small-sized grits. |

PLATE 132

Period III Pottery From Areas B and D: Decorated Bodies (*cont.*). Scale 2:5.

Plate 133. Period III Pottery From Areas A, D, and E: Metallic Ware Bowls and Jars, and Miscellaneous Rare Painted Sherds. Scale 2:5.

|   | MRN | CONTEXT | FCN | WARE | FORM | TYPE | DECO. | WARE/REMARKS |
|---|---|---|---|---|---|---|---|---|
| A | 15311 | D56-0491/92-019 | D156 | 02 | 1612 | Unass. Bowl | Ring Bns. | Dense gray-black clay; no visible tempering; traces of ring burnishing on interior and exterior. |
| B | 17293 | D66-1210-083 | D725 | 02 | 1636 | Bowl 6 | Ring Bns. | Dense dark brown clay, gray core; minute white grits visible; ring burnished on interior and exterior. |
| C | 3108 | D76-03-002 | 029 | 02 | 1171 | Bowl 8b | Ring Bns. | Dense gray clay; no visible tempering; faint traces of ring burnishing on exterior. |
| D | 14778 | D23-0279-004 | D105 | 02 | 019a | Unass. Bowl | Ring Bns. | Dense brownish-buff clay grading to orange on exterior; faint traces of ring burnishing on exterior. |
| E | 15809 | D23-0192-013 | D186 | 02 | 1606 | Bowl 8b | — | Dense gray clay; no visible tempering except scattered small-sized white grits. |
| F | 3911 | D44-04-018 | 070 | 02 | 813 | Jar 22 | — | Dense reddish clay grading to grayish towards exterior; occasional scattered small-sized white grits. |
| G | 4804 | E04-01-002 | 004 | 02 | 906 | Jar 1 | Ring Bns. | Dense gray clay; no visible tempering; ring burnished on exterior. |
| H | 001 | A01-02-002 | 003 | 02 | 195 | Jar 1 | — | Dense gray clay; no visible tempering; no preserved traces on exterior burnishing. |
| I | 3892 | D34-0178-002 | 027 | 02 | C-16 | Jar 1 | Ring Bns. | Dense gray clay; occasional scattered white grits; light horizontal ring burnish on exterior; (= KH 1981/48). |
| J | — | Area D Provenance lost | — | 02 | 599 | Jar 14 | — | Dense gray clay; occasional scattered white grits; light gray exterior; unburnished. |
| K | 15190 | D66-0827-083 | D485 | 02 | 620 | Jar 15a | — | Dense gray clay; occasional scattered black grits; unburnished. |
| L | 15902 | D66-0829-087 | D510 | 02 | 1600 | Unass. Jar | Ring Bns. | Dense gray clay; no visible tempering; faint traces of ring burnishing on exterior. |
| M | 615 | D66-02-003 | 062 | 02 | 116 | Jar 24a | — | Dense brown clay; occasional scattered white grits. |
| N | 3393 | D54-05-014 | 053 | 02 | 695 | Jar 29 | 023 | Dense gray clay; occasional scattered small-sized white grits. |
| O | 8279 | D35-0242-008 | 189 | 02 | C-36 | Jar 29 | Ring Bns. | Dense brownish clay, exterior mottled black-brownish; occasional scattered small white grits; ring burnishing on neck; (= KH 1982/121). |
| P | 878 | D66-05-001 | 098 | 24 | 120 | Jar 26b | — | Buff clay; small-sized white grits; greenish-buff on exterior, black paint. |
| Q | 2725 | D45-01-003 | 013 | 24 | 121 | Unass. Jar | — | Rather dense brownish-buff clay; small-sized grits; lighter brownish-buff slip on exterior; brown paint. |
| R | 8484 | D35-0373-010 | D210 | 24 | — | Unass. Body | 190 | Reddish-buff clay; small- and medium-sized white grits, brown paint. |
| S | 6291 | D44-0178-026 | 193 | 21 | 1158 | Unass. Body | — | Dense gray clay; tempered primarily with very finely-chopped chaff and a few scattered white grits. |
| T | 2725 | D45-01-003 | 013 | 24 | 120 | Jar 26b | — | Light yellowish-buff clay; small-sized black grits; on exterior, self slip of same color as clay but lighter; dark brown paint. |

PLATE 133

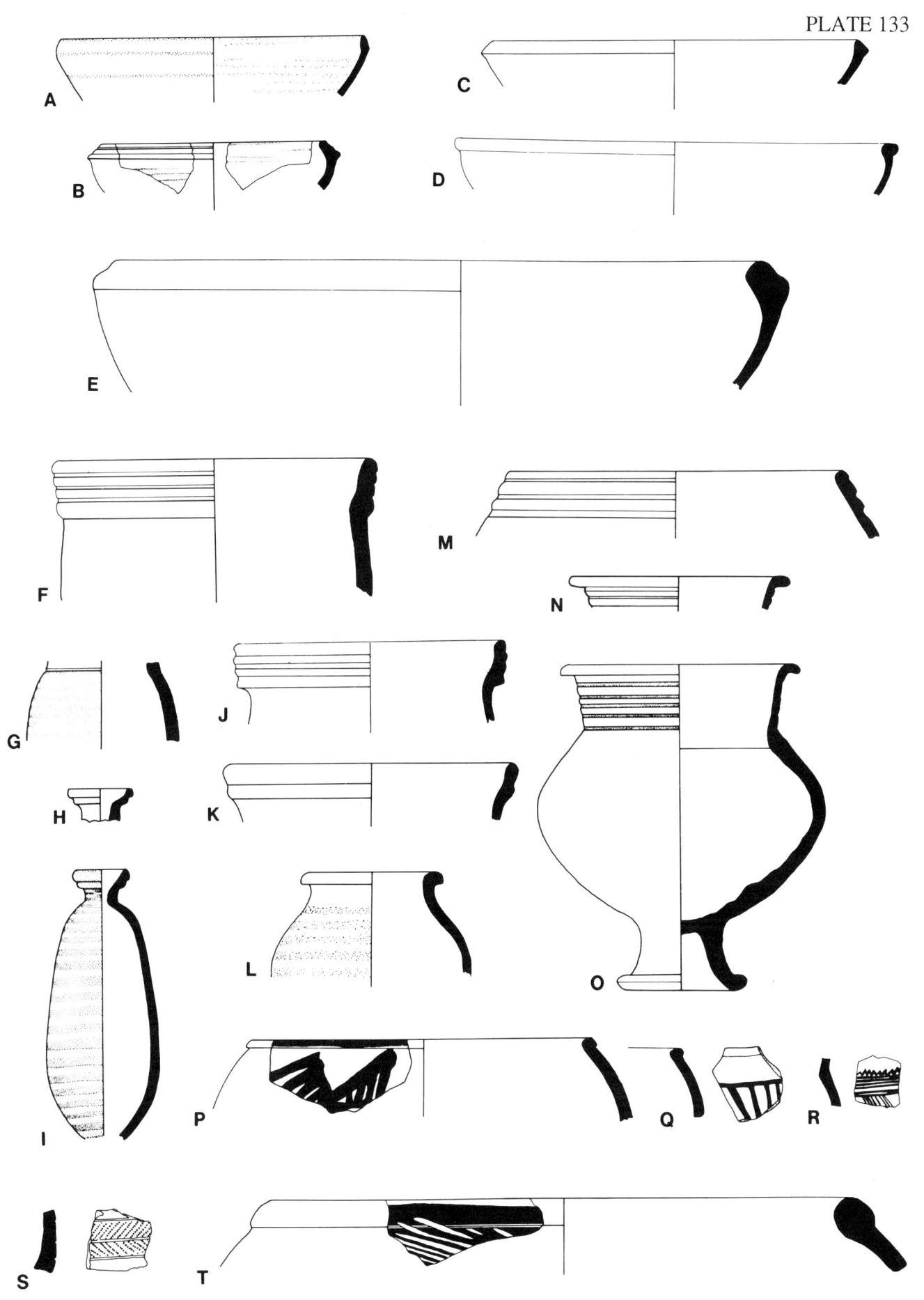

Period III Pottery From Areas A, D, and E: Metallic Ware Bowls and Jars, and Miscellaneous Rare Painted Sherds. Scale 2:5.

Plate 134. Period III Pottery From Area D: Ware Group II Bowls. Scale 2:5.

|   | MRN | CONTEXT | FCN | WARE | FORM | TYPE | DECO. | WARE/REMARKS |
|---|---|---|---|---|---|---|---|---|
| A | 5019 | D54-05-014 | 102 | 21 | 897 | Unass. Jar | 622 | Dense brown clay; tempered with finely-chopped chaff; a few grits visible. |
| B | 541 | D66-03-002 | 049 | 09 | 155 | Bowl 16 | — | Brownish clay; tempered with a combination of medium-sized white grits and quartz flakes; surfaces are black. |
| C | 16550 | D36-0242-006 | 459 | 09 | 1614 | Bowl 17 | — | Dense gray clay; a few scattered white grits and quartz flakes; exterior is mottled gray and brown. |
| D | 15073 | D25-0191-003 | 190 | 09 | 1628 | Bowl 17 | — | Dense grayish clay; a few scattered medium-sized white grits and quartz flakes. |
| E | 17095 | D56-03-030 | — | 09 | 1668 | Unass. Bowl | — | Reddish-brown clay; tempered with medium-sized white grits and quartz flakes. |
| F | 2724 | D44-03-012 | 043 | 09 | 0636 | Unass. Bowl | Bns. | Orange-buff clay; small- and medium-sized white grits; exterior surface mottled brownish-orange and grayish; burnished. |
| G | 5864 | D44-05-017 | 063 | 09 | 1306 | Unass. Bowl | — | Dense brownish clay; medium-sized white grits and quartz flakes visible; exterior is mottled brown and black. |
| H | 15828 | D23-0285/95-013 | D205 | 09 | 1605 | Unass. Bowl | Bns. | Red clay; gritty with medium-sized gray grits and quartz flakes; exterior mottled red and gray, lightly burnished. |
| I | 3392 | D53-01-002 | 013 | 09 | 1244 | Unass. Jar | — | Reddish clay; small-sized white grits, quartz flakes and larger-sized black grits visible; exterior is rough. |

PLATE 134

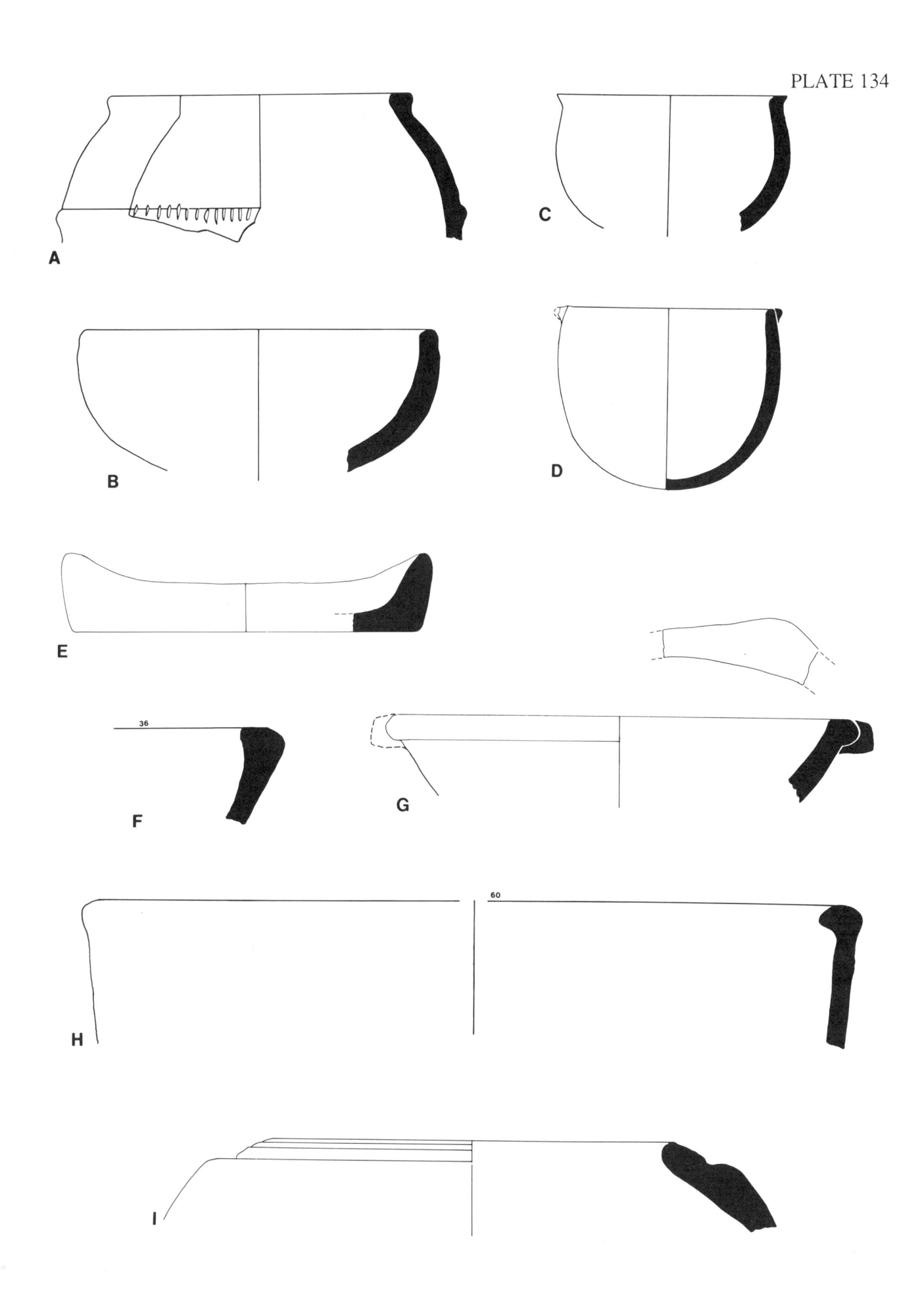

Period III Pottery From Area D: Ware Group II Bowls. Scale 2:5.

Plate 135. Period III Pottery From Areas A, B, and D: Ware Group II Jars. Scale 2:5.

|   | MRN | CONTEXT | FCN | WARE | FORM | TYPE | DECO. | WARE/REMARKS |
|---|---|---|---|---|---|---|---|---|
| A | 15892 | D23-03-020 | 257 | 09 | 228 | Jar 30 | Bns. | Brownish clay; tempered with medium-sized gray grits and quartz flakes; exterior mottled brown and black; lightly burnished. |
| B | 10012 | D42-02-001 | 206 | 09 | 1514 | Jar 30 | Bns. | Fairly dense gray clay; white grits and a few scattered quartz flakes visible; exterior orangish mottled gray. |
| C | 15722 | D23-0299-021 | 284 | 09 | 228 | Jar 30 | Bns. | Gray clay; small- and medium-sized white and gray grits, occasional scattered quartz flakes; exterior mottled gray and brown; lightly burnished. |
| D | 19005 | B72-0202-009 | 079 | 09 | 1514 | Jar 30 | Bns. | Brownish clay, prominent gray core; quartz flakes very prominent; exterior is grayish and burnished. |
| E | 12882 | A01-05-032 | 071 | 09 | 228 | Jar 30 | Bns. | Reddish clay; very gritty with medium-sized white grits prominent; some crushed shell used in tempering; exterior mottled brown and gray; lightly burnished. |
| F | 825 | A02-02-026 | 079 | 09 | 228 | Jar 30 | Bns. | Brownish clay; gritty with large and medium-sized white grits; exterior is brownish-buff; lightly burnished. |
| G | 17879 | D38-04-018 | D066 | 09 | 150 | Jar 31a | Bns. | Brownish clay; medium-sized gray grits, occasional small-sized pebbles also used as tempering; quartz flakes prominent; exterior mottled in several shades of brown; lightly burnished. |
| H | 15081 | D35-0501-028 | 762 | 09 | 150 | Jar 31a | Bns. | Brownish-orange clay; gritty with numerous medium- and large-sized white grits and quartz flakes visible; exterior light brown; very lightly burnished. |
| I | 17856 | D66-1095-096 | D876 | 09 | 150 | Jar 31a | — | Gray clay grading to orange on exterior surface; medium-sized white grits, quartz flakes visible. |
| J | 2225 | D45-01-003 | 008 | 09 | 150 | Jar 31a | — | Orange clay; medium- to large-sized white and gray grits, quartz flakes visible; unburnished. |

PLATE 135

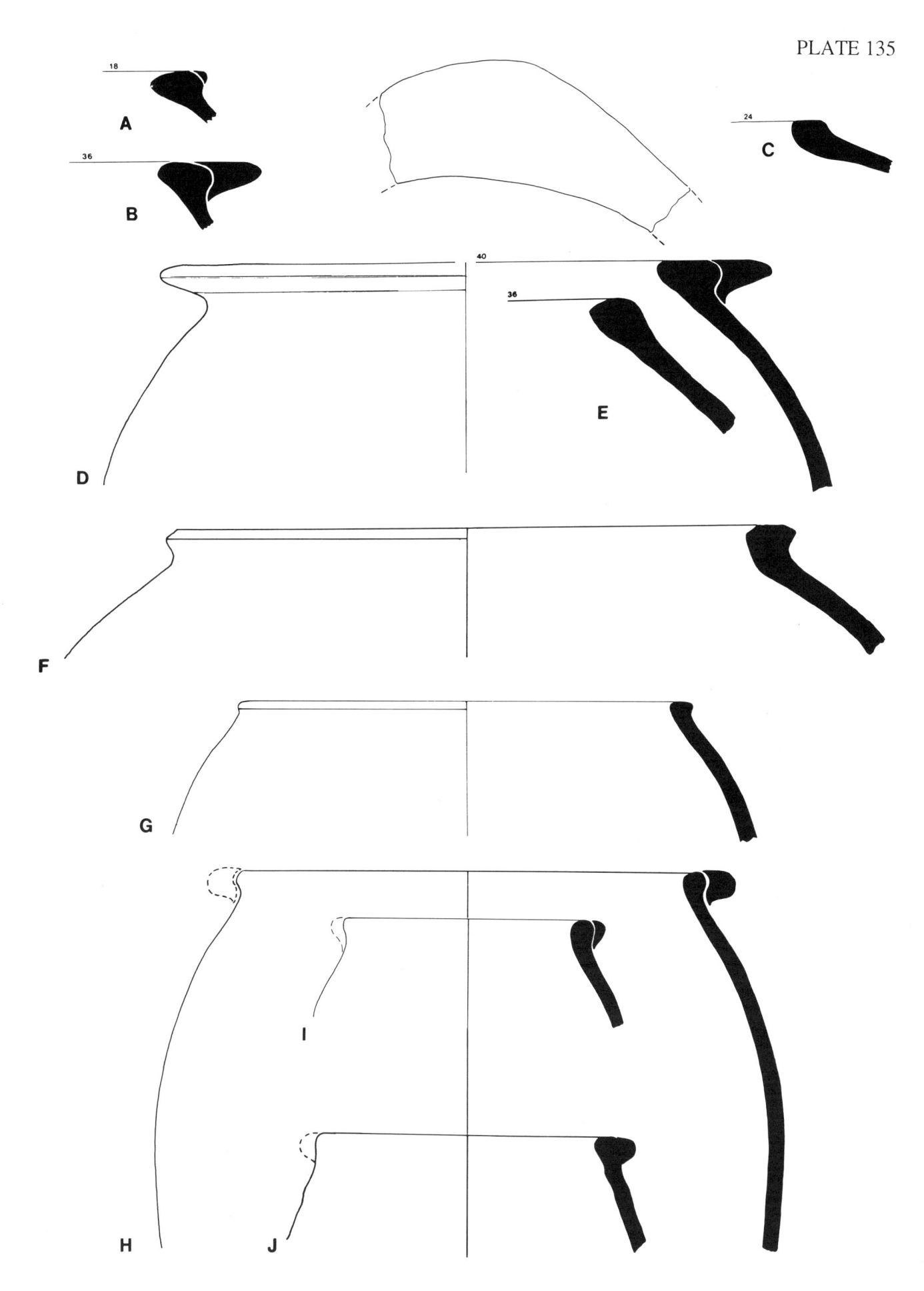

Period III Pottery From Areas A, B, and D: Ware Group II Jars. Scale 2:5.

Plate 136. Period III Pottery From Areas A and D: Ware Group II Jars (*cont.*). Scale 2:5.

|   | MRN | CONTEXT | FCN | WARE | FORM | TYPE | DECO. | WARE/REMARKS |
|---|---|---|---|---|---|---|---|---|
| A | 2730 | D65-03-001 | 058 | 09 | 151 | Jar 31b | — | Reddish-brownish clay, dark gray core; large white grits; exterior mottled reddish, pinkish, and brownish; unburnished. |
| B | 12895 | A01-05-016 | 084 | 09 | 151 | Jar 31b | Bns. | Reddish clay; medium-sized gray grits and quartz flakes used as tempering; exterior mottled orange and brown; highly burnished. |
| C | 17169 | D56-0471-031 | D266 | 09 | 151 | Jar 31b | Bns. | Brownish clay grading to gray towards interior surface; medium-sized grits and quartz flakes visible; both surfaces lightly burnished. |
| D | 4936 | D44-05-017 | 122 | 09 | 1188 | Jar 32 | — | Reddish clay grading to gray towards surfaces; large- and medium-sized white grits; unburnished. |
| E | 1637 | D66-06-042 | 203 | 09 | 293 | Jar 32 | — | Orange clay, gray core; white grits and quartz flakes visible; unburnished. |
| F | 2492 | D66-07-054 | 270 | 09 | 293 | Jar 32 | — | Brownish-buff clay; medium-sized white grits and quartz flakes used as tempering; unburnished. |
| G | 870 | D66-04-016 | 100 | 09 | 293 | Jar 32 | — | Brownish-buff clay; medium- and large-sized white grits. |
| H | 870 | D66-04-016 | 100 | 09 | 293 | Jar 32 | Bns. | Grayish clay; medium- and large-sized grits, some quartz flakes; exterior is grayish and lightly burnished. |
| I | 8740 | D35-0375-010 | 257 | 09 | 640 | Jar 32 | 600 | Brownish-buff clay; gritty with medium-sized black and white grits and quartz flakes visible; on exterior a large blackened burnt patch. |
| J | 2656 | D65-02-006 | 052 | 09 | 640 | Jar 32 | Bns. 600 | Gray clay; gritty with white and gray grits visible; exterior mottled brownish and gray; lightly burnished. |
| K | 7010 | D66-1097-002 | D609 | 09 | 640a | Jar 32 | Bns. 600 | Brownish clay, gray core; gritty with white and gray grits and quartz flakes visible; exterior grayish and lightly burnished or smoothed. |
| L | 7698 | D35-0107-002 | 009 | 09 | 293 | Jar 32 | — | Brownish clay; gritty with medium-sized grits. |

PLATE 136

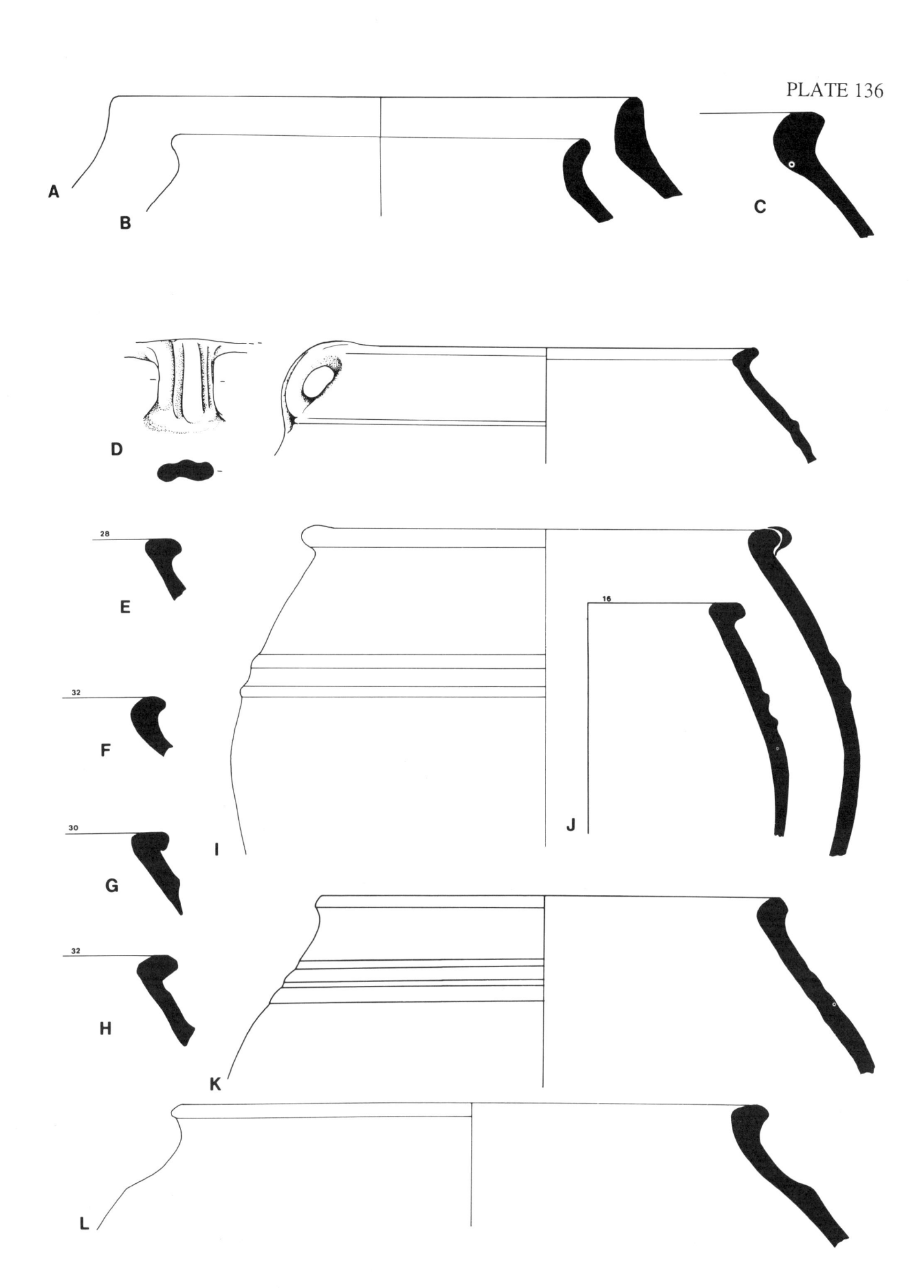

Period III Pottery From Areas A and D: Ware Group II Jars (*cont.*). Scale 2:5.

Plate 137. Period II Pottery From Area D: Glazed Bowls. Scale 2:5.

|   | MRN | CONTEXT | FCN | WARE | FORM | TYPE | DECO. | WARE/REMARKS |
|---|---|---|---|---|---|---|---|---|
| A | 2290 | D55-02-006 | 024 | 22 | C-69 | — | Glazed | Dense orange clay; occasional scattered small-sized white grits; exterior covered with uniform yellow glaze. |
| B | 3498 | D54-01-013 | 060 | 22 | 1245 | — | Glazed | Dense orange-buff clay; small-sized white grits; splashes of yellow glaze on exterior. |
| C | 1398 | D56-03-002 | 029 | 22 | 1245 | — | Glazed | Dense orange clay; somewhat gritty with white grits visible; on interior, uniform blue-green glaze; on exterior, yellow glaze splashed. |
| D | 1398 | D56-03-002 | 029 | 22 | 410 | — | Glazed | Dense orange clay; small-sized white grits; on exterior, splashes of cream-white glaze; on interior, white-cream glaze towards top of vessel and green glaze towards base. |
| E | 15028 | D53-05-001 | 056 | 22 | 1623 | — | Glazed | Dense orange/light brownish-buff clay; small-sized white grits; surface splashes of cream-white glaze on exterior; on interior, irregular pattern formed by diagonal bonds of cream-white and black glaze. |
| F | 1709 | D66-06-044 | 215 | 22 | 549 | — | Glazed | Dense brownish-buff/orange clay; small-sized grits; on interior, uniform yellow glaze, on exterior, splashes of yellow glaze. |
| G | 2481 | D42-01-003 | 012 | 22 | 1341 | — | Glazed | Dense reddish-buff/orange clay; small-sized white grits; both surfaces covered with cream-white glaze; on exterior, glaze has been scraped away in places and occasionally a coat of green glaze has been added on top. |
| H | 3394 | D54-06-001 | 055 | 22 | 730 | — | Glazed | Dense orange clay; small-sized white grits; both surfaces covered with cream-white glaze; on exterior, rim covered with dark green glaze; interior covered with irregular swirl in shades of brown, green, and olive green glaze. |
| I | 3395 | D65-04-001 | 083 | 22 | 1343 | — | Glazed | Dense brownish-buff clay; small-sized white grits; both surfaces covered with coat of cream-white glaze; a second coat of greenish-blue glaze spread uniformly over the first; the glaze is lighter and whiter where thin, and increasingly bluish where thicker; (= KH 1981/104). |

PLATE 137

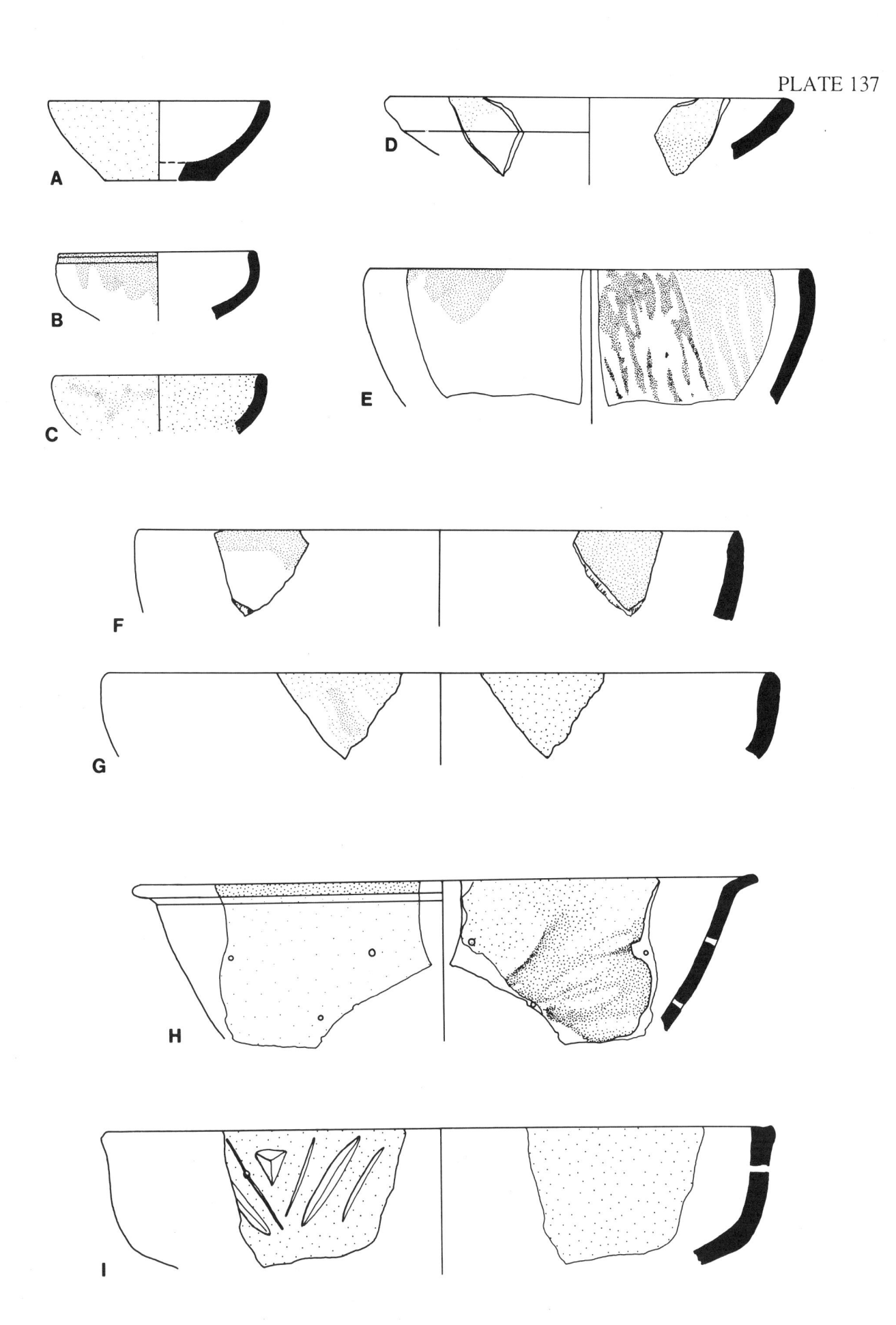

Period II Pottery From Area D: Glazed Bowls. Scale 2:5.

Plate 138. Period II Pottery From Area D: Glazed Bowls (*cont.*), Jars, and Lamp. Scale 2:5.

|   | MRN | CONTEXT | FCN | WARE | FORM | TYPE | DECO. | WARE/REMARKS |
|---|-----|---------|-----|------|------|------|-------|--------------|
| A | 10000 | D56-01-003 | 055 | 22 | 1343 | — | Glazed | Dense orange clay; small-sized white grits; bluish-greenish glaze covers both surfaces. |
| B | 8494 | D55-04-001 | 087 | 22 | 1343 | — | Glazed | Dense yellowish clay; small-sized grits; surfaces covered with coat of cream-white glaze over which a second coat of greenish glaze has been applied. |
| C | 2584 | D66-06-002 | 267 | 22 | 1343 | — | Glazed | Dense orange clay; small-sized white grits; surfaces covered with uniform greenish glaze. |
| D | 9041 | D55-05-021 | 208 | 22 | 1357 | — | Glazed | Orange clay; small-sized white grits; surfaces covered with uniform coat of green glaze. |
| E | 15431 | D25-0637-021 | D231 | 22 | 1534 | — | Glazed | Dense orange clay; small-sized grits; exterior covered with uniform coat of greenish glaze; (=KH 1983/161). |
| F | 3723 | D53-02-001 | 020 | 22 | 1343 | — | Glazed | Dense orange clay; small-sized white grits; both surfaces covered with uniform coat of cream-white glaze; a second coat of greenish glaze was applied over both surfaces under horizontal bands of darker greenish glaze visible on interior. |
| G | 3723 | D53-02-001 | 020 | 22 | 1243 | — | Glazed | Rather porous greenish-buff clay; small-sized grits; coat of greenish glaze applied over initial coat of cream-white glaze; darker towards rim. |
| H | 5811 | D43-04-001 | 049 | 22 | 1343 | — | Glazed | Orange clay; small-sized grits; coat of greenish glaze applied over initial coat of cream-white glaze; thinner on exterior, thicker on interior. |
| I | 9041 | D55-05-021 | 208 | 22 | 1343 | — | Glazed | Yellowish clay; small-sized grits; uniform coat of olive green glaze applied over initial coat of cream glaze; lighter on patches where thinner. |
| J | 3177 | D54-04-013 | 050 | 22 | 760 | — | Glazed | Buff clay; small-sized grits; exterior covered with aquamarine blue glaze irregularly applied. |
| K | 2486 | D54-04-001 | 024 | 22 | C-38 | — | Glazed | Dense orange clay; exterior covered with uniform coat of cream glaze and irregular splashes of green glaze. |
| L | 4837 | D55-03-009 | 055 | 22 | 1175 | — | Glazed | Dense orange clay; small-sized grits; glazed only on interior with pattern achieved by an initial coat of cream glaze covered in sections with patches of green glaze; a number of depressions on exterior. |
| M | 8876 | D55-0466-019 | 132 | 22 | 1620 | — | Glazed | Dense greenish-buff clay; small-sized grits; both surfaces covered by greenish glaze with patches mottled bluish. |

PLATE 138

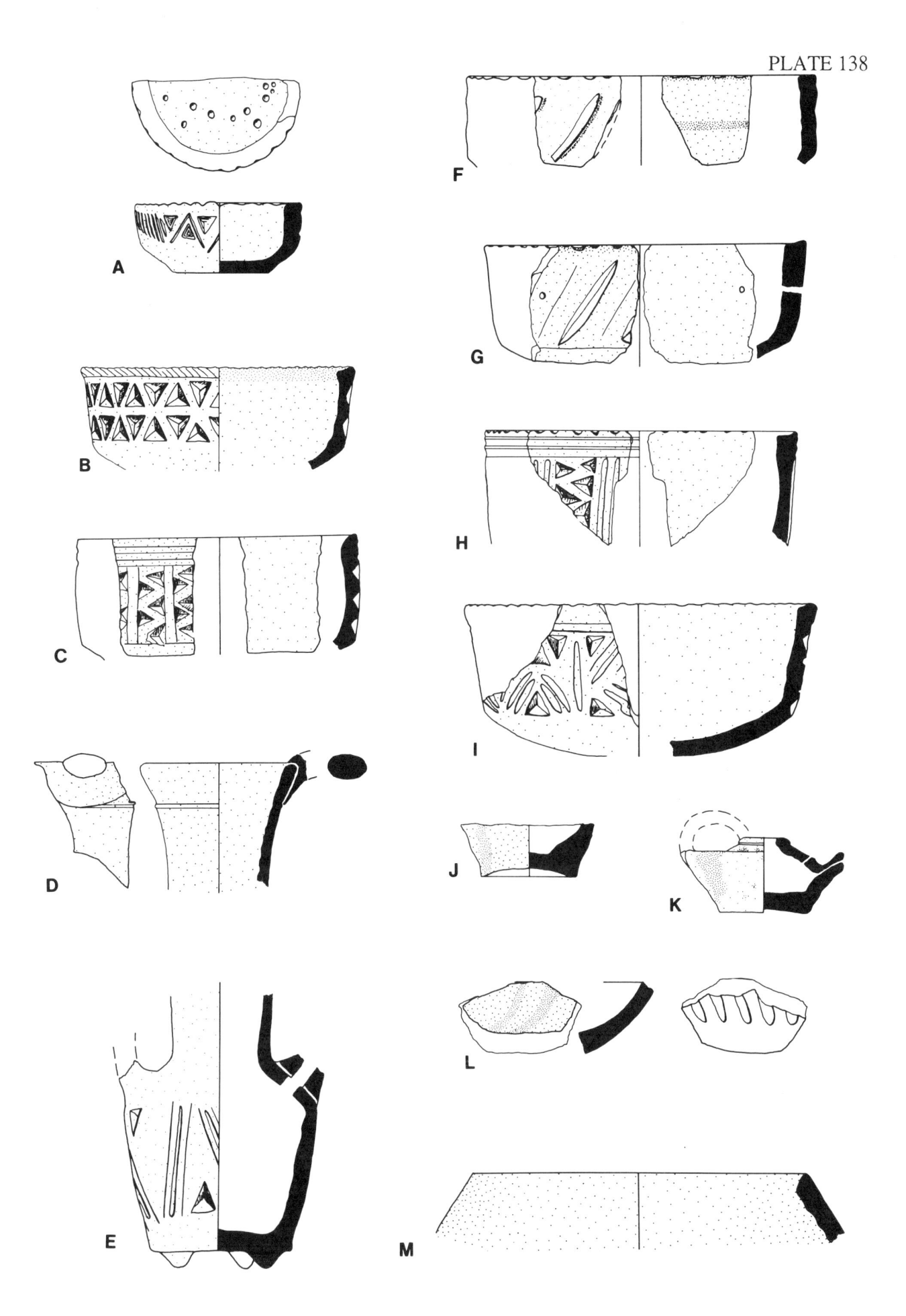

Period II Pottery From Area D: Glazed Bowls (*cont.*), Jars, and Lamp. Scale 2:5.

Plate 139. Period II Pottery From Area D: Plain Simple Ware and Cream Ware Bowls. Scale 2:5.

|   | MRN | CONTEXT | FCN | WARE | FORM | TYPE | DECO. | WARE/REMARKS |
|---|---|---|---|---|---|---|---|---|
| A | 1630 | D46-01-004 | 017 | 04 | 570 | — | — | Orange-buff clay; small-sized white grits; possibly a glaze ware form but, if so, traces of glaze did not survive. |
| B | 5807 | D34-01-002 | 010 | 04 | 560 | — | — | Orange clay; small-sized grits; possibly a glazed form but, if so, traces of glaze did not survive. |
| C | 8712 | D55-04-018 | 097 | 04 | 1349 | — | — | Fairly dense grayish/brownish-buff clay; small-sized grits. |
| D | 1956 | D66-07-050 | 238 | 04 | 529 | — | — | Dense dark brown clay; small-sized white grits; loop handle attached to rim. |
| E | 10040 | D55-02-039 | 308 | 04 | 1619 | — | 351 | Fairly dense brownish-buff clay; small-sized black grits; on interior, imprinted and incised decoration; on exterior, fire smudged. |
| F | 9013 | D55-05-001 | 160 | 04 | 1358 | — | 350 | Fairly dense light brownish-buff clay; small-sized grits; incised decoration on exterior. |
| G | 15212 | D25-0556-011 | D258 | 04 | 1633 | — | — | Light brownish-buff clay, pale reddish core; fairly gritty with small white and gray grits, also a few scattered larger-sized white angular grits visible. |
| H | 3568 | D53-02-001 | 022 | 04 | 754 | — | — | Gritty buff clay; small-sized grits. |
| I | 5811 | D43-04-011 | 049 | 04 | 1339 | — | — | Dense orange clay, gray core; small-sized white grits. |
| J | 14307 | D56-04-013 | 072 | 04 | 1626 | — | 622 | Somewhat porous orange clay; small-sized grits, some white; exterior brownish, fire smudged in places. |
| K | 2653 | D45-01-003 | 010 | 04 | 691 | — | — | Buff clay; small-sized white grits. |
| L | 14307 | D56-04-013 | 072 | 52 | 1625 | — | — | Rather porous cream clay; small- and medium-sized grits. |
| M | 9121 | D55-05-021 | 217 | 04 | — | — | 352 | Light brownish-buff clay; small-sized black and white grits. |
| N | 3487 | D54-06-015 | 058 | 04 | — | — | — | Reddish-buff clay; small-sized grits; cream slip on exterior; root of handle. |

PLATE 139

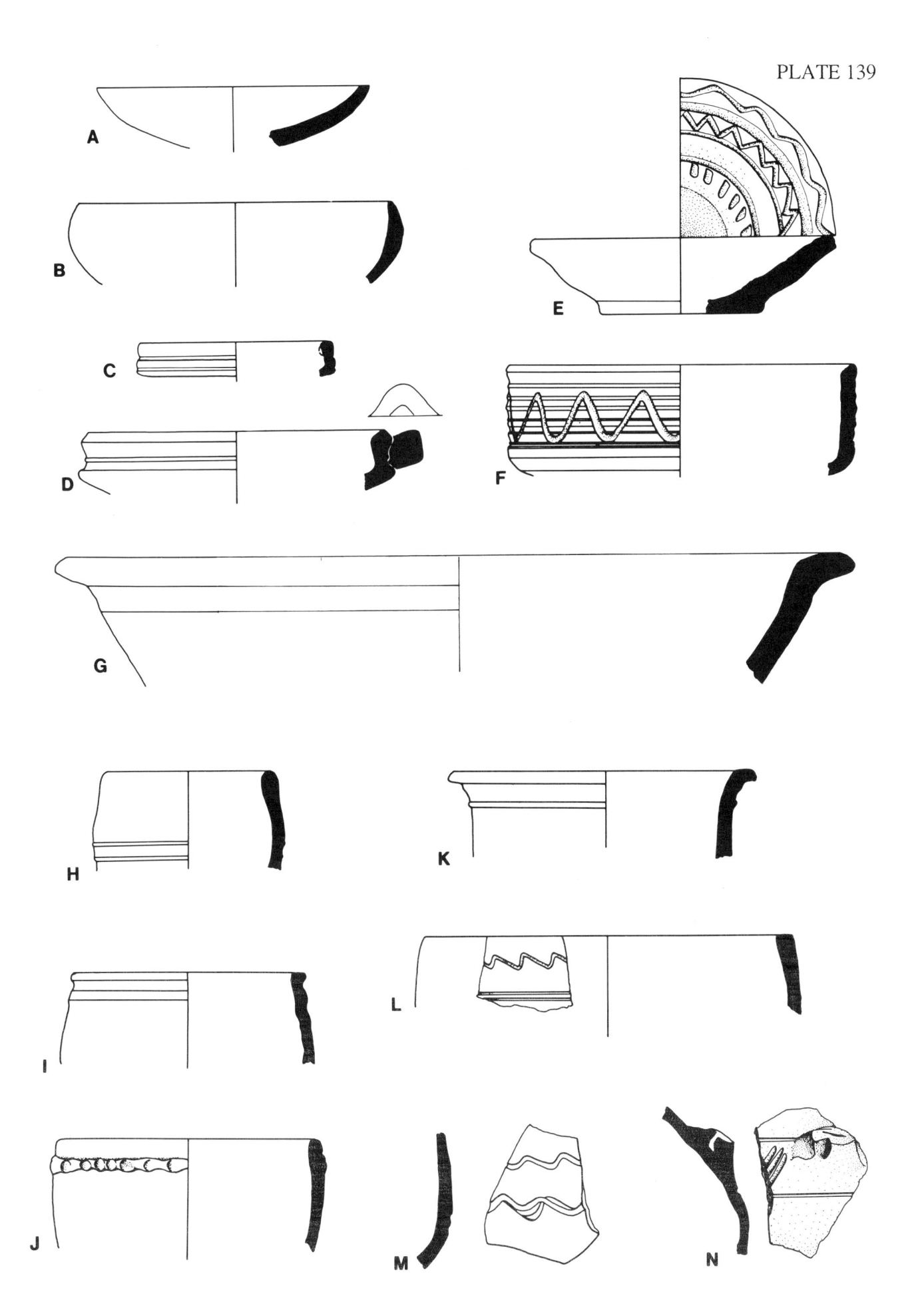

Period II Pottery From Area D: Plain Simple Ware and Cream Ware Bowls. Scale 2:5.

Plate 140. Period II Pottery From Area D: Plain Simple Ware and Cream Ware Jars. Scale 2:5.

|   | MRN | CONTEXT | FCN | WARE | FORM | TYPE | DECO. | WARE/REMARKS |
|---|---|---|---|---|---|---|---|---|
| A | 4802 | D55-01-004 | 057 | 52 | 1194 | — | — | Light buff clay; small-sized grits. |
| B | 8494 | D55-04-001 | 087 | 52 | 1345 | — | — | Porous light greenish-buff clay; small-sized grits. |
| C | 5359 | D54-06-024 | 119 | 52 | 1223 | — | — | Soft, porous cream clay; small-sized black grits. |
| D | 1398 | D56-03-002 | 029 | 52 | 405 | — | — | Porous light greenish-buff clay; small-sized grits. |
| E | 2167 + 2293 | D65-01-002 + D65-01-005 | 009 + 022 | 04 | 556 | — | — | Orange clay, brownish-buff core; small-sized white grits; imprinted and excised decoration on exterior. |
| F | 14313 | D56-02-015 | 078 | 04 | 289 | — | — | Dense brownish-buff clay; small-sized grits; greenish-buff slip on surface. |
| G | 7156 | D76-02-036 | 197 | 52 | 1127 | — | 023 | Greenish-buff clay; small-sized grits; fast wheel striations visible on exterior and interior; intrusive in Period III pit. |
| H | 3723 | D53-02-001 | 020 | 52 | — | — | 541 | Porous light greenish-buff clay; small-sized grits. |
| I | 15212 | D25-0556-011 | D258 | 52 | 1631 | — | — | Greenish-buff/cream clay; small-sized grits, some white but red and gray ones also visible. |
| J | 15434 | D36-06-016 | D313 | 52 | 1637 | — | — | Cream-buff clay; small-sized grits, some gray and white visible. |
| K | 2487 | D55-02-006 | 026 | 52 | 605 | — | — | Porous greenish-buff clay; small-sized grits. |
| L | 8725 | D55-0454-019 | 110 | 52 | 1354 | — | — | Porous greenish-buff clay; small-sized grits. |
| M | 2164 | D54-03-001 | 017 | 04 | 621 | — | — | Fairly dense orange-reddish clay, gray core; small-sized grits. |
| N | 2586 | D76-02-001 | 005 | 04 | 621 | — | — | Dense brownish-buff clay grading to orange on exterior and gray towards interior. |

PLATE 140

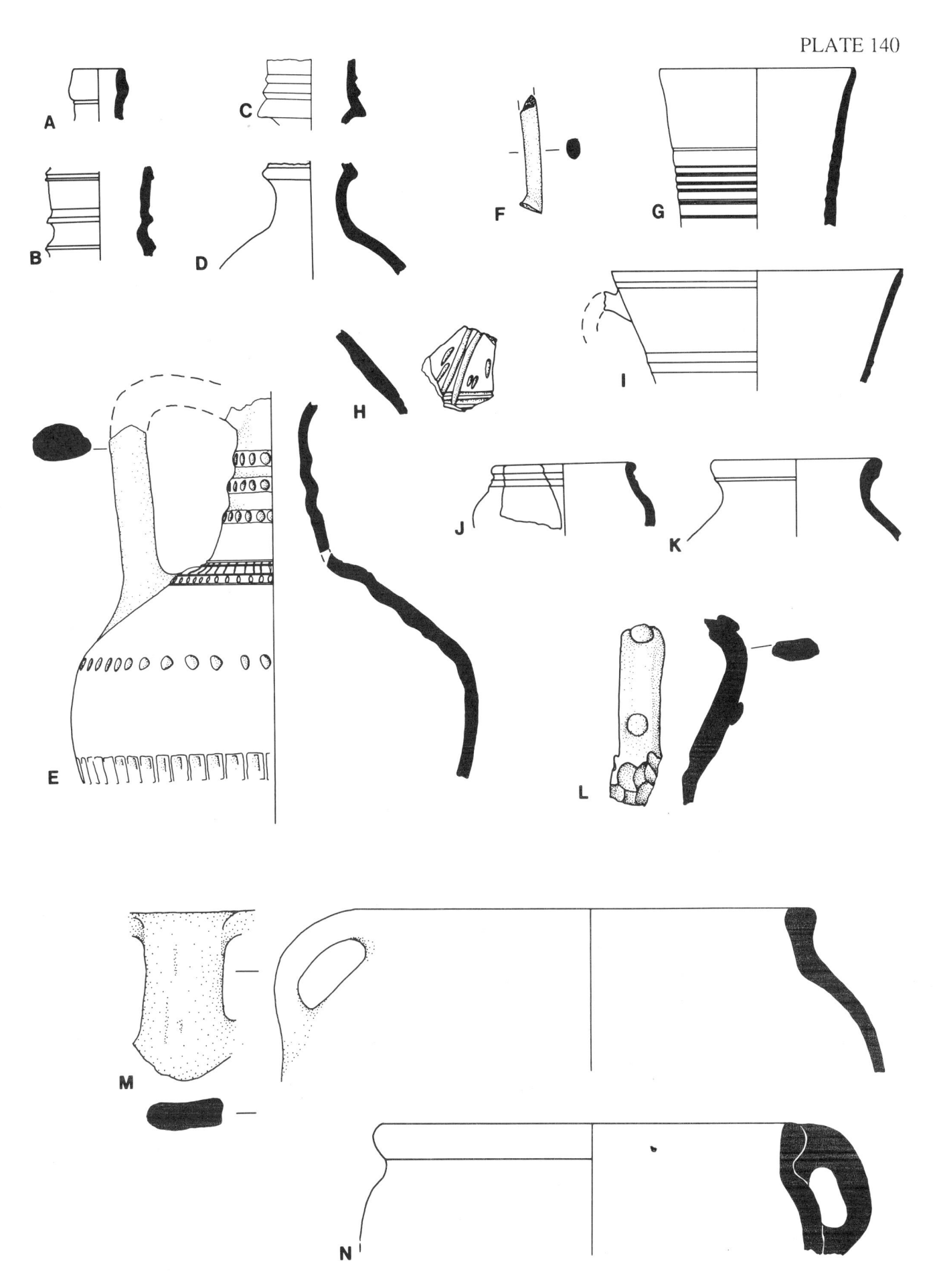

Period II Pottery From Area D: Plain Simple Ware and Cream Ware Jars. Scale 2:5.

Plate 141. Period II Pottery From Areas B and D: Plain Simple Ware Amphorae. Scale 2:5.

|   | MRN | CONTEXT | FCN | WARE | FORM | TYPE | DECO. | WARE/REMARKS |
|---|---|---|---|---|---|---|---|---|
| A | 5019 | D54-05-014 | 102 | 04 | 899 | — | — | Light grayish-buff clay; small-sized gray and white grits. |
| B | 8717 | D55-04-018 | D099 | 04 | 1351 | — | — | Fairly dense buff clay; small-sized grits. |
| C | 15110 | D66-0817-083 | D416 | 04 | 1618 | — | — | Cream-buff clay; small-sized grits; out of context, intrusive in Period III deposits. |
| D | 604 | B03-06-002 | 023 | 04 | 252 | — | — | Buff clay; small-sized white grits. |
| E | 2481 | D42-01-003 | 012 | 04 | 1340 | — | — | Fairly dense orange clay; small-sized black grits. |
| F | 3896 | D76-04-002 | 060 | 04 | 820 | — | — | Brownish-buff clay; small-sized white grits. |
| G | 8725 | D55-0454-019 | 110 | 04 | 1353 | — | — | Fairly dense brownish-buff clay, orange core; small-sized grits. |
| H | 830 | D66-05-001 | 090 | 04 | 252 | — | — | Light reddish-buff clay; small-sized grits. |
| I | 6088 | D54-06-025 | 136 | 04 | 1101 | — | — | Dense orange clay; small-sized white grits. |
| J | 265 | D66-02-004 | 012 | 04 | 252 | — | — | Brownish-buff clay; small- and medium-sized grits. |
| K | 358 | D66-03-001 | 030 | 04 | 82 | — | — | Brownish-buff clay; small-sized grits. |

PLATE 141

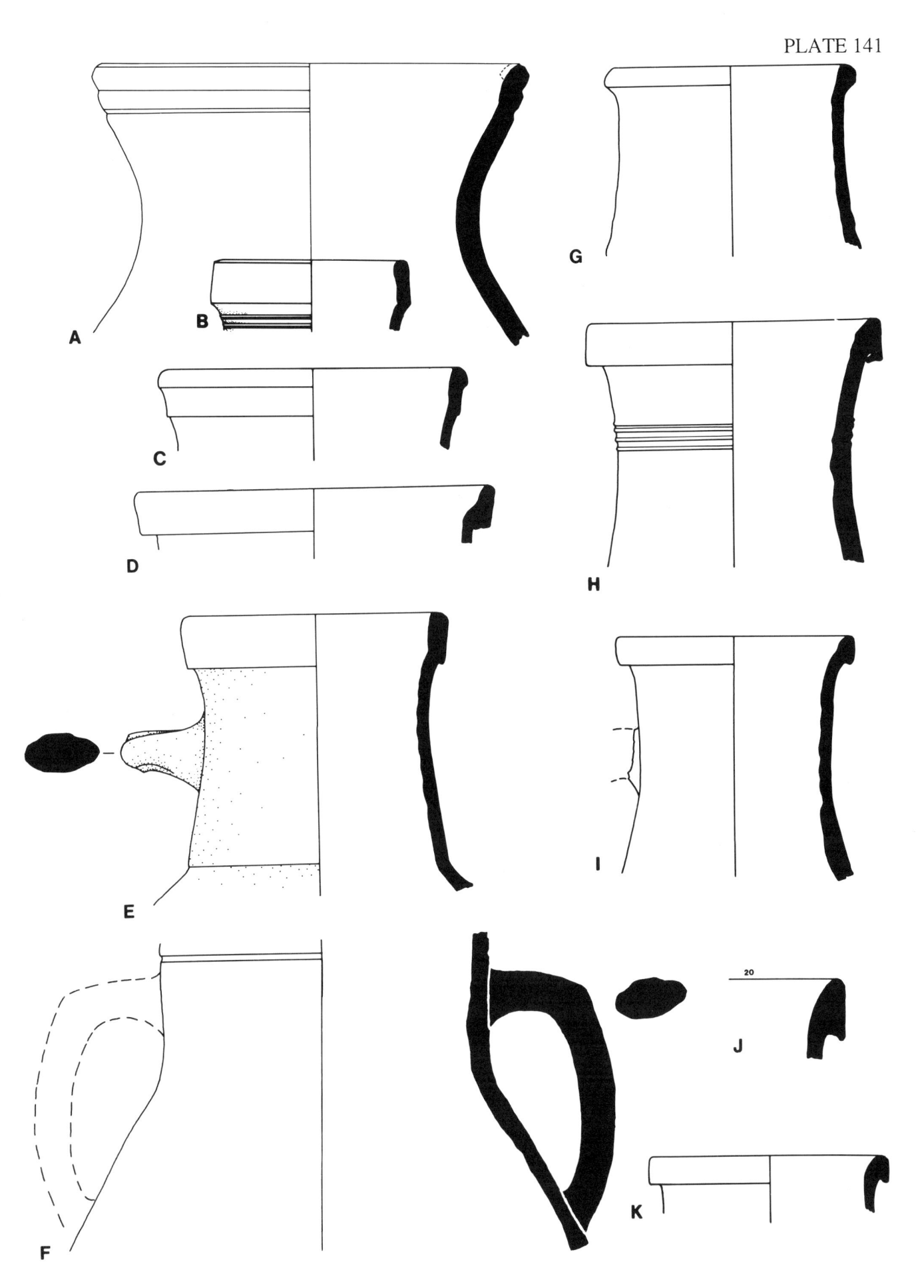

Period II Pottery From Areas B and D: Plain Simple Ware Amphorae. Scale 2:5.

Plate 142. Period II and Early First Millennium A.D. Pottery From Area D: Plain Simple Wares (A–E), "Scroll Painted" (G and H), and Gritty Red (I). Scale 2:5.

|   | MRN | CONTEXT | FCN | WARE | FORM | TYPE | DECO. | WARE/REMARKS |
|---|---|---|---|---|---|---|---|---|
| A | 3766 | D53-02-003 | 027 | 04 | 1208 | — | — | Dense orange clay, gray core; small-sized grits; interior is gray; small fragment of handle root preserved on shoulder. |
| B | 8494 | D55-04-001 | 087 | 04 | 1349 | — | — | Reddish-buff clay; small-sized white grits. |
| C | 15631 | D56-07-019 | D208 | 04 | 1624 | — | — | Dense orange-buff clay; no visible tempering; possibly a glazed ware piece but, if so, no traces of glaze visible. |
| D | 1711 | D66-06-045 | 222 | 04 | 546 | — | — | Gritty brownish-buff clay; small- and medium-sized grits prominent; fast wheel corrugations visible on interior. |
| E | 5811 | D43-04-001 | 049 | 04 | 1350 | — | — | Brownish-buff clay; small-sized black grits. |
| F | 8708 | D34-0383-010 | 121 | 04 | 1653 | — | — | Dense light brownish-buff clay; small red and black grits; out of context, intrusive in Period III deposits. |
| G | 15755 | D37-03-007 | D051 | 20 | 1649 | — | — | Porous light buff clay; small-sized black grits; a few air pockets visible; brown paint; out of context, intrusive in Period III deposits. |
| H | 14683 | D56-04-013 | 113 | 20 | 1647 | — | — | Dense light brownish-buff clay; small-sized black grits; faint traces of paint preserved on rim; out of context, intrusive in Period III deposits. |
| I | 9223 | D45-0445-015 | 155 | 26 | 1617 | — | — | Gritty brick red clay; small-sized grits prominent; out of context, intrusive in Period III deposits. |

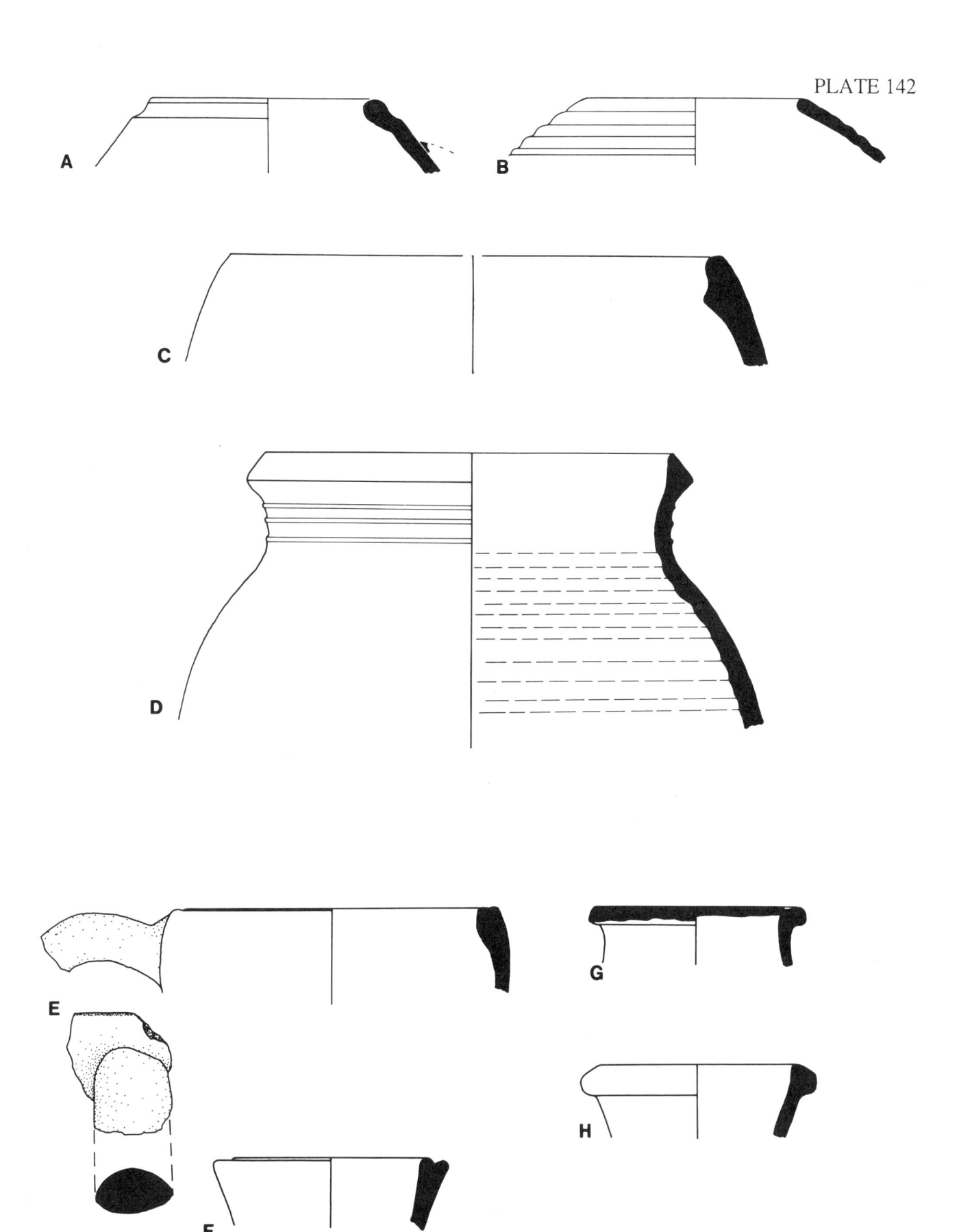

PLATE 142

Period II and Early First Millennium A.D. Pottery From Area D: Plain Simple Wares (A–E), "Scroll Painted" (G and H), and Gritty Red (I). Scale 2:5.

Plate 143. Period II Pottery From Area D: Cooking Pot Ware Vessels. Scale 2:5.

|   | MRN | CONTEXT | FCN | WARE | FORM | TYPE | DECO. | WARE/REMARKS |
|---|---|---|---|---|---|---|---|---|
| A | 172 | D66-02-002 | 003 | 19 | 201 | — | — | Brownish clay; small-sized grits, white ones prominent. |
| B | 878 + 879 | D66-05-001 + D66-05-017 | 098 + 106 | 19 | 172 | — | — | Black-dark brown clay; large-sized white grits prominent; gray-black slip on exterior. |
| C | 15212 | D25-0556-011 | D258 | 19 | 1632 | — | — | Brownish clay; gritty with small-sized white grits prominent. |
| D | 2012 | D66-07-052 | D248 | 19 | 1154a | — | — | Orange-red clay, brown core; medium-sized white grits; red slip on exterior. |
| E | 6088 | D54-06-025 | 136 | 19 | 1154 | — | — | Orange-reddish clay, gray core; white grits prominent; red slip on exterior. |
| F | 16461 | D57-01-001 | 005 | 19 | 1154a | — | — | Soft, porous dark orange-brownish clay; small- and medium-sized white grits; exterior brown mottled black (from fire?) in places. |
| G | 932 | D66-05-017 | 111 | 19 | 201a | — | — | Brownish clay; gritty with white grits prominent; exterior near rim smudged black from fire. |
| H | 5012 | D54-06-015 | 105 | 13 | 1216 | — | — | Brownish clay, darker brown core; tempered with finely-chopped chaff; rough, possibly handmade. |
| I | 5012 | D54-06-015 | 105 | 19 | 1215 | — | — | Brown-gray clay; tempered with a combination of medium-sized angular white grits and quartz flakes; brown on surface. |
| J | 856 | D66-04-016 | 092 | 19 | 243 | — | — | Reddish clay; gritty with medium- and large-sized white grits visible. |
| K | 274 | D66-02-003 | 009 | 19 | 202 | — | — | Brick red clay; small- and medium-sized white grits; exterior mottled black from fire. |
| L | 172 | D66-02-002 | 003 | 19 | 130 |  | — | Brick red clay; gritty with small- and medium-sized white grits visible; exterior covered with thick black slip. |

PLATE 143

Period II Pottery From Area D: Cooking Pot Ware Vessels. Scale 2:5.

PLATE 144

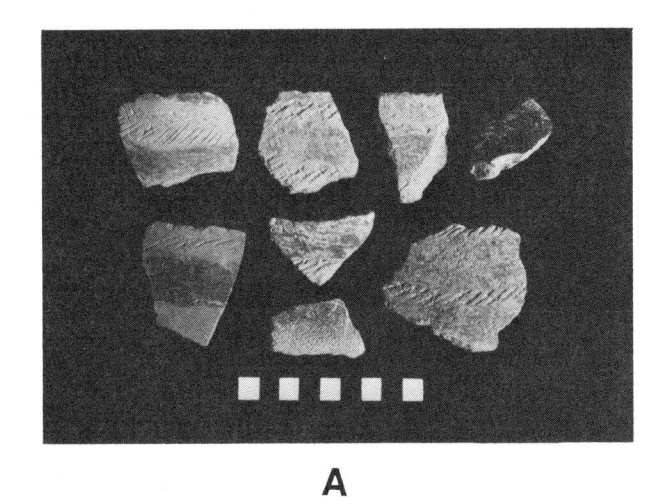

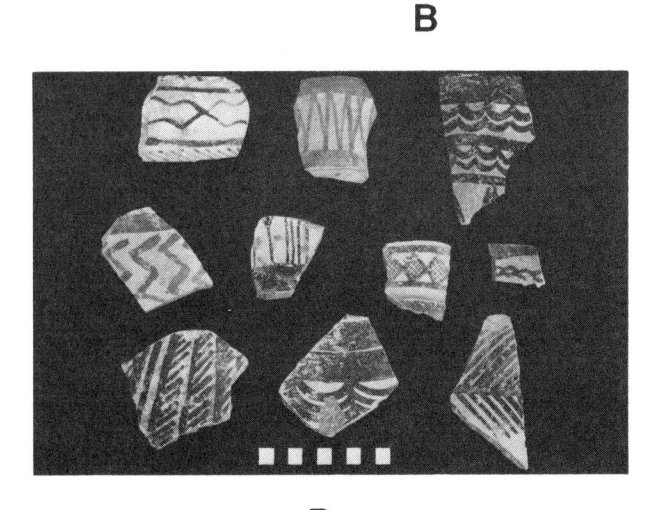

(*A*) Neolithic Washed and Impressed Ware From Areas A and C01 [Extrusive in Periods VIII, VII, V, and IV Deposits]. (*B*) Period VIII, Halaf Painted Pottery [Wares 32 and 38] from Areas A and C01 [Extrusive: top row left, and bottom row]. (*C*) Period VIII, Halaf Painted Pottery from Area A. (*D*) Period VIII, Halaf Painted Pottery from Area A. (*E*) Period VII, Middle Chalcolithic Painted Pottery [Ware 31] From Area C01. (*F*) Period VII, Middle Chalcolithic Chaff/Straw-Tempered Pottery [Ware 13/14] from Area C01.

PLATE 145

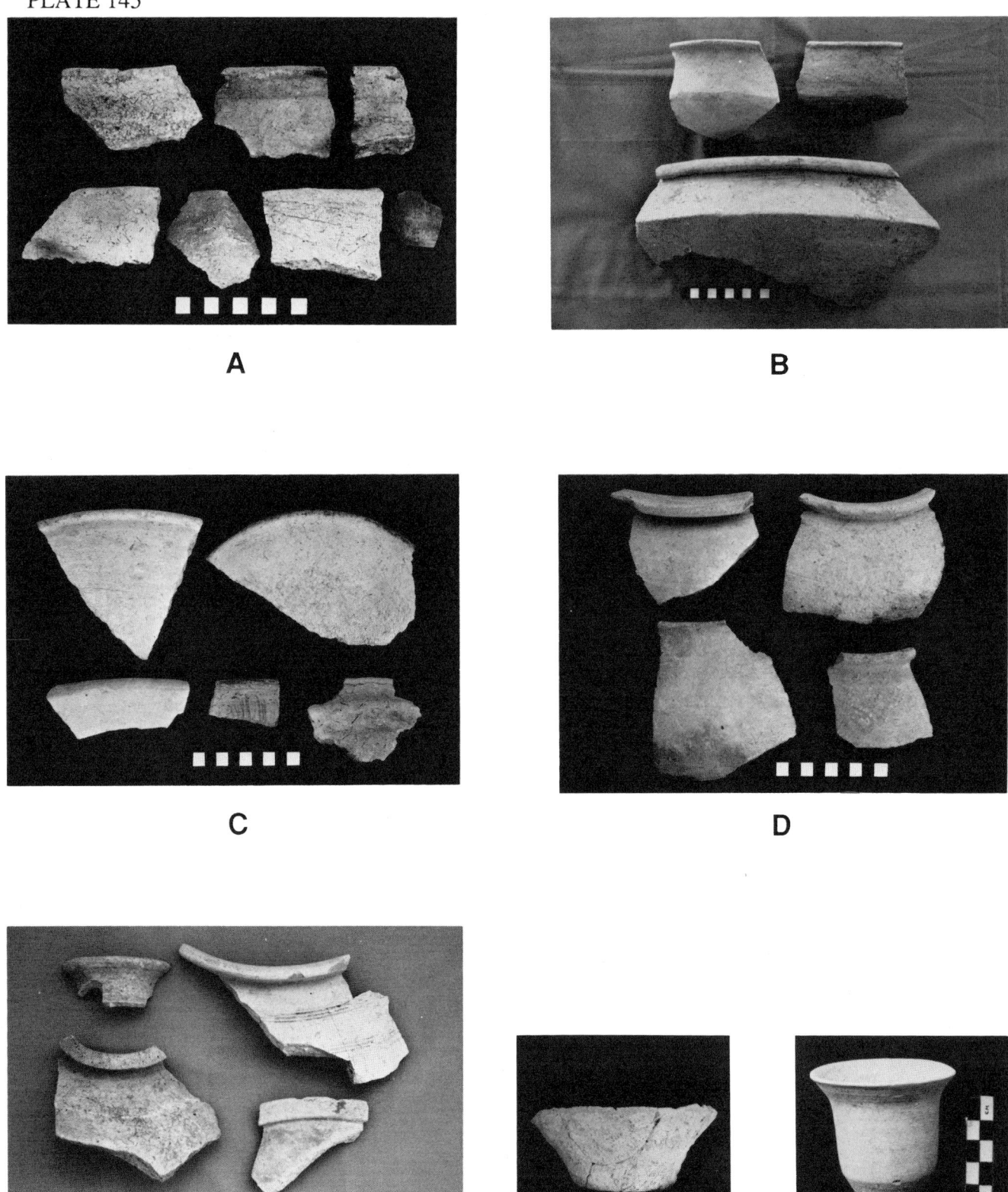

(*A*) Period VI, Late Chalcolithic Chaff/Straw-Tempered Pottery [Ware 13/14] From Pit 203, Area C01. (*B*) Period VI, Late Chalcolithic Chaff/Straw-Tempered Carinated Vessels [Jar 20a] From Area A. (*C*) Period VI, Late Chalcolithic Chaff/Straw-Tempered Ware Platters [Bowl 26] From Areas A and C01. (*D*) Period VI, Late Chalcolithic Chaff/Straw-Tempered Jars From Area A. (*E*) Period VI, Late Chalcolithic Plain Simple Ware [Ware 04] Jars From Areas A and C01. (*F*) Period VI, Late Chalcolithic Beveled Rim Bowl [Ware 17] From Area A [= KH 1983/166]. (*G*) Period VI, Late Chalcolithic Plain Simple Ware Cup From Area C01 [= Plate 19: I].

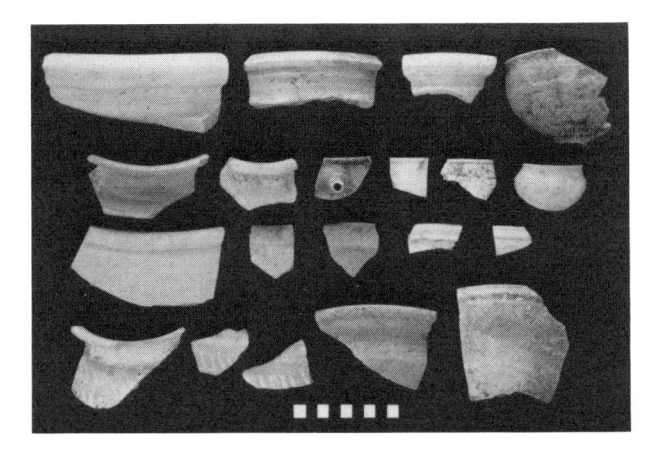

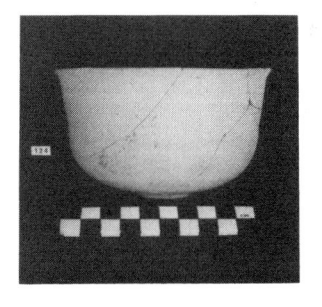

PLATE 146

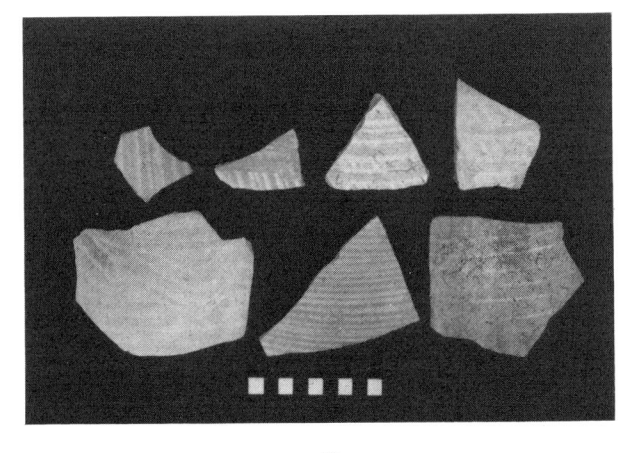

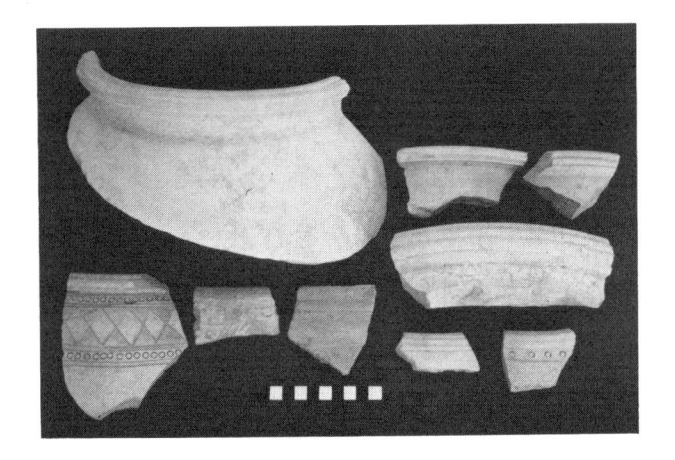

(A) Period VB, Plain Simple Ware [Ware 04] From Area C01, Phases 3 and 4. (B) Period VA, Plain Simple and Dense Wares [Wares 04 and 03] From Area C01, Phases 8–10. (C) Comparison of Periods V and IV Reserved Slip Wares. Period V [Top Row]: Diagonal, From Area C01. Period IV [Bottom Row]: Horizontal, From Area A. (D) Cyma-Recta Cup Found Inside Oven 169 in Area C01, Phases 9 and 10 [= KH 1982/124]. (E) Periods IVA–B, Plain Simple and Karababa Painted Wares [Wares 04 and 08] Grooved Rim Jars. (F) Period IV, Metallic Ware [Ware 02].

PLATE 147

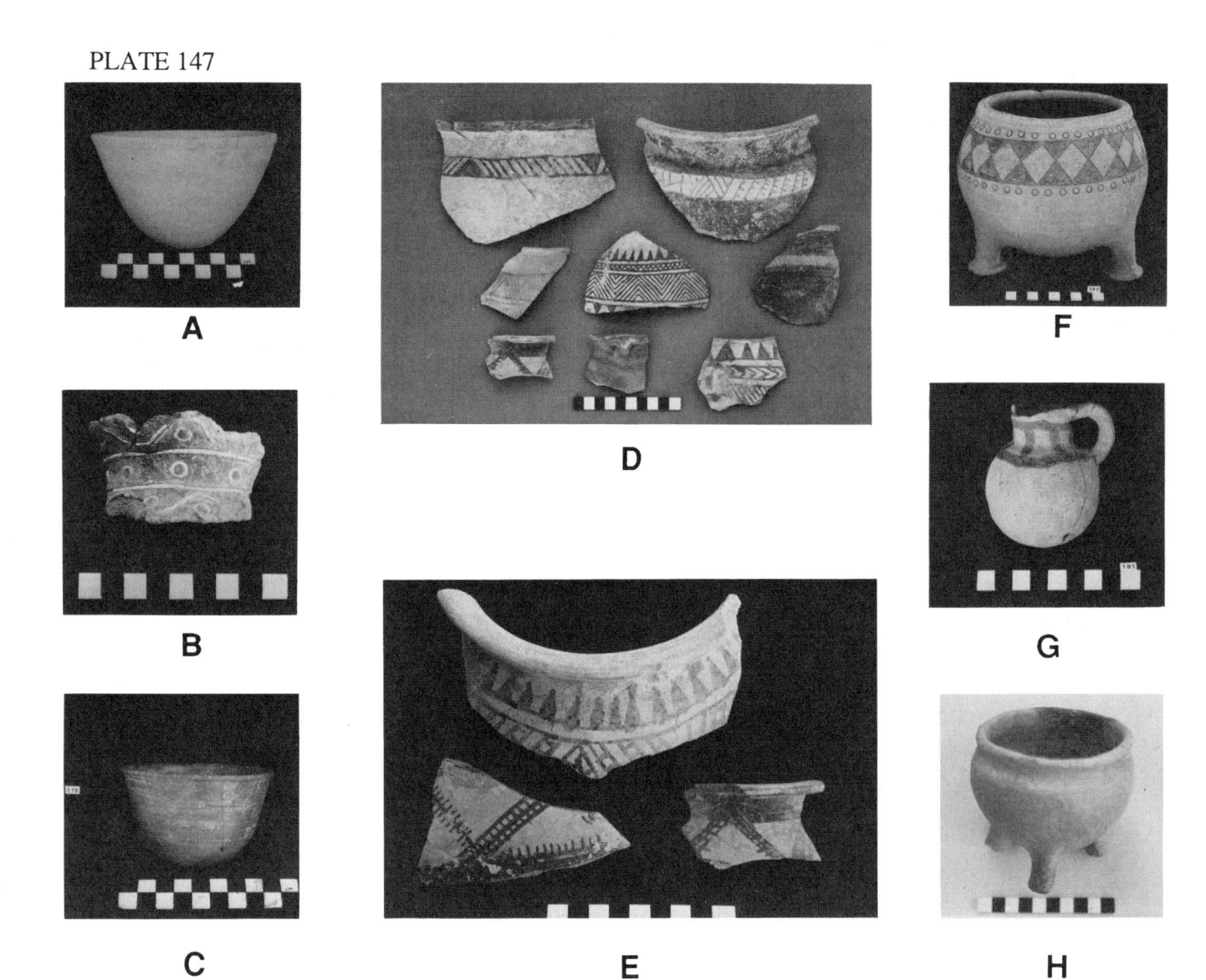

(*A*) Period IV, Plain Simple Ware [Ware 04] Cup [Bowl 1e, = Plate 53: V]. (*B*) Period IV, White Incrusted Gray Ware [Ware 10] Stand [= Plate 90: H]. (*C*) Period IV, Metallic Ware [Ware 02] Cup [Bowl 1e, = Plate 77: D]. (*D*) Period IV, Karababa Painted Ware Sherds [Ware 08]. (*E*) Period IV, Karababa Painted Ware Sherds. (*F*) Period IVA Karababa Painted Ware Tripod From Area B [= Fig. 134: B]. (*G*) Period IV, Karababa Painted Ware Handled Jar [= Plate 89: B]. (*H*) Period IVA, Cooking Pot Ware [Ware 18] Tripod From Area B [= Plate 90: B]. (*I*) Periods IVA–B, Combed Wash Ware [Ware 07] Sherds. (*J*) Period IV, Band Painted Ware [Ware 01].

PLATE 148

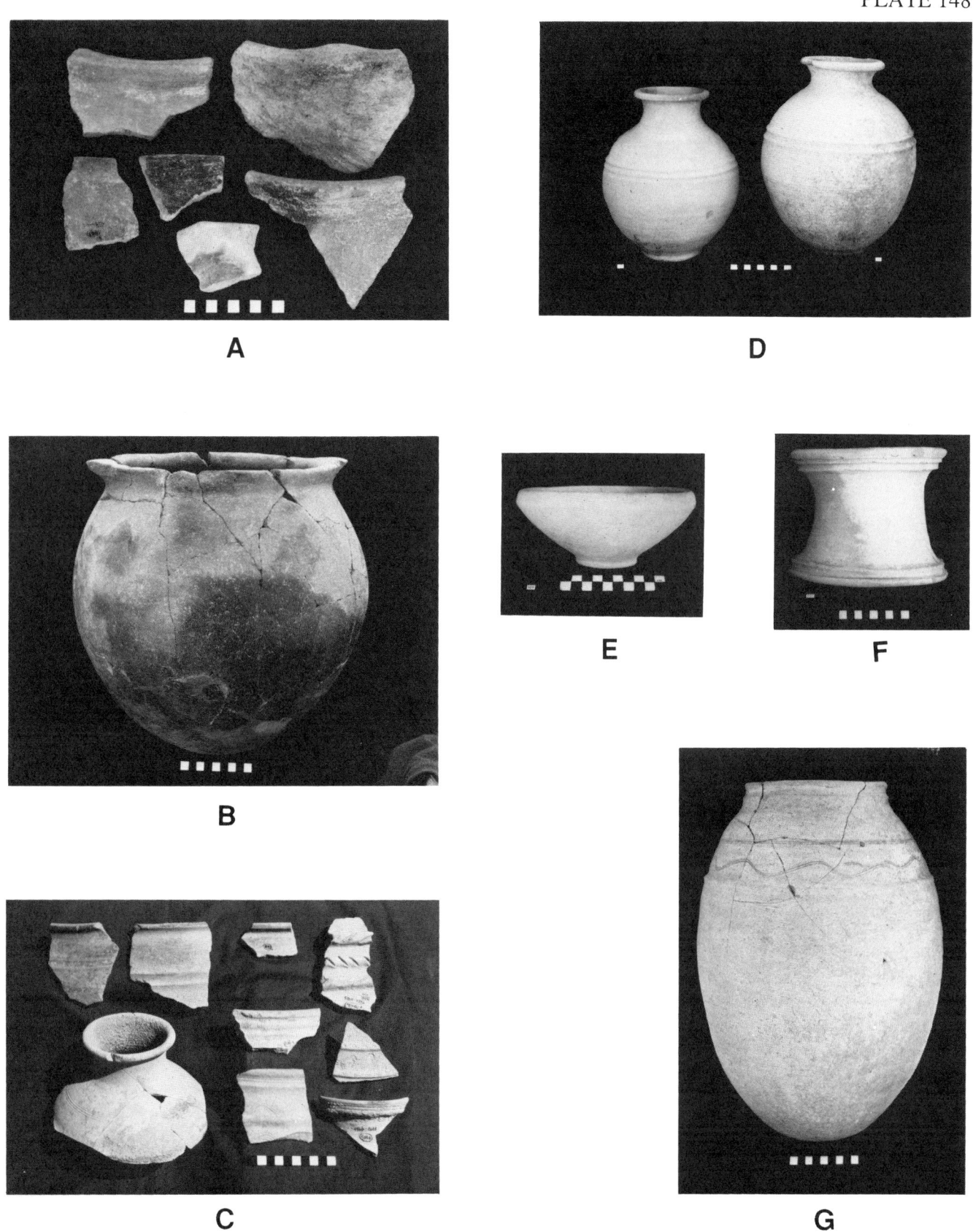

(A) Period IV, Cooking Pot Ware [Ware 09] Sherds. (B) Period IV, Cooking Pot Ware Jar [= KH 1981/105]. (C) Period III, Representative Plain Simple Ware and Cooking Pot Ware [Wares 04 and 09] Sherds From Area D, Building Phase II Deposits. (D) Period III, Plain Simple Ware Jars [Jar 12b; Left = Plate 111: C, Right = Plate 111: D] From Area D. (E) Period III, Plain Simple Ware Bowl From Area D [= Plate 98: M]. (F) Period III, Plain Simple Ware Stand From Area D [= Plate 129: N]. (G) Period III, Plain Simple Ware Barrel From Area D [= KH 1981/57].

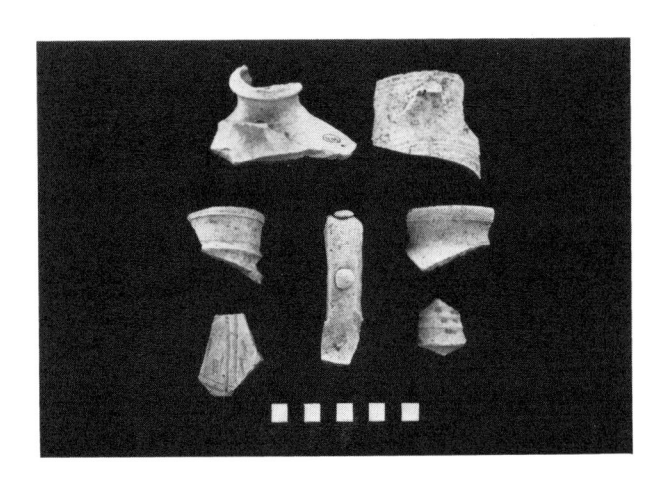

PLATE 149

*(A)* Period III, Cooking Pot Ware [Ware 09] Sherds From Area D. *(B)* Period III, Plain Simple Ware [Ware 04] Barrel Shapes From Area D. *(C)* Period III, Metallic Ware [Ware 02] Jar From Area D [= Plate 133: O]. *(D)* Period III, Metallic Ware "Syrian Bottle" From Area D [= Plate 133: I]. *(E)* Period III, Rare Painted Sherds [Ware 24], and Unique Vegetal-Tempered Ware Sherd [Ware 21] with Punctated Decoration [Bottom Row] From Area D. *(F)* Period II, Abbasid Cream Ware [Ware 52].

PLATE 150

(*A*) Period II, Plain Simple Ware [Ware 04]. (*B*) Period II, Glazed Ware [Ware 22].

Plate 151. Human (A–C) and Animal Figurines (D–J) From Period IV Levels, Areas A, B, and C. Scale 3:5.

|   | MRN | CONTEXT | FCN | PERIOD | PHASE | DESCRIPTION/REMARKS |
|---|---|---|---|---|---|---|
| A | 20729 | B02-04-018 | 490 | IVA | — | Hip fragment of a female figurine; sharply accentuated bulging hips, pubic area articulated with incisions and punctures; sand-tempered Plain Simple Ware (10YR 8/2); (= KH 1984/198). |
| B | 7247 | C55-03-016 | 656 | IVB | — | Upper torso of stalk-like figurine with spotted snake on collar entwined around neck; sand-tempered Plain Simple Ware; buff clay with greenish slip on exterior. |
| C | 7229 | C35-05-003 | 305 | IVB | — | Headless torso of stalk-like figurine; painted but paint is badly eroded; skirt articulated by parallel vertical and horizontal red painted bands fringed by hanging loops; necklace or loop-like collar along the neck; fine sand-tempered Plain Simple Ware; paste is light brownish-buff (10YR 5/3); paint is red (10YR 4/8). |
| D | 11341 | A05-08-037 | 117 | IVA | 16–17 | Torso fragment of hollow figurine, bovid(?); legs are rendered by means of short stumps, tail is clearly articulated; sand-tempered light gray (10YR 7/2) paste; greenish paint. |
| E | 4611 | C55-04-012 | 301 | IVB | — | Quadruped; decorated with finger nail incisions along the neck and below the belly; sand-tempered light brownish-buff Plain Simple Ware; (= KH 1981/74). |
| F | 16063 | A01-06-029 | 188 | IVA | 20 | Head fragment of horned animal, bovid(?); eyes accentuated by means of a pellet of clay punctured in the middle; buff Plain Simple Ware (10YR 8/2), burnished; (= KH 1983/160). |
| G | 19002 | B01-05-010/017 | 197 | IVA | — | Quadruped with tail flipped over its left haunch, dog(?); eyes, nozzle, and tail, tool impressed; brown painted stripes over body (10YR 4/4); buff Plain Simple Ware (5Y 8/1); (= KH 1984/174). |
| H | 3044 | C56-0748-001 | 111 | IV | — | Animal figurine of pig or porcupine(?); eyes depicted by means of punctures; serrated back and articulated nipples; badly eroded stripes of gray-brown paint over body; sand-tempered Plain Simple Ware paste; out of context in plow zone deposits but assignable to Period IV on the basis of general provenance; (= KH 1981/35). |
| I | 5620 + 6625 | C55-06-012 + C55-05-025 | 447 + 605 | IVB | — | Horned animal figurine, bovid; on surface badly eroded stripes of reddish-yellowish paint (5YR 6/6); fine sand-tempered pinkish Plain Simple Ware paste (7.5YR 8/2); (=KH 1981/88 + KH 1981/111). |
| J | 11238 | A04-07-057 | 288 | IVA | 17 | Quadruped, rather indistinct animal figurine, sheep(?); sand-tempered grayish Plain Simple Ware paste (10YR 7/2); exterior surface slightly burnt. |

PLATE 151

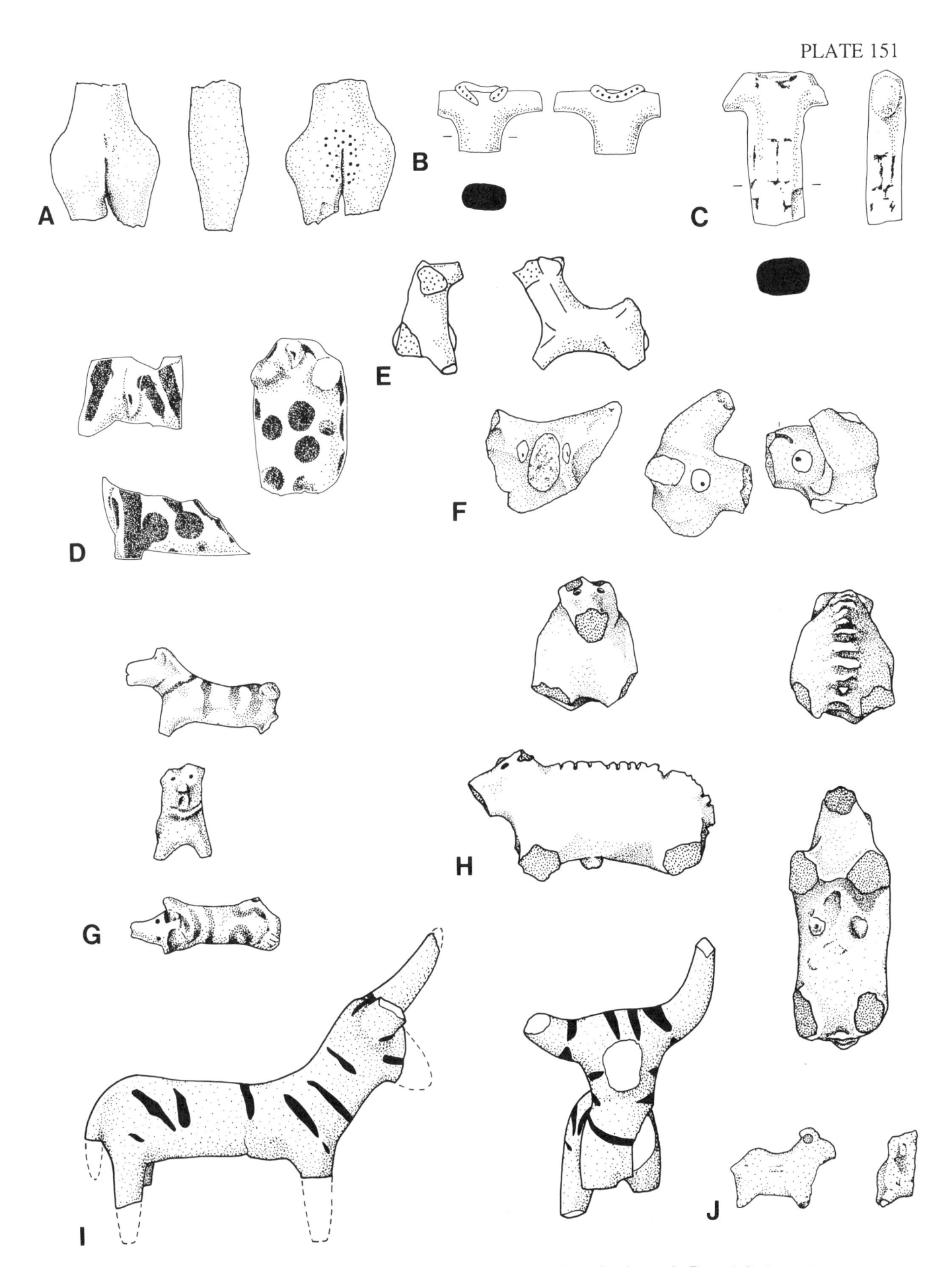

Human (A–C) and Animal Figurines (D–J) From Period IV Levels, Areas A, B, and C. Scale 3:5.

Plate 152. Human (A) and Animal Figurines (B–K) From Period III Levels, Areas A and D. Scale 3:5.

|   | MRN | CONTEXT | FCN | PERIOD | PHASE | DESCRIPTION/REMARKS |
|---|---|---|---|---|---|---|
| A | 17600 | D56-0491-018 | 341 | III | — | Headless torso of stalk-like figurine; modeled protuberance indicates at least one breast; covered with irregular parallel bands of red paint (2.5YR 5/6); navel or vagina indicated by indentation at the bottom of the stalk; sand-tempered, pinkish-buff Plain Simple Ware paste (5YR 7/4); (= KH 1984/187). |
| B | 2666 | D76-01-002 | 014 | III | — | Quadruped with vertical tail, dog(?) or sheep (?); sand-tempered buff Plain Simple Ware paste; (= KH 1981/31). |
| C | 1683 | A08-01-002 | 057 | — | — | Fragment of hollow figurine, possibly a bird, but head and wing are missing; surface covered with thin vertical and horizontal incision; sand-tempered Plain Simple Ware paste covered with cream slip; out of context in slope wash; possibly Period III or IV; (= KH 1981/20). |
| D | 17161 | D77-01-004 | 020 | III | — | Forepart fragment of horned quadruped, bovid; traces of orifice through nozzle; eyes formed by impressing a hollow tube, possibly a reed; mixed sand and chaff-tempered grayish paste; traces of burning on exterior surface; (= KH 1984/182). |
| E | 17400 | D65-0637-050 | D280 | III | — | Forepart fragment of quadruped, horned(?); short stubby legs and pointed snout; straw-tempered paste, light reddish gray in color (5YR 6/2); (= KH 1984/185). |
| F | 3920 | D34-01-002 | 024 | III | — | Forepart fragment of horned animal; bent horn, sheep(?), ram(?); coarse straw-tempered paste; exterior surface blackened by fire. |
| G | 14740 | D23-03-002 | 066 | III | — | Forepart of horned animal, bovid; eyes delineated by means of punctations; sand-tempered Plain Simple Ware paste, fairly rough; light gray in color (5Y 7/2). |
| H | 070 | A02-0209-002 | 004 | III | 22 | Quadruped with solid stalk-like legs, dog(?); spout-like opening through nozzle and near right haunch; eyes indicated by means of two punctures; surface covered with stripes of brownish-orange paint; greenish Plain Simple Ware paste; (= KH 1980/3). |
| I | 14429 | D36-04-011 | 140 | III | — | Forepart fragment of horned quadruped, elongated snout suggests a sheep; sand-tempered Plain Simple Ware paste, light grayish-buff in color (5Y 7/2). |
| J | 2431 | D66-0751-054 | 272 | III | — | Small quadruped; pinched snout, sheep(?); sand-tempered Plain Simple Ware paste; exterior surface blackened by fire; (= KH 1981/26). |
| K | 5290 | D54-0556-014 | 108 | III | — | Two-headed horned animal with heads at opposite extremes of torso; possibly a depiction of a cow giving birth; chaff-tempered reddish-buff paste, fairly rough; (= KH 1981/85). |

PLATE 152

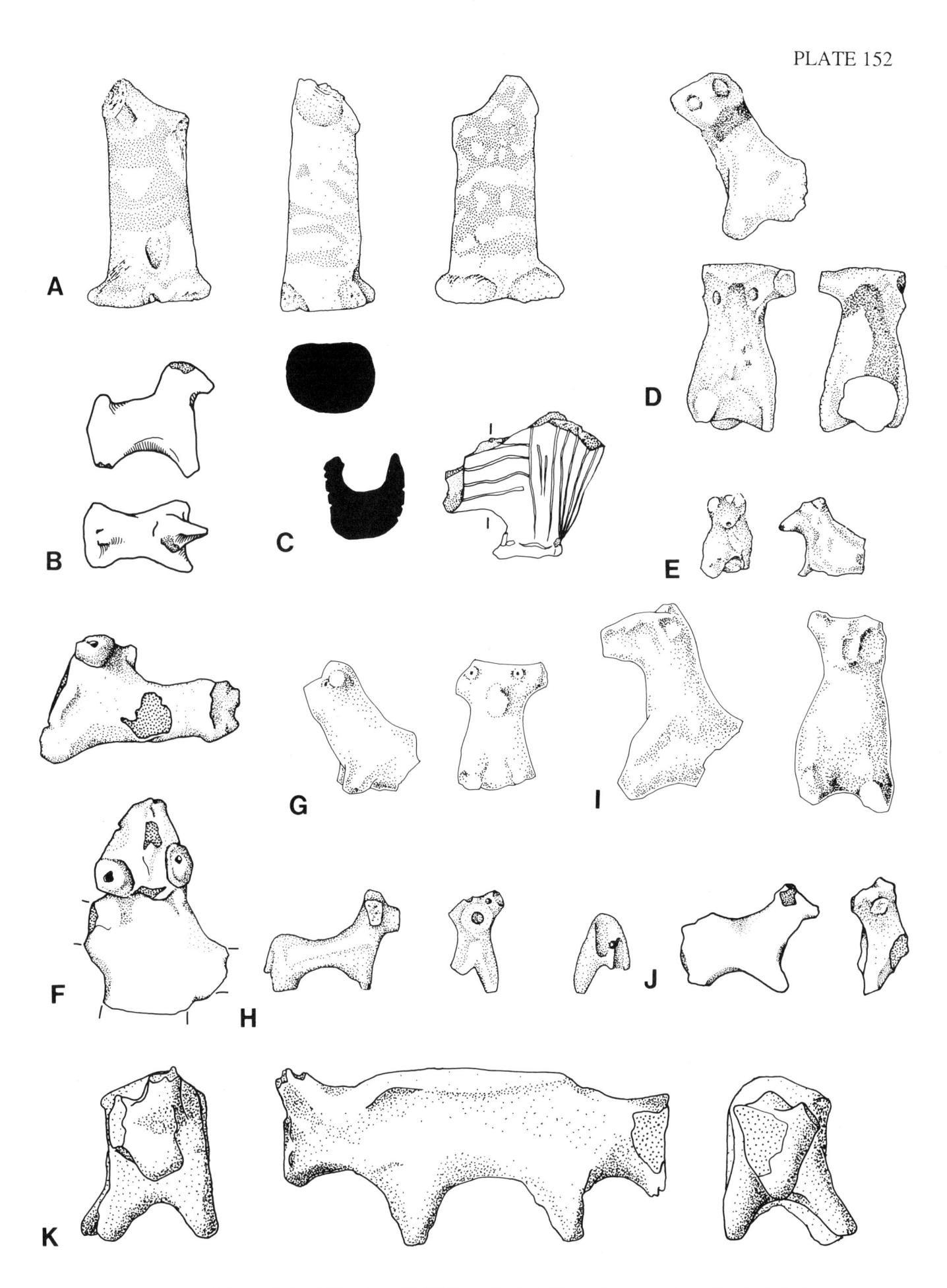

Human (A) and Animal Figurines (B–K) From Period III Levels, Areas A and D. Scale 3:5.

Plate 153. Figurines From Periods III and IV Levels, Areas A, B, C, and D.

|   | *MRN* | *Context* | *FCN* | *Period* | *Phase* | *Description/Remarks* |
|---|---|---|---|---|---|---|
| A | 070 | A02-0209-002 | 004 | III | 22 | = plate 152:H. |
| B | 19002 | B01-05-010/017 | 197 | IVA | — | = plate 151:G. |
| C | 5620 + 6625 | C55-06-012 + C55-05-025 | 447 + 605 | IVB | — | = plate 151:I. |
| D | 17909 | A04-10-101 | 593 | IVB-C | Pre-13 | Coarse grit and chaff-tempered ware; exterior surface charred black; one "horn" broken; height = 1.96 cm, diameter at base = 1.49 cm; (= KH 1984/197). |
| E | 5290 | D54-0556-014 | 108 | III | — | = plate 152:K. |
| F | 17600 | D56-0491-018 | 341 | III | — | = plate 152:A. |

PLATE 153

A

B

C

D

E

F

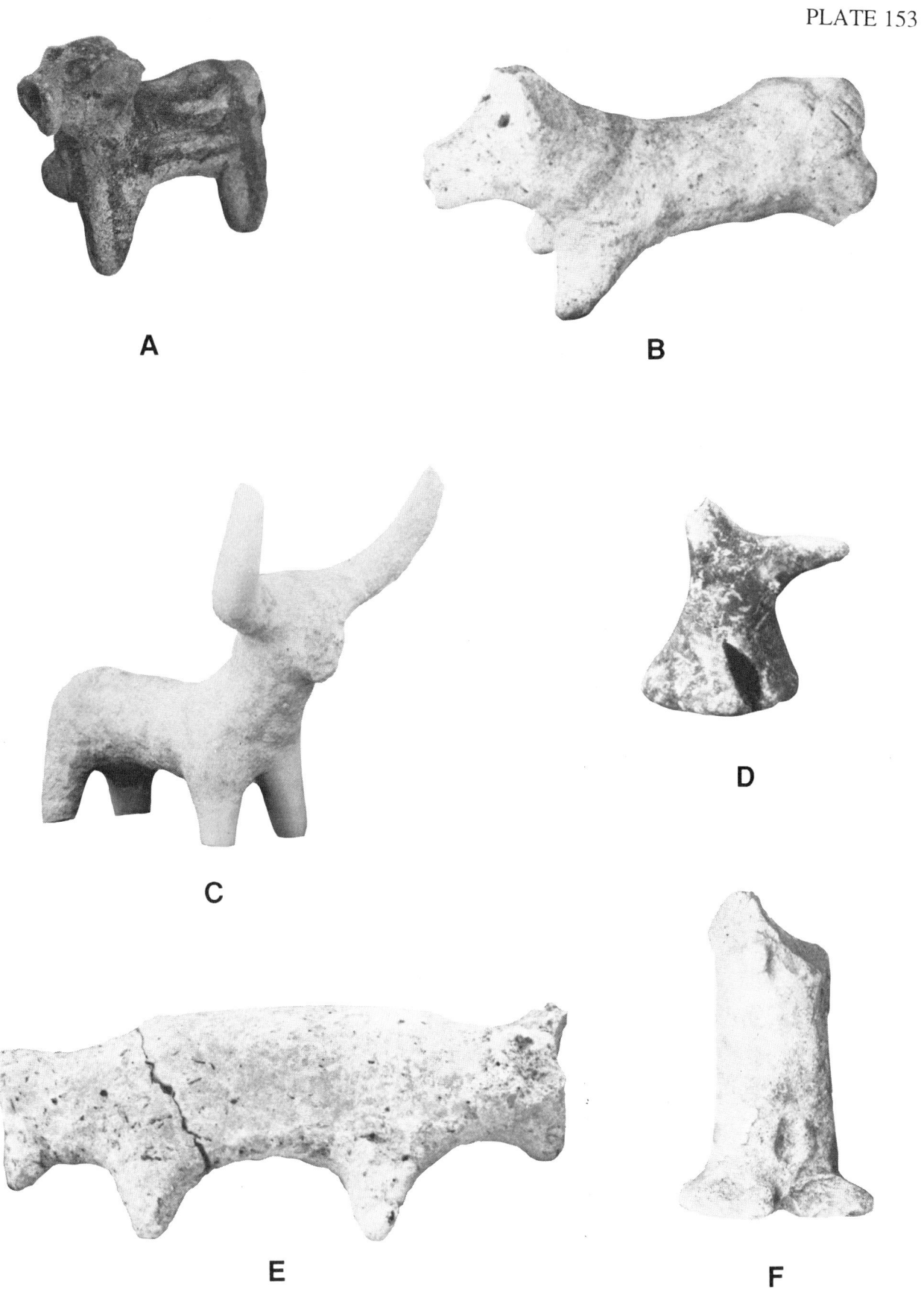

Figurines From Periods III and IV Levels, Areas A, B, C, and D.

Plate 154. Theriomorphic Vessels From Periods III and IV Levels, Areas A, C, and D. Scale 2:5.

|   | *MRN* | *Context* | *FCN* | *Period* | *Phase* | *Description/Remarks* |
|---|---|---|---|---|---|---|
| A | 3919 | D34-0188-002 | 020 | III | — | Theriomorphic vessel in the shape of a ram; brownish-buff Plain Simple Ware; (= KH 1981/46). |
| B | 3328 | C35-02-022 | 050 | IVB | — | Head of theriomorphic vessel, apparently a horned animal; Plain Simple Ware; (= KH 1981/41). |
| C | 7511 | A07-0772-027 | 251 | IVA-B | 15 | Torso fragment of theriomorphic vessel; rough cylindrical shape with two orifices on top for attachment of spout/head; reddish-buff Plain Simple Ware with buff slip on exterior (10YR 8/3); (= KH 1982/117). |

PLATE 154

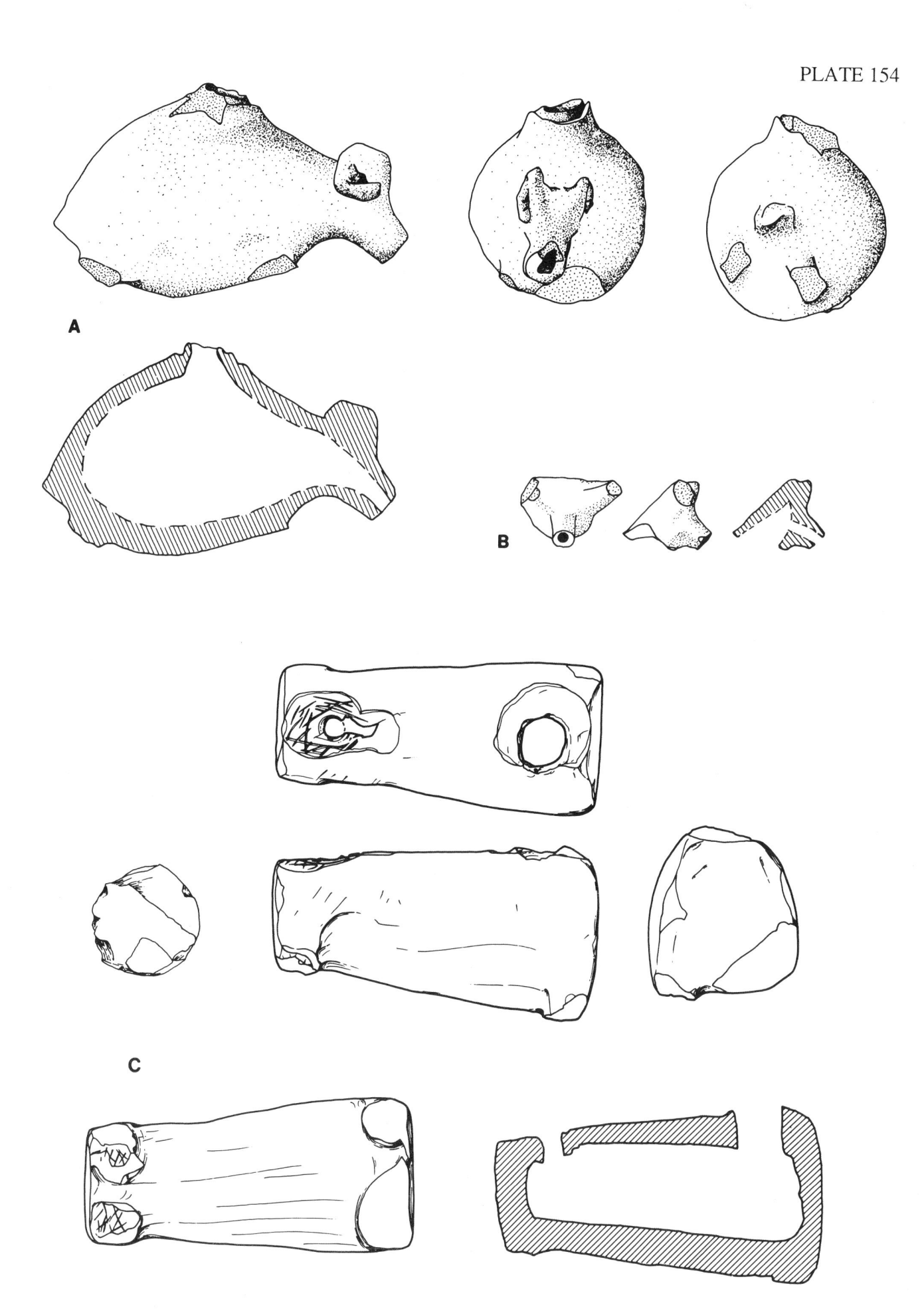

Theriomorphic Vessels From Periods III and IV Levels, Areas A, C, and D. Scale 2:5.

Plate 155. Terracotta Implements From Diverse Periods, Areas A–C, C01, and D: Spindle Whorls (A–C), "Chariot Wheels" (D–L), Beads (M and N), Perforated Roundels (O–W, Y, Z, and BB), and Scrapers (X, AA, and CC–EE). Scale 2:5.

|    | MRN | CONTEXT | FCN | PERIOD | PHASE | DESCRIPTION/REMARKS |
|----|-----|---------|-----|--------|-------|---------------------|
| A | 6570 | C01-0178-120 | 1631 | VIA | 2 | Terracotta spindle whorl; reddish-brownish Plain Simple Ware paste (5YR 6/4). |
| B | 11491 | A07-1972-085 | 799 | VIA | 7 | Terracotta spindle whorl; brownish-buff Plain Simple Ware paste (10YR 5/4). |
| C | 2753 | C45-07-024 | 278 | IVB | — | Terracotta spindle whorl; (= KH 1981/34). |
| D | 17914 | A04-1032/42-101 | 599 | IVB-C | — | Terracotta spindle whorl/"chariot wheel"; coarse straw- and grit-tempered paste, grayish in color (5YR 3/1); exterior, fire blackened; (= KH 1984/192). |
| E | 9096 | D55-05-021 | 210 | III | — | Terracotta spindle whorl/"chariot wheel"; brownish-buff Plain Simple Ware paste (10YR 7/3); (= KH 1982/125). |
| F | 8309 | A04-08-050 | 234 | IV | — | Terracotta spindle whorl/"chariot wheel"; bone awl tip was found lodged in central perforation, presumably the spindle rod, or alternately the axle of a toy chariot; fine dense brownish-buff Plain Simple Ware paste (10YR 8/3); spoke-like pattern formed by bands of reddish-brown paint (5YR 6/4) on both surfaces; (= KH 1982/122). |
| G | 17910 | A04-10-101 | 594 | IVB-C | — | Terracotta spindle whorl/"chariot wheel"; coarse straw- and grit-tempered paste; dark gray clay (5YR 3/1); (= KH 1984/188). |
| H | 1511 | C01-0189-049 | 417 | IVB | 12 | Terracotta spindle whorl/"chariot wheel"; buff, Plain Simple Ware paste; (= KH 1981/16). |
| I | 681 | B01-05-012 | 193 | IVA | — | Terracotta spindle whorl/"chariot wheel"; buff, Plain Simple Ware paste; small-sized grits; (= KH 1980/8). |
| J | 983 | D56-0168-001 | 003 | III | — | Terracotta spindle whorl/"chariot wheel"; buff, Plain Simple Ware paste; brownish-buff slip over exterior; (= KH 1981/13). |
| K | 5213 | C55-05-014 | 315 | IVB | — | Terracotta spindle whorl/"chariot wheel"; buff, Plain Simple Ware paste; (= KH 1981/84). |
| L | 14613 | D25-05-015 | 211 | III | — | Terracotta spindle whorl/"chariot wheel"; gritty buff, Plain Simple Ware (10YR 8/2); incised decoration on surfaces; (= KH 1983/146). |
| M | 15651 | D25-0557-011 | D284 | III | — | Terracotta perforated roundel. |
| N | 981 | C45-03-001 | 067 | IV | — | Faceted perforated disc bead; buff, Plain Simple Ware paste; (= KH 1981/18). |
| O | 11679 | A07-2091-095 | D900 | IVB? |  | Terracotta perforated roundel; pinkish-buff Plain Simple Ware paste (5YR 7/4); from a mixed Periods VIII-VIB lot, presumably Period VIB in date. |
| P | 6589 | C01-0167/77-126 | 1837 | VIA? | 1/2 | Terracotta perforated roundel; from a mixed Period VII-VIA lot, presumably VIA in date. |
| Q | 11520 | A07-1970-089 | 815 | VIB | 6 | Terracotta perforated roundel; straw-tempered ware covered with burnished red wash. |
| R | 11168 | A07-1691-075 | 723 | VIA | 9 | Terracotta perforated roundel. |
| S | 7923 | A07-14-060 | 446 | IVC or VIA | 10/11 | Terracotta perforated roundel; reddish-buff Plain Simple Ware paste (5YR 7/6); from a locus of uncertain stratification between phases 10 and 11 in Area A; associated ceramics are late Chalcolithic. |
| T | 13164 | C01-1027/28/29-174 | D2661 | VA | 8 | Terracotta perforated roundel. |
| U | 8898 | C01-09-160 | D2340 | IVB | 11 | Terracotta perforated roundel; chaff-tempered late Chalcolithic ware. |
| V | 3886 | D76-04-002 | 056 | III | — | Terracotta perforated roundel. |
| W | 7239 | C01-0169/79/89-130 | 1971 | VII | 1 | Terracotta perforated roundel; straw-tempered ware; found together with MRN 7239 (plate 155:DD). |
| X | 15667 | D25-0354-011 | D294 | III | — | Terracotta perforated roundel. |
| Y | 7021 | C56-06-031 | 406 | IVB | — | Terracotta perforated roundel. |
| Z | 17229 | D66-1201-083 | D678 | III | — | Terracotta perforated roundel. |
| AA | 15661 | D25-0568-022 | D291 | III | — | Terracotta roundel. |
| BB | 8265 | A07-1592-078 | 526 | VIA | 8 | Terracotta perforated roundel; pinkish-buff Plain Simple Ware paste (7.5YR 7/4). |
| CC | 15290 | D25-0569-023 | D274 | III | — | Terracotta roundel. |
| DD | 7239 | C01-0169/79/89-130 | 1971 | VII | 1 | Terracotta roundel; straw-tempered ware; found together with MRN 7239 (plate 155:W). |
| EE | 11403 | A08-10-037 | 362 | VIA | 8 | Terracotta roundel; made out of a painted Halaf sherd (Ware 38); dense reddish-buff clay; brown paint. |

PLATE 155

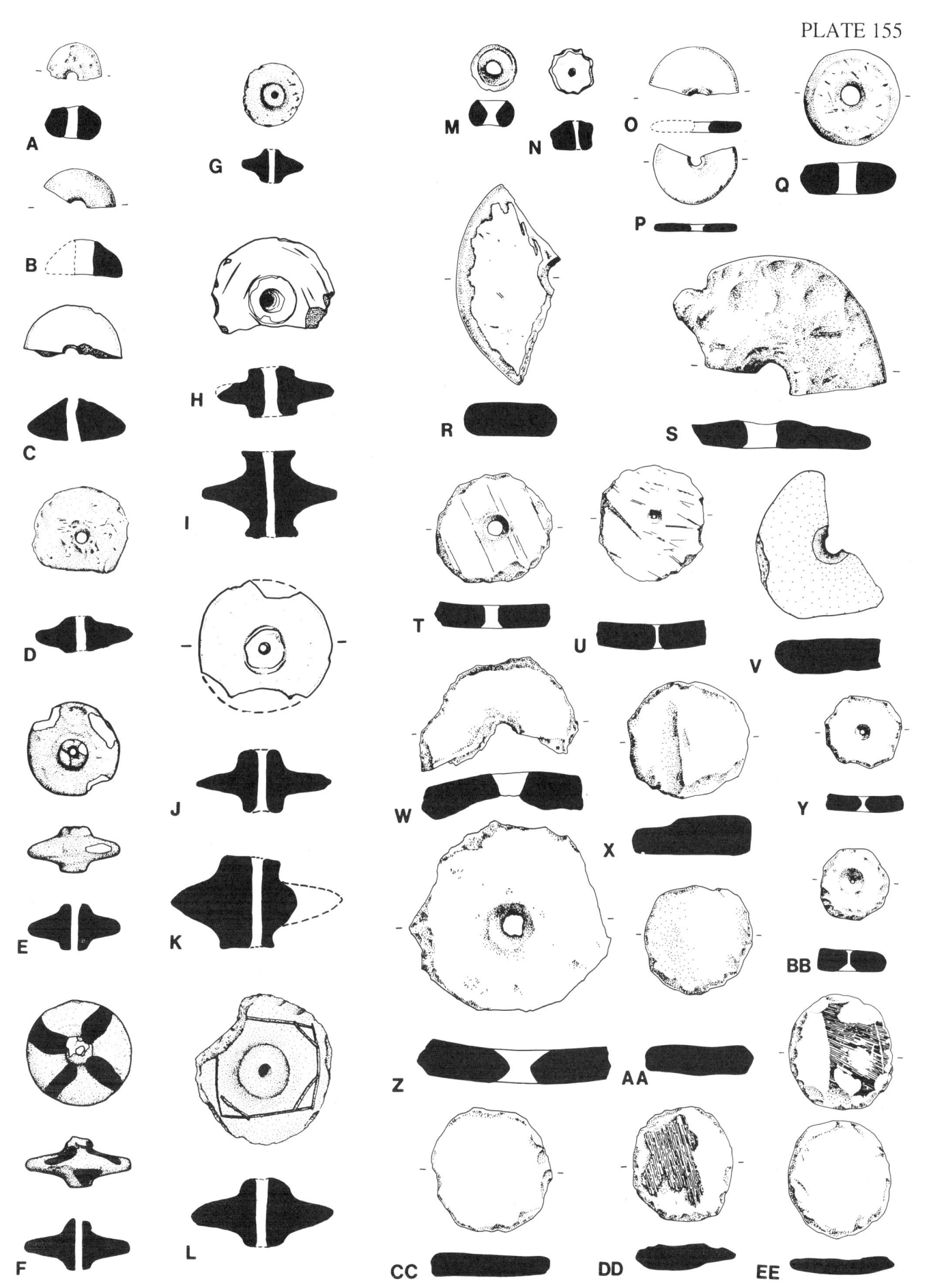

Terracotta Implements From Diverse Periods, Areas A–C, C01, and D: Spindle Whorls (A–C), "Chariot Wheels" (D–L), Beads (M and N), Perforated Roundels (O–W, Y, Z, and BB), and Scrapers (X, AA, and CC–EE). Scale 2:5.

Plate 156. Terracotta Implements From Diverse Periods, Areas A–C, C01, D, and G: Spools (A and B), Tokens/"Gaming Pieces" (C–E), Stand (H), Spoon (I), Crucibles (J and K), Clay Nails (L–O and Q), Model House (P), and Unassigned (G and M). Scale 2:5.

|   | MRN | CONTEXT | FCN | PERIOD | PHASE | DESCRIPTION/REMARKS |
|---|---|---|---|---|---|---|
| A | 11539 | A08-0501-046 | 427 | VIA | 7 | Spool; cream/light brownish-buff Plain Simple Ware paste (2.5Y 8/2, 10YR 7/3); top and bottom surfaces appear worn, presumably from use. |
| B | 19112 | B01-05-025 | 273 | IVA | — | Spool; terracotta, pinkish-buff Plain Simple Ware paste. |
| C | 1348 | A08-01-001 | 003 | — | — | "Gaming piece"/counter; terracotta, solid core; exterior charred black; (= KH 1981/100); out of context in slope wash. |
| D | 4989 | C55-05-014 | 320 | IVB | — | "Gaming piece"/counter; terracotta, solid core; exterior charred black; (= KH 1981/98). |
| E | 4562 | C55-05-012 | D284 | IVB | — | "Gaming piece"/counter; terracotta, solid core; exterior charred black; (= KH 1981/98). |
| F | 10985 | D43-06-020 | 110 | III | — | "Gaming piece"/counter; terracotta, solid core; dark gray clay with quartz inclusions; exterior charred black. |
| G | 4990 | C55-05-014 | 314 | IVB | — | Unbaked clay disk with central finger(?) impression; pinkish paste (7.5YR 8/2). |
| H | 14185 | D36-03-001 | 093 | II/III | — | Solid rectangular object = hearth stand(?), andiron(?); side surfaces decorated with incised lines, perhaps a stylized face(?); tempered with grits and quartz flakes; Cooking Pot Ware; (= KH 1983/153); out of context in plow zone. |
| I | 12638 | A07-24-102 | 1106 | VIII | 4 | Ladle; coarse straw-tempered ware, charred black; (= KH 1983/140). |
| J | 7226 | C45-01-001 | 314 | IV | — | Crucible/lamp(?); dense brown clay; no visible tempering; handmade. |
| K | 9204 | D55-0557-023 | 218 | III | — | Crucible/lamp(?); coarse straw-tempered ware; exterior and interior mottled black from fire; on exterior, six knobs; (= KH 1982/126). |
| L | 19611 | G64-0217-012 | 139 | IV | — | Terracotta object; buff Plain Simple Ware paste. |
| M | 17851 | D36-0354-006 | 531 | III | — | Terracotta disc; pinkish-gray Plain Simple Ware paste (5YR 7/2); on interior of convex side, randomly spaced tool punctures; (= KH 1984/191). |
| N | 6254 | C01-0168-120 | 1617 | VIA | 2 | Terracotta head of "nail"; (= KH 1981/96). |
| O | 2750 | C01-0169-072 | 731 | V | 10 | Terracotta head of "nail," presumably for architectural use; chaff-tempered paste; (= KH 1981/32). |
| P | 6628 | C35-0362-005 | 245 | IVB | — | Architectural model(?); buff Plain Simple Ware paste; gritty; buff slip on surface, dark red paint; circular opening may designate door and rectangular slits may represent windows; (= KH 1981/96). |
| Q | 1684 | C45-05-028 | 249 | IVB | — | Massive rectangular terracotta peg, presumably for architectural use; (= KH 1981/21). |

PLATE 155

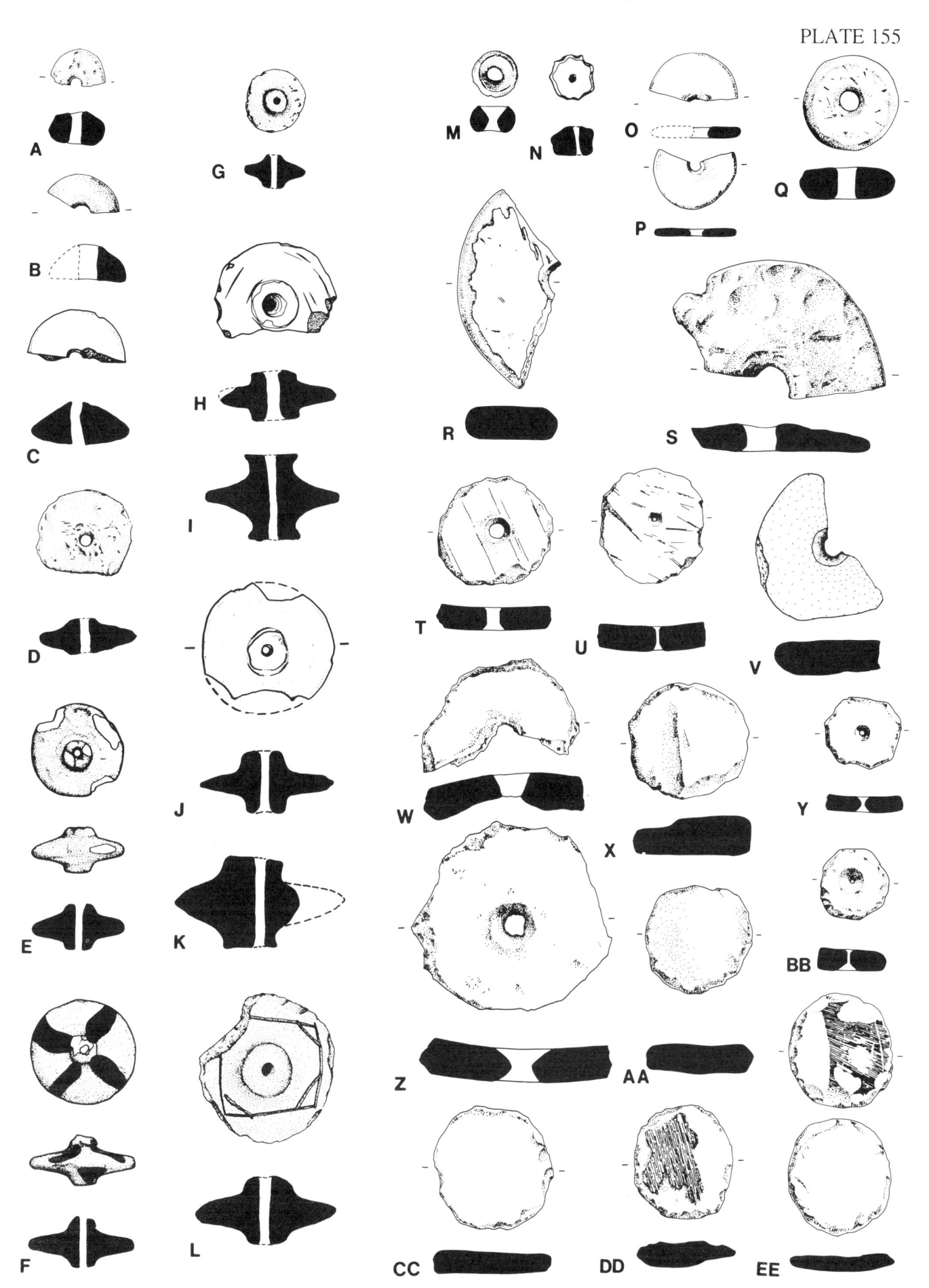

Terracotta Implements From Diverse Periods, Areas A–C, C01, and D: Spindle Whorls (A–C), "Chariot Wheels" (D–L), Beads (M and N), Perforated Roundels (O–W, Y, Z, and BB), and Scrapers (X, AA, and CC–EE). Scale 2:5.

Plate 156. Terracotta Implements From Diverse Periods, Areas A–C, C01, D, and G: Spools (A and B), Tokens/"Gaming Pieces" (C–E), Stand (H), Spoon (I), Crucibles (J and K), Clay Nails (L–O and Q), Model House (P), and Unassigned (G and M). Scale 2:5.

|   | MRN | CONTEXT | FCN | PERIOD | PHASE | DESCRIPTION/REMARKS |
|---|---|---|---|---|---|---|
| A | 11539 | A08-0501-046 | 427 | VIA | 7 | Spool; cream/light brownish-buff Plain Simple Ware paste (2.5Y 8/2, 10YR 7/3); top and bottom surfaces appear worn, presumably from use. |
| B | 19112 | B01-05-025 | 273 | IVA | — | Spool; terracotta, pinkish-buff Plain Simple Ware paste. |
| C | 1348 | A08-01-001 | 003 | — | — | "Gaming piece"/counter; terracotta, solid core; exterior charred black; (= KH 1981/100); out of context in slope wash. |
| D | 4989 | C55-05-014 | 320 | IVB | — | "Gaming piece"/counter; terracotta, solid core; exterior charred black; (= KH 1981/98). |
| E | 4562 | C55-05-012 | D284 | IVB | — | "Gaming piece"/counter; terracotta, solid core; exterior charred black; (= KH 1981/98). |
| F | 10985 | D43-06-020 | 110 | III | — | "Gaming piece"/counter; terracotta, solid core; dark gray clay with quartz inclusions; exterior charred black. |
| G | 4990 | C55-05-014 | 314 | IVB | — | Unbaked clay disk with central finger(?) impression; pinkish paste (7.5YR 8/2). |
| H | 14185 | D36-03-001 | 093 | II/III | — | Solid rectangular object = hearth stand(?), andiron(?); side surfaces decorated with incised lines, perhaps a stylized face(?); tempered with grits and quartz flakes; Cooking Pot Ware; (= KH 1983/153); out of context in plow zone. |
| I | 12638 | A07-24-102 | 1106 | VIII | 4 | Ladle; coarse straw-tempered ware, charred black; (= KH 1983/140). |
| J | 7226 | C45-01-001 | 314 | IV | — | Crucible/lamp(?); dense brown clay; no visible tempering; handmade. |
| K | 9204 | D55-0557-023 | 218 | III | — | Crucible/lamp(?); coarse straw-tempered ware; exterior and interior mottled black from fire; on exterior, six knobs; (= KH 1982/126). |
| L | 19611 | G64-0217-012 | 139 | IV | — | Terracotta object; buff Plain Simple Ware paste. |
| M | 17851 | D36-0354-006 | 531 | III | — | Terracotta disc; pinkish-gray Plain Simple Ware paste (5YR 7/2); on interior of convex side, randomly spaced tool punctures; (= KH 1984/191). |
| N | 6254 | C01-0168-120 | 1617 | VIA | 2 | Terracotta head of "nail"; (= KH 1981/96). |
| O | 2750 | C01-0169-072 | 731 | V | 10 | Terracotta head of "nail," presumably for architectural use; chaff-tempered paste; (= KH 1981/32). |
| P | 6628 | C35-0362-005 | 245 | IVB | — | Architectural model(?); buff Plain Simple Ware paste; gritty; buff slip on surface, dark red paint; circular opening may designate door and rectangular slits may represent windows; (= KH 1981/96). |
| Q | 1684 | C45-05-028 | 249 | IVB | — | Massive rectangular terracotta peg, presumably for architectural use; (= KH 1981/21). |

PLATE 156

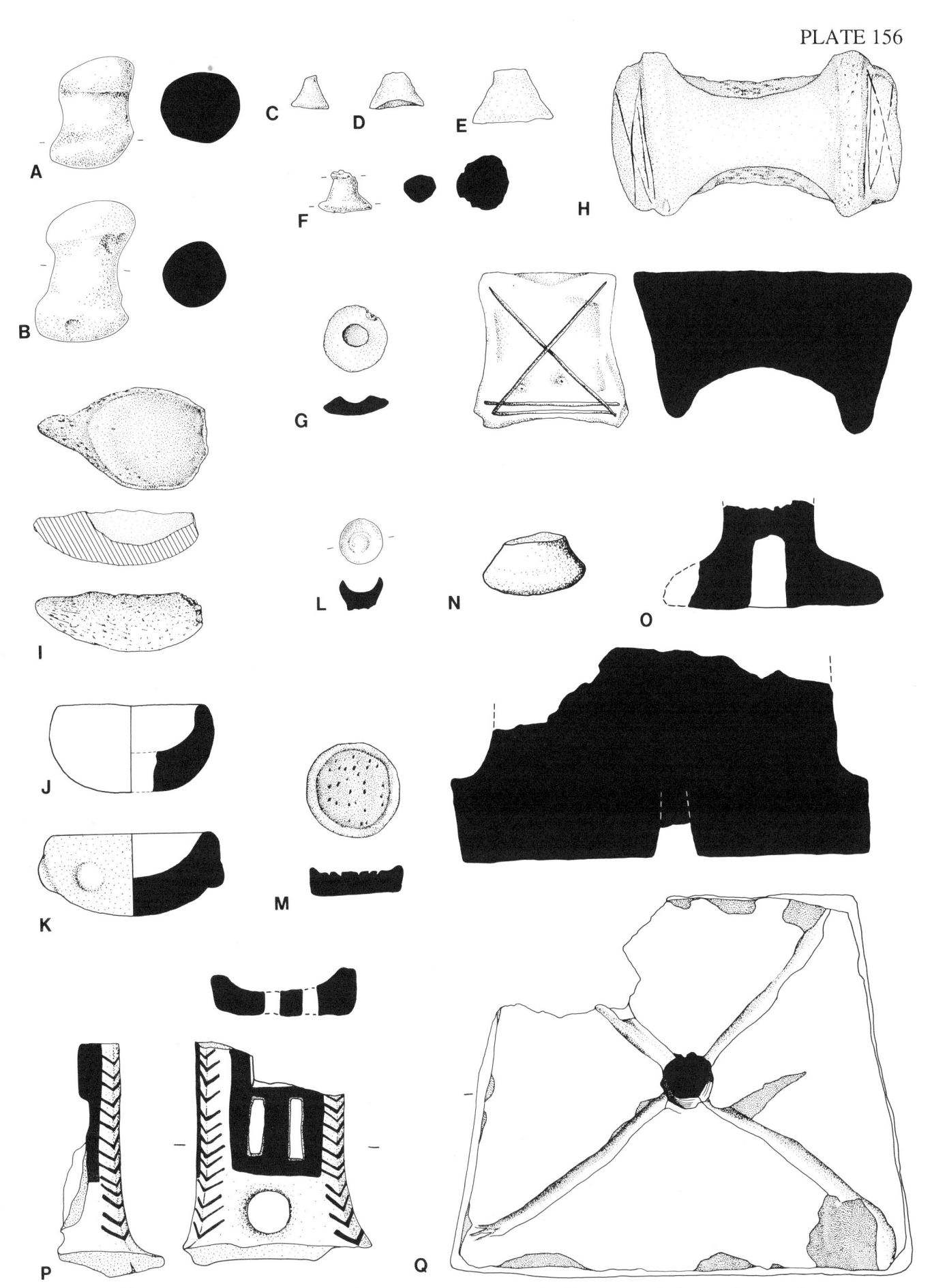

Terracotta Implements From Diverse Periods, Areas A–C, C01, D, and G: Spools (A and B), Tokens/"Gaming Pieces" (C–E), Stand (H), Spoon (I), Crucibles (J and K), Clay Nails (L–O and Q), Model House (P), and Unassigned (G and M). Scale 2:5.

Plate 157. Painted and Unpainted Lids From Periods III and IV Levels, Areas A, C, and D. Scale 3:5.

|   | MRN | CONTEXT | FCN | PERIOD | PHASE | DESCRIPTION/REMARKS |
|---|---|---|---|---|---|---|
| A | 7283 | C45-07-021 | 326 | IVB | — | Terracotta lid; buff Plain Simple Ware paste. |
| B | 885 | C45-02-002 | 052 | IV | — | Terracotta lid; Plain Simple Ware paste; reddish-brownish paint; (= KH 1981/15). |
| C | 7187 | D76-02-032 | 201 | III | — | Terracotta lid; Plain Simple Ware paste; red paint; (= KH 1982/115). |
| D | 17651 | A05-0552/62-067 | 293 | IVB | 13(?) | Terracotta lid; buff Plain Simple Ware; incised zigzag decoration. |
| E | 1040 | Surface, Area of Trench D66 | — | — | — | Terracotta lid; (= KH 1981/10). |
| F | 982 | D66-0525-017 | 119 | III | — | Terracotta lid; (= KH 1981/14). |
| G | 5200 | C56-03-028 | 297 | IVB | — | Terracotta lid; (= KH 1981/78). |
| H | 3116 | C55-08-003 | 181 | IV | — | Terracotta lid; (= KH 1981/44). |
| I | 3917 | C46-05-008 | 082 | IV | — | Terracotta lid; (= KH 1981/44). |

PLATE 157

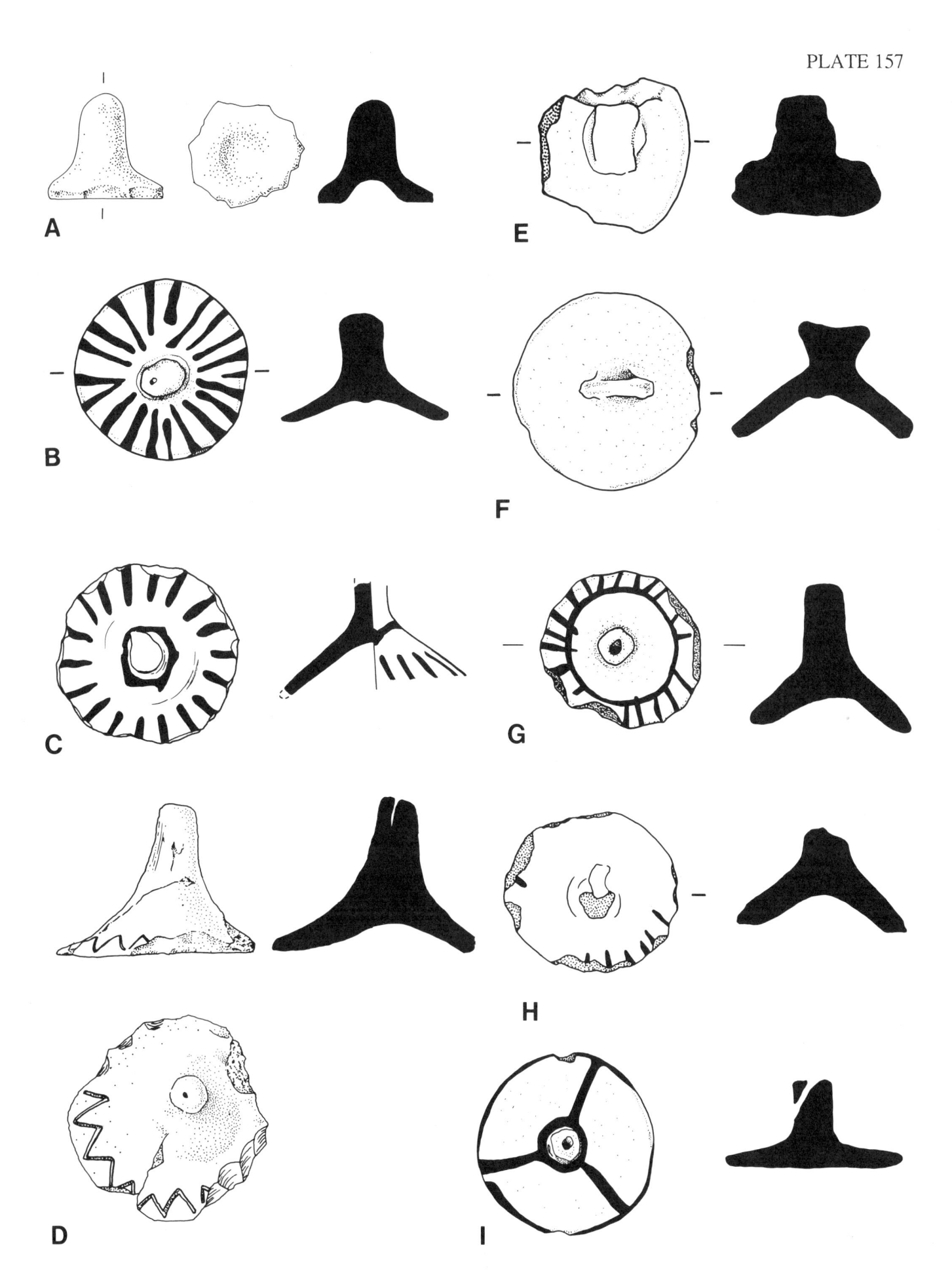

Painted and Unpainted Lids From Periods III and IV Levels, Areas A, C, and D. Scale 3:5.

Plate 158. Terracotta Implements From Diverse Periods, Areas A, C, C01, and D: Lids (A and B), Spoon (E), Stand (F), Perforated Brick (G), and Unassigned (C and D). Scale Indicated.

|   | MRN | CONTEXT | FCN | PERIOD | PHASE | DESCRIPTION/REMARKS |
|---|---|---|---|---|---|---|
| A | 7187 | D76-02-032 | 201 | III | — | = plate 157:C. |
| B | 885 | C45-02-002 | 052 | IV | — | = plate 157:B. |
| C | 12912 | A01-0512/13-016 | 100 | III | 21 | Reddish-brown Plain Simple Ware paste; as preserved: long side = 10.45 cm, short side = 9.05 cm; width = 6.3 cm. |
| D | 4565 | C56-08-022 | 246 | IV | — | Reddish Cooking Pot Ware, mottled black; gritty with medium- and large-sized white grits and quartz flakes prominent; as preserved: long side = 10.7 cm, short side = 8.9 cm, width = 4.6 cm. |
| E | 12638 | A07-24-102 | 1106 | VIII | 4 | = plate 156:I. |
| F | 14185 | D36-03-001 | 093 | II/III | — | = plate 156:H. |
| G | 13221 | C01-0939-175 | 2718 | V A | 7 | Baked brick; interior reddish in color; exterior mottled gray and brown; height = 8 cm, width = 17.5 cm, length = 20 cm. |

PLATE 158

A

B

C

D

E

F

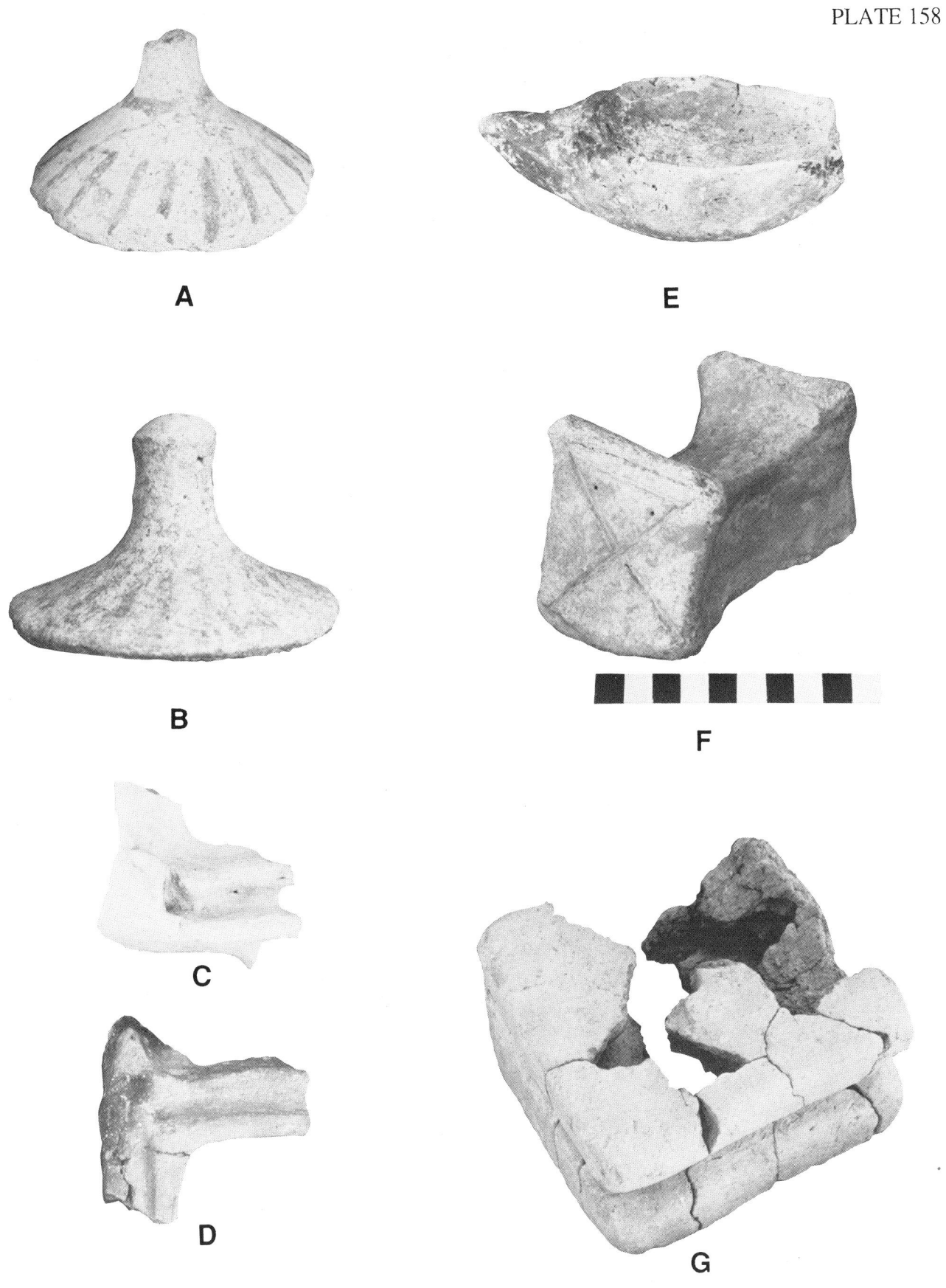

G

Terracotta Implements From Diverse Periods, Areas A, C, C01, and D: Lids (A and B), Spoon (E), Stand (F), Perforated Brick (G), and Unassigned (C and D). Scale Indicated.

Plate 159. Copper Implements From Diverse Periods, Areas C, C01, D, and F:
Pins (A–D, F, H, and I), Needles (E and G), and a Lead Coil (J). Scale 4:5.

|   | *MRN* | *Context* | *FCN* | *Period* | *Phase* | *Description/Remarks* |
|---|---|---|---|---|---|---|
| A | 3921 | C01-0189-095 | 1269 | VIA | 2 | Copper/bronze pin with zoomorphic finial, possibly a bird with outstretched wings or perhaps two birds flanking the square cross-section; from a mixed Periods VII/VI group in Area C01, presumably VIA in date; (= KH 1981/49); see also plate 161:J. |
| B | 3121 | C01-0178-074 | 928 | VA | 9 | Copper/bronze pin with round cross-section; (= KH 1981/39); see also plate 161:I. |
| C | 13155 | C01-0957-172 | 2630 | VA | 7 | Copper/bronze pin with mushroom-shaped head; traces of vestigial loop just below the head on the shank; round cross-section; found inside a hearth in Area C01, Phase 7; (= KH 1983/141); see also plate 161:G. |
| D | 12080 | F01-05-040 | 220 | IVB | 10 | Copper/bronze pin with perforated shank; top twisted and bent into a hook; perforation executed on flanged, lozenge-shaped shaft; otherwise, round cross-section; upper part of pin twisted at least three times; square cross-section; (= KH 1983/154); see also plate 161:E. |
| E | 14914 | D36-0567-012 | 290 | III | — | Copper/bronze pin; shank has a round cross-section and a lozenge shaped eyelet; (= KH 1983/148); see also plate 161:F. |
| F | 19404 | D76-0131-008 | 060 | III | — | Copper/bronze pin with mushroom shaped head; immediately below head, faint traces of horizontal incisions or grooves; perforated shank with round cross-section; (= KH 1984/195); see also plate 161:A. |
| G | 6631 | C35-0371-005 | D255 | IVB | — | Copper/bronze fish hook; eyelet manufactured by twisting wire into loop; (= KH 1981/109); see also plate 161:D. |
| H | 6632 | C35-0372-005 | 269 | IVB | — | Copper/bronze pin or needle; shank perforated on upper end; (= KH 1981/110); see also plate 161:C. |
| I | 17162 | D77-01-004 | 021 | III | — | Copper/bronze pin with slightly swollen head; perforated shank has round cross-section; possibly bent on purpose to form a hook in antiquity; (= KH 1984/196); see also plate 161:B. |
| J | 15895 | D23-01-012 | 259 | III | — | Bent length of lead; round cross-section; coiled on top. |

PLATE 159

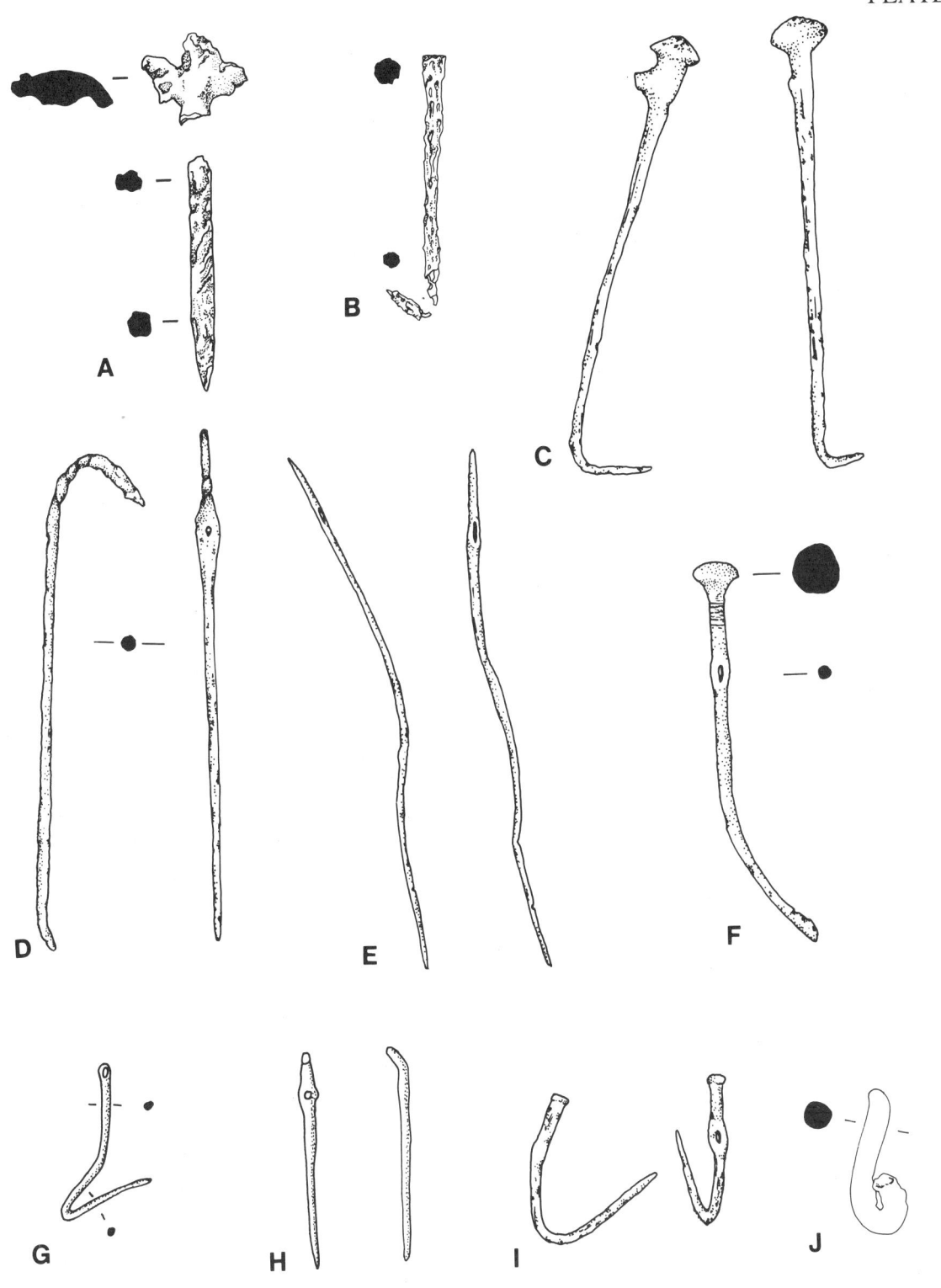

Copper Implements From Diverse Periods, Areas C, C01, D, and F: Pins (A–D, F, H, and I),
Needles (E and G), and a Lead Coil (J). Scale 4:5.

Plate 160. Iron Implements From Period II Levels, Area D. Scale 3:5.

|   | MRN | CONTEXT | FCN | PERIOD | PHASE | DESCRIPTION/REMARKS |
|---|---|---|---|---|---|---|
| A | 15027 | D53-03-001 | 055 | II | — | Iron spike, attached to cylindrical haft with open slit; see also plate 161:BB. |
| B | 776 | D66-04-016 | 096 | II | — | Iron adze; see also plate 161:JJ. |
| C | 8918 | D55-05-001 | 150 | II | — | Iron bracelet; see also plate 161:GG. |
| D | 14206 | D43-07-020 | 128 | II | — | Iron fragment, perhaps a fibula or ring; see also plate 161:V. |
| E | 15416 | D15-01-002 | D013 | II | — | Iron nail; see also plate 161:AA. |
| F | 2286 | D65-01-004 | 016 | II | — | Iron nail; see also plate 161:S. |
| G | 3953 | D65-04-023 | 098 | II | — | Tool with splayed edge; possibly for gouging; see also plate 161:L. |
| H | 9273 | D55-0579-027 | 289 | II | — | Iron pin; see also plate 161:O. |
| I | 14228 | D23-01-002 | 009 | II | — | Iron arrowhead(?); found together with a second identical piece; point tapers to a rather dull edge; shaft is bent; (= KH 1983/143). |
| J | 15251 | D37-03-007 | D046 | II | — | Iron spike or chisel; see also plate 161:K. |
| K | 14316 | D56-02-015 | 081 | II | — | Iron pin; see also plate 161:N. |

PLATE 160

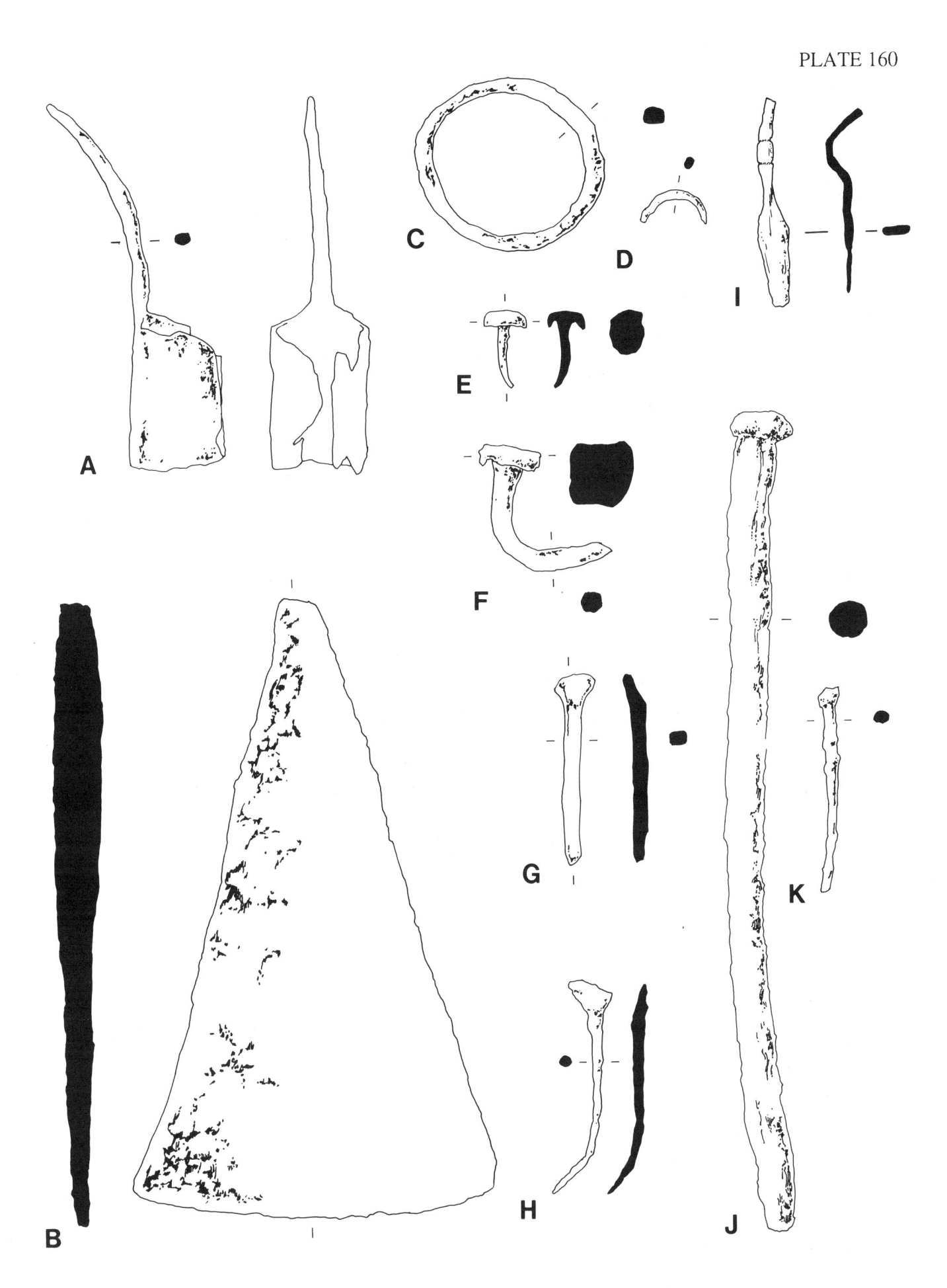

Iron Implements From Period II Levels, Area D. Scale 3:5.

Plate 161. Copper Implements (A–J) From Diverse Periods, Areas C, C01, D and F; Iron Implements (K–LL) From Period II Levels, Areas C and D. Scale Indicated.

|   | MRN | Context | FCN | Period | Phase | Description/Remarks |
|---|---|---|---|---|---|---|
| A | 19404 | D76-0131-008 | 060 | III | — | = plate 159:F. |
| B | 17162 | D77-01-004 | 021 | III | — | = plate 159:I. |
| C | 6632 | C35-0372-005 | 269 | IVB | — | = plate 159:H. |
| D | 6631 | C35-0371-005 | D255 | IVB | — | = plate 159:G. |
| E | 12080 | F01-05-040 | 220 | IVB | 10 | = plate 159:D. |
| F | 14914 | D36-0567-012 | 290 | III | — | = plate 159:E. |
| G | 13155 | C01-0957-172 | 2630 | VA | 7 | = plate 159:C. |
| H | 6630 | C55-0370-005 | D228 | IVB | — | Copper/bronze badly eroded shank fragment of pin; (= KH 1981/108). |
| I | 3121 | C01-0178-074 | 928 | VA | 9 | = plate 159:B. |
| J | 3921 | C01-0189-095 | 1269 | VIA | 2 | = plate 159:A. |
| K | 15251 | D37-03-007 | D046 | II | — | = plate 160:J. |
| L | 3953 | D65-04-023 | 098 | II | — | = plate 160:G. |
| M | 2088 | D65-0100-002 | 008 | II | — | Iron nail shaft; square cross-section. |
| N | 14316 | D56-02-015 | 081 | II | — | = plate 160:K. |
| O | 9273 | D55-0579-027 | 289 | II | — | = plate 160:H. |
| P | 15058 | D26-01-001 | 011 | II | — | Iron nail with disk shaped head; square cross-section. |
| Q | 984 | D66-0525-0 | 116 | II | — | Iron nail with disk shaped head; square cross-section. |
| R | 10174 | D35-07-001 | 386 | II | — | Iron nail; circular head, square cross-section. |
| S | 2286 | D65-01-004 | 016 | II | — | = plate 160:F. |
| T | 15409 | D46-04-001 | 076 | II | — | Iron nail or pin. |
| U | 14665 | D45-0636/46-026 | D314 | II | — | Iron nail with wedge-shaped head; square cross-section. |
| V | 14206 | D43-07-020 | 128 | II | — | = plate 160:D. |
| W | 15009 | D54-08-001 | 162 | II | — | Iron nail shaft fragment; square cross-section. |
| X | 8984 | D55-0455-019 | 169 | II | — | Flat headed iron nail; square cross-section. |
| Y | 10122 | D55-06-001 | 329 | II | — | Iron nail fragment; flat head, round cross-section. |
| Z | 14626 | D36-0497-012 | D206 | II | — | Iron nail; flat head, square cross-section. |
| AA | 15416 | D15-01-002 | D013 | II | — | = plate 160:E. |
| BB | 15027 | D53-03-001 | 055 | II | — | = plate 160:A. |
| CC | 5212 | D66-02-009 | 053 | II | — | Iron disk fragment; wedge-shaped as preserved, tabular form; width 0.3 cm. |
| DD | 14575 | D37-01-001 | 006 | II | — | Iron disk fragment; wedge-shaped as preserved, tabular form; width 0.3 cm. |
| EE | 6654 | D65-05-030 | 194 | II | — | Iron disk fragment; half of a circular tabular form; width 9.3 cm. |
| FF | 14620 | D25-05-001 | 207 | II | — | Iron; flat, slender sliver of metal with tang; razor(?). |
| GG | 8918 | D55-05-001 | 150 | II | — | = plate 160:C. |
| HH | 3045 | D76-04-001 | 028 | II | — | Iron fragment of nail head. |
| II | 2745 | D45-01-003 | 015 | II | — | Iron; semi-circular disk fragment. |
| JJ | 776 | D66-04-016 | 096 | II | — | = plate 160:B. |
| KK | 2424 | C56-0242-001 | 034 | — | — | Iron; fragment of tool, possibly a chisel; rectangular cross-section. |
| LL | 5183 | C55-0765-011 | D367 | — | — | Iron nail or chisel; flat head with groove, semi-circular cross-section; from an Area C, Period IVB complex pebble surface (fig. 121: Unit 13), presumably intrusive. |

PLATE 161

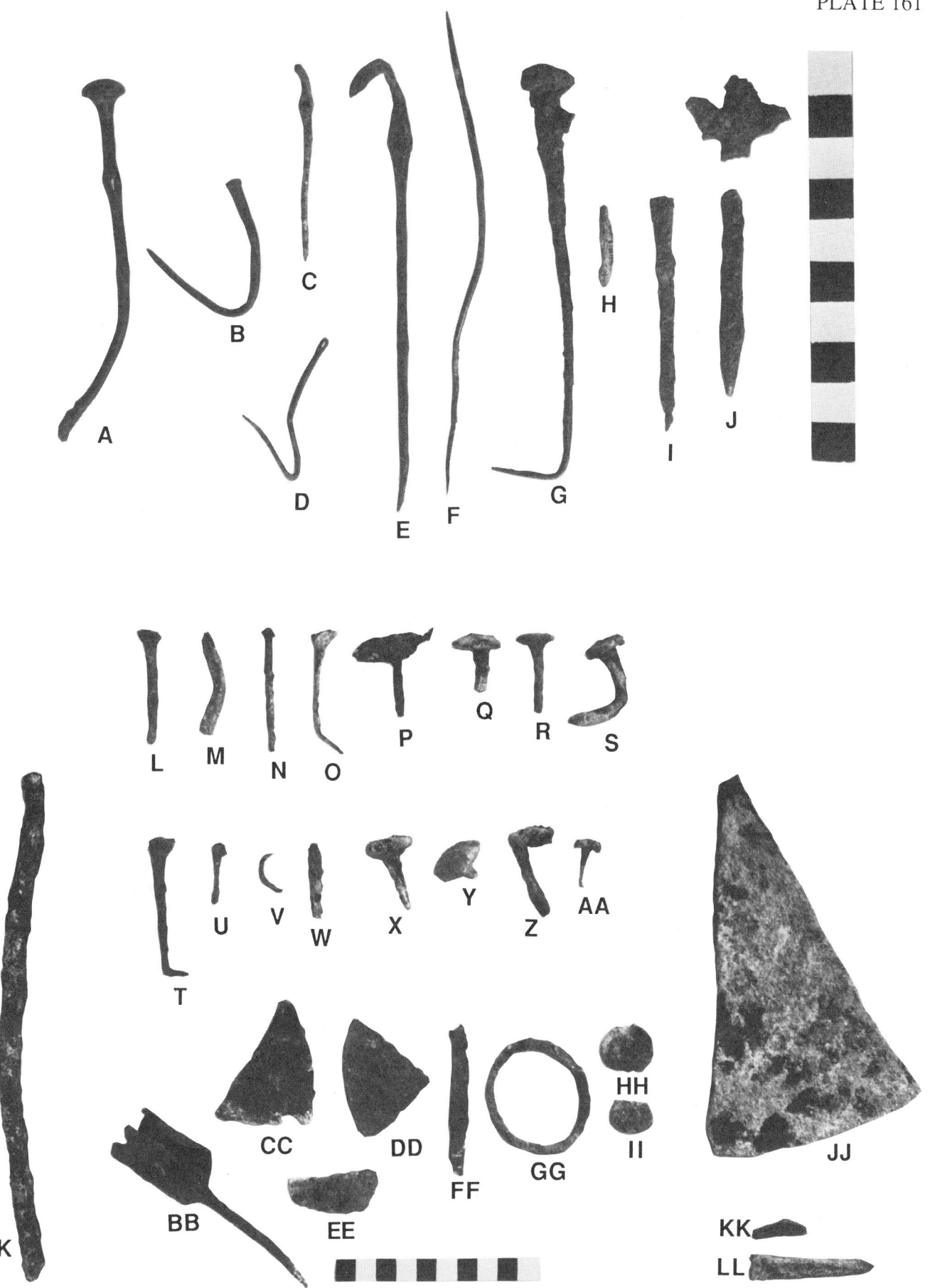

Copper Implements (A–J) From Diverse Periods, Areas C, C01, D, and F; Iron Implements (K–LL) From Period II Levels, Areas C and D. Scale Indicated.

Plate 162. Bone Implements From Diverse Periods, Areas A, B, C01, and D: Bead (B), Pins (D and E), Horn Core (F), Awls and Awl Fragments (G–I and K–M), Needle (J), Spatula (N), and Unassigned (A and C). Scales: (A, C–I, and K–N) 3:5; (B and J) 6:5.

| | MRN | CONTEXT | FCN | PERIOD | PHASE | DESCRIPTION/REMARKS |
|---|---|---|---|---|---|---|
| A | 8674 | A07-15-069 | 556 | VIA | 10 | Worked bone; carved fragment of unknown function, perhaps part of figurine(?); left proximal metatarsal of cow; see also plate 163:H. |
| B | 9315 | A08-07-029 | 304 | VIA | 9 | Bone bead, carved out of hollow, cylindrical bird bone shaft; faint transverse incisions near one end; glossy polished exterior; edges rounded; see also plate 163:F; from same locus as plate 163:E. |
| C | 1512 | D56-0248-001 | 036 | II/III | — | Worked bone; solid fragment of carved artifact; function unknown, perhaps an ornament; rounded head; deeply incised transverse grooves along shaft; polished; see also plate 163:D. |
| D | 13583 | C01-0927/37/28/38-196 | D3080 | VB | 3 | Bone pin or miniature spoon; carved out of an unidentifiable, dense, long bone shaft; highly polished; carefully made diagonal incisions on shaft immediately below head/scoop, round cross-section; artifact is brown in color but mottled black and gray in places, presumably from fire; found inside an ashy pit in Area C01, Phase 3 (fig. 70); (= KH 1983/157); see also plate 163:A, J. |
| E | 13337 | C01-1027-180 | 2834 | VA | 6 | Bone pin; carved out of an unidentifiable, dense, long bone shaft; highly polished; flat nail-like head; found on exterior surface area (Unit 6.3) of Area C01, Phase 6 (fig. 73); (= KH 1983/156); see also plate 163:B, from same locus as plate 162:H, below. |
| F | 17743 | A04-10-099 | 584 | IVB | 13 | Worked bone; sawed-off, smoothed horn core shaft and tip; function unknown; found inside Room 13.8 in Area A, Phase 13 (fig. 16); (= KH 1984/189); see also plate 163:I. |
| G | 12421 | A08-14-067 | 675 | VIII | 4 | Bone awl; carved out of left distal tibia of small ruminant, possibly gazelle; fire blackened, presumably deliberate for hardening; polished to a high gloss along shaft and on tip; diagonal and longitudinal striations on anterior and posterior surfaces of shaft from use or from shaping the implement; flattened on anterior side; (= KH 1983/155); see also plate 163:T. |
| H | 13323 | C01-0937-180 | 2820 | VA | 6 | Bone awl; made from right metacarpal of gazelle; surface highly polished towards point; point surface well smoothed and all edges rounded from use; found on exterior surface area (Unit 6.3) in Area C01, Phase 6 (fig. 73); from same locus as plate 162:E, above; (= KH 1983/164); see also plate 163:EE, KK. |
| I | 13373a | C01-09-183 | 2870 | VA-B | 5 | Bone awl; carved out of unfused distal metacarpal of small ruminant, perhaps gazelle; lower shaft towards point highly polished; somewhat carved-in, triangular shape along shaft, in cross-section; found together with plate 163:AA; see also plate 163:BB. |
| J | 13139 | C01-0959-088 | D2646 | VA | 7 | Bone implement, presumably a needle; carved fragment with perforation near top; surface highly polished throughout; hole drilled from both sides of shaft; found on exterior surface Area 7.4 in Area C01, Phase 7 (fig. 78); from same locus as plate 163:DD; see also plate 163:C. |
| K | 11596 | A04-07-065 | 403 | IVB | 14 | Bone awl; equid second metapodial; carved primarily at the point; natural shape of bone lends itself to use as a boring tool; point polished from use; see also plate 163:X. |
| L | 5926 | A06-05-031 | 153 | IVB | 13 | Bone awl; shaft and point fragment; carved from probably small ruminant metapodial; highly polished; thin, flattened, tubular shape; found on floor inside Unit 13.1 in Area A, Phase 13 (fig. 16); (= KH 1981/97); see also plate 163:B. |
| M | 20499 | B82-0152/62-002 | 051 | IVA or III | — | Bone awl; carved from half of a distal metapodial of a ruminant; (= KH 1984/190); see also plate 163:Z. |
| N | 13191 | C01-1017/18/19-173 | 2688 | VA | 8 | Bone implement, probably a smoother or scraper; longitudinal shaft carved from long bone probably of a small ruminant; one end of implement part of unfused diaphysis of long bone; other end thin, flat, polished from use; not pointed; see also plate 163:JJ. |

PLATE 162

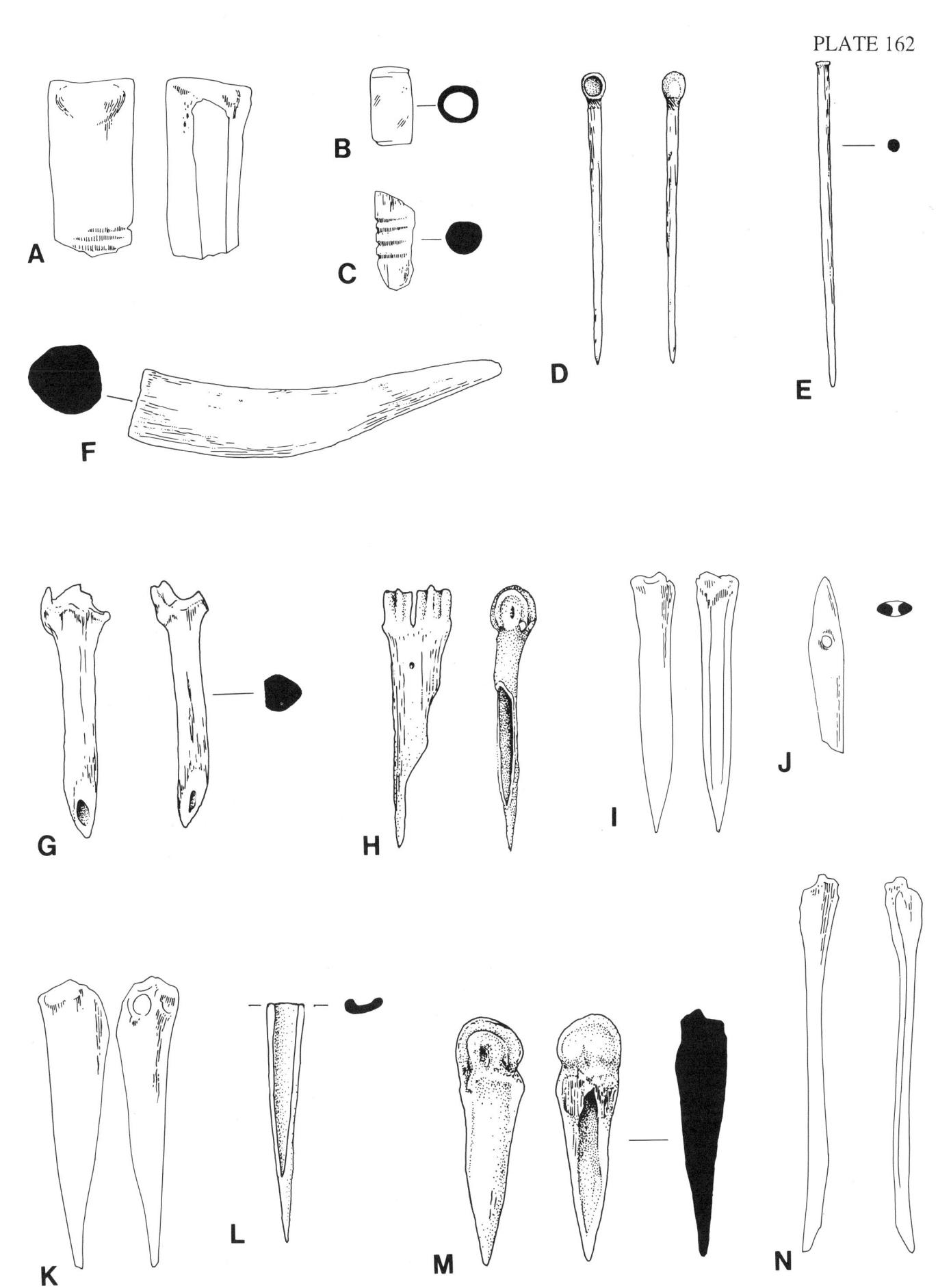

Bone Implements From Diverse Periods, Areas A, B, C01, and D: Bead (B), Pins (D and E), Horn Core (F),
Awls and Awl Fragments (G–I and K–M), Needle (J), Spatula (N), and Unassigned (A and C).
Scales: (A, C–I, and K–N) 3:5; (B and J) 6:5.

Plate 163. Bone Implements From Diverse Periods, Areas A, B, C, C01, and D. Scales Indicated.

|   | MRN | CONTEXT | FCN | PERIOD | PHASE | DESCRIPTION/REMARKS |
|---|---|---|---|---|---|---|
| A | 13583 | C01-0927/37/28/38-196 | D3080 | VB | 3 | = plate 162:D. |
| B | 13337 | C01-1027-180 | 2834 | VA | 6 | = plate 162:E. |
| C | 13139 | C01-0959-088 | D2646 | VA | 7 | = plate 162:J. |
| D | 1512 | D56-0248-001 | 036 | II/III | — | = plate 162:C. |
| E | 9306 | A08-07-029 | 296 | VIA | 9 | Bead; probably bone but could be shell instead; cylindrical, tiny; ca. 0.2 cm in diameter and 0.2 cm in length; white with black smudges from fire; from same locus as plate 163:F, below. |
| F | 9315 | A08-07-029 | 304 | VIA | 9 | = plate 162:B. |
| G | 7182 | C55-0439-011 | D674 | IVB | — | Bone bead, ornament(?); carved out of cylindrical limb shaft of small vertebrate; ends blunt from carving and smoothing; small groove incised near one end; fragmentary; tubular shaft broken in half longitudinally. |
| H | 8674 | A07-15-069 | 556 | VIA | 10 | = plate 162:A. |
| I | 17743 | A04-10-099 | 584 | IVB | 13 | = plate 162:F. |
| J | 13583 | C01-0927/37/28/38-196 | D3080 | VB | 3 | Enlarged view of upper portion of plate 162:D and plate 163:A. |
| K | 7268 | C35-02-006 | 318 | IV | — | Worked bone, small fragment of implement; probably from lower shaft of awl. |
| L | 7265 | C35-03-005 | 315 | IVB | — | Worked bone, small fragment of implement; probably awl point. |
| M | 7264 | C35-02-015 | 314 | IVB | — | Worked bone, small fragment of implement; probably awl point; possible metapodial of small ruminant; polished. |
| N | 6253 | C55-05-014 | 501 | IVB | — | Worked bone, small fragment of implement; probably awl point; possible equid metapodial; polished. |
| O | 7188 | C550-03-007 | 680 | IVB | — | Worked bone, small fragment of implement; probably from lower shaft of awl; possible metapodial of small ruminant; upper shaft flattened in cross-section; polished. |
| P | 7259 | C45-01-007 | 321 | IVB | — | Worked bone, small fragment of implement; probably from lower shaft of awl; longitudinal striations. |
| Q | 16478 | D35-0949-033 | 792 | III | — | Worked bone, small fragment of implement; probably awl point; polished. |
| R | 7192 | A09-03-013 | 238 | Slope Wash | — | Worked bone, fragment of implement; probably awl; possible metapodial of small ruminant; upper shaft flattened in cross-section; polished. |
| S | 7198 | A09-05-012 | 240 | VIA-B | 6-7 | Worked bone(?); fragment of possible implement, probably awl; rib of large mammal; smooth, tapered to a point, but no obvious traces of carving; shape could be natural, the result of fracture. |
| T | 12421 | A08-14-067 | 675 | VIII | 4 | = plate 162:G. |
| U | 7686 | A07-1190-042 | 396 | IVA-B | 15 | Worked bone; fragment of implement, probably awl; possible metapodial of small ruminant; shaft dark brown-gray in color; tip black, presumably from fire hardening; polished to a high gloss; upper shaft semi-circular in shape; found inside pits in Unit 15.2 of Area A, Phase 15 (fig. 18). |
| V | 5926 | A06-05-031 | 153 | IVB | 13 | = plate 162:L. |
| W | 11320 | A04-07-068 | 375 | IVB | 14 | Worked bone; shaft and point fragment of a heavy, crude but sharp awl; made from humerus of large mammal; exterior surface and interior longitudinal groove polished; finger-hold positions suggested by polishing. |
| X | 11596 | A04-07-065 | 403 | IVB | 14 | = plate 162:K. |
| Y | 17817 | A05-0552-051 | 388 | IV | Post-14/Pre-16 | Worked bone; small fragment of implement, probably awl point. |
| Z | 20499 | B82-0152/62-002 | 051 | IVA or III | — | = plate 162:M. |

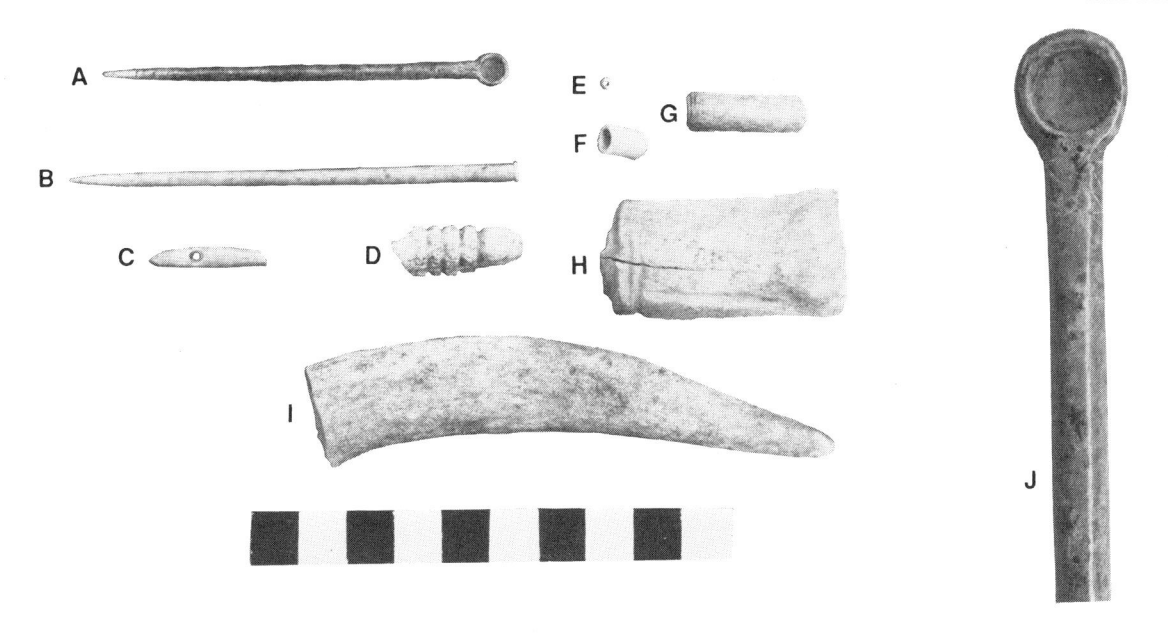

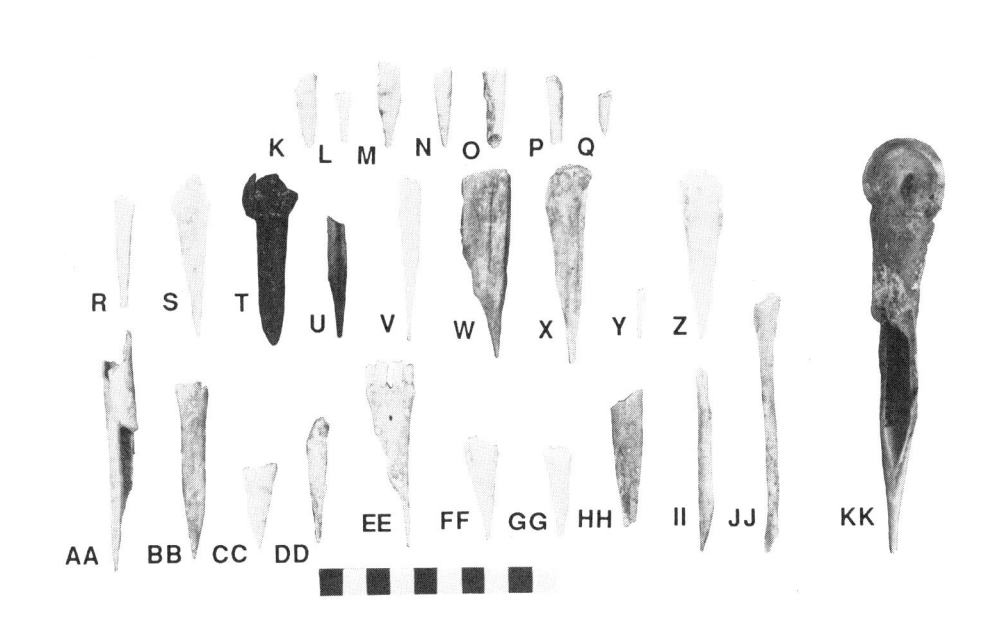

PLATE 163

Bone Implements From Diverse Periods, Areas A, B, C, C01, and D. Scales Indicated.

Plate 163. Bone Implements From Diverse Periods, Areas A, B, C, C01, and D. Scales Indicated. (*cont.*).

| | MRN | CONTEXT | FCN | PERIOD | PHASE | DESCRIPTION/REMARKS |
|---|---|---|---|---|---|---|
| AA | 13373b | C01-09-183 | 2870 | VA-B | 5 | Worked bone; shaft and point fragment of implement, probably awl; made from tibia of small ruminant; shape could be result of natural fracture, but upper shaft polished as if from use; found together with plate 163:BB, below. |
| BB | 13373a | C01-09-183 | 2870 | VA-B | 5 | = plate 162:I. |
| CC | 8535 | C01-0939-156 | 2261 | VA | 10 | Worked bone, probably an awl; carved possibly from femur of small ruminant; triangular, half-conical shape, from diaphysis of bone to awl point; polished. |
| DD | 17818 | C01-0957-088 | 3279 | VA | 7 | Worked bone, fragment of implement, probably awl point; from same locus as plate 162:J. |
| EE | 13323 | C01-0937-180 | 2820 | VA | 6 | = plate 162:H. |
| FF | 1080 | C45-01-007 | 113 | IVB | — | Worked bone, probably an awl; carved probably from distal metapodial of small ruminant; triangular, almost conical shape, from fused diaphysis of bone to awl point; polished. |
| GG | 1879 | C01-0168-048 | 537 | IVB | 12 | Worked bone, probably an awl; carved possibly from distal metapodial of small ruminant; almost conical shape at diaphysis of bone; flattened toward point; polished; found on floor of Unit 12.1 of Area C01, Phase 12 (fig. 78). |
| HH | 5621 | C01-0177-092 | 1370 | VA | 6 | Worked bone; fragment of implement, probably awl; possible metapodial of small ruminant; almost tabular shape, back side of shaft shows transverse carving striations from flattening; highly polished. |
| II | 7241 | C01-0187/88/89-078 | 1972 | VA | 9 | Worked bone; shaft and point fragment of implement, possibly a needle; carved from long bone shaft of small ruminant; shaft not consistently thin and tapered as for pins, but point is sharp and therefore smoothing/scraping tool not suggested; polished or smoothed surface the result of normal weathering(?). |
| JJ | 13191 | C01-1017/18/19-173 | 2688 | VA | 8 | = plate 162:N. |
| KK | 13323 | C01-0937-180 | 2820 | VA | 6 | Enlarged view of plate 162:H and plate 163:EE. |

Plate 164. Marine and Worked Shells From Diverse Periods, Areas A–D and F–H: Scales: (A–C, E–H and J) 1:1; (D and I) 2:1; (K–V) Indicated.

| | MRN | CONTEXT | FCN | PERIOD | PHASE | DESCRIPTION/REMARKS |
|---|---|---|---|---|---|---|
| A | 5799 | C55-06-012 | 494 | IV | — | *Venus*; ground down, hole at umbo (umbonal view). |
| B | 5872 | D45-0332-007 | 083 | III | — | *Glycymeris*; ground down, hole at umbo (umbonal view). |
| C | 7189 | C35-05-009 | 304 | IVB | — | *Conus*; water worn, ground down, hole at apex (apical view). |
| D | 20505 | G64-06-024 | 208 | IV | — | *Arcularia*; open body. |
| E | 5188 | C55-0765-011 | 381 | IVB | — | *Nerita*; ground down and holed at apex, worn (apical view). |
| F | 12424 | A07-1972-085 | 959 | VIA | 7 | *Murex trunculus*; lacking apex, ground down on several surfaces. |
| G | 4273 | C55-05-007 | 201 | IVB | — | *Murex brandaris*; worn; no distal end. |
| H | 19229 | H62-0192-008 | 089 | III | — | *Strombus*; worn; recent hole on body. |
| I | 19256 | B02-02-011 | D232 | IVA | — | Mother of pearl; presumably from *unio*; winged figure pendant. |
| J | 11333 | A04-08-069 | 388 | IVB | 14 | *Conus*; whorl bead. |
| K | 15274 | D37-03-007 | 049 | II/III | — | *Conus*; whorl bead; carefully ground down. |
| L | 11333 | A04-08-069 | 388 | IVB | 14 | = plate 164:J, above. |
| M | 12262 | F01-05-063 | 353 | IVC/VI | — | *Unio*; holed bead. |
| N | 12734 | A05-0552-051 | 185 | IVA | Post 14 | *Unio*; ring fragment. |
| O | 12526 | A08-13-069 | 724 | VIII | 3 | *Semicassis* lip fragment; rounded off, smoothed; broken hole at top, presumably a pendant. |
| P | 20205 | G64-06-024 | 208 | IV | — | = plate 164:D, above. |
| Q | 19505 | B82-0116/17-006 | 110 | IVA | — | *Arcularia*; open body. |
| R | 9304 | A07-14-060 | 557 | IVC/VIA | 10/11 | *Unio*; holed pendant; hole drilled from inside. |
| S | 2751 | C01-0938-069/073 | 823 | IVB | 13 | *Unio*; holed pendant; hole drilled from one side. |
| T | 2746 | D44-03-012 | 040 | III | — | *Unio*; holed pendant; hole drilled from outside. |
| U | 19256 | B02-02-011 | D232 | IVA | — | = plate 164:I, above. |
| V | 19744 | B02-0406/07-037 | 377 | IVA | — | Pearl (probably fresh water). |

PLATE 164

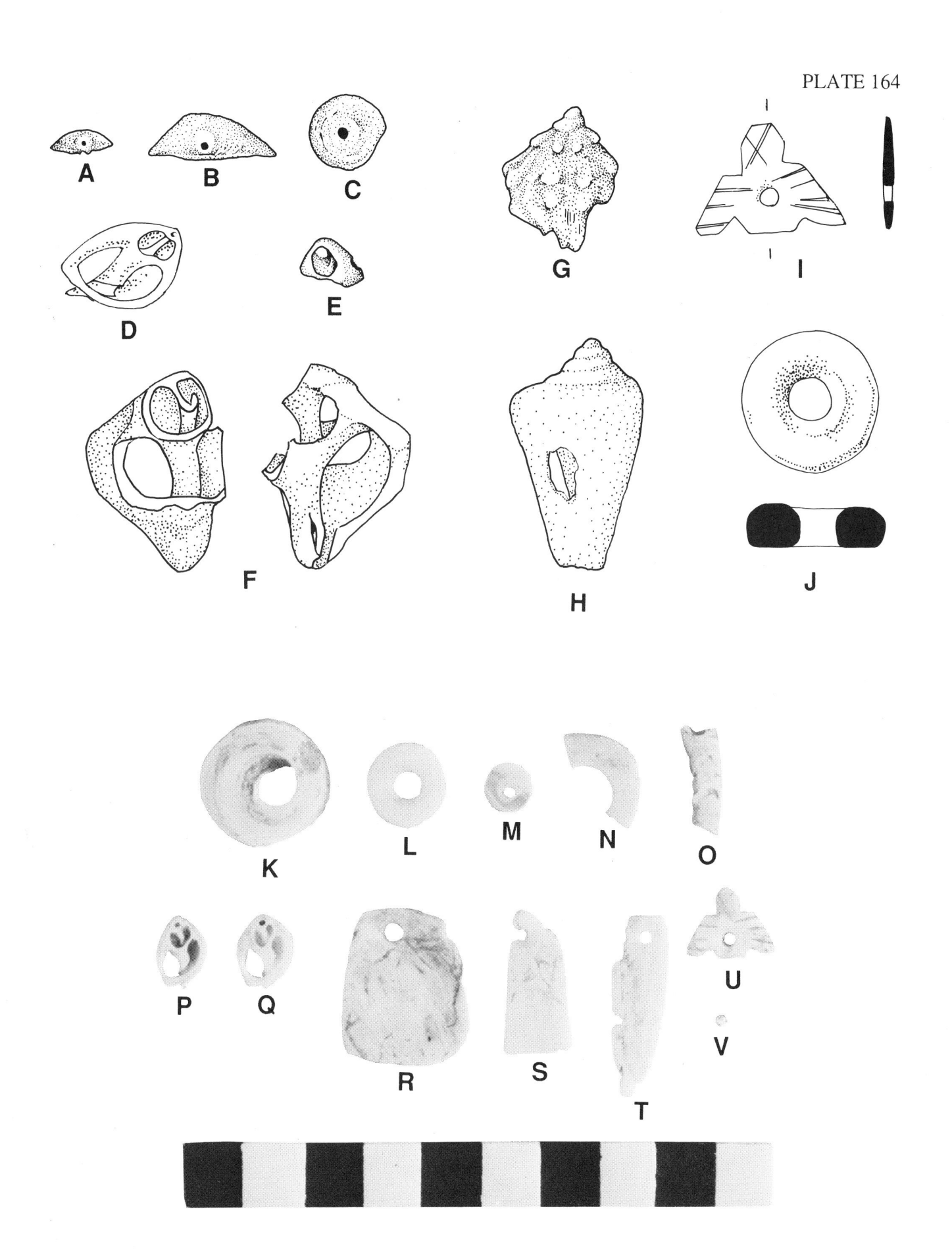

Marine and Worked Shells From Diverse Periods, Areas A–D and F–H.
Scales: (A–C, E–H, and J) 1:1; (D and I) 2:1; (K–V) Indicated.

Plate 165. Stone Vessels From Period VIII Levels, Area A (A–C); Registered Ground Stone (D–U) and Chipped Stone (V–BB) Artifacts From Diverse Periods, Areas A–C, C01, and F. Scales: (A–T and W–BB) 2:5; (U and V) 4:5.

|   | MRN | CONTEXT | FCN | PERIOD | PHASE | DESCRIPTION/REMARKS |
|---|---|---|---|---|---|---|
| A | 12423 | A07-19-098 | 958 | VIII | 4 | Stone vessel; steatite/chlorite dark blue stone; (= KH 1983/137); see also plate 166:E. |
| B | 12422 | A08-1141-058 | 676 | VIII | 5 | Stone vessel; steatite/chlorite dark blue stone; (= KH 1983/136); see also plate 166:F. |
| C | 11850 + 12569 | A08-0511-051 + A08-12-074 | D544 + 761 | VIA VIII | 7 1 | Stone vessel; steatite/chlorite dark blue stone; broken into two fragments, one recovered in a late Chalcolithic pit and the other, presumably in situ, in a Period VIII level; (= KH 1983/138); see also plate 166:G. |
| D | 2434 | C01-0177-072 | 769 | VA | 10 | Small faceted limestone bead; found on floor (fig. 76: Area C01, Phase 10, Unit 10.2); (= KH 1981/28). |
| E | 3923 | C55-08-009 | 208 | IV | — | Small limestone roundel; (= KH 1981/70). |
| F | 4272 | C01-0188-091 | D1158 | VA | 7 | Small limestone roundel; (= KH 1981/62). |
| G | 3970 | C46-07-003 | — | IV | — | Pendant; carved out of a river cobble; (= KH 1981/71). |
| H | 12091 | F01-05-040 | 231 | IVB | 10 | Stone fragment, perhaps part of a pendant(?); (= KH 1983/162). |
| I | 4271 | C46-05-010 | 098 | IV | — | Perforated limestone fragment, pendant(?); (= KH 1981/61). |
| J | 4559 | C55-0569-011 | 272 | IVB | — | Perforated stone roundel; (= KH 1981/89). |
| K | 11513 | A08-0502-046 | 410 | VIA | 7 | Black stone spindle whorl; (= KH 1983/132). |
| L | 8987 | C01-1007/17/08/18-164 | D2396 | VA | 9 | Limestone spindle whorl; found on the floor of an Area C01, Phase 9 room (fig. 75: Unit 9.1); (= KH 1982/123). |
| M | 13697 | C01-0948-201 | 3229 | VIA | 2 | Veined stone "macehead"; found on an Area C01, Phase 2 surface (fig. 69); (= KH 1983/159). |
| N | 2623 | C35-01-001 | 003 | IV | — | Perforated stone, limestone; (= KH 1981/37). |
| O | 1043 | C01-0169-009 | 235 | IVB | 13 | Limestone "macehead"; found on the floor of an Area C01, Phase 13 room (fig. 79: Unit 13.1); from same floor as an identical example (MRN 694: KH 1980/9), not illustrated. |
| P | 3689 | A07-0750-022 | 181 | IVA-B | 15 | Stone loomweight; (= KH 1981/53). |
| Q | 5991 + 7138 | C55-07-020 + C55-07-037 | 482 + 677 | IVB | — | Stone adze; (= KH 1983/173). |
| R | 11720 | A08-10-050 | 486 | IVA-B | 15? | Stone adze; found discarded inside a Period IV well in Area A; (= KH 1983/133). |
| S | 12040 | F01-05-029 | 180 | IVB | 12 | Limestone adze; (= KH 1983/163). |
| T | 5191 | C55-0795-011 | 388 | IVB | — | Stone adze; (= KH 1981/76). |
| U | 19050 | B02-04-001 | 200 | — | — | Vesicular basalt, black; (= KH 1984/199). |
| V | 2752 | C55-07-003 | 165 | IV | — | Flint arrowhead; translucent brown stone; (= KH 1981/33). |
| W | 1347 | C01-1027-033 | 309 | IVB | 14 | Flint arrowhead; translucent brown stone; found on floor/suprafloor deposits inside Room 14.3 in Area C01, Phase 14 (fig. 80); (= KH 1981/17). |
| X | 6450 | C01-1007-124 | D1750 | IVB | 12 | Obsidian bladelet; (= KH 1981/114). |
| Y | 6882 | C01-0177-128 | 1914 | VII | 1 | Obsidian bladelet; (= KH 1981/113). |
| Z | 3922 | C55-08-009 | 207 | IV | — | Obsidian bladelet; (= KH 1981/50). |
| AA | 1041 | Surface, Area of Trench A08 | 187 | — | — | Flint blade; (= KH 1981/11). |
| BB | 2194 | C01-0188-067 | 690 | VA | 10 | Flint blade; cortex fragment still attached on side; (= KH 1981/24). |

PLATE 165

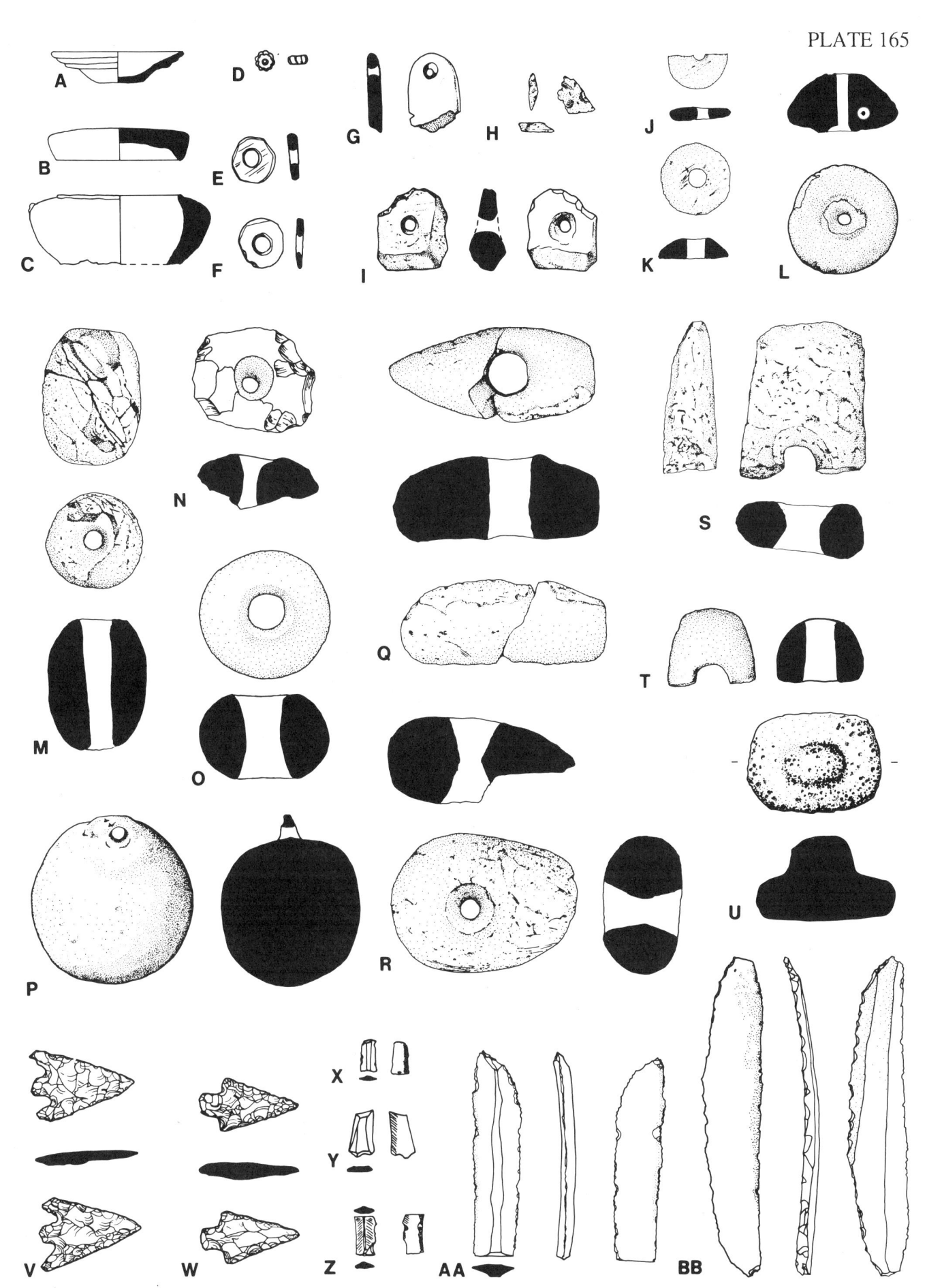

Stone Vessels From Period VIII Levels, Area A (A–C); Registered Ground Stone (D–U) and Chipped Stone (V–BB) Artifacts From Diverse Periods, Areas A–C, C01, and F. Scales: (A–T and W–BB) 2:5; (U and V) 4:5.

Plate 166. Ground and Chipped Stone Artifacts From Diverse Periods, Areas A, B, C01, and D. Scales Indicated.

|   | *MRN* | *Context* | *FCN* | *Period* | *Phase* | *Description/Remarks* |
|---|---|---|---|---|---|---|
| A | 11513 | A08-0502-046 | 410 | VIA | 7 | = plate 165:K. |
| B | 19050 | B02-04-001 | 200 | — | — | = plate 165:U. |
| C | 13697 | C01-0948-201 | 3229 | VIA | 2 | = plate 165:M. |
| D | 14317 | D56-02-015 | 082 | III | — | Flint arrowhead, tip broken; brown translucent stone; (= KH 1983/144). |
| E | 12423 | A07-19-098 | 958 | VIII | 4 | = plate 165:A. |
| F | 12422 | A07-1141-058 | 676 | VIII | 5 | = plate 165:B. |
| G | 11850 + 12569 | A08-0511-051 + A08-12-074 | D544 + 761 | VIA VIII | 7 1 | = plate 165:C. |
| H | 12570 | A07-2492-107 | 1019 | VIII | 3 | Bifacial dagger; translucent brown stone, cortex-covered butt; found on floor inside *Tholos* 3.1 in Area A, Phase 3; (= KH 1983/139). |

PLATE 166

Ground and Chipped Stone Artifacts From Diverse Periods, Areas A, B, C01, and D. Scales Indicated.

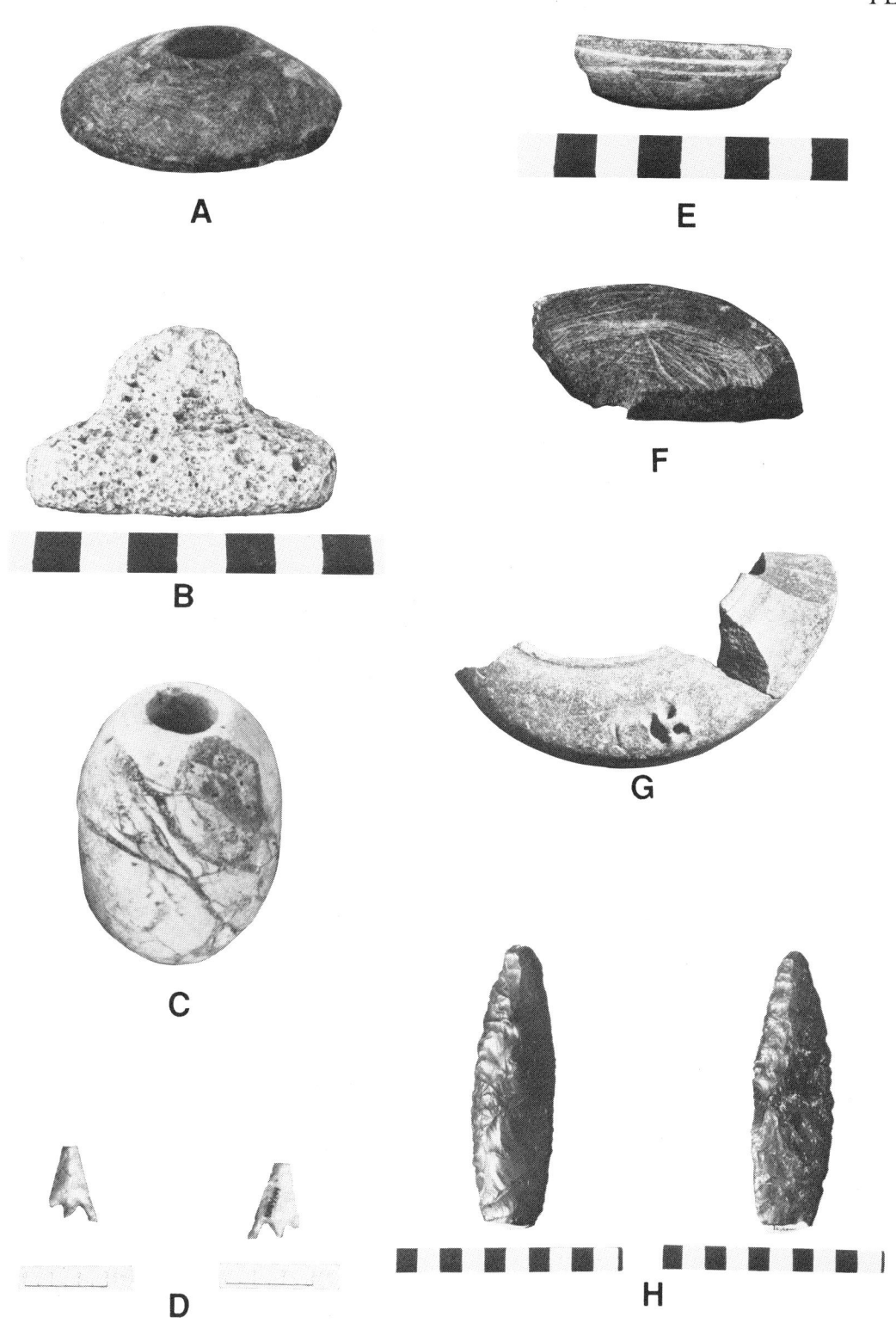

Plate 167. Seals (A–C, H, and I), Sealing (G), Stoppers (D and E), and "Tablet" (F) From Diverse Periods, Areas A, C, C01, D, E, and F. Scales: (A–E and G–I) 3:5; (F) 6:5.

|   | MRN | CONTEXT | FCN | PERIOD | PHASE | DESCRIPTION/REMARKS |
|---|---|---|---|---|---|---|
| A | 11939 | F01-05-022 | 079 | IVB | 12/13 | Stone stamp seal fragment; on reverse, loop handle; flat tabular square shape; irregular crosshatched incised design; dolorite or diorite; black (2.5YR 2.5/0); (= KH 1983/134); see also plate 168:G. |
| B | 5619 | E44-0115-006 | 024 | III | — | Cylinder seal; very worn, perhaps an heirloom reused in a later context as a bead; irregular crosshatched design; black serpentine; (= KH 1981/87); see also plate 168:F. |
| C | 6629 | C56-0993-035 | 425 | IVB | — | Stamp seal with stalk handle; broken lengthwise; design: irregular crosshatch/zigzag within a rectangular frame; pink limestone; (= KH 1981/107); see also plate 168:H, I. |
| D | 8686 | C01-1018-145 | 2275 | VA | 10 | Clay jar stopper(?); dense unfired clay, light gray (10YR 7/2); found inside a room (Unit 10.1); from same locus, another possible jar stopper, plate 167: E, below. |
| E | 8114 | C01-1008/18/28-145 | 2093 | VA | 10 | Clay jar stopper; dense clay with no visible inclusions used as temper; fragment still preserves impression of vessel rim on its surface; apparently fired, presumably secondarily; light gray clay (7.5YR 8/4); from same locus, another possible jar stopper, plate 167:D, above. |
| F | 8673 | A07-1592-072 | 555 | VIA | 9 | Rectangular tablet-like object; rounded edges broken at one corner; dense unfired clay with no inclusions visible as tempering; rather heavy; longitudinal and transverse sections taken from preliminary field sketches and enlarged to actual size, not a carefully made measured drawing; length = 3.6 cm, width = 3.2 cm, thickness = 1.75 cm, weight = 21.85 gm. |
| G | 9301 | C01-0937/38-159 | 2495 | IVB or VA | 10/11 | Seal impression on clay; clay is black-brown in color and dense with no visible tempering; impressed with circular stamp seal design; a circle divided into quadrants(?); on reverse faint traces of coiled rope(?); however, since the sealing is fairly flat it is not part of a door sealing; (= KH 1982/127); see also plate 168:E. |
| H | 2432 | D42-02-002 | 009 | II | — | Single-sided stamp seal, white limestone; (= KH 1981/27). |
| I | 15017 | D54-08-038 | 166 | II | — | Double-sided stamp seal, white limestone; (= KH 1983/149). |

PLATE 167

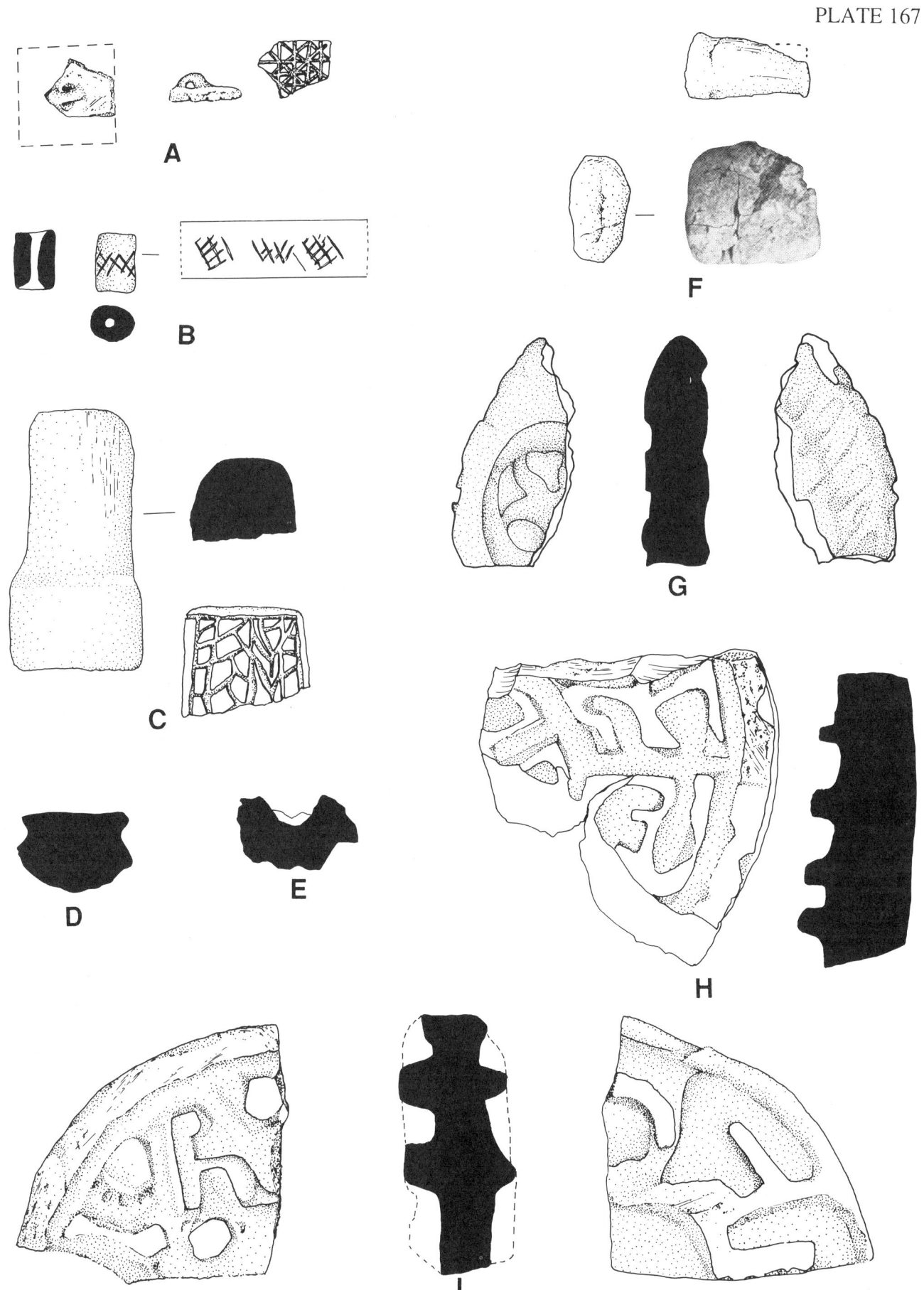

Seals (A–C, H, and I), Sealing (G), Stoppers (D and E), and "Tablet" (F) From Diverse Periods,
Areas A, C, C01, D, E, and F. Scales: (A–E and G–I) 3:5; (F) 6:5.

Plate 168. Seals and Sealings From Diverse Periods, Areas A, C, C01, D, E, and F.

|   | MRN | CONTEXT | FCN | PERIOD | PHASE | DESCRIPTION/REMARKS |
|---|---|---|---|---|---|---|
| A | 11386 | A04-07-078 | 435 | IVB | 14 | Seal impression on clay, possibly a door sealing; obverse: two impressions of a single circular stamp seal; design: interlocking triangles with solid triangular filler motifs; reverse: two spiral cord impressions; preserved dimensions: length = 3.9 cm, width = 3.5 cm, thickness = 2 cm; found inside Room 14.3 in Area A, Phase 14 (fig. 17); (= KH 1983/131); other views, see also plate 168:B and C, below. |
| B | 11386 | A04-07-078 | 435 | IVB | 14 | Another view of plate 168:A, above, and C, below. |
| C | 11386 | A04-07-078 | 435 | IVB | 14 | Another view of plate 168:A and B, above. |
| D | 15017 | D54-08-038 | 166 | II | — | = plate 167:I. |
| E | 9301 | C01-0937/38-159 | 2495 | IVB or VA | 10/11 | = plate 167:G. |
| F | 5619 | E44-0115-006 | 024 | III | — | = plate 167:B. |
| G | 11939 | F01-05-022 | 079 | IVB | 12/13 | = plate 167:A. |
| H | 6629 | C56-0993-035 | 425 | IVB | — | = plate 167:C. |
| I | 6629 | C56-0993-035 | 425 | IVB | — | Enlarged view of design of plate 168:H, above. |

PLATE 168

Seals and Sealings From Diverse Periods, Areas A, C, C01, D, E, and F.

Plate 169. Roman and Ottoman Coins From Area D. Scales: (A) 2:1; (B and C) 3:2.

|   | MRN | Context | FCN | Period | Phase | Description/Remarks |
|---|---|---|---|---|---|---|
| A | 14200 | D43-06-020 | 122 | — | — | Late Roman coin, AE 4 of Arcadius; draped bust with pearl diadem facing right; obverse legend: DN ARCADIUS PF AVG. Reverse: victory dragging a captive and holding a trophy with + in the field; reverse legends: SALVS REI PUBLICAE; in exergue, ANTB; struck at Antioch (officina B) between A.D. 383 and 392; diameter: = 1.3 cm; (= KH 1983/142). |
| B | 10996 | D43-07-001 | 118 | — | — | Large bronze Roman coin of Nerva (AE 22); struck at Antioch; the portrait is rather crude and the reverse is the typical SC wreath of Antioch; obverse legends not preserved; diameter = 2.8 cm; (= KH 1983/158). |
| C | 14484 | D16-0096-000 | 001 | — | — | Late nineteenth century Ottoman coin; Tugra of Abdulhamed II; diameter = 2.4 cm; (= KH 1983/145). |

PLATE 169

Roman and Ottoman Coins From Area D. Scales: (A) 2:1; (B and C) 3:2.

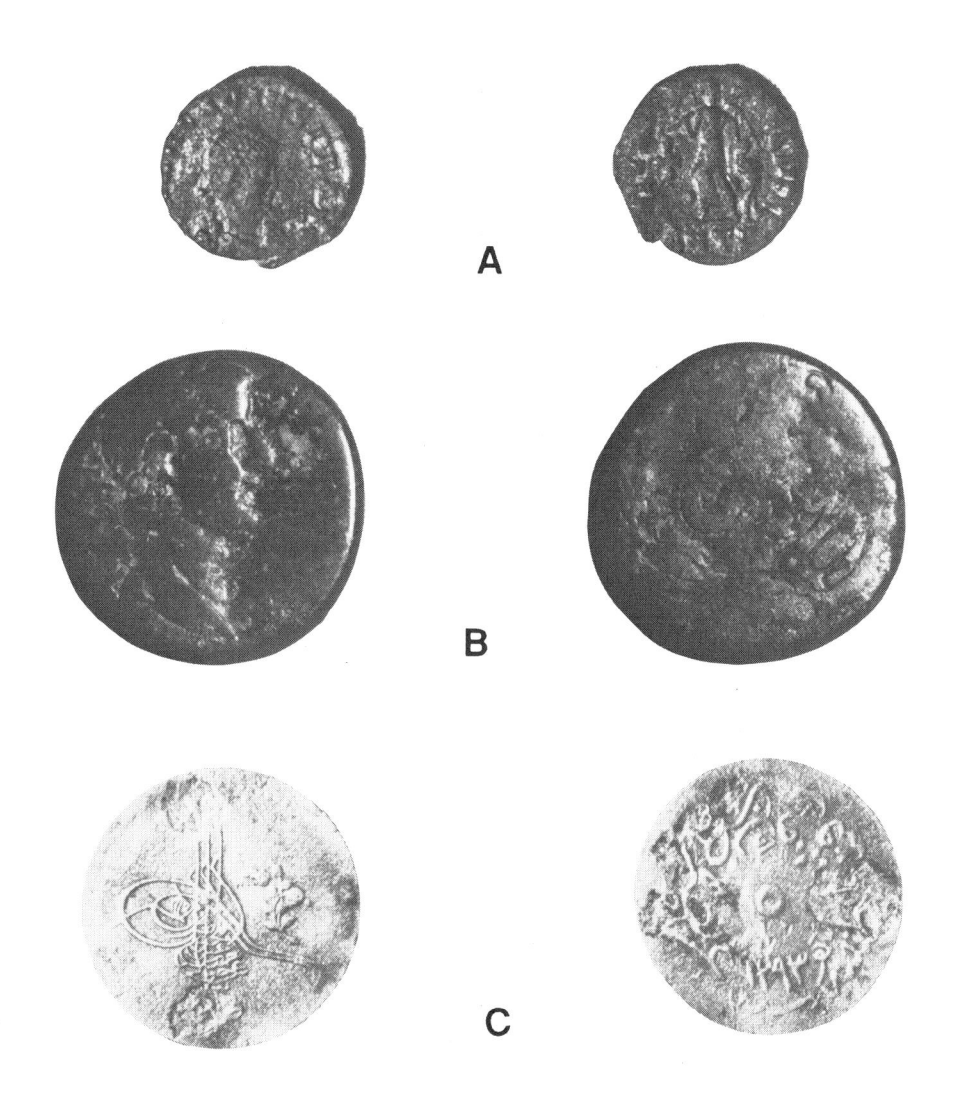